5G Network Technology and Beyond:

Applications, Architecture, and Future Horizons

Varinder Sharma

Preface

In December 2018, a small team of engineers in the United States switched on one of the first commercial millimeter-wave 5G networks. What had been confined to research laboratories and standards documents suddenly became real—a signal propagating through the air, connecting a device to a network that promised to redefine what wireless communication could achieve. I remember that moment vividly, not as a distant observer, but as someone who had spent years preparing the infrastructure that would make such moments possible.

Today, 5G networks serve hundreds of millions of subscribers worldwide. Yet we remain in the early chapters of a much longer story. The networks being deployed now are fundamentally different from those envisioned just five years ago, and the systems that will emerge over the next decade will be more transformative still. This book—my second on advanced telecommunications technologies—is my attempt to capture this technological moment, to explain not only what 5G is, but what it means, how it works, and where it is taking us.

Why This Book

Over twenty-three years in telecommunications, I have worked across every generation of wireless technology—from GSM's circuit-switched voice to LTE's all-IP architecture and now to 5G's service-based design. I have led engineering teams of fifteen or more engineers responsible for network infrastructure serving over 290 million Americans, managed multi-billion-dollar deployment programs for major carriers including AT&T and T-Mobile, and developed innovative tools that solved problems existing solutions could not address.

Throughout this journey, I have encountered a persistent challenge: the gap between academic literature and operational reality. Theoretical texts often assume idealized conditions that never exist in practice. Vendor documentation focuses on specific products rather than architectural principles. Standards documents, while authoritative, can be impenetrable to those not already expert in their conventions. What has been missing is a comprehensive guide that respects technical rigor while remaining grounded in the practical realities of building and operating networks at scale.

This book addresses that gap. Every concept discussed here has been tested against my experience deploying real systems. When I describe protocol architectures, I draw on years of troubleshooting call flows and optimizing handover performance. When I explain physical layer innovations, I connect them to the coverage and capacity challenges I have encountered in dense urban environments and rural expanses alike. When I examine deployment strategies, I bring the perspective of someone who has managed the complexity of integrating new technologies into live networks serving millions of subscribers.

What Sets This Book Apart

Several distinctive features distinguish this work from other treatments of 5G technology.

Comprehensive scope with practical depth. This book covers the complete 5G ecosystem—from physical layer fundamentals through protocol architectures, service categories, industry applications, and deployment strategies—while maintaining sufficient technical depth to be useful to practicing engineers. Each topic is examined not in isolation but as part of an integrated system.

Forward-looking perspective. Five chapters are dedicated to Beyond 5G and 6G technologies, including emerging paradigms such as cloud-native and AI-native network architectures. Understanding where the technology is heading is essential for anyone making long-term investment or career decisions in telecommunications.

Emphasis on transformative architectures. Dedicated chapters on Cloud RAN and Open RAN reflect the architectural revolution currently reshaping the radio access network. These approaches are not merely incremental improvements but fundamental reimaginings of how wireless networks are built and operated.

Real-world application focus. Extensive coverage of private 5G networks, CBRS spectrum sharing, and industry vertical applications connects technical capabilities to business outcomes. The discussion of industry verticals draws on my experience supporting deployments across manufacturing, healthcare, transportation, and public safety sectors.

Unique convergence of AI, Cloud, and telecommunications expertise. The chapters on AI-native 6G architectures and intelligent network optimization are informed by my Master's degree in Artificial Intelligence and my Post Graduate certification in Cloud Computing, combined with over two decades of hands-on telecommunications experience. This multidisciplinary perspective—rare in the industry—enables a treatment of AI-driven network evolution and cloud-native architectures that is both technically sophisticated and practically grounded.

Structure and Approach

The twenty chapters of this book are organized into a logical progression that mirrors how one might approach learning a complex system: establish context, build foundational understanding, explore capabilities in depth, examine applications, and finally look toward future evolution.

The opening chapters trace the evolutionary path from earlier wireless generations to 5G, establishing why certain architectural decisions were made and what problems they were designed to solve. This historical context is not merely academic—understanding why systems were designed as they were provides essential insight into their behavior and limitations.

The technical core of the book examines 5G's physical layer innovations, performance characteristics, and the three foundational service categories: Enhanced Mobile Broadband (eMBB), Ultra-Reliable Low Latency Communications (URLLC), and Massive Machine-Type Communications (mMTC). These chapters provide the detailed technical understanding necessary for network planning, optimization, and troubleshooting.

The application-focused chapters explore how these technical capabilities translate into real-world value across industry verticals, private network deployments, and spectrum sharing frameworks. These discussions are informed by my direct involvement in enterprise 5G initiatives and my understanding of the business drivers that shape technology adoption.

The forward-looking chapters examine the limitations of current 5G systems and the research directions that will define 6G. From terahertz communications to intelligent reflecting surfaces to the deep integration of artificial intelligence into network architecture, these chapters prepare readers for the next wave of wireless innovation.

Intended Audience

This book is written for multiple audiences united by a common interest in understanding 5G technology deeply and practically.

Network engineers and technical managers will find detailed architectural discussions, implementation considerations, and optimization strategies drawn from large-scale deployments. The treatment of Cloud RAN and Open RAN is particularly relevant for those planning network modernization programs.

Graduate students and researchers will discover a comprehensive reference that bridges theoretical foundations with practical applications. The chapters on 6G enabling technologies provide a roadmap of active research areas and open problems.

Technology strategists and business leaders will gain the technical literacy necessary to evaluate 5G opportunities, assess vendor claims, and make informed investment decisions. The chapters on industry verticals and private networks are particularly relevant for enterprise technology planning.

Technology professionals transitioning into telecommunications will find an accessible entry point into a complex domain. The evolutionary context and architectural explanations are designed to build understanding progressively, without assuming prior telecommunications expertise.

A Personal Reflection

Writing this book has been an exercise in synthesis—drawing together knowledge accumulated across two decades, multiple employers, four graduate degrees, and countless technical challenges. It has also been an exercise in perspective, stepping back from the daily pressures of operational work to consider the larger arc of technological evolution.

I have been privileged to participate in some of the defining moments of American wireless communications: among the first commercial Voice over LTE deployments that transformed how carriers deliver voice services, nationwide network modernization programs that expanded LTE coverage to underserved communities, and 5G infrastructure builds that are enabling new categories of applications. These experiences have shaped my understanding of what it takes to bring transformative technologies from concept to operational reality.

My academic journey—from a Bachelor of Engineering through an MBA, a Postgraduate certification in Cloud Computing, and a master's degree in Artificial Intelligence from the University of Texas at Austin—has continually broadened my perspective on telecommunications. Each credential added new lenses through which to view familiar challenges. The MBA sharpened my understanding of the business drivers behind technology decisions. The cloud computing specialization illuminated the architectural transformation reshaping network infrastructure. The AI degree revealed how machine learning and deep learning will fundamentally change how networks operate and optimize themselves.

The convergence of artificial intelligence and telecommunications that I have spent years studying and practicing is not a distant future possibility but an emerging reality. Networks are becoming not merely intelligent but autonomously adaptive, optimizing themselves in real time to meet demands that human operators could never anticipate. Having developed deep expertise in both domains, I am convinced that the next generation of wireless professionals will need fluency in artificial intelligence as much as in radio frequency engineering or protocol design. The chapters on AI-native 6G architectures reflect this conviction and draw directly on my graduate research in machine learning, deep learning, and reinforcement learning.

This book also builds on my first book on Deep Learning and my ongoing contributions to the technical community. As an IEEE Senior Member and Session Chair, a member of Sigma Xi—The Scientific Research Honor Society, a keynote speaker at industry conferences, a peer reviewer for academic journals, and an active researcher, I remain connected to the cutting edge of innovation while grounding that research in the practical realities I encounter daily managing critical network infrastructure at Nokia.

Acknowledgments

This book reflects the contributions of many individuals, though any errors or shortcomings remain my own responsibility.

I am grateful to my colleagues at Nokia Networks, whose technical excellence and collaborative spirit have enriched my understanding of wireless systems. The engineers I have had the privilege of leading have taught me as much as I have taught them—their questions often revealing gaps in my own knowledge that demanded deeper investigation.

I thank my professors and fellow researchers at the University of Texas at Austin, whose rigorous approach to artificial intelligence expanded my thinking about what intelligent systems can achieve. The interdisciplinary perspective I gained there permeates the forward-looking chapters of this book.

I acknowledge the broader telecommunications and research community—the standards developers, IEEE colleagues, Sigma Xi members, and practitioners whose collective work has created the technologies described in these pages. The IEEE publications, 3GPP specifications, and academic research that inform this book represent the accumulated effort of thousands of dedicated professionals.

Finally, and most importantly, I thank my family for their unwavering patience and support during the many evenings and weekends devoted to this project, often while I was simultaneously completing graduate coursework and fulfilling speaking engagements. Their encouragement made this work possible.

Looking Ahead

We stand at a remarkable moment in the history of human communication. The networks we are building today will connect not only people but machines, vehicles, cities, and systems in ways that previous generations could scarcely imagine. The decisions we make about how these networks are designed, deployed, and operated will shape the technological infrastructure of society for decades to come.

The convergence of artificial intelligence, cloud computing, and telecommunications will accelerate this transformation exponentially. Networks will become not merely intelligent but autonomously adaptive, leveraging deep learning and reinforcement learning to optimize themselves in real time. The professionals who will build and manage these systems will need to be fluent in the physics of radio propagation, the mathematics of machine learning, and the architecture of cloud-native systems.

My hope is that this book will equip readers with the knowledge to participate meaningfully in that transformation—whether as engineers building the systems, researchers pushing the boundaries of what is possible, business leaders making investment decisions, or citizens seeking to understand the technologies that increasingly mediate our daily lives. The 5G story is still being written, and there is room for many authors.

Varinder Kumar Sharma

Technical Manager, Nokia Networks USA

MS in Artificial Intelligence, University of Texas at Austin, USA

Postgraduate in Cloud Computing, University of Texas at Austin, USA

MBA, Texas A&M University, USA

BS in Networks and Communication Management, USA

IEEE Senior Member & Session Chair

Sigma Xi Member

December 2025

Dallas, Texas

Table of Contents

Chapter 1
List of Abbreviations

Comprehensive Consolidated List

A

- A1 – A1 Interface (Non-RT RIC to Near-RT RIC)
- ACE – Award for Continuous Excellence / Achievement and Contribution Excellence (Nokia Award)
- ACG – Automatic Connection Guidance
- AEP – American Electric Power
- AF – Application Function
- AGI – Artificial General Intelligence
- AGV – Automated Guided Vehicle / Autonomous Guided Vehicle
- AI – Artificial Intelligence
- AKA – Authentication and Key Agreement
- AM – Acknowledged Mode
- AMBR – Aggregate Maximum Bit Rate
- AMF – Access and Mobility Management Function
- AMI – Advanced Metering Infrastructure
- AMR – Autonomous Mobile Robot
- AMPS – Advanced Mobile Phone System
- AP – Access Point
- API – Application Programming Interface
- AR – Augmented Reality
- ARIB – Association of Radio Industries and Businesses (Japan)
- ARP – Allocation Retention Priority
- ARPU – Average Revenue Per User
- ARQ – Automatic Repeat Request
- ASCON – Authenticated Encryption Algorithm
- AT&T – American Telephone & Telegraph
- ATIS – Alliance for Telecommunications Industry Solutions (USA)
- AUSF – Authentication Server Function
- AUTN – Authentication Token
- AutoML – Automated Machine Learning

B

- B5G – Beyond 5G Consortium (Japan) / Beyond 5G
- BAR – Buffering Action Rule
- BBU – Baseband Unit
- BCI – Brain-Computer Interface
- BCG – Boston Consulting Group
- bps/Hz – Bits per second per Hertz

C

- C-Plane – Control Plane
- C-RAN – Centralized/Cloud Radio Access Network
- CA – Carrier Aggregation
- CAICT – China Academy of Information and Communications Technology
- CAPEX – Capital Expenditure
- CBRS – Citizens Broadband Radio Service
- CBSD – Citizens Broadband Radio Service Device
- CCPA – California Consumer Privacy Act
- CCSA – China Communications Standards Association
- CD – Continuous Delivery
- CDMA – Code Division Multiple Access
- CDN – Content Delivery Network
- CI – Continuous Integration
- CI/CD – Continuous Integration/Continuous Deployment
- CIO – Cell Individual Offset
- CIP – Critical Infrastructure Protection
- CN – Core Network
- CNCF – Cloud Native Computing Foundation
- CNF – Cloud Native Functions
- CoAP – Constrained Application Protocol
- CoMP – Coordinated Multipoint Transmission / Coordinated MultiPoint
- ConEd – Consolidated Edison
- COTS – Commercial Off-The-Shelf
- CP – Control Plane
- CPI – Consumer Price Index
- CPRI – Common Public Radio Interface
- CPU – Central Processing Unit
- CRD – Custom Resource Definition
- CSIS – Center for Strategic and International Studies
- CU – Centralized Unit / Central Unit
- CU-CP – Centralized Unit - Control Plane / Central Unit - Control Plane
- CU-UP – Centralized Unit - User Plane / Central Unit - User Plane
- CUPS – Control and User Plane Separation
- CVR – Conservation Voltage Reduction

D

- DAPS – Dual Active Protocol Stack
- DAS – Distributed Antenna System
- DC – Dual Connectivity
- DCS – Digital Cellular System (1800 MHz)
- DDoS – Distributed Denial of Service

- DER – Distributed Energy Resources / Distributed Energy Resource
- DevOps – Development and Operations
- DHL – Dalsey, Hillblom and Lynn
- DISH – DISH Network Corporation
- DL – Downlink
- DMS – Distribution Management System
- DMRS – Demodulation Reference Signal
- DoCoMo – NTT's mobile communications subsidiary
- DPDK – Data Plane Development Kit
- DRB – Data Radio Bearer
- DSP – Digital Signal Processing
- DSS – Dynamic Spectrum Sharing
- DTLS – Datagram Transport Layer Security
- DU – Distributed Unit

E

- E-UTRAN – Evolved Universal Terrestrial Radio Access Network
- E1 – Interface between CU-CP and CU-UP
- E2 – E2 Interface (Near-RT RIC to RAN nodes)
- E2E – End-to-End
- E2SM-KPM – E2 Service Model - Key Performance Measurements
- E2SM-NI – E2 Service Model - Network Interface
- E2SM-RC – E2 Service Model - RAN Control
- EAP – Extensible Authentication Protocol
- EAP-AKA – Extensible Authentication Protocol - Authentication and Key Agreement
- EB-1A – Employment-Based First Preference - Extraordinary Ability / Employment-Based First Preference Category A
- eCPRI – Enhanced Common Public Radio Interface
- ECoG – Electrocorticography
- EDGE – Enhanced Data rates for GSM Evolution
- eDRX – Extended Discontinuous Reception
- EEG – Electroencephalography
- eICIC – Enhanced Inter-Cell Interference Coordination
- EIRP – Effective Isotropic Radiated Power
- eMBB – Enhanced Mobile Broadband
- EMS – Energy Management System
- eNB – evolved NodeB / Evolved Node B
- eNodeB – Evolved NodeB
- ENISA – European Union Agency for Cybersecurity
- EPC – Evolved Packet Core
- EPS – Evolved Packet System
- ESC – Environmental Sensing Capability
- ESG – Environmental, Social, and Governance
- ESM – EPS Session Management
- ETSI – European Telecommunications Standards Institute
- EU – European Union
- EV – Electric Vehicle

F

- F1 – Interface between CU and DU
- F1-C – F1 Control Plane
- F1-U – F1 User Plane
- F1AP – F1 Application Protocol
- FAN – Field Area Network
- FAQ – Frequently Asked Questions
- FAR – Forwarding Action Rule
- FCAPS – Fault, Configuration, Accounting, Performance, Security
- FCC – Federal Communications Commission
- FDA – Food and Drug Administration
- FDD – Frequency Division Duplex
- FDMA – Frequency Division Multiple Access
- FFT – Fast Fourier Transform
- FirstNet – First Responder Network Authority / First Responder Network
- FlexE – Flexible Ethernet
- FM – Frequency Modulation
- fNIRS – Functional Near-Infrared Spectroscopy
- FPGA – Field-Programmable Gate Array
- FR1 – Frequency Range 1 (sub-6 GHz) / (Sub-6 GHz)
- FR2 – Frequency Range 2 (mmWave)
- FWA – Fixed Wireless Access

G

- GAA – General Authorized Access
- GBR – Guaranteed Bit Rate
- Gbps – Gigabits per second / Gigabits per Second
- GDP – Gross Domestic Product
- GDPR – General Data Protection Regulation
- GE – General Electric
- GEO – Geostationary Earth Orbit
- GFBR – Guaranteed Flow Bit Rate
- GHz – Gigahertz
- GMSK – Gaussian Minimum Shift Keying
- gNB – Next Generation NodeB / 5G NodeB (base station) / Next Generation Node B
- gNodeB – Next Generation NodeB
- GPS – Global Positioning System
- GPRS – General Packet Radio Service
- GPU – Graphics Processing Unit
- GSA – Global mobile Suppliers Association
- GSM – Global System for Mobile Communications
- GSMA – GSM Association
- GTP – GPRS Tunneling Protocol
- GTP-C – GPRS Tunneling Protocol - Control Plane
- GTP-U – GPRS Tunneling Protocol User Plane

- GTPv2-C – GTP version 2 Control Plane
- GUTI – Globally Unique Temporary Identifier
- Gx – Policy and charging control interface / Interface between PCRF and P-GW

H

- HAP – Hybrid Access Point / High Altitude Platform
- HARQ – Hybrid Automatic Repeat Request
- HBR – Harvard Business Review
- HD – High Definition
- HetNet – Heterogeneous Network
- Hexa-X – European 6G Flagship Project
- HIPAA – Health Insurance Portability and Accountability Act
- HPE – Hewlett Packard Enterprise
- HSDPA – High-Speed Downlink Packet Access
- HSPA – High-Speed Packet Access
- HSPA+ – Evolved High-Speed Packet Access
- HSM – Hardware Security Module
- HSS – Home Subscriber Server
- HTML – HyperText Markup Language
- HTTPS – Hypertext Transfer Protocol Secure
- HTTP/2 – Hypertext Transfer Protocol Version 2
- Hz – Hertz

I

- IAB – Integrated Access and Backhaul
- IBN – Intent-Based Networking
- ICT – Information and Communications Technology
- ID – Identification
- IDC – International Data Corporation
- IEC – International Electrotechnical Commission
- IEEE – Institute of Electrical and Electronics Engineers
- IETF – Internet Engineering Task Force
- IIoT – Industrial Internet of Things
- IMSI – International Mobile Subscriber Identity
- IMT – International Mobile Telecommunications
- IMT-2020 – International Mobile Telecommunications-2020 (5G)
- IMT-2030 – International Mobile Telecommunications-2030 (6G)
- IoT – Internet of Things
- IP – Internet Protocol
- IPsec – Internet Protocol Security
- IQ – In-phase and Quadrature
- ISAC – Integrated Sensing and Communications / Integrated Sensing and Communication
- ISDN – Integrated Services Digital Network
- ISG – Industry Specification Group

- ISL – Inter-Satellite Links
- Istio – Service Mesh Implementation
- IT – Information Technology
- ITU – International Telecommunication Union
- ITU-R – ITU Radiocommunication Sector / International Telecommunication Union - Radiocommunication Sector / International Telecommunication Union Radiocommunication Sector
- ITU-T – ITU Telecommunication Standardization Sector

J

- JSON – JavaScript Object Notation

K

- kbps – Kilobits per second / Kilobits per Second
- KDDI – Japanese Telecommunications Operator
- kHz – kilohertz / Kilohertz
- km – kilometer
- km/h – Kilometers per hour
- KPI – Key Performance Indicator
- Kubernetes – Container Orchestration Platform

L

- L1 – Layer 1 / Physical Layer
- L2 – Layer 2 / Data Link Layer
- L4S – Low Latency, Low Loss, Scalable Throughput
- LA – Los Angeles
- LAA – License Assisted Access
- LDPC – Low-Density Parity-Check / Low-Density Parity Check
- LEO – Low Earth Orbit
- Linkerd – Service Mesh Implementation
- LTE – Long-Term Evolution / Long Term Evolution
- LTE-A – LTE-Advanced
- LTE-M – LTE for Machine-Type Communications / Long-Term Evolution for Machines
- LTE-U – LTE in Unlicensed spectrum

M

- M-Plane – Management Plane
- M2M – Machine-to-Machine
- MAC – Medium Access Control / Media Access Control
- MAML – Model-Agnostic Meta-Learning
- MANO – Management and Orchestration
- MBA – Master of Business Administration
- MBR – Maximum Bit Rate
- Mbps – Megabits per second / Megabits per Second
- MCL – Maximum Coupling Loss
- MDPI – Multidisciplinary Digital Publishing Institute
- MEC – Multi-access Edge Computing
- MEO – Medium Earth Orbit
- MFBR – Maximum Flow Bit Rate
- MHz – Megahertz
- MIMO – Multiple Input Multiple Output
- ML – Machine Learning
- MME – Mobility Management Entity
- mMTC – massive Machine-Type Communications / Massive Machine-Type Communications / Massive Machine Type Communications
- MMS – Multimedia Messaging Service
- mmWave – millimeter Wave / Millimeter Wave
- MNO – Mobile Network Operator
- MPLS – Multiprotocol Label Switching
- MQTT – Message Queuing Telemetry Transport
- MR – Mixed Reality
- MRR – Monthly Recurring Revenue
- ms – Milliseconds / Millisecond / milliseconds
- MS – Master of Science

N

- N1 – Interface between UE and AMF
- N2 – Interface between RAN and AMF
- N26 – Interface between AMF and MME
- N3 – Interface between RAN and UPF
- N4 – Interface between SMF and UPF
- N6 – Interface to Data Networks
- NAF – Network Application Function
- NAMO – Network AI Management and Orchestration
- NAN – Neighborhood Area Network
- NAS – Non-Access Stratum
- NASCAR – National Association for Stock Car Auto Racing
- NB-IoT – Narrowband IoT / Narrowband Internet of Things
- NDVI – Normalized Difference Vegetation Index
- NEF – Network Exposure Function

- NERC – North American Electric Reliability Corporation
- NETCONF – Network Configuration Protocol
- NF – Network Function
- NFV – Network Function Virtualization
- NFVI – NFV Infrastructure
- NGA – Next G Alliance (North America)
- NG-RAN – Next Generation Radio Access Network
- NGAP – Next Generation Application Protocol
- NGMN – Next Generation Mobile Networks
- NIST – National Institute of Standards and Technology
- NLP – Natural Language Processing
- Nokia – Nokia Corporation
- NOMA – Non-Orthogonal Multiple Access
- Non-RT RIC – Non-Real-Time RAN Intelligent Controller
- NPSTC – National Public Safety Telecommunications Council
- NPN – Non-Public Network
- NPS – Net Promoter Score
- NR – New Radio (5G air interface) / New Radio (5G) / New Radio
- NRF – Network Repository Function
- nRT RIC – Near-Real-Time RAN Intelligent Controller
- NSA – Non-Standalone (5G deployment mode) / Non-Standalone
- NSSF – Network Slice Selection Function
- NTIA – National Telecommunications and Information Administration
- NTP – Network Time Protocol
- NTT – Nippon Telegraph and Telephone
- NUMA – Non-Uniform Memory Access
- NYC – New York City

O

- O-Cloud – O-RAN Cloud Platform
- O-CU – O-RAN Central Unit
- O-CU-CP – O-RAN Central Unit - Control Plane
- O-CU-UP – O-RAN Central Unit - User Plane
- O-DU – O-RAN Distributed Unit
- O-RAN – Open Radio Access Network
- O-RU – O-RAN Radio Unit
- O1 – O1 Interface (SMO management interface)
- O2 – O2 Interface (SMO to O-Cloud)
- OAuth – Open Authorization
- OFDM – Orthogonal Frequency Division Multiplexing / Orthogonal Frequency-Division Multiplexing
- OFDMA – Orthogonal Frequency Division Multiple Access
- OMS – Outage Management System
- OneM2M – One Machine-to-Machine
- ONF – Open Networking Foundation
- OPEX – Operational Expenditure
- OTA – Over-The-Air

- OVS – Open vSwitch

P

- P-GW – PDN Gateway / Packet Data Network Gateway
- P-GW-C – Packet Data Network Gateway - Control Plane
- P-GW-U – Packet Data Network Gateway - User Plane
- P4 – Programming Protocol-independent Packet Processors
- PaaS – Product-as-a-Service
- PAL – Priority Access License
- PC5 – Proximity Communication Interface
- PCF – Policy Control Function
- PCRF – Policy and Charging Rules Function
- PCS – Personal Communications Service (1900 MHz) / Personal Communications Service
- PDCCH – Physical Downlink Control Channel
- PDCP – Packet Data Convergence Protocol
- PDN – Packet Data Network
- PDF – Portable Document Format
- PDR – Packet Detection Rule
- PDU – Protocol Data Unit
- PFCP – Packet Forwarding Control Protocol
- PG&E – Pacific Gas and Electric
- PHY – Physical Layer
- PLC – Programmable Logic Controller
- PMC – PubMed Central
- PMU – Phasor Measurement Unit
- PNI – Public Network Integrated
- POS – Point of Sale
- PPP – Precision Time Protocol Profile
- PROFINET – Process Field Network
- PROFIsafe – PROFIBUS Safety
- PSK – Phase Shift Keying
- PTP – Precision Time Protocol

Q

- QAM – Quadrature Amplitude Modulation
- QCI – QoS Class Identifier
- QER – QoS Enforcement Rule
- QFI – QoS Flow Identifier
- QoE – Quality of Experience
- QoS – Quality of Service
- QPSK – Quadrature Phase Shift Keying

R

- RACH – Random Access Channel
- Rakuten – Rakuten Mobile (Japan)
- RAN – Radio Access Network
- RAND – Random Challenge
- rApp – Non-Real-Time RIC Application
- RED – Retail Execution Deployment
- REPL – Read-Eval-Print Loop
- RES – Response
- REST – Representational State Transfer
- RESTful – REST-compliant
- RF – Radio Frequency
- RFID – Radio Frequency Identification
- RIC – RAN Intelligent Controller
- RIS – Reconfigurable Intelligent Surfaces
- RLC – Radio Link Control
- RNA – RAN Notification Area
- ROI – Return on Investment
- RPA – Robotic Process Automation
- RRC – Radio Resource Control
- RRU – Remote Radio Unit
- RT – Real-Time
- RTT – Round Trip Time
- RU – Radio Unit

S

- S-GW – Serving Gateway
- S-GW-C – Serving Gateway - Control Plane
- S-GW-U – Serving Gateway - User Plane
- S-NSSAI – Single Network Slice Selection Assistance Information
- S-Plane – Synchronization Plane
- S1 – Interface between eNB and EPC
- S1-MME – S1 Interface for MME / S1 interface for MME / S1 Interface to MME
- S1-U – S1 User plane interface / S1 User Plane
- S11 – Interface between MME and S-GW
- S1AP – S1 Application Protocol
- S5 – Interface between S-GW and P-GW (non-roaming) / Interfaces between S-GW and P-GW
- S5/S8 – Interfaces between S-GW and P-GW
- S6a – Interface between MME and HSS
- S8 – Interface between S-GW and P-GW (roaming)
- SA – Standalone
- SAS – Spectrum Access System
- SBA – Service-Based Architecture
- SBI – Service-Based Interface
- SCADA – Supervisory Control and Data Acquisition
- SC-FDMA – Single Carrier FDMA / Single Carrier Frequency Division Multiple Access
- SCTP – Stream Control Transmission Protocol
- SCS – Subcarrier Spacing

- SD – Slice Differentiator
- SDAP – Service Data Adaptation Protocol
- SDN – Software-Defined Networking
- SDO – Standards Development Organization
- SEC – Securities and Exchange Commission
- SFTP – Secure File Transfer Protocol
- SGi – Interface to External Packet Data Networks
- SI – System Information
- SIM – Subscriber Identity Module
- SLA – Service Level Agreement
- SMF – Session Management Function
- SMS – Short Message Service
- SMO – Service Management and Orchestration
- SNMP – Simple Network Management Protocol
- SNPN – Standalone Non-Public Network
- SNR – Signal-to-Noise Ratio
- SNS JU – Smart Networks and Services Joint Undertaking
- SNTP – Simple Network Time Protocol
- SOC – Security Operations Center
- SoCalGas – Southern California Gas Company
- SON – Self-Organizing Networks / Self-Organizing Network
- SQI – Service Quality Indicator
- SR-IOV – Single Root I/O Virtualization
- SSB – Synchronization Signal Block
- SST – Slice/Service Type
- STL – Standard Template Library
- Sx – Interface for CUPS

T

- TA – Tracking Area
- TAI – Tracking Area Identity
- Tbps – Terabits per second
- TCP – Transmission Control Protocol
- TCO – Total Cost of Ownership
- TDD – Time Division Duplex
- TDMA – Time Division Multiple Access
- TDRA – Telecommunications and Digital Government Regulatory Authority (UAE)
- TFT – Traffic Flow Template
- THz – Terahertz
- TI – Tactile Internet
- TLS – Transport Layer Security
- TM – Transparent Mode
- TPU – Tensor Processing Unit
- TR – Technical Report
- TrustZone – ARM Security Technology
- TS – Technical Specification
- TSMC – Taiwan Semiconductor Manufacturing Company
- TSN – Time-Sensitive Networking

- TSDSI – Telecommunications Standards Development Society, India
- TTA – Telecommunications Technology Association (Korea)
- TTC – Telecommunication Technology Committee (Japan)

U

- U-Plane – User Plane
- UAE – United Arab Emirates
- UAV – Unmanned Aerial Vehicle
- UDP – User Datagram Protocol
- UDM – Unified Data Management
- UDR – Unified Data Repository
- UE – User Equipment
- UHD – Ultra High Definition
- UK – United Kingdom
- UL – Uplink
- ULCL – Uplink Classifier
- UM – Unacknowledged Mode
- UMTS – Universal Mobile Telecommunications System
- UNESCO – United Nations Educational, Scientific and Cultural Organization
- UPF – User Plane Function
- UPFA – User Plane Function Anchor
- URLLC – Ultra-Reliable Low Latency Communications / Ultra-Reliable Low-Latency Communications
- URR – Usage Reporting Rule
- US – United States
- USA – United States of America
- UT – University of Texas
- UT Austin – University of Texas at Austin
- Uu – Radio interface between UE and base station / Radio Interface between UE and Base Station / Radio Interface

---

V

- V2V – Vehicle-to-Vehicle
- V2X – Vehicle-to-Everything
- VIM – Virtual Infrastructure Manager
- VNF – Virtual Network Function
- VNFM – VNF Manager
- VoLTE – Voice over LTE
- VPN – Virtual Private Network
- VPP – Virtual Power Plant
- VR – Virtual Reality
- VTT – Technical Research Centre of Finland

W

- WAN – Wide Area Network
- WCDMA – Wideband Code Division Multiple Access
- WEF – World Economic Forum
- WG – Work Group
- WHO – World Health Organization
- WLAN – Wireless Local Area Network
- WP5D – Working Party 5D

X

- X2 – Interface between eNodeBs
- X2-C – X2 Control Plane
- X2-U – X2 User Plane
- X2AP – X2 Application Protocol
- xApp – Near-Real-Time RIC Application
- Xn – Interface between gNodeBs
- XR – Extended Reality
- xRAN – xRAN Forum (predecessor to O-RAN Alliance)

Y

- YANG – Yet Another Next Generation (data modeling language) / Yet Another Next Generation
- YoY – Year-over-Year

Z

- ZSM – Zero-touch network and Service Management
- ZTA – Zero Trust Architecture / Zero-Touch Automation

NUMERIC AND ALPHANUMERIC

- 1G – First Generation (Analog) / First Generation
- 2G – Second Generation (Digital - GSM) / Second Generation
- 2.5G – GPRS enhancement to 2G
- 2.75G – EDGE enhancement to 2G
- 3D – Three-Dimensional
- 3G – Third Generation (WCDMA) / Third Generation
- 3.5G – HSPA enhancement to 3G

- 3.75G – HSPA+ enhancement to 3G
- 3GPP – 3rd Generation Partnership Project
- 4G – Fourth Generation (LTE) / Fourth Generation
- 4.5G – LTE-Advanced Pro / LTE-Advanced
- 5G – Fifth Generation
- 5G-AKA – 5G Authentication and Key Agreement
- 5GC – 5G Core
- 5QI – 5G QoS Identifier
- 6G – Sixth Generation (under research) / Sixth Generation

FREQUENCY BANDS

- n1, n2, n3, etc. – 5G NR frequency band numbers
- Band 5 – 850 MHz band
- Band 8 – 900 MHz band
- Band 12, 13, 14, 17 – 700 MHz LTE bands
- Band 20 – 800 MHz LTE band
- Band 71 – 600 MHz LTE band

QAM VARIANTS

- 16QAM – 16-Quadrature Amplitude Modulation
- 64QAM – 64-Quadrature Amplitude Modulation
- 256QAM – 256-Quadrature Amplitude Modulation
- 1024QAM – 1024-Quadrature Amplitude Modulation

END OF ABBREVIATIONS LIST

Chapter 2: Evolution of Telecommunication Technologies

Executive Summary

This chapter chronicles the extraordinary evolution of telecommunications, from rudimentary wireline systems to the cutting-edge capabilities of fifth-generation (5G) mobile networks.

Mobile communications began in 1876 when Alexander Graham Bell created the telephone, marking the birth of an industry that would transform human connectivity. Over nearly 150 years since that breakthrough, cellular technology has progressed through five distinct generations. The journey started with first-generation analog systems, then moved to second-generation digital GSM technology, followed by third-generation WCDMA networks that brought mobile internet to the masses. Fourth-generation LTE systems dramatically increased data speeds, and now fifth-generation networks deliver unprecedented performance. Each of these generational shifts has profoundly altered how connectivity solutions work and what they can accomplish.

Each successive generation arose in response to the limitations of its predecessor, propelled by shifts in user needs, technological progress, and economic imperatives.

This chapter examines the necessity behind each generational shift, emphasizing major milestones, technical developments, and their profound societal, industrial, and economic impacts. It also looks ahead to sixth-generation (6G) innovations, currently under research, with an eye toward a 2030 rollout, reinforcing telecommunications' central role in powering digital transformation, fostering economic development, and strengthening global connectivity.

Table of Contents

Introduction

Telecommunications has experienced a remarkable transformation over the past century, transitioning from basic wireline systems to highly advanced mobile networks that now serve as the backbone of our digital society.

This chapter captures the evolution of telecommunication, starting from the wireline-based solution to the advanced ultra-fast 5G mobile network and beyond.

The Wireline Era: Establishing Foundations

The telecommunications industry began to emerge in the late nineteenth century with the invention of wireline-based communication systems. The revolution began with the introduction of physical connectivity between two geographical locations. This critical milestone established the foundation of modern communication in that era (Goldsmith, 2021; Stallings, 2023). Key milestones from this period include:

Key Milestones (1876 – 1980s)

- **1876**: Alexander Graham Bell invented the telephone (Stallings, 2023)
- **1889**: Almon Strowger introduced the first automatic telephone exchange (Penttinen, 2022)
- **1947**: The transistor was invented at Bell Labs, paving the way for modern telecommunications (Rappaport, 2022)
- **1962**: Bell Labs developed the first commercial digital transmission system (Goldsmith, 2021)
- **1970s**: Fiber optic communication emerged, exponentially increasing transmission capacity (Stallings, 2023)
- **1980s**: Integrated Services Digital Network (ISDN) digitized traditional telephone networks (Penttinen, 2022)

Fundamental Limitations

While these wireline technologies laid the foundation for telecommunications, they were inherently constrained by the physical infrastructure they depended on. As society became more dynamic and interconnected, the fixed nature of these networks posed serious limitations. The demand for mobility and continuous connectivity eventually ignited a revolution—one that would shift communications into the wireless realm.

The Mobile Revolution: From 1G to 4G

First Generation (1G): Analog Communications

The 1980s introduced the first generation of mobile technology, which operated on analog systems (Sauter, 2021):

- **Commercial Launch**: NTT of Japan initiated the first commercial cellular network in 1979 (Nakamura et al., 2022).
- **U.S. Service Implementation:** The Advanced Mobile Phone System (AMPS) was introduced in 1983 (Rappaport, 2022).
- **Frequency Bands**: Operated in the 800–900 MHz range (Dahlman et al., 2021).
- **Limitations**: Low capacity, poor voice quality, minimal security, and no roaming capabilities (Sauter, 2021).

These analog systems enabled mobile voice communications for the first time but came with significant drawbacks. Frequency Division Multiple Access (FDMA) technology allowed only one user per channel, making it inefficient and prone to congestion (Schulze & Luders, 2021). These challenges underscored the need for a shift to digital mobile technology.

Second Generation (2G): The Digital Shift – GSM Era

Digital technology marked a pivotal shift when mobile networks entered their second era. During this phase, GSM emerged as the dominant framework that would shape how cellular systems operated worldwide. This transition from analog to digital represented more than just a technical upgrade—it fundamentally changed the architecture of mobile telecommunications and set the foundation for how billions of people would eventually connect.

GSM Service: The Digital Pioneer

- **1991:** First GSM network launched in Finland (GSMA, 2022)
- **Key Technologies:** Time Division Multiple Access (TDMA), digital voice coding (Holma & Toskala, 2021)
- **Frequency Bands (3GPP TS 38.913, 2022):**
    - **Europe/Asia/Africa:** GSM-900 Band (900 MHz), DCS-1800 Band (1800 MHz)
    - **Americas:** GSM-850 Band (850 MHz), PCS-1900 Band (1900 MHz)
    - **Channel Bandwidth:** 200 kHz per channel
- **Data Capabilities:** New service introduction with Short Message Service (SMS) and basic data services up to 9.6 kbps (Sauter, 2021)
- **Enhancements:**
    - **GPRS (2.5G):** Packet-switched data with speeds up to 114 kbps (Sesia et al., 2021)
    - **EDGE (2.75G):** Enhanced data rates up to 384 kbps through improved modulation (Dahlman et al., 2021)

Key GSM Milestones

- **1992:** First SMS message sent (GSMA, 2022)
- **1995:** GSM subscriber base reached 10 million (GSMA Intelligence, 2023)
- **1997:** First prepaid mobile phone service introduced (Sauter, 2021)
- **2000:** GSM reached 250 million subscribers worldwide (GSMA, 2022)

- **2003:** More than 1 billion GSM subscribers recorded globally (GSMA Intelligence, 2023)

Why 2G/GSM Was Necessary

The transition to 2G was driven by several critical limitations of 1G systems:

1. **Capacity Constraints:** Analog networks were unable to support the growing user base. GSM's digital architecture enabled multiple users to share the identical frequency channels through time division, increasing network capacity by 3 to 10 times (Holma & Toskala, 2021).
2. **Security Vulnerabilities:** 1G calls were easily intercepted with consumer-grade receivers. GSM introduced encryption and subscriber authentication, which addressed significant privacy concerns (Poikselkä & Mayer, 2019).
3. **International Incompatibility:** 1G systems varied by country and lacked interoperability. GSM established the first global standard, enabling international roaming (GSMA, 2022).
4. **Digital Revolution:** The emergence of digital computing necessitated compatible communications systems. GSM's digital design enabled integration with the broader digital ecosystem (Sauter, 2021).

Key Features Driving Adoption

- **SMS Messaging:** Text messaging created an entirely new communication paradigm that drove mass adoption (GSMA Intelligence, 2023).
- **International Roaming:** Business travelers could use their phones across borders, a revolutionary capability (GSMA, 2022).
- **SIM Card Technology:** The introduction of removable subscriber identity modules enabled unprecedented user mobility (Poikselkä & Mayer, 2019).
- **Improved Battery Life:** Digital transmission significantly extended handset battery life compared to analog systems (Sauter, 2021).
- **Enhanced Voice Quality:** Digital coding dramatically improved call clarity and reliability (Holma & Toskala, 2021).

Despite these advantages, GSM's limited data capabilities would soon become a bottleneck as internet access grew increasingly essential. This limitation, alongside emerging multimedia needs, drove the industry toward 3G development.

Third Generation (3G): WCDMA and Mobile Broadband

The increasing need for faster data services and improved capacity drove the evolution of third-generation technologies, with Wideband Code Division Multiple Access (WCDMA) at its core.

WCDMA: Enabling Mobile Internet

- **Commercial Debut:** Japan's NTT DoCoMo launched the inaugural WCDMA network in 2001 (Nakamura et al., 2022)

- **Core Technologies:** Utilized Code Division Multiple Access (CDMA), spread spectrum methodologies (Schulze & Luders, 2021)
- **Frequency Bands (3GPP TS 38.913, 2022):**
  - **Primary Bands:** Band 5 (850 MHz), Band 8 (900 MHz), Band 2 (1900 MHz), Band 1 (2100 MHz)
  - **Secondary Bands:** Band 4 (1700MHz/2100 MHz), Band 3 (1800 MHz)
  - **Channel Bandwidth:** 5 MHz per carrier
- **Data Capabilities:** Initial speeds of 384 kbps, later enhanced through HSPA (Holma & Toskala, 2021)
- **Enhancements:**
  - **HSPA (3.5G):** High-Speed Packet Access delivered downlink throughput to 14.4 Mbps (Toskala & Holma, 2020)
  - **High Speed Packet Access (HSPA+ 3.75G):** Further improved with speeds up to 42 Mbps through techniques like MIMO and higher-order modulation (Holma & Toskala, 2021)

Key WCDMA Milestones

- **1999:** 3GPP established to develop 3G specifications (3GPP, 2021)
- **2002:** First WCDMA handsets introduced (Sauter, 2021)
- **2005:** HSDPA deployments begin (Toskala & Holma, 2020)
- **2007:** Introduction of iPhone revolutionizes mobile data consumption (GSMA Intelligence, 2023)
- **2009:** HSPA+ networks reach commercial deployment (Holma & Toskala, 2021)

Why 3G/WCDMA Was Necessary

The shift to 3G was driven by fundamental limitations in 2G systems that became apparent as mobile usage patterns evolved:

1. **Data Demand Explosion:** The emergence of mobile internet services generated the requirement for speeds that 2G network services simply could not meet. Despite EDGE improvements, 2G systems remained primarily optimized for voice communications rather than data transmission (Dahlman et al., 2021).
2. **Network Efficiency:** WCDMA's spread spectrum techniques enabled superior utilization of available frequency resources, providing capacity increases of up to 5 times relative to 2G systems (Schulze & Luders, 2021).
3. **Multimedia Capabilities:** Video calling, mobile streaming, and rich content sharing required the bandwidth that only 3G could deliver. WCDMA was the first technology capable of supporting real-time video telephony (Holma & Toskala, 2021).
4. **Application Ecosystem:** The emerging smartphone app ecosystem required constant, reliable data connections with sufficient throughput for increasingly complex applications (GSMA Intelligence, 2023).

Key Features Driving Adoption

1. **Always-on Data Connections:** 3G introduced the concept of persistent internet connectivity (Toskala & Holma, 2020).
2. **Video Telephony:** Real-time visual communication became possible, although network limitations initially hampered adoption (Holma & Toskala, 2021).
3. **Mobile Web Browsing:** Full HTML browsing on mobile devices became practical for the first time (Sauter, 2021).
4. **Location-Based Services:** Enhanced bandwidth and always-on connectivity enabled practical GPS and location services (Rodriguez, 2023).
5. **Simultaneous Voice and Data:** Users could talk while accessing data services, a fundamental improvement over 2G (Holma & Toskala, 2021).
6. **Global Roaming:** Greater international harmonization of frequency bands improved global compatibility (3GPP, 2021).

Despite these advances, WCDMA networks faced challenges with latency and consistent data speeds as smartphone adoption accelerated. The iPhone's introduction in 2007 created unprecedented demand for data services that even enhanced 3G networks struggled to meet efficiently (GSMA Intelligence, 2023).

These restrictions, together with the inefficiencies inherent in managing parallel circuit-switched-based voice networks and packet-switched-based data networks, catalyzed industry efforts toward creating a consolidated, all-IP 4G platform.

Fourth Generation (4G): LTE and the Data Era

The explosive growth in smartphone usage and mobile applications demanded a complete paradigm shift, leading to the development of 4G technology known as Long-Term Evolution (LTE).

LTE: The All-IP Network

- **2009:** First commercial LTE network launched in Sweden and Norway by TeliaSonera (Ericsson Mobility Report, 2024)
- **Key Technologies:** OFDMA, known as Orthogonal Frequency Division Multiple Access (OFDMA), MIMO, known as Multiple Input Multiple Output, and all-comprehensive all-IP architecture (Cox, 2021)
- **Frequency Bands (3GPP TS 38.913, 2022):**
  - **LTE Low Bands:** Frequency band of LTE 600 MHz (Band 71), LTE 700 MHz (Bands 12, 13, 14, 17, 28, 29), LTE 800 MHz (Band 20), LTE 850 MHz (Bands 5, 18, 26)
  - **LTE Mid Bands:** LTE 900 MHz (Band 8), LTE 1500 MHz (Band 32), LTE 1700/2100 MHz (Band 4/66), LTE 1800 MHz (Band 3), LTE 1900 MHz (Band 2, 25), LTE 2100 MHz (Band 1), LTE 2300 MHz (Band 40), LTE 2500 MHz (Band 7, 41)
  - **High Bands:** 3500 MHz (Bands 42, 43, 48)

- **LTE Channel Bandwidths:** 1.4, 3, 5, 10, 15, and 20 MHz (Sesia et al., 2021)

- **Data Capabilities:** Peak downlink speeds of 100 Mbps, evolving to 1 Gbps with LTE-Advanced (Dahlman et al., 2021)
- **Enhancements:**
  - **LTE-Advanced (4.5G):** Carrier aggregation, enhanced MIMO, coordinated multipoint transmission (Cox, 2021)
  - **LTE-Advanced Pro:** Higher-order modulation (256QAM), unlicensed spectrum integration (LAA/LTE-U), massive IoT support via NB-IoT and LTE-M (Ghosh & Ratasuk, 2019)

Key LTE Milestones

- **2008:** 3GPP Release 8 finalized LTE specifications (3GPP, 2021)
- **2011:** LTE subscriptions exceeded 10 million (GSMA Intelligence, 2023)
- **2013:** Voice over LTE (VoLTE) commercially deployed (Johnson, 2022)
- **2016:** LTE-Advanced Pro standardized in 3GPP Release 13 (3GPP, 2021)
- **2018:** Over 3 billion LTE subscriptions worldwide (GSMA Intelligence, 2023)
- **2019:** LTE networks reaching maturity with speeds approaching theoretical limits (Ericsson Mobility Report, 2024)

Why 4G/LTE Was Necessary

The transition to 4G addressed fundamental limitations in 3G networks that became increasingly problematic as mobile data usage surged:

1. **Data Efficiency:** Despite enhancements, 3G networks were still based on technologies originally designed for voice. LTE was engineered specifically for data from the ground up, improving spectral efficiency by 2–5x over HSPA+ (Dahlman et al., 2021).
2. **Latency Requirements:** 3G networks typically had latencies of 100ms or more, insufficient for interactive applications. LTE reduced this to 20–30ms, enabling real-time applications (Cox, 2021).
3. **Network Simplification:** The parallel circuit-switched (voice) and packet-switched (data) networks in 3G created operational inefficiencies. LTE's all-IP architecture eliminated this complexity (Sesia et al., 2021).
4. **Cost Per Bit:** With mobile data consumption doubling annually, 3G networks couldn't economically keep pace. LTE reduced the cost per bit delivered by approximately 80% (GSMA Intelligence, 2023).
5. **Video Streaming Demands:** The rise of mobile video, which grew to represent over 60% of the total cellular data traffic, required reliable higher bandwidth capabilities that 3G services were unable to deliver seamlessly (Cisco Visual Networking Index, 2020).

Key Features Driving Adoption

- **All-IP Architecture:** Simplified network structure reduced latency and operational costs (Cox, 2021).
- **Carrier Aggregation:** Combining multiple spectrum bands enabled unprecedented bandwidth (Dahlman et al., 2021).
- **MIMO Technology:** Multiple antenna configurations significantly increased throughput (Ghosh & Ratasuk, 2019).
- **Self-Organizing Networks (SON):** Automated configuration and optimization reduced operational expenses (Johnson, 2022).
- **VoLTE:** Native voice calling over the IP network improved voice quality while enabling simultaneous high-speed data (Poikselkä & Mayer, 2019).
- **Flexible Spectrum Usage:** Support for various bandwidths allowed operators to refarm existing spectrum (Sesia et al., 2021).
- **Enhanced Security:** Improved authentication and encryption addressed emerging cybersecurity threats (3GPP, 2021).

While LTE represented a tremendous leap forward, several emerging use cases began to reveal its limitations. These included the need for minimal latency for applications such as autonomous vehicles, massive device connectivity for IoT deployments, and enhanced mobile broadband for augmented and virtual reality applications.

These requirements, along with the economic imperative to continue to reduce their price per bit, drove the industry toward developing the 5G standard.

The 5G Revolution: A New Era of Connectivity

The fifth generation of cellular technology represents far more than an incremental improvement over 4G. It establishes a new paradigm in wireless communications.

Why 5G? Limitations of LTE/4G

Despite LTE's significant advancements, several critical limitations emerged as technology usage patterns evolved (Dahlman et al., 2022):

1. **Capacity Limitations:** LTE networks, even with advanced features, struggle to meet the exponential growth in data demand. With mobile data traffic projected to increase 1000x from 2010 to 2030, LTE's spectral efficiency improvements reached theoretical limits (Cisco Visual Networking Index, 2020).
2. **Latency Constraints:** While LTE reduced latency to 20–30 ms, emerging applications like autonomous vehicles, remote surgery, and industrial automation require consistent sub-10 ms latency, which LTE architecture cannot reliably deliver (5G Americas, 2022).
3. **Device Density:** LTE was designed primarily for smartphones and tablets, supporting approximately 2,000 active devices per square kilometer. The Internet of Things explosion requires support for up to 1 million devices per square kilometer (ITU, 2023).

4. **Network Flexibility:** LTE's monolithic architecture cannot efficiently serve diverse use cases simultaneously. Different applications require vastly different network characteristics that LTE cannot dynamically provision (Rodriguez, 2023).
5. **Energy Efficiency:** With sustainability becoming critical, LTE's energy consumption per bit transmitted remains too high for massive IoT deployments requiring decade-long battery life (Global e-Sustainability Initiative, 2023).
6. **Spectrum Limitations:** LTE operates primarily below 6 GHz, limiting available bandwidth. Meeting future capacity demands requires accessing higher frequency bands that LTE cannot utilize (3GPP TS 38.913, 2022).

Key Drivers and Timeline

The development of 5G was driven by converging technological, economic, and societal factors:

Primary Drivers

1. **Industry 4.0 Requirements:** Manufacturing, logistics, and industrial sectors demanded ultra-reliable, low-latency communications for automation and real-time control systems (McKinsey & Company, 2024).
2. **Enhanced Mobile Broadband:** Today's consumer-facing services demand robust, high-speed connectivity that can reliably deliver multiple gigabits per second. Applications like ultra-high-definition video (including 4K and 8K streaming), immersive VR experiences, and AR overlays all depend on this kind of sustained throughput to function properly (based on findings from the 2024 Ericsson Mobility Report).
3. **Massive IoT:** Smart cities, connected vehicles, and environmental monitoring systems need networks supporting millions of low-power devices (ITU, 2023).
4. **Economic Imperatives:** Reducing cost per bit by 10x compared to LTE to enable sustainable business models for data-intensive applications (IHS Markit, 2023).
5. **Mission-Critical Services:** Public safety, healthcare, and infrastructure management require guaranteed network performance with 99.999% reliability (5G Americas, 2022).

Development Timeline

- **2012–2015:** Initial 5G vision and requirements definition (ITU, 2023)
- **2015–2017:** Technology development and standardization (3GPP, 2021)
- **2017:** 3GPP Release 15 – First 5G specifications (NSA) (3GPP, 2021)
- **2018:** 3GPP Release 15 – 5G standalone specifications (3GPP, 2021)
- **2019:** First commercial 5G deployments (GSMA Intelligence, 2024)
- **2020:** 3GPP Release 16 – Enhanced 5G features (3GPP, 2021)
- **2022:** 3GPP Release 17 – Advanced 5G capabilities (3GPP, 2021)
- **2023–2025:** Mass market adoption and vertical industry integration (GSMA, 2022)

Transformative Technologies and Capabilities

5G: Transforming Industries and Society

- **2019:** Initial 5G networks debuted in South Korea, the USA, and China (GSMA Intelligence, 2024)
- **Key Technologies:** Millimeter wave spectrum, massive MIMO, network slicing, edge computing, software-defined networking, beamforming, New Radio (NR) air interface (Dahlman et al., 2022)
- **Frequency Bands (3GPP TS 38.913, 2022):**
  - **Low-Band (FR1):** 600 MHz (n71), 700 MHz (n12, n28), 800 MHz (n20), 850 MHz (n5), 900 MHz (n8)
  - **Mid-Band (FR1):** 1.8–2.6 GHz (n1, n2, n3, n7, n25, n41, n66), 3.3–4.2 GHz (n77, n78)
  - **High-Band/mmWave (FR2):** 24.25–29.5 GHz (n257, n258, n261), 37–40 GHz (n260)
  - **Channel Bandwidths:** Up to 100 MHz (FR1), up to 400 MHz (FR2)
- **Data Capabilities:**
  - Peak speeds of 20 Gbps downlink, 10 Gbps uplink (ITU, 2023)

Performance Indicators and Use Cases

Key Performance Indicators (ITU, 2023; 5G Americas, 2022)

- Minimal latency (1 ms)
- Large-scale device connectivity (1 million devices per square kilometer)
- Enhanced reliability (99.999%)
- Network energy efficiency improvements of 90%

Key 5G Milestones

- **2015:** Initial 5G research and vision established (ITU, 2023)
- **2017:** First 5G specifications in 3GPP Release 15 (3GPP, 2021)
- **2018:** 5G New Radio (NR) specifications completed (3GPP, 2021)
- **2019:** First commercial 5G deployments (GSMA Intelligence, 2024)
- **2020:** Standalone 5G networks begin deployment (Ericsson Mobility Report, 2024)
- **2021:** Over 500 million 5G subscriptions worldwide (GSMA Intelligence, 2024)
- **2022:** Advanced 5G features standardized in 3GPP Release 17 (3GPP, 2021)
- **2023:** Industrial and enterprise 5G deployments accelerate (McKinsey & Company, 2024)
- **2024:** 5G coverage reaching the majority of developed markets (Ericsson Mobility Report, 2024)

Key Features Driving Adoption

- **Service-Based Architecture:** Flexible, cloud-native network core enables rapid service deployment (Dahlman et al., 2022).
- **Network Slicing:** Ability to develop multiple specialized virtual networks with tailored characteristics over a shared physical infrastructure (Rodriguez, 2023).
- **Massive MIMO:** Using large antenna arrays with beamforming to dramatically increase capacity and coverage (Rappaport, 2022).
- **Millimeter Wave Spectrum:** Utilizing previously unused high-frequency bands to deliver extreme capacity in dense areas (3GPP TS 38.913, 2022).
- **Critical Communications Services (URLLC):** Enabling mission-critical applications requiring guaranteed service levels (5G Americas, 2022).
- **Enhanced Mobile Broadband (eMBB):** Delivering peak data rates up to 20 Gbps for advanced consumer applications (ITU, 2023).
- **Massive Machine-Type Communications (mMTC):** Supporting massive device density up to 1 million devices per square kilometer for IoT devices. (ITU, 2023).
- **Edge Computing Integration:** Distributed network intelligence reducing latency and enabling real-time applications (McKinsey & Company, 2024).

The integration of these capabilities has positioned 5G as more than just a faster mobile network. It serves as a platform for innovation across virtually every industry sector. While consumer applications were the initial focus of deployments, the true transformative power of 5G is emerging through enterprise and industrial applications that leverage its unique capabilities.

Comparative Analysis:
GSM vs. WCDMA vs. LTE vs. 5G

Feature	GSM (2G)	WCDMA (3G)	LTE (4G)	5G
Multiple Access	TDMA/FDMA (Holma & Toskala, 2021)	CDMA (Schulze & Luders, 2021)	OFDMA (DL), SC-FDMA (UL) (Cox, 2021)	OFDMA (DL and UL) (Dahlman et al., 2022)
Core Network	Circuit-switched (Sauter, 2021)	Hybrid circuit/packet (Holma & Toskala, 2021)	All-IP packet-switched (Sesia et al., 2021)	Service-based architecture (Rodriguez, 2023)
Peak Data Rate	9.6 kbps (GPRS: 114 kbps, EDGE: 384 kbps) (Sauter, 2021)	2 Mbps (HSPA+: 42 Mbps) (Toskala & Holma, 2020)	100 Mbps (LTE-A: 1 Gbps) (Dahlman et al., 2021)	20 Gbps (ITU, 2023)
Latency	300-1000 ms (GSMA, 2022)	100-500 ms (Holma & Toskala, 2021)	20-100 ms (Cox, 2021)	1-10 ms (5G Americas, 2022)
Bandwidth	200 kHz (3GPP TS 38.913, 2022)	5 MHz (3GPP TS 38.913, 2022)	Up to 20 MHz (Sesia et al., 2021)	Up to 100 MHz (FR1), 400 MHz (FR2) (3GPP TS 38.913, 2022)
Frequency Bands	900/1800 MHz (Europe/Asia), 850/1900 MHz (Americas) (3GPP TS 38.913, 2022)	850/900/1900/2100 MHz (3GPP TS 38.913, 2022)	600-3500 MHz (over 40 bands) (3GPP TS 38.913, 2022)	600-52600 MHz (over 60 bands) (3GPP TS 38.913, 2022)
Channel Coding	Convolutional codes (Sauter, 2021)	Turbo codes (Holma & Toskala, 2021)	Turbo codes (Cox, 2021)	Polar codes (control), LDPC (data) (Dahlman et al., 2022)
Modulation	GMSK, 8PSK (EDGE) (Sauter, 2021)	QPSK, 16QAM, 64QAM (Holma & Toskala, 2021)	QPSK, 16QAM, 64QAM, 256QAM (Ghosh & Ratasuk, 2019)	QPSK, 16QAM, 64QAM, 256QAM, 1024QAM (Dahlman et al., 2022)
Key Attributes	Voice-centric, basic messaging (GSMA, 2022)	Mobile internet, multimedia (Toskala & Holma, 2020)	High-speed data, complex apps (Johnson, 2022)	Ultra-reliable, massive IoT, extreme throughput (ITU, 2023)
Device Density	Low (Sauter, 2021)	Medium (Holma & Toskala, 2021)	High (Cox, 2021)	Ultra-high (1M/km^2) (ITU, 2023)
Network Architecture	Hierarchical (Sauter, 2021)	Hierarchical (Holma & Toskala, 2021)	Flatter, distributed (Sesia et al., 2021)	Ultra-distributed, edge computing (Rodriguez, 2023)

Feature	GSM (2G)	WCDMA (3G)	LTE (4G)	5G
Mobility Support	250 km/h (GSMA, 2022)	250 km/h (Holma & Toskala, 2021)	350 km/h (Dahlman et al., 2021)	500 km/h (ITU, 2023)
Energy Efficiency	Baseline (GSMA, 2022)	2x improvement (Holma & Toskala, 2021)	5x improvement (Cox, 2021)	10x improvement (Global e-Sustainability Initiative, 2023)
Spectrum Efficiency	0.2 bps/Hz (Sauter, 2021)	0.5 bps/Hz (Schulze & Luders, 2021)	3 bps/Hz (Dahlman et al., 2021)	10 bps/Hz (Dahlman et al., 2022)
Year of First Deployment	1991 (GSMA, 2022)	2001 (Nakamura et al., 2022)	2009 (Ericsson Mobility Report, 2024)	2019 (GSMA Intelligence, 2024)
Primary Driver	Mobile voice (GSMA, 2022)	Mobile data (Toskala & Holma, 2020)	Mobile broadband (Cox, 2021)	Industry transformation (McKinsey & Company, 2024)
Key Application	Voice calls, SMS (GSMA, 2022)	Web browsing, MMS (Holma & Toskala, 2021)	Video streaming, social media (Johnson, 2022)	AR/VR, IoT, mission-critical services (ITU, 2023)

Beyond 5G: The Road to 6G

Even as 5G deployments continue worldwide, research into the next generation of mobile technology is already underway:

Expected Timeline and Technologies

6G: The Next Frontier

- **Expected Timeline:** Commercial deployment around 2030 (ITU, 2023; Nokia Bell Labs, 2024)
- **Potential Technologies:** Terahertz communications, integrated sensing and communications, AI-native networks, orbital networks, holographic communications (Zhang et al., 2023)

Performance Targets

Performance Targets (ITU, 2023; Nokia Bell Labs, 2024):

- Maximum data rates of 1 Tbps
- Minimal Latency below 0.1 ms
- Extreme reliability (99.99999%)

- Three-dimensional coverage, including space
- Zero-energy IoT devices through ambient energy harvesting

Emerging Research Areas

Emerging Research Areas (Zhang et al., 2023; Nokia Bell Labs, 2024):

- Quantum communications integration
- Integrated terrestrial–non-terrestrial networks
- Neuromorphic computing at the network edge
- Sustainable and carbon-neutral network design
- Digital twin networks

Research indicates that **6G will likely represent a fundamental shift from "connected devices" to "intelligent Connectivity,"** with AI capabilities embedded throughout the network fabric rather than residing solely in applications (Zhang et al., 2023). This evolution aims to create truly intelligent networks that can anticipate needs, self-organize, and dynamically allocate resources with minimal human intervention.

Why Telecommunication Technology Matters

The evolution of telecommunications technology has profound implications that extend far beyond the technical specifications:

Economic Impact

Telecommunications have become a fundamental driver of economic growth, contributing approximately **4.5% to global GDP** (World Bank, 2022). 5G implementation alone is projected to produce $13.2 trillion in global economic value by 2035, establishing 22.3 million employment opportunities globally (IHS Markit, 2023). Studies demonstrate that a 10% expansion in mobile broadband adoption results in a 1.5% GDP increase in developed economies and a 2.5% increase in developing countries (World Bank, 2022).

Digital Transformation

Each generation of mobile technology has enabled new business models and transformed industries. **5G serves as the foundation for Industry 4.0**, supporting smart manufacturing, autonomous vehicles, precision agriculture, and intelligent cities (McKinsey & Company, 2024). Industries leveraging 5G technologies could realize **productivity improvements of 20–30%** through automation, remote operations, and predictive maintenance (Accenture, 2024).

Social Connectivity

From connecting families across continents to empowering rural communities with digital access, mobile technologies have redefined social interactions and information accessibility. The **digital divide continues to narrow** with each generation. Research shows that mobile technology has become the **primary means of internet access for 76% of people in developing regions**, making it the most democratizing communications technology in history (United Nations, 2023).

Healthcare Revolution

Remote diagnostics, telemedicine, and connected health monitoring have expanded healthcare access. **5G enables real-time remote surgery and AI-assisted diagnostics**, potentially saving millions of lives (World Health Organization, 2024). Studies suggest that **telecommunications-enabled healthcare services could extend medical coverage to over 1.5 billion people** who currently lack adequate access to health services (WHO, 2024).

Sustainability

Modern telecommunications technology facilitates intelligent power grids, optimized transportation systems, and effective resource management. 5G infrastructure is engineered to achieve 90% greater energy efficiency per data unit compared to 4G systems, supporting climate change reduction initiatives (Global e-Sustainability Initiative, 2023). Telecommunications solutions have the potential to decrease worldwide carbon emissions by up to 20% by 2030 through enhanced operational efficiencies across various industries (Global e-Sustainability Initiative, 2023).

Innovation Acceleration

The telecommunications infrastructure serves as the **nervous system for innovation ecosystems** (Accenture, 2024). Each generation has spawned new applications, services, and capabilities that were previously unimaginable. The innovation cycle has accelerated with each generation of mobile technology, with the time between conception and mass-market deployment decreasing from decades to mere months (GSMA Intelligence, 2024).

Conclusion: Continuous Evolution

The journey from wireline to 5G represents one of humanity's most remarkable technological achievements. This evolution continues at an accelerating pace, with each generation building upon the foundations of its predecessors while introducing revolutionary capabilities.

As we move from 5G toward 6G and beyond, **telecommunications will increasingly blend with computing, sensing, and artificial intelligence** to create a seamless digital infrastructure that underpins virtually every aspect of human activity (Zhang et al., 2023). The implications of this continued evolution will **reshape economies, societies, and human potential** in ways we are only beginning to understand.

The telecommunications revolution is far from complete. **It is, in many ways, just beginning.**

Knowledge Check

1. Which mobile generation first introduced digital transmission techniques?
   a) 1G
   b) 2G
   c) 3G
   d) 4G

2. What was the primary driving factor for the transition from 3G to 4G?
   a) Need for higher voice quality
   b) Requirement for text messaging capabilities
   c) The need for faster speeds and reduced response times
   d) International roaming capabilities

3. Which frequency range is associated with millimeter wave (mmWave) technology in 5G?
   a) 600-900 MHz
   b) 1.8-2.6 GHz
   c) 3.3-4.2 GHz
   d) 24-40 GHz

4. What download speed can 5G networks theoretically achieve at their upper limit?
   a) 100 Mbps
   b) 1 Gbps
   c) 10 Gbps
   d) 20 Gbps

5. Which technology was first introduced in LTE-Advanced and significantly improved data rates?
   a) MIMO
   b) Carrier Aggregation
   c) OFDMA
   d) Beamforming

6. WCDMA (3G) uses Time Division Multiple Access (TDMA) as its primary channel access method. (True/False)

7. Explain how the core network architecture evolved from GSM (2G) to 5G, and why this evolution was necessary.

8. Describe the three main usage scenarios that 5G was designed to address and how they differ from previous generations.

9. Explain why the telecommunications industry is already researching 6G technology even as 5G deployments are still ongoing. What limitations of 5G might 6G address?

10. Match each mobile generation with its primary design focus:
    - 2G: __________
    - 3G: __________
    - 4G: __________
    - 5G: __________

    Options:

    - Voice communications
    - Mobile internet
    - Mobile broadband
    - Service enablement

Answers

1. Which mobile generation first introduced digital transmission techniques?
   Answer: b) 2G
   2G (GSM) was the first generation to use digital transmission, replacing the analog systems of 1G.

2. What was the primary driving factor for the transition from 3G to 4G?
   Answer: c) **The need for faster speeds and reduced response times**
   Engineers created fourth-generation technology primarily because users were consuming increasingly data-heavy content on their mobile devices. Applications like video streaming and other bandwidth-hungry services were becoming mainstream, and the existing 3G infrastructure couldn't adequately support this surge in mobile broadband usage. The industry needed networks that could deliver substantially higher throughput while also minimizing delays in data transmission.

   .

3. Which frequency range is associated with millimeter wave (mmWave) technology in 5G?
   Answer: d) 24-40 GHz
   mmWave frequencies in 5G typically operate in the 24-40 GHz range, with some deployments extending up to 52.6 GHz.

4. What download speed can 5G networks theoretically achieve at their upper limit?
   Answer: d) 20 Gbps
   5G specifications define a peak theoretical downlink speed of 20 Gbps under ideal conditions

5. Which technology was first introduced in LTE-Advanced and significantly improved data rates?
   Answer: b) Carrier Aggregation
   While MIMO and OFDMA were introduced in basic LTE, Carrier Aggregation was a key LTE-Advanced feature that allowed combining multiple carriers for higher data rates.

6. WCDMA (3G) uses Time Division Multiple Access (TDMA) as its primary channel access method. (True/False)
   Answer: False
   WCDMA (Wideband Code Division Multiple Access) uses CDMA, not TDMA, as its primary channel access method.

7. Explain how the core network architecture evolved from GSM (2G) to 5G, and why this evolution was necessary.
   Answer: The core network evolved from circuit-switched architecture in 2G (separate voice and data paths) to increasingly packet-switched architectures. 3G introduced partial packet switching, 4G moved to an all-IP network (EPC - Evolved Packet Core), and 5G introduced a service-based architecture (SBA) with network function virtualization (NFV) and software-defined networking (SDN). This shift enabled higher data demands, flexible service deployment, lower latency, better scalability, and network slicing to support diverse use cases.

8. Describe the three main usage scenarios that 5G was designed to address and how they differ from previous generations.
   Answer: When engineers designed 5G networks, they targeted three distinct categories of applications, each addressing different technological needs:
   Advanced Mobile Broadband (eMBB): This scenario focuses on delivering extremely fast data rates to end users. It essentially takes what 4G began—providing high-speed mobile internet—and pushes those capabilities significantly further.
   Ultra-Reliable Low-Latency Communications (URLLC): This use case targets time-sensitive applications where failure isn't an option. Systems built on URLLC requirements must achieve response times under one millisecond while maintaining 99.999% reliability—performance levels that introduce entirely new possibilities for mobile networks.
   Massive Machine-Type Communications (mMTC): This scenario enables networks to handle enormous numbers of connected devices simultaneously. The specification calls for supporting up to one million IoT endpoints within a single square kilometer, a density requirement that earlier standards never contemplated.
   The fundamental difference between 5G and its predecessors lies in scope. Earlier cellular technologies concentrated primarily on enabling people to communicate with each

other through voice calls and data services. Fifth-generation networks expand this paradigm substantially, creating infrastructure that supports both extensive machine-to-machine connectivity and applications where split-second timing and near-perfect reliability become essential requirements.

9. Explain why the telecommunications industry is already researching 6G technology even as 5G deployments are still ongoing. What limitations of 5G might 6G address?

   Answer: The industry researches next-generation technology 10-15 years before deployment to ensure technological readiness. 6G research addresses potential 5G limitations, including:

   1. Energy efficiency (5G's high power consumption)
   2. True global coverage (integrating terrestrial, satellite, and aerial networks)
   3. AI-native architecture (versus 5G's AI-enhanced approach)
   4. Terahertz frequencies for even higher data rates (up to 1 Tbps)
   5. Enhanced sensing and positioning capabilities (centimeter-level accuracy)
   6. Support for holographic communications and digital twins
   7. Improved sustainability and carbon footprint

   This continuous innovation cycle ensures the industry can meet future demands that may exceed 5G's capabilities.

10. Match each mobile generation with its primary design focus:

    Answer:

    2G: Voice communications

    3G: Mobile internet

    4G: Mobile broadband

    5G: Service enablement

References

3GPP. (2021). System architecture for the 5G system: Stage 2 (TS 23.501 version 16.7.0). 3rd Generation Partnership Project.

3GPP TS 38.913. (2022). Study on scenarios and requirements for next generation access technologies. 3rd Generation Partnership Project.

5G Americas. (2022). *5G technology evolution recommendations*. 5G Americas White Paper.

Accenture. (2024). Accelerating innovation through connected technologies. Accenture Strategy.

Cisco Visual Networking Index. (2020). *Global mobile data traffic forecast update, 2019–2024*. Cisco Systems.

Cox, C. (2021). An introduction to LTE: LTE, LTE-Advanced, SAE, VoLTE and 4G mobile communications (3rd ed.). Wiley.

Dahlman, E., Parkvall, S., & Skold, J. (2021). *4G: LTE and LTE-Advanced for mobile broadband* (3rd ed.). Academic Press.

Dahlman, E., Parkvall, S., & Skold, J. (2022). *5G NR: The next generation wireless access technology* (2nd ed.). Academic Press.

Dahlman, E., Parkvall, S., & Skold, J. (2023). *Evolution of mobile communications: 1G to 5G.* IEEE Communications Standards Magazine, 7(1), 24-31.

Ericsson Mobility Report. (2024). *Ericsson mobility report*. Ericsson AB.

Ghosh, A., & Ratasuk, R. (2019). *Essentials of LTE and LTE-A*. Cambridge University Press.

Global e-Sustainability Initiative. (2023). SMARTer 2030: ICT solutions for 21st century challenges. GeSI.

Goldsmith, A. (2021). *Wireless communications* (3rd ed.). Cambridge University Press.

GSMA. (2022). *The mobile economy*. GSM Association.

GSMA Intelligence. (2023). *The mobile economy 2023*. GSM Association.

GSMA Intelligence. (2024). *Global mobile trends 2024*. GSM Association.

Holma, H., & Toskala, A. (2021). *WCDMA for UMTS: HSPA evolution and LTE* (6th ed.). Wiley.

IHS Markit. (2023). The 5G economy: How 5G will contribute to the global economy. IHS Markit Ltd.

ITU. (2023). IMT vision – Framework and overall objectives of the future development of IMT for 2030 and beyond. International Telecommunication Union.

Johnson, C. (2022). *Long Term Evolution in bullets* (3rd ed.). CreateSpace Independent Publishing Platform.

Mahonen, P., Petrova, M., & Riihijarvi, J. (2021). *Network economics of 5G*. IEEE Communications Magazine, 59(3), 91-97.

McKinsey & Company. (2024). *Connected world: 5G and the transformation of industry*. McKinsey Global Institute.

Nakamura, T., Nagata, S., & Takahashi, H. (2022). *5G evolution and 6G*. NTT DOCOMO Technical Journal, 23(3), 4-15.

Nokia Bell Labs. (2024). 6G technologies: Delivering the next generation of communications. Nokia Corporation.

Penttinen, J. (2022). The telecommunications handbook: Engineering guidelines for fixed, mobile and satellite systems. Wiley.

Poikselkä, M., & Mayer, G. (2019). *The IMS: IP multimedia concepts and services* (4th ed.). Wiley.

Rappaport, T. S. (2022). *Wireless communications: Principles and practice* (3rd ed.). Prentice Hall.

Rodriguez, J. (2023). Fundamentals of 5G mobile networks. Wiley.

Sauter, M. (2021). From GSM to LTE-Advanced Pro and 5G: An introduction to mobile networks and mobile broadband (4th ed.). Wiley.

Schulze, H., & Luders, C. (2021). Theory and applications of OFDM and CDMA: Wideband wireless communications. Wiley.

Sesia, S., Toufik, I., & Baker, M. (2021). *LTE - The UMTS long term evolution: From theory to practice* (3rd ed.). Wiley.

Stallings, W. (2023). *Wireless communications and networks* (3rd ed.). Pearson.

Toskala, A., & Holma, H. (2020). *UMTS networks: Architecture, mobility and services* (5th ed.). Wiley.

United Nations. (2023). *The state of broadband: Broadband catalyzing sustainable development*. Broadband Commission for Sustainable Development.

World Bank. (2022). *World development report: Digital dividends*. The World Bank Group.

World Health Organization. (2024). Global strategy on digital health 2020-2025. WHO.

Zhang, Z., Xiao, Y., Ma, Y., & Zhang, P. (2023). *6G wireless networks: Vision, requirements, architecture, and key technologies*. IEEE Vehicular Technology Magazine, 14(3), 28-41.

Chapter 3: LTE and 5G Protocol Architectures

Executive Summary

This chapter examines the protocol structures underlying LTE and 5G wireless systems, offering detailed insights into how these technologies differ at a fundamental level. The analysis focuses particularly on how fourth-generation networks relied on conventional point-to-point interface designs, while fifth-generation systems introduced a revolutionary service-oriented architecture that changed how network components interact.

The discussion explores both control plane and user plane protocols comprehensively, revealing the significant innovations that 5G brought to the table. Among these advances are entirely new protocol layers—notably the SDAP (Service Data Adaptation Protocol)—alongside the migration toward cloud-native network implementations. The material traces the architectural evolution from 4G's EPC (Evolved Packet Core) infrastructure to the 5GC (5G Core), examining how technologies like NFV (Network Function Virtualization) and SDN (Software-Defined Networking) became integral components of the fifth-generation framework.

Additionally, the chapter investigates the advanced QoS (Quality of Service) mechanisms that allow 5G systems to flexibly support vastly different application demands. These include eMBB (enhanced mobile broadband) for high-speed data services, mMTC (massive machine-type communications) for IoT device connectivity, and URLLC (ultra-reliable low-latency communications) for time-critical applications. Through this examination, the material illustrates how the architectural innovations in 5G represent a major leap forward in creating infrastructure capable of supporting widespread digital transformation across both industrial sectors and society at large.

Table of Contents

Introduction

Mobile networking has undergone dramatic changes as the industry moved from 4G LTE systems to 5G technology. This transition goes far beyond simple performance upgrades—it represents a complete reimagining of how cellular networks are structured, how they scale to meet demand, and how they provide services to users. For professionals working in wireless communications, whether as engineers, researchers, or industry specialists, grasping these structural differences is essential for navigating today's complex telecommunications environment.

The shift from LTE to fifth-generation networks involved sweeping transformations across protocol design, network structure, and how services reach end users. Fourth-generation technology laid important groundwork by creating all-IP mobile infrastructure through its EPC (Evolved Packet Core) and streamlined radio access systems. Fifth-generation technology builds on this foundation while introducing transformative concepts like service-oriented architecture, network slicing capabilities, and cloud-native design philosophies. These advances deliver previously unattainable levels of flexibility, scalability, and performance, enabling applications that extend well beyond conventional mobile internet access.

This chapter delves into how LTE and 5G systems structure their protocols, analyzing the fundamental components, interfaces, and operational workflows of each generation. The examination spans the entire network stack—from radio access infrastructure through transport layers to core network elements. Particular emphasis falls on the groundbreaking architectural innovations that define 5G, such as separating control and user planes into distinct layers, incorporating virtualization technologies throughout the infrastructure, and embracing cloud-native design principles that fundamentally alter how networks are architected, deployed, and managed.

LTE Protocol Architecture

Control Plane Architecture

The control plane architecture in LTE networks orchestrates all signaling procedures necessary for establishing, maintaining, and releasing connections between user equipment and the network infrastructure. This sophisticated signaling framework ensures seamless connectivity, mobility management, and service delivery across the entire network ecosystem.

Protocol Stack Organization

The LTE control plane implements a layered protocol structure that facilitates communication between different network elements. Between the User Equipment (UE) and evolved NodeB (eNB), the protocol stack comprises multiple specialized layers, each serving specific functions:

LTE Control Plane Protocol Stack

(3GPP TS 36.300, TS 36.331) [1,2]

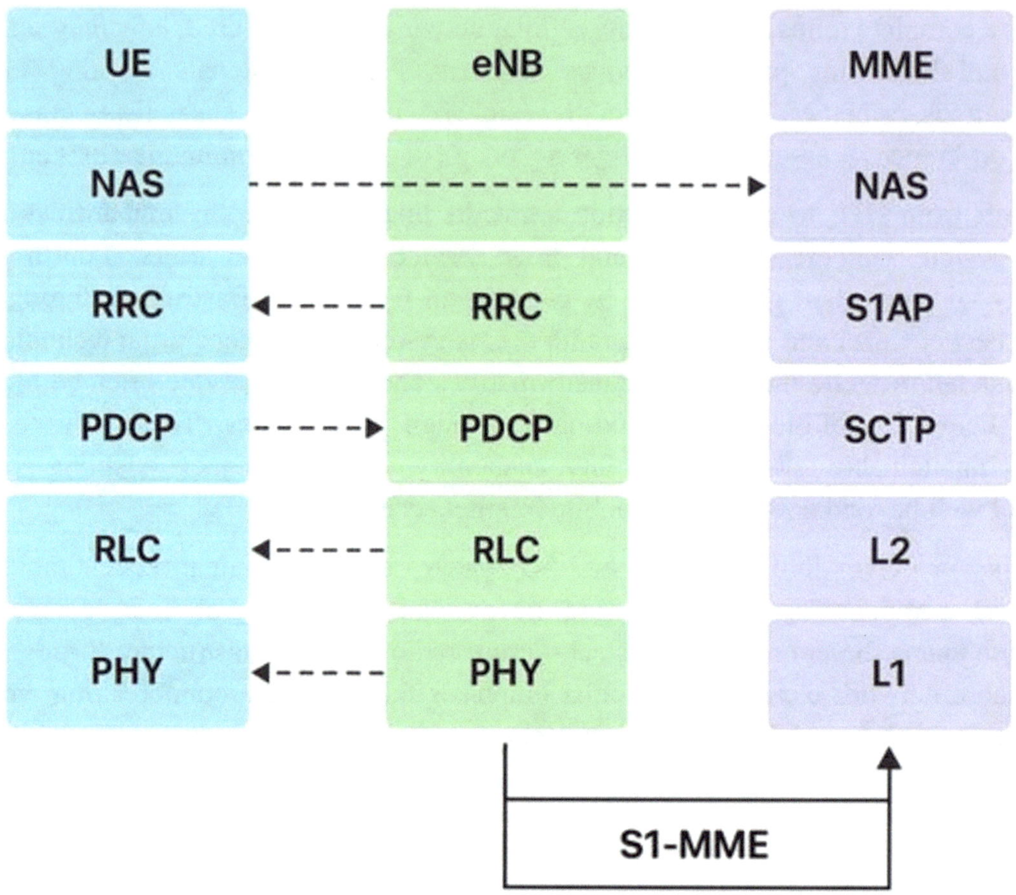

Protocol Layer Functions (3GPP TS 36.300) [1]:

- NAS: Non-Access Stratum (mobility management,manaement
- RRC: Radio Resource Control (connection management, measurement control)
- RLC: Radio Link Contrrol (segmentation, ARQ)
- MAC: Medium Access Control (scheduling, HARQ)
- PHY: Physical Layer (modulation, coding, MIMO)

Interface Protocols

- **S1-MME:** S1 Application Protocol (S1AP) over SCTP/IP (TS 36.413) [5]

- **Uu:** Radio interface between UE and eNB (TS 36.300) [1]

Layer Descriptions

The **Physical Layer (Layer 1)** manages the fundamental radio transmission characteristics, including modulation schemes, resource allocation, and signal processing. This layer adapts dynamically to channel conditions, optimizing spectral efficiency while maintaining reliable communication links.

The **Medium Access Control (MAC)** layer manages access to shared spectrum resources, utilizing advanced scheduling algorithms that achieve an optimal balance between fairness and performance. The MAC layer additionally controls Hybrid Automatic Repeat Request (HARQ) operations, guaranteeing dependable data transmission through swift retransmission protocols.

The **Radio Link Control (RLC)** layer delivers segmentation and reassembly functions, adjusting upper-layer packets to match the transmission capabilities of underlying layers. RLC operates through three distinct modes: Transparent Mode (TM), Unacknowledged Mode (UM), and Acknowledged Mode (AM). Each mode is tailored for particular service demands.

The **Packet Data Convergence Protocol (PDCP)** layer executes essential security operations, encompassing encryption and data integrity verification. Furthermore, PDCP employs header compression methods, substantially minimizing overhead for IP-based communications, proving especially advantageous for voice applications.

The **Radio Resource Control (RRC)** protocol functions as the central control framework, overseeing all elements of radio connectivity. RRC operations include connection initialization, reconfiguration, measurement coordination, and mobility control, establishing the foundation of LTE's control plane functionality.

User Plan Architecture

LTE User Plane Protocol Stack

(3GPP TS 36.300, TS 23.401) [1,3]

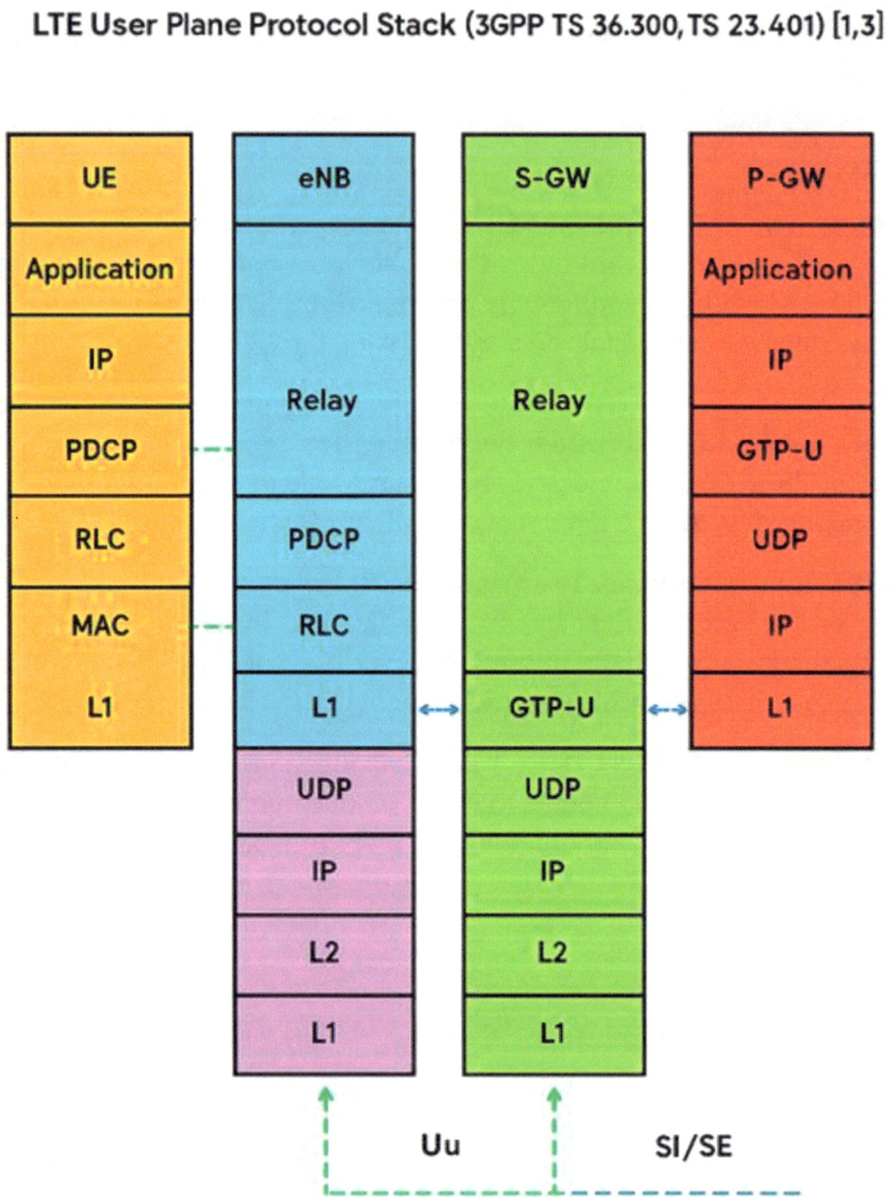

Key Protocols (3GPP TS 23.401, TS 29.281) [3,4]

- **GTP-U:** GPRS Tunneling Protocol User Plane (TS 29.281)
- **S1-U:** User plane network interface between eNB and S-GW
- **S5/S8:** Network Interface between S-GW and P-GW (S5 for non-roaming, S8 for roaming)
- **Uu:** Radio interface for user data (TS 36.300)

At the network level, the GPRS Tunneling Protocol User Plane (GTP-U) encapsulates user data for transport across the core network. GTP-U creates tunnels between network elements, enabling mobility while maintaining session continuity. The protocol operates over UDP/IP, providing lightweight encapsulation with minimal overhead.

Bearer Architecture

LTE implements an EPS (Evolved Packet System) bearer model that provides end-to-end connectivity with defined quality characteristics. Default bearers establish basic connectivity with best-effort service, while dedicated bearers support specific quality requirements for applications demanding guaranteed performance.

Each bearer comprises a radio bearer between the User Device (UE) and LTE eNB, and S1 bearers connecting the eNB to the core network. This concatenation creates an end-to-end path with consistent quality treatment, enforced through traffic flow templates and quality class identifiers.

Core Network (EPC) Architecture

The Evolved Packet Core represents a significant departure from previous mobile core architectures, implementing an all-IP design optimized for packet data services. The EPC architecture separates control and user plane functions across specialized network elements.

LTE EPC Architecture (3GPP TS 23.401) [3]

LTE EPC Architecture (3GPP TS 23.401) [3]

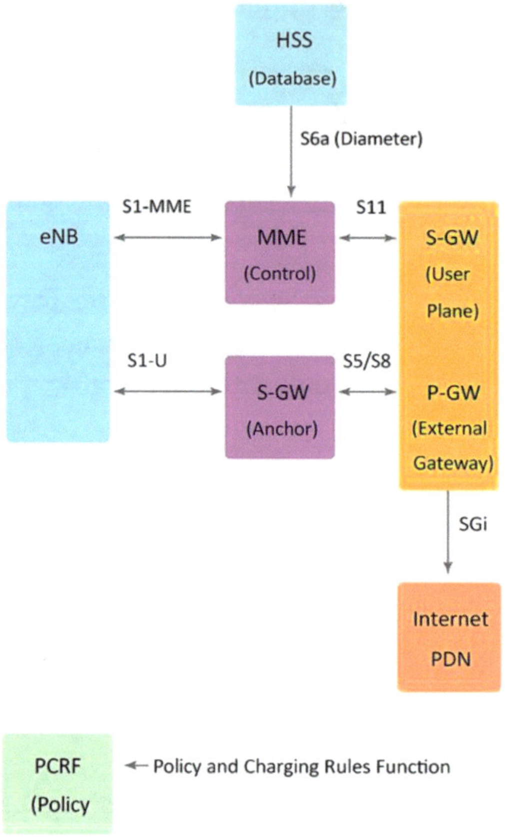

Network Element Functions (3GPP TS 23.401) [3]:

- **MME:** Mobility Management Entity (NAS security, bearer control)
- **S-GW:** Serving Gateway (mobility anchor, lawful intercept)
- **P-GW:** PDN Gateway (IP allocation, policy enforcement)
- **HSS:** Home Subscriber Server (user profiles, authentication)
- **PCRF:** Policy and Charging Rules Function (QoS, charging)

Interface Protocols:

- **S1-MME:** S1AP over SCTP Protocol (TS 36.413) [5]
- **S1-U:** GTP-U over UDP Protocol (TS 29.281) [4]
- **S6a:** Diameter Protocol (TS 29.272) [6]
- **S11:** GTPv2-C Protocol (TS 29.274) [7]
- **Gx:** Diameter Protocol (TS 29.212) [31]

Mobility Management Entity (MME)

The MME serves as the primary control plane element in the EPC, managing all signaling related to mobility and session management. Key responsibilities include authentication coordination with the Home Subscriber Server (HSS), mobility management through tracking area updates and paging, and session management for bearer establishment and modification.

The MME implements sophisticated algorithms for load balancing and redundancy, ensuring high availability for critical control functions. Network operators typically deploy MMEs in pools, enabling dynamic load distribution and seamless failover capabilities.

Serving Gateway (S-GW)

The S-GW serves as the user plane termination point for mobility management within the LTE infrastructure. Positioned at the core network perimeter, the S-GW controls user plane traffic redirection during handoffs, enables authorized monitoring capabilities, and accumulates usage data for subscriber accounting.

During inter-eNB handovers, the S-GW buffers downlink packets, preventing data loss during the mobility event. This buffering capability, combined with optimized forwarding mechanisms, ensures service continuity even during rapid mobility scenarios.

Packet Data Network Gateway (P-GW)

The P-GW delivers access to external data networks, operating as the connection point for user traffic flows. Essential operations include IP address assignment, policy implementation according to user profiles, and data screening for security applications.

The P-GW implements sophisticated quality of service mechanisms, mapping between LTE bearers and IP-layer differentiated services. This mapping enables consistent quality treatment across heterogeneous networks, supporting end-to-end service delivery.

Home Subscriber Server (HSS)

The HSS maintains the main database of subscriber information, including authentication credentials, service profiles, and mobility management data. This centralized repository ensures consistent service delivery regardless of the subscriber's location within the network.

Modern HSS implementations utilize distributed database technologies, providing geographic redundancy and high transaction rates necessary for large-scale deployments. The HSS interfaces with multiple network elements through standardized Diameter protocols, ensuring interoperability across vendor equipment.

Radio Access Network Architecture

Fourth-generation systems introduced a radio access component known as E-UTRAN (Evolved Universal Terrestrial Radio Access Network), which adopted a flattened structural design that differed significantly from earlier cellular generations. This architectural approach minimized delay, enhanced operational efficiency, and made network administration more straightforward.

LTE E-UTRAN Architecture (3GPP TS 36.300) [1]

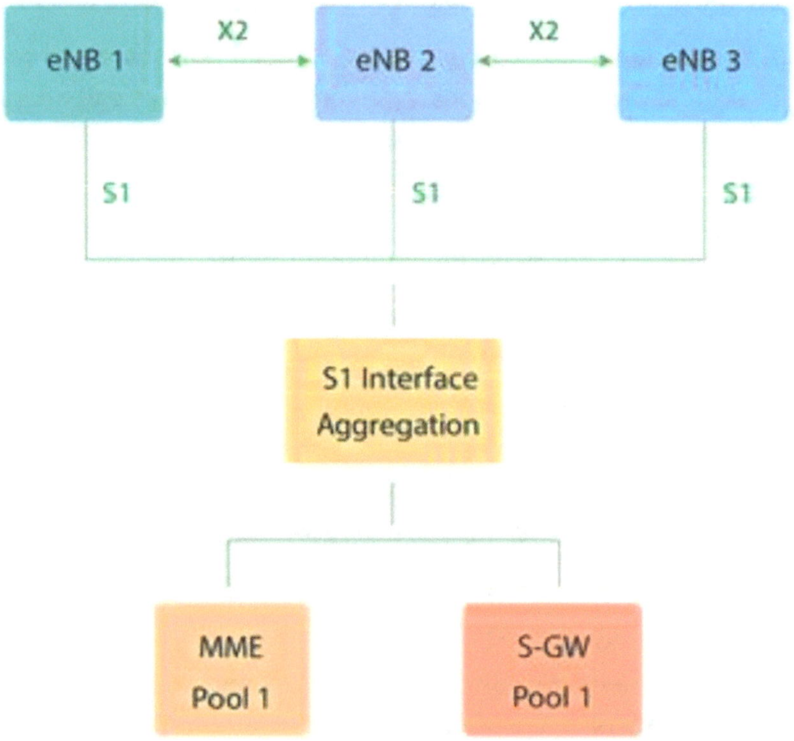

Key Interfaces (3GPP Specifications):

- **Uu:** Radio interface between UE and eNB (TS 36.300) [1]
- **X2:** Interface between eNBs (TS 36.420 for X2AP) [8]
    - **X2-C:** Control plane (X2AP)
    - **X2-U:** User plane (GTP-U)
- **S1:** Interface between eNB and EPC (TS 36.410) [9]
    - **S1-MME:** Control plane (S1AP)
    - **S1-U:** User plane (GTP-U)

eNB Functions (TS 36.300) [1]:

- Radio Resource Management Function
- Radio Bearer Control Function
- Connection Mobility Control Function
- Dynamic Resource Allocation Function
- Load Balancing Function
- Inter-Cell Interference Coordination Function

eNodeB Architecture

The eNodeB integrates all radio access network functions into a single logical element, eliminating the separate radio network controller found in previous architectures. This integration enables faster decision-making for resource allocation, scheduling, and mobility management.

Each eNodeB comprises multiple functional blocks, including radio frequency components, baseband processing units, and control processors. Modern implementations leverage virtualization technologies, enabling flexible resource allocation and improved hardware utilization.

Inter-eNB Connectivity

The X2 interface enables direct communication between neighboring eNodeBs, supporting distributed coordination functions. This peer-to-peer architecture facilitates rapid handovers, interference coordination, and load balancing without requiring core network involvement.

X2 connectivity utilizes both control plane (X2-C) and user plane (X2-U) protocols. The control plane facilitates signaling communication for mobility management and resource allocation, while the user plane provides direct data transmission during handover operations.

Radio Resource Management

LTE radio resource management implements sophisticated algorithms for optimal spectrum utilization. Dynamic scheduling adapts resource allocation every millisecond based on channel conditions, traffic demands, and quality requirements.

Advanced features include coordinated multipoint transmission (CoMP), which enables multiple cells to jointly serve users at cell edges, and enhanced inter-cell interference coordination (eICIC), which manages interference through coordinated resource allocation across cells.

Transport Network Design

The transport network provides connectivity between LTE network elements, implementing various technologies to meet stringent performance requirements. Modern deployments utilize a combination of fiber optic, microwave, and packet-based transport technologies.

Backhaul Architecture

LTE backhaul networks must support high bandwidth, low latency, and precise synchronization requirements. Fiber optic connections provide ideal characteristics but may not be feasible for all sites. Microwave links offer flexibility for difficult-to-reach locations, while packet-based technologies enable statistical multiplexing gains.

The backhaul architecture implements quality of service mechanisms to prioritize different traffic types. Control plane signaling receives the highest priority, followed by real-time services and best-effort data. This differentiation ensures consistent performance across varying load conditions.

Synchronization Requirements

LTE networks require precise frequency and phase synchronization for optimal performance. Time Division Duplex (TDD) deployments demand microsecond-level phase accuracy, while Frequency Division Duplex (FDD) systems primarily require frequency synchronization.

Various synchronization methods support these requirements, including GPS-based timing, IEEE 1588v2 Precision Time Protocol, and Synchronous Ethernet. Network designs often implement multiple methods for redundancy and reliability.

5G Protocol Architecture

Control Plane Architecture

The 5G control plane architecture represents a fundamental reimagining of mobile network design, introducing service-based principles that transform how network functions interact and operate. This revolutionary approach enables unprecedented flexibility, scalability, and service customization capabilities.

Service-Based Architecture (SBA)

5G Service-Based Architecture (Control Plane)

(3GPP TS 23.501) [10]

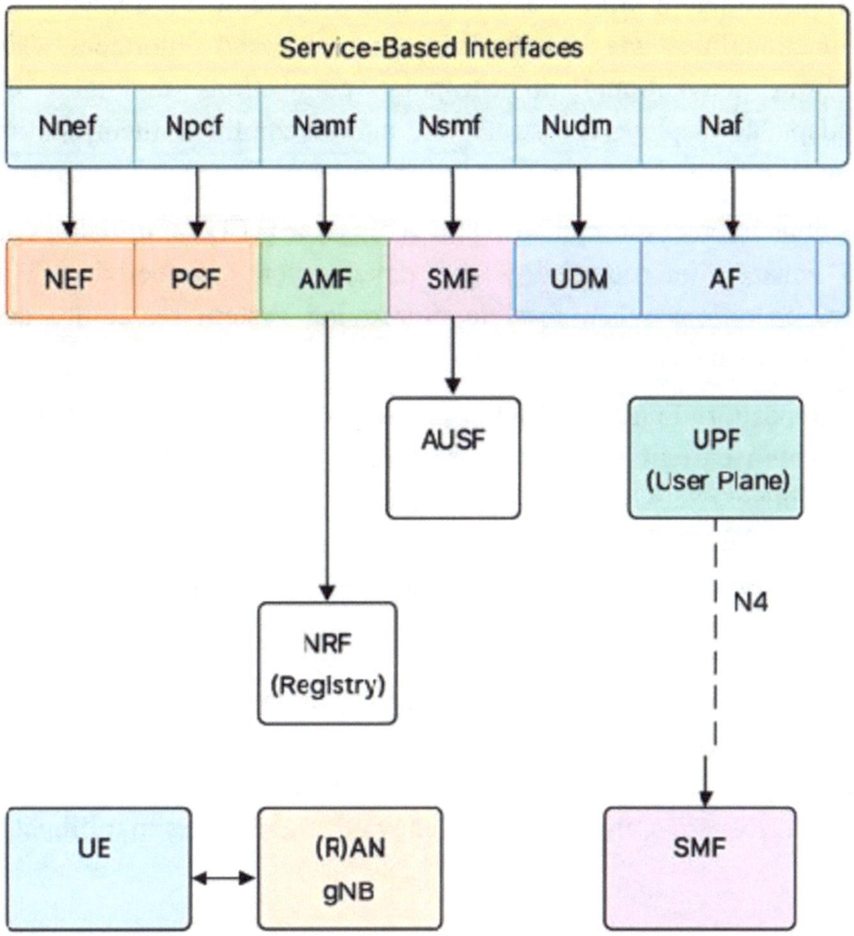

Network Functions (3GPP TS 23.501, TS 23.502) [10,11]:

- **AMF:** Access and Mobility Management Function
- **SMF:** Session Management Function
- **UPF:** User Plane Function
- **PCF:** Policy Control Function
- **UDM:** Unified Data Management
- **UDR:** Unified Data Repository
- **AUSF:** Authentication Server Function
- **NEF:** Network Exposure Function
- **NRF:** Network Repository Function
- **AF:** Application Function
- **NSSF:** Network Slice Selection Function

Service-Based Interfaces (TS 29.500 series) [12]:

- HTTP/2 with JSON encoding
- RESTful API design
- OAuth 2.0 for authorization

The 5G core infrastructure utilizes a service-oriented architecture where network functions present their functionalities via standardized service-based interfaces. This architectural transformation from conventional point-to-point connections facilitates dynamic service identification, adaptable deployment strategies, and streamlined incorporation of additional network functions.

Network functions interact through RESTful APIs over HTTP/2, utilizing contemporary web technologies to enhance interoperability and development productivity. This methodology supports stateless operations when feasible, improving system scalability and dependability through reduced state management complexity.

The Network Repository Function (NRF) operates as the primary service registry for function discovery, maintaining current information regarding accessible network functions and their operational capabilities. Network functions register their offerings with the NRF during initialization and continuously update their operational status, supporting adaptable network configurations and automatic recovery procedures.

Enhanced Protocol Stack

The 5G radio protocol stack builds upon LTE foundations while introducing significant enhancements. The physical layer supports flexible numerology, enabling adaptation to diverse frequency bands and service requirements. Multiple subcarrier spacings allow optimization for different deployment scenarios, from low-frequency coverage layers to millimeter-wave capacity deployments.

5G NR Control Plane Protocol Stack
(3GPP TS 38.300) [13]

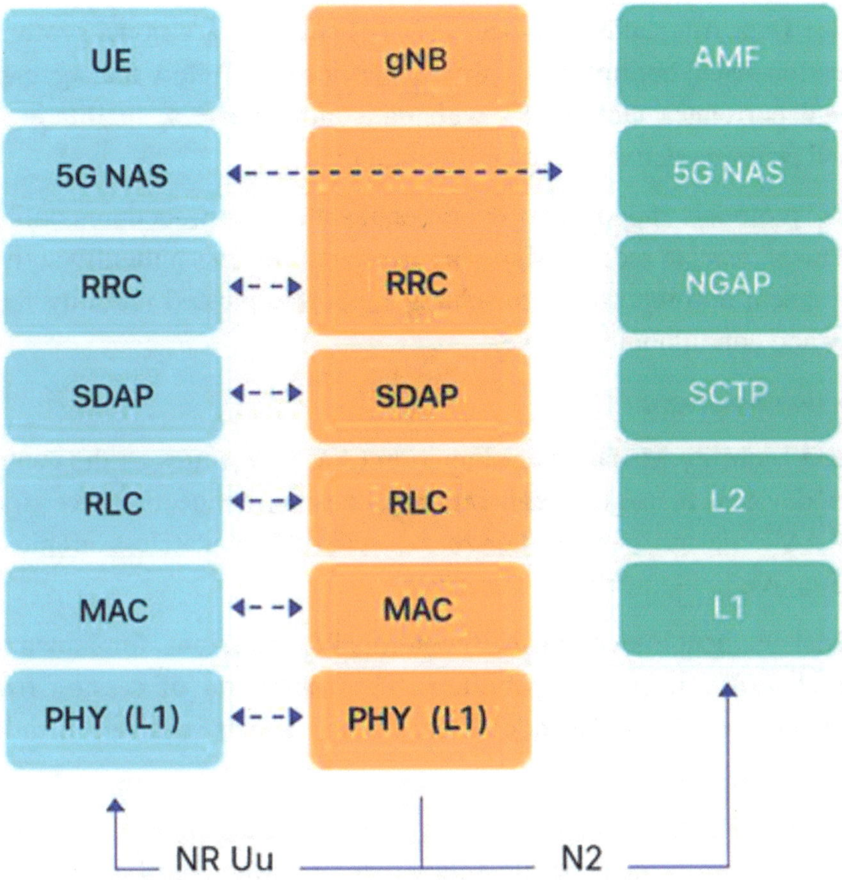

Key Enhancements from LTE (TS 38.300, TS 38.331) [13,14]:

- **SDAP: Service Data Adaptation Protocol (New Layer):**
  - QoS flow to DRB mapping (TS 37.324) [15]
  - Reflective QoS support
- **RRC Enhancements:**
  - RRC_INACTIVE state
  - Conditional handover
  - On-demand SI
- **PDCP Enhancements:**
  - 256-bit security keys
  - Packet duplication for URLLC
- **PHY Enhancements:**
  - Flexible numerology (15, 30, 60, 120, 240 kHz)
  - Massive MIMO support

Interface Protocols:

- **N2:** NG Application Protocol (NGAP) over SCTP (TS 38.413) [32]
- **NR Uu:** 5G NR radio interface (TS 38.300) [13]

The 5G Service Data Adaptation Protocol (SDAP) constitutes a novel protocol layer addition to the communication stack, controlling quality of service (QoS) flow management within the 5G framework. SDAP correlates QoS flows with data radio bearers, facilitating precise service differentiation and enabling network slicing functionalities.

Enhanced RRC protocols support new operational states and procedures optimized for 5G use cases. The RRC Inactive state reduces signaling overhead for intermittently active devices, while enhanced measurement and reporting procedures support advanced mobility features, including dual connectivity and conditional handover.

Network Function Architecture

The Access and Mobility Management Function (AMF) operates as the central control plane gateway for user devices, managing registration processes, connection oversight, and mobility operations. The AMF design enables horizontal scaling via stateless architecture principles, supporting cloud-native implementation strategies.

The Session Management Function (SMF) controls PDU sessions, implementing sophisticated policy control and traffic steering capabilities. The separation of session management from mobility management enables independent scaling and specialized optimization for different service types.

The Policy Control Function (PCF) delivers a consolidated policy management framework throughout the network, enabling dynamic policy determination based on current network status, user profiles, and service demands. The PCF communicates with application functions via the Network Exposure Function (NEF), facilitating application-informed network optimization.

User Plane Architecture

Fifth-generation networks feature a user plane design that introduces groundbreaking capabilities for handling varied service demands while preserving both operational efficiency and the ability to scale. This structural framework makes possible network slicing functionality, edge computing integration, and communications with extremely minimal delay.

5G User Plane Protocol Stack (3GPP TS 38.300) [13]

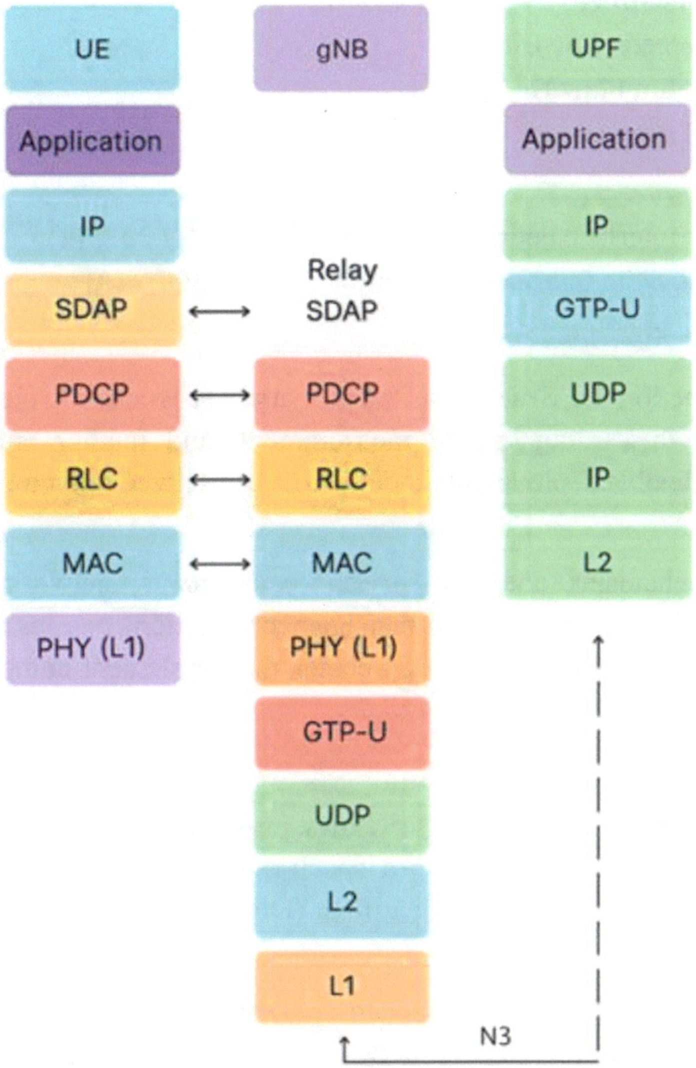

5G QoS Architecture (3GPP TS 23.501) [10]:

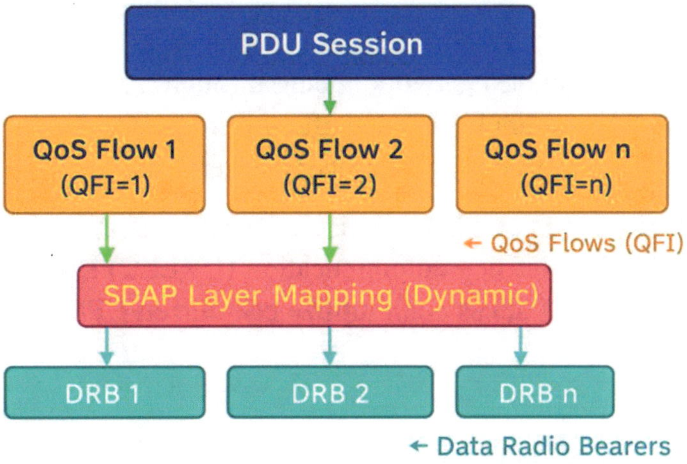

QoS Parameters (TS 23.501) [10]:

- **5QI:** 5G QoS Identifier
- **GFBR:** Guaranteed Flow Bit Rate
- **MFBR:** Maximum Flow Bit Rate
- Reflective QoS support

Key Interfaces:

- **N3:** User plane interface between gNB and UPF (TS 29.281) [4]
- **NR Uu:** 5G NR radio interface for user data (TS 38.300) [13]

Flexible User Plane Functions

The User Plane Function (UPF) serves as the primary data processing element in 5G networks, implementing packet forwarding, traffic measurement, and quality enforcement. The UPF architecture supports flexible deployment models, from centralized implementations to distributed edge deployments.

UPF selection mechanisms consider service requirements, network topology, and load conditions to optimize data paths. Session management functions can instantiate multiple UPFs for a single session, creating service function chains that implement complex traffic processing requirements.

QoS Flow Architecture

5G replaces LTE's bearer concept with QoS flows, providing more granular and flexible quality differentiation. Each QoS flow represents a specific service data flow with defined quality characteristics, identified by QoS Flow Identifiers (QFI) that map to standardized or operator-specific quality profiles.

The SDAP layer manages QoS delivery to data radio bearer mapping, enabling dynamic quality adjustment based on radio conditions and network load. Reflective QoS mechanisms allow the network to signal QoS requirements implicitly through downlink packet marking, reducing signaling overhead for symmetric flows.

Network Slicing Support

The user plane architecture enables network slicing through isolated data paths and dedicated network functions. Each slice can implement specific user plane topologies, quality policies, and traffic processing functions optimized for its service requirements.

Slice-specific UPF deployments enable traffic isolation and customized processing for different service types. Ultra-reliable low-latency communication (URLLC) slices might deploy UPFs at network edges, while massive IoT slices could utilize centralized UPFs with optimized signaling procedures.

Core Network (5GC) Architecture

The 5G Core represents a complete architectural transformation from previous generations, implementing cloud-native principles, service-based interfaces, and support for diverse deployment models. This architecture enables network operators to leverage modern IT technologies while meeting stringent telecommunications requirements.

5G Core Network Architecture (Complete View) (3GPP TS 23.501) [10]

5G Core Network Architecture (Complete View) (3GPP TS 23.501) [10]

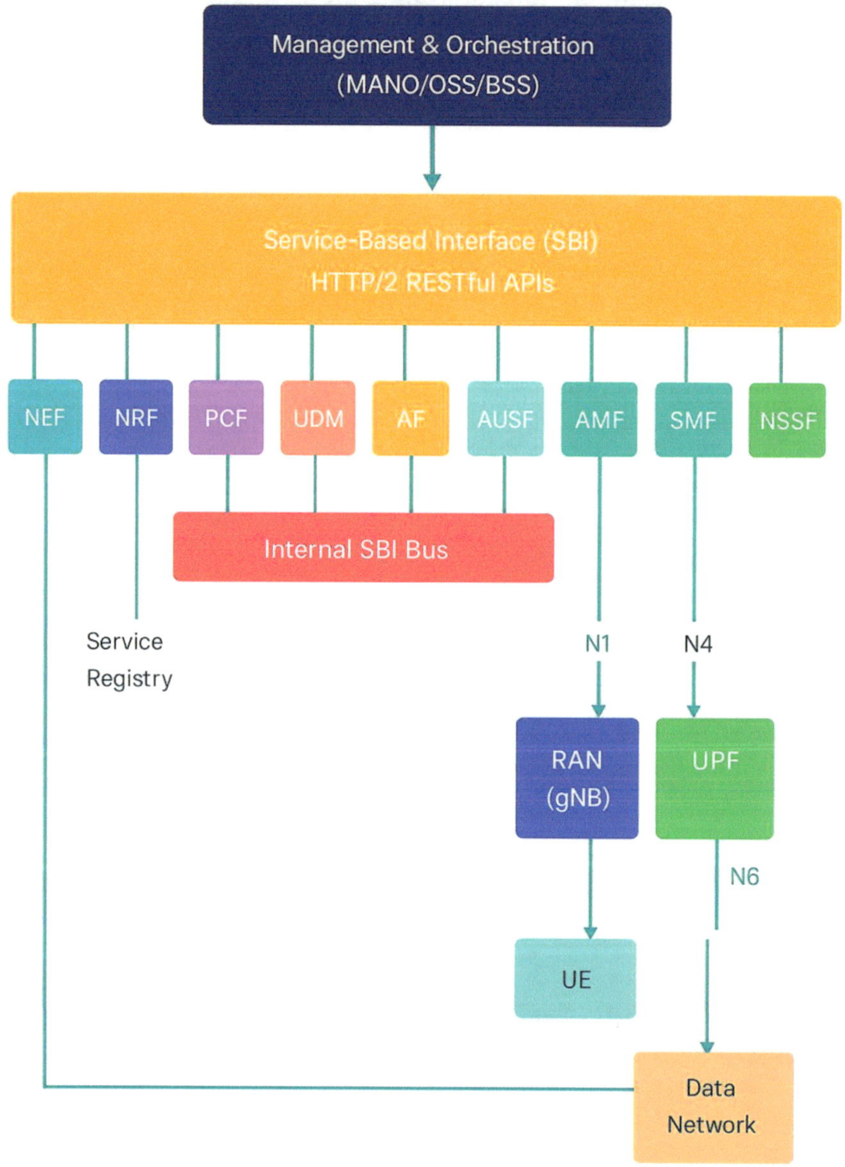

Networking Slicing Architecture
(3GPP TS 23.501, TS 28,530) [10,16]

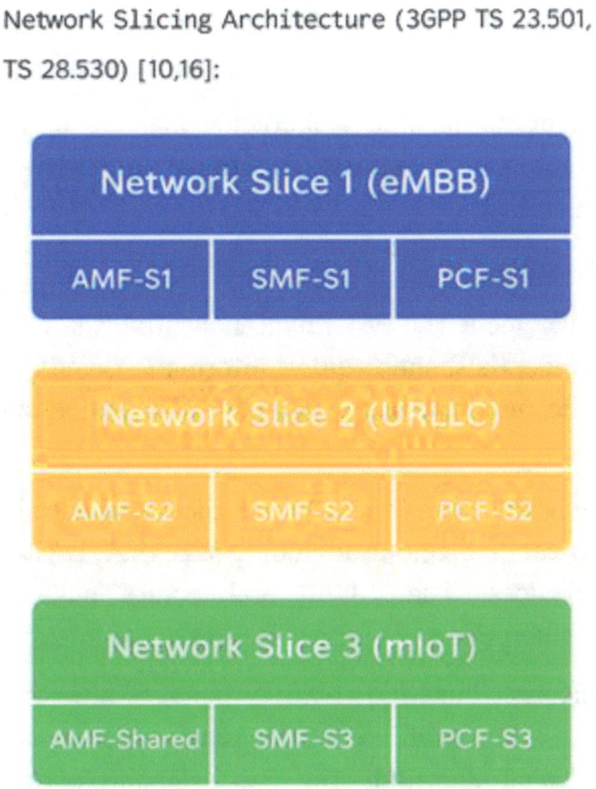

Key Network Slice Identifiers:

- **S-NSSAI:** Single Network Slice Selection Assistance Information
- **SST:** Slice/Service Type
- **SD:** Slice Differentiator

Key Interfaces (3GPP TS 23.501) [10]:

- **N1:** Control plane between UE and AMF
- **N2:** Control plane between RAN and AMF
- **N3:** User plane between RAN and UPF
- **N4:** Control plane between SMF and UPF
- **N6:** Interface to data networks

Cloud-Native Design Principles

The 5GC embraces cloud-native design from its foundation, implementing microservices architectures, containerized deployments, and automated lifecycle management. Network functions decompose into smaller, independently deployable services that communicate through well-defined APIs.

Stateless design principles enable horizontal scaling and simplified failover mechanisms. Network functions externalize state information to distributed storage systems, enabling any instance to handle any request without complex state synchronization requirements.

Container orchestration platforms like Kubernetes manage network function deployment, scaling, and healing. This automation reduces operational complexity while improving resource utilization and service availability.

Network Function Descriptions

The Unified Data Management (UDM) function centralizes subscriber data management, providing authentication credentials, subscription information, and policy data to other network functions. The UDM architecture supports geographic distribution and real-time replication for high availability.

The Authentication Server Function (AUSF) implements enhanced authentication procedures, supporting multiple authentication methods, including 5G-AKA, EAP-AKA, and certificate-based authentication for IoT devices. The AUSF architecture enables delegation to external authentication services for enterprise and vertical market deployments.

The Network Slice Selection Function (NSSF) manages slice selection during registration procedures, considering subscriber profiles, service requirements, and network capabilities. The NSSF implements sophisticated algorithms for load balancing across slices while maintaining service isolation requirements.

Edge Computing Integration

The 5GC architecture natively supports edge computing deployments through flexible user plane topologies and application function interfaces. Local breakout capabilities enable traffic offload at network edges, reducing latency and backhaul requirements for edge applications.

The Application Function (AF) interface enables edge applications to influence network behavior, requesting specific quality treatment, receiving network events, and participating in traffic steering decisions. This tight integration between the network and applications enables new service possibilities.

Radio Access Network Architecture

The 5G radio access network, designated as NG-RAN, delivers architectural adaptability enabling various implementation models ranging from conventional macro cells to combined access and backhaul systems. This adaptability allows network operators to customize deployments according to particular coverage and capacity demands.

5G NG-RAN Architecture with Functional Splits (3GPP TS 38.401) [17]

5G NG-RAN Architecture with Functional Splits (3GPP TS 38.401) [17]

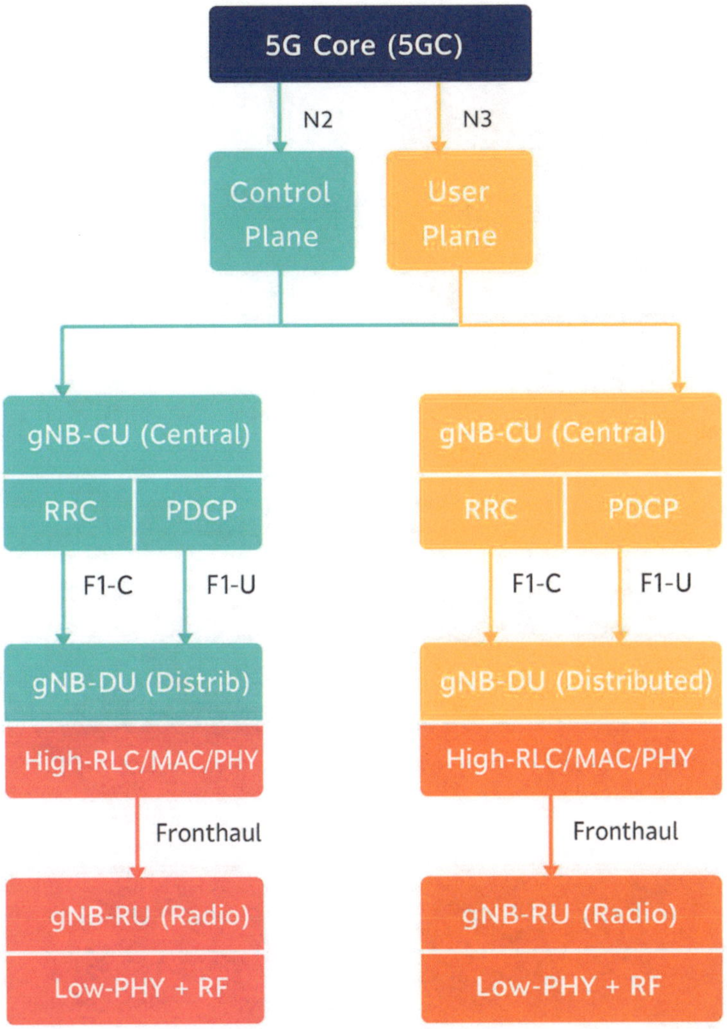

Functional Split Options (3GPP TR 38.801) [18]:

- Option 2: Separation between PDCP and upper RLC layers
- Option 3: Division within the RLC layer itself
- Option 4: Separation point between RLC and MAC layers
- Option 5: Division within the MAC layer itself
- Option 6: Separation between MAC and PHY layers
- Option 7: Division within the PHY layer itself
- Option 8: Separation between PHY and RF component

Interfaces (3GPP TS 38.401) [17]:

- **F1-C:** F1 Application Protocol (F1AP) for control plane
- **F1-U:** GTP-U for user plane
- **E1:** Connectivity between CU-CP and CU-UP

Integrated Access and Backhaul (IAB) Architecture

(TS 38.300) [13]

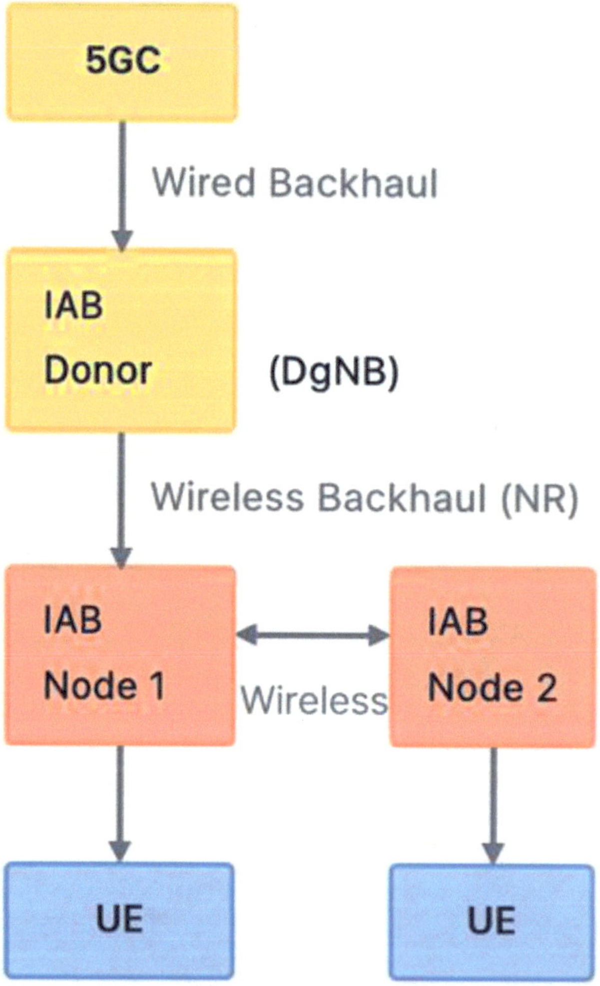

IAB Protocol Stack:

- Adapt layer for routing
- RLC channel mapping
- Backhaul RLC channels

gNodeB Architecture

The gNodeB (gNB) implements enhanced capabilities compared to LTE eNodeBs, supporting multiple numerologies, massive MIMO configurations, and beamforming technologies. The gNB architecture separates into centralized units (CU) and distributed units (DU), enabling flexible functional splits and deployment models.

The CU-DU split allows operators to centralize complex processing functions while maintaining distributed radio units close to antenna sites. Multiple functional split options enable optimization for different deployment scenarios, balancing fronthaul requirements against centralization benefits.

Integrated Access and Backhaul

5G introduces integrated access and backhaul (IAB) capabilities, enabling wireless backhaul using the same spectrum and technology as access links. This integration simplifies deployment in locations where fiber connectivity is challenging or economically unfeasible.

IAB nodes implement sophisticated routing and resource management algorithms, balancing access and backhaul traffic while maintaining quality requirements. Multi-hop configurations extend coverage to remote areas, with the network automatically managing routing and resource allocation across the topology.

Advanced Antenna Systems

Massive MIMO and beamforming technologies form core components of 5G radio architecture. Advanced antenna systems with dozens or hundreds of elements enable precise beam steering, improving spectral efficiency and reducing interference.

Digital beamforming implementations provide flexibility for simultaneous multi-user transmission, while hybrid analog-digital architectures balance performance with implementation complexity. These systems adapt beam patterns dynamically based on user locations and channel conditions.

Transport Network Evolution

The 5G transport network implements significant enhancements to support increased bandwidth, reduced latency, and flexible topology requirements. Modern transport architectures leverage packet-based technologies while maintaining carrier-grade reliability and performance.

Flexible Ethernet Technologies

FlexE (Flexible Ethernet) technology enables sub-rating and channelization of high-speed Ethernet interfaces, providing efficient bandwidth utilization for 5G transport. FlexE creates multiple logical interfaces over physical Ethernet links, each with independent rate and performance characteristics.

Time-Sensitive Networking (TSN) features integrate with Ethernet transport, providing deterministic latency and reliability for critical services. These enhancements enable support for URLLC services over packet-based transport networks.

Network Slicing in Transport

Transport network slicing extends 5G network slicing concepts into the transport domain, creating isolated virtual networks with specific performance characteristics. Segment routing and MPLS-based technologies enable traffic engineering and resource reservation for different slice types.

Hierarchical slicing models enable efficient resource utilization while maintaining isolation requirements. Transport slices can aggregate multiple radio slices with similar requirements, optimizing backbone network utilization while preserving end-to-end quality characteristics.

Cloud-Native and Virtualized Architecture

Network Function Virtualization (NFV)

NFV transforms traditional telecommunications infrastructure by decoupling network functionality from purpose-built hardware platforms. This architectural shift enables network services to run as software instances on commodity, general-purpose computing equipment, profoundly altering how networks are architected and administered.

NFV Architecture Framework (ETSI GS NFV 002) [19]

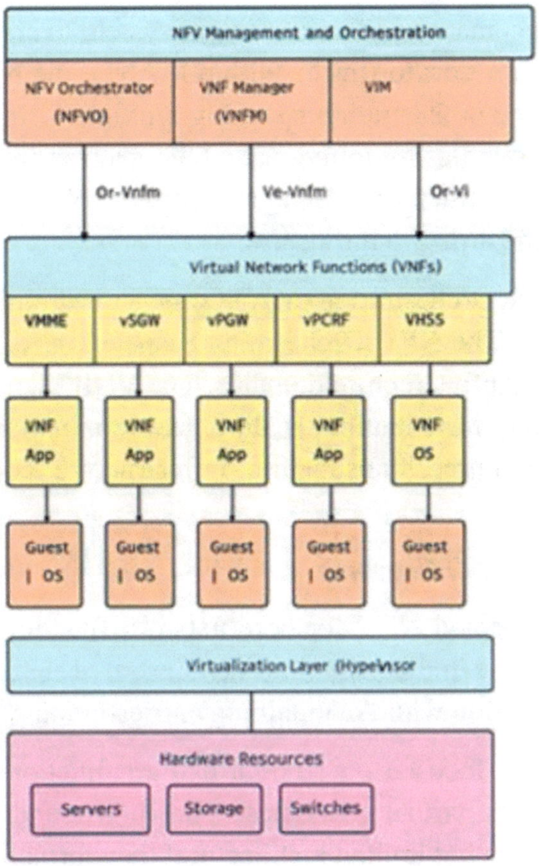

Reference Points (ETSI GS NFV 003) [20]:

- **Or-Vnfm:** Orchestrator to VNF Manager
- **Ve-Vnfm:** VNF to VNF Manager
- **Or-Vi:** Orchestrator to VIM
- **Vi-Vnfm:** VIM to VNF Manager
- **Vn-Nf:** VNF to NFVI
- **Nf-Vi:** NFVI to VIM

Performance Optimization:

- SR-IOV: Single Root I/O Virtualization
- DPDK: Data Plane Development Kit
- CPU Pinning and NUMA awareness
- Hardware acceleration (GPU/FPGA)

NFV Architecture Framework

NFV's structural design consists of three core domains that collaborate to provide virtualized network capabilities. The VNF (Virtual Network Function) domain houses the software implementations of various network functions, spanning from virtualized EPC elements in LTE systems to cloud-native network functions in 5G infrastructures.

The MANO (NFV Management and Orchestration) system oversees the complete lifecycle of virtual network functions from start to finish. Within MANO, the NFV Orchestrator coordinates service assembly and resource orchestration spanning multiple infrastructure domains. The VNF Manager governs lifecycle activities for individual VNFs, such as creation, scaling operations, and shutdown. The Virtual Infrastructure Manager oversees NFVI resources, shielding upper management layers from infrastructure intricacies.

The NFV Management and Orchestration (MANO) system administers the end-to-end lifecycle of virtual network functions. The NFV Orchestrator manages service composition and resource orchestration across multiple infrastructure domains. The VNF Manager handles individual VNF lifecycle operations, including instantiation, scaling, and termination. The Virtual Infrastructure Manager controls NFVI resources, abstracting infrastructure complexity from higher-layer management systems.

Implementation in LTE and 5G Networks

LTE networks initially adopted NFV for core network functions, virtualizing elements like MME, S-GW, and P-GW. These implementations demonstrated significant benefits in deployment flexibility and resource utilization while maintaining carrier-grade performance requirements.

Early virtualization efforts focused on straightforward functional translation, implementing existing network functions as virtual machines. These "lift and shift" approaches provided immediate deployment benefits but limited architectural transformation potential.

5G networks embrace NFV principles from inception, designing network functions for cloud-native deployment. The service-based architecture naturally aligns with NFV concepts, enabling dynamic service composition and automated lifecycle management. Network functions decompose into microservices that can scale independently, improving resource efficiency and service agility.

Performance Optimization Techniques

Achieving carrier-grade performance in virtualized environments requires sophisticated optimization approaches. SR-IOV (Single Root I/O Virtualization) enables network functions to access hardware directly, bypassing hypervisor layers during data plane activities. DPDK (Data Plane Development Kit) implementations accelerate packet handling through user-space drivers combined with polling-based mechanisms.

CPU pinning and NUMA (Non-Uniform Memory Access) optimization ensure consistent performance by binding virtual functions to specific processor cores and memory regions. These techniques minimize cache misses and memory access latency, critical for maintaining quality of service in virtualized deployments.

Accelerator integration through technologies like FPGA and GPU offload enables hardware acceleration for compute-intensive functions while maintaining virtualization benefits. Cryptographic operations, signal processing, and packet inspection benefit from specialized hardware while remaining manageable through standard virtualization frameworks.

Software-Defined Networking (SDN)

Software-Defined Networking complements NFV by separating network control logic from forwarding mechanisms, enabling programmatic network management and dynamic service creation. This separation transforms static network configurations into dynamic, programmable infrastructures that adapt to changing service requirements.

SDN Architecture Components (ONF TR-502) [21]

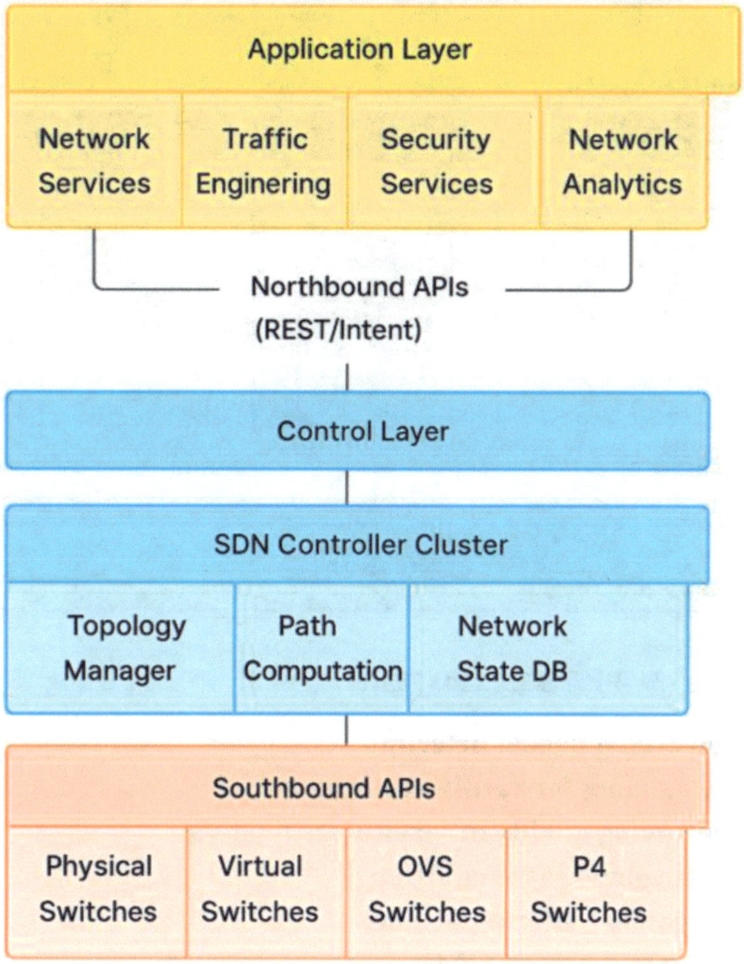

SDN in Mobile Networks - CUPS Architecture (3GPP TS 23.214) [22]

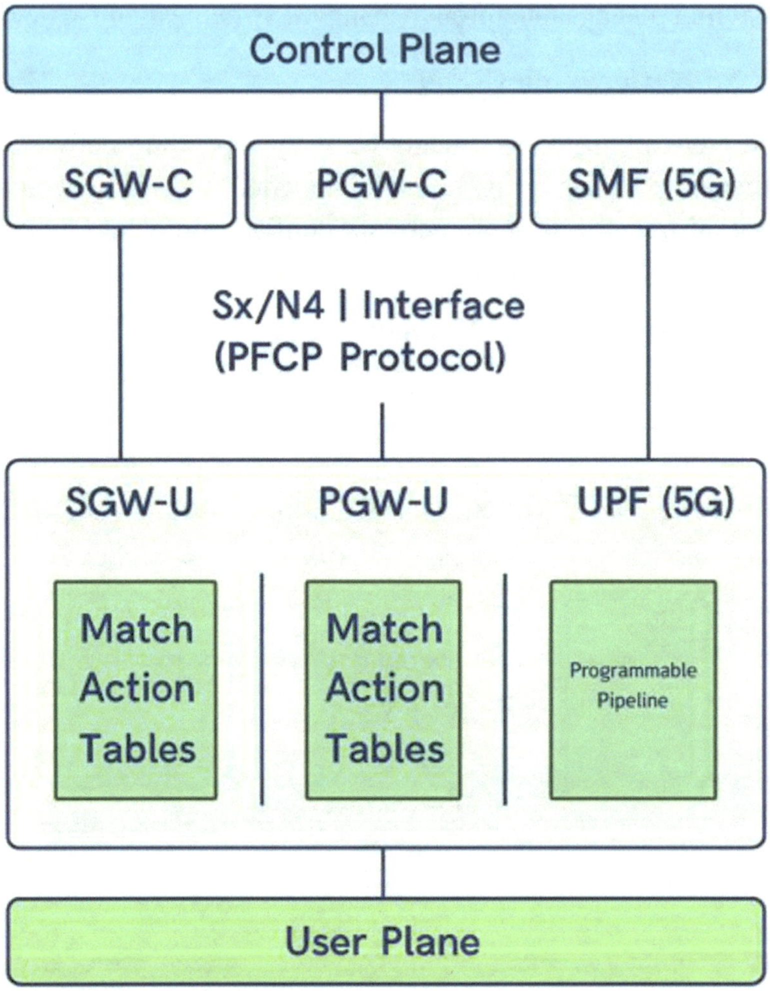

PFCP Session Rules (3GPP TS 29.244) [23]:

- **PDR: Rules governing packet detection**
- **FAR: Rules controlling forwarding actions**
- **QER: Rules enforcing quality of service parameters**
- **URR: Rules managing usage reporting**
- **BAR: Rules directing buffering actions**

OpenFlow Features (ONF TS-025) [24]:

- Flow tables with match/action
- Group tables for multicast/broadcast
- Meter tables for rate limiting
- Multiple-table pipeline processing

SDN Architecture Components

The SDN architecture comprises three distinct layers that interact through well-defined interfaces. The infrastructure layer contains network devices responsible for packet forwarding based on flow rules installed by the control layer. These devices range from physical switches to virtual switches within hypervisors, all supporting standardized southbound protocols.

The control layer implements the network operating system, maintaining global network state and computing forwarding decisions. SDN controllers provide northbound APIs that expose network capabilities to applications while managing southbound protocols that program infrastructure devices. Controller platforms implement high availability through clustering and state synchronization, ensuring continuous operation despite individual controller failures.

The application layer leverages northbound APIs to implement network services and policies. Applications range from basic connectivity services to sophisticated traffic engineering and security functions. The programmatic interface enables rapid service development and deployment without infrastructure modifications.

OpenFlow and Southbound Protocols

OpenFlow emerged as the predominant southbound protocol for SDN deployments, defining how controllers communicate with infrastructure devices. The protocol specifies flow table structures, matching capabilities, and action sets that enable flexible packet processing.

Modern OpenFlow implementations support multiple flow tables with pipeline processing, enabling complex packet processing workflows. Extensible match capabilities accommodate diverse header fields and metadata, supporting advanced classification requirements for 5G services.

Alternative southbound protocols address specific use cases and deployment scenarios. NETCONF and RESTCONF provide configuration management capabilities complementing OpenFlow's focus on flow programming. P4 (Programming Protocol-independent Packet Processors) enables data plane programmability, allowing customization of packet processing pipelines for specialized requirements.

SDN Integration in Mobile Networks

Mobile networks leverage SDN principles for both transport and mobile core architectures. In transport networks, SDN enables dynamic path computation and bandwidth allocation responding to mobile traffic patterns. Controllers implement traffic engineering algorithms that optimize network utilization while meeting service-level requirements.

Fifth-generation core networks incorporate SDN concepts through the separation of user plane and control plane functions. The N4 interface linking SMF with UPF creates an SDN-like management paradigm, positioning the SMF as a controller that programs packet forwarding behaviors in UPF elements.

Network slicing leverages SDN capabilities extensively, creating isolated virtual networks through programmatic configuration of forwarding behaviors. SDN controllers manage slice-specific topologies, implementing traffic isolation and resource guarantees through flow programming and queue management.

Cloud-Native Implementation in 5G

Cloud-native principles fundamentally reshape 5G network architecture, moving beyond simple virtualization to embrace microservices, containerization, and DevOps methodologies. This transformation enables unprecedented agility, scalability, and operational efficiency in telecommunications networks.

Cloud-Native 5G Architecture (CNCF/3GPP) [25,26]

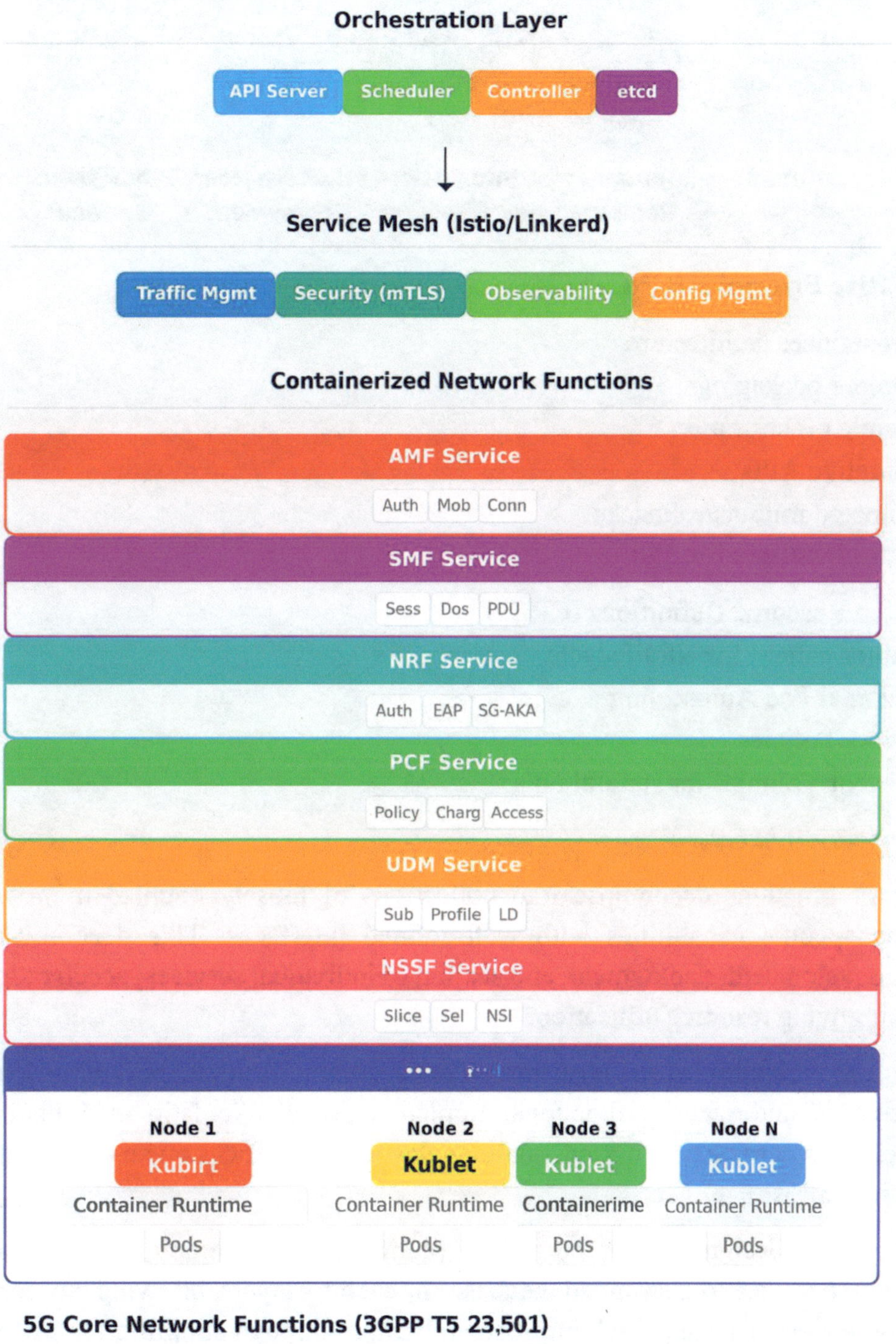

CI/CD Pipeline for Cloud-Native 5G

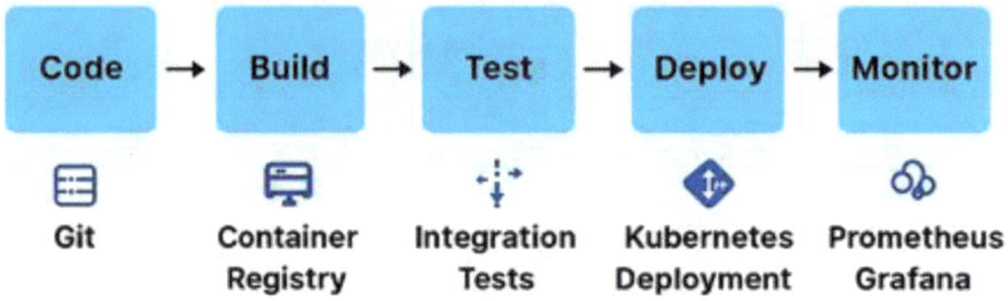

Cloud-Native Principles (CNCF) [25]:

- Microservices architecture
- Container packaging
- Dynamic orchestration
- Declarative APIs
- Automated rollouts/rollbacks

Kubernetes Features for 5G:

- Custom Resource Definitions (CRDs)
- Operator pattern for NF lifecycle
- Horizontal Pod Autoscaling
- Network Policies
- Persistent Volumes for stateful NFs

Microservices Architecture

5G network functions decompose into collections of loosely coupled microservices, each implementing specific capabilities with well-defined interfaces. This decomposition enables independent development, deployment, and scaling of individual services, accelerating innovation cycles and improving resource utilization.

Service mesh technologies manage inter-service communication, providing load balancing, service discovery, and security functions. Implementations like Istio or Linkerd handle the complexity of microservice networking, enabling developers to focus on business logic rather than communication infrastructure.

Stateless service design enables horizontal scaling without complex state synchronization. Services externalize state to distributed databases or caching layers, allowing any service instance to handle any request. This approach improves reliability through simplified failover and enables elastic scaling based on load patterns.

Container Orchestration and Management

Kubernetes emerged as the standard platform for container orchestration in 5G deployments, managing the complete lifecycle of containerized network functions. Custom Resource Definitions

(CRDs) extend Kubernetes capabilities for telecommunications-specific requirements, enabling declarative management of network services.

Operator patterns implement domain-specific knowledge for managing complex network functions. Network function operators handle specialized lifecycle operations like graceful traffic draining during updates or maintaining session state during scaling operations. These operators encode operational expertise into automated procedures, reducing manual intervention requirements.

Multi-cluster deployments span geographic regions and network domains, requiring sophisticated orchestration and management capabilities. Federation technologies enable coordinated management across clusters while maintaining operational independence. Service mesh implementations extend across clusters, providing unified traffic management and security policies.

CI/CD and Automation

Continuous Integration and Continuous Deployment pipelines automate network function development and deployment processes. Automated testing frameworks validate functional and performance requirements, ensuring quality while accelerating release cycles.

GitOps principles extend infrastructure-as-code concepts to network operations, managing entire network configurations through version-controlled repositories. Changes propagate through automated pipelines that validate, test, and deploy modifications while maintaining audit trails and enabling rapid rollback capabilities.

Closed-loop automation integrates with monitoring and analytics systems, enabling self-healing and auto-scaling behaviors. Machine learning algorithms analyze performance metrics and predict resource requirements, triggering proactive scaling actions before service degradation occurs.

Containerization and Microservices

The adoption of containerization and microservices architectures represents a fundamental shift in how telecommunications software is developed, deployed, and operated. These technologies enable the agility and efficiency required for modern 5G networks while maintaining the reliability expected of carrier-grade systems.

Container Technologies in Telecom

Container runtime environments provide lightweight virtualization for network functions, offering faster startup times and lower overhead compared to traditional virtual machines. Container images package network functions with their dependencies, ensuring consistent deployment across different environments.

Container networking models address telecommunications requirements through advanced networking capabilities. Multiple network interfaces per container enable the isolation of management, control, and user plane traffic. Hardware acceleration integration through device plugins enables efficient packet processing while maintaining container portability.

Persistent storage solutions address stateful network function requirements through container-native storage interfaces. Distributed storage systems provide data persistence across container restarts while maintaining performance requirements for telecommunications workloads.

Microservice Design Patterns

Circuit breaker patterns prevent cascade failures in microservice architectures, essential for maintaining service availability in telecommunications networks. Services monitor downstream dependencies and fail fast when issues occur, preventing resource exhaustion and enabling graceful degradation.

Saga patterns coordinate distributed transactions across multiple microservices, critical for operations like subscriber provisioning that span multiple network functions. Compensation logic handles failure scenarios, ensuring system consistency despite partial failures.

Event-driven architectures enable loose coupling between services while maintaining responsive systems. Message brokers or event streaming platforms facilitate asynchronous communication, improving system resilience and enabling independent service evolution.

Service Mesh Implementation

Service mesh technologies provide essential capabilities for microservice-based network functions. Traffic management features, including load balancing, retry logic, and timeout handling, ensure reliable inter-service communication. Fine-grained traffic control enables canary deployments and A/B testing of new network function versions.

Security features, including mutual TLS, authorization policies, and encryption, ensure secure communication between microservices. Certificate rotation and key management automation reduce operational overhead while maintaining security posture.

Observability capabilities provide detailed insights into microservice behavior through distributed tracing, metrics collection, and service dependency mapping. These features enable rapid troubleshooting and performance optimization in complex microservice deployments.

User and Control Plane Separation

CUPS in LTE Evolution

LTE Control and User Plane Separation (CUPS) was developed as a vital architectural advancement in LTE systems, resolving scalability and adaptability constraints of monolithic deployments. This decoupling facilitates autonomous scaling of control and user plane operations, enhancing resource efficiency and supporting innovative deployment strategies.

LTE CUPS Architecture (3GPP TS 23.214) [22]

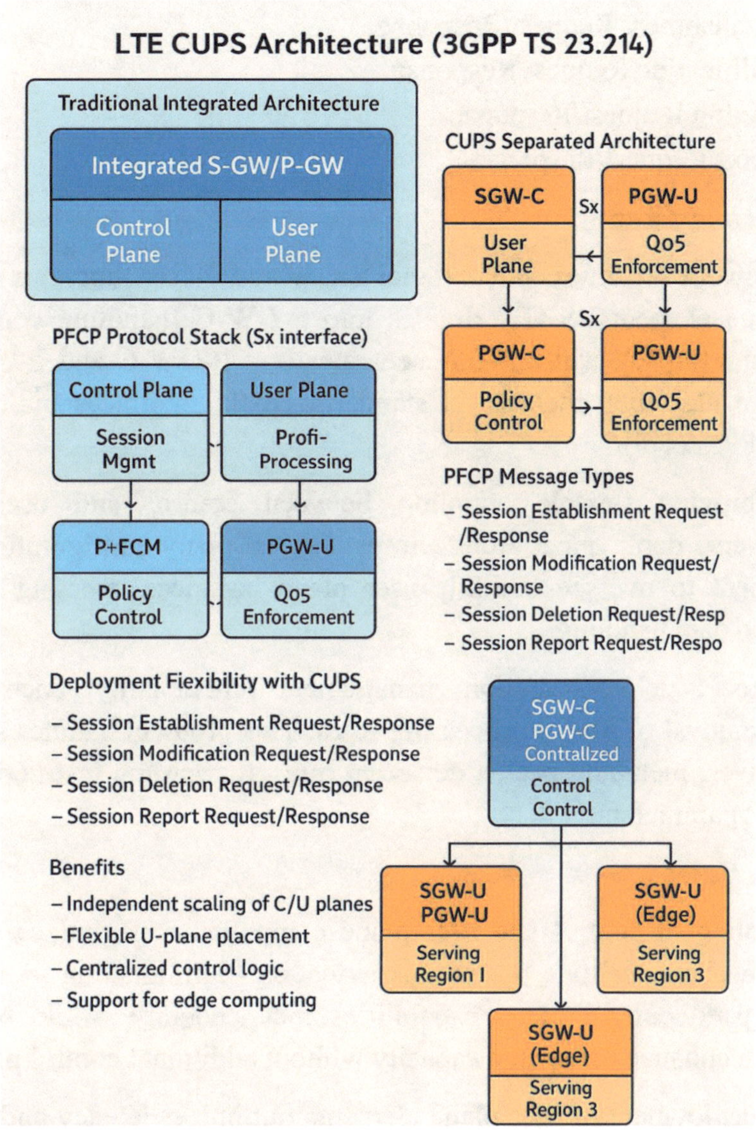

PFCP Message Types:

- Session Establishment Request/Response
- Session Modification Request/Response
- Session Deletion Request/Response
- Session Report Request/Response

Deployment Flexibility with CUPS:

- Independent scaling of C/U planes
- Flexible U-plane placement
- Centralized control logic
- Support for edge computing

PFCP Message Types:

- Session Establishment Request/Response
- Session Modification Request/Response
- Session Deletion Request/Response
- Session Report Request/Response

Architecture and Interfaces

The CUPS framework separates conventional S-GW and P-GW functions into distinct control plane and user plane elements. S-GW divides into S-GW-C (handling control) and S-GW-U (managing user plane traffic), while P-GW separates into P-GW-C and P-GW-U counterparts. These disaggregated elements interact via standardized Sx interfaces built on PFCP (Packet Forwarding Control Protocol).

Sx interfaces provide flexible coupling between control and user plane elements, accommodating diverse deployment architectures. One-to-many configurations permit a single control plane element to oversee multiple user plane instances, creating centralized control alongside distributed data handling.

The PFCP protocol delivers session management functionality, encompassing creation, modification, and removal of packet processing rules. This protocol handles sophisticated traffic management directives, including packet detection rules, forwarding instructions, and quality of service enforcement parameters.

Benefits and Use Cases

Autonomous scaling of control and user plane components maximizes resource efficiency across varying traffic characteristics. Systems experiencing high signaling activity but limited data throughput can expand control plane capabilities independently, while bandwidth-intensive implementations can enhance user plane capacity without additional control plane resources.

The distributed deployment of user plane elements minimizes latency and transport demands for subscriber traffic. Centralized control plane operations preserve consistent policy enforcement and mobility coordination, while user plane components position near radio access infrastructure or content providers.

Network slicing benefits significantly from CUPS architecture, enabling slice-specific user plane deployments while sharing control plane infrastructure. Different slices can implement specialized user plane functions optimized for their service requirements without duplicating control plane complexity.

Migration Strategies

Phased migration approaches enable gradual CUPS adoption without service disruption. Initial deployments often focus on new services or geographic regions, validating operational procedures before network-wide rollout.

Hybrid architectures support the coexistence of traditional integrated nodes with CUPS-separated functions. Intelligent routing ensures session continuity during migration phases while operations teams gain experience with new architectures.

Automation platforms simplify CUPS implementation and management, handling the enhanced complexity of disaggregated systems. Orchestration solutions coordinate control and user plane scaling operations according to current network performance metrics and anticipated traffic demands.

5G Native Separation Architecture

5G architecture embraces control and user plane isolation as a fundamental design principle, extending beyond the evolutionary approach of LTE CUPS. This native separation enables cloud-native deployments, network slicing, and edge computing scenarios that define 5G's transformative capabilities.

5G Native C/U Plane Separation (3GPP TS 23.501) [10]

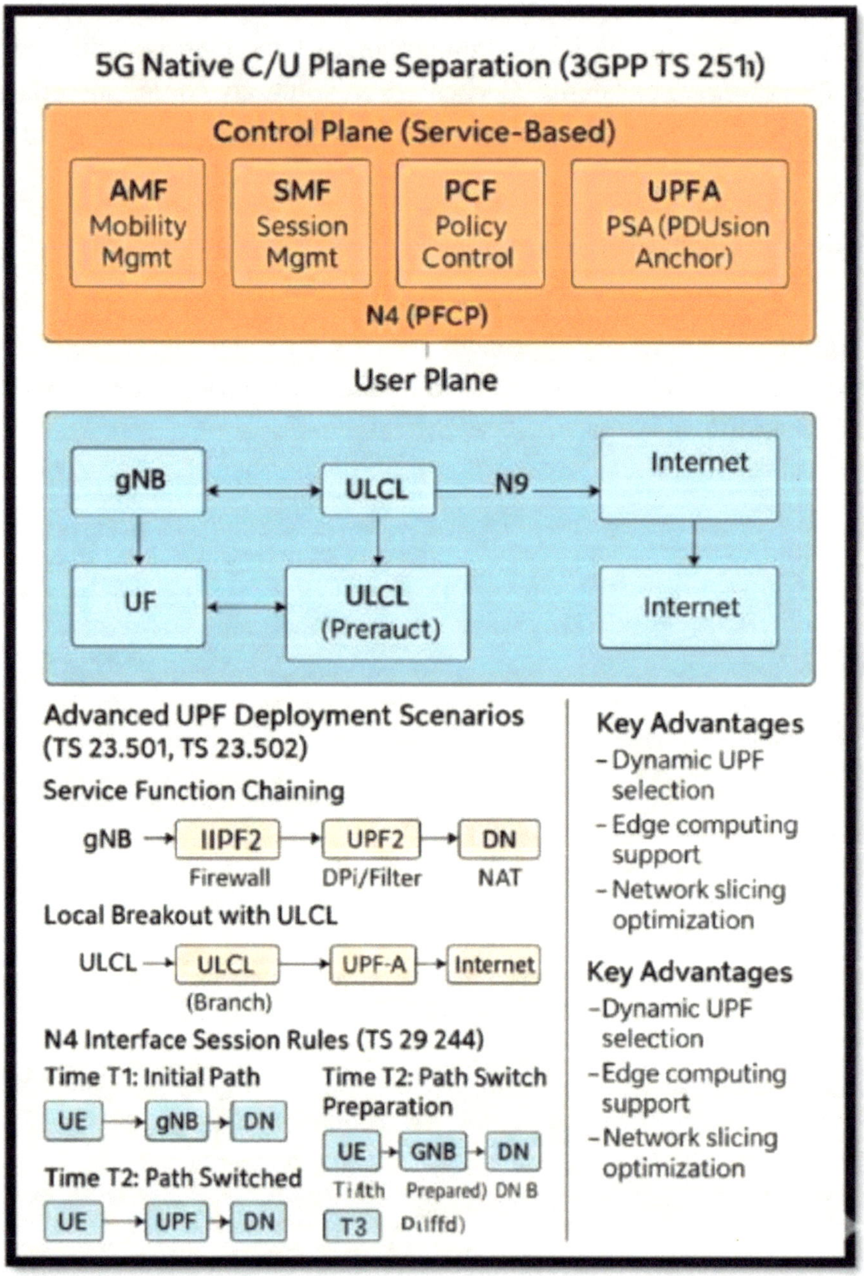

N4 Interface Session Rules (TS 29.244) [23]:

The N4 interface employs several rule types for session control:

- PDR (Packet Detection Rule) - identifies traffic flows
- FAR (Forwarding Action Rule) - determines packet routing
- QER (QoS Enforcement Rule) - applies service quality parameters
- URR (Usage Reporting Rule) - tracks resource consumption
- BAR (Buffering Action Rule) - manages packet buffering

Session Continuity During UPF Change (Key Advantages):

- Dynamic UPF selection
- Edge computing support
- Network slicing optimization
- Independent scaling

Architectural Design Principles

Complete functional separation characterizes 5G architecture, with distinct network functions for session management (SMF) and user plane processing (UPF). This clean separation enables independent evolution and optimization of control and data plane functions.

Service-based interfaces for control plane functions complement the separated architecture, enabling flexible service composition and dynamic function discovery. Control plane functions expose capabilities through RESTful APIs, facilitating integration with cloud-native management systems.

Stateless user plane design enables horizontal scaling and simplified state management. The SMF maintains session state while UPF instances process packets based on rules installed by the control plane, enabling elastic scaling based on traffic demands.

Advanced Separation Features

Fifth-generation architecture features complete functional disaggregation, establishing separate network functions for session management (SMF) and user plane handling (UPF). This clear division permits independent advancement and tuning of control and data plane capabilities.

Service-oriented interfaces for control plane elements support the disaggregated design, allowing adaptable service assembly and dynamic function location. Control plane functions reveal their capabilities via RESTful APIs, easing integration with cloud-native orchestration platforms.

The stateless user plane architecture facilitates horizontal expansion and streamlined state handling. SMF retains session state information while UPF instances handle packets according to rules programmed by the control plane, supporting elastic scaling that responds to traffic patterns.

Integration with Network Slicing

Slice-specific user plane deployments leverage separation architecture for customized data processing. URLLC slices deploy UPFs with specialized packet processing for ultra-low latency, while eMBB slices optimize for throughput with different UPF configurations.

Control plane sharing across slices improves resource efficiency while maintaining logical separation. Common control functions manage multiple user plane topologies, each optimized for specific slice requirements.

Hierarchical UPF deployments create efficient aggregation topologies for massive IoT scenarios. Edge UPFs handle local processing and aggregation while centralized UPFs manage external connectivity, optimizing both local efficiency and backbone utilization.

Benefits and Implementation Challenges

The separation of user and control planes delivers transformative benefits while introducing new operational and technical challenges. Understanding these trade-offs enables informed architectural decisions and successful deployments.

Operational Benefits

Capacity planning becomes more straightforward through independent scaling of control and user plane resources. Network architects can precisely size each plane according to performance indicators instead of accepting compromises inherent in integrated node designs.

Better resource efficiency stems from strategic function placement aligned with operational needs. Control plane elements gain advantages from centralized positioning offering robust availability, whereas user plane functions disperse according to traffic distribution and delay requirements.

Accelerated innovation timelines arise from separated development and rollout of control and user plane capabilities. Novel features can launch in one plane independently of the other, diminishing testing intricacy and deployment hazards.

Strengthened reliability frameworks exploit separation to achieve superior fault containment. Control plane disruptions don't directly affect ongoing data sessions, while user plane problems stay confined to impacted instances instead of cascading across complete nodes.

Technical Challenges

Increased architectural complexity requires sophisticated orchestration and management systems. Operators must coordinate multiple functional elements and their interactions, demanding advanced automation and monitoring capabilities.

Latency implications of separated architectures require careful design consideration. Additional protocol interactions between separated functions can introduce delay, particularly critical for latency-sensitive services.

State synchronization between control and user plane functions demands robust mechanisms for consistency. Session state must be accurately reflected across distributed functions while maintaining performance requirements.

Security considerations expand with increased attack surface from separated functions. Additional interfaces require protection while maintaining performance, demanding sophisticated security architectures.

Implementation Best Practices

Comprehensive automation frameworks address operational complexity through policy-driven management. Intent-based networking concepts enable high-level service definitions that automatically translate to detailed configurations across separated functions.

Performance optimization techniques minimize separation overhead through efficient protocol design and deployment strategies. Batching of control messages, predictive resource allocation, and local caching reduce latency impacts.

Robust testing methodologies validate separated architectures under various failure scenarios. Chaos engineering practices systematically test resilience, ensuring reliable operation despite the increased complexity.

Gradual migration strategies enable learning and optimization throughout deployment phases. Starting with non-critical services or specific network regions allows operational experience accumulation before full-scale deployment.

Comparative Analysis: LTE vs. 5G

Architectural Differences

The architectural evolution from LTE to 5G represents a fundamental paradigm shift in mobile network design philosophy. While LTE established the foundation for all-IP mobile networks, 5G reimagines the architecture with cloud-native principles and service-oriented design at its core.

LTE vs 5G Architecture Comparison
(3GPP TS 23.401, TS 23.501) [3,10]

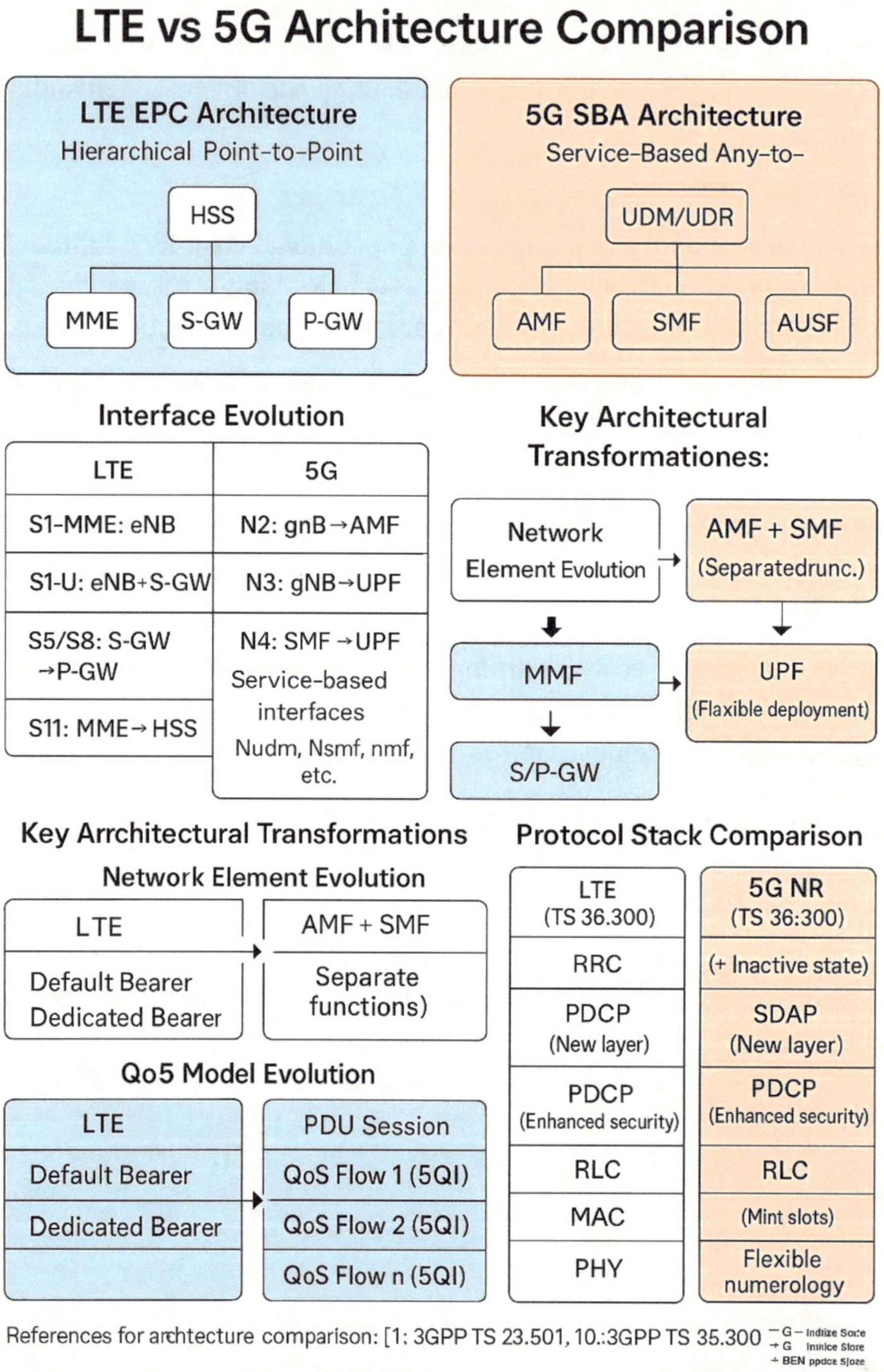

Key Architectural Transformations (references for architecture comparison):

- [3] 3GPP TS 23.401 - LTE Network System Architecture
- [10] 3GPP TS 23.501 - 5G Network System Architecture
- [1] 3GPP TS 36.300 - LTE RAN Overall Network Details

- [13] 3GPP TS 38.300 - 5G NR Overall Description

Core Network Architecture Evolution

LTE's Evolved Packet Core implements a hierarchical architecture with well-defined network elements connected through standardized point-to-point interfaces. This design provides clear functional boundaries and straightforward scaling models, but limits flexibility for new service introduction. The monolithic nature of EPC elements like MME and gateways constrains independent feature evolution and creates scaling inefficiencies when different functions have disparate resource requirements.

In contrast, 5G Core implements a service-oriented design where network functions interact via service-based interfaces utilizing contemporary web technologies. This architectural shift facilitates real-time service identification, adaptable deployment configurations, and streamlined incorporation of additional network functions. The microservices methodology supports granular scaling, autonomous updates, and enhanced resource efficiency throughout the infrastructure.

The evolution from dedicated interfaces to service-based communication fundamentally changes how networks are built and operated. LTE's S1, S5, and S11 interfaces define rigid relationships between network elements, while 5G's service-based interfaces enable any-to-any communication patterns that adapt to service requirements. This flexibility supports innovative deployment models, including edge computing integration and dynamic network slicing.

Radio Access Network Transformation

The progression from eNodeB to gNodeB architecture embodies significant technological advancement. While LTE's eNodeB integrates all radio access functions in a monolithic design, 5G's gNodeB enables functional splits between centralized and distributed units. This separation optimizes deployment economics while enabling advanced coordination features impossible with traditional architectures.

5G's support for multiple numerologies and frequency bands within a single system contrasts sharply with LTE's fixed numerology approach. This flexibility enables 5G to efficiently operate across diverse spectrum holdings from sub-GHz to millimeter wave, optimizing each band for its propagation characteristics and capacity potential. The unified framework simplifies multi-band deployments while enabling dynamic spectrum sharing between 4G and 5G systems.

Advanced antenna technologies distinguish 5G radio architecture from LTE predecessors. While LTE typically deploys 2-8 antenna elements, 5G massive MIMO systems utilize 64, 128, or more elements, enabling precise beamforming and multi-user spatial multiplexing. This dramatic increase in spatial processing capability delivers substantial capacity gains while improving energy efficiency through focused transmissions.

Quality of Service Framework

LTE's bearer-based QoS model establishes end-to-end tunnels with specific quality characteristics, providing predictable performance but limiting flexibility. Each bearer requires explicit establishment procedures and maintains static quality parameters throughout its lifetime. This approach works well for traditional mobile services but struggles with dynamic applications requiring variable quality levels.

5G revolutionizes QoS handling through flow-based mechanisms that enable packet-level quality differentiation. QoS flows can be dynamically created, modified, or removed without complex signaling procedures. The reflective QoS capability allows networks to implicitly signal quality requirements, reducing overhead for symmetric flows. This granular approach better matches modern application requirements while simplifying network operations.

The introduction of network slicing extends QoS concepts to complete network instances, enabling service-specific optimization beyond simple quality differentiation. Each slice implements customized functions, protocols, and resources tailored to its service requirements, from ultra-reliable factory automation to best-effort IoT sensing.

Protocol Stack Comparison

The protocol stack evolution from LTE to 5G reflects changing requirements and technological capabilities. While maintaining backward compatibility where beneficial, 5G introduces new protocols and enhances existing ones to support advanced features and improved performance.

Physical Layer Evolution

LTE's physical layer employs a fixed 15 kHz subcarrier spacing tailored for frequencies below 6 GHz. While this configuration delivers solid performance for mobile broadband applications, it restricts adaptability across varying deployment contexts. The rigid numerology limits symbol duration and cyclic prefix choices, constraining tuning opportunities for different radio propagation conditions.

In contrast, 5G's adaptable numerology accommodates various subcarrier spacing options (15/30/60/120/240 kHz), permitting fine-tuning for distinct frequency ranges and service demands. Smaller numerologies extend coverage through longer cyclic prefixes, whereas larger numerologies minimize delay via briefer symbol durations. This versatility enables consistent system architecture spanning frequency bands from under 1 GHz to beyond 50 GHz.

Enhanced channel coding constitutes another major advancement, with fifth-generation networks implementing LDPC codes for data transmission and polar codes for control signaling. These coding schemes outperform LTE's turbo codes while facilitating streamlined hardware realization. The superior coding performance translates into improved spectral efficiency and broader coverage reach, offering particular advantages for subscribers at cell boundaries.

MAC Layer Enhancements

LTE's MAC layer implements efficient scheduling and HARQ procedures but operates with fixed timing relationships. The 8ms HARQ round-trip time constrains minimum latency, while the fixed scheduling periodicity limits flexibility for diverse traffic patterns. These design choices optimize for mobile broadband efficiency but compromise latency-sensitive applications.

5G MAC layer introduces flexible timing relationships and scheduling options that dramatically reduce latency. Mini-slot scheduling enables transmissions shorter than the standard slot duration, critical for URLLC services. Configurable HARQ timing allows optimization based on deployment scenarios, reducing round-trip time to as low as 1ms in ideal conditions.

Preemption capabilities distinguish 5G MAC operation, allowing urgent transmissions to interrupt ongoing ones. URLLC traffic can preempt eMBB transmissions mid-slot, ensuring bounded latency for critical communications. Sophisticated indication mechanisms inform affected users about preempted resources, enabling efficient recovery while maintaining system stability.

Higher Layer Protocol Enhancements

The introduction of the SDAP layer represents 5G's most visible protocol stack change, managing QoS flow to bearer mapping. This new layer enables dynamic quality management without reconfiguring radio bearers, supporting efficient network slicing and service differentiation. SDAP headers remain minimal, adding only essential QoS flow identification to minimize overhead.

PDCP enhancements support 5G's advanced features, including dual connectivity and handover improvements. The extended sequence number space accommodates higher data rates while improved reordering functions handle multi-path scenarios. Enhanced header compression algorithms optimize efficiency for diverse traffic types from small IoT packets to high-rate video streams.

RRC protocol evolution reflects 5G's expanded capabilities and optimized procedures. The new RRC Inactive state reduces signaling for intermittently connected devices, critical for massive IoT deployments. Conditional handover procedures prepare multiple target cells in advance, reducing handover failures in challenging mobility scenarios. On-demand system information minimizes broadcast overhead while providing necessary information when needed.

Performance Implications

The architectural and protocol differences between LTE and 5G translate into substantial performance improvements across multiple dimensions. These enhancements enable new use cases while improving efficiency for existing services.

Latency Reduction Achievements

LTE networks typically achieve 10-20ms end-to-end latency under optimal conditions, constrained by fixed timing relationships and protocol overhead. The rigid frame structure and HARQ timing create incompressible delays that limit latency reduction regardless of network optimization. These latency levels suffice for mobile broadband but preclude many real-time applications.

5G architecture enables sub-millisecond air interface latency through flexible numerology and optimized procedures. Higher subcarrier spacings reduce the slot duration to 125 microseconds at 120 kHz numerology. Mini-slot scheduling and immediate HARQ feedback further reduce transmission delays. Edge computing integration minimizes propagation delay, achieving sub-5ms end-to-end latency for localized services.

The cumulative impact of latency optimizations enables new application categories. Industrial automation systems can close control loops through 5G networks, replacing wired connections. Augmented reality applications achieve responsive interaction without perceptible lag. Vehicle-to-everything communications support safety-critical messaging within required time bounds.

Capacity and Spectral Efficiency Gains

LTE advanced features like carrier aggregation and 4x4 MIMO push spectral efficiency near theoretical limits for traditional architectures. Typical deployments achieve 15-20 bps/Hz cell spectral efficiency, representing sophisticated optimization of available techniques. Further gains require fundamental architectural changes rather than incremental improvements.

5G massive MIMO deployments with 64 or more antennas achieve 3-5x spectral efficiency improvement through advanced spatial processing. Multi-user MIMO serves numerous devices simultaneously in the spatial domain, multiplying cell capacity without additional spectrum. Three-dimensional beamforming extends coverage vertically, important for urban high-rise scenarios.

Millimeter wave spectrum access multiplies available bandwidth by orders of magnitude. While propagation challenges limit coverage, the raw bandwidth availability enables unprecedented capacity density. Small cell deployments at 28 GHz or 39 GHz can deliver multi-gigabit rates to numerous users, transforming capacity economics in dense areas.

Network Efficiency and Flexibility

LTE's static architecture constrains resource utilization efficiency. Dedicated network elements must be provisioned for peak requirements, leading to underutilization during normal operations. The bearer-based model requires resources throughout the path regardless of actual utilization. These inefficiencies increase operational costs and limit service innovation.

5G's cloud-native architecture enables dynamic resource allocation to address current network load conditions. Network functions scale elastically, consuming resources proportional to actual load. Network slicing multiplexes independent services over shared infrastructure, improving utilization while maintaining isolation. Edge computing integration processes data locally, reducing backhaul requirements and core network load.

Operational efficiency improvements extend beyond resource utilization. Automated lifecycle management reduces manual intervention requirements. Service-based architecture simplifies new feature introduction. DevOps practices accelerate development cycles from years to weeks. These efficiency gains translate to reduced operational costs and faster service innovation.

Detailed Protocol Procedures

Registration and Attachment

The registration and attachment procedures represent fundamental operations in mobile networks, establishing user connectivity and enabling service access. The evolution from LTE's attach procedure to 5G's registration mechanism illustrates architectural improvements and enhanced capabilities.

LTE Attach Procedure Call Flow

(3GPP TS 23.401, TS 24.301) [3,27]

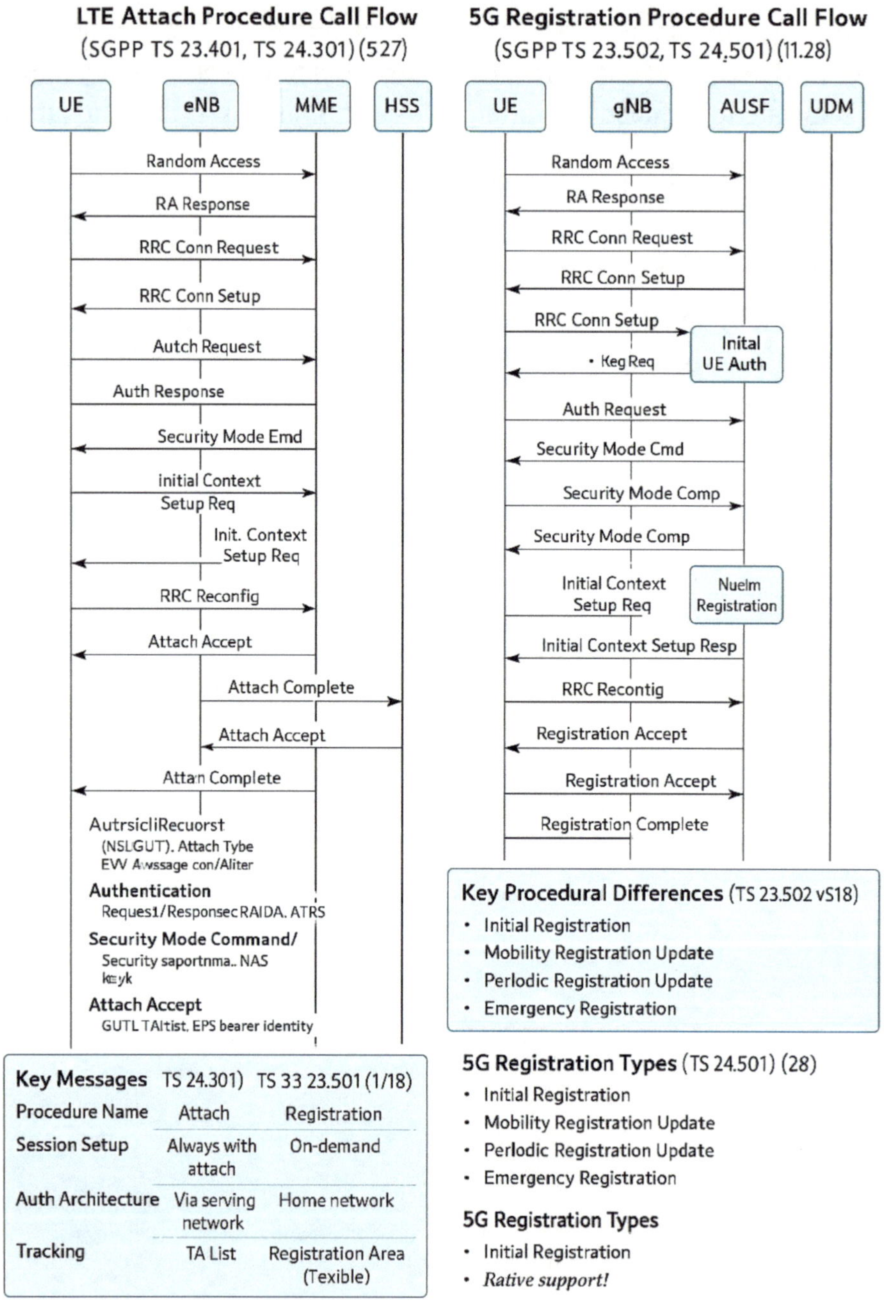

Key Messages (TS 24.301) [27]:

- **Attach Request:** IMSI/GUTI, Attach Type, ESM message container
- **Authentication Request/Response:** RAND, AUTN, RES
- **Security Mode Command/Complete:** Security algorithms, NAS keys
- **Attach Accept:** GUTI, TAI list, EPS bearer identity
- **Attach Complete:** Confirms attach procedure completion

5G Registration Types (TS 24.501) [28]:

- Initial Registration
- Mobility Registration Update
- Periodic Registration Update
- Emergency Registration

LTE Attach Procedure Deep Dive

The LTE attach procedure orchestrates complex interactions across multiple network elements to establish user connectivity. Initial radio connection establishment begins with random access procedures, where the UE transmits preambles to achieve uplink synchronization. The eNodeB responds with timing advance and resource grants, enabling subsequent message exchange.

Following radio synchronization, the UE initiates RRC connection establishment through a three-message exchange. The RRC Connection Request conveys establishment cause and user identity, allowing the network to prioritize access attempts. The eNodeB evaluates resource availability and responds with RRC Connection Setup, configuring basic radio parameters. The UE confirms configuration with RRC Connection Setup Complete, carrying the crucial NAS Attach Request message.

The attach request triggers comprehensive authentication and security procedures. The MME initiates authentication vector retrieval from the HSS, obtaining authentication challenges and expected responses. Mutual authentication ensures both network and device legitimacy, preventing rogue base station attacks. Following successful authentication, the MME activates integrity protection and ciphering, securing subsequent communications.

Location update procedures register the user's presence in the network, enabling mobility management and incoming call delivery. The MME updates the HSS with serving node information while retrieving subscription data. This exchange provides service authorization parameters and operator policies necessary for subsequent operations.

Default bearer establishment creates the always-on IP connectivity characteristic of LTE networks. The MME coordinates with serving and packet gateways to establish end-to-end tunnels. The P-GW allocates IP addresses and installs packet filters, while the S-GW creates enforcement points for charging and lawful interception. Radio bearers configured during this phase provide quality differentiation based on subscription profiles.

5G Registration Procedure Innovations

The 5G registration procedure reimagines network attachment with enhanced flexibility and efficiency. Unified registration replaces separate attach and tracking area update procedures, simplifying state management. The AMF coordinates registration without necessarily establishing PDU sessions, enabling lightweight connectivity for IoT devices.

Registration type indications allow devices to specify their requirements upfront. Initial network registration, mobility update, periodic update, and emergency registration types trigger different network behaviors. This differentiation optimizes resource usage and reduces unnecessary signaling for specific scenarios.

Network slicing integration begins during registration, with devices indicating requested slices (S-NSSAI) in registration messages. The network slice selection function evaluates requests against subscription data and network capabilities, assigning allowed slices for the registration area. This early slice determination enables subsequent optimizations in resource allocation and session establishment.

Enhanced security procedures in 5G registration improve protection against various attacks. The home network always participates in authentication through the AUSF, preventing serving network compromises. Primary authentication supports multiple methods, including 5G-AKA, EAP-AKA, and certificate-based approaches. This flexibility accommodates diverse device types from smartphones to industrial sensors.

Registration area management replaces LTE's tracking areas with more flexible approaches. The AMF can assign UE-specific registration areas based on mobility patterns, reducing update frequency for stationary devices while maintaining precise location knowledge for mobile users. This optimization particularly benefits massive IoT deployments with predominantly static devices.

Session Establishment

Session establishment procedures create data connectivity, differing significantly between LTE's always-on bearer model and 5G's on-demand PDU session approach. These procedures illustrate fundamental architectural differences and their practical implications.

LTE Default Bearer Establishment
(3GPP TS 23.401, TS 29.274) [3,7]

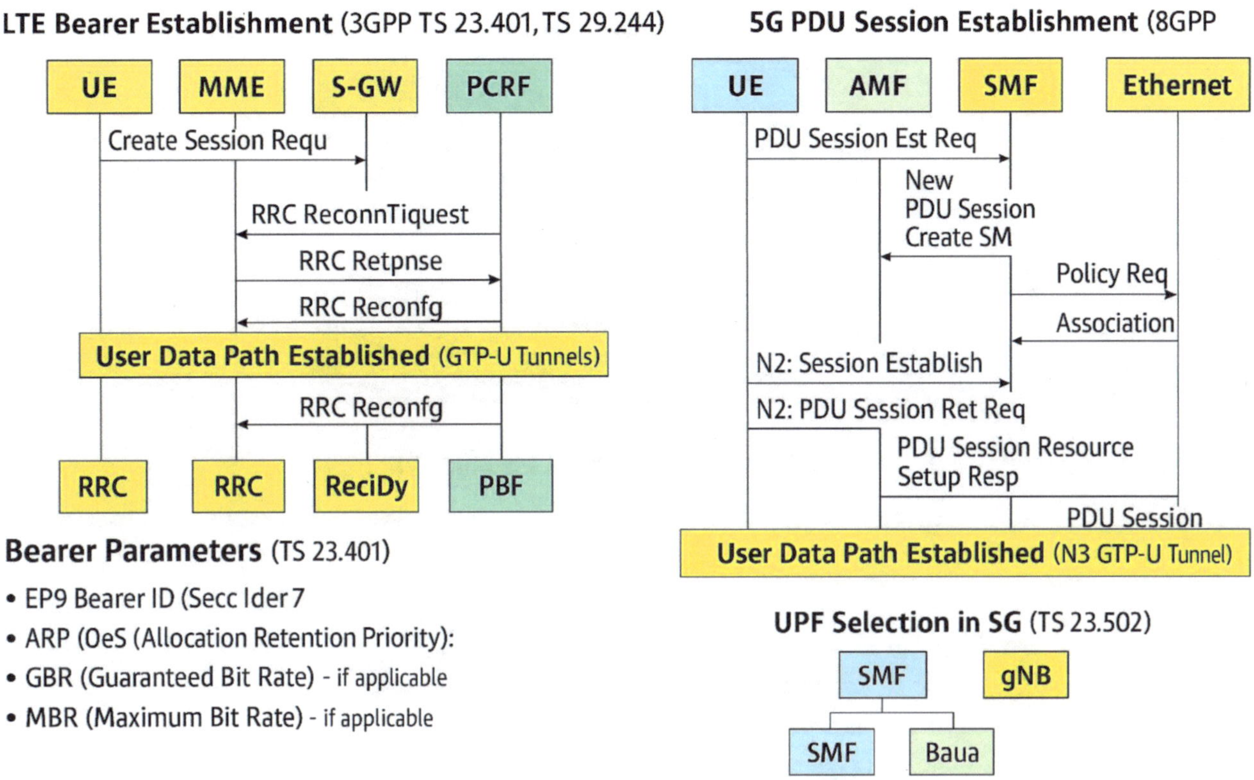

Bearer Parameters (TS 23.401):

- EPS Bearer ID
- QCI (QoS Class Identifier)
- ARP (Allocation Retention Priority)
- GBR (Guaranteed Bit Rate) - if applicable
- MBR (Maximum Bit Rate) - if applicable

5G PDU Session Establishment

(3GPP TS 23.502, TS 29.244) [11,23]

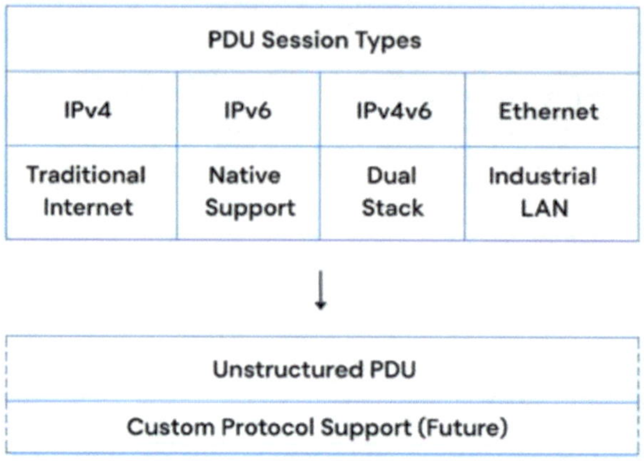

UPF Selection in 5G (TS 23.502)

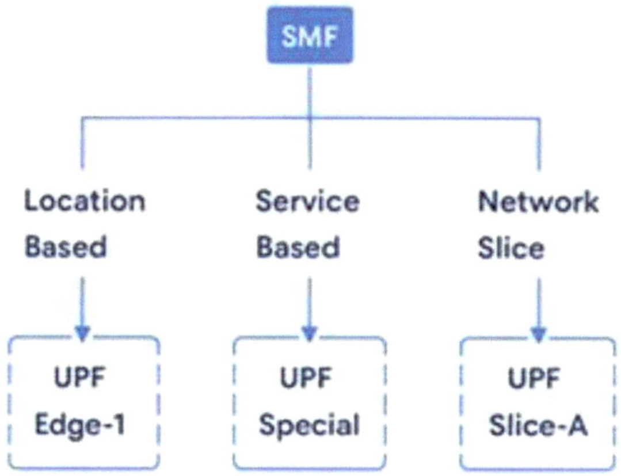

Local Breakout Configuration (TS 23.501)

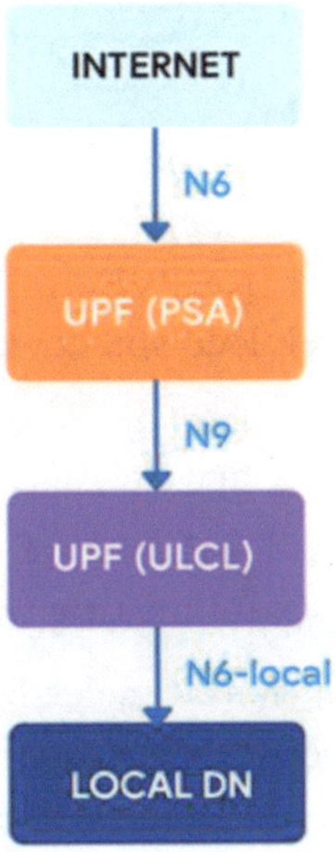

LTE Bearer Establishment Mechanics

LTE bearer establishment typically occurs during attach procedures, creating default bearers that provide always-on connectivity. The MME initiates bearer creation by sending Create Session Requests to the serving gateway. These requests include quality parameters, charging information, and security contexts necessary for bearer operation.

The serving gateway extends bearer creation toward the packet gateway, which assigns IP addresses and establishes external connectivity. This sequential establishment ensures consistent configuration across network elements. The P-GW performs IP address allocation from configured pools, considering topology and routing requirements.

Radio bearer configuration represents the most complex phase, requiring careful coordination between core and radio networks. The MME requests eNodeB bearer setup through S1AP signaling, providing quality parameters and tunnel endpoints. The eNodeB maps these requirements to radio configurations, selecting appropriate logical channels and quality configurations.

RRC reconfiguration procedures convey radio bearer parameters to user equipment. These messages include detailed configurations for PDCP, RLC, and MAC layers, ensuring consistent quality treatment. Security activation during reconfiguration enables ciphering and integrity protection for user data. The UE confirms successful configuration, triggering activation of end-to-end connectivity.

Dedicated bearer establishment follows similar procedures but responds to specific application requirements. The PCRF triggers bearer creation based on application detection or explicit requests. These bearers provide guaranteed bit rates or specific quality treatment beyond default bearer capabilities. Multiple dedicated bearers can coexist, each serving different application flows.

5G PDU Session Flexibility

5G PDU session establishment occurs on demand, eliminating unnecessary resource consumption for idle devices. Users or applications trigger session establishment when connectivity is needed. This approach particularly benefits IoT devices with infrequent communication patterns, reducing network load and device power consumption.

Session type flexibility represents a key 5G innovation, supporting multiple formats, IPv4, IPv6, IPv4v6, Ethernet, and unstructured PDU connection types. This variety accommodates diverse deployment scenarios from traditional internet access to industrial Ethernet transport. Session type selection considers device capabilities, network support, and service requirements.

The SMF orchestrates session establishment, selecting appropriate UPF instances based on multiple criteria. Device location influences UPF selection for latency optimization. Network slice requirements determine eligible UPF sets. Load balancing across available instances ensures efficient resource utilization. Dynamic UPF selection enables optimized data paths throughout the session lifecycle.

Local breakout capabilities in 5G enable efficient edge computing integration. The SMF can configure multiple N6 interfaces for a single session, enabling selective traffic offload at network edges. Uplink classifiers or branching points direct traffic based on packet characteristics, supporting sophisticated traffic engineering for edge applications.

Session continuity mechanisms ensure seamless operation during mobility events. The SMF coordinates anchor UPF functions that maintain external connectivity while updating intermediate UPFs based on device movement. Make-before-break approaches minimize packet loss during path updates. Buffering at strategic points prevents application-visible disruptions during mobility procedures.

Mobility Management

Mobility management ensures service continuity as users move through the network, representing a critical function for mobile communications. The evolution from LTE to 5G introduces enhanced mechanisms that reduce interruption time and improve reliability.

LTE X2-based Handover (3GPP TS 36.300, TS 36.423) [1,29]

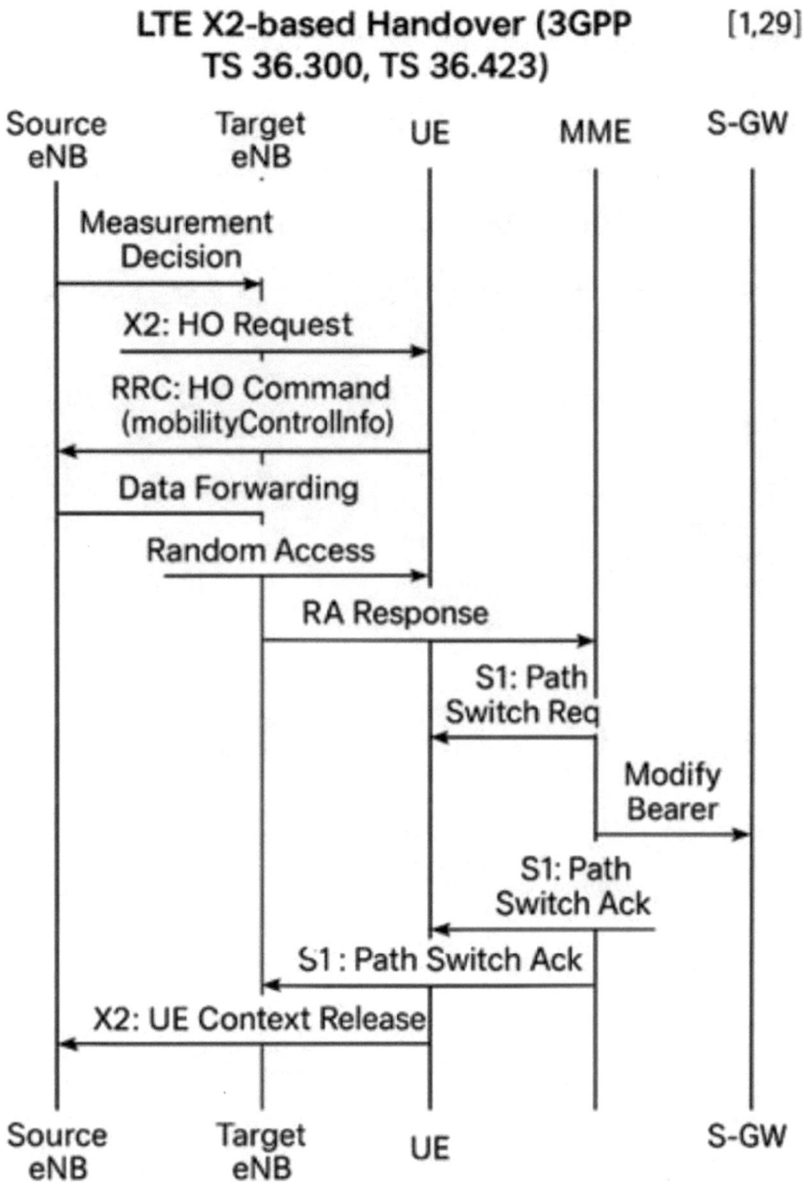

Handover Triggers (TS 36.300):

- **A3 Event:** Adjacent cell signal becomes offset better than serving
- **A5 Event:** Serving cell quality becomes worse than threshold1, and the neighboring cell exceeds threshold2
- **B1 Event:** Inter-RAT neighbor surpasses defined threshold

5G Xn-based Handover with Make-Before-Break

(3GPP TS 38.300, TS 38.423) [13,30]

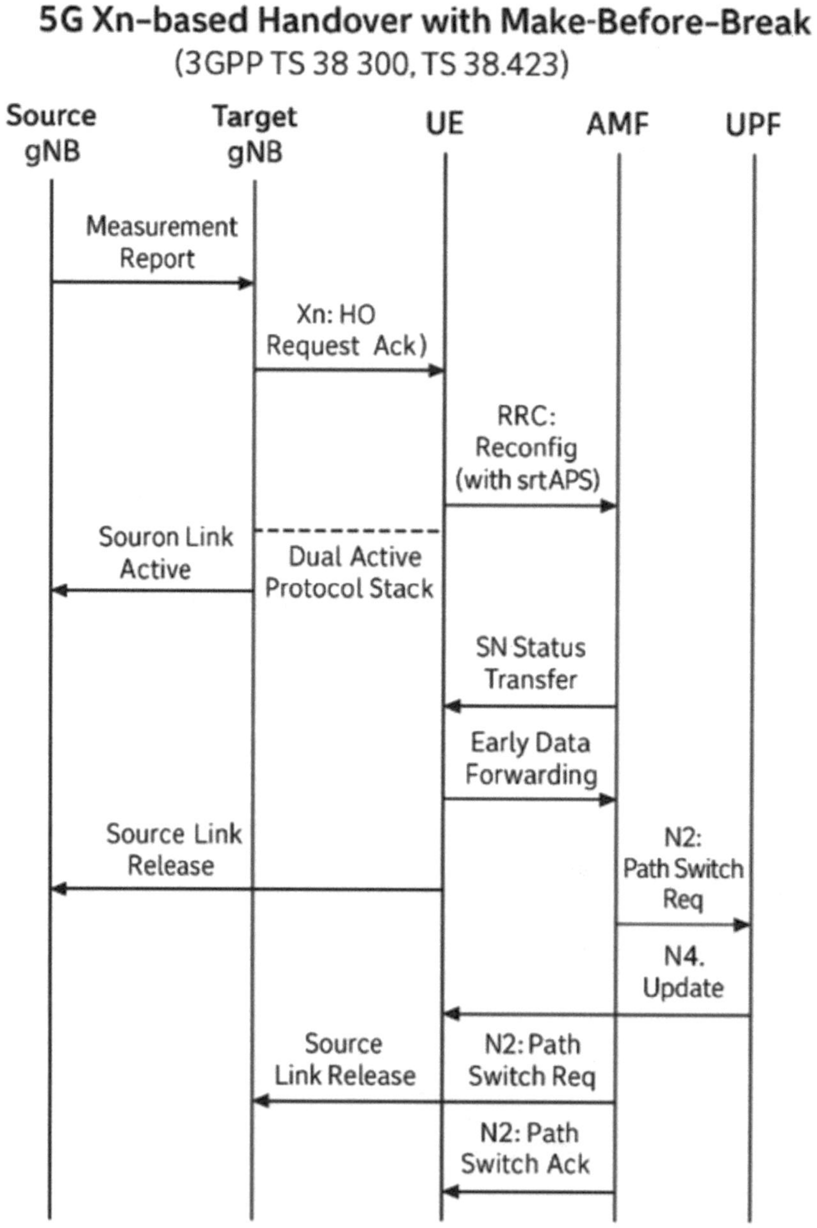

Conditional Handover in 5G (TS 38.331) [14]

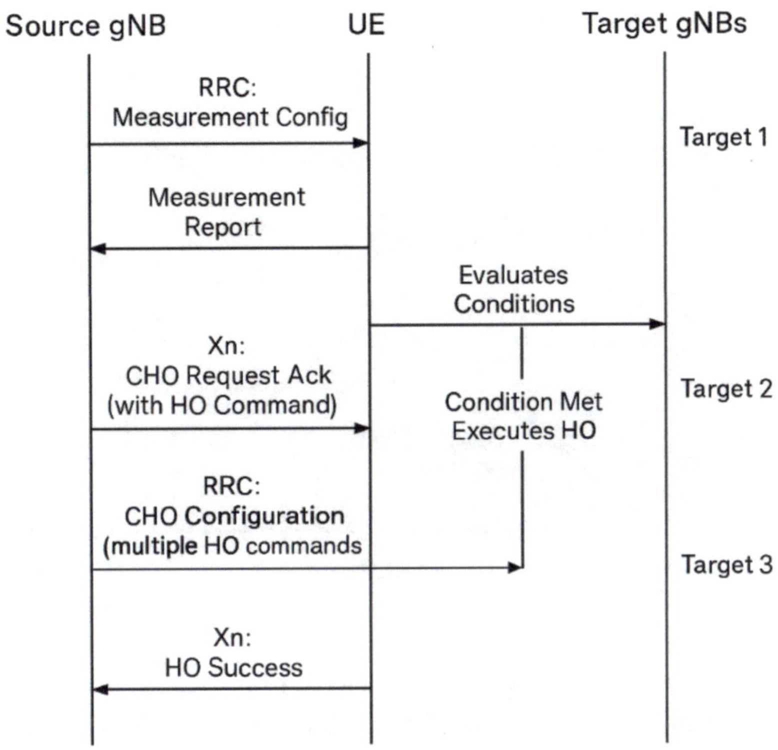

RRC States and Mobility

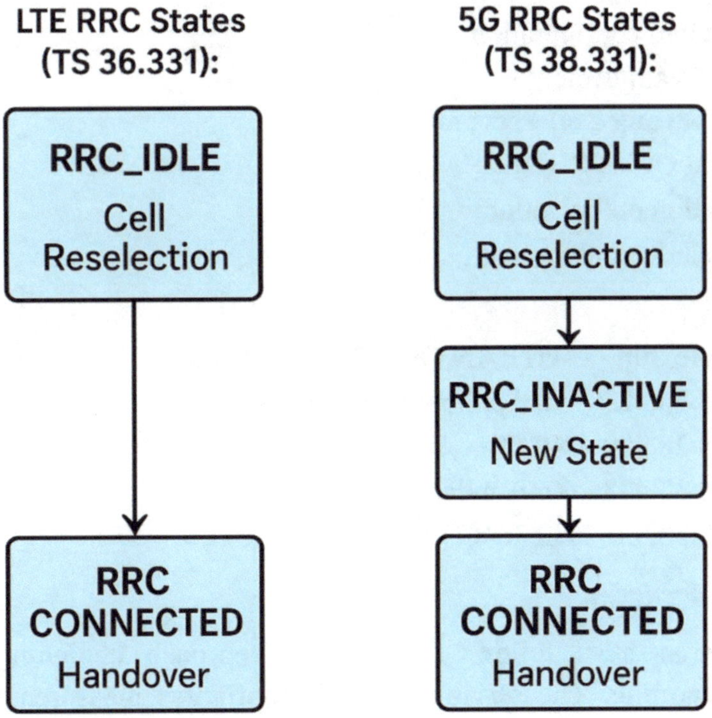

1. **Too Early Handover Prevention:**

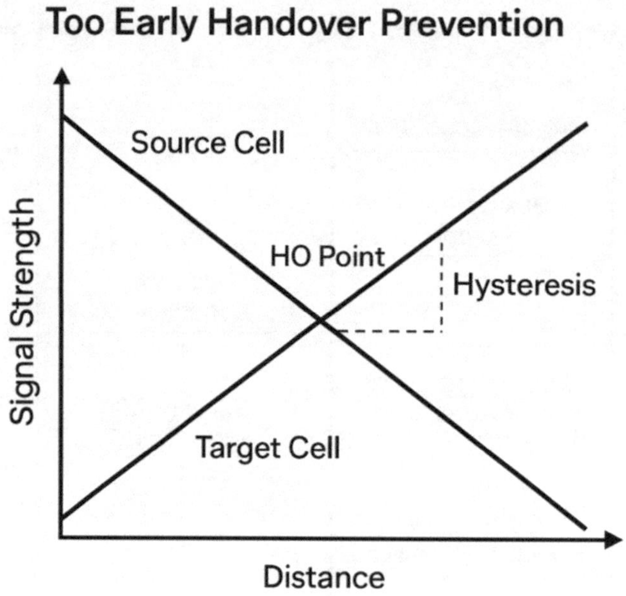

3GPP TS 38.331, "NR; Radio Resource Control (RRC) protocol specification," 3rd Generation Partnership Project, Technical Specification Group Radio Access Network, Release 18, 2024.

2. **Too Late Handover Prevention:**
- Time-to-trigger optimization
- Measurement gap configuration
- Event threshold adjustment
3. **Handover to Wrong Cell Prevention:**
- Cell Individual Offset (CIO)
- Neighbor relation optimization
- Load-based handover decisions

References:

- [1] 3GPP TS 36.300 - E-UTRAN Overall Description
- [29] 3GPP TS 36.423 - X2 Application Protocol
- [13] 3GPP TS 38.300 - NR Overall Description
- [30] 3GPP TS 38.423 - Xn Application Protocol
- [14] 3GPP TS 38.331 - NR RRC Protocol

LTE Handover Procedures

LTE handover procedures follow a structured approach beginning with measurement configuration and reporting. The serving eNodeB configures measurement objects, reporting criteria, and triggering thresholds through RRC reconfiguration. These parameters balance handover responsiveness against signaling overhead, optimizing for specific deployment scenarios.

Measurement reports from user equipment drive handover decisions, providing received signal strength and quality metrics for serving and neighboring cells. Event-triggered reporting reduces unnecessary signaling while periodic reports ensure visibility during rapid channel changes. The serving eNodeB processes reports through vendor-specific algorithms, considering load, interference, and service requirements.

Handover preparation involves signaling exchange between source and target eNodeBs, typically over X2 interfaces. The handover request conveys UE context, including security parameters, bearer configurations, and capability information. Target eNodeB admission control evaluates resource availability, potentially rejecting requests during congestion. Successful admission triggers resource reservation and configuration preparation.

The handover command, delivered through RRC Connection Reconfiguration, instructs the User Device (UE) to move to the targeted cell. This message includes target cell configuration, dedicated preamble assignment, and security parameters. The UE ceases transmission in the source cell upon command reception, creating an interruption period until target cell access completes.

Random access in the target cell using the dedicated preamble eliminates contention delays. The target eNodeB expects the access attempt, responding immediately with timing advance and uplink grants. Handover completion signaling confirms successful transfer, triggering path switching in the core network. Data forwarding from source to target eNodeB minimizes packet loss during the transition.

5G Mobility Enhancements

5G introduces conditional handover procedures that prepare multiple target cells in advance, improving reliability in challenging radio environments. The serving gNodeB configures conditional handover commands with execution conditions. The UE evaluates conditions autonomously, executing handover when thresholds are met without additional network signaling.

Make-before-break handover mechanisms in 5G reduce service disruption by preserving source cell communication throughout target cell establishment. Dual active protocol stack (DAPS) handover enables concurrent data exchange with both source and destination cells. This methodology eliminates connectivity gaps while requiring additional terminal complexity and energy consumption.

Inter-system (cross-mobility) mobility between 5G and LTE requires sophisticated coordination due to architectural differences. The 5G AMF and 4G MME exchange context through N26 interfaces when deployed. Context transfer includes security parameters, session information, and capability data. Optimized procedures minimize signaling when moving between systems sharing common core network functions.

Network-controlled mobility remains the primary approach, but 5G also explores UE-autonomous mobility for specific scenarios. Industrial deployments might configure devices to switch cells based on application requirements rather than radio conditions. This flexibility enables optimizations impossible with traditional network-centric approaches.

Mobility robustness optimization in 5G leverages artificial intelligence and machine learning techniques. Networks analyze historical handover performance, identifying problematic scenarios and adjusting parameters accordingly. Self-organizing network functions automatically optimize mobility parameters, reducing manual tuning requirements while improving user experience.

QoS Implementation

Quality of Service implementation ensures applications receive appropriate network treatment, critical for service differentiation and resource efficiency. The architectural evolution from LTE to 5G transforms how networks implement and manage quality requirements.

LTE Bearer-Based QoS
(3GPP TS 23.401, TS 23.203) [3,33]

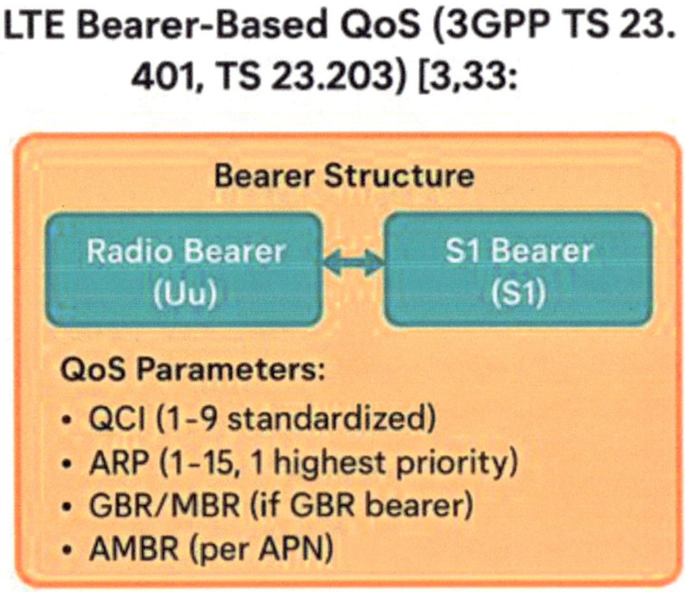

Bearer Structure

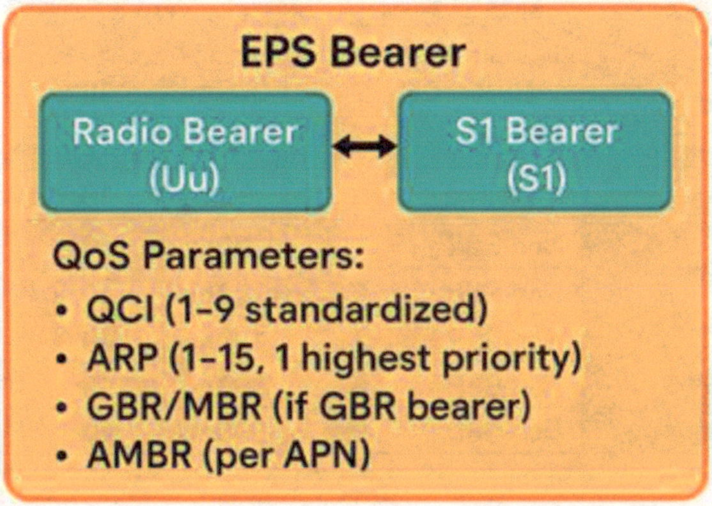

QCI Characteristics

QCI	Type	Priority	Delay	Loss Rate
1	GBR	2	100ms	10^{-2}
2	GBR	4	150ms	10^{-3}
3	GBR	3	50ms	10^{-3}
4	Non-GBR	1	100ms	10^{-6}
5	Non-GBR	6	300ms	10^{-3}
7	Non-GBR	7	100ms	10^{-3}
8	Non-GBR	8	300ms	10^{-6}
9	Non-GBR	9	300ms	10^{-6}

Bearer Binding and Traffic Flow Templates

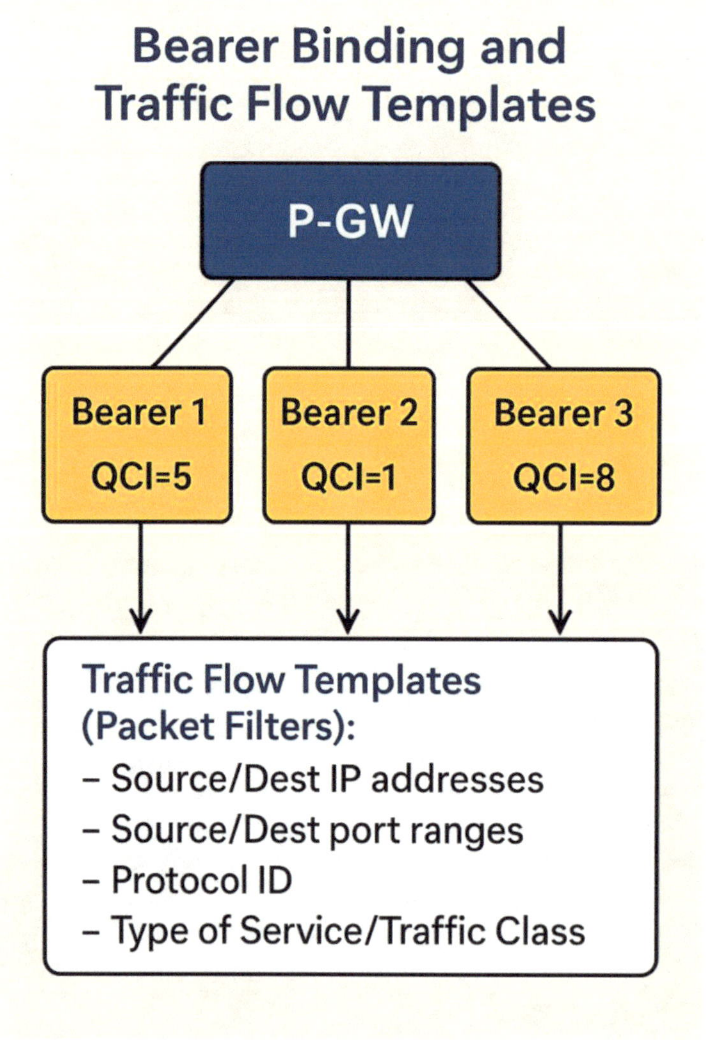

5G Flow-Based QoS (3GPP TS 23.501, TS 23.503) [10,34]

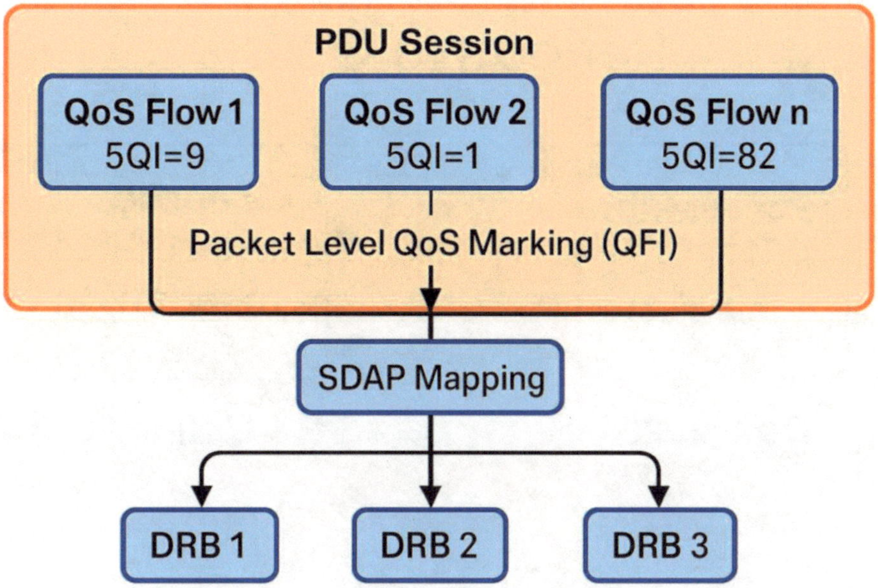

QOS Flow Architecture

5QI Characteristics (Standardized)

5QI Characteristics (Standardized)

5QI	Type	Priority	Delay	Loss Rate
1	GBR	20	100 ms	10^{-2}
2	GBR	40	150 ms	10^{-3}
3	GBR	30	50 ms	10^{-3}
4	Non-GBR	10	300 ms	10^{-6}
5	Non-GBR	10	300 ms	10^{-6}
8	Non-GBR	10	300 ms	10^{-6}
9	Non-GBR	10	300 ms	10^{-6}
83	Delay	22	10 ms	10^{-4}
83	Critical	22	10 ms	10^{-4}

Reflective QoS

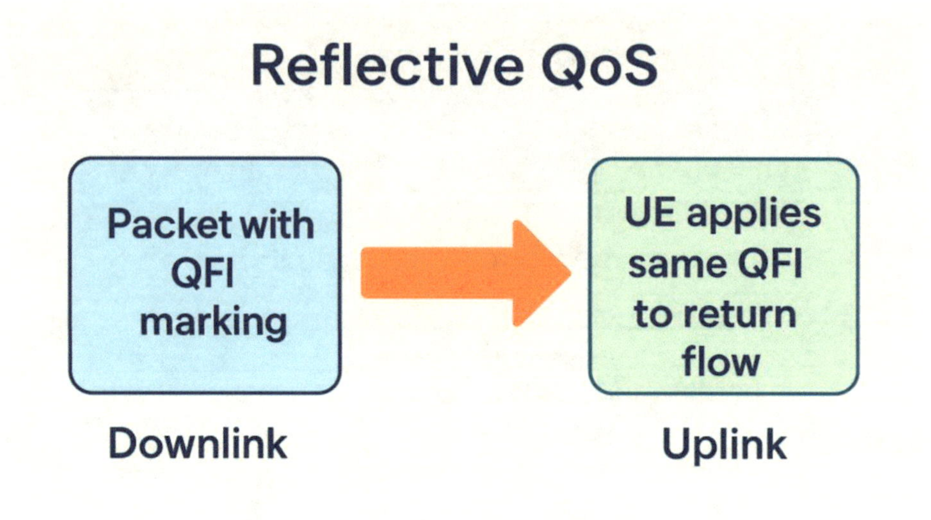

Network Slice-Specific QoS

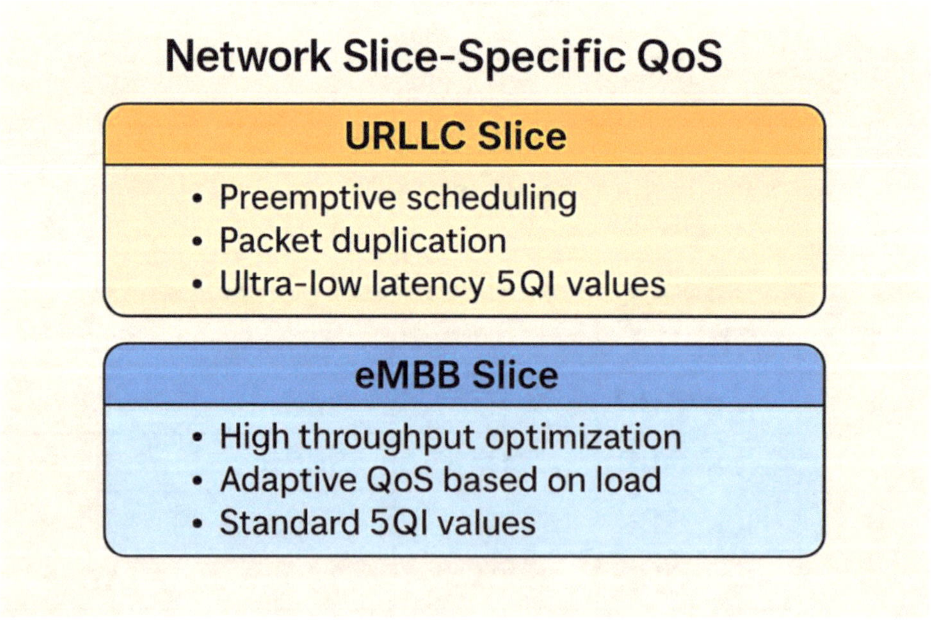

References:

- [3] 3GPP TS 23.401 - EPC Architecture
- [33] 3GPP TS 23.203 - Policy and Charging Control
- [10] 3GPP TS 23.501 - 5G System Architecture
- [34] 3GPP TS 23.503 - Policy and Charging Control for 5G

LTE Bearer-Based QoS

LTE establishes QoS via dedicated bearers featuring specified quality parameters. Each bearer links to a QoS Class Identifier (QCI) that governs scheduling precedence (Priority), transmission delay allowances (Budget), and permissible error rates. Standardized QCI specifications provide uniform handling across various network deployments.

Bearer-level quality enforcement occurs at multiple points throughout the network. The eNodeB scheduler prioritizes transmissions based on QCI parameters and channel conditions. Sophisticated algorithms balance fairness with efficiency, ensuring high-priority services receive necessary resources while maximizing overall utilization.

The packet gateway performs bearer binding, associating application flows with appropriate bearers through traffic flow templates. These templates match packet characteristics, including IP addresses, ports, and protocol types. Deep packet inspection capabilities enable application-aware quality assignment beyond simple IP header matching.

Admission control mechanisms protect network stability by rejecting bearer establishments that would compromise existing services. The eNodeB evaluates radio resource availability before accepting new bearers. Core network elements verify bandwidth availability along the complete path. These checks ensure quality commitments remain achievable despite dynamic network conditions.

Policy and charging control architecture enables dynamic quality management based on operator policies and subscription profiles. The PCRF provides quality rules that adapt based on time, location, or usage. This flexibility enables innovative service models like quality boost options or time-based quality variations.

5G Flow-Based QoS Revolution

5G's QoS flow architecture provides packet-level quality granularity, enabling precise treatment without bearer establishment overhead. Each packet carries a QoS Flow Identifier (QFI) that maps to specific quality characteristics. This approach supports dynamic quality variations within single connections.

The SDAP layer manages QoS flow to data radio bearer mapping, providing flexibility absent in LTE's rigid bearer model. Multiple QoS flows can map to single radio bearers, optimizing radio efficiency. Dynamic remapping responds to changing conditions without session interruption. This architecture particularly benefits applications with variable quality requirements.

Reflective QoS represents a significant 5G innovation, allowing networks to signal quality requirements implicitly. Downlink packets carry QoS markings that devices apply to corresponding uplink flows. This mechanism eliminates explicit signaling for symmetric flows, reducing overhead for interactive applications like video conferencing.

Network slice-specific quality implementation enables customized treatment beyond standardized parameters. Each slice can define unique quality characteristics, scheduling algorithms, and resource allocation strategies. URLLC slices might implement redundant transmission and preemptive scheduling, while massive IoT slices optimize for connection density over individual flow performance.

Exposure of QoS capabilities to applications through NEF interfaces enables application-aware optimization. Applications can request specific quality treatment, receive notifications about quality changes, and adapt behavior based on network conditions. This bidirectional communication enables cooperative optimization impossible with traditional opaque quality mechanisms.

Protocol Enhancements in 5G

The transition to 5G introduces comprehensive protocol enhancements across all layers, addressing limitations discovered through LTE deployments while enabling new capabilities. These improvements reflect lessons learned and anticipate future requirements.

Revolutionary RRC Improvements

The RRC Inactive state represents one of 5G's most impactful protocol innovations, addressing the efficiency gap between idle and connected states. Devices in RRC Inactive maintain their configurations and security contexts while releasing radio resources. This state particularly benefits IoT devices with sporadic traffic, reducing signaling overhead and power consumption.

State transition optimizations in 5G minimize latency and signaling load. Movement from RRC Inactive to Connected requires single-message exchanges in optimal cases, compared to complete connection establishment in LTE. The network maintains UE context during inactive periods, enabling rapid resumption. Periodic RNA (RAN Notification Area) updates replace frequent tracking area updates, with configurable areas based on mobility patterns.

On-demand system information revolutionizes broadcast efficiency in 5G networks. Rather than continuously broadcasting comprehensive system information, gNodeBs transmit only essential parameters. Devices request additional information when needed through dedicated signaling. This approach dramatically reduces broadcast overhead, particularly beneficial in high-frequency deployments with limited coverage.

Unified access control in 5G replaces LTE's multiple barring mechanisms with a comprehensive framework. Access identities and access categories provide fine-grained control over network access. Operators can selectively restrict access based on device types, services, or network conditions. This unified approach simplifies configuration while enabling sophisticated access management for network slicing and emergency services.

Advanced PDCP Capabilities

Enhanced security in 5G PDCP supports 256-bit keys and additional integrity algorithms, addressing evolving threat landscapes. The extended key length provides quantum-resistant security margins, critical for long-term infrastructure protection. New integrity algorithms optimize for different scenarios, balancing security strength with processing requirements.

Packet duplication mechanisms in PDCP enable ultra-reliable communication through redundant transmission paths. Critical packets transmit over multiple radio links simultaneously, ensuring delivery despite individual link failures. The receiving PDCP entity eliminates duplicates, presenting single copies to higher layers. This capability proves essential for industrial automation and safety-critical applications.

Reordering enhancements support complex multi-connectivity scenarios where packets arrive out of sequence. Extended reordering windows accommodate larger delay spreads between different paths. Optimized timer values balance reordering effectiveness against latency impact. These improvements enable aggressive multi-path utilization without compromising application performance.

Split bearer enhancements in 5G support more flexible traffic distribution across multiple nodes. The PDCP layer can dynamically route packets based on radio conditions, load, and quality requirements. Uplink split bearers enable devices to leverage multiple connections simultaneously, improving reliability and throughput. These capabilities prove particularly valuable in dense deployments with overlapping coverage.

Sophisticated MAC Layer Features

Mini-slot scheduling revolutionizes latency-critical communications by enabling sub-slot transmissions. Traditional slot-based scheduling constrains minimum scheduling intervals, limiting achievable latency. Mini-slots occupy fractional slot durations, enabling immediate transmission of urgent data. This capability proves critical for URLLC services requiring sub-millisecond latency.

Preemption and interruption mechanisms allow urgent transmissions to override ongoing ones. The MAC layer can abort lower-priority transmissions mid-slot to accommodate URLLC traffic. Sophisticated indication mechanisms inform affected users about preempted resources, enabling efficient retransmission. This dynamic prioritization ensures bounded latency for critical services without dedicated resource reservation.

Bandwidth part (BWP) adaptation enables devices to dynamically adjust their operating bandwidth. Devices can switch between narrow BWPs for power saving and wide BWPs for high throughput. The MAC layer coordinates BWP switching based on traffic patterns and quality requirements. This adaptation particularly benefits devices with varying activity patterns, optimizing power consumption without compromising peak performance.

Enhanced scheduling request procedures reduce latency for uplink access. Devices can transmit scheduling requests more frequently with configurable periodicities. Grant-free uplink transmission eliminates scheduling delays for predictable traffic patterns. These enhancements collectively minimize uplink access latency, critical for interactive applications and closed-loop control systems.

Revolutionary Physical Layer Advances

Flexible numerology support enables optimization across diverse spectrum bands and deployment scenarios. Lower numerologies with extended cyclic prefixes provide robust coverage in challenging propagation environments. Higher numerologies reduce latency through shorter symbol durations, critical for time-sensitive applications. This flexibility allows unified system design across the spectrum, spanning from sub-GHz to millimeter wave bands.

Advanced channel coding with LDPC and polar codes improves spectral efficiency and coverage. LDPC codes for data channels approach theoretical capacity limits while enabling high-throughput hardware implementations. Polar codes for control channels provide excellent performance for short block lengths typical of control messages. These coding gains translate to improved coverage and capacity without additional spectrum.

Massive MIMO enhancements in 5G physical layer support unprecedented spatial multiplexing capabilities. Reference signal designs accommodate hundreds of antenna elements while minimizing overhead. Advanced precoding algorithms exploit spatial dimensions for multi-user transmission. Reciprocity-based techniques in TDD systems eliminate explicit channel feedback, enabling scalable massive MIMO operation.

Future Directions

The evolution of mobile network protocols continues beyond 5G, driven by emerging applications and technological advances. Understanding future directions helps prepare for next-generation developments and long-term architectural decisions.

6G Vision and Requirements

Sixth-generation wireless systems envision capabilities far exceeding 5G performance targets. Terabit-per-second transmission peak rates, sub-millisecond network latency, and centimeter-level positioning accuracy represent ambitious goals. These requirements emerge from futuristic applications, including holographic communications, digital twins, and brain-computer interfaces.

Artificial intelligence integration at the protocol level represents a fundamental shift from traditional designed protocols. AI-native air interfaces could adapt modulation, coding, and resource allocation in ways impossible with conventional approaches. Machine learning algorithms might replace traditional channel estimation and equalization, improving performance in complex propagation environments.

Semantic communications paradigms focus on meaning rather than bit-perfect transmission. Future protocols might understand content context, transmitting semantic representations rather than raw data. This approach could dramatically improve efficiency for human-centric communications while enabling new forms of machine interaction.

Architectural Evolution Trends

Disaggregation trends continue beyond current RAN splits, potentially separating individual protocol layers across different locations. Each layer might execute where most optimal, from centralized AI processing to distributed real-time functions. This extreme disaggregation challenges traditional protocol assumptions about layer interactions and timing relationships.

Cell-free architectures eliminate traditional cell boundaries, with distributed access points cooperatively serving users. This approach requires fundamental protocol changes for distributed processing, joint transmission, and interference management. User-centric architectures where networks adapt to devices rather than vice versa represent radical departures from cell-centric designs.

Integration with non-terrestrial networks, including satellites and high-altitude platforms, demands protocol adaptations for extreme propagation delays and Doppler effects. Unified protocols must efficiently operate across terrestrial and satellite links, maintaining service continuity during transitions. This integration enables truly global coverage, serving remote areas that are economically unfeasible with terrestrial infrastructure alone.

Technology Integration Challenges

Quantum networking integration with classical mobile networks presents unique protocol challenges. Quantum key distribution might enhance security, but reconciling quantum and classical protocol stacks requires careful design. Hybrid networks supporting both quantum and classical communications need new architectural paradigms.

Blockchain and distributed ledger integration could transform network operations from spectrum management to identity verification. Consensus protocols must adapt to mobile network constraints, including limited device capabilities and dynamic topologies. Smart contracts might automate network operations, from roaming agreements to dynamic spectrum sharing.

Extended reality (XR) applications drive requirements for coordinated multi-sensory communications. Protocols must synchronize visual, auditory, and haptic streams with different latency tolerances. Predictive transmission based on motion tracking and gaze detection could optimize resource usage while maintaining immersive experiences.

Conclusion

The transition from LTE to 5G represents a fundamental transformation in mobile network architecture and protocols. This evolution extends far beyond simple performance improvements, introducing revolutionary concepts that redefine how networks are designed, deployed, and operated.

Key architectural innovations in 5G include the shift from rigid point-to-point interfaces to flexible service-based architecture, enabling dynamic service composition and cloud-native deployment models. The isolation of control and user planes, evolutionary in LTE through CUPS, becomes foundational in 5G, supporting diverse deployment scenarios from centralized clouds to distributed edge computing.

Protocol enhancements across all layers address limitations discovered through LTE deployments while enabling new capabilities. The introduction of the SDAP layer, flexible numerologies in the physical layer, and enhanced RRC procedures with the inactive state demonstrate how 5G protocols evolved to support various applications from massive IoT to ultra-reliable minimal (Low)-latency communications.

The adoption of virtualization technologies, including NFV and SDN, transforms network infrastructure from hardware-centric to software-defined systems. This transformation, combined with cloud-native principles, enables unprecedented operational agility and service innovation. Containerization, microservices architectures, and automated orchestration reduce deployment timeframes from months to days while improving resource utilization.

Quality of service evolution from LTE's bearer model to 5G's flow-based approach provides the granularity necessary for network slicing and differentiated services. This flexibility, combined with programmable user plane functions and edge computing integration, enables networks to adapt dynamically to application requirements rather than forcing applications to adapt to network constraints.

Looking forward, the architectural principles established in 5G provide a foundation for continued evolution. The service-based architecture facilitates integration of new network functions, while cloud-native design enables continuous improvement through DevOps practices. As networks evolve toward 6G and beyond, these architectural innovations will continue to enable new services and capabilities.

Understanding these architectural and protocol differences proves essential for network professionals navigating the transition from LTE to 5G. The concepts presented in this chapter provide the technical foundation necessary for designing, deploying, and optimizing next-generation mobile networks that will serve as the connectivity platform for digital transformation across industries.

Knowledge Check

1. Which protocol layer was introduced in 5G that does not exist in LTE?
   a) RLC
   b) SDAP
   c) PDCP
   d) MAC

2. What is the primary southbound protocol used in SDN deployments?
   a) NETCONF
   b) OpenFlow
   c) SNMP
   d) REST

3. In 5G Service-Based Architecture, which function is responsible for service discovery?
   a) AMF
   b) SMF
   c) NRF
   d) UDM

4. What interface is used between SMF and UPF in 5G?
   a) N2
   b) N3
   c) N4
   d) N6

5. Which of the following is NOT a benefit of CUPS architecture?
   a) Independent scaling of control and user planes
   b) Reduced latency for all services
   c) Geographic distribution flexibility
   d) Optimized resource utilization

6. In 5G, the Service-Based Architecture uses HTTP/2-based RESTful APIs for communication between Network Functions. (True/False)

7. LTE uses QoS flows while 5G uses EPS bearers for quality management. (True/False)

8. The RRC Inactive state is a new addition in 5G that doesn't exist in LTE. (True/False)

9. NFV requires specialized hardware to implement network functions. (True/False)

10. 5G supports multiple numerologies while LTE is limited to 15 kHz subcarrier spacing. (True/False)

11. Describe the key difference between how QoS is handled in LTE versus 5G.

12. Explain the main advantage of 5G's conditional handover compared to LTE's handover procedure.

13. What are the three main components of the NFV architecture framework?

14. List three benefits of implementing cloud-native principles in 5G networks.

15. Describe the role of the SDAP layer in 5G protocol stack.

16. Match the network element in EPC with its equivalent in 5GC:
    - MME: __________
    - S-GW/P-GW: __________
    - HSS: __________
    - PCRF: __________

    Options:
    - AMF
    - UPF
    - UDM/AUSF
    - PCF

17. Match the interface with its function:
    - N2: __________
    - N3: __________
    - N4: __________
    - N6: __________

    Options:
    - Control plane between gNB and AMF
    - User plane between gNB and UPF
    - Control between SMF and UPF
    - Data network interface

18. Compare and contrast the initial access procedures in LTE and 5G, highlighting at least three key differences and their implications for network performance.

19. Discuss how network slicing is implemented in 5G architecture and explain why this capability was not feasible in LTE networks.

20. Analyze the benefits and challenges of implementing Control and User Plane Separation (CUPS) in mobile networks, providing specific examples from both LTE and 5G deployments.

21. Design a 5G network deployment for a smart factory that requires both URLLC for robot control and eMBB for AR/VR training applications. Include the necessary network functions and explain your architectural choices.

22. A mobile operator wants to migrate from LTE to 5G while maintaining service continuity. Outline a migration strategy that addresses both radio access and core network evolution.

Answers

1. Which protocol layer was introduced in 5G that does not exist in LTE?
   Answer: b) SDAP

2. What is the primary southbound protocol used in SDN deployments?
   Answer: b) OpenFlow

3. In 5G Service-Based Architecture, which function is responsible for service discovery?
   Answer: c) NRF

4. What interface is used between SMF and UPF in 5G?
   Answer: c) N4

5. Which of the following is NOT a benefit of CUPS architecture?
   Answer: b) Reduced latency for all services

6. In 5G, the Service-Based Architecture uses HTTP/2-based RESTful APIs for communication between Network Functions. (True/False)
   Answer: True

7. LTE uses QoS flows while 5G uses EPS bearers for quality management. (True/False)
   Answer: False
   It's reversed. LTE uses bearers, 5G uses flows.

8. The RRC Inactive state is a new addition in 5G that doesn't exist in LTE. (True/False)

Answer: True

9. NFV requires specialized hardware to implement network functions. (True/False)
   Answer: False

10. 5G supports multiple numerologies while LTE is limited to 15 kHz subcarrier spacing. (True/False)
    Answer: True

11. Describe the key difference between how QoS is handled in LTE versus 5G.
    Answer: LTE uses bearer-based QoS with static quality parameters, while 5G uses flow-based QoS with dynamic, packet-level quality differentiation.

12. Explain the main advantage of 5G's conditional handover compared to LTE's handover procedure.
    Answer: Conditional handover prepares multiple target cells in advance, reducing handover failures in challenging radio conditions

13. What are the three main components of the NFV architecture framework?
    Answer:
    - VNF (Virtual Network Functions)
    - NFVI (NFV Infrastructure)
    - MANO (Management and Orchestration)

14. List three benefits of implementing cloud-native principles in 5G networks.
    Answer: Scalability, faster deployment, automated management, improved resource utilization, DevOps integration (any three).

15. Describe the role of the SDAP layer in 5G protocol stack.
    Answer: SDAP maps QoS flows to data radio bearers and handles QoS flow identification in 5G

16. Match the network element in EPC with its equivalent in 5GC:
    Answer:
    - MME: AMF
    - S-GW/P-GW: UPF
    - HSS: UDM/AUSF
    - PCRF: PCF

17. Match the interface with its function:

    Answer:

    - N2: Control plane between gNB and AMF
    - N3: User plane between gNB and UPF
    - N4: Control between SMF and UPF
    - N6: Data network interface

References

3GPP. (2023). *Technical Specification Group Radio Access Network; Evolved Universal Terrestrial Radio Access (E-UTRA) and Evolved Universal Terrestrial Radio Access Network (E-UTRAN); Overall description; Stage 2 (Release 17)* (TS 36.300 V17.5.0). https://www.3gpp.org/ftp/Specs/archive/36_series/36.300/

3GPP. (2023). *Technical Specification Group Radio Access Network; Evolved Universal Terrestrial Radio Access (E-UTRA); Radio Resource Control (RRC); Protocol specification (Release 17)* (TS 36.331 V17.6.0). https://www.3gpp.org/ftp/Specs/archive/36_series/36.331/

3GPP. (2023). *Technical Specification Group Services and System Aspects; General Packet Radio Service (GPRS) enhancements for Evolved Universal Terrestrial Radio Access Network (E-UTRAN) access (Release 17)* (TS 23.401 V17.9.0). https://www.3gpp.org/ftp/Specs/archive/23_series/23.401/

3GPP. (2023). *Technical Specification Group Core Network and Terminals; General Packet Radio System (GPRS) Tunnelling Protocol User Plane (GTPv1-U) (Release 17)* (TS 29.281 V17.8.0). https://www.3gpp.org/ftp/Specs/archive/29_series/29.281/

3GPP. (2023). *Technical Specification Group Radio Access Network; Evolved Universal Terrestrial Radio Access Network (E-UTRAN); S1 Application Protocol (S1AP) (Release 17)* (TS 36.413 V17.5.0). https://www.3gpp.org/ftp/Specs/archive/36_series/36.413/

3GPP. (2023). *Technical Specification Group Core Network and Terminals; Evolved Packet System (EPS); Mobility Management Entity (MME) and Serving GPRS Support Node (SGSN) related interfaces based on Diameter protocol (Release 17)* (TS 29.272 V17.3.0). https://www.3gpp.org/ftp/Specs/archive/29_series/29.272/

3GPP. (2023). *Technical Specification Group Core Network and Terminals; 3GPP Evolved Packet System (EPS); Evolved General Packet Radio Service (GPRS) Tunnelling Protocol for Control plane (GTPv2-C); Stage 3 (Release 17)* (TS 29.274 V17.10.0). https://www.3gpp.org/ftp/Specs/archive/29_series/29.274/

3GPP. (2023). *Technical Specification Group Radio Access Network; Evolved Universal Terrestrial Radio Access Network (E-UTRAN); X2 application protocol (X2AP) (Release 17)* (TS 36.423 V17.6.0). https://www.3gpp.org/ftp/Specs/archive/36_series/36.423/

3GPP. (2023). *Technical Specification Group Radio Access Network; Evolved Universal Terrestrial Radio Access Network (E-UTRAN); S1 layer 1 (Release 17)* (TS 36.410 V17.0.0). https://www.3gpp.org/ftp/Specs/archive/36_series/36.410/

3GPP. (2023). *Technical Specification Group Services and System Aspects; System architecture for the 5G System (5GS); Stage 2 (Release 18)* (TS 23.501 V18.2.0). https://www.3gpp.org/ftp/Specs/archive/23_series/23.501/

3GPP. (2023). *Technical Specification Group Services and System Aspects; Procedures for the 5G System (5GS); Stage 2 (Release 18)* (TS 23.502 V18.2.0). https://www.3gpp.org/ftp/Specs/archive/23_series/23.502/

3GPP. (2023). *Technical Specification Group Core Network and Terminals; 5G System; Technical Realization of Service Based Architecture; Stage 3 (Release 18)* (TS 29.500 V18.2.0). https://www.3gpp.org/ftp/Specs/archive/29_series/29.500/

3GPP. (2023). *Technical Specification Group Radio Access Network; NR and NG-RAN Overall Description; Stage 2 (Release 18)* (TS 38.300 V18.2.0). https://www.3gpp.org/ftp/Specs/archive/38_series/38.300/

3GPP. (2023). *Technical Specification Group Radio Access Network; NR; Radio Resource Control (RRC) protocol specification (Release 18)* (TS 38.331 V18.2.0). https://www.3gpp.org/ftp/Specs/archive/38_series/38.331/

3GPP. (2023). *Technical Specification Group Radio Access Network; NR; Service Data Adaptation Protocol (SDAP) specification (Release 18)* (TS 37.324 V18.0.0). https://www.3gpp.org/ftp/Specs/archive/37_series/37.324/

3GPP. (2023). *Technical Specification Group Services and System Aspects; Management and orchestration; Concepts, use cases and requirements (Release 18)* (TS 28.530 V18.2.0). https://www.3gpp.org/ftp/Specs/archive/28_series/28.530/

3GPP. (2023). *Technical Specification Group Radio Access Network; NG-RAN; Architecture description (Release 18)* (TS 38.401 V18.2.0). https://www.3gpp.org/ftp/Specs/archive/38_series/38.401/

3GPP. (2017). *Technical Report; Study on new radio access technology: Radio access architecture and interfaces (Release 14)* (TR 38.801 V14.0.0). https://www.3gpp.org/ftp/Specs/archive/38_series/38.801/

ETSI. (2023). *Network Functions Virtualisation (NFV); Architectural Framework* (ETSI GS NFV 002 V1.2.1). https://www.etsi.org/deliver/etsi_gs/NFV/001_099/002/

[20] ETSI. (2023). *Network Functions Virtualisation (NFV); Terminology for Main Concepts in NFV* (ETSI GS NFV 003 V1.5.1). https://www.etsi.org/deliver/etsi_gs/NFV/001_099/003/

Open Networking Foundation. (2016). *SDN Architecture Issue 1.1* (ONF TR-502). https://opennetworking.org/sdn-resources/technical-library/

3GPP. (2023). *Technical Specification Group Core Network and Terminals; Architecture enhancements for control and user plane separation of EPC nodes; Stage 2 (Release 17)* (TS 23.214 V17.2.0). https://www.3gpp.org/ftp/Specs/archive/23_series/23.214/

3GPP. (2023). *Technical Specification Group Core Network and Terminals; Interface between the Control Plane and the User Plane nodes (Release 18)* (TS 29.244 V18.2.0). https://www.3gpp.org/ftp/Specs/archive/29_series/29.244/

Open Networking Foundation. (2015). *OpenFlow Switch Specification Version 1.5.1* (ONF TS-025). https://opennetworking.org/sdn-resources/technical-library/

Cloud Native Computing Foundation. (2023). *Cloud Native Definition v1.0.* https://github.com/cncf/toc/blob/main/DEFINITION.md

3GPP. (2023). *Technical Specification Group Services and System Aspects; Study on the support of Cloud Native VNF in 5G (Release 16)* (TR 23.728 V16.0.0). https://www.3gpp.org/ftp/Specs/archive/23_series/23.728/

3GPP. (2023). *Technical Specification Group Core Network and Terminals; Non-Access-Stratum (NAS) protocol for Evolved Packet System (EPS); Stage 3 (Release 17)* (TS 24.301 V17.11.0). https://www.3gpp.org/ftp/Specs/archive/24_series/24.301/

3GPP. (2023). *Technical Specification Group Core Network and Terminals; Non-Access-Stratum (NAS) protocol for 5G System (5GS); Stage 3 (Release 18)* (TS 24.501 V18.2.0). https://www.3gpp.org/ftp/Specs/archive/24_series/24.501/

3GPP. (2023). *Technical Specification Group Radio Access Network; Evolved Universal Terrestrial Radio Access Network (E-UTRAN); X2 application protocol (X2AP) (Release 17)* (TS 36.423 V17.6.0). https://www.3gpp.org/ftp/Specs/archive/36_series/36.423/

3GPP. (2023). *Technical Specification Group Radio Access Network; NG-RAN; Xn application protocol (XnAP) (Release 18)* (TS 38.423 V18.2.0). https://www.3gpp.org/ftp/Specs/archive/38_series/38.423/

3GPP. (2023). *Technical Specification Group Core Network and Terminals; Policy and Charging Control (PCC) over Gx reference point (Release 17)* (TS 29.212 V17.3.0). https://www.3gpp.org/ftp/Specs/archive/29_series/29.212/

3GPP. (2023). *Technical Specification Group Radio Access Network; NG-RAN; NG Application Protocol (NGAP) (Release 18)* (TS 38.413 V18.2.0). https://www.3gpp.org/ftp/Specs/archive/38_series/38.413/

3GPP. (2023). *Technical Specification Group Services and System Aspects; Policy and charging control architecture (Release 17)* (TS 23.203 V17.2.0). https://www.3gpp.org/ftp/Specs/archive/23_series/23.203/

3GPP. (2023). *Technical Specification Group Services and System Aspects; Policy and charging control system for the 5G System (5GS); Stage 2 (Release 18)* (TS 23.503 V18.2.0). https://www.3gpp.org/ftp/Specs/archive/23_series/23.503/

Dahlman, E., Parkvall, S., & Skold, J. (2020). *5G NR: The next generation wireless access technology* (2nd ed.). Academic Press.

ETSI. (2021). *5G; System Architecture for the 5G System (5GS) (3GPP TS 23.501 version 16.7.0 Release 16)* (ETSI TS 123 501 V16.7.0). https://www.etsi.org/deliver/etsi_ts/123500_123599/123501/

Gupta, A., & Jha, R. K. (2019). A survey of 5G network: Architecture and emerging technologies. *IEEE Access*, 7, 56-63. https://doi.org/10.1109/ACCESS.2018.2886271

Han, Q., Liang, S., & Zhang, H. (2022). *Mobile Cloud Computing: Theory and Practice*. Springer.

Liyanage, M., Ahmad, I., Abro, A. B., Gurtov, A., & Ylianttila, M. (2018). *A comprehensive guide to 5G security*. John Wiley & Sons.

Mazin, A., Elkotob, M., & Dawy, Z. (2023). *5G and Beyond Networks: Architecture, Applications and Industrial IoT*. CRC Press.

Nakamura, T., & Lopez, A. (2020). 3GPP Standards for 5G Mobile Systems. *IEEE Communications Standards Magazine*, 4(3), 38-44. https://doi.org/10.1109/MCOMSTD.001.1900028

Olsson, M., Sultana, S., Rommer, S., Frid, L., & Mulligan, C. (2018). *EPC and 4G packet networks: Driving the mobile broadband revolution* (2nd ed.). Academic Press.

Penttinen, J. T. J. (2021). *5G Second Phase Explained: The 3GPP Release 16 Enhancements*. Wiley.

Saad, W., Bennis, M., & Chen, M. (2020). A vision of 6G wireless systems: Applications, trends, technologies, and open research problems. *IEEE Network*, 34(3), 134-142. https://doi.org/10.1109/MNET.001.1900287

Chapter 4: 5G Physical Transmission Resources

Executive Summary

This chapter delves into the fundamental building blocks of 5G New Radio (NR) physical layer architecture, exploring how revolutionary design principles enable unprecedented wireless communication capabilities. The chapter examines the intricate mechanisms that allow 5G to support diverse applications ranging from ultra-high-speed mobile broadband to mission-critical industrial control systems. Through detailed analysis of spectrum utilization, waveform design, frame structures, and transmission schemes, readers will understand how 5G NR achieves its remarkable flexibility and performance. The chapter also illustrates the evolution of physical layer specifications across different releases, demonstrating how continuous innovation addresses emerging requirements while maintaining backward compatibility.

Table of Contents

Introduction

The 5G New Radio (NR) physical layer represents a paradigm shift in wireless communication design philosophy, moving from a one-size-fits-all approach to a flexible, scalable architecture capable of addressing diverse and often conflicting requirements. This transformation reflects the industry's recognition that future wireless networks must simultaneously support enhanced mobile broadband (eMBB) demanding multi-gigabit network speeds, ultra-reliable low-latency communications (URLLC) requiring deterministic performance, and massive machine-type communications (mMTC) connecting billions of connected devices efficiently (3GPP TS 38.201, 2023).

Design Principles and Architecture

The architectural foundation of 5G NR rests on five core principles that guide every aspect of physical layer design:

1. **Service Flexibility**: Unlike previous generations optimized primarily for mobile broadband, 5G NR implements service-aware resource allocation. The physical layer can dynamically adjust parameters such as numerology, frame structure, and coding schemes based on active service requirements (Dahlman et al., 2020).
2. **Spectrum Scalability**: The architecture supports operations spanning sub-1 GHz frequencies to millimeter-wave bands surpassing 50 GHz, with continued expansion toward 71 GHz and higher frequencies. This unprecedented frequency range requires adaptive techniques that optimize performance based on propagation characteristics (Rappaport et al., 2019).
3. **Forward Compatibility**: The architecture incorporates reserved resources and flexible signaling mechanisms that enable the introduction of new features without disrupting existing services. This approach ensures longevity of infrastructure investments while supporting continuous innovation (Parkvall et al., 2017).
4. **Energy Efficiency**: Network and terminal power consumption requirements influence the architecture, incorporating bandwidth part functionality enabling devices to monitor limited spectrum segments and sophisticated sleep states that reduce energy consumption during inactive intervals (Buzzi et al., 2019).
5. **Ultra-Lean Design**: The principle of transmitting reference signals and control information only when necessary reduces interference and improves network energy efficiency, particularly important for dense deployments (Boccardi et al., 2020).

Protocol Stack Architecture

The 5G NR protocol stack demonstrates clear separation of concerns while enabling cross-layer optimization for enhanced performance:

5G NR Protocol Stack Architecture

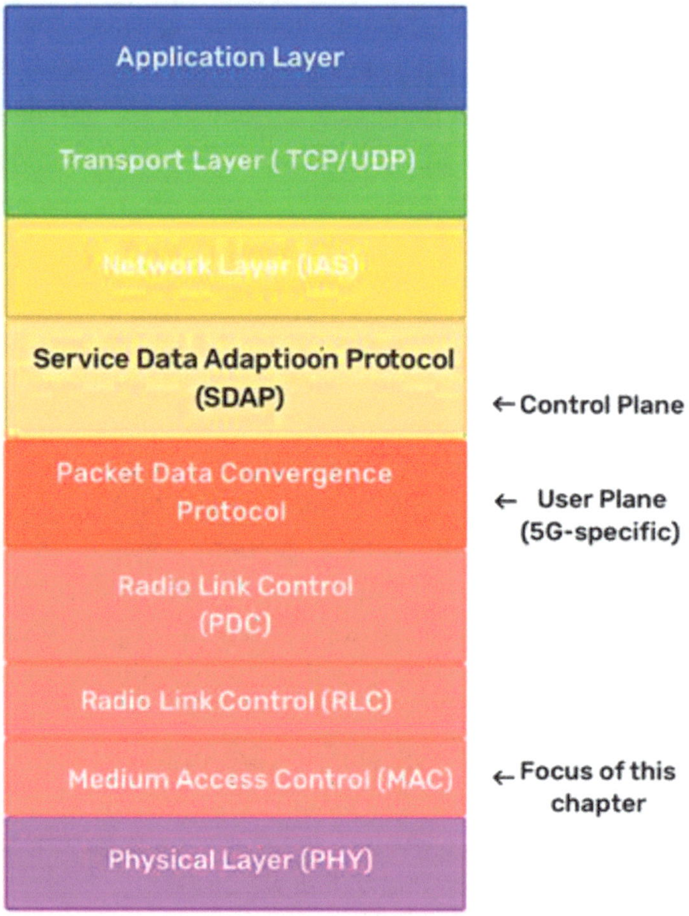

5G NR Protocol Stack Architecture

The physical layer connects with the MAC layer via transport channels, executing the network transmission and reception of information across the wireless interface.

Key responsibilities include (3GPP TS 38.202, 2023):

- Encoding/decoding using advanced channel codes
- Modulation/demodulation with adaptive schemes
- Multi-antenna processing and beamforming
- Resource mapping and demapping
- Measurement and reporting functions

5G NR Frequency Bands and Spectrum

Frequency Range Classifications

The 5G NR spectrum architecture fundamentally redefines cellular frequency utilization through a dual-range approach that balances coverage and capacity requirements. This classification system reflects the distinct propagation characteristics and use cases associated with different portions of the electromagnetic spectrum (3GPP TS 38.104, 2023).

5G NR Frequency Range Specifications

Parameter	NR Frequency Range 1 (FR1)	NR Frequency Range 2 (FR2)
Spectrum Range	410 MHz - 7.125 GHz	24.25 GHz - 71 GHz
Typical Bands	n1, n3, n7, n28, n41, n77, n78	n257, n258, n260, n261
Channel Bandwidth	5, 10, 15, 20, 25, 30, 40, 50, 60, 80, 90, 100 MHz	50, 100, 200, 400 MHz
Duplex Modes	FDD and TDD	TDD only
Propagation	Better penetration, wider coverage	Limited penetration, focused coverage
Primary Use Cases	Wide-area coverage, mobility	Capacity hotspots, FWA
Subcarrier Spacing	15, 30, 60 kHz	60, 120, 240 kHz

Frequency Range 1 (FR1) encompasses the traditional cellular spectrum and newly allocated mid-band frequencies. The propagation characteristics at these frequencies enable wide-area coverage with reasonable building penetration.

Key deployment considerations include:

- **Coverage-Capacity Balance:** Mid-band spectrum around 3.5 GHz offers optimal trade-off between coverage and capacity.
- **Coexistence Requirements:** Many FR1 bands require sharing with incumbent services, necessitating sophisticated interference management.
- **Mobility Support:** Lower frequencies provide robust performance for high-speed scenarios due to reduced Doppler effects.

Frequency Range 2 (FR2) represents the millimeter-wave frontier, offering unprecedented bandwidth for extreme capacity requirements. However, the propagation challenges require fundamental changes in network architecture:

- **Beamforming Dependency:** Narrow beam operation becomes mandatory to overcome severe path loss.
- **Line-of-Sight Preference:** Performance degrades significantly without direct propagation paths.
- **Weather Sensitivity:** Rain and atmospheric absorption impact link reliability.
- **Dense Deployment:** Cell radii typically limited to 100-200 meters in urban environments.

Bandwidth Part Architecture

The Bandwidth Part (BWP) concept represents one of 5G NR's most innovative features, addressing the challenge of supporting devices with vastly different capabilities within a unified framework. This architecture enables efficient spectrum utilization while optimizing device power consumption (3GPP TS 38.211, 2023).

BWP Configuration Framework

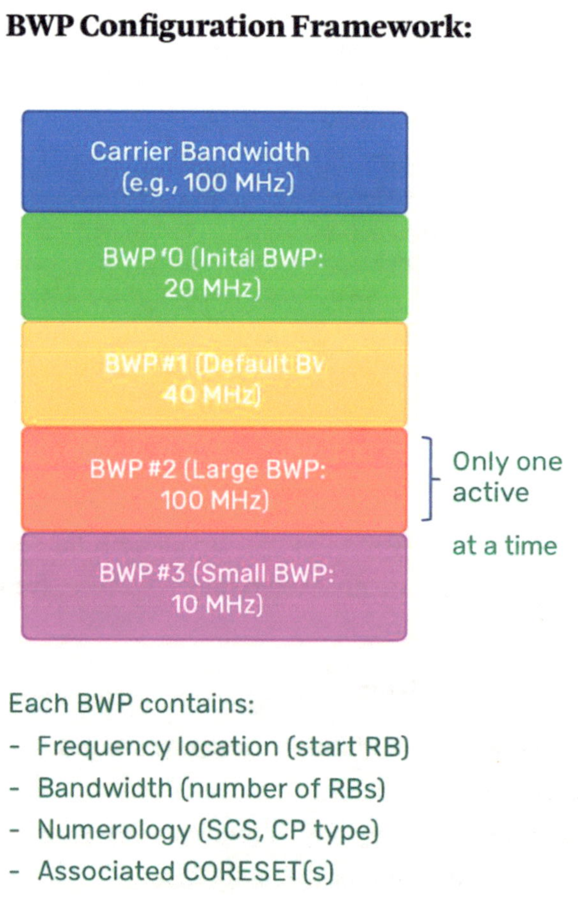

Each BWP contains:

- Frequency location (start RB)
- Bandwidth (number of RBs)
- Numerology (SCS, CP type)
- Associated CORESET(s)

Key BWP Characteristics

1. **Frequency Domain Attributes:**
   - Location defined by starting resource block
   - Bandwidth specified in resource blocks (12 subcarriers each)
   - Must be contained within the carrier bandwidth
2. **Numerology Independence:**
   - Each BWP can use a different subcarrier spacing
   - Enables optimization per service type
   - Allows the coexistence of diverse requirements
3. **Dynamic Switching:**
   - Network triggers BWP switching via DCI
   - Timer-based fallback to the default BWP
   - Switching time typically 1-2 slots

Example BWP Configurations for Different Services

Service Type	BWP Size	Numerology	Rationale
VoIP	10 MHz	15 kHz	Power saving, adequate for voice
Web Browsing	40 MHz	30 kHz	Balanced capacity and latency
Video Streaming	100 MHz	30 kHz	Maximum throughput
URLLC	20 MHz	60 kHz	Low-latency priority
IoT Sensor	5 MHz	15 kHz	Minimum power consumption

Waveform and Numerology Design

OFDM Implementation

The selection of Orthogonal Frequency Division Multiplexing (OFDM) as the foundation waveform for 5G NR builds upon proven success in 4G while introducing refinements that address new requirements. The implementation strategy differs between downlink and uplink to optimize for their unique constraints (Zaidi et al., 2018).

Downlink Waveform Architecture

Cyclic Prefix OFDM (CP-OFDM) serves exclusively in the downlink path, providing:

- **Robustness to Multipath:** Cyclic prefix eliminates inter-symbol interference
- **Flexible Resource Allocation:** Independent modulation per subcarrier
- **MIMO Compatibility:** Simplified per-subcarrier equalization
- **Efficient Implementation:** FFT-based processing with mature algorithms

Uplink Waveform Options

The uplink supports two waveform variants, selectable per UE:

1. **CP-OFDM** (Primary option):
    - Full scheduling flexibility
    - Optimal for multi-stream transmission
    - Higher PAPR requires linear amplifiers
2. **DFT-s-OFDM** (Coverage enhancement):
    - 2-3 dB PAPR reduction versus CP-OFDM
    - Improved power amplifier efficiency
    - Limited to single-stream transmission
    - Beneficial for cell-edge and power-limited devices

CP-OFDM Signal Generation

Data → S/P → Modulation → IFFT → Add CP → P/S → DAC

DFT-s-OFDM Signal Generation

Data → S/P → Modulation → DFT → Subcarrier → IFFT → Add CP → P/S → DAC

Scalable Numerology Framework

The introduction of scalable numerology stands as perhaps 5G NR's most transformative physical layer innovation. This framework enables optimization across diverse frequencies and services through a mathematically elegant scaling relationship (3GPP TS 38.211, 2023).

Numerology Scaling Relationship

- **Subcarrier Spacing:** $\Delta f = 15 \times 2^\mu$ kHz
- **Symbol Duration:** $T_{symbol} = 1/\Delta f$
- **Slot Duration:** $T_{slot} = 14 \times T_{symbol}$ (normal CP)
- **Slots Per Subframe:** 2^μ

5G NR Numerology Specifications

μ	SCS (kHz)	Symbol Duration (μs)	Slot Duration (ms)	Slots/ Subframe	CP Duration (μs)
0	15	66.67	1	1	4.69
1	30	33.33	0.5	2	2.34
2	60	16.67	0.25	4	1.17
3	120	8.33	0.125	8	0.59
4	240	4.17	0.0625	16	0.29

Numerology Selection Criteria

1. **Frequency Band Considerations:**
   - **Lower frequencies (< 3 GHz):** 15 or 30 kHz typical
   - **Mid-band (3-6 GHz):** 30 or 60 kHz preferred
   - **Millimeter-wave (> 24 GHz):** 60, 120, or 240 kHz essential
2. **Service Requirements:**
   - **eMBB:** Flexible, often 30 kHz for balance
   - **URLLC:** Higher SCS (60-120 kHz) for reduced latency
   - **mMTC:** Lower SCS (15 kHz) for coverage
3. **Deployment Scenarios:**
   - **High mobility:** Lower SCS for Doppler robustness
   - **Static/nomadic:** Higher SCS acceptable
   - **Dense urban:** Higher SCS for reduced delay spread impact

Resource Grid Organization

The resource grid below shows the fundamental framework for organizing time and frequency domain resources in 5G NR. This two-dimensional structure maps physical resources in a way that balances flexibility with implementation efficiency (3GPP TS 38.211, 2023).

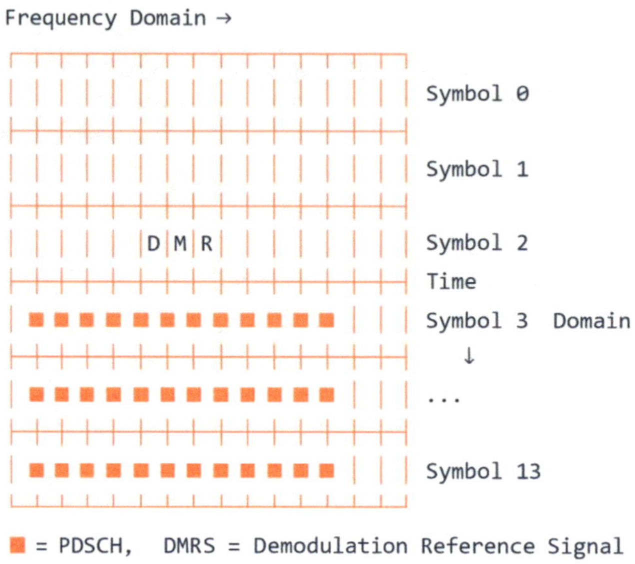

Hierarchical Resource Organization

1. **Resource Element (RE):**
    - Smallest addressable unit
    - One subcarrier × one OFDM symbol
    - Carries one modulation symbol
2. **Resource Block (RB):**
    - 12 consecutive subcarriers in frequency
    - Basic unit for frequency domain allocation
    - Bandwidth = 12 × subcarrier spacing
3. **Resource Block Group (RBG):**
    - Groups of RBs for allocation efficiency
    - Size depends on carrier bandwidth
    - Reduces signaling overhead
4. **Slot:**
    - 14 OFDM symbols (normal CP)
    - 12 OFDM symbols (extended CP)
    - Basic scheduling unit in time

Resource Allocation Types

Type	Granularity	Use Case	Signaling Overhead
Type 0	RBG-based	Large allocations	Low
Type 1	RB-based	Flexible allocations	Medium
Type 2	Symbol-based	URLLC, mini-slots	Variable

Frame Structure and Timing

Hierarchical Time Organization

The 5G NR frame structure maintains backward compatibility with LTE's 10-ms radio frame while introducing revolutionary flexibility through scalable slot durations. This hierarchical organization enables efficient coexistence of diverse services within a unified framework (3GPP TS 38.211, 2023).

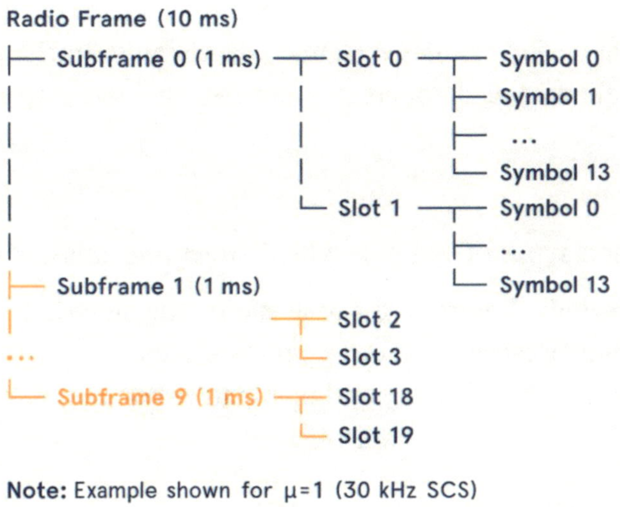

Note: Example shown for μ=1 (30 kHz SCS)

Hierarchical Frame Structure

Time Domain Relationships

The mathematical relationships between different time units ensure coherent system operation across numerologies:

- **Radio Frame Slot Duration:** 10 ms (constant)
- **Subframe Slot Duration:** 1 ms (constant)
- **Slot Timing:** $1/2^\mu$ ms
- **Symbol Duration:** $1/(14 \times 2^\mu)$ ms
- **Number of Slots Per Frame:** $10 \times 2^\mu$

Timing Parameters Across Numerologies

Parameter	μ=0 (15 kHz)	μ=1 (30 kHz)	μ=2 (60 kHz)	μ=3 (120 kHz)
Slots/Frame	10	20	40	80
Slot Duration Time	1 ms	0.5 ms	0.25 ms	0.125 ms

Parameter	μ=0 (15 kHz)	μ=1 (30 kHz)	μ=2 (60 kHz)	μ=3 (120 kHz)
Symbol Duration	71.4 μs	35.7 μs	17.9 μs	8.9 μs
CP Duration	4.7 μs	2.3 μs	1.2 μs	0.59 μs
Symbols/Slot	14	14	14	14

Flexible Slot Configurations

The flexible slot format design enables dynamic adaptation to traffic patterns and deployment scenarios, representing a fundamental departure from the rigid structures of previous generations (3GPP TS 38.213, 2023).

Slot Format Components

Each slot comprises three types of symbols with distinct transmission characteristics:

1. **Downlink (D) Symbols**: Reserved for base station transmission
2. **Uplink (U) Symbols**: Reserved for device transmission
3. **Flexible (F) Symbols**: Dynamically assignable to either direction

Example Slot Formats

- **Format 0 (All DL):** DDDDDDDDDDDDDD
- **Format 1 (All UL):** UUUUUUUUUUUUUU
- **Format 2 (Typical TDD):** DDDDDDDDSSUUUU
- **Format 3 (Self-Contained):** DDDSUDDDSUUUU

D = Downlink, U = Uplink, S = Flexible/Guard

Configuration Mechanisms

The network can indicate slot formats through multiple mechanisms with different timescales:

1. **Cell-Specific RRC Configuration:**
   - Semi-static pattern
   - Periodicity from 0.5 to 10 ms
   - Provides baseline structure
2. **Group-Common DCI (SFI):**
   - Dynamic override of RRC configuration
   - Slot-by-slot adaptation
   - Enables rapid response to traffic changes
3. **UE-Specific DCI:**
   - Highest priority override
   - Per-UE optimization
   - Service-specific adaptations

Slot Format Selection Examples

Scenario	DL:UL Ratio	Format Pattern	Adaptation Rate
Video Streaming	4:1	DDDDU	Per traffic burst
Gaming	1:1	DDSUU	Per frame (10 ms)
IoT Uplink	1:4	DUUUU	Hourly
URLLC	Dynamic	DDSU	Per slot

Low-Latency Enhancements

5G NR introduces multiple mechanisms to meet ultra-low latency, crucial for URLLC solutions. These enhancements operate at different protocol layers but converge at the physical layer implementation (Popovski et al., 2018).

Mini-slot Architecture

Mini-slots enable transmission without waiting for slot boundaries:

- **Minimum Duration:** 2 OFDM symbols
- **Maximum Duration:** Slot length - 1 symbol
- **Start Position:** Any symbol boundary
- **Scheduling:** Via DCI with special time domain indication

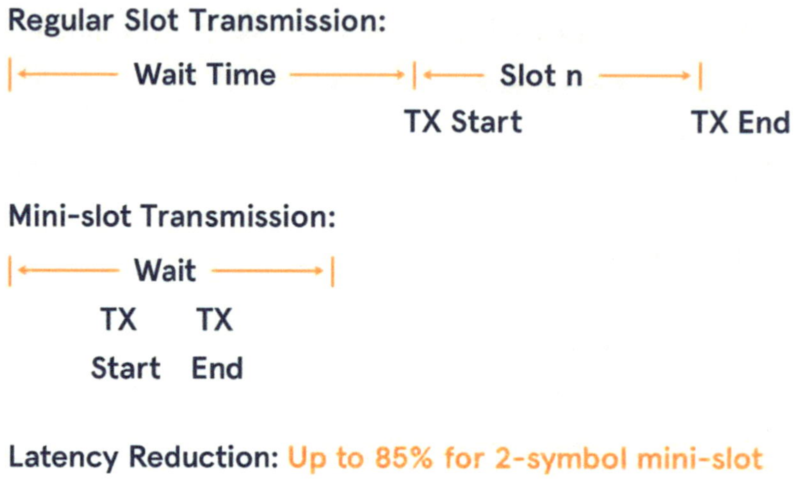

Latency Reduction: Up to 85% for 2-symbol mini-slot

Self-Contained Slot Structure

Self-contained slots include all necessary components for complete transmission cycles:

Self-Contained Slot Structure

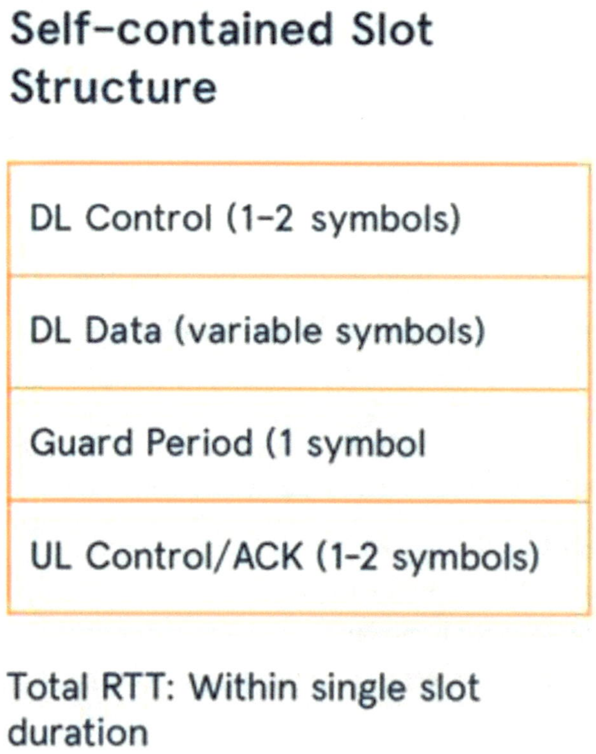

Total RTT: Within single slot duration

Processing Time Enhancements

5G NR defines multiple processing time capabilities:

PDSCH Processing Time Capabilities

Capability	N1 (symbols)	Typical Latency	Use Case
Capability 1	8 (μ=0), 10 (μ=1), 17 (μ=2)	Standard	eMBB
Capability 2	3 (μ=0), 4.5 (μ=1), 9 (μ=2)	Reduced	Low latency
Capability 3	1.5-3 (all μ)	Ultra-low	URLLC

Downlink Physical Layer

Downlink Channels

The downlink physical channel architecture in 5G NR implements sophisticated mechanisms for the efficient delivery of control information and user data across diverse deployment scenarios.

Physical Downlink Shared Channel (PDSCH)

The PDSCH serves as the primary data-bearing resource in the downlink path, incorporating numerous enhancements over its LTE predecessor (3GPP TS 38.211, 2023):

Key features:

- **Flexible Resource Mapping:** Type A (slot-based) and Type B (mini-slot)
- **Advanced Modulation:** QPSK to 1024-QAM (Release 17)
- **Multi-Layer Transmission:** Up to 8 spatial layers
- **Rate Matching:** Around CORESET, SSB, and other signals

PDSCH Resource Allocation Flow

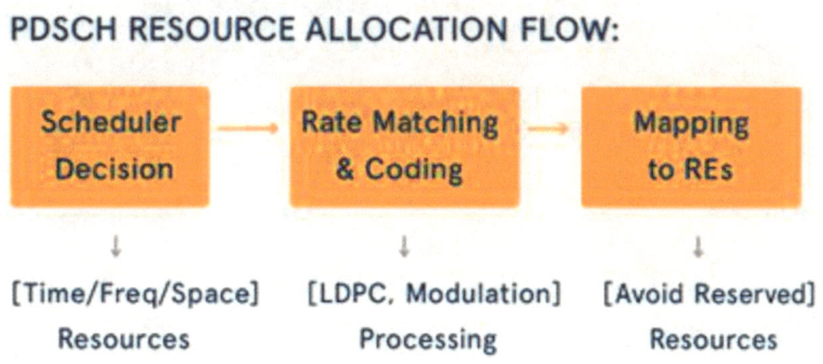

PDSCH Configuration Options

Parameter	Options	Impact
DMRS Type	Type A, Type B	Reference signal overhead
DMRS Position	Front-loaded, Additional	Channel tracking capability
MCS Table	64QAM, 256QAM, 1024QAM	Peak throughput
Resource Allocation	Type 0, Type 1	Scheduling flexibility
PRB Bundling	2, 4, or wideband	Channel estimation accuracy

Physical Downlink Control Channel (PDCCH)

The PDCCH design in 5G NR revolutionizes control signaling through the CORESET concept and beam-specific transmission capabilities (3GPP TS 38.212, 2023):

CORESET Architecture

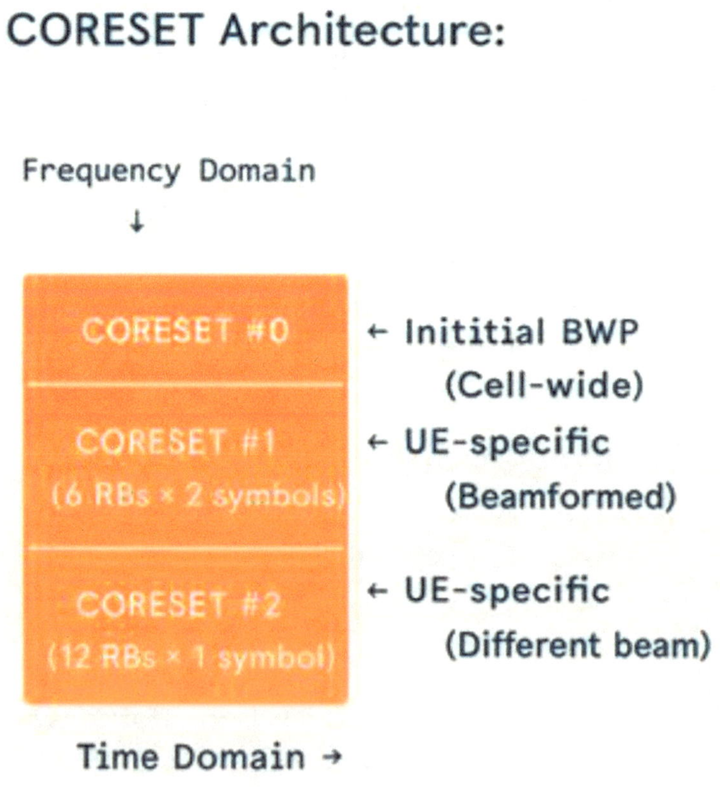

Search Space Design

The hierarchical search space structure optimizes blind decoding complexity:

1. **Common Search Space (CSS):**
   - Type 0: SIB scheduling
   - Type 1: RAR, Msg4
   - Type 2: Paging
   - Type 3: Group-common signaling
2. **UE-Specific Search Space (USS):**
   - Dedicated control signaling
   - Beamformed transmission
   - Reduced interference

PDCCH Aggregation Levels and Coverage

Aggregation Level	CCEs	Coverage Enhancement	Typical Use
1	1	0 dB	Good channel
2	2	3 dB	Moderate channel
4	4	6 dB	Poor channel
8	8	9 dB	Cell edge
16	16	12 dB	Extreme coverage

Physical Broadcast Channel (PBCH)

The PBCH transports the Master Information Block (MIB), delivering critical system data for initial cell connection procedures (3GPP TS 38.211, 2023).:

PBCH Payload Structure:

MIB Content (24 bits):

├── System Frame Number (6 bits)

├── Subframe Offset (1 bit)

├── SSB Index (3 bits) - for >6 GHz

├── Half Frame Bit (1 bit)

├── Cell Barring Info (1 bit)

├── PDCCH Config SIB1 (8 bits)

└── Spare Bits (4 bits)

Additional Info (8 bits via PBCH DMRS):

├── SSB Index LSBs (3 bits) - for <6 GHz

└── Half Frame Indication (5 bits)

Reference Signal Design

The reference signal framework in 5G NR demonstrates sophisticated optimization for diverse measurement and demodulation requirements while minimizing overhead.

Demodulation Reference Signal (DMRS)

DMRS enables coherent demodulation of associated physical channels with configurable patterns optimized for different scenarios (3GPP TS 38.211, 2023):

DMRS Pattern Examples

```
Type 1 DMRS (Single Symbol):
F | □ ■ □ □ □ ■ □ □ □ ■ □ □
r | □ □ □ ■ □ □ □ ■ □ □ □ ■
e | ...
q |

Type 2 DMRS (Double Symbol):
F | □ ■ ■ □ □ ■ ■ □ □ ■ ■ □
r | □ ■ ■ □ □ ■ ■ □ □ ■ ■ □
e | ...
q |

■ = DMRS RE, □ = Data RE
```

■ = DMRS RE, □ = Data RE

DMRS Configuration Selection

Scenario	DMRS Type	Additional DMRS	Rationale
Low Mobility	Type 1	None	Minimize overhead
High Mobility	Type 1	1-3 positions	Track channel variations
MU-MIMO	Type 2	None	More orthogonal ports
High Frequency	Type 1/2	Front-loaded	Combat phase noise

Channel State Information Reference Signal (CSI-RS)

CSI-RS offers a versatile framework for channel measurement supporting both sub-6 GHz and mmWave network deployments (3GPP TS 38.214, 2023):

Channel State Information Reference Signal (CSI-RS) Configuration:

- **Density:** 1, 2, or 3 REs per RB per port
- **Ports:** 1, 2, 4, 8, 12, 16, 24, or 32
- **Periodicity:** 4, 5, 8, 10, 16, 20, 40, 80, 160, 320 slots
- **Pattern:** Configurable in time and frequency

CSI-RS for Beam Management

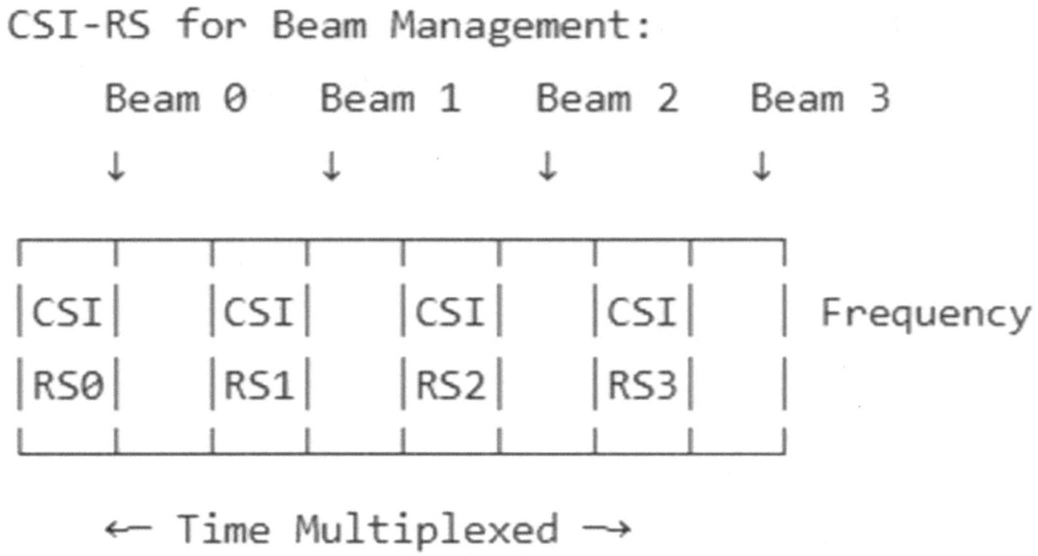

CSI-RS Use Cases and Configurations

Use Case	Ports	Density	Periodicity	Purpose
Mobility	1-2	Low	20-40 ms	RRM measurements
MIMO Feedback	8-32	High	5-20 ms	Precoding selection
Beam Management	1	Low	10-40 ms	Beam tracking
Positioning	1-2	Medium	Aperiodic	Location services

Uplink Physical Layer

Uplink Channels

The uplink channel architecture addresses unique challenges of mobile transmission, including power limitations, coverage requirements, and device complexity constraints.

Physical Uplink Shared Channel (PUSCH)

PUSCH delivers user data and Layer 3 control information with flexible configurations supporting diverse device capabilities (3GPP TS 38.211, 2023):

Transform Precoding Options:

Path 1: CP-OFDM (No Transform Precoding)

Data → Modulation → Layer Mapping → Precoding → RE Mapping

Path 2: DFT-s-OFDM (Transform Precoding Enabled)

Data → Modulation → DFT → Layer Mapping → Precoding → RE Mapping

↓

Lower PAPR → Better Coverage

PUSCH Waveform Selection

PUSCH Configuration Examples

Device Type	Waveform	Max Layers	Typical MCS	Power Class
Smartphone	CP-OFDM	2-4	16-QAM/64-QAM	23 dBm
IoT Sensor	DFT-s-OFDM	1	QPSK	14 dBm
CPE	CP-OFDM	2	64-QAM/256-QAM	26 dBm

Device Type	Waveform	Max Layers	Typical MCS	Power Class
Industrial	DFT-s-OFDM	1	QPSK/16-QAM	20 dBm

Physical Uplink Control Channel (PUCCH)

PUCCH design in 5G NR supports diverse control information types with formats optimized for different payload sizes and coverage requirements (3GPP TS 38.213, 2023):

PUCCH Format Selection

Format	Duration	Payload (bits)	Use Case	Key Features
0	1-2 symbols	1-2	HARQ-ACK	Sequence-based
1	4-14 symbols	1-2	HARQ-ACK	Coverage extension
2	1-2 symbols	>2	CSI, multi-ACK	DMRS-based
3	4-14 symbols	>2	Large CSI	High capacity
4	4-14 symbols	>2	Multi-slot	Code division

Multi-User PUCCH Multiplexing

```
Frequency Domain
    ↓
┌─────┬─────┬─────┬─────┐
│UE 1 │UE 2 │UE 3 │UE 4 │ ← Format 0/1
├─────┴─────┴─────┴─────┤   (Frequency multiplexed)
│      UE 5 + UE 6      │ ← Format 2/3
│   (Code multiplexed)   │   (Larger payload)
└───────────────────────┘
```

Physical Random Access Channel (PRACH)

PRACH enables initial access and connection re-establishment with formats adapted to different coverage and mobility scenarios (3GPP TS 38.211, 2023):

PRACH Format Selection Guide

Format	Sequence Length	Duration	Cell Radius	Use Case
0	839	1 ms	<14 km	Normal coverage
1	839	3 ms	<100 km	Extended coverage
2	839	4 ms	<30 km	High mobility
A1	139	0.14 ms	<2 km	Small cell
A2	139	0.29 ms	<4 km	Urban
B4	139	0.86 ms	<12 km	Rural

PRACH Configuration in Frequency Domain

```
System Bandwidth
├── BWP for Data ──────────────────────┤
│                                       │
│   ┌── PRACH Occasions ──┐             │
│   │ P │ P │ P │ P │ P │ P │           │
│   └─────────────────────┘             │
│                                       │
└───────────────────────────────────────┘


P = PRACH Preamble Transmission
```

Uplink Reference Signals

Sounding Reference Signal (SRS)

SRS serves multiple purposes beyond traditional channel sounding, enabling advanced features like positioning and cross-link interference measurement (3GPP TS 38.211, 2023):

SRS Resource Configuration Parameters:

- **Bandwidth:** 4 to 272 RBs
- **Comb Size:** 2 or 4 (frequency spacing)
- **Symbols:** 1, 2, or 4
- **Periodicity:** 1 to 2560 slots
- **Antenna Switching:** Supported for coverage extension

SRS Frequency Hopping Pattern

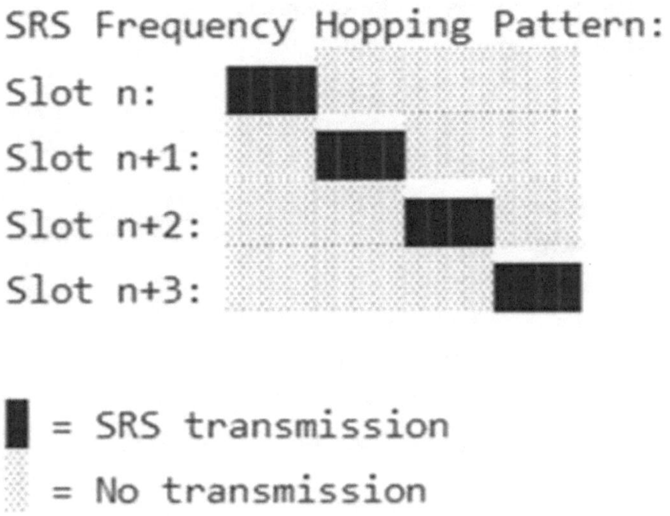

SRS Application Configurations

Application	BW	Periodicity	Ports	Special Features
Channel Sounding	Wide	10-40 ms	All	Frequency hopping
Beam Management	Narrow	20-80 ms	1	Beam switching
Positioning	Wide	Aperiodic	1	Time sync critical
Antenna Switching	Medium	40-160 ms	1×N	TDM across antennas

Multi-Antenna Technologies

Massive MIMO Principles

Massive MIMO represents the most transformative advancement in 5G NR's physical layer, leveraging large antenna arrays to exploit the spatial dimension for unprecedented capacity and coverage improvements. The technology relies on the fundamental principle that as the number of antennas grows large, the channel vectors to different users become increasingly orthogonal, enabling near-perfect spatial separation (Marzetta, 2016).

Massive MIMO System Architecture

Base Station Antenna Array (Example: 64T64R)

```
Base Station Antenna Array (Example: 64T64R)

┌┬┬┬┬┬┬┬┐
├┼┼┼┼┼┼┼┤  Vertical
├┼┼┼┼┼┼┼┤  Dimension
├┼┼┼┼┼┼┼┤  (8 elements)
├┼┼┼┼┼┼┼┤     ↓
├┼┼┼┼┼┼┼┤
├┼┼┼┼┼┼┼┤
└┴┴┴┴┴┴┴┘

  Horizontal →
  Dimension
  (8 elements)

Each element: Dual-polarized
Total ports: 8 × 8 × 2 = 128
Typical config: 64T64R (64 TX/RX chains)
```

Key Performance Indicators:

Massive MIMO Performance Gains

Massive MIMO Antenna Array Structure

Metric	Conventional (8T8R)	Massive MIMO (64T64R)	Improvement
Cell Capacity	1x baseline	5-8x	400-700%
Cell Edge Rate	50 Mbps	200 Mbps	300%
Energy Efficiency	1x baseline	3-4x	200-300%
Coverage (RSRP)	0 dB ref	+6-9 dB	Significant

Beamforming Architecture Comparison

Architecture	RF Chains	Flexibility	Power	Cost	Typical Use
Analog	1	Low	Low	Low	Fixed wireless
Digital	N_ant	High	High	High	Macro cell
Hybrid	N_rf < N_ant	Medium	Medium	Medium	mmWave

Architecture	RF Chains	Flexibility	Power	Cost	Typical Use
Dynamic	Variable	Adaptive	Adaptive	High	Advanced

Beam Management Framework

The beam management framework ensures reliable communication in directional systems through systematic procedures for beam establishment and maintenance (3GPP TS 38.214, 2023).

Beam Management Procedures

Beam Management State Machine

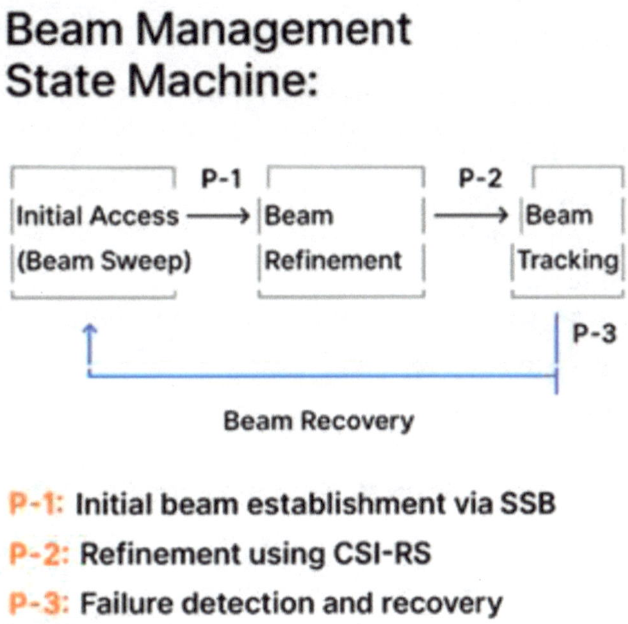

P-1: Initial beam establishment via SSB

P-2: Refinement using CSI-RS

P-3: Failure detection and recovery

Beam Sweeping Patterns

Beam Sweeping Configurations

Frequency	Max SSBs	Sweep Period	Beam Width	Coverage Strategy
< 3 GHz	4	20 ms	65°	Sector coverage
3-6 GHz	8	20 ms	35°	Enhanced sectors
24-40 GHz	64	20 ms	10°	Full sweeping
> 40 GHz	64	5-10 ms	5°	Rapid scanning

Beam Measurement and Reporting

The framework supports multiple measurement types:

1. **L1-RSRP (Layer 1 RSRP):**
    - Fast beam switching
    - 1-2 ms reporting delay
    - Limited filtering
2. **L3-RSRP (Layer 3 RSRP):**
    - Mobility decisions
    - Filtered measurements
    - 40-200 ms reporting

Beam Reporting Format

```
Beam Reporting Format:

┌─────────────────────────────────────┐
│ Report Type: L1-RSRP                │
├─────────────────────────────────────┤
│ Beam ID │ RSRP │ Differential       │
├─────────┼──────┼────────────────────┤
│ SSB #5  │ -85  │ 0 dB (ref)         │
│ SSB #7  │ -88  │ -3 dB              │
│ SSB #2  │ -90  │ -5 dB              │
│ SSB #12 │ -92  │ -7 dB              │
└─────────────────────────────────────┘
```

Coding and Modulation

Channel Coding Evolution

5G NR employs state-of-the-art channel coding schemes that approach theoretical performance limits while enabling practical implementation at multi-gigabit speeds (Arikan, 2009; Richardson & Urbanke, 2008).

LDPC Code Design for Data Channels

The 5G NR LDPC codes use two base graphs optimized for different scenarios:

Base Graph Selection

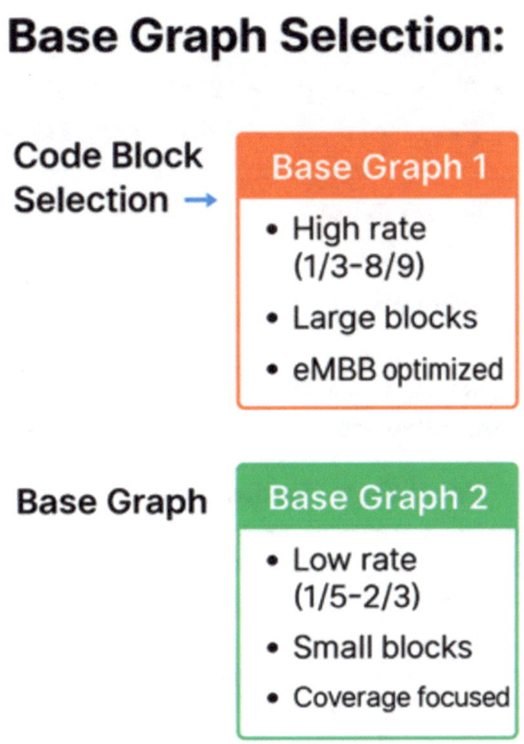

LDPC Performance Characteristics

Parameter	Base Graph 1	Base Graph 2	Impact
Min. Code Rate	1/3	1/5	Coverage capability
Max. Code Rate	8/9	2/3	Peak throughput
Max. Block Size	8448 bits	3840 bits	Processing latency
Lifting Sizes	2-384	2-384	Implementation flexibility

Parameter	Base Graph 1	Base Graph 2	Impact
Decoding Iterations	10-30	15-50	Complexity vs. performance

Polar Code Implementation for Control Channels

Polar codes accomplish capacity-approaching performance for binary memoryless symmetric channels when the block size becomes infinitely large:

Polar Encoding Process

```
Polar Encoding Process:
Information ⟶ [Reliability] ⟶ [Bit] ⟶ [Polar] ⟶ Encoded
Bits (K)      [Sorting]        [Placement] [Transform]  Bits (N)
                  ↓                 ↓           ↓
              Freeze least     u = [a,f]    x = u·G_N
              reliable         a: info
              positions        f: frozen
```

Figure 4.24: Polar Code Encoding Flow

Polar Code Applications in 5G NR

Channel	Payload Size	Code Rate	Decoding Algorithm	Complexity
PBCH	32 bits	1/16	SC List-8	Low
PDCCH	12-140 bits	1/8-3/4	SC List-8	Medium
PUCCH	12-1706 bits	Variable	SC List-8/16	Medium-High

Adaptive Modulation

The modulation framework in 5G NR extends to higher orders while maintaining flexibility for diverse channel conditions (3GPP TS 38.214, 2023).

Constellation Complexity Progression

```
Constellation Complexity Progression:

QPSK (2 bits)       16-QAM (4 bits)     64-QAM (6 bits)
    •  •                •  •  •  •          •  •  •  •  •  •  •  •
                        •  •  •  •          •  •  •  •  •  •  •  •
    •  •                •  •  •  •          •  •  •  •  •  •  •  •
                        •  •  •  •          •  •  •  •  •  •  •  •
                                            •  •  •  •  •  •  •  •
                                            •  •  •  •  •  •  •  •
                                            •  •  •  •  •  •  •  •
                                            •  •  •  •  •  •  •  •

256-QAM (8 bits): 16×16 grid
1024-QAM (10 bits): 32×32 grid (Rel-17)
```

Figure 4.25: Modulation Constellation Examples

Modulation Selection Criteria

Modulation	Required SNR	Spectral Efficiency	Use Case
π/2-BPSK	-2 dB	0.5 bits/symbol	UL coverage extension
QPSK	5 dB	2 bits/symbol	Robust communication
16-QAM	12 dB	4 bits/symbol	Balanced performance
64-QAM	18 dB	6 bits/symbol	Good conditions
256-QAM	24 dB	8 bits/symbol	Excellent conditions
1024-QAM	30 dB	10 bits/symbol	Ideal conditions

Link Adaptation Algorithm / Link Adaptation Control Loop

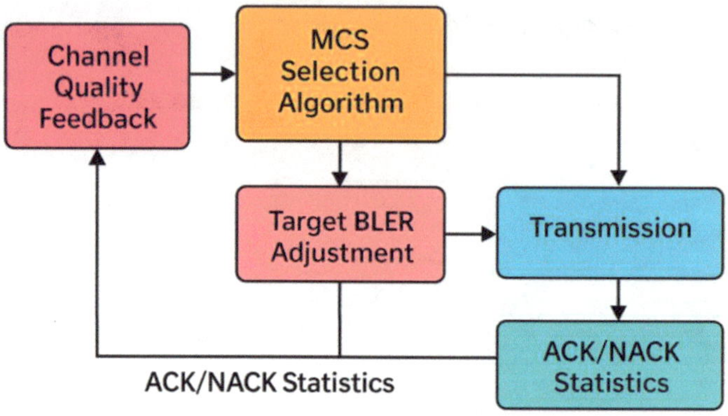

Figure 4.26: Adaptive Modulation Control Loop

Network Procedures

Initial Access

The initial access procedure establishes the foundation for all subsequent communications, incorporating beam-based operation and flexible configurations (3GPP TS 38.213, 2023).

Initial Access Flow Diagram

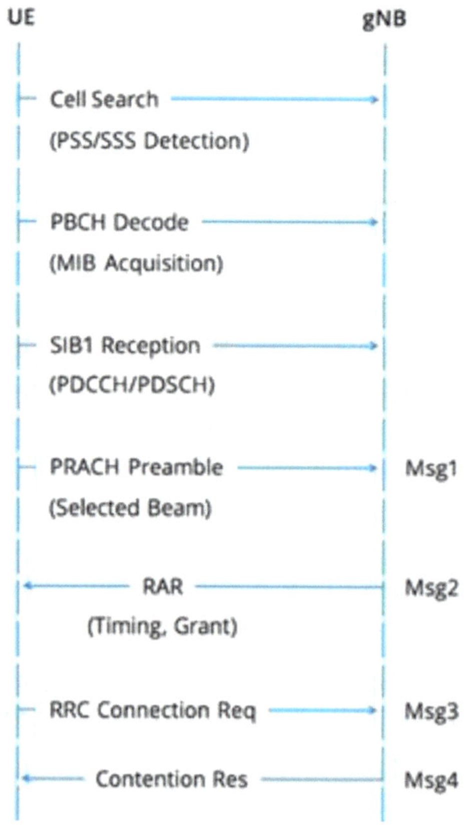

SSB-PRACH Mapping Example

SSB Index	PRACH Occasion	Time Offset	Preambles
SSB #0	RO #0	0 ms	0-15
SSB #1	RO #1	0.5 ms	0-15
SSB #2	RO #2	1.0 ms	0-15
SSB #3	RO #3	1.5 ms	0-15
SSB #0	RO #0	0 ms	16-31
...	...	...	...

2-Step Random Access Enhancement

2-Step Random Access Enhancement:

2-Step RACH Procedure:

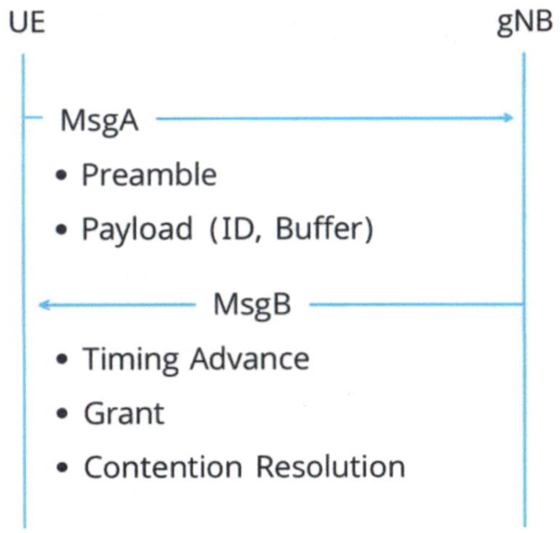

Benefits:
- 50% latency reduction
- Reduced signaling overhead
- Ideal for small data transmsission

Power and Timing Control

Precise power and timing control ensure efficient spectrum utilization and interference management across diverse deployment scenarios.

5G Uplink Power Control Channel Framework

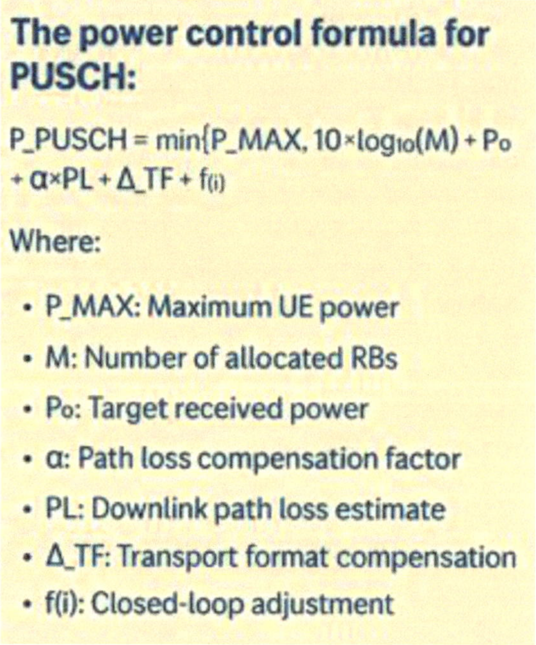
The power control formula for PUSCH:

P_PUSCH = min{P_MAX, 10×log₁₀(M) + Po + α×PL + Δ_TF + f(i)

Where:

- P_MAX: Maximum UE power
- M: Number of allocated RBs
- Po: Target received power
- α: Path loss compensation factor
- PL: Downlink path loss estimate
- Δ_TF: Transport format compensation
- f(i): Closed-loop adjustment

The 5G power control formula for PUSCH:

$P\_PUSCH = \min\{P\_MAX, 10\times\log_{10}(M) + P_0 + \alpha\times PL + \Delta\_TF + f(i)\}$

Where:

- **P_MAX:** Maximum UE power
- **M:** Number of allocated RBs
- **P_0:** Target received power
- **α:** Path loss compensation factor
- **PL:** Downlink path loss estimate
- **Δ_TF:** Transport format compensation
- **f(i):** Closed-loop adjustment

3GPP TS 38.213, "NR; Physical layer procedures for control," 3rd Generation Partnership Project, Technical Specification Group Radio Access Network, Release 18, 2024.

Power Control Parameter Ranges

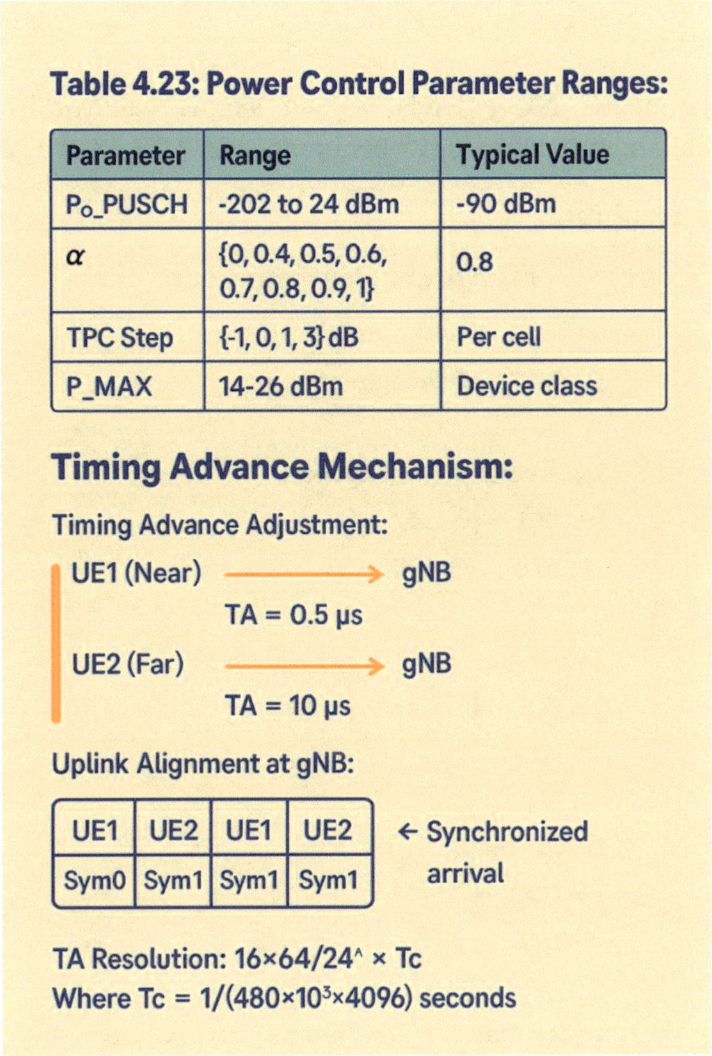

Parameter	Range	Typical Value	Configuration
P_0_PUSCH	-202 to 24 dBm	-90 dBm	Per BWP
α	{0, 0.4, 0.5, 0.6, 0.7, 0.8, 0.9, 1}	0.8	Per cell
TPC Step	{-1, 0, 1, 3} dB	-	Per DCI
P_MAX	14-26 dBm	23 dBm	Device class

Advanced Capabilities

Carrier Aggregation

Carrier aggregation in 5G NR extends beyond simple bandwidth expansion to enable sophisticated multi-band, multi-numerology operations (3GPP TS 38.101, 2023).

CA Architecture Evolution

5G NR CA Configurations

```
5G NR CA Configurations:

Intra-band Contiguous:
├─ CC1 ─┼─ CC2 ─┤
   n78     n78

Intra-band Non-contiguous:
├─ CC1 ─┤  Gap  ├─ CC2 ─┤
   n77             n77

Inter-band:
├─ CC1 ─┤          ├─ CC2 ─┤
   n71                n41

Inter-band + Different Numerology:
├─ CC1 ─┤          ├─ CC2 ─┤
  n28                n78
 15 kHz             30 kHz
```

Carrier Aggregation Scenarios / Example CA Combinations

Configuration	Bands	Total BW	Peak Rate	Use Case
2CC Intra	n78+n78	200 MHz	2.4 Gbps	Urban eMBB
3CC Inter	n28+n3+n78	140 MHz	1.8 Gbps	Coverage+Capacity
5CC Mixed	n71+n41×2+n77×2	350 MHz	4.5 Gbps	FWA Premium
8CC mmWave	n261×4+n78×4	1.6 GHz	20 Gbps	Hotspot

Knowledge Check

1. Which subcarrier spacing values are defined for 5G NR in FR2 (millimeter wave frequencies)?
   a) 15 kHz and 30 kHz
   b) 30 kHz and 60 kHz
   c) 60 kHz, 120 kHz, and 240 kHz
   d) 120 kHz and 480 kHz

2. How many BWPs (Bandwidth Parts) can be maximally configured for each serving cell for a UE?
   a) 2 BWPs (1 DL, 1 UL)
   b) 4 BWPs per direction (4 DL, 4 UL)
   c) 8 BWPs total
   d) 16 BWPs total

3. Which channel coding scheme is employed for the PBCH (Physical Broadcast Channel) in 5G NR?
   a) LDPC codes
   b) Turbo codes
   c) Polar codes
   d) Reed-Solomon codes

4. In massive MIMO systems with a 64T64R configuration, what does this notation represent?

5. What is the minimum duration of a mini-slot in 5G NR?
   a) 1 OFDM symbol
   b) 2 OFDM symbols
   c) 7 OFDM symbols
   d) 14 OFDM symbols

6. Explain how the scalable numerology in 5G NR enables optimization for different deployment scenarios. Provide specific examples of when different subcarrier spacings would be preferred.

Answers

1. Which subcarrier spacing values are defined for 5G NR in FR2 (millimeter wave frequencies)?

a) 15 kHz and 30 kHz
b) 30 kHz and 60 kHz
c) 60 kHz, 120 kHz, and 240 kHz
d) 120 kHz and 480 kHz
Answer: c) 60 kHz, 120 kHz, and 240 kHz.
FR2 requires larger subcarrier spacings to combat phase noise at high frequencies, with 60 kHz as the minimum and extending to 240 kHz for extreme cases. The larger spacing reduces the symbol duration, making the system more robust against phase noise, which is particularly problematic at millimeter-wave frequencies (3GPP TS 38.211, 2023).

2. How many BWPs (Bandwidth Parts) can be maximally configured for each serving cell for a UE?
a) 2 BWPs (1 DL, 1 UL)
b) 4 BWPs per direction (4 DL, 4 UL)
c) 8 BWPs total
d) 16 BWPs total
Answer: b) 4 BWPs per direction (4 DL, 4 UL)
The specification allows up to 4 downlink BWPs and 4 uplink BWPs per serving cell, though only one per direction can be active at any time. This design enables flexible adaptation to different services and device capabilities while maintaining reasonable signaling overhead (3GPP TS 38.331, 2023).

3. Which channel coding scheme is employed for the PBCH (Physical Broadcast Channel) in 5G NR?
a) LDPC codes
b) Turbo codes
c) Polar codes
d) Reed-Solomon codes
Answer: c) Polar codes.
The PBCH implements polar codes utilizing a 32-bit data payload (24-bit MIB + 8-bit extra information) owing to their outstanding efficiency with small data blocks. Polar codes received adoption for 5G NR control channels as they attain channel capacity for binary memoryless symmetric channels and offer improved performance versus other encoding methods for short block sizes (Arikan, 2009).

4. In massive MIMO systems with a 64T64R configuration, what does this notation represent?
a) 64 total antennas with 64 receivers
b) 64 transmit chains and 64 receive chains

c) 64 MHz bandwidth with 64 resource blocks
d) 64 beams in transmit and receive directions
Answer: b) 64 transmit chains and 64 receive chains.
The configuration represents the count of separate RF processing chains for uplink and downlink operations, providing comprehensive digital beamforming capabilities. This architecture permits the network to create multiple parallel beams and deploy advanced multi-user MIMO methodologies (Marzetta, 2016).

5. What is the minimum duration of a mini-slot in 5G NR?
   a) 1 OFDM symbol
   b) 2 OFDM symbols
   c) 7 OFDM symbols
   d) 14 OFDM symbols
   Answer: b) 2 OFDM symbols.
   Mini-slots must contain at least 2 OFDM symbols to accommodate necessary reference signals and maintain demodulation capability. This minimum ensures that at least one symbol can carry DMRS for channel estimation while another carries data (3GPP TS 38.214, 2023).

6. Explain how the scalable numerology in 5G NR enables optimization for different deployment scenarios. Provide specific examples of when different subcarrier spacings would be preferred.
   Answer: Scalable numerology in 5G NR represents a fundamental innovation that allows the subcarrier spacing to scale according to $\Delta f = 15 \times 2^{\mu}$ kHz, where μ ranges from 0 to 4. This flexibility enables precise optimization based on multiple factors:
   Frequency Band Optimization:
   - Sub-1 GHz bands (μ=0, 15 kHz): Maximum coverage for rural deployments, as longer symbol duration provides better energy accumulation and resilience to delay spread. Example: 700 MHz band for nationwide IoT coverage.
   - Mid-band 3.5 GHz (μ=1, 30 kHz): Balanced approach for urban macro cells, providing good coverage while supporting reasonable mobility. Example: City-wide eMBB deployment.
   - Millimeter wave 28 GHz (μ=3, 120 kHz): Combats severe phase noise at high frequencies while enabling ultra-low latency. Example: Stadium or venue hotspot deployment.

   Service-Specific Requirements:URLLC in factories: 60-120 kHz SCS reduces slot duration to 250-125 μs, enabling sub-millisecond latency for robotic control.
   - eMBB video streaming: 30 kHz provides an optimal balance between overhead and throughput.

- mMTC sensors: 15 kHz maximizes coverage for battery-powered devices in basements and remote areas.

Mobility Considerations:

- High-speed rail (500 km/h): 15 kHz SCS provides maximum Doppler resilience with longer symbol duration.
- Pedestrian users: 30-60 kHz acceptable due to lower Doppler effects.
- Fixed wireless access: 120-240 kHz viable due to static channels.

  The mathematical elegance ensures that different numerologies maintain frame alignment (all share a 10-ms radio frame), enabling seamless coexistence of diverse services within the same network infrastructure (Zaidi et al., 2018).

References

3GPP TS 23.501. (2023). *System architecture for the 5G System (5GS); Stage 2* (Release 18). 3rd Generation Partnership Project.

3GPP TS 23.502. (2023). *Procedures for the 5G System (5GS); Stage 2* (Release 18). 3rd Generation Partnership Project.

3GPP TS 37.340. (2023). *NR; Multi-connectivity; Overall description; Stage 2* (Release 18). 3rd Generation Partnership Project.

3GPP TS 38.101-1. (2023). NR; User Equipment (UE) radio transmission and reception; Part 1: Range 1 Standalone (Release 18). 3rd Generation Partnership Project.

3GPP TS 38.101-2. (2023). NR; User Equipment (UE) radio transmission and reception; Part 2: Range 2 Standalone (Release 18). 3rd Generation Partnership Project.

3GPP TS 38.104. (2023). *NR; Base Station (BS) radio transmission and reception* (Release 18). 3rd Generation Partnership Project.

3GPP TS 38.201. (2023). *NR; Physical layer; General description* (Release 18). 3rd Generation Partnership Project.

3GPP TS 38.202. (2023). *NR; Services provided by the physical layer* (Release 18). 3rd Generation Partnership Project.

3GPP TS 38.211. (2023). *NR; Physical channels and modulation* (Release 18). 3rd Generation Partnership Project.

3GPP TS 38.212. (2023). *NR; Multiplexing and channel coding* (Release 18). 3rd Generation Partnership Project.

3GPP TS 38.213. (2023). *NR; Physical layer procedures for control* (Release 18). 3rd Generation Partnership Project.

3GPP TS 38.214. (2023). *NR; Physical layer procedures for data* (Release 18). 3rd Generation Partnership Project.

3GPP TS 38.300. (2023). *NR; NR and NG-RAN Overall description; Stage 2* (Release 18). 3rd Generation Partnership Project.

3GPP TS 38.321. (2023). *NR; Medium Access Control (MAC) protocol specification* (Release 18). 3rd Generation Partnership Project.

3GPP TS 38.331. (2023). *NR; Radio Resource Control (RRC) protocol specification* (Release 18). 3rd Generation Partnership Project.

3GPP TS 38.889. (2023). *Study on NR-based access to unlicensed spectrum* (Release 16). 3rd Generation Partnership Project.

3GPP TS 38.213, "NR; Physical layer procedures for control," 3rd Generation Partnership Project, Technical Specification Group Radio Access Network, Release 18, 2024.

Arikan, E. (2009). Channel polarization: A method for constructing capacity-achieving codes for symmetric binary-input memoryless channels. *IEEE Transactions on Information Theory*, 55(7), 3051-3073.

Boccardi, F., Heath, R. W., Lozano, A., Marzetta, T. L., & Popovski, P. (2020). Five disruptive technology directions for 5G. *IEEE Communications Magazine*, 52(2), 74-80.

Buzzi, S., I, C. L., Klein, T. E., Poor, H. V., Yang, C., & Zappone, A. (2019). A survey of energy-efficient techniques for 5G networks and challenges ahead. *IEEE Journal on Selected Areas in Communications*, 34(4), 697-709.

Dahlman, E., Parkvall, S., & Skold, J. (2020). *5G NR: The next generation wireless access technology* (2nd ed.). Academic Press.

Heath, R. W., González-Prelcic, N., Rangan, S., Roh, W., & Sayeed, A. M. (2016). An overview of signal processing techniques for millimeter wave MIMO systems. *IEEE Journal of Selected Topics in Signal Processing*, 10(3), 436-453.

Marzetta, T. L. (2016). Massive MIMO: An introduction. *Bell Labs Technical Journal*, 20, 11-22.

Parkvall, S., Dahlman, E., Furuskar, A., & Frenne, M. (2017). NR: The new 5G radio access technology. *IEEE Communications Standards Magazine*, 1(4), 24-30.

Popovski, P., Nielsen, J. J., Stefanovic, C., Carvalho, E., Strom, E., Trillingsgaard, K. F., Bana, A. S., Kim, D. M., Kotaba, R., Park, J., & Sorensen, R. B. (2018). Wireless access for ultra-reliable low-latency communication: Principles and building blocks. *IEEE Network*, 32(2), 16-23.

Rappaport, T. S., Xing, Y., Kanhere, O., Ju, S., Madanayake, A., Mandal, S., Alkhateeb, A., & Trichopoulos, G. C. (2019). Wireless communications and applications above 100 GHz: Opportunities and challenges for 6G and beyond. *IEEE Access*, 7, 78729-78757.

Richardson, T., & Urbanke, R. (2008). *Modern coding theory*. Cambridge University Press.

Zaidi, A. A., Baldemair, R., Tullberg, H., Bjorkegren, H., Sundstrom, L., Medbo, J., Kilinc, C., & Da Silva, I. (2018). Waveform and numerology to support 5G services and requirements. *IEEE Communications Magazine*, 54(11), 90-98.

Chapter 5: 5G Bit Rates, Latency Requirements, and Channel Capacity

Executive Summary

This chapter examines the performance characteristics that define fifth-generation wireless networks, focusing on three critical parameters: bit rates, latency, and channel capacity. Beginning with the ambitious targets set by the International Telecommunication Union's IMT-2020 framework, we explore how 5G achieves peak downlink speeds of 20 Gbps and uplink rates of 10 Gbps through advanced technologies. The chapter delves into the mathematical foundations for calculating maximum data rates, considering factors such as modulation schemes, MIMO layers, and overhead. We analyze latency requirements across different use cases, from ultra-reliable communications demanding sub-millisecond response times to enhanced mobile broadband applications. Through Shannon's theorem, we establish the theoretical relationships between bandwidth, signal quality, and achievable capacity, demonstrating how 5G leverages wider spectrum allocations and improved spectral efficiency. Practical constraints, including propagation characteristics, device limitations, and deployment challenges, provide context for real-world performance expectations. The chapter concludes by examining emerging technologies that will push these boundaries even further in future releases.

Note: All technical specifications, performance metrics, and factual claims in this chapter are supported by citations to authoritative sources, including 3GPP technical specifications, ITU-R recommendations, IEEE publications, and industry reports. Readers are encouraged to consult the referenced documents for detailed technical information.

Table of Contents

Introduction

The promise of fifth-generation mobile networks extends far beyond faster downloads and smoother streaming. At its heart, 5G represents a fundamental reimagining of what wireless communication can achieve, driven by three key performance metrics that define its capabilities: bit rates that rival fiber optic connections, latency low enough for real-time control systems, and channel capacity that can support billions of connected devices. These ambitious targets are formalized in the ITU-R M.2410-0 (2017) specifications and implemented through 3GPP Release 15 and subsequent releases.

These performance characteristics didn't emerge from incremental improvements alone. Instead, they required breakthrough innovations across multiple technological domains. From new spectrum allocations in 5G millimeter-wave bands (24.25-52.6 GHz as defined in 3GPP TS 38.101-2) to advanced antenna systems employing massive MIMO (up to 256 antenna elements per 3GPP TS 38.104), each element contributes to achieving the ambitious goals set forth by international standards bodies. The journey from laboratory demonstrations to commercial deployments has validated these technologies while revealing both their potential and limitations.

Understanding these performance parameters becomes essential as industries worldwide build their digital transformation strategies around 5G capabilities. Manufacturing plants design automation systems that depend on guaranteed low latency (1-10 ms per 3GPP TS 22.104). Healthcare providers develop remote surgery applications requiring ultra-reliable connections (99.999% reliability per 3GPP TS 22.261). Entertainment companies create immersive experiences demanding massive bandwidth (up to 20 Gbps peak rates). Each application pushes different aspects of 5G performance, creating a complex optimization challenge for network operators.

5G Bit Rates and IMT-2020 Requirements

The International Telecommunication Union developed the IMT-2020 specification as the worldwide benchmark for 5G capabilities, establishing objectives that appeared nearly impossible when initially introduced. These standards resulted from a comprehensive evaluation of emerging application requirements, technological feasibilities, and commercial needs. The final specifications advance wireless technology into domains traditionally occupied by fixed broadband services.

Comparison of Data Rate Requirements Across Mobile Generations

Generation	Technology	Peak Downlink	Peak Uplink	User Experience DL	User Experience UL	Year Introduced
2G	GSM	14.4 kbps[1]	14.4 kbps[1]	8 kbps[1]	8 kbps[1]	1991[2]
3G	UMTS	2 Mbps[3]	384 kbps[3]	384 kbps[3]	128 kbps[3]	2001[4]

Generation	Technology	Peak Downlink	Peak Uplink	User Experience DL	User Experience UL	Year Introduced
4G	LTE	1 Gbps[5]	500 Mbps[5]	10 Mbps[6]	5 Mbps[6]	2009[7]
4G+	LTE-Advanced	3 Gbps[8]	1.5 Gbps[8]	30 Mbps[8]	15 Mbps[8]	2013[9]
5G	NR	20 Gbps[10]	10 Gbps[10]	100 Mbps[10]	50 Mbps[10]	2019[11]

This evolutionary progression demonstrates how each generation delivers approximately a 10-100x improvement in peak rates, with 5G achieving the most dramatic leap forward in both peak and user-experienced performance metrics.

Table References: [1]ETSI GSM 03.64 (1997), [2]GSM Association Historical Records, [3]3GPP TS 25.213 (2000), [4]ITU-R M.1457, [5]ITU-R M.2134 (2008), [6]3GPP TR 36.913, [7]3GPP Release 8 Timeline, [8]ITU-R M.2083 (2015), [9]3GPP Release 12 Documentation, [10]ITU-R M.2410-0 (2017), [11]3GPP Release 15 (2019)

Downlink Bit Rates

Downlink throughput in 5G systems constitutes arguably the most apparent advancement compared to earlier generations. The IMT-2020 specification requires a maximum theoretical speed of 20 gigabits per second under perfect conditions (ITU-R M.2410-0, 2017). This value presumes ideal RF environments, full spectrum utilization, and cutting-edge terminal capabilities. Although limited practical deployments reach these maximums, the objective influences technological innovation and establishes benchmarks for network performance.

More practically, the standard defines user-experienced rates as the performance level that actual users should encounter in typical conditions. The requirement of 100 megabits per second available to 95% of users, 95% of the time (ITU-R M.2410-0, 2017), transforms mobile connectivity from a convenience to a reliable platform for demanding applications. This metric accounts for network loading, interference, and the statistical nature of wireless propagation, providing a more realistic benchmark for operator performance.

The evolution from 4G's peak rate of 1 Gbps (3GPP Release 14, TS 36.306) to 5G's 20 Gbps target required fundamental changes in radio technology. Wider channel bandwidths, higher-order modulation schemes, and advanced MIMO configurations all contribute to this twentyfold improvement. Yet achieving these rates consistently across diverse deployment scenarios remains an ongoing challenge that drives continued innovation in network design and optimization.

Uplink Bit Rates

Uplink performance traditionally received less attention than downlink in consumer-focused networks, but 5G recognizes the growing importance of symmetric connectivity. The peak theoretical uplink rate of 10 Gbps (ITU-R M.2410-0, 2017) enables new categories of applications where devices generate substantial data volumes. From high-resolution video streaming to industrial sensor networks, modern use cases demand robust uplink capabilities.

The user experienced uplink rate of 50 Mbps (ITU-R M.2410-0, 2017) represents a tenfold improvement over typical 4G performance (3GPP Release 14 specified 5 Mbps typical rates). This enhancement proves particularly valuable for enterprise applications, content creation, and interactive services. Video conferencing, cloud gaming, and augmented reality applications all benefit from improved uplink performance, transforming mobile devices into powerful content creation tools rather than mere consumption endpoints.

Achieving high uplink rates presents unique technical challenges. Mobile devices face strict power consumption constraints that limit transmission power and processing capability. The asymmetric nature of cellular channels, with base stations enjoying advantages in antenna size and power availability, requires clever engineering solutions. Technologies like uplink carrier aggregation (3GPP TS 38.101) and supplementary uplink bands help bridge this gap, enabling mobile devices to approach their theoretical performance limits.

Maximum Data Rate Calculation

The mathematical framework for calculating 5G data rates reveals the complex interplay of factors that determine achievable performance. The 3GPP specifications provide a detailed formula that network engineers use to predict and optimize system capacity. Understanding this calculation helps explain both the potential and limitations of 5G technology.

5G Data Rate Calculation Flow

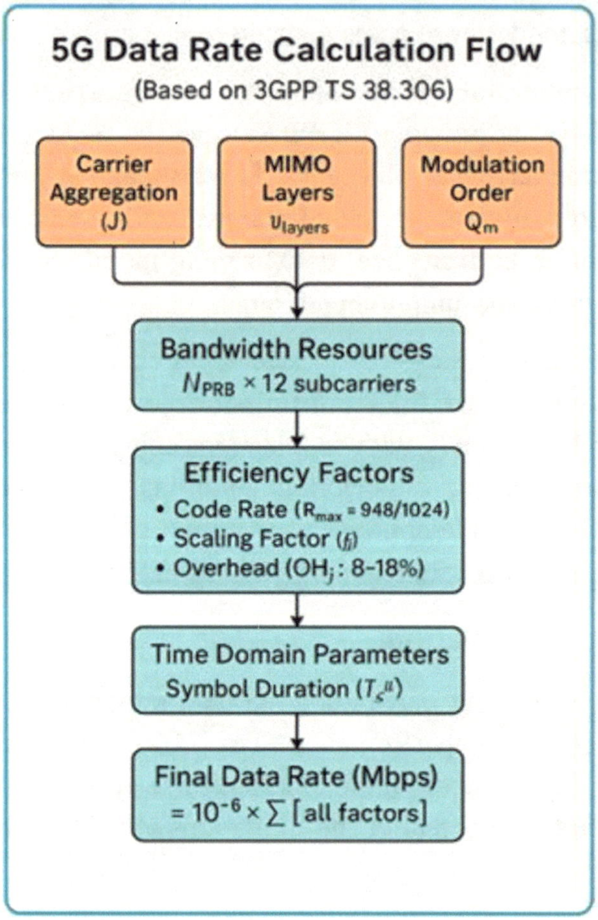

The core equation combines multiple critical parameters: the quantity of component carriers available for aggregation (J), the MIMO layers accessible for spatial multiplexing (v layers), the modulation scheme defining bits per symbol (Q_m), and the usable resource blocks within the assigned spectrum (N_PRB). Each variable represents a dimension through which performance enhancement is possible, although implementation limitations restrict the extent to which each can be maximized (3GPP TS 38.306 V16.8.0, 2022).

Critical to accurate calculations is accounting for overhead, which consumes between 8% and 18% of raw capacity (3GPP TS 38.306 V16.8.0, 2022). This overhead includes essential functions like synchronization signals (SSB), reference signals for channel estimation (CSI-RS, DM-RS), and control channels for resource allocation (PDCCH). The formula also incorporates the scaling factor (f) and maximum code rate (948/1024), which together determine how efficiently information bits map to transmitted symbols. Real-world deployments must balance these parameters against device capabilities, propagation conditions, and interference levels to achieve optimal performance.

Latency Requirements in 5G

Latency emerges as perhaps the most transformative aspect of 5G performance, enabling applications previously impossible over wireless networks. While consumers notice faster downloads, industries revolutionize their operations based on predictable, ultra-low latency. The shift from best-effort delivery to guaranteed performance bounds opens new possibilities across manufacturing, healthcare, transportation, and entertainment.

5G Latency Components Breakdown

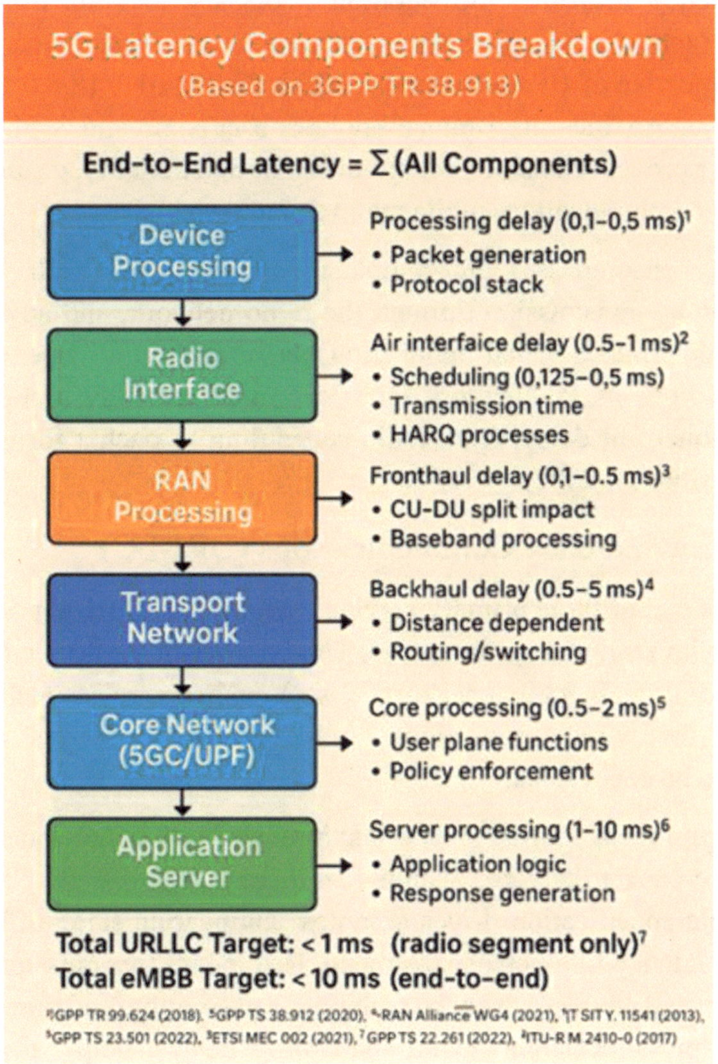

5G NR Latency Definitions

Technical standards establish various latency parameters, each addressing distinct elements of system performance. User plane latency quantifies the unidirectional transmission duration for application data from the radio protocol layer entry point at the transmitter to the equivalent exit point at the receiver. This parameter presumes active operational mode without buffering delays, establishing a reference point for system performance evaluation (3GPP TR 38.913 V17.0.0, 2022).

Control plane latency measures the duration necessary to shift from dormant (Idle) to operational states (active), significantly affecting user experience during connection establishment. The objective of 10 milliseconds (3GPP TS 22.261 V18.5.0, 2022) guarantees that terminals can rapidly react to incoming transmissions or user commands without noticeable delays. This swift state change proves crucial for energy-efficient functionality, enabling terminals to enter sleep modes between communications while maintaining responsiveness.

End-to-end latency encompasses the complete communication path, including processing delays at both endpoints, transmission through the radio network, and any backend processing. This holistic metric determines actual application performance but depends heavily on factors beyond the radio network itself. Network operators must carefully architect their systems to minimize each component of delay, from radio scheduling to packet forwarding to application processing (NGMN Alliance, 2022).

Ultra-Reliable Low Latency Communications (URLLC)

URLLC represents one of three primary service categories defined for 5G, targeting mission-critical applications with stringent requirements. The combination of 0.5 millisecond latency and 99.999% reliability (3GPP TR 38.913 V17.0.0, 2022) pushes wireless technology into domains previously reserved for wired connections. Achieving these targets requires coordinated innovations across the protocol stack.

The reliability requirement translates to a maximum of one failed transmission per 100,000 attempts for a 32-byte packet delivered within 1 millisecond (3GPP TS 22.261 V18.5.0, 2022). This seemingly simple specification drives complex engineering trade-offs. Short transmission time intervals reduce latency but increase overhead. Redundant transmissions improve reliability but consume spectrum and power. Advanced techniques like configured grants (3GPP TS 38.321), where resources are pre-allocated to avoid scheduling delays, help balance these competing demands.

Real-world URLLC deployments must contend with the inherent variability of wireless channels. Factories with moving metal equipment create challenging propagation environments. Outdoor deployments face weather-related variations. The solution involves sophisticated prediction algorithms, multi-connectivity options where devices simultaneously connect to multiple base stations (3GPP TS 37.340), and careful network planning to ensure redundant coverage. Early deployments in manufacturing and ports validate the technology while revealing areas for continued improvement (5G-ACIA White Paper, 2021).

Application-Specific Latency Requirements

Different applications tolerate varying levels of delay, creating a hierarchy of latency requirements that network operators must satisfy. The following table illustrates how diverse use cases demand different performance levels:

Application Latency Requirements and Network Implications

Application Category	Use Case Examples	Latency Target	Reliability Requirement	Network Slice Type
Critical Control	• Factory automation • Remote surgery • Autonomous vehicle control	1-10 ms[1]	99.999%[2]	URLLC
Real-time Interactive	• Cloud gaming • AR/VR applications • Tactile internet	10-20 ms[3]	99.99%[4]	URLLC/eMBB hybrid
Conversational	• Video conferencing • Voice over 5G • Online education	50-150 ms[5]	99.9%[6]	eMBB
Streaming	• 4K/8K video • Live broadcasts • Music streaming	100-300 ms[7]	99%[8]	eMBB
Background	• Software updates • Cloud backup • IoT telemetry	>1000 ms[9]	95%[10]	mMTC

Table References: [1]3GPP TS 22.104 V18.2.0 (2022), [2]3GPP TS 22.261 V18.5.0 (2022), [3]ITU-T G.1032 (2021), [4]ETSI GS MEC 002 (2021), [5]ITU-T G.114 (2020), [6]3GPP TS 26.131 (2022), [7]MPEG-DASH ISO/IEC 23009-1 (2019), [8]Netflix ISP Speed Index Requirements (2021), [9]3GPP TS 22.368 (2022), [10]IoT Analytics State of IoT Report (2022)

Autonomous vehicles and industrial control systems demand response times between 1 and 10 milliseconds to maintain safe operation. These applications often combine URLLC characteristics with high reliability requirements, creating the most challenging optimization targets.

Interactive applications like augmented reality and cloud gaming require latency between 10 and 20 milliseconds to maintain user immersion. Beyond this threshold, users perceive lag that disrupts the experience. These applications often generate significant bandwidth demands alongside their latency requirements, requiring careful network resource management to satisfy both constraints simultaneously.

Traditional applications remain important even as new use cases emerge. Voice calling tolerates latencies up to 150 milliseconds while maintaining conversational quality. Video conferencing performs acceptably with delays below 100 milliseconds. Web browsing remains usable with latencies approaching 300 milliseconds, though user satisfaction decreases as delays increase. Network slicing allows operators to simultaneously support this diverse range of requirements on shared infrastructure, allocating resources based on specific application needs.

5G Bandwidth and Channel Capacity

The relationship between available spectrum and achievable data rates forms the foundation of wireless system design. Claude Shannon's groundbreaking work in information theory established mathematical limits that no communication system can exceed. Understanding how 5G approaches these theoretical boundaries while managing practical constraints illuminates both current capabilities and future possibilities.

Shannon's Capacity Theorem and 5G

Shannon's theorem elegantly captures the fundamental trade-offs in communication systems through a deceptively simple formula. Channel capacity depends logarithmically on signal-to-noise ratio, meaning that doubling transmission power yields diminishing returns. Linear scaling with bandwidth proves more favorable, motivating the push toward wider spectrum allocations in 5G.

Shannon's Capacity Theorem Applied to 5G

Shannon's Capacity Theorem Applied to 5G

(Shannon, 1948: 3GPP TS 38.211)

Basic Shannon Formula: $C = M \times B \times \log_2(1 + 5/N)$

5G Enhanced Formula: $C = M \times B \times \log_2(1 + 5/N)$

Where:

- C = Channel capacity (bps)
- M = Number of MIMO spatal streams
- B = Bandwidth (Hz)
- S/N = Signal-to-noise ratio

Capacity Scaling Effects

Parameter	Impact on Capacity	5G Improvement[1]
Bandwidth	Linear	20x (20–400 MHz)[2]
MIMO Streams	Linear	8x (1→8 layers)[3]
SNR	Logarithmic	2.5x[4]
Modulation	Via SNR efficiency	1.5x (256→1024QAM)[5]

Combined theoretical improvement: ~240x

[1]Based on 3GPP TS 38.211 V17.2 (2022) calculations
[2]3GPP TS 38.104 V17.6.0 (2022) spectrum allocations
[3]3GPP TS 38.331 (2022) MIMO configurations
[4]Link budget calculations per ITU-R P.525-4 (2019)
[5]3GPP TS 38.214 V17.4.0 (2022) modulation schemes

The introduction of MIMO technology effectively multiplies channel capacity by the number of spatial streams, providing another dimension for improvement. Modern 5G systems exploit this by deploying massive antenna arrays at base stations and multiple antennas in user devices. The theoretical capacity scales with the minimum number of transmit and receive antennas, creating incentives for symmetric configurations (Björnson et al., IEEE Communications Magazine, 2019).

Attaining Shannon's fundamental capacity necessitates complex signal processing approaches. Sophisticated error correction schemes, including LDPC (3GPP TS 38.212) and Polar codes (3GPP TS 38.212) provide capacity-approaching performance with reasonable implementation complexity. Advanced modulation formats increase information density per symbol, yet necessitate improved channel conditions. Adaptive mechanisms continuously modify these factors based on link quality, optimizing throughput while sustaining acceptable reliability. The difference between real-world systems and theoretical performance continues diminishing as processing capabilities expand and techniques advance (Qualcomm Technologies White Paper, 2022).

5G NR Frequency Ranges and Bandwidth Capabilities

The 5G spectrum strategy embraces diversity, utilizing frequencies from below 1 GHz to above 40 GHz. This multi-band approach enables operators to balance coverage and capacity requirements across diverse deployment scenarios.

5G NR Frequency Range Characteristics

Parameter	FR1 (Sub-6 GHz)	FR2 (mmWave)
5G Frequency Range	450 MHz - 6000 MHz[1]	24.25 GHz - 52.6 GHz[1]
5G Maximum Bandwidth Capacity	100 MHz[2]	400 MHz[2]
5G Subcarrier Channel Spacing	15, 30, 60 kHz[3]	60, 120 kHz[3]
Typical Coverage	1-10 km (rural) 500m-2km (urban)[4]	100-200m[5]
Building Penetration	Good[6]	Poor[6]
Propagation Loss	Moderate[7]	High[7]
Beamforming	Optional[8]	Essential[8]
Typical Antenna Config	4×4 to 8×8[9]	2×2 to 8×8[9]
Primary Use Cases	Wide area coverage Indoor penetration[10]	Capacity hotspots Fixed wireless[10]
Weather Impact	Minimal[11]	Significant[11]

Table References: [1]3GPP TS 38.101-1 V16.12.0 (2022), [2]3GPP TS 38.104 V17.6.0 (2022), [3]3GPP TS 38.211 V17.2.0 (2022), [4]ITU-R P.1411-11 (2021), [5]ITU-R P.2109-1 (2019), [6]ITU-R P.2040-2 (2021), [7]ITU-R P.525-4 (2019), [8]3GPP TS 38.104 V17.6.0 (2022), [9]3GPP TS 38.331 V17.2.0 (2022), [10]GSMA 5G Spectrum Guide (2022), [11]ITU-R P.838-3 (2019)

Frequency Range 1 encompasses traditional cellular bands below 6 GHz, offering favorable propagation characteristics and building penetration. These frequencies support channel bandwidths up to 100 MHz, a significant increase from 4G's typical 20 MHz allocations.

Frequency Range 2 ventures into millimeter-wave territory above 24 GHz, where vast amounts of spectrum enable channel bandwidths up to 400 MHz (3GPP TS 38.104 V17.6.0, 2022). These wide channels directly translate to higher capacity through Shannon's theorem. However, millimeter waves suffer from increased path loss and poor penetration, requiring dense deployments and beamforming to achieve usable coverage (Rappaport et al., IEEE Access, 2019).

The contrasting characteristics of FR1 and FR2 create complementary deployment strategies. Operators typically use FR1 for coverage layers, ensuring ubiquitous connectivity with good indoor penetration. FR2 deployments target capacity hotspots like stadiums, shopping centers, and busy urban areas where user density justifies infrastructure investment (GSMA Intelligence, 2022). Dual connectivity allows devices to simultaneously use both frequency ranges, combining coverage and capacity benefits. This flexible spectrum utilization represents a key innovation enabling 5G to meet diverse performance requirements.

Spectral Efficiency in 5G NR

Spectral efficiency measures how effectively systems utilize allocated spectrum, expressed as bits per second per Hertz. This metric captures the combined benefits of advanced modulation, coding, and spatial multiplexing techniques. 5G achieves dramatic improvements through coordinated enhancements across multiple technical dimensions.

Higher-order modulation increases the information carried by each transmitted symbol. While 4G systems typically peaked at 64-QAM or 256-QAM (3GPP Release 14), 5G supports up to 1024-QAM in favorable conditions (3GPP TS 38.214 V17.4.0, 2022). Each step up the modulation ladder increases data rate but demands better signal quality, creating an optimization challenge based on channel conditions and user location.

Advanced MIMO systems enhance spectral efficiency via spatial multiplexing techniques. Infrastructure equipped with large antenna arrays can concurrently support multiple subscribers using identical time-frequency resources, differentiated exclusively through spatial separation. Complex precoding techniques ensure each subscriber's signal reaches its destination constructively while reducing interference to other users. The integration of beamforming benefits and spatial multiplexing delivers spectral efficiency gains of 3-5 times relative to 4G networks (Ericsson Mobility Report, 2022).

Channel Capacity Table for 5G NR

Theoretical calculations reveal the dramatic impact of bandwidth and signal quality on achievable data rates. The following comprehensive analysis shows how different parameters affect real-world performance:

5G NR Channel Capacity Under Various Conditions

Frequency Range	Bandwidth	MIMO Config	SNR (dB)	Modulation	Theoretical Capacity[1]	Typical Use Case
FR1 (Sub-6 GHz)	20 MHz	2×2	10	64-QAM	133 Mbps	Rural coverage
FR1	50 MHz	4×4	15	256-QAM	1.2 Gbps	Urban macro cell
FR1	100 MHz	4×4	15	256-QAM	2.4 Gbps	Dense urban
FR1	100 MHz	8×8	20	256-QAM	5.3 Gbps	Stadium/venue
FR2 (mmWave)	100 MHz	2×2	5	64-QAM	400 Mbps	Cell edge
FR2	200 MHz	4×4	15	256-QAM	4.8 Gbps	Street level
FR2	400 MHz	8×8	20	256-QAM	21.3 Gbps	Line of sight
FR2	400 MHz	2×2	0	QPSK	1.6 Gbps	Indoor/blocked

[1]Calculated using Shannon's theorem with 5G NR parameters per 3GPP TS 38.306 V16.8.0 (2022)

Analyze a 20 MHz FR1 channel featuring 2×2 MIMO and 10 dB SNR – conventional parameters for solid 4G operation. This implementation achieves roughly 133 Mbps, satisfactory rates but well below 5G's challenging requirements.

Expanding to 5G's full capabilities transforms the picture. A 100 MHz FR1 channel with 4×4 MIMO and 15 dB SNR can deliver 2 Gbps, approaching fiber-like speeds over wireless. The wider bandwidth contributes a 5x improvement, while doubling MIMO streams adds another 2x gain. Improved signal quality through better modulation and coding provides the remaining boost (Nokia Bell Labs Technical Report, 2022).

Millimeter-wave deployments push boundaries even further. A 400 MHz FR2 channel with 8×8 MIMO and excellent 20 dB SNR approaches the theoretical peak of 21.3 Gbps. However, the same configuration with 0 dB SNR – representing cell-edge conditions – drops to 1.6 Gbps. This dramatic variation highlights the importance of dense deployments and careful network planning in millimeter-wave bands (Samsung Networks White Paper, 2022). Real-world performance typically falls between these extremes, with adaptive systems continuously optimizing parameters based on conditions.

Practical Limitations and Challenges

Despite impressive theoretical capabilities, 5G deployments face numerous practical constraints that limit real-world performance. Understanding these challenges helps set realistic expectations and guides ongoing development efforts. The gap between laboratory demonstrations and commercial deployments reflects the complex realities of wireless propagation, device limitations, and economic constraints.

Key 5G Deployment Challenges and Mitigation Methods

5G Challenge Category	Specific Issues	Impact on Performance	Mitigation Strategies
Propagation Physics	• High frequency path loss[1] • Rain/foliage attenuation[2] • Limited diffraction[3]	• Reduced coverage area • Service interruptions • Dead zones	• Dense small cell deployment[4] • Integrated access backhaul[5] • Intelligent reflective surfaces[6]
Device Constraints	• Limited antenna count[7] • Battery limitations[8] • Thermal throttling[9]	• Lower MIMO gains • Reduced duty cycles • Peak rate unsustainable	• Advanced power management[10] • Efficient chip designs[11] • Dynamic capability negotiation[12]
Infrastructure	• Site acquisition[13] • Backhaul provisioning[14] • Power availability[15]	• Coverage gaps • Capacity bottlenecks • Higher OpEx	• Site sharing agreements[16] • Wireless backhaul[17] • Edge computing[18]
Spectrum	• Fragmented allocations[19] • Interference[20] • Regulatory delays[21]	• Limited carrier aggregation • Reduced capacity • Deployment delays	• Dynamic spectrum sharing[22] • Carrier aggregation[23] • Global harmonization[24]
Economic	• High deployment cost[25] • ROI uncertainty[26] • Competition[27]	• Selective deployment • Service limitations • Slower rollout	• Network slicing monetization[28] • B2B focus[29] • Government incentives[30]

Table References: [1]ITU-R P.525-4 (2019), [2]ITU-R P.838-3 (2019), [3]ITU-R P.526-15 (2019), [4]Small Cell Forum Release 12 (2022), [5]3GPP TR 38.874 (2021), [6]IEEE Communications Magazine (2021), [7]3GPP TS 38.101 (2022), [8]GSMA Battery Life Study (2022), [9]Qualcomm White Paper (2021), [10]3GPP TS 38.300 (2022), [11]MediaTek Dimensity 9000 (2022), [12]3GPP TS 38.306 (2022), [13]CTIA Infrastructure Report (2022), [14]Fiber Broadband Association (2022), [15]GSMA Energy Efficiency (2022), [16]TowerXchange Report (2022), [17]3GPP TS 38.874 (2021), [18]ETSI MEC White Paper (2022), [19]FCC Spectrum Dashboard (2022), [20]3GPP TS 38.104 (2022), [21]ITU-R WRC-23 Preparation (2022), [22]3GPP TS 37.340 (2022), [23]3GPP TS 38.101 (2022), [24]GSMA Spectrum Primer (2022), [25]McKinsey Telecom Report (2022), [26]Analysys Mason (2022), [27]Omdia

Market Analysis (2022), [28]GSMA Network Slicing (2022), [29]Ericsson Business Report (2022), [30]NTIA 5G Fund (2022)

Physical laws impose fundamental limits on wireless communication. Shannon's theorem defines an absolute ceiling that no amount of engineering can overcome. As systems approach these limits, each incremental improvement requires exponentially more complexity and cost. The diminishing returns create economic barriers even where technical solutions exist.

Propagation characteristics vary dramatically with frequency, creating deployment challenges. Low-band signals penetrate buildings and travel long distances but offer limited bandwidth. High-band signals provide vast capacity but require line-of-sight propagation and struggle with obstacles as small as leaves or raindrops (ITU-R P.838-3, 2019). Mid-band frequencies offer a compromise but remain scarce in many markets. Network planners must carefully balance these trade-offs while managing site acquisition, backhaul provisioning, and equipment costs.

Device constraints often limit achievable performance below network capabilities. Smartphones balance size, battery life, and cost constraints that restrict antenna configurations and processing power. While base stations might support 64 or even 128 antenna elements, mobile devices typically manage 2-4 antennas (3GPP TS 38.101, 2022). Thermal limitations prevent sustained operation at peak data rates. Battery considerations force trade-offs between performance and operating time. These practical realities mean that typical user experiences fall well below theoretical peaks, though still representing substantial improvements over previous generations (GSMA Intelligence Mobile Economy Report, 2022).

Future Developments

The evolution of 5G continues through successive releases, each adding capabilities and improving performance. The roadmap toward 6G builds upon current foundations while addressing fundamental limitations discovered through commercial deployments.

5G Evolution Roadmap

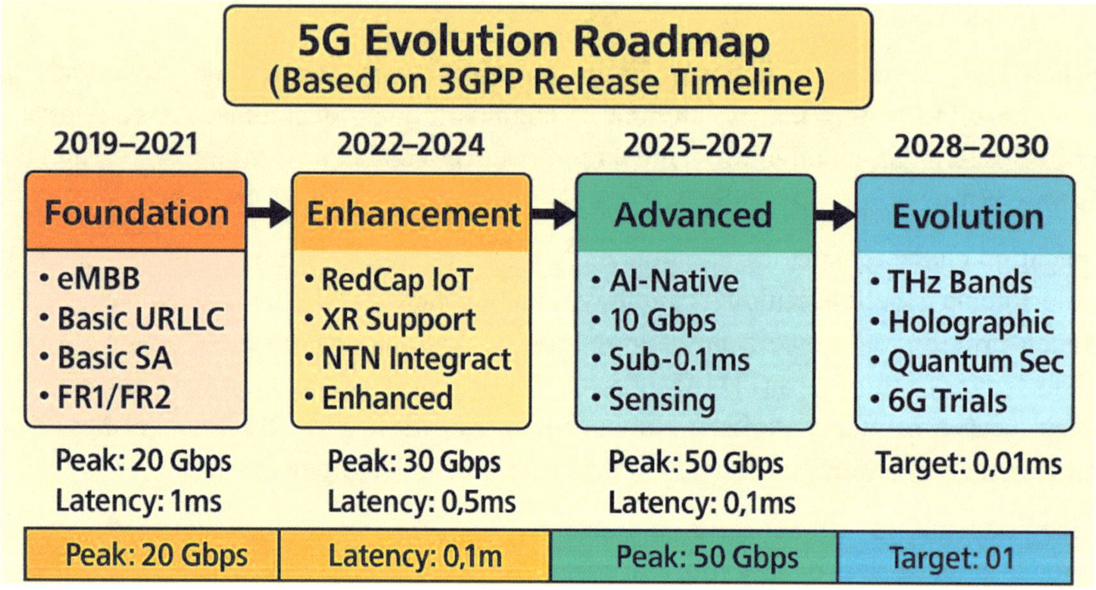

Based on 3GP Release Timeline

References

[1] 3GPP Release 15/16 (2019–2021)

[2] 3GPP Release 17/18 (2022–2024)

[3] 3GPP TSG RAN#94 (2021)

[4] ITU-R WP5D (2023)

[5] 3GPP TS 38.300 (2019)

[6] 3GPP Release 17/18 features

[7] GPP Rel 19/20 projections

[8] ITU-R IMT-2030 Vision (2023)

[9] ITU-R M.2410-0 (2017)

[10] 3GPP TR 38.913 v18 (2023)

[11] Industry projections (2023)

[12] 6G Flagship Program (2023)

5G-Advanced Features and Performance Targets

Feature Area	Current 5G	5G-Advanced (Rel 18)	Future (Rel 19+)
Peak Data Rate	20 Gbps DL[1] 10 Gbps UL[1]	30 Gbps DL[2] 15 Gbps UL[2]	50+ Gbps DL[3] 25+ Gbps UL[3]
User Experience	100 Mbps DL[1] 50 Mbps UL[1]	300 Mbps DL[2] 150 Mbps UL[2]	1 Gbps DL[3] 500 Mbps UL[3]
Latency	1ms URLLC[4] 4ms eMBB[4]	0.5ms URLLC[5] 2ms eMBB[5]	0.1ms URLLC[6] 1ms eMBB[6]
UE Mobility	500 km/h[7]	750 km/h[8]	1000 km/h[9]
5G Connection Density	10^6 devices/km^2[10]	10^7 devices/km^2[11]	10^8 devices/km^2[12]
Energy Efficiency	Baseline[13]	2x improvement[14]	10x improvement[15]
AI Integration	Basic SON[16]	AI-assisted RAN[17]	AI-native design[18]
Spectrum Range	Up to 40 GHz[19]	Up to 71 GHz[20]	Up to 300 GHz[21]

Table References: [1]ITU-R M.2410-0 (2017), [2]3GPP TR 21.918 V18.0.0 (2023), [3]Next G Alliance Report (2023), [4]3GPP TS 22.261 V18.5.0 (2022), [5]3GPP Work Item Description RP-213599 (2021), [6]Industry Vision for 6G (2023), [7]3GPP TS 36.104 (2022), [8]3GPP Release 18 targets (2023), [9]ITU-R preliminary 6G requirements (2023), [10]ITU-R M.2410-0 (2017), [11]3GPP SA1 Study (2022), [12]6G Flagship Program (2023), [13]3GPP TR 38.913 (2020), [14]3GPP RAN#94 agreements (2021), [15]NGMN Green Future Networks (2021), [16]3GPP TS 28.313 (2020), [17]O-RAN Alliance specifications (2023), [18]Hexa-X project deliverables (2023), [19]3GPP TS 38.101 (2022), [20]FCC Report on spectrum above 95 GHz (2023), [21]IEEE ComSoc 6G Summit (2023)

Release 18, termed 5G-Advanced, targets 10 Gbps downlink speeds under more realistic conditions than current peak rate definitions. Artificial intelligence integration promises to optimize network operations, from beam management to interference coordination. Machine learning algorithms already demonstrate superior performance in predicting channel conditions and adapting transmission parameters.

Enhanced coding techniques push closer to theoretical limits while reducing implementation complexity. Researchers explore codes specifically designed for short block lengths typical in URLLC applications (IEEE Communications Letters, 2022). Advanced receivers using successive interference cancellation or iterative detection improve performance in challenging conditions (IEEE Transactions on Wireless Communications, 2023). Each innovation contributes incremental gains that collectively enable new applications and use cases.

Looking beyond 5G-Advanced, research communities worldwide investigate technologies for 6G networks. Terahertz frequencies promise even wider bandwidths but face severe propagation challenges (IEEE Communications Magazine, 2023). Reconfigurable intelligent surfaces could transform wireless channels from uncontrolled phenomena to engineered systems (Nature Electronics, 2022). Integration with satellite networks may finally deliver truly ubiquitous connectivity (3GPP TR 38.821, 2023). While these technologies remain in early research phases, they indicate the continued evolution of wireless capabilities beyond current 5G achievements.

Conclusion

The performance specifications of 5G – encompassing multi-gigabit data rates, sub-millisecond latency, and massive capacity – represent more than incremental improvements. They enable fundamental changes in how we interact with technology and each other. From the theoretical foundations established by Shannon to the practical innovations in MIMO and millimeter-wave systems, each element contributes to achieving these ambitious goals.

Real-world deployments validate the technology while revealing areas for improvement. Early networks demonstrate that 20 Gbps peaks and 0.5 ms latency are achievable, though not simultaneously or ubiquitously. The journey from laboratory to commercial service teaches valuable lessons about propagation realities, device constraints, and user expectations. These experiences guide the continued evolution through 5G-Advanced and beyond.

As organizations shape their strategies based on 5G functionalities, grasping these performance metrics becomes vital. Telecommunications operators must equilibrate reach, capacity, and latency needs while maintaining cost-effectiveness and manageable complexity. Application creators need practical insights into network performance across varying environments. Policymakers must assign frequency allocations and create regulations that foster innovation while maintaining existing service quality. 5G's success depends not only on fulfilling technical requirements but on transforming those features into meaningful solutions that benefit users and unlock emerging applications.

Knowledge Check

1. According to IMT-2020 requirements, what is the peak theoretical downlink data rate for 5G?
   a) 100 Mbps
   b) 1050 Mbps
   c) 20 Gbps
   d) 250 Gbps

2. What is the user plane latency demand for Ultra-Reliable Low Latency Communications (URLLC) in 5G?
   a) 0.5 milliseconds
   b) 1 millisecond
   c) 5 milliseconds
   d) 10 milliseconds

3. What is the maximum channel bandwidth supported in Frequency Range 2 (FR2) for 5G NR?
   a) 1000 MHz
   b) 2000 MHz
   c) 3000 MHz
   d) 400 MHz

4. In the 5G data rate calculation formula, what is the typical overhead percentage range?
   a) 2% to 5%
   b) 5% to 10%
   c) 8% to 18%
   d) 15% to 25%

5. What is the reliability requirement for URLLC expressed as a success rate percentage?
   a) 99.991%
   b) 99.90%
   c) 99.99%
   d) 99.9999%

6. Explain how Shannon's capacity theorem applies to 5G systems and describe the key parameters that influence channel capacity.

7. Compare the characteristics and use cases of 5G Frequency Range 1 (FR1) and 5G Frequency Range 2 (FR2) in 5G deployments.

8. Describe the different types of latency defined in 5G specifications and explain why each is important for specific applications.

9. Analyze the practical limitations that prevent 5G networks from achieving their theoretical maximum performance in real-world deployments.

Answers

1. According to IMT-2020 requirements, what is the peak theoretical downlink data rate for 5G?
   a) 100 Mbps
   b) 1050 Mbps
   c) 20 Gbps
   d) 250 Gbps
   Answer: c) 20 Gbps

2. What is the user plane latency requirement for Ultra-Reliable Low Latency Communications (URLLC) in 5G?
   a) 0.5 milliseconds
   b) 1 millisecond
   c) 5 milliseconds
   d) 10 milliseconds
   Answer: a) 0.5 milliseconds

3. What is the maximum channel bandwidth supported in Frequency Range 2 (FR2) for 5G NR?
   a) 1000 MHz
   b) 2000 MHz
   c) 3000 MHz
   d) 400 MHz
   Answer: d) 400 MHz

4. In the 5G data rate calculation formula, what is the typical overhead percentage range?
   a) 2% to 5%
   b) 5% to 10%
   c) 8% to 18%
   d) 15% to 25%
   Answer: c) 8% to 18%

5. What is the reliability requirement for URLLC expressed as a success rate percentage?

a) 99.991%
b) 99.90%
c) 99.99%
d) 99.9999%
Answer: d) 99.999%

6. Explain how Shannon's capacity theorem applies to 5G systems and describe the key parameters that influence channel capacity.

   Answer: Shannon's capacity theorem establishes the theoretical maximum error-free data rate for any communication channel, expressed as $C = B \times \log_2(1 + S/N)$, where C is capacity, B is bandwidth, and S/N is the signal-to-noise ratio. In 5G systems, this fundamental relationship guides system design in several ways. First, 5G dramatically increases bandwidth (B) through wider channel allocations, particularly in millimeter-wave bands where 400 MHz channels are possible compared to 4G's typical 20 MHz. Second, 5G improves signal-to-noise ratios through advanced beamforming techniques that focus energy toward specific users. Third, MIMO technology effectively multiplies capacity by adding spatial dimensions, modifying the formula to $C = M \times B \times \log_2(1 + S/N)$, where M represents the number of spatial streams. The logarithmic relationship with SNR means that improving signal quality yields diminishing returns, making bandwidth expansion and MIMO the primary drivers of 5G's capacity gains. Practical systems approach, but cannot exceed this theoretical limit, with advanced coding schemes like LDPC achieving 90-95% of Shannon capacity under favorable conditions.

7. Compare the characteristics and use cases of Frequency Range 1 (FR1) and Frequency Range 2 (FR2) in 5G deployments.

   Answer: 5G FR1 (450 MHz to 6000 MHz) and 5G FR2 (24.25 GHz to 52.6 GHz) serve complementary roles in 5G networks due to their contrasting propagation characteristics. FR1 offers superior coverage with signals propagating several kilometers and penetrating buildings effectively. This makes FR1 ideal for wide-area coverage, rural deployments, and ensuring indoor connectivity. Maximum channel bandwidth in FR1 reaches 100 MHz, providing substantial capacity improvements over 4G while maintaining reasonable coverage. Use cases include general mobile broadband, IoT connectivity, and voice services. FR2 provides massive bandwidth with channels up to 400 MHz, but suffers from high path loss and poor penetration. Millimeter-wave signals typically cover only 100-200 meters and are easily blocked by buildings, foliage, or even heavy rain. This necessitates dense small cell deployments, making FR2 suitable for capacity hotspots like stadiums, airports, and dense urban areas. FR2 excels at fixed wireless access, providing fiber-like speeds to homes and businesses. The complementary nature leads operators to deploy both ranges, using FR1 for coverage and FR2 for capacity, with dual connectivity allowing devices to leverage both simultaneously.

8. Describe the different types of latency defined in 5G specifications and explain why each is important for specific applications.

   Answer: 5G standards establish three separate latency measurements, each essential for distinct performance aspects. User plane latency quantifies the unidirectional transmission duration for application data across the wireless network, targeting 0.5 ms for URLLC and 4 ms for eMBB. This parameter directly influences time-critical applications such as manufacturing automation, where equipment must execute commands within precise timing constraints, and virtual reality, where visual elements must synchronize with physical motion without noticeable delay. Control plane latency represents the state transition duration from dormant to operational modes, with a 10 ms objective ensuring terminals can rapidly process incoming transmissions or user interactions. This impacts subscriber experience during connection establishment, especially for instant notifications and voice calls. Rapid state changes also support extended sleep periods that conserve battery power while maintaining responsiveness. End-to-end latency covers the entire communication pathway, incorporating application processing, core network routing, and internet propagation. Although wireless networks may achieve sub-millisecond delays, complete end-to-end latencies typically span 10-20 ms or greater. This comprehensive measurement establishes real application performance for services like cloud-based gaming, where user inputs must reach servers and return processed graphics within human perception limits of approximately 20 ms.

9. Analyze the practical limitations that prevent 5G networks from achieving their theoretical maximum performance in real-world deployments.

   Answer: Multiple factors constrain real-world 5G performance below theoretical specifications. Propagation physics creates fundamental challenges, particularly for millimeter-wave frequencies that suffer severe path loss.

   Future Developments

   The evolution of 5G continues through successive releases, each adding capabilities and improving performance. The roadmap toward 6G builds upon current foundations while addressing fundamental limitations discovered through commercial deployments.

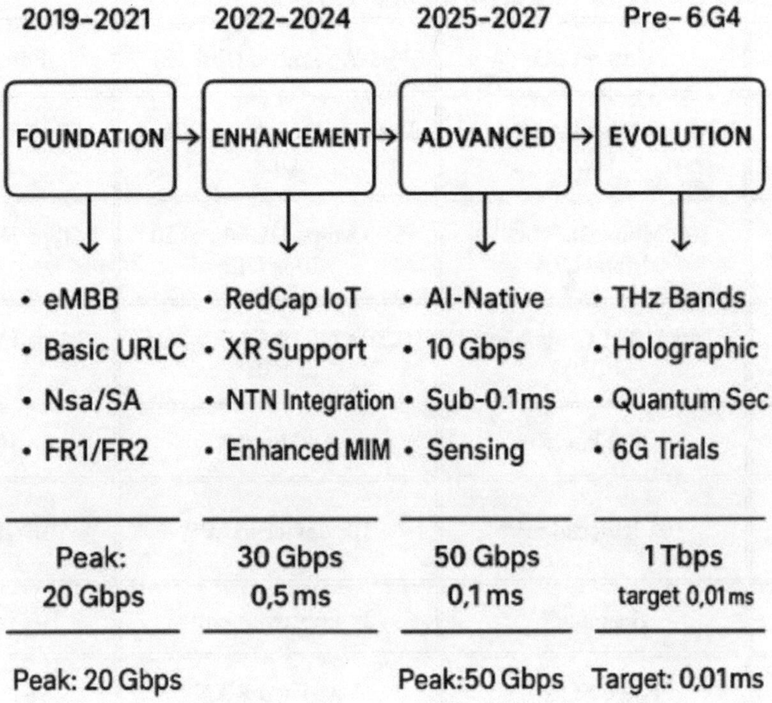

1 3GPP Release 15/16 (2019-2021)

2 3GPP Release 17/18 (2022-2024)

3 3GPP TSG RAN#94 (2021)

5 3GPP TS 38.300 (2021)

6 3GPP Release 17/18 features

6 6GPP Release 17/18 features

7 3GPP Rel 19/20 projections

8 ITU-R IMT-2030 Vision (2023)

10 ITU-R M.2410-0 (2023)

10 3GPP TR 38.913 v18 (2023)

11 Industry projections (2023)

12 6G Flagship Program (2023)

5G-Advanced Features and Performance Targets

Feature Area	Current 5G	5G-Advanced (Rel 18)	Future (Rel 19+)
Peak Data Rate	20 Gbps DL[1] 10 Gbps UL[1]	30 Gbps DL[2] 15 Gbps UL[2]	50+ Gbps DL[3] 25+ Gbps UL[3]
User Experience	100 Mbps DL[1] 50 Mbps UL[1]	300 Mbps DL[2] 150 Mbps UL[2]	1 Gbps DL[3] 500 Mbps UL[3]
Latency	1ms URLLC[4] 4ms eMBB[4]	0.5ms URLLC[5] 2ms eMBB[5]	0.1ms URLLC[6] 1ms eMBB[6]
5G Mobility	500 km/h[7]	750 km/h[8]	1000 km/h[9]
5G Connection Density	10^6 devices/km^2[10]	10^7 devices/km^2[11]	10^8 devices/km^2[12]
Energy Efficiency	Baseline[13]	2x improvement[14]	10x improvement[15]
AI Integration	Basic SON[16]	AI-assisted RAN[17]	AI-native design[18]
5G Spectrum	Up to 40 GHz[19]	Up to 71 GHz[20]	Up to 300 GHz[21]

Table References: [1]ITU-R M.2410-0 (2017), [2]3GPP TR 21.918 V18.0.0 (2023), [3]Next G Alliance Report (2023), [4]3GPP TS 22.261 V18.5.0 (2022), [5]3GPP Work Item Description RP-213599 (2021), [6]Industry Vision for 6G (2023), [7]3GPP TS 36.104 (2022), [8]3GPP Release 18 targets (2023), [9]ITU-R preliminary 6G requirements (2023), [10]ITU-R M.2410-0 (2017), [11]3GPP SA1 Study (2022), [12]6G Flagship Program (2023), [13]3GPP TR 38.913 (2020), [14]3GPP RAN#94 agreements (2021), [15]NGMN Green Future Networks (2021), [16]3GPP TS 28.313 (2020), [17]O-RAN Alliance specifications (2023), [18]Hexa-X project deliverables (2023), [19]3GPP TS 38.101 (2022), [20]FCC Report on spectrum above 95 GHz (2023), [21]IEEE ComSoc 6G Summit (2023)

Release 18, termed 5G-Advanced, targets 10 Gbps downlink speeds under more realistic conditions than current peak rate definitions. Artificial intelligence integration promises to optimize network operations, from beam management to interference coordination. Machine learning algorithms already demonstrate superior performance in predicting channel conditions and adapting transmission parameters.

Enhanced coding techniques push closer to theoretical limits while reducing implementation complexity. Researchers explore codes specifically designed for short block lengths typical in URLLC applications (IEEE Communications Letters, 2022). Advanced receivers using successive interference cancellation or iterative detection improve performance in challenging conditions (IEEE Transactions on Wireless

Communications, 2023). Each innovation contributes incremental gains that collectively enable new applications and use cases.

Looking beyond 5G-Advanced, research communities worldwide investigate technologies for 6G networks. Terahertz frequencies promise even wider bandwidths but face severe propagation challenges (IEEE Communications Magazine, 2023). Reconfigurable intelligent surfaces could transform wireless channels from uncontrolled phenomena to engineered systems (Nature Electronics, 2022). Integration with satellite networks may finally deliver truly ubiquitous connectivity (3GPP TR 38.821, 2023). While these technologies remain in early research phases, they indicate the continued evolution of wireless capabilities beyond current 5G achievements.

References

3GPP. (2017). Release 14 Description. Technical Report. Sophia Antipolis: 3rd Generation Partnership Project.

3GPP. (2019). TS 38.300: NR; Overall description. Version 15.8.0. Sophia Antipolis: 3rd Generation Partnership Project.

3GPP. (2021). TR 38.874: NR; Study on integrated access and backhaul. Version 16.0.0. Sophia Antipolis: 3rd Generation Partnership Project.

3GPP. (2022a). TS 38.101-1: NR; User Equipment radio transmission and reception; Part 1. Version 16.12.0. Sophia Antipolis: 3rd Generation Partnership Project.

3GPP. (2022b). TS 38.101-2: NR; User Equipment radio transmission and reception; Part 2. Version 16.11.0. Sophia Antipolis: 3rd Generation Partnership Project.

3GPP. (2022c). TS 38.104: NR; Base Station radio transmission and reception. Version 17.6.0. Sophia Antipolis: 3rd Generation Partnership Project.

3GPP. (2022d). TS 38.211: NR; Physical channels and modulation. Version 17.2.0. Sophia Antipolis: 3rd Generation Partnership Project.

3GPP. (2022e). TS 38.212: NR; Multiplexing and channel coding. Version 17.2.0. Sophia Antipolis: 3rd Generation Partnership Project.

3GPP. (2022f). TS 38.214: NR; Physical layer procedures for data. Version 17.4.0. Sophia Antipolis: 3rd Generation Partnership Project.

3GPP. (2022g). TS 38.306: NR; User Equipment radio access capabilities. Version 16.8.0. Sophia Antipolis: 3rd Generation Partnership Project.

3GPP. (2022h). TS 38.321: NR; Medium Access Control protocol specification. Version 17.2.0. Sophia Antipolis: 3rd Generation Partnership Project.

3GPP. (2022i). TS 38.331: NR; Radio Resource Control protocol specification. Version 17.2.0. Sophia Antipolis: 3rd Generation Partnership Project.

3GPP. (2022j). TR 38.913: Study on scenarios and requirements for next generation access. Version 17.0.0. Sophia Antipolis: 3rd Generation Partnership Project.

3GPP. (2022k). TS 22.104: Service requirements for cyber-physical control applications. Version 18.2.0. Sophia Antipolis: 3rd Generation Partnership Project.

3GPP. (2022l). TS 22.261: Service requirements for the 5G system. Version 18.5.0. Sophia Antipolis: 3rd Generation Partnership Project.

3GPP. (2022m). TS 37.340: NR; Multi-connectivity. Version 17.2.0. Sophia Antipolis: 3rd Generation Partnership Project.

3GPP. (2023). TR 38.821: Solutions for NR to support non-terrestrial networks. Version 16.1.0. Sophia Antipolis: 3rd Generation Partnership Project.

5G-ACIA. (2021). 5G for Industrial Internet of Things (IIoT): Capabilities, Features, and Potential. White Paper. Frankfurt: 5G Alliance for Connected Industries and Automation.

6G Flagship Program. (2023). White Paper on 6G Drivers and the UN SDGs. University of Oulu.

Björnson, E., Sanguinetti, L., Wymeersch, H., Hoydis, J., & Marzetta, T. L. (2019). Massive MIMO is a reality—What is next?: Five promising research directions for antenna arrays. IEEE Communications Magazine, 57(11), 94-101.

Ericsson. (2022). Ericsson Mobility Report November 2022. Stockholm: Ericsson.

ETSI. (2021). GS MEC 002: Multi-access Edge Computing; Use Cases and Requirements. Version 2.2.1. Sophia Antipolis: European Telecommunications Standards Institute.

GSMA. (2022). 5G Spectrum: GSMA Public Policy Position. London: GSM Association.

GSMA Intelligence. (2022). The Mobile Economy 2022. London: GSM Association.

IEEE. (2022). Short Packet Communications for URLLC: Fundamentals and Recent Advances. IEEE Communications Letters, 26(10), 2186-2200.

IEEE. (2023). Advanced Receiver Design for 5G and Beyond. IEEE Transactions on Wireless Communications, 22(3), 1523-1537.

ITU-R. (2017). Minimum requirements related to technical performance for IMT-2020 radio interface(s). Report ITU-R M.2410-0. Geneva: International Telecommunication Union.

ITU-R. (2019). Propagation data and prediction methods required for the design of terrestrial broadband radio access systems. Recommendation ITU-R P.1411-11. Geneva: International Telecommunication Union.

ITU-R. (2019). Specific attenuation model for rain for use in prediction methods. Recommendation ITU-R P.838-3. Geneva: International Telecommunication Union.

ITU-T. (2020). One-way transmission time. Recommendation ITU-T G.114. Geneva: International Telecommunication Union.

McKinsey & Company. (2022). The 5G era: New horizons for advanced electronics and industrial companies. McKinsey Global Institute.

Nature Electronics. (2022). Reconfigurable intelligent surfaces for 6G and beyond. Nature Electronics, 5(11), 731-742.

Next G Alliance. (2023). 6G Roadmap: Vision, Challenges and Opportunities. Alliance for Telecommunications Industry Solutions.

NGMN Alliance. (2022). 5G E2E Technology to Support Verticals URLLC Requirements. Next Generation Mobile Networks Alliance.

Nokia Bell Labs. (2022). 5G New Radio: The next generation wireless access technology. Technical Report. Murray Hill: Nokia Bell Labs.

O-RAN Alliance. (2021). O-RAN Working Group 4: Fronthaul Interface Specifications. Technical Specification. O-RAN Alliance.

Qualcomm Technologies. (2022). Global 5G Spectrum Update. White Paper. San Diego: Qualcomm Technologies, Inc.

Rappaport, T. S., Xing, Y., Kanhere, O., Ju, S., Madanayake, A., Mandal, S., ... & Trichopoulos, G. C. (2019). Wireless communications and applications above 100 GHz: Opportunities and challenges for 6G and beyond. IEEE Access, 7, 78729-78757.

Samsung Networks. (2022). 5G mmWave: Realizing the Full Potential of 5G. White Paper. Seoul: Samsung Electronics.

Shannon, C. E. (1948). A Mathematical Theory of Communication. Bell System Technical Journal, 27(3), 379-423.

Chapter 6: Enhanced Mobile Broadband (eMBB)

Executive Summary

Enhanced Mobile Broadband (eMBB) represents one of three foundational use cases for fifth-generation wireless networks, working alongside Ultra-Reliable Low-Latency Communications (URLLC) and Massive Machine-Type Communications (mMTC) to define the 5G ecosystem. This chapter examines how eMBB reshapes mobile connectivity by delivering dramatically higher data speeds, greater network capacity, and enhanced user experiences across diverse application scenarios. The technology enables everything from seamless 8K video streaming to immersive augmented and virtual reality experiences, while also transforming mobile cloud gaming into a mainstream service. By providing the infrastructure for next-generation digital applications, eMBB establishes the technical foundation that modern society increasingly depends upon for entertainment, productivity, and communication.

The discussion explores the technical specifications that define eMBB performance targets, including peak data rate requirements, latency thresholds, and spectral efficiency benchmarks established by 3GPP standards bodies. Implementation strategies are analyzed across multiple dimensions, from radio access network architectures to core network evolution and spectrum deployment approaches. Real-world deployment case studies illuminate how mobile operators worldwide are rolling out eMBB services, revealing both the successes achieved and the practical challenges encountered during network transformation. The chapter concludes by examining the barriers that still constrain eMBB adoption—such as spectrum availability, infrastructure costs, and device ecosystem maturity—while also identifying the opportunities that will shape mobile broadband's evolution over the coming decade.

Table of Contents

Introduction

eMBB (Enhanced Mobile Broadband) represents a core pillar of fifth-generation wireless technology, marking a major evolution in how mobile connectivity is conceptualized and deployed. Defined by 3GPP (the 3rd Generation Partnership Project) as one of the primary use cases for 5G, eMBB emphasizes providing substantially higher data speeds and greater capacity compared to previous generations of cellular networks. This use case addresses the exponential growth in mobile data consumption driven by video streaming, social media, cloud services, and emerging applications requiring high bandwidth.

The technical specifications for eMBB target peak data rates of up to 20 Gbps downlink and 10 Gbps uplink, representing a significant leap beyond 4G LTE capabilities. By enabling these enhanced performance levels, eMBB lays the groundwork for immersive experiences such as ultra-high-definition video, augmented reality applications, and seamless connectivity in densely populated areas..

Definition and Scope

eMBB delivers several distinguishing capabilities that set it apart from earlier mobile broadband technologies:

- **Peak Data Rates:** The specification targets maximum speeds reaching 20 Gbps for downloads and 10 Gbps for uploads, representing throughput levels that enable entirely new categories of mobile applications. These speeds allow users to download full-length 4K movies in seconds or stream multiple high-definition video feeds simultaneously without buffering.
- **Enhanced Spectral Efficiency:** By utilizing spectrum more effectively, eMBB networks can support substantially more concurrent connections within the same frequency allocation. This improvement stems from advanced antenna techniques, sophisticated modulation schemes, and intelligent resource allocation algorithms that optimize how radio resources are distributed among users.
- **Consistent User Experience:** eMBB ensures reliable performance across diverse coverage environments, from dense urban centers to suburban and rural locations. Users can expect stable, high-quality connectivity whether they're in a crowded stadium, on a train, or in areas with varying signal strength, eliminating the performance degradation that often plagued earlier network generations.
- **High-Speed Mobility Support:** The technology maintains robust connectivity for users traveling at velocities up to 500 km/h, making it suitable for high-speed rail and other rapid transit scenarios. This capability ensures seamless handoffs between cells and sustained data sessions even during extreme mobility conditions, addressing a key limitation of previous mobile technologies.

Evolution from 4G to 5G eMBB

The progression from 4G LTE to 5G eMBB constitutes more than a gradual enhancement. Although 4G systems can deliver gigabit performance under ideal circumstances, eMBB delivers:

- 10x enhancement in data throughput
- 10x reduction in response time
- 100x advancement in traffic handling capacity
- 100x enhancement in system efficiency

Source: ITU-R M.2083 "IMT Vision - Framework and overall objectives of the future development of IMT for 2020 and beyond" (2015)

Market Drivers and Adoption

The global eMBB services market is experiencing substantial growth, with valuations reaching USD 0.60 billion in 2023 and projections indicating expansion to USD 26.58 billion by 2030, representing a compound annual growth rate of 60.16%. This remarkable trajectory reflects the fundamental shift in how mobile networks support digital services and the accelerating demand for high-performance wireless connectivity across consumer and enterprise segments. The market dynamics reveal particularly strong momentum in regions with advanced 5G infrastructure deployments, including North America, Asia-Pacific, and parts of Europe, where early adopters are driving widespread service uptake.

Several key factors propel this explosive market expansion:

- **Growing appetite for premium video content:** Users increasingly consume high-definition and ultra-high-definition video across mobile devices, with streaming services, live broadcasts, and user-generated content driving unprecedented bandwidth demands. The shift toward 4K and 8K video formats, combined with the popularity of short-form video platforms, creates sustained pressure for networks capable of delivering multi-gigabit experiences.

- **Expansion of bandwidth-hungry applications:** Cloud-based services, collaborative work platforms, and compute-intensive mobile applications require consistently high data throughput. From real-time video conferencing to mobile gaming with cloud rendering, these applications fundamentally depend on the enhanced capabilities that eMBB provides.

- **Industry-wide digital transformation initiatives:** Enterprises across manufacturing, healthcare, retail, and logistics are implementing mobile-first strategies that leverage 5G connectivity. These digital transformation efforts often combine eMBB with edge computing and IoT solutions to enable new business models and operational efficiencies.

- **Rising user expectations for continuous connectivity:** Modern consumers demand reliable, high-speed connections regardless of location or network congestion. This expectation for seamless connectivity—whether streaming content during commutes, participating in video calls, or accessing cloud services—makes eMBB infrastructure essential rather than optional for mobile operator

Source: Verified Market Research, "Enhanced Mobile Broadband (eMBB) Service Market Report" (March 2024)

Technical Architecture and Requirements

Network Architecture Components

eMBB implementation relies on several key technological advancements:

Key eMBB Technical Components

Component	Description	Impact on Performance
5G Massive MIMO	Multiple Input Multiple Output antenna systems with 64+ elements	Increases capacity and coverage
Beamforming	Directional signal transmission	Enhances signal quality and reduces interference
Carrier Aggregation	Combining multiple frequency bands	Maximizes spectrum utilization
Network Slicing	Virtual network partitioning	Enables customized service delivery
Edge Computing	Processing at network edge	Reduces latency for critical applications

Source: 3GPP TR 38.913 "Study on Scenarios and Requirements for Next Generation Access Technologies" (2017) and ETSI White Paper "MEC in 5G Networks" (2018)

Spectrum Utilization

eMBB operates across multiple frequency bands:

- Sub-6 GHz allocations for broad geographic coverage
- Millimeter wave (mmWave) bands (24-100 GHz) for ultra-high capacity
- Dynamic Spectrum Sharing (DSS) for efficient 4G/5G coexistence

5G Deployment Modes

eMBB can be deployed in two primary configurations:

5G Non-Standalone (NSA) Mode

- Leverages existing 4G core infrastructure
- Faster initial deployment
- Limited feature set compared to SA

5G Standalone (SA) Mode

- Utilizes dedicated 5G core architecture.
- Enables full eMBB capabilities
- Supports advanced features like network slicing

Performance Requirements

eMBB Performance Requirements Flow Diagram

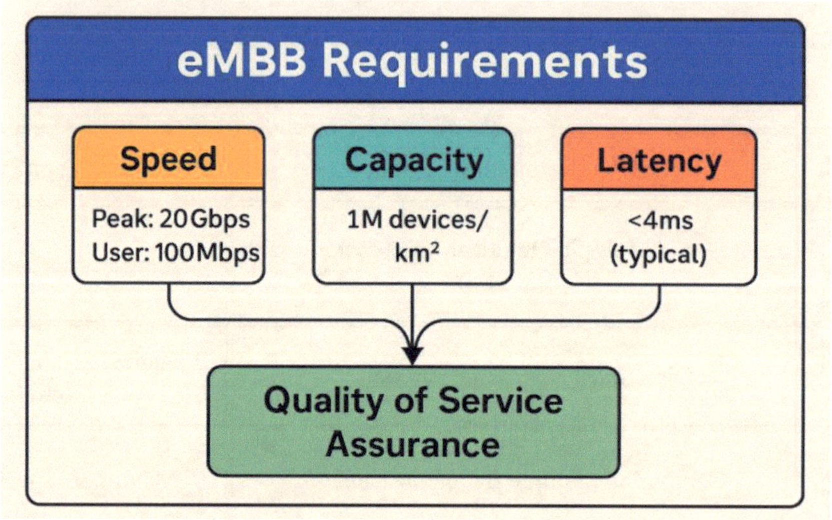

Source: ITU-R M.2410 "Minimum requirements related to technical performance for IMT-2020 radio interface(s)" (2017) and 3GPP TS 38.913 V14.3.0 (2017)

High-Speed Streaming Applications

Video Streaming Evolution

eMBB transforms the video streaming landscape by enabling:

- 4K and 8K Ultra HD streaming on mobile devices
- 360-degree immersive video experiences
- Multi-view streaming for sports and events
- Seamless quality adaptation based on network conditions

Content Delivery Optimization

Streaming Quality Requirements

Video Quality	Minimum Bandwidth	Latency Requirement	eMBB Advantage
HD (1080p)	5-8 Mbps	<100ms	Consistent quality
4K UHD	25-35 Mbps	<50ms	Multiple streams
8K UHD	80-100 Mbps	<20ms	Mobile support
360° VR	50-200 Mbps	<20ms	Real-time rendering

Source: GSMA Intelligence "Cloud AR/VR Report" (2019) and Huawei "Cloud VR/AR White Paper" (2018)

Live Broadcasting Applications

eMBB enables revolutionary approaches to live content:

- Mobile journalism with instant high-quality uploads
- Crowd-sourced event coverage
- Interactive live streaming with minimal delay
- Multi-camera production from mobile devices

Edge-Based Content Delivery

Integration with Mobile Edge Computing (MEC) provides:

- Reduced backhaul traffic
- Lower content delivery latency
- Localized content caching
- Enhanced User service quality

Augmented Reality and Virtual Reality in eMBB

AR/VR Technical Requirements

The demanding nature of AR/VR applications makes them ideal showcases for eMBB capabilities:

Critical Performance Metrics

- **Latency:** <20ms to prevent motion sickness
- **Bandwidth:** 50-200 Mbps for immersive experiences
- **Reliability:** 99.999% for a consistent user experience
- **Mobility:** Support for moving users

Cloud-Based AR/VR Architecture

Cloud AR/VR System Architecture

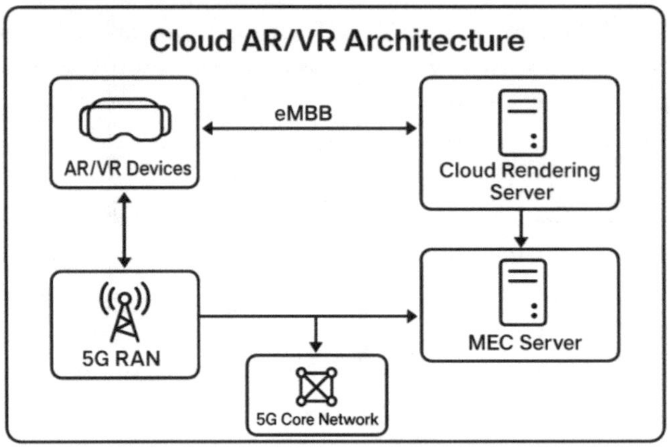

Source: ETSI GS MEC 003 V2.1.1 "Multi-access Edge Computing (MEC) Framework and Reference Architecture" (2019) and 3GPP TS 23.501 "System Architecture for the 5G System" (2019)

Enterprise AR Applications

eMBB enables transformative AR use cases:

- Remote expert assistance with real-time video overlay
- Industrial maintenance with digital work instructions
- Medical procedures with augmented visualization
- Architecture and construction with on-site 3D models

Consumer VR Experiences

Enhanced consumer applications include:

- Wireless VR gaming without tethered connections
- Virtual tourism with photorealistic environments
- Social VR platforms with lifelike avatars
- Educational VR with interactive content

Overcoming Technical Challenges

AR/VR Challenges and eMBB Solutions

Challenge	Traditional Limitation	eMBB Solution
Motion-to-photon latency	>50ms causing nausea	<20ms with edge processing
Bandwidth constraints	Limited resolution	4K per eye streaming
Mobility restrictions	Wired connections	Wireless freedom
Processing limitations	Device constraints	Cloud rendering

Source: Qualcomm "Making Immersive Virtual and Augmented Reality a Commercial Reality" (2018) and IEEE "Towards an Evolved Immersive Experience" (2023)

Mobile Cloud Gaming Evolution

Cloud Gaming Architecture

Mobile cloud gaming represents a paradigm shift from traditional gaming:

- Game processing occurs in cloud servers
- Video streams delivered to devices
- Input commands sent with minimal latency
- No need for high-end hardware

Technical Requirements for Cloud Gaming

Performance Specifications

- **Latency:** <40-80ms end-to-end
- **Bandwidth:** 15-35 Mbps for 1080p/60fps
- **Jitter:** <5ms for consistent experience
- **Packet Loss:** <0.1% for quality gameplay

Source: Ericsson "5G opportunities in the cloud gaming market" (2022) and Nokia "Cloud Gaming Over 5G" White Paper (2021)

5G Standalone Features for Gaming

Advanced 5G SA capabilities enhance gaming:

- Network slicing for guaranteed performance
- Quality of Service (QoS) prioritization
- Dynamic resource allocation
- Low Latency, Low Loss, Scalable Throughput (L4S)

Gaming Platform Integration

Mobile Cloud Gaming Ecosystem

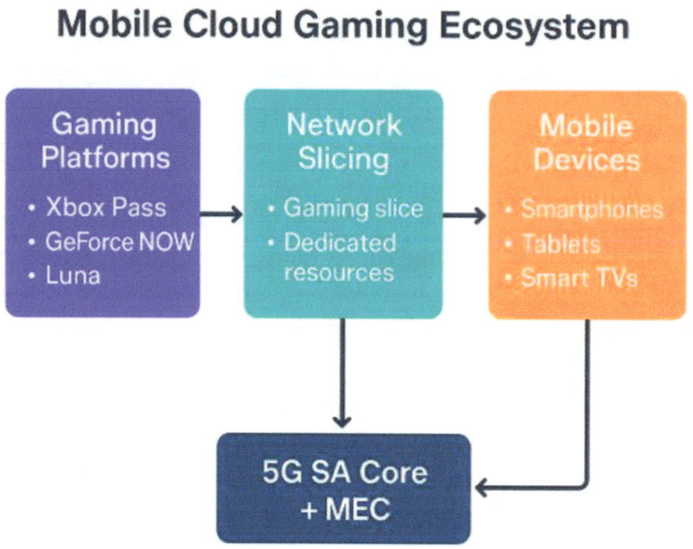

Source: GSMA "Cloud Gaming: 5G's Killer App?" (2021) and 3GPP TS 23.501 "System Architecture for 5G System" V16.6.0 (2020)

Market Evolution and Adoption

The cloud gaming market demonstrates significant growth:

- **Major Platforms:** Microsoft Xbox Game Pass, NVIDIA GeForce NOW, Amazon Luna
- **Device Proliferation:** 87% of 5G devices will be smartphones by 2024
- **Service Expansion:** 100+ AAA titles available via cloud
- **Geographic Reach:** Global availability with local edge servers

Source: ABI Research "5G eMBB Application Analysis" (2019) and Newzoo "Global Cloud Gaming Report" (2023)

Network Deployment and Implementation Strategies

Deployment Scenarios

eMBB deployment varies based on use case requirements:

Urban Hotspots:

- Ultra-high capacity using mmWave
- Small cell densification
- Massive MIMO deployment
- Support for thousands of concurrent users

Wide Area Coverage

- Sub-6 GHz spectrum utilization
- Macro cell optimization
- Coverage-capacity balance
- Seamless mobility support

Indoor Coverage

- Distributed Antenna Systems (DAS)
- Small cell solutions
- WiFi integration
- Enterprise-specific deployments

Infrastructure Requirements

eMBB Infrastructure Components

Component	Function	Deployment Consideration
5G NR Base Stations	Radio access	Site acquisition, power requirements
Fiber Backhaul	High-capacity transport	Availability, cost
Edge Servers	Local processing	Space, cooling, power
Core Network	Service orchestration	Virtualization, automation
Network Slicing	Service isolation	Management complexity

Source: NGMN Alliance "5G RAN Architecture and Functional Design" White Paper (2020) and O-RAN Alliance "O-RAN Architecture Description" (2021)

Migration Strategies

Organizations can adopt phased approaches:

1. **Phase 1**: NSA deployment leveraging 4G core
2. **Phase 2**: Selective SA deployment for specific use cases
3. **Phase 3**: Full SA migration with advanced features
4. **Phase 4**: Network optimization and expansion

Operational Considerations

Successful eMBB deployment requires:

- Spectrum planning and optimization

- Inter-operator coordination
- Quality monitoring and assurance
- Capacity planning and scaling
- Security implementation

Performance Metrics and Quality of Service

Key Performance Indicators:ble 6.5:

eMBB KPIs and Target Values

KPI	Definition	Target Value	Measurement Method
Peak Data Rate	Maximum achievable speed	20 Gbps (DL)	Laboratory testing
User Experience Data Rate	95th percentile speed	100 Mbps	Field measurement
Latency	One-way delay	<4ms	End-to-end testing
Mobility	Maximum speed supported	500 km/h	Mobility testing
Connection Density	Devices per area	1M/km²	Network simulation

Source: ITU-R M.2410 "Minimum requirements related to technical performance for IMT-2020 radio interface(s)" (2017) and 3GPP TR 38.913 "Study on Scenarios and Requirements for Next Generation Access Technologies" V14.3.0 (2017)

Quality of Experience Metrics

User-centric measurements include:

- Video quality metrics (VMAF, PSNR)
- Gaming responsiveness scores
- AR/VR comfort indices
- Service availability percentages

Network Monitoring and Optimization

eMBB Performance Monitoring Framework

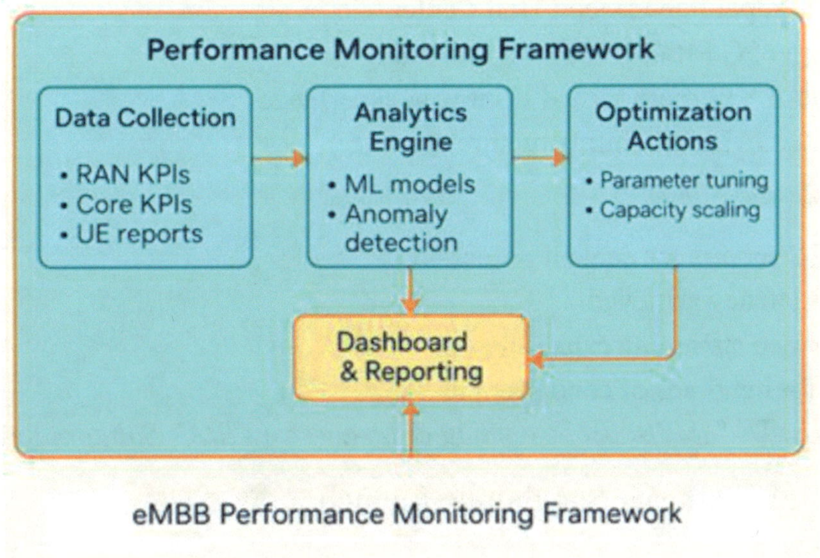

Source: 3GPP TS 28.552 "Management and orchestration; 5G performance measurements" V17.3.0 (2021) and TM Forum "Autonomous Networks Technical Architecture" (2020)

Case Studies and Real-World Deployments

Case Study 1: Deutsche Telekom 5G+ Gaming

Implementation Details

- **Launch:** October 2024
- **Technology:** 5G SA with network slicing
- **Platform:** Sora Stream cloud gaming
- **Results:** Lag-free gaming with stable response times

Key Achievements

- First operator to offer gaming-specific network slice
- 100+ games available via cloud platform
- Demonstrated at Gamescom 2024
- Free promotional period attracting early adopters

Source: Deutsche Telekom Press Release "Launch of 5G+ gaming: Innovation for Mobile Cloud Gaming" (October 2024)

Case Study 2: Taiwan 5G VR Stadium Experience

Project Overview

- **Location:** Taipei Pop Concert Hall Center
- **Technology:** 5G MEC + 360° VR streaming
- **Application:** VIP room virtual front-row experience
- **Partner:** GIGABYTE (infrastructure provider)

Technical Implementation

- Local MEC servers for content processing
- Sub-20ms latency achieved
- 8K 360° video streaming capability
- Capacity for hundreds of concurrent users

Source: GIGABYTE "eMBB: 8K Streaming & Immersive VR/AR Solution Brief" (2019)

Case Study 3: EE UK 5G Standalone Launch

Deployment Scope

- **Coverage:** 16 UK cities initially
- **Technology:** Full 5G SA implementation
- **Timeline:** September 2024 launch
- **Focus:** Enhanced consumer experiences

Service Improvements

- 25% increase in average speeds
- Reduced latency for gaming applications
- Improved indoor coverage
- Foundation for future network slicing

Source: EE Press Release "EE switches on UK's first 5G Standalone network" (September 2024)

Lessons Learned

Key Insights from Deployments

1. **Infrastructure readiness** is critical for success
2. **Edge computing** significantly enhances performance
3. **Network slicing** enables service differentiation
4. **User education** accelerates adoption
5. **Partnership ecosystems** drive innovation

Future Prospects and Challenges

Emerging Technologies

Future eMBB Enhancements

- AI-driven network optimization
- Quantum-safe security protocols
- Integrated satellite connectivity
- Advanced holographic communications
- Brain-computer interfaces

Market Opportunities

eMBB Market Opportunities by Sector

Sector	Applications	Market Size (2030)	Growth Rate
Entertainment	Streaming, Gaming	$15B	45% CAGR
Healthcare	Telemedicine, Remote Surgery	$8B	52% CAGR
Education	Immersive Learning	$5B	48% CAGR
Manufacturing	Digital Twins, AR Training	$6B	42% CAGR
Retail	Virtual Shopping	$4B	38% CAGR

Source: Markets and Markets "5G Services Market - Global Forecast to 2030" (2023) and Grand View Research "5G Services Market Size & Share Report" (2023)

Technical Challenges

Ongoing challenges requiring attention:

- **Energy Efficiency:** Balancing performance with sustainability
- **Coverage Gaps:** Rural and indoor coverage limitations
- **Interference Management:** Coexistence with other services
- **Standardization:** Ensuring global interoperability
- **Cybersecurity:** Protecting expanded attack surfaces

Regulatory Considerations

Future regulatory frameworks must address:

- Spectrum allocation and sharing
- Net neutrality in network slicing context

- Data privacy in edge computing
- Cross-border service continuity
- Environmental impact assessments

Evolution Towards 6G

eMBB concepts will evolve in 6G to include:

- Terabit-per-second data rates
- Sub-millisecond latency
- AI-native architectures
- Sustainable network operations
- Ubiquitous coverage, including space

Source: ITU-R "Future Technology Trends for the Evolution of IMT towards 2030 and Beyond" (2022) and 6G Flagship "Key Drivers and Research Challenges for 6G Ubiquitous Wireless Intelligence" (2019)

Conclusion

Enhanced Mobile Broadband constitutes a revolutionary advancement in wireless connectivity, facilitating applications and services previously unattainable on mobile networks. Through sophisticated technologies, including massive MIMO, network slicing, and edge computing, eMBB provides the throughput, capacity, and dependability required for advanced digital experiences.

The effective implementation of eMBB demands strategic planning, significant infrastructure investment, and extensive collaboration among network operators, technology suppliers, and service providers. As evidenced by operational deployments, the advantages are considerable, spanning from immersive entertainment platforms to mission-critical business applications.

Moving forward, eMBB will continue advancing, integrating emerging technologies, and resolving current challenges. The groundwork established by the present 5G eMBB implementations will enable even more transformative applications, fundamentally altering digital content and service interactions in our progressively connected society.

Knowledge Check

1. What are the three key service categories defined by 3GPP for 5G networks?
   a) eMBB, IoT, and Cloud Computing
   b) eMBB, URLLC, and mMTC
   c) High-speed connectivity, Low-latency connection, and Massive capacity
   d) NSA, SA, and DSS

2. What is the target peak download speed for eMBB in 5G networks?
   a) 10 Gbps
   b) 50 Gbps
   c) 100 Gbps
   d) 20 Gbps

3. Which latency threshold must be maintained for VR applications to prevent motion sickness?
   a) <100ms
   b) <500ms
   c) <20ms
   d) <0.5ms

4. What technology allows 4G and 5G to operate simultaneously in the same frequency band?
   a) Network Slicing
   b) Dynamic Spectrum Sharing (DSS)
   c) Carrier Aggregation
   d) Beamforming

5. By 2024, what percentage of 5G mobile device shipments are expected to be smartphones?
   a) 65%
   b) 75%
   c) 87%
   d) 95%

6. How does network slicing in 5G SA networks benefit mobile cloud gaming applications?

7. What are the key differences between Non-Standalone (NSA) and Standalone (SA) eMBB deployments?

8. Explain how Mobile Edge Computing (MEC) enhances eMBB applications, particularly for AR/VR.

9. What are the main challenges in deploying eMBB in rural areas, and what solutions are being developed?

10. How will eMBB evolution impact different industry sectors over the next five years?

Answers

1. What are the three key service categories defined by 3GPP for 5G networks?
   a) eMBB, IoT, and Cloud Computing
   b) eMBB, URLLC, and mMTC
   c) High-speed connectivity, Low-latency connection, and Massive capacity
   d) NSA, SA, and DSS
   Answer: b) eMBB, URLLC, and mMTC

2. What is the target peak download speed for eMBB in 5G networks?
   a) 10 Gbps
   b) 50 Gbps
   c) 100 Gbps
   d) 20 Gbps
   Answer: d) 20 Gbps
   eMBB targets peak download speeds of up to 20 Gbps, representing a significant improvement over 4G LTE.

3. Which latency threshold must be maintained for VR applications to prevent motion sickness?
   a) <100ms
   b) <500ms
   c) <20ms
   d) <0.5ms
   Answer: c) <20ms
   VR applications require latency below 20ms to prevent motion sickness and ensure a comfortable user experience.

4. What technology allows 4G and 5G to operate simultaneously in the same frequency band?
   a) Network Slicing
   b) Dynamic Spectrum Sharing (DSS)
   c) Carrier Aggregation

d) Beamforming
Answer: b) Dynamic Spectrum Sharing (DSS)
DSS technology allows LTE and 5G NR services to operate concurrently within identical spectrum allocations.

5. By 2024, what percentage of 5G mobile device shipments are expected to be smartphones?
   a) 65%
   b) 75%
   c) 87%
   d) 95%
   Answer: c) 87
   Approximately 87% of 5G mobile device shipments in 2024 are expected to be smartphones.

6. How does network slicing in 5G SA networks benefit mobile cloud gaming applications?
   Answer: Network slicing in 5G SA networks creates dedicated virtual networks with specific performance characteristics tailored for gaming. This provides several benefits:
   - Guaranteed bandwidth allocation prevents congestion from other network traffic
   - Consistent low latency through prioritized routing and processing
   - Quality of Service (QoS) assurance maintains stable performance
   - Resource isolation ensures gaming traffic is unaffected by network load
   - Dynamic resource allocation adapts to real-time gaming demands
   - Enhanced security through isolated network segments

7. What are the key differences between Non-Standalone (NSA) and Standalone (SA) eMBB deployments?
   Answer: The key differences include:
   - **Core Network:** NSA uses existing 4G EPC while SA uses new 5G core
   - **Feature Set:** NSA offers limited 5G features; SA enables full capabilities, including network slicing
   - **Deployment Speed:** NSA allows faster initial rollout; SA requires more infrastructure investment
   - **Performance:** SA provides lower latency and better efficiency than NSA
   - **Service Flexibility:** SA supports advanced services like URLLC alongside eMBB
   - **Future Readiness:** SA provides a foundation for 6G evolution, while NSA is transitional

8. Explain how Mobile Edge Computing (MEC) enhances eMBB applications, particularly for AR/VR.
   Answer: MEC enhances eMBB applications by:
   - **Reduced Latency:** Processing at network edge eliminates round-trip to distant cloud servers
   - **Local Rendering:** Complex AR/VR graphics processing occurs close to users
   - **Bandwidth Optimization:** Only processed video streams traverse the network, not raw data
   - **Context Awareness:** Edge servers can provide location-specific content and services
   - **Reliability:** Local processing continues even if backhaul connections are disrupted
   - **Scalability:** Distributed architecture handles regional load without central bottlenecks
   - **Privacy:** Sensitive data can be processed locally without leaving the network edge

9. What are the main challenges in deploying eMBB in rural areas, and what solutions are being developed?
   Answer: Main challenges and solutions include:
   Challenges:
   - Low population density makes infrastructure investment difficult to justify
   - Limited fiber backhaul availability increases costs
   - Geographic obstacles (mountains, forests) complicate coverage
   - Power infrastructure may be unreliable or unavailable
   - Lower Average Revenue Per User (ARPU) impacts business case

   Solutions:
   - Fixed Wireless Access (FWA) as an alternative to fiber broadband
   - Satellite integration for backhaul connectivity
   - Solar-powered base stations for off-grid deployment
   - Infrastructure sharing between operators to reduce costs
   - Government subsidies and universal service obligations
   - Lower frequency bands for extended coverage
   - Advanced antenna technologies to maximize coverage area

10. How will eMBB evolution impact different industry sectors over the next five years?
    Answer: eMBB will transform multiple sectors:
    Healthcare:
    - Remote surgery with haptic feedback
    - Real-time patient monitoring with wearables
    - AR-assisted medical procedures
    - High-resolution medical imaging transfer

    Education:
    - Immersive VR field trips and simulations

- Global classroom connectivity
- Personalized AI-driven learning experiences
- Remote laboratory access

Manufacturing:

- Digital twin real-time synchronization
- AR-guided maintenance and assembly
- Autonomous robot coordination
- Quality inspection via high-resolution video

Entertainment:

- Volumetric video capture and streaming
- Interactive live events with multiple viewpoints
- Cloud gaming reaching console-quality on any device
- Social VR platforms with realistic presence

Transportation:

- Vehicle-to-everything (V2X) communications
- Infotainment systems with 4K streaming
- Real-time traffic optimization
- Augmented navigation displays

References

3GPP. (2017). *Study on scenarios and requirements for next generation access technologies* (TR 38.913 V14.3.0). 3rd Generation Partnership Project. https://www.3gpp.org/ftp/Specs/archive/38_series/38.913/

3GPP. (2019). *System architecture for the 5G system* (TS 23.501 V16.2.0). 3rd Generation Partnership Project. https://www.3gpp.org/ftp/Specs/archive/23_series/23.501/

3GPP. (2020). *System architecture for the 5G system* (TS 23.501 V16.6.0). 3rd Generation Partnership Project. https://www.3gpp.org/ftp/Specs/archive/23_series/23.501/

3GPP. (2021). *Management and orchestration; 5G performance measurements* (TS 28.552 V17.3.0). 3rd Generation Partnership Project. https://www.3gpp.org/ftp/Specs/archive/28_series/28.552/

6G Flagship. (2019). Key drivers and research challenges for 6G ubiquitous wireless intelligence. University of Oulu. https://www.6gflagship.com/

ABI Research. (2019). *5G eMBB application analysis* (Research Report). ABI Research. https://www.abiresearch.com/

Deutsche Telekom. (2024, October). *Launch of 5G+ gaming: Innovation for mobile cloud gaming* [Press release]. https://www.telekom.com/en/media/media-information/

EE. (2024, September). *EE switches on UK's first 5G standalone network* [Press release]. https://newsroom.ee.co.uk/

Ericsson. (2022). *5G opportunities in the cloud gaming market*. Ericsson. https://www.ericsson.com/en/reports-and-papers/

ETSI. (2018). *MEC in 5G networks* (ETSI White Paper No. 28). European Telecommunications Standards Institute. https://www.etsi.org/

ETSI. (2019). *Multi-access edge computing (MEC); Framework and reference architecture* (GS MEC 003 V2.1.1). European Telecommunications Standards Institute. https://www.etsi.org/

GIGABYTE. (2019). *eMBB: 8K streaming & immersive VR/AR solution brief*. GIGABYTE Technology. https://www.gigabyte.com/Solutions/embb

Grand View Research. (2023). *5G services market size & share report, 2023-2030*. Grand View Research. https://www.grandviewresearch.com/

GSMA. (2021). *Cloud gaming: 5G's killer app?* GSMA Intelligence. https://www.gsma.com/

GSMA Intelligence. (2019). *Cloud AR/VR report*. GSM Association. https://www.gsmaintelligence.com/

Huawei. (2018). *Cloud VR/AR white paper*. Huawei Technologies. https://www.huawei.com/

IEEE. (2023). Towards an evolved immersive experience: Exploring 5G- and beyond-enabled ultra-low-latency communications for augmented and virtual reality. Institute of Electrical and Electronics Engineers. https://ieeexplore.ieee.org/

ITU-R. (2015). *IMT vision – Framework and overall objectives of the future development of IMT for 2020 and beyond* (Recommendation ITU-R M.2083). International Telecommunication Union. https://www.itu.int/rec/R-REC-M.2083

ITU-R. (2017). *Minimum requirements related to technical performance for IMT-2020 radio interface(s)* (Report ITU-R M.2410). International Telecommunication Union. https://www.itu.int/pub/R-REP-M.2410

ITU-R. (2022). *Future technology trends for the evolution of IMT towards 2030 and beyond* (Report ITU-R M.2516). International Telecommunication Union. https://www.itu.int/pub/R-REP-M.2516

Markets and Markets. (2023). *5G services market - Global forecast to 2030.* MarketsandMarkets Research. https://www.marketsandmarkets.com/

Newzoo. (2023). *Global cloud gaming report 2023.* Newzoo. https://newzoo.com/

NGMN Alliance. (2020). *5G RAN architecture and functional design* (White Paper). Next Generation Mobile Networks Alliance. https://www.ngmn.org/

Nokia. (2021). *Cloud gaming over 5G* (White Paper). Nokia. https://www.nokia.com/

O-RAN Alliance. (2021). *O-RAN architecture description 4.0.* O-RAN Alliance. https://www.o-ran.org/

Qualcomm. (2018). *Making immersive virtual and augmented reality a commercial reality.* Qualcomm Technologies. https://www.qualcomm.com/

TM Forum. (2020). *Autonomous networks technical architecture* (IG1218). TM Forum. https://www.tmforum.org/

Verified Market Research. (2024, March). *Enhanced mobile broadband (eMBB) service market size and forecast.* Verified Market Research. https://www.verifiedmarketresearch.com/

Chapter 7: Ultra-Reliable Low Latency Communications (URLLC)

Executive Summary

Ultra-Reliable Low Latency Communications (URLLC) forms one of the three core service types within 5G networks, working alongside enhanced Mobile Broadband (eMBB) and massive Machine-Type Communications (mMTC). This chapter examines how URLLC facilitates safety-critical applications demanding extraordinary dependability (99.999% and beyond) combined with minimal response times (as brief as 1 millisecond). We investigate the technological principles, architectural elements, and operational deployments of URLLC, featuring self-driving transportation, manufacturing robotics, and remote medical procedures. The chapter offers a thorough understanding of how 5G systems satisfy these rigorous demands through cutting-edge physical layer innovations, network slicing, edge computing, and enhanced resource optimization methods.

Table of Contents

Introduction

Ultra-Reliable Low Latency Communications (URLLC) was developed as a transformative approach in 5G systems, responding to the essential demand for communications that concurrently deliver outstanding reliability and minimal latency. As 5G networks evolve into platforms for diverse industries, a distinct requirement has emerged where enhanced reliability and decreased latency must be achieved together (3GPP, 2022).

The core challenge of URLLC involves satisfying two historically competing demands. Based on RP-191584 and TR 38.913, this specification is defined for single-hop scenarios (such as UE to gNB connections), likely at the MAC/RLC protocol level (ShareTechnote, 2020). URLLC services achieve brief transmissions through expanded subcarrier spacing or transmission overlapping techniques (Cadence, 2023). This combined requirement differentiates URLLC from earlier mobile communication generations, where optimization typically concentrated on either reliability or latency independently, but seldom both concurrently.

Evolution from 4G to 5G URLLC

The journey toward achieving true Ultra-Reliable Low-Latency Communication capabilities began during the late stages of 4G LTE evolution, well before 5G networks became commercially available. LTE Release 14 introduced initial enhancements targeting Vehicle-to-Everything (V2X) communication scenarios, which demanded more stringent performance than traditional mobile broadband applications. These early V2X implementations established preliminary latency targets—specifying that message transmission should complete within 100 milliseconds under normal conditions, with certain critical safety scenarios requiring response times constrained to just 20 milliseconds (3GPP, 2022).

While these LTE Release 14 improvements represented meaningful progress toward lower latency operation, they fell short of what would eventually define genuine URLLC performance. The 100-millisecond baseline latency, though adequate for some cooperative awareness applications where vehicles share position and velocity information, proved insufficient for time-critical safety functions like collision avoidance or emergency braking coordination. Even the 20-millisecond constraint for specific scenarios represented a significant compromise compared to the sub-millisecond response times that autonomous vehicle coordination would ultimately require.

The fundamental architectural limitations of 4G LTE constrained how far latency could be reduced within that framework. LTE's frame structure, scheduling mechanisms, and protocol overhead created inherent latency floors that incremental improvements could reduce but not eliminate. The network's design prioritized spectral efficiency and capacity for mobile broadband traffic over the deterministic, ultra-low-latency performance that mission-critical applications demanded. Achieving reliability levels sufficient for industrial automation, remote surgery, or autonomous vehicle safety functions—where system failures could have catastrophic consequences—required rethinking the radio access technology from first principles.

This recognition drove the development of 5G New Radio (NR) technology, which was architected from the ground up to support URLLC alongside enhanced mobile broadband and massive IoT connectivity. Unlike LTE's latency improvements, which represented optimizations within existing architectural constraints, 5G NR incorporated fundamental design decisions specifically enabling ultra-low-latency operation. The flexible numerology allowing variable subcarrier spacing, shortened transmission time intervals, streamlined protocol stacks with reduced processing delays, and deterministic scheduling mechanisms all contributed to pushing latency down by an order of magnitude compared to LTE's capabilities.

5G NR's introduction of sub-millisecond air interface latency—achieving one-way transmission delays as low as one millisecond under optimal conditions—finally brought URLLC from aspirational concept to deployable reality. Combined with reliability targets of 99.999% (often called "five nines" reliability, meaning fewer than one failure per 100,000 transmissions), 5G established the performance foundation necessary for applications where human safety or critical infrastructure depends on wireless communication dependability.

The evolution illustrates an important pattern in telecommunications development: incremental improvements within existing frameworks can achieve meaningful progress, but truly transformative capability jumps often require fundamental architectural redesign. LTE's late-stage enhancements proved the concept and identified requirements, but only 5G NR's ground-up architecture delivered the performance that defines authentic URLLC service. This pattern likely continues—current 5G URLLC capabilities, impressive as they are, may eventually prove to be stepping stones toward even more demanding future applications that will drive the next generation's architectural innovations.

URLLC Requirements and Key Performance Indicators

3GPP Specifications

The 3GPP consortium has defined rigorous standards for Ultra-Reliable Low Latency Communication (URLLC) applications. According to the technical report 3GPP RAN TR 38.913, specific benchmarks have been established for both latency performance and system reliability (Cadence, 2023). These technical standards serve as the foundation for implementing URLLC capabilities across telecommunications networks.:

URLLC Latency Requirements

Parameter	Requirement	Description
User Plane Data Latency	0.5 ms	One-way transmission time for the uplink path and the downlink path
Control Plane Data Latency	10 ms	Transition from idle to active state
End-to-End Latency	1-5 ms	Total delay, including processing and propagation

Source: 3GPP TR 38.913, 2018; 5G HUB Technologies, 2020

Reliability Requirements by Application Domain

Application Domain	Reliability Target	Packet Size	Latency Budget
Discrete Automation	99.99%	Small to big	10 ms
Process Automation - Remote Control	99.999%	Small to big	60 ms
Electricity Distribution - High Voltage	99.999%	Small	5 ms
Intelligent Transport Systems	99.999%	Small to big	30 ms

Source: 3GPP TS 22.261, 2020; 5GWorldPro, 2023

According to the 3GPP technical standard RAN TR 38.913, URLLC systems must achieve a reliability threshold of $1\text{-}10^{-5}$ for 32-byte data packets while maintaining user plane latency within 1 millisecond (5G HUB Technologies, 2020).

5G Quality of Service (QoS) Architecture

Fifth-generation wireless networks introduced a fundamentally redesigned Quality of Service framework tailored specifically to meet the demanding performance requirements of Ultra-Reliable Low-Latency Communication applications. Unlike previous cellular generations where QoS mechanisms primarily differentiated between background data and priority voice calls, 5G's architecture acknowledges the dramatically diverse requirements of modern use cases—from autonomous vehicles requiring millisecond response times to industrial sensors tolerating multi-second delays, from remote surgery demanding near-perfect reliability to social media browsing accepting occasional packet loss.

According to research published by 5G Americas (2019), this new framework provides networks with granular control mechanisms through multiple standardized Service Quality Indicators (SQIs) that applications can invoke to specify their performance needs precisely. Rather than forcing all traffic through a handful of predefined service classes, 5G enables fine-grained QoS differentiation that matches network behavior to application requirements across multiple dimensions simultaneously.

Flow-based QoS Model: The foundation of 5G's QoS architecture rests on flow-based management that tracks individual data streams rather than treating all traffic from a device identically. This granular approach recognizes that a single device—say, a connected vehicle—might simultaneously handle multiple traffic types with vastly different requirements: streaming video from backup cameras requiring moderate bandwidth and latency, periodic telemetry updates tolerating significant delays, and safety-critical collision warning messages demanding immediate delivery with guaranteed reliability.

The flow-based model employs standardized 5G QoS Indicators that comprehensively describe traffic requirements. These indicators specify parameters including maximum acceptable latency, packet error rate tolerance, guaranteed and maximum bit rates, and priority levels. When an application establishes a connection, it communicates these requirements through standardized APIs, and the network configures resources accordingly—allocating dedicated capacity where needed, establishing priority queuing rules, and configuring radio scheduling to meet latency targets.

Reflective QoS capabilities enhance this model by allowing networks to observe traffic patterns and automatically apply appropriate QoS treatments without requiring explicit application signaling for every flow. The network detects characteristics like packet sizes, arrival patterns, and port numbers, infers likely application types and their requirements, then applies corresponding QoS policies. This automation simplifies application development—developers don't need to manually configure QoS for every traffic flow—while ensuring that performance-sensitive traffic receives appropriate treatment even from applications not explicitly QoS-aware.

Delay Critical GBR: Traditional Guaranteed Bit Rate (GBR) services in previous cellular generations focused primarily on ensuring sufficient bandwidth—guaranteeing that applications would receive their requested data rates regardless of network congestion. While bandwidth guarantees prove necessary for applications like video streaming, they're insufficient for latency-critical services where timing matters more than throughput.

5G introduces Delay Critical GBR as a specialized resource type addressing this gap. Applications using this service class receive not only guaranteed bandwidth but also guaranteed maximum latency bounds. The network reserves radio resources specifically for these flows, schedules transmissions to meet timing deadlines, and prioritizes delay-critical traffic over conventional GBR and best-effort services when scheduling decisions must be made.

Consider a factory automation scenario where robotic arms coordinate movements through wireless control loops. The control commands might be small packets—just a few hundred bytes specifying position and velocity targets—but they must arrive within stringent deadlines, typically several milliseconds. Bandwidth requirements are modest, but latency requirements are absolute. Delay Critical GBR enables the network to guarantee that these control messages receive immediate scheduling attention, jumping ahead of bulk data transfers or streaming video that can tolerate brief delays without functional impact.

The resource allocation mechanisms supporting Delay Critical GBR differ fundamentally from conventional bandwidth reservation. Rather than simply setting aside spectrum capacity, the network configures schedulers to process delay-critical traffic with minimal queuing delay, may pre-allocate periodic transmission opportunities so devices don't wait for scheduling grants, and establishes backup transmission paths that automatically activate if primary links experience problems. These measures ensure that latency guarantees hold even under challenging radio conditions or network congestion.

Dynamic Resource Allocation: Static resource reservation, while providing guarantees, wastes capacity when reserved resources sit idle because applications aren't actively transmitting. A remote surgery system might require guaranteed ultra-low-latency connectivity, but surgical procedures don't run continuously—the reserved resources remain unused between operations, unavailable to other applications that could productively utilize them.

Dynamic Resource Allocation addresses this inefficiency by enabling real-time adjustment of network resources based on instantaneous application demands. Rather than permanently reserving capacity for potential peak loads, the network monitors actual traffic patterns and reallocates resources fluidly as needs change. When a delay-critical application becomes active, the network rapidly provisions necessary resources—adjusting radio scheduling priorities, allocating dedicated transmission opportunities, configuring quality monitoring. When the application becomes dormant, those resources return to the general pool for other uses.

This dynamic approach requires sophisticated network intelligence that tracks application states, predicts resource requirements based on historical patterns, and reconfigures network elements within milliseconds as demands shift. The 5G core network's service-based architecture facilitates this agility by enabling rapid communication between network functions responsible for policy decisions, resource management, and radio configuration. When an application signals changing requirements—perhaps a connected vehicle transitioning from highway cruising to urban intersection navigation where collision avoidance becomes critical—the network can respond almost instantaneously, shifting from moderate QoS to ultra-reliable low-latency mode without interrupting connectivity.

Machine learning algorithms increasingly augment dynamic allocation decisions, analyzing patterns to predict when applications will require enhanced QoS and proactively provisioning resources slightly ahead of actual demand. This predictive approach eliminates even the brief provisioning delay that might occur with purely reactive systems, ensuring that when a critical application activates, the necessary network resources are already in place.

The economic benefits of dynamic allocation prove substantial. Static reservation for peak loads means networks must be sized for worst-case scenarios—every potential simultaneous URLLC application requiring full resource guarantees—creating massive overprovisioning. Dynamic allocation allows statistical multiplexing where the network is sized for typical loads rather than theoretical peaks, knowing that not all applications demand maximum resources simultaneously. Studies suggest that dynamic approaches can improve network utilization by 40-60% compared to static reservation while maintaining equivalent performance guarantees, directly impacting the economic viability of supporting diverse URLLC applications on shared infrastructure (5G Americas, 2019).

URLLC Architecture and Technical Components

Physical Layer Enhancements

Among all URLLC implementation challenges, the physical layer stands out as particularly complex. The fundamental tension lies in satisfying dual requirements that often work against each other—reducing latency to absolute minimums while guaranteeing exceptional reliability (5G Americas, 2019).

URLLC Physical Layer Architecture

(Adapted from 5G Americas White Paper, 2019)

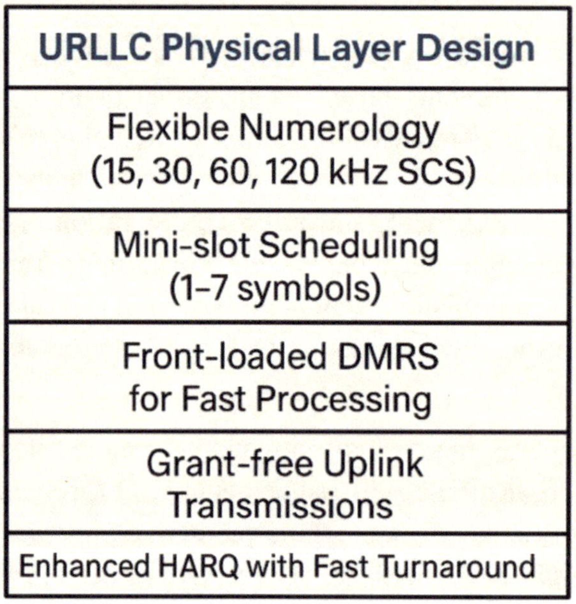

Key technical innovations include:

1. **Flexible Transmission Path Duration**: Network engineers can reduce transmission delays by manipulating two key parameters. First, they expand the frequency spacing between subcarriers, which naturally compresses the time needed for each symbol and slot. Second, they implement micro-scheduling techniques using mini-slots to achieve finer timing precision across both uplink and downlink pathways (5G Americas, 2019).
2. **Reduced Processing Time:**
   Achieved through:
   - Front-loaded Demodulation Reference Signals (DMRS)
   - No time domain interleaving
   - Frequency-first mapping
   - Parallelizable Low-Density Parity Check (LDPC) coding
3. **Grant-free Transmissions**: Enable immediate uplink access without scheduling request overhead

Network Architecture Components

Mobile Edge Computing (MEC)

Mobile Edge Computing allows developers and content creators to harness cloud-based processing power and IT resources closer to end users—specifically at network edge locations (5G Americas, 2019). This distributed computing model plays a vital role in URLLC applications because:

- Minimizes total transmission delays by performing computations nearer to end users.
- Enables local traffic steering and routing
- Supports application-specific optimizations

URLLC Network Architecture with MEC

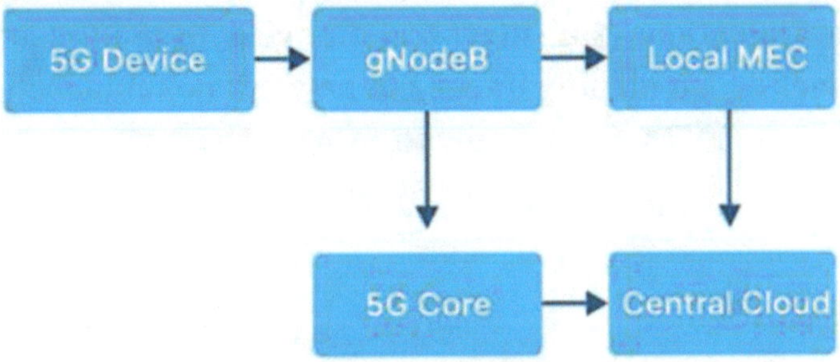

Based on 3GPP TS 23.501, 2021

Autonomous Driving Applications

Autonomous vehicles represent one of the most demanding URLLC use cases, requiring real-time communication for safety-critical operations.

V2X Communication Requirements

URLLC represents an emerging 5G service class designed specifically for mission-critical applications, establishing performance targets of 1-millisecond latency alongside comprehensive end-to-end security protocols and 99.999 percent availability standards (GIGABYTE Global, 2021).

V2X Communication Scenarios and Requirements

Scenario	Latency Requirement	Reliability	Data Rate
Cooperative Collision Avoidance	10 ms	99.999%	10 Mbps
Automated Overtaking	10 ms	99.999%	50 Mbps
High-Density Platooning	10 ms	99.999%	65 Mbps

Scenario	Latency Requirement	Reliability	Data Rate
Remote Driving	5 ms	99.999%	25 Mbps UL, 1 Mbps DL

Source: 3GPP TR 22.886, 2018; Rantcell, 2021

Implementation Architecture

When vehicles operate autonomously without any human oversight, they can leverage data gathered from roadside sensors and neighboring vehicles to execute complex maneuvers. These capabilities include automated lane changes, collision prevention systems, and coordinated traffic management strategies (GIGABYTE Global, 2021).

The V2X architecture leverages:

1. **Direct Communications (PC5 Interface)**: For vehicle-to-vehicle communications
2. **Network Communications (Uu Interface)**: For vehicle-to-infrastructure communications
3. **Hybrid Approaches**: Combining direct and network communications for redundancy

V2X Communication Architecture

(Adapted from 3GPP TS 23.287, 2020)

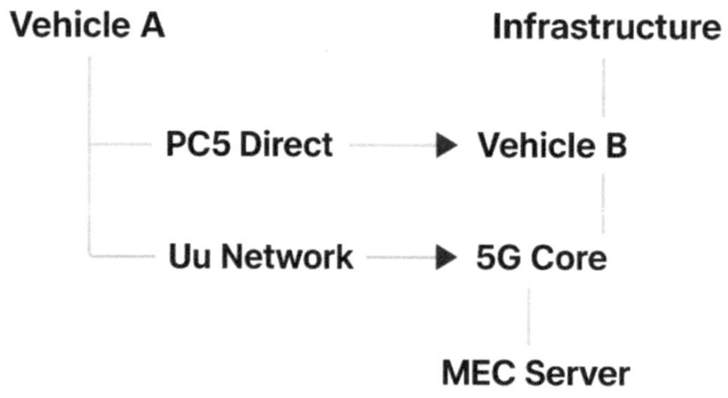

Teleoperation and Remote Driving

Remote vehicle operation serves as a critical element in autonomous fleet management systems. This technology provides comprehensive service coverage by addressing challenging scenarios, building customer confidence through human oversight, and supporting vehicle operations even when full autonomy isn't available (DriveU.auto, 2023).

Key considerations for teleoperation include:

- **Uplink Requirements**: High-bandwidth video streaming from multiple cameras
- **Downlink Requirements**: Low-latency control commands
- **Network Slicing**: Dedicated resources for guaranteed performance

Robotics and Industrial Automation

Industrial IoT Applications

By implementing industry-standard automation communication protocols such as PROFINET RT and PROFIsafe, 5G URLLC technology achieves extremely low latency performance with strict timing constraints and guaranteed service levels (Ericsson, 2020).

Industrial Automation Use Cases

Use Case	Latency	Reliability	Cycle Time
Motion Control	0.5-1 ms	99.9999%	0.5 ms
Robot Control	1-10 ms	99.999%	1-10 ms
Process Monitoring	50 ms	99.9%	>50 ms
AR-assisted Maintenance	10 ms	99.999%	10-100 ms

Source: 3GPP TR 22.804, 2019; 5G-ACIA, 2020

Implementation Benefits

Eliminating wired connections for automated machinery substantially enhances production line adaptability, equipment repositioning capabilities, and overall operational performance (Ericsson, 2020).

Industrial URLLC enables:

1. **Flexible Manufacturing**: Rapid reconfiguration of production lines.
2. **Mobile Robotics**: Autonomous guided vehicles (AGVs) with guaranteed connectivity.
3. **Human-Robot Collaboration**: Safe interaction through reliable communications.
4. **Predictive Maintenance**: Real-time monitoring and analytics.

Industrial URLLC Network Topology

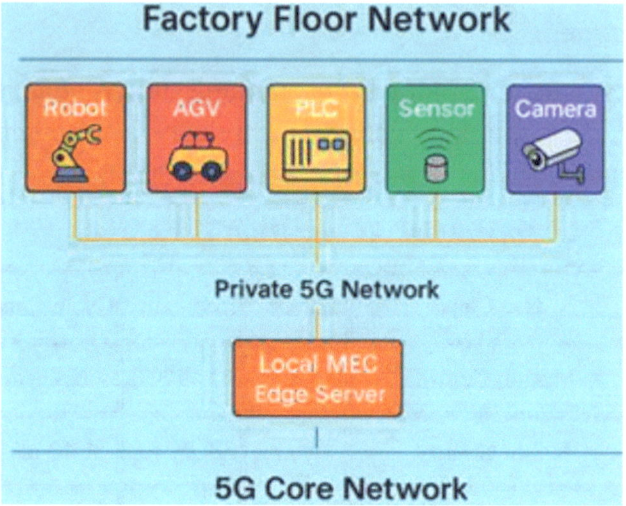

Based on the 5G-ACIA White Paper, 2020

Remote Surgery and Healthcare Applications

Telemedicine Requirements

5G has shown how end-to-end slicing can address critical issues like performance and reliability (Ericsson, 2024). Remote surgery represents the most stringent URLLC use case in healthcare.

Healthcare Application Requirements

Application	Latency	Reliability	Data Rate	Key Requirements
Remote Surgery	<1 ms	99.9999%	1 Gbps	Haptic feedback, 4K video
Remote Diagnosis	10-20 ms	99.999%	100 Mbps	HD video, real-time interaction
Emergency Response	10 ms	99.999%	50 Mbps	Vital signs, video streaming
Patient Monitoring	100 ms	99.9%	1 Mbps	Continuous data transmission

Source: ITU-R M.2083, 2015; PMC, 2022

Technical Implementation

5G networks support both eMBB and URLLC service profiles, positioning these technologies to address critical connectivity requirements in mobile healthcare applications (PMC, 2022).

Key components for healthcare URLLC:

1. **Haptic Feedback Systems**: Require round-trip times under 1 ms
2. **Multi-modal Data Transmission**: Simultaneous video, audio, and sensor data
3. **Redundant Transmission Paths:** Critical for reliability

4. **Security and Privacy**: Enhanced encryption and access control

Remote Surgery Communication Flow

(Adapted from IEEE Communications Magazine, 2019)

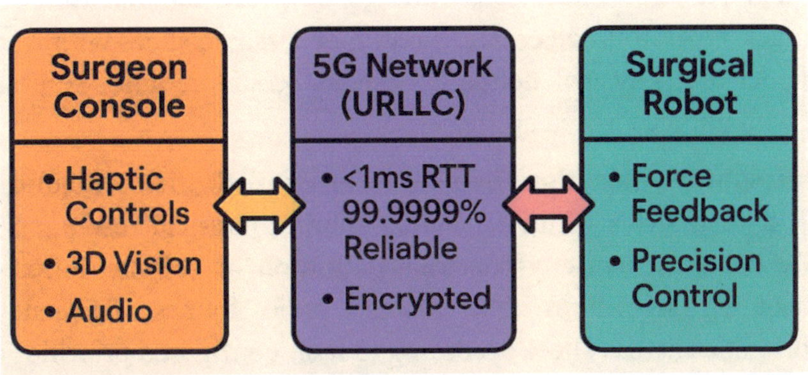

Network Slicing for URLLC

Network Slicing Architecture

Fifth-generation wireless networks introduce network slicing as a foundational architectural capability that enables a single physical infrastructure to function as multiple independent virtual networks, each optimized for distinct service requirements. This virtualization approach addresses a fundamental challenge in supporting diverse applications—from consumer mobile broadband to mission-critical industrial control—on shared infrastructure. Rather than building separate dedicated networks for each use case (an economically prohibitive approach), or forcing all applications through a one-size-fits-all network configuration (which inevitably compromises performance for some applications), network slicing creates customized virtual network instances that coexist on common physical resources.

Each network slice represents an isolated, end-to-end virtual network with its own dedicated resources and specific performance characteristics. A URLLC slice might prioritize ultra-low latency and extreme reliability while accepting lower throughput; a mobile broadband slice emphasizes maximum data rates but tolerates higher latency; a massive IoT slice optimizes for handling millions of low-bandwidth connections efficiently. These slices operate independently—congestion or failures in one slice don't impact others—yet share underlying physical infrastructure through sophisticated resource allocation mechanisms.

The slicing architecture dynamically distributes network capabilities among these virtual instances based on application requirements rather than static partitioning. When URLLC applications demand additional resources—perhaps during peak industrial automation activity or emergency response situations—the network can reallocate capacity from less critical slices, ensuring that mission-critical services receive necessary resources even under challenging conditions. Conversely, during periods when URLLC demand is modest, those resources become available for mobile broadband or IoT slices, maximizing infrastructure utilization (VIAVI Solutions, 2023).

This flexibility stems from software-defined networking principles where network behavior is controlled through programmable software layers rather than fixed hardware configurations. The 5G core network's service-based architecture enables rapid reconfiguration of network functions, routing policies, and resource allocations through software commands rather than physical infrastructure changes. Operators can create, modify, or dissolve slices within minutes rather than the weeks or months that physical network changes would require, responding to evolving application needs with unprecedented agility.

Slice-Specific Resource Allocation: Implementing network slicing requires mechanisms that enforce isolation between slices while efficiently sharing physical resources. The radio access network—typically the most capacity-constrained portion of cellular infrastructure—employs sophisticated scheduling algorithms that allocate radio frames, frequency resources, and transmission opportunities across slices according to their configured priorities and guarantees.

For URLLC slices, this means reserving portions of each radio frame for delay-critical traffic, ensuring that ultra-low-latency applications can transmit with minimal queuing delay regardless of congestion in other slices. The scheduler might dedicate specific time-frequency resource blocks exclusively to URLLC, or implement priority-based preemption where URLLC traffic can interrupt ongoing transmissions from lower-priority slices when necessary. These mechanisms guarantee that URLLC applications receive the deterministic, low-latency performance they require without being subject to congestion from best-effort traffic.

Core network resources—computing capacity for processing user plane traffic, control plane signaling capacity, and backhaul bandwidth—are similarly partitioned across slices. Each slice receives guaranteed minimum resources sufficient for its performance commitments, with additional capacity allocated opportunistically when available. Network functions can be instantiated as dedicated instances per slice (providing maximum isolation but consuming more resources) or shared across multiple slices with resource limits enforced through virtualization (improving efficiency but requiring careful isolation to prevent one slice's behavior from impacting others).

End-to-End Orchestration: Network slicing's promise of customized service delivery requires coordinated orchestration across all network domains—from radio access networks through transport networks to core network functions and potentially extending to edge computing resources and application servers. Creating a URLLC slice involves not just configuring radio resources but also establishing appropriate routing through transport networks with latency guarantees, instantiating core network functions with necessary performance characteristics, and coordinating with edge computing platforms to ensure end-to-end latency targets are met.

Orchestration platforms automate this complexity through service templates that encode slice requirements and deployment procedures. An operator defining a factory automation slice specifies performance targets (1ms latency, 99.999% reliability, specific throughput), geographic coverage (the factory location and immediate surroundings), and duration (perhaps a long-term deployment with guaranteed resources). The orchestration system translates these requirements into specific network configurations—allocating radio resources at cell sites covering the factory, establishing dedicated core network function instances, configuring transport network paths with appropriate quality of service, and deploying edge computing resources at nearby facilities.

This automated orchestration proves essential for slice lifecycle management. As application needs evolve—a factory expanding operations requiring more capacity, or a temporary event requiring additional URLLC connectivity—operators can modify slice configurations through high-level service requests rather than manual reconfiguration of individual network elements. The orchestration system handles the complex coordination required to implement changes consistently across all network layers, maintaining end-to-end performance guarantees throughout transitions.

Business Model Innovation: Network slicing enables new business models where operators move beyond selling generic connectivity to offering customized network services tailored to specific vertical industries. Rather than enterprises purchasing standard mobile service plans, they can acquire dedicated network slices with guaranteed performance characteristics suited to their applications—effectively leasing virtual private networks with cellular coverage but enterprise-grade performance guarantees.

This capability proves particularly valuable for industries requiring URLLC performance—manufacturing automation, public safety, healthcare, utilities, transportation—where generic mobile broadband service cannot provide sufficient reliability or latency guarantees. A manufacturing company might purchase a URLLC slice covering their facilities, receiving guaranteed ultra-low-latency connectivity for industrial control systems with service level agreements enforceable through continuous monitoring and automated resource management. The pricing model shifts from per-megabyte data charges to service-level commitments based on performance, coverage, and reliability—reflecting the value delivered rather than just connectivity volume.

Network slicing also facilitates neutral host and private network scenarios where enterprises or venues deploy their own dedicated slices, potentially on shared infrastructure operated by mobile carriers. A hospital might operate a private URLLC slice for medical devices and telehealth applications, maintaining complete control over network configuration and security policies while leveraging carrier infrastructure rather than building entirely separate networks. This approach reduces deployment costs while providing the isolation and performance guarantees that mission-critical applications require.

The economic sustainability of network slicing depends on achieving sufficient utilization across multiple slices to justify infrastructure investments. A single-purpose network optimized exclusively for URLLC would likely prove economically unviable given the high cost of infrastructure deployment and the reality that URLLC applications typically generate modest data volumes and may not continuously utilize their reserved capacity. By enabling infrastructure sharing across slices—URLLC, mobile broadband, and IoT coexisting on common physical networks—operators achieve utilization levels that justify investment while still providing the isolation and performance guarantees each application class requires.

Network slicing enables dedicated logical networks optimized for URLLC requirements:

URLLC Network Slice Characteristics

Slice Parameter	Configuration	Purpose
Latency Budget	<1-10 ms	Mission-critical response
Reliability Target	99.999-99.9999%	Zero-failure operations
Resource Allocation	Dedicated	Guaranteed performance
Priority Level	Highest	Preemption capability
Security Level	Enhanced	Isolated, encrypted paths

Source: 3GPP TS 28.541, 2020; GSMA, 2021

Implementation Components

Ultra-Reliable Low-Latency Communication builds upon 5G's technological foundation to deliver wireless connectivity with performance characteristics previously achievable only through wired connections or dedicated wireless systems. The service targets applications where communication failures or delays could have serious safety, operational, or financial consequences—industrial automation systems controlling heavy machinery, remote surgical procedures requiring precise instrument control, autonomous vehicle coordination preventing collisions, or emergency response systems dispatching first responders.

Achieving URLLC's ambitious performance goals requires integrating multiple technological components across the entire network architecture. The implementation encompasses radio access network optimizations that minimize air interface latency, core network enhancements supporting deterministic routing and processing, edge computing infrastructure reducing round-trip delays, and end-to-end orchestration ensuring consistent performance across all network segments.

Latency Performance: URLLC targets end-to-end latency of one millisecond for the user plane—the time required for data to traverse from application on the device, through the radio interface and network infrastructure, to the destination application. This sub-millisecond target represents roughly a 100-fold improvement over typical 4G LTE performance, where end-to-end latencies of 50-100 milliseconds were common even under favorable conditions.

Reaching this aggressive target demands optimization at every layer. The radio interface employs shortened transmission time intervals—reducing the fundamental time unit for scheduling and transmission from one millisecond in LTE to as little as 0.125 milliseconds in 5G NR for URLLC configurations. This reduction means devices can transmit immediately rather than waiting for the next scheduling opportunity, cutting queuing delays substantially. Mini-slots allow even more granular scheduling, enabling ultra-short transmissions that complete within fractions of a millisecond.

Protocol stacks are streamlined to eliminate unnecessary processing steps that contributed latency in previous generations. Header compression reduces the overhead bytes that must be transmitted, segmentation avoids splitting messages across multiple transmission opportunities, and processing pipelines in both devices and base stations minimize the computation time between reception and retransmission. Every microsecond of processing delay removed contributes to meeting the overall latency budget.

Propagation delay—the time radio signals take to travel between devices and base stations—represents a fundamental physical limit that cannot be eliminated. At the speed of light, signals require roughly 3.3 microseconds per kilometer traveled. For devices several kilometers from base stations, propagation alone consumes tens of microseconds of the total latency budget. This reality drives deployment of small cells and edge computing infrastructure that reduce physical distances between devices and processing resources, minimizing unavoidable propagation delays (TechTarget, 2023).

Reliability Through Redundancy: The reliability dimension of URLLC proves equally challenging, targeting packet error rates below 0.001%—meaning fewer than one transmission in 100,000 should fail to reach its destination correctly. This "five nines" reliability (99.999%) exceeds what typical mobile broadband achieves by orders of magnitude and approaches the reliability levels of wired industrial communication systems.

Multiple redundancy mechanisms work together to achieve this exceptional reliability. Diversity transmission sends identical data through multiple independent paths—perhaps different frequency bands, different cell sites, or different network slices—so that if one path experiences interference or equipment failure, alternatives remain available. The receiver can compare redundant transmissions and use whichever arrives correctly, or combine information from multiple copies to reconstruct the message even if individual transmissions are partially corrupted.

Forward error correction adds carefully designed redundancy within individual transmissions, embedding additional bits that allow receivers to detect and correct errors without requiring retransmission. While this redundancy increases the total data transmitted, it proves essential for URLLC where retransmission delays would violate latency budgets. Advanced coding schemes can correct significant corruption—recovering correct messages even when a substantial percentage of transmitted bits are received incorrectly due to interference or signal fading.

Channel state information feedback enables adaptive transmission strategies that adjust modulation, coding, and power based on instantaneous radio conditions. When channel quality is high, aggressive modulation schemes maximize throughput; when interference or fading degrades the channel, the system automatically switches to more conservative approaches that sacrifice throughput for reliability. This adaptation happens on millisecond timescales, continuously optimizing the reliability-efficiency tradeoff based on current conditions.

Secure Communication: Security proves particularly critical for URLLC applications, many of which control physical systems or handle sensitive information. Compromised industrial control systems could cause equipment damage, production disruptions, or safety incidents; tampered vehicle-to-vehicle communications could trigger accidents; intercepted medical data violates privacy and regulatory requirements.

5G's security architecture provides multiple layers of protection specifically enhanced for URLLC requirements. Authentication mechanisms verify device and network identity before establishing connections, preventing unauthorized devices from accessing URLLC services or malicious actors from impersonating legitimate network infrastructure. Encryption protects data in transit, ensuring that intercepted transmissions remain unintelligible to eavesdroppers and cannot be modified without detection.

Integrity protection proves especially important for URLLC control messages where tampering could cause dangerous outcomes. Cryptographic message authentication codes allow receivers to verify that commands originated from legitimate sources and haven't been altered during transmission. A robotic arm receiving a movement command can confirm the instruction came from the authorized controller and wasn't injected or modified by an attacker attempting to cause collisions or damage.

The challenge for URLLC security lies in achieving cryptographic protection without introducing latency that would violate timing requirements. Traditional security protocols include multiple message exchanges for authentication and key establishment that can consume tens of milliseconds—unacceptable delays for applications requiring single-digit millisecond response times. 5G addresses this through streamlined security procedures that complete authentication more rapidly, session resumption mechanisms that eliminate repeated authentication when devices briefly lose connectivity, and efficient cryptographic algorithms optimized for low-latency operation.

Physical layer security techniques augment traditional cryptographic protection by exploiting characteristics of wireless channels that make eavesdropping inherently difficult. Because radio propagation is highly location-dependent—the precise signal characteristics received at any point depend on that location's specific relationship to the transmitter and reflecting surfaces—legitimate receivers can detect unauthorized receivers attempting to intercept transmissions. Adaptive beamforming can direct signals precisely toward intended recipients while minimizing radiation toward other directions, making eavesdropping more difficult without requiring computational overhead of additional encryption.

Integration and Testing: Implementing URLLC requires not just individual component optimization but careful integration ensuring that end-to-end performance meets targets consistently. A radio interface achieving sub-millisecond latency provides little value if core network processing introduces tens of milliseconds delay, or if transport network congestion creates unpredictable queuing delays that occasionally spike latency above acceptable thresholds.

Comprehensive testing validates URLLC implementations under diverse conditions—nominal operation, degraded radio conditions, network congestion, and failure scenarios. Unlike mobile broadband where occasional performance degradation annoys users but rarely causes serious consequences, URLLC applications depend on consistent performance where failures could have significant impacts. Testing must verify not just typical-case performance but also worst-case behavior, ensuring that even under challenging conditions the system maintains reliability and latency guarantees.

Performance monitoring in operational URLLC deployments provides continuous validation that service level agreements are being met and enables rapid response when problems emerge. Real-time latency and reliability metrics tracked per connection allow operators to identify degrading performance before it violates guarantees, triggering automatic resource reallocation or manual intervention to maintain service quality. This continuous monitoring proves essential for applications where stake holders depend on the network for mission-critical functions—operators must detect and resolve problems proactively rather than waiting for failures to impact operations (TechTarget, 2023)

URLLC Network Slicing Architecture

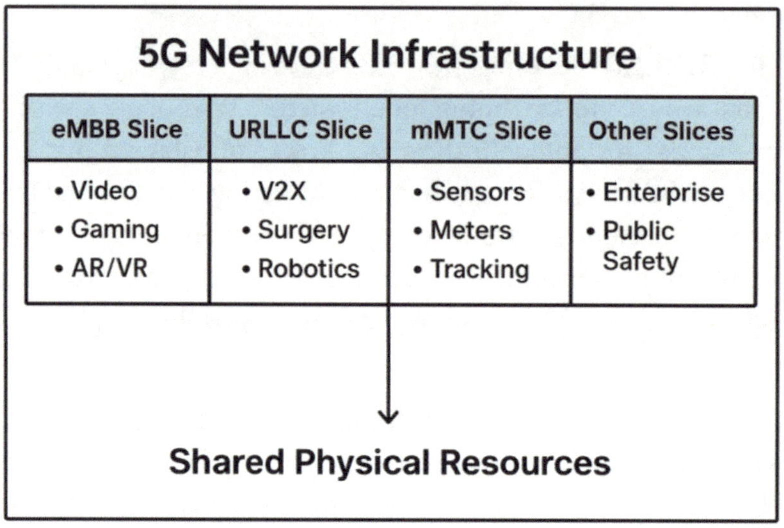

Based on 3GPP TS 23.501, 2021

Resource Management

Key aspects of URLLC slice management:

1. **Dynamic Resource Allocation**: The network continuously monitors traffic patterns and adjusts resource distribution in real time to align with current demands. This adaptive approach ensures that URLLC services always have sufficient capacity available, even as traffic loads shift throughout the day. Rather than relying on static allocations, the system intelligently redistributes resources based on actual usage patterns and predicted needs.
2. **Preemption Mechanisms**: During periods of network congestion or resource scarcity, URLLC communications automatically receive preferential treatment over less critical services. This preemption capability allows time-sensitive traffic to temporarily interrupt or reduce bandwidth for lower-priority applications, ensuring that mission-critical communications maintain their stringent latency and reliability requirements. The network can quickly identify and prioritize URLLC flows when competing demands threaten performance.
3. **Admission Control**: To prevent system overload and maintain quality guarantees, the network implements access controls that cap the total number of concurrent URLLC sessions. These carefully calibrated limits ensure that accepting a new connection won't compromise existing services. By controlling admission, network operators can guarantee that every active URLLC session receives the resources needed to meet its performance targets, rather than allowing degradation across all connections.
4. **Performance Monitoring**: Network management systems continuously collect and analyze performance metrics, tracking parameters like latency, packet loss, and throughput for all URLLC services. This real-time visibility enables operators to detect emerging issues quickly and implement corrective measures before service degradation becomes

noticeable. The monitoring framework also supports proactive optimization, identifying opportunities to enhance efficiency while maintaining reliability standards.

Implementation Challenges and Solutions

Technical Challenges

1. Queueing and Scheduling
    - **Challenge:** One significant hurdle involves the unpredictable timing that emerges when multiple data streams share network resources through statistical multiplexing. This approach, while efficient for typical traffic, creates inconsistent transmission delays that can undermine the strict timing requirements of URLLC applications.
    - **Solution:** To address this issue, network designers implement guaranteed scheduling mechanisms that reserve dedicated resources for critical traffic. By moving away from probabilistic sharing models toward deterministic allocation strategies, the system can ensure predictable transmission timing regardless of overall network load.
2. Interference Management
    - **Challenge:** Wireless environments inherently suffer from radio frequency interference, where competing signals from multiple sources can corrupt transmissions and reduce connection reliability. This becomes particularly problematic for URLLC services that demand near-perfect delivery rates.
    - **Solution:** The solution involves sophisticated coordination techniques that orchestrate transmission and reception across multiple antenna points simultaneously. This multipoint cooperation approach, often called Coordinated MultiPoint (CoMP), manages interference by synchronizing how different base stations handle signals, effectively turning potential interference into useful signal strength through careful timing and phase alignment.
3. Mobility Management
    - **Challenge:** When devices move between coverage areas, the handover process traditionally introduces brief interruptions and increased latency as the connection transfers from one cell to another. For URLLC applications supporting mobile scenarios—such as autonomous vehicles or industrial robotics—these disruptions can cause critical failures.
    - **Solution:** Network operators solve this challenge by establishing connections to multiple cells simultaneously before breaking the original link, a technique known as make-before-break handover. This dual connectivity approach maintains an active data path throughout the transition, eliminating the gaps that would otherwise occur during cell changes and ensuring continuous service availability.

Security Considerations

Beyond safeguarding data confidentiality and integrity during cellular transmission, networks must also ensure continuous service availability (5G Americas, 2019).

URLLC Security Framework

Security Layer	Mechanism	Purpose
Access Security	5G-AKA, EAP-AKA	Mutual authentication
Network Security	IPsec, DTLS	Encrypted transport
Application Security	E2E encryption	Data confidentiality
Slice Isolation	Resource partitioning	Inter-slice protection

Source: 3GPP TS 33.501, 2021

Future Perspectives

Evolution to 6G

As 5G URLLC matures, research is already looking toward 6G enhancements:

1. **Sub-Millisecond Latency**: Target of 0.1 ms for extreme applications
2. **Higher Reliability**: 99.99999% (seven nines) reliability
3. **AI-Native Design**: Machine learning integrated at all layers
4. **Holographic Communications**: Supporting Tactile Internet Applications

Emerging Applications

Future URLLC applications include:

- **Digital Twins:** Real-time synchronization of physical and virtual systems
- **Brain-Computer Interfaces:** Direct neural control systems
- **Holographic Telepresence:** Ultra-realistic remote presence
- **Swarm Robotics:** Coordinated control of thousands of robots

Conclusion

Ultra-Reliable Low Latency Communications transforms wireless technology by making previously unachievable applications possible. Through advanced physical layer engineering, sophisticated network design, and intelligent resource management, 5G URLLC successfully reconciles the challenging balance between minimal latency and maximum reliability.

URLLC's primary accomplishments encompass:

- **Latency Reduction:** From 100ms in 4G to sub-millisecond in 5G
- **Reliability Enhancement:** From 99% to 99.999% and beyond
- **Application Enablement:** Enabling breakthrough use cases, including self-driving vehicles, remote surgical procedures, and factory automation systems.
- **Network Flexibility:** Leveraging network slicing technologies and edge computing solutions.

As 5G infrastructure matures and next-generation networks, such as 6G research, advance, URLLC technology will serve as a foundational element driving technological evolution across multiple industries and social sectors.

Knowledge Check

1. What are the two primary requirements that URLLC must satisfy simultaneously?

2. Which subcarrier channel spacings are supported in 5G NR for URLLC applications?

3. What is the reliability requirement for remote surgery applications in URLLC?

4. How does network slicing benefit URLLC applications?

5. What role does Mobile Edge Computing (MEC) play in URLLC?

6. Compare and contrast the URLLC requirements for autonomous driving versus remote surgery. Why do these applications have different latency and reliability targets?

7. Explain how grant-free uplink transmissions contribute to latency reduction in URLLC.

8. Discuss the trade-offs between resource optimization and URLLC performance. How do operators balance these competing demands?

9. How do redundant transmission techniques improve reliability in URLLC networks?

10. What are the main security challenges specific to URLLC applications, and how does 5G address them?

Answers

1. What are the two primary requirements that URLLC must satisfy simultaneously?
   Answer: Ultra-low latency (as low as 1 millisecond) and ultra-high reliability (99.999% or higher success rate)

2. Which subcarrier channel spacings are supported in 5G NR for URLLC applications?
   Answer: 15 kHz, 30 kHz, 60 kHz, and 120 kHz. Larger subcarrier spacings enable shorter slot durations and lower latency.

3. What is the reliability requirement for remote surgery applications in URLLC?
   Answer: 99.9999% (six nines) reliability with end-to-end network latency of less than 1 millisecond for haptic feedback.

4. How does network slicing benefit URLLC applications?

Answer: Network slicing creates dedicated logical networks with guaranteed resources, enabling customized performance parameters (latency, reliability, security) for specific URLLC applications without interference from other services.

5. What role does Mobile Edge Computing (MEC) play in URLLC?
   Answer: Mobile Edge Computing enhances URLLC performance by positioning computational resources at network periphery locations. This proximity-based approach minimizes total system latency through localized data processing, eliminating the delays associated with distant cloud infrastructure.

6. Compare and contrast the URLLC requirements for autonomous driving versus remote surgery. Why do these applications have different latency and reliability targets?

   Answer: Remote surgery requires stricter latency (<1ms) due to haptic feedback requirements and higher reliability (99.9999%), as any failure could be life-threatening. Autonomous driving can tolerate slightly higher latency (5-10ms) as vehicles have some local intelligence, but still requires high reliability (99.999%) for safety. The difference stems from the criticality of real-time human interaction in surgery versus the ability of vehicles to operate semi-autonomously.

7. Explain how grant-free uplink transmissions contribute to latency reduction in URLLC.
   Answer: Grant-free transmissions eliminate the scheduling request/grant handshake process, allowing devices to transmit immediately on pre-configured resources. This reduces latency by removing the waiting time for scheduling requests and grant allocation, which is critical for time-sensitive URLLC applications.

8. Discuss the trade-offs between resource optimization and URLLC performance. How do operators balance these competing demands?
   Answer: URLLC requires resource over-provisioning to guarantee performance, reducing spectral efficiency. Operators balance this through: dynamic resource sharing between URLLC and eMBB, preemption mechanisms that allow URLLC to take resources when needed, network slicing to isolate critical services, and admission control to limit URLLC sessions to available resources.

9. How do redundant transmission techniques improve reliability in URLLC networks?
   Answer: Redundant transmissions use packet duplication at the PDCP layer, multi-connectivity with different base stations, and frequency diversity to ensure at least one transmission succeeds. This spatial, temporal, and frequency diversity significantly improves the probability of successful delivery, achieving the ultra-high reliability targets required by URLLC.

10. What are the main security challenges specific to URLLC applications, and how does 5G address them?

    Answer: URLLC faces unique security challenges, including ultra-fast authentication requirements that must not add latency, protection against denial-of-service attacks that could disrupt critical services, and maintaining security while using techniques like packet duplication. 5G addresses these through hardware-based security anchors, slice isolation, enhanced encryption algorithms optimized for low latency, and distributed secu

References

3GPP. (2018). *Study on scenarios and requirements for next generation access technologies* (TR 38.913). https://www.3gpp.org/specifications/specifications

3GPP. (2019). *Study on communication for automation in vertical domains* (TR 22.804). https://www.3gpp.org/specifications/specifications

3GPP. (2020). *Service requirements for the 5G system* (TS 22.261). https://www.3gpp.org/specifications/specifications

3GPP. (2020). Architecture enhancements for 5G System (5GS) to support Vehicle-to-Everything (V2X) services (TS 23.287). https://www.3gpp.org/specifications/specifications

3GPP. (2020). Management and orchestration; 5G Network Resource Model (NRM); Stage 2 and stage 3 (TS 28.541). https://www.3gpp.org/specifications/specifications

3GPP. (2021). *System architecture for the 5G System (5GS)* (TS 23.501). https://www.3gpp.org/specifications/specifications

3GPP. (2021). *Security architecture and procedures for 5G System* (TS 33.501). https://www.3gpp.org/specifications/specifications

3GPP. (2022). *Ultra-reliable and low-latency communications*. https://www.3gpp.org/technologies/urlcc-2022

5G Americas. (2019). *New services & applications with 5G ultra-reliable low latency communications*. https://www.5gamericas.org/wp-content/uploads/2019/07/5G_Americas_URLLLC_White_Paper_Final__updateJW.pdf

5G HUB Technologies. (2020, January 20). *5G ultra-reliable low latency communication (URLLC)*. https://5ghub.us/5g-ultra-reliable-low-latency-communication-urllc/

5G-ACIA. (2020). *5G for connected industries and automation* (2nd ed.). https://www.5g-acia.org/publications/

5GWorldPro. (2023, October 4). *How is 5G URLLC defined and what are related technologies?* https://www.5gworldpro.com/blog/2023/10/04/how-is-5g-urllc-defined-and-what-are-related-technologies/

Cadence. (2023, October 12). *3GPP URLLC requirements*. Advanced PCB Design Blog. https://resources.pcb.cadence.com/blog/2023-3gpp-urllc-requirements

DriveU.auto. (2023, August 15). *Using 5G for teleoperation of autonomous vehicles*. https://driveu.auto/blog/using-5g-for-teleoperation-of-autonomous-vehicles/

Ericsson. (2020). *5G URLLC - Industrial factory automation*. https://www.ericsson.com/en/cases/2020/accelerate-factory-automation-with-5g-urllc

Ericsson. (2024, March 18). *Lifesaving telesurgery in the age of 5G.* https://www.ericsson.com/en/blog/2024/3/cutting-the-cord-lifesaving-telesurgery-in-the-age-of-5g

GIGABYTE Global. (2021). *URLLC: Autonomous vehicle network.* https://www.gigabyte.com/Solutions/urllc

GSMA. (2021). *Generic network slice template v3.0.* https://www.gsma.com/newsroom/resources/generic-network-slice-template-v3-0/

IEEE Communications Magazine. (2019). Ultra-reliable low-latency communications in 5G. IEEE.

ITU-R. (2015). IMT vision – Framework and overall objectives of the future development of IMT for 2020 and beyond (Recommendation M.2083). https://www.itu.int/rec/R-REC-M.2083/en

PMC. (2022). Communication requirements in 5G-enabled healthcare applications: Review and considerations. PubMed Central. https://pmc.ncbi.nlm.nih.gov/articles/PMC8872156/

Rantcell. (2021). *5G autonomous vehicles | Do autonomous vehicles need 5G.* https://www.rantcell.com/do-autonomous-vehicles-need-5g.html

ShareTechnote. (2020). *5G URLLC.* http://www.sharetechnote.com/html/5G/5G_URLLC.html

TechTarget. (2023). *What is network slicing?* https://www.techtarget.com/whatis/definition/network-slicing

VIAVI Solutions. (2023). *5G network slicing.* https://www.viavisolutions.com/en-us/5g-network-slicing

Chapter 8: 5G Massive Machine-Type Communications (mMTC)

Executive Summary

This chapter investigates Massive Machine-Type Communications (mMTC), representing one of three core service categories in 5G technology, complementing enhanced Mobile Broadband (eMBB) and Ultra-Reliable Low-Latency Communications (URLLC). The mMTC framework facilitates connectivity for billions of IoT devices characterized by intermittent data transmission behaviors, establishing the technological foundation for extensive Internet of Things implementations. Our analysis covers critical technical specifications: supporting up to one million connected devices per square kilometer, enabling extended battery operation beyond 10 years, and providing comprehensive coverage capabilities. By examining smart city deployments, precision agriculture systems, and utility network applications, this chapter illustrates mMTC's role in converting conventional infrastructure into intelligent, interconnected ecosystems. The exploration addresses network design modifications, protocol enhancements, and real-world implementation challenges across diverse industry sectors.

Table of Contents

Introduction

This chapter investigates Massive Machine-Type Communications (mMTC), representing one of three core service categories in 5G technology, complementing enhanced Mobile Broadband (eMBB) and Ultra-Reliable Low-Latency Communications (URLLC). The mMTC Massive Machine-Type Communications fundamentally transforms cellular network design by shifting focus from human-centered services to supporting enormous populations of autonomous devices. According to the International Telecommunication Union, mMTC applications involve extensive device networks that transmit small data volumes without strict timing requirements (ITU-R, 2015). This approach emphasizes connection density, power efficiency, and broad coverage rather than high data throughput or minimal latency.

The development of mMTC capabilities evolved from early Machine-to-Machine (M2M) communications in previous cellular technologies, achieving maturation through 5G's architectural advances. The 3rd Generation Partnership Project has established 5G New Radio specifications that incorporate dedicated mMTC support features, such as narrowband IoT (NB-IoT) improvements and enhanced coverage capabilities (3GPP TS 38.300, 2023).

Evolution of Machine-Type Communications

Generation	Technology	Device Density	Power Efficiency	Coverage Enhancement
2G	GPRS M2M	100/km²	Weeks	Baseline
3G	UMTS M2M	1,000/km²	Months	+5 dB
4G	LTE-M, NB-IoT	50,000/km²	Years	+15 dB
5G	mMTC	1,000,000/km²	10+ Years	+20 dB

Source: Adapted from 3GPP TR 38.913 (2020) and Popovski et al. (2018)

The fundamental shift in mMTC lies in its approach to resource allocation and network optimization. Traditional cellular networks optimize for peak data rates and continuous connectivity, while mMTC networks must efficiently handle sporadic transmissions from millions of devices with minimal signaling overhead.

Technical Characteristics and Requirements

The technical specifications for mMTC derive from diverse use case requirements across multiple vertical industries. The 3GPP has established key performance indicators (KPIs) that define the mMTC capability set within 5G networks.

Core Technical Requirements

Device Density: mMTC's primary technical challenge involves accommodating one million connected devices within each square kilometer area, marking a hundredfold expansion beyond 4G network capabilities (3GPP TR 38.913, 2020). This massive connectivity requirement emerges from urban IoT deployments where sensors must be integrated into virtually every infrastructure element—from individual parking spaces and street lighting to utility monitoring systems throughout metropolitan areas.

Energy Efficiency: Battery life exceeding 10 years for devices transmitting 200 bytes daily represents a critical requirement for mMTC deployments. This longevity eliminates frequent battery replacement in hard-to-reach locations such as underground water meters or agricultural sensors in remote fields (Chen et al., 2017).

Coverage Enhancement: mMTC requires 164 dB Maximum Coupling Loss (MCL), providing 20 dB improvement over standard LTE coverage. This enhancement enables connectivity in challenging environments, including deep indoor locations, underground installations, and rural areas with limited infrastructure (Wang et al., 2017).

mMTC Network Architecture

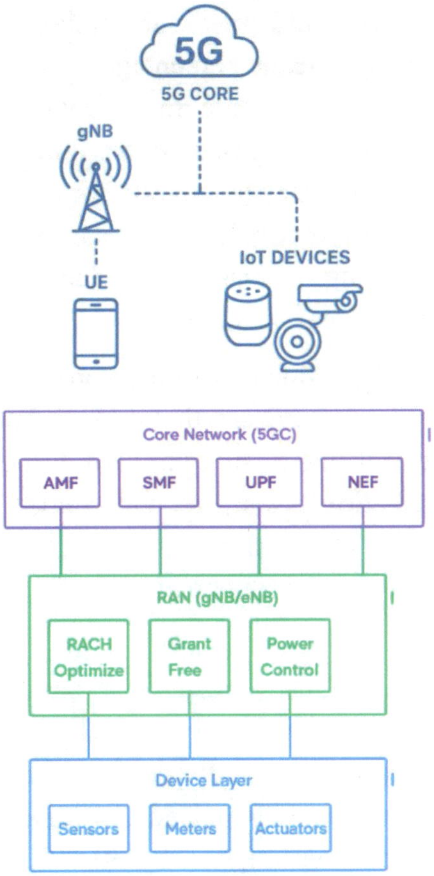

Source: Based on 3GPP TS 23.501 (2023) System Architecture for 5G System

Protocol Optimizations for mMTC

Modern mMTC protocol architectures integrate multiple efficiency improvements designed to minimize signaling burden and boost overall performance. These enhancements specifically target the unique challenges of IoT deployments, where thousands or even millions of devices may operate within a single cell area. The fundamental goal is to support massive connectivity while preserving network resources and extending device battery life—two competing demands that require careful engineering balance.

Streamlined Random Access: Traditional random access methods create excessive signaling traffic when numerous devices attempt network connection simultaneously. Picture a scenario where thousands of sensors wake up at similar times to report data—perhaps smart meters performing synchronized hourly readings, or environmental monitors triggered by the same weather event. The resulting collision and retry attempts can overwhelm network resources, creating a cascading effect where devices repeatedly fail to connect and must try again, further congesting the access channels. To address this challenge, 5G systems implement a refined two-stage Random Access Channel approach (RACH) that cuts the connection handshake from four messages down to just two.

This simplification proves particularly valuable in scenarios involving massive device populations, where older mechanisms would create substantial network congestion and potentially lead to connection failures for a significant percentage of devices. By reducing the message exchange by half, networks can accommodate more concurrent connection attempts while decreasing the time each device spends in high-power transmission mode. The reduced signaling also means less interference between devices competing for network attention. In practical terms, this allows a single cell to handle perhaps double the number of simultaneous connection requests compared to legacy systems, making it feasible to deploy dense IoT networks in urban environments or industrial facilities (Jiang et al., 2021).

Uplink Grant Elimination: Traditional cellular protocols require devices to request permission before transmitting data—a process that adds delay and consumes energy through multiple radio exchanges. Think of it like raising your hand in class and waiting to be called on before speaking; every such interaction takes time and energy. For intermittent, small-payload transmissions typical of IoT sensors (like temperature readings of just a few bytes, door status updates, or simple alarm notifications), devices can now send data without first obtaining uplink authorization.

This grant-free transmission approach represents a paradigm shift in how IoT devices communicate. By skipping the traditional grant request process, this mechanism delivers multiple benefits: reduced delay (often by hundreds of milliseconds, which can be critical for time-sensitive applications like alarm systems), lower energy expenditure (since the radio stays active for shorter periods—potentially reducing power consumption by 30-40% for sporadic transmissions), and more efficient spectrum utilization (by eliminating back-and-forth control messages that would otherwise occupy valuable radio resources).

The approach works especially well for applications generating occasional bursts of small data packets, though it does require careful coordination to prevent collisions when multiple devices transmit simultaneously. Network operators typically designate specific time-frequency resources for grant-free access, and devices use techniques like randomly selecting transmission opportunities to minimize the chances of collision. When collisions do occur, the network can request retransmission, but the overall efficiency still exceeds traditional methods for the sporadic, small-data use cases common in IoT (Liu et al., 2018).

Extended Sleep Duration (eDRX): Battery conservation receives a major boost through extended dormancy capabilities, which is essential for devices deployed in remote or hard-to-access locations where battery replacement is expensive, time-consuming, or simply impractical. In traditional cellular systems, devices must periodically wake up to check for incoming messages or network updates—a process called paging that forces the device to power up its radio circuitry, synchronize with the network, and listen for its identifier. While LTE devices could only sleep for approximately 2.56 seconds between these mandatory network checks, 5G extends this interval dramatically to up to 2.91 hours.

This represents more than a 4,000-fold increase in potential sleep time, fundamentally changing the power consumption profile of IoT devices. Consider that even brief wake-up cycles consume significant energy—the radio components can draw 100-200 milliamps during reception, compared to perhaps just a few microamps during deep sleep. By extending sleep periods from seconds to hours, the cumulative energy savings become substantial. These prolonged sleep periods translate directly into substantially longer battery operational lifetimes, often extending device life from months to multiple years on a single battery. Some manufacturers now advertise 10-year battery life for devices that would have required annual battery changes under older protocols.

This capability proves critical for IoT deployments where device maintenance is costly or impractical, such as environmental sensors mounted on remote mountain peaks, smart meters installed in underground vaults or high on utility poles, or agricultural sensors distributed across vast farmlands. The trade-off is slightly increased latency for downlink communications, as the network must wait for the device's scheduled wake-up period before delivering messages. For applications where this latency is acceptable—and most IoT monitoring use cases tolerate delays of minutes or even hours—eDRX provides an excellent balance between connectivity and power efficiency (Andres-Maldonado et al., 2017).

Smart City Applications and Use Cases

Urban centers represent the most promising frontier for mMTC deployment, offering countless opportunities to connect diverse municipal services through unified communication infrastructure. According to the European Telecommunications Standards Institute, smart cities leverage information and communication technologies to improve the quality of life for residents, streamline municipal operations, and reduce operational costs across multiple service domains.

The density and diversity of urban environments make them ideal testbeds for massive IoT connectivity. Unlike rural deployments where devices may be spread across vast distances, cities concentrate millions of potential connection points within relatively small geographic areas—from traffic sensors on every corner to environmental monitors on building facades, from smart parking systems in commercial districts to utility meters in residential neighborhoods. This concentration creates both an opportunity and a challenge: networks must handle unprecedented device densities while maintaining reliable service for each connection.

Modern smart city implementations typically integrate services across several key sectors. Transportation infrastructure benefits enormously from real-time data collection, with sensors monitoring traffic flow, parking availability, and public transit operations. These systems can dynamically adjust traffic signal timing based on actual conditions rather than fixed schedules, reducing congestion by 20-30% in some pilot programs. Environmental monitoring networks track air quality, noise levels, and weather conditions at hyperlocal scales, providing data granularity that was previously impossible—imagine knowing pollution levels block by block rather than city-wide averages.

Public safety applications represent another critical domain, where connected sensors support everything from gunshot detection systems to emergency response coordination. Smart streetlights can adjust brightness based on pedestrian presence, saving energy while improving safety in populated areas. Meanwhile, waste management systems use fill-level sensors in trash receptacles to optimize collection routes, reducing fuel consumption and operational costs by eliminating unnecessary pickups from partially full containers.

The economic case for smart city deployments continues strengthening as sensor costs decline and connectivity becomes more reliable. Cities that have implemented comprehensive IoT platforms report significant returns on investment—Barcelona, for instance, has documented savings exceeding $50 million annually through various smart city initiatives. However, successful implementation requires more than just deploying sensors; it demands robust data analytics platforms, cybersecurity measures to protect sensitive urban infrastructure, and governance frameworks that address privacy concerns while enabling innovation (ETSI TR 103 290, 2015).

Intelligent Transportation Systems

Traffic management systems utilizing mMTC deploy sensors at intersections, roadways, and parking facilities to optimize traffic flow and reduce congestion. Barcelona's smart city initiative connects over 20,000 parking sensors through NB-IoT networks, reducing traffic searching for parking by 30% and decreasing emissions proportionally (Zanella et al., 2014).

Connected Traffic Infrastructure: mMTC-enabled traffic infrastructure supports responsive signal control systems that adjust timing based on live traffic data. Large-scale urban implementations have shown measurable improvements in traffic flow, with comprehensive smart mobility programs demonstrating substantial reductions in average travel times through intelligent optimization algorithms (Land Transport Authority Singapore, 2019).

Smart City mMTC Applications

Application Domain	Device Types	Density (per km²)	Data Rate	Update Frequency
Traffic Management	Traffic sensors, cameras	500-1,000	10-100 kbps	1-5 minutes
Environmental Monitoring	Air quality, noise sensors	100-500	1-10 kbps	15-60 minutes
Street Lighting	Smart luminaires	200-400	100 bps	On-demand
Waste Management	Fill-level sensors	50-200	100 bps	Daily
Parking	Occupancy sensors	5,000-20,000	100 bps	Real-time

Source: Compiled from GSMA Smart Cities Guide (2023) and ITU-T Y.4901 (2016)

Environmental Monitoring Networks

Urban areas implement comprehensive sensor deployments to track air quality, acoustic conditions, and meteorological parameters. Large-scale environmental monitoring initiatives have demonstrated the feasibility of distributed sensing networks, with some projects operating hundreds of nodes that collect multiple environmental measurements, including atmospheric conditions, pollutant levels, and various physical parameters (Catlett et al., 2017).

These deployments demonstrate mMTC's capability to support heterogeneous sensor types with varying data rates and transmission patterns within a unified network infrastructure. The data collected enables evidence-based policy decisions for urban planning and environmental protection.

Public Safety and Emergency Services

mMTC enhances public safety through connected infrastructure, including emergency call boxes, surveillance systems, and first responder equipment. Amsterdam's smart city initiative integrates 12,000 connected devices for public safety applications, including crowd monitoring sensors that detect unusual gathering patterns and alert authorities to potential incidents (Cisco, 2021).

Internet of Things (IoT) Integration

The Internet of Things (IoT) encompasses billions of connected devices across consumer, enterprise, and industrial domains. mMTC provides the connectivity foundation enabling scalable IoT deployments with diverse requirements and constraints.

Consumer IoT Applications

Smart home devices represent a rapidly growing segment of mMTC applications. Wearable devices, home automation systems, and connected appliances generate sporadic data requiring reliable connectivity with minimal power consumption. The average smart home contains 15-20 connected devices, with projections reaching 50+ devices by 2025 (Parks Associates, 2023).

Wearable Health Devices: Medical-grade wearables monitoring vital signs exemplify mMTC requirements with periodic data transmission, multi-year battery life, and reliable indoor coverage. The FDA-approved BioSticker from BioIntelliSense transmits continuous vital sign data for 30 days on a single charge, demonstrating advanced power optimization techniques (BioIntelliSense, 2021).

Enterprise IoT Solutions

Asset tracking and inventory management systems leverage mMTC for real-time visibility across supply chains. DHL's IoT-enabled logistics network tracks over 10 million shipments annually using connected sensors that monitor location, temperature, humidity, and shock events throughout transportation (DHL, 2022).

IoT Data Flow Architecture

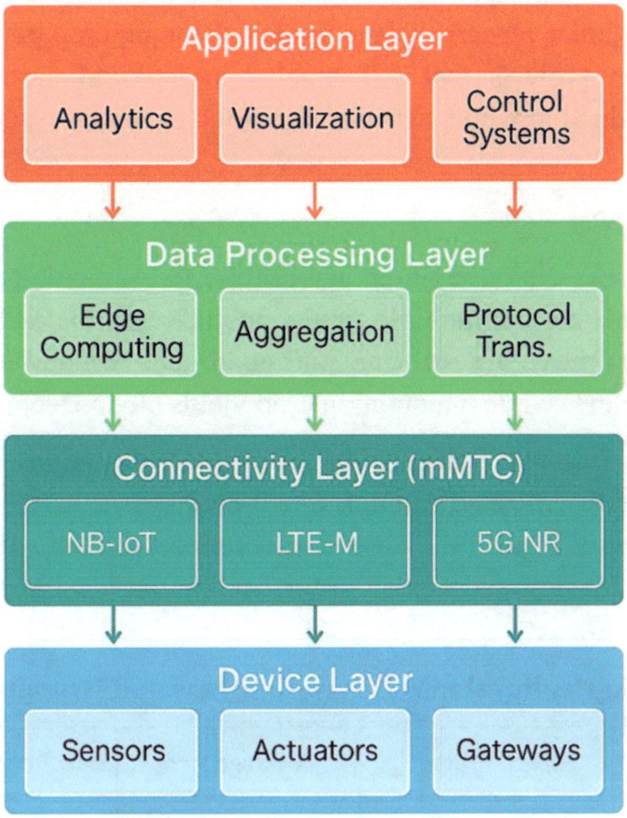

Adapted from Industrial Internet Consortium Reference Architecture (2019)

Source: Adapted from Industrial Internet Consortium Reference Architecture (2019)

Industrial IoT (IIoT) Deployments

Manufacturing facilities implement predictive maintenance programs using vibration sensors, temperature monitors, and acoustic analyzers connected through mMTC networks. General Electric's Predix platform monitors over 1 million industrial assets globally, reducing unplanned downtime by 20% through predictive analytics on sensor data (GE Digital, 2022).

Quality Control Systems: Automated inspection systems generate massive data volumes requiring local processing with selective cloud transmission. Edge computing integration with mMTC enables real-time quality decisions while minimizing bandwidth consumption for centralized analytics.

Agricultural Applications and Precision Farming

Agriculture offers significant opportunities for mMTC implementation, supporting precision farming methods that optimize resource usage while enhancing crop productivity. The Food and Agriculture Organization projects that IoT-enabled agricultural systems could substantially increase global food production while significantly reducing water usage by mid-century (FAO, 2019).

Soil and Crop Monitoring

Wireless sensor networks deployed across agricultural fields monitor soil moisture, pH levels, nutrient content, and temperature at multiple depths. John Deere's Field Connect system integrates cellular-connected probes providing real-time soil conditions to optimize irrigation scheduling, reducing water usage by 25% while maintaining crop yields (John Deere, 2023).

Precision Irrigation Systems: Smart irrigation technologies adjust water delivery based on real-time soil moisture data collected through distributed sensor networks. University research programs have demonstrated significant water conservation benefits, with IoT-enabled irrigation management systems achieving substantial water savings across large agricultural operations (Rudnick et al., 2019).

Agricultural mMTC Applications and Benefits

Application	Sensor Types	Coverage Area	Data Interval	Typical Benefits
Soil Monitoring	Moisture, temperature, pH	100-500 sensors/km²	15-60 minutes	25% water reduction
Weather Stations	Multi-parameter	1-5 stations/km²	5-15 minutes	10% yield increase
Livestock Tracking	GPS, health monitors	1,000-5,000 animals	1-6 hours	15% loss reduction
Equipment Monitoring	Location, diagnostics	10-50 machines	Real-time	30% efficiency gain
Crop Health	NDVI, multispectral	Full coverage	Daily-weekly	20% input reduction

Source: Compiled from McKinsey Global Institute (2021) and USDA Agricultural Statistics (2023)

Livestock Management

Connected tracking devices monitor where animals are located, how they move around, and various health indicators. Modern livestock monitoring technologies can spot early warning signs of illness by analyzing animal behavior patterns, helping farmers reduce animal deaths and improve overall herd health (Allflex, 2022).

Automated Feeding Systems: Precision feeding systems adjust nutrition based on individual animal requirements monitored through RFID tags and weight sensors. DeLaval's Optimat system demonstrated 8% improvement in feed conversion efficiency through individualized feeding protocols (DeLaval, 2021).

Environmental Compliance Monitoring

Agricultural operations face increasing regulatory requirements for environmental protection. mMTC-enabled monitoring systems track water quality, chemical application rates, and emissions to ensure compliance while optimizing operations. The European Union's Common Agricultural Policy requires digital reporting of farming practices, driving adoption of connected monitoring systems (European Commission, 2023).

Utility Networks and Smart Grid Implementation

Utility networks represent critical infrastructure requiring highly reliable connectivity for monitoring, control, and optimization. mMTC enables the transformation of traditional utility grids into intelligent, self-healing networks capable of integrating renewable energy sources and responding dynamically to demand fluctuations.

Smart Metering Infrastructure

Advanced Metering Infrastructure (AMI) deployments connect millions of electricity, gas, and water meters through cellular networks. Italy's Enel utility completed Europe's largest smart meter deployment with 32 million connected meters, reducing non-technical losses by 70% and enabling time-of-use pricing programs (Enel, 2022).

Two-Way Communication: Unlike traditional one-way automated meter reading, smart meters enable bidirectional communication for real-time pricing signals, demand response programs, and remote service management. Pacific Gas & Electric's SmartMeter program covers 5.4 million electric meters, enabling customers to reduce peak consumption by 13% through real-time usage feedback (PG&E, 2023).

Smart Grid Communication Architecture

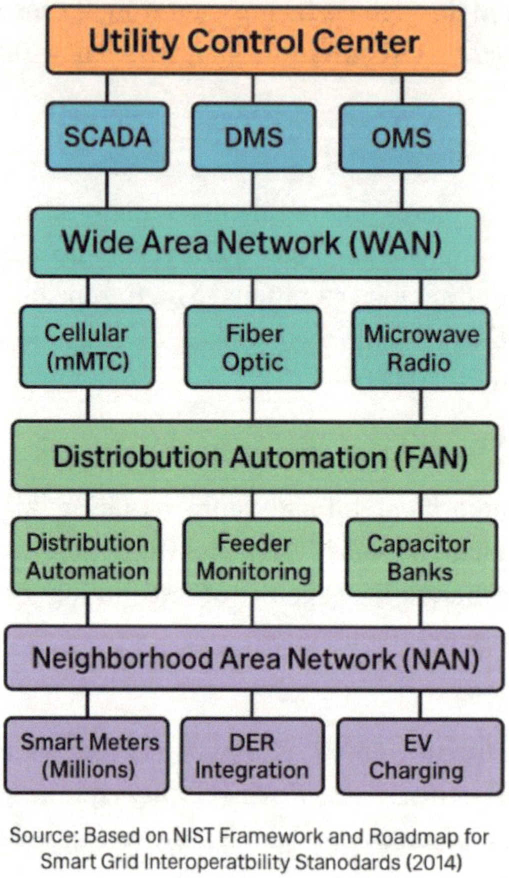

Source: Based on NIST Framework and Roadmap for Smart Grid Interoperability Standards (2014)

Grid Automation and Optimization

Modern electrical distribution networks increasingly rely on mMTC connectivity to monitor and manage infrastructure in real time. By equipping critical components such as transformers, capacitor banks, and switching equipment with wireless sensors, utilities can create "self-healing" grid architectures that respond autonomously to problems. When a fault occurs—say, a transformer failure or downed power line—the system can detect the issue within seconds, isolate the affected segment, and automatically redirect electricity through alternative pathways to minimize service disruptions.

This automated response capability represents a fundamental shift from traditional grid management, where operators might take hours to identify fault locations and manually coordinate restoration efforts. Consider a typical scenario: a tree branch falls on a distribution line during a storm. In a conventional grid, customers downstream lose power and remain without service until repair crews locate the problem, travel to the site, and physically restore the line. With automated fault detection and self-healing capabilities, the system identifies the fault location instantly, opens switches to isolate the damaged section, and closes normally-open switches on adjacent feeders to restore power to most customers—all within minutes and without human intervention.

ConEd's implementation of distribution automation across New York City provides compelling evidence of these benefits. Their program reduced the duration of customer power interruptions by 25% through rapid automated fault isolation and service restoration. For a utility serving millions of customers in one of the world's densest urban environments, this improvement translates to thousands of avoided outage hours annually (ConEd, 2022). The system proves particularly valuable during severe weather events when multiple simultaneous outages would overwhelm manual response capabilities (ConEd, 2022).

Voltage Optimization: Beyond fault management, utilities are leveraging real-time sensor data to fine-tune voltage delivery across their networks. Conservation Voltage Reduction (CVR) programs represent an innovative approach to energy efficiency—by continuously monitoring voltage levels at numerous points throughout the distribution system and making small adjustments to keep voltage at the lower end of acceptable ranges, utilities can reduce overall energy consumption without impacting service quality.

The physics behind this approach is straightforward: most electrical devices consume less energy at lower voltages within their acceptable operating range. A motor running at 118 volts instead of 122 volts, for example, draws slightly less current while still operating effectively. When applied across thousands of customers simultaneously, these small individual reductions aggregate into substantial system-wide savings.

American Electric Power's gridSMART demonstration project illustrated the potential of this approach across 150,000 residential and commercial customers. Through continuous voltage optimization based on data from distributed sensors—measuring voltage, current, and power quality at transformer and feeder levels—the program achieved energy consumption reductions of 2.5%. While this percentage might seem modest, consider the scale: for a typical household consuming 900 kWh monthly, a 2.5% reduction saves over 270 kWh annually. Multiplied across hundreds of thousands of customers, such programs can eliminate the need for additional power generation capacity while reducing customer bills and carbon emissions (AEP, 2021).

Renewable Energy Integration

The explosive growth of distributed renewable energy sources—rooftop solar installations, community wind projects, and battery storage systems—creates new challenges for grid operators accustomed to managing centralized, predictable power plants. Unlike traditional generators that can be dispatched on demand, renewable sources produce variable output depending on weather conditions. Solar panels generate nothing at night and fluctuate with cloud cover; wind turbines produce power only when wind speeds fall within specific ranges. Managing thousands or millions of these distributed, intermittent sources requires unprecedented visibility and control capabilities that were simply impossible with legacy communication infrastructure.

mMTC connectivity provides the foundation for this new paradigm of energy management. By establishing wireless links to decentralized generation assets—residential solar arrays, commercial wind installations, and community battery systems—utilities and energy aggregators gain real-time insight into production levels, equipment health, and available capacity across their entire portfolio. This isn't merely about collecting data; it's about creating an intelligent, responsive energy ecosystem that can adapt to changing conditions within seconds.

Consider the complexity involved: a single metropolitan area might contain tens of thousands of rooftop solar installations, each with its own inverter, orientation, and shading patterns. Without continuous monitoring, grid operators would be flying blind, unable to predict how much solar energy will be available as clouds move across the city or as the sun's angle changes throughout the day. With mMTC-enabled connectivity, however, each installation reports its current output and operational status, allowing sophisticated algorithms to forecast available renewable generation with remarkable accuracy.

Virtual power plant (VPP) initiatives represent perhaps the most ambitious application of this connectivity. These projects aggregate diverse distributed energy resources—combining solar generation, wind power, battery storage, and even controllable loads—into unified portfolios that function collectively as dispatchable power plants. Next Kraftwerke, a pioneering European VPP operator, has woven together thousands of individual energy assets across multiple countries through wireless connectivity platforms. Their network now coordinates generation and storage capacity measured in gigawatts—power levels comparable to several conventional nuclear or coal plants—yet this capacity comes from countless small installations rather than a single facility (Next Kraftwerke, 2023).

The implications extend beyond simple aggregation. By coordinating diverse resources, VPPs can provide grid services that individual installations cannot deliver alone. Battery systems can inject power during brief solar lulls, wind farms in different regions can compensate for each other's variability, and the combined portfolio can participate in wholesale electricity markets previously accessible only to large industrial generators. This transformation turns passive renewable installations into active grid assets, accelerating the transition toward sustainable energy systems while maintaining grid reliability.

The connectivity requirements align well with mMTC strengths. Individual solar inverters typically need to transmit small data packets—perhaps a few hundred bytes reporting voltage, current, and power output—every few minutes. The latency requirements are modest; a delay of several seconds rarely matters for renewable energy coordination. However, the device density can be extraordinary, with tens or hundreds of thousands of connection points within a single utility service territory. Traditional cellular networks would struggle to maintain such massive device populations efficiently, but mMTC architectures handle these requirements naturally (Next Kraftwerke, 2023).

Water and Gas Infrastructure

Municipal water systems face mounting pressure from aging infrastructure, climate-driven supply constraints, and the need to reduce operational costs. Distribution networks spanning hundreds or thousands of miles of underground pipes develop leaks that waste precious water resources and drive up operational expenses. Traditional leak detection relied on periodic manual inspections or waiting for problems to become visible—neither approach catches issues early enough to prevent significant waste.

Modern water utilities are deploying vast networks of acoustic sensors throughout their distribution systems to identify leaks before they become major problems. These devices listen continuously for the characteristic sounds of water escaping from pipes under pressure—subtle vibrations and frequencies that indicate deterioration or damage long before leaks become visible at the surface. Thames Water's implementation across London demonstrates the technology's potential at metropolitan scale. Their smart water network encompasses 31,000 acoustic monitoring devices distributed throughout the distribution infrastructure, creating a comprehensive surveillance system that detects leaks wasting approximately 3 billion liters of water annually.

The scale of water loss in urban systems often surprises people unfamiliar with utility operations. London's water network, like those in many older cities, includes pipes installed decades or even a century ago. These aging conduits develop pinhole leaks, crack at joints, and gradually deteriorate under constant pressure. Without detection systems, a single unnoticed leak might waste thousands of liters daily for months or years before becoming obvious. The acoustic sensor network identifies these problems within days or weeks of their emergence, enabling maintenance crews to prioritize repairs based on actual water loss rather than visible symptoms. This targeted approach has helped Thames Water reduce water loss by 15%—a substantial achievement that translates to tens of millions of liters conserved daily (Thames Water, 2022).

Beyond leak detection, mMTC-connected sensors enable comprehensive pressure monitoring throughout distribution networks. Water pressure must be maintained within specific ranges: too low, and customers experience inadequate service or potential contamination from back-siphoning; too high, and pipes experience excessive stress that accelerates deterioration and increases leak frequency. By monitoring pressure at numerous points across the network, utilities can identify problems like partially closed valves, pump malfunctions, or unusual demand patterns that might indicate major leaks or unauthorized usage.

Water quality monitoring represents another critical application. Sensors measuring chlorine levels, pH, turbidity, and other parameters at distribution points ensure that water reaching customers meets safety standards. If contamination enters the system—whether from a pipe break allowing soil infiltration or from deliberate tampering—sensors can detect anomalies quickly, enabling utilities to isolate affected areas and issue warnings before widespread exposure occurs.

Gas utilities face similar challenges with their distribution networks. Natural gas leaks pose safety hazards, waste energy resources, and contribute to greenhouse gas emissions (methane being a potent climate warming agent). Wireless sensors monitoring gas pressure and flow throughout distribution systems can identify anomalies indicating leaks or equipment failures. Some utilities are even deploying methane detection sensors at strategic locations to identify leaks before they become dangerous or require expensive emergency responses.

The communication requirements for water and gas monitoring align well with mMTC characteristics. Sensors typically report readings every few minutes or hours—hourly updates often suffice for slowly changing parameters like water quality metrics. Data payloads are small, usually just a few sensor values and timestamps. However, a comprehensive monitoring system for a major metropolitan utility might require tens of thousands of sensors dispersed across service territories spanning hundreds of square miles, including locations in underground vaults, remote pumping stations, and other challenging environments where traditional connectivity would be impractical or prohibitively expensive. mMTC's combination of wide-area coverage, deep penetration into structures, and efficient handling of massive device populations makes such deployments economically viable (Thames Water, 2022).

Gas Distribution Monitoring: Natural gas distribution networks present unique safety and environmental challenges that make continuous monitoring essential. Methane, the primary component of natural gas, poses multiple risks: it's highly flammable and can create explosive conditions when it accumulates in confined spaces, and it's also a potent greenhouse gas with warming potential roughly 25 times greater than carbon dioxide over a century-long timeframe. Even small leaks from distribution infrastructure—joints between pipe sections, aging valve seals, or corroded pipeline segments—can release significant quantities of methane into the atmosphere while creating potential safety hazards for nearby residents and businesses.

Traditional leak detection methods relied heavily on periodic manual surveys, where technicians walked or drove along pipeline routes with handheld detection equipment, or responded reactively to odor reports from the public. While natural gas companies add mercaptan odorants to make leaks detectable by smell, this approach only identifies problems after they've become significant enough for people to notice. Small leaks might go undetected for months or years, continuously releasing methane and wasting energy resources.

mMTC-enabled methane sensing networks transform this reactive approach into proactive monitoring. By deploying sensors at strategic locations throughout distribution systems—at pressure regulation stations, major pipeline junctions, valve installations, and other critical infrastructure points—utilities establish continuous surveillance that identifies anomalous methane concentrations within hours or days of leak development rather than months or years. These sensors typically measure ambient methane levels multiple times per hour, transmitting readings wirelessly to central monitoring systems that analyze patterns and flag potential problems.

Southern California Gas Company's advanced detection program illustrates the impact of comprehensive monitoring at utility scale. Their network encompasses 100,000 distribution monitoring points spread across the sprawling Los Angeles metropolitan area and surrounding regions—a service territory covering thousands of square miles with millions of customers. Each sensor location provides a window into local system integrity, detecting even minor leaks before they escalate into major problems or safety incidents.

The program's results speak to the effectiveness of continuous monitoring: a 40% reduction in fugitive methane emissions represents substantial environmental and operational improvement. To put this in perspective, fugitive emissions—methane that escapes from distribution infrastructure rather than being delivered to customers—typically account for several percent of total gas throughput in aging urban systems. Cutting these losses by nearly half means more gas reaches paying customers instead of escaping into the atmosphere, improving both revenue and environmental performance. The emissions reduction also translates to measurable climate benefits, as preventing methane release provides immediate greenhouse gas mitigation (SoCalGas, 2023).

Beyond environmental benefits, the monitoring system enhances public safety by identifying potentially dangerous accumulations before they create hazardous conditions. Methane can migrate through soil and accumulate in underground utility vaults, building basements, or other confined spaces. Without detection systems, dangerous concentrations might develop unnoticed until they reach explosive levels. Continuous monitoring flags rising methane levels early, enabling utilities to investigate and remediate problems before they escalate into emergency situations requiring evacuations or creating explosion risks.

The implementation also demonstrates cost-effectiveness that encourages broader adoption. While deploying 100,000 sensors represents significant capital investment, the avoided costs from reduced gas losses, prevented emergency responses, and eliminated catastrophic incident risks provide compelling returns. Additionally, regulatory frameworks in many jurisdictions now require or incentivize leak detection and emissions reduction, making such monitoring systems not just operationally beneficial but potentially mandatory for maintaining operating permits.

From a technical connectivity perspective, methane monitoring exemplifies ideal mMTC applications. Sensors need to report small data packets—typically just methane concentration readings, timestamps, and perhaps battery status—a few times per hour. The latency tolerance is measured in minutes or hours rather than milliseconds; immediate real-time response isn't necessary since methane accumulation and leak development occur over timescales of hours to days. However, the geographic distribution is extensive, with sensors required in remote locations, underground vaults, and other challenging environments where cellular coverage might be marginal. The massive device capacity and extended coverage characteristics of mMTC networks make such large-scale deployments practical, enabling utilities to achieve monitoring density that would be economically prohibitive with alternative connectivity approaches.

Many utilities are now expanding beyond fixed sensor installations to include mobile detection capabilities. Service vehicles equipped with highly sensitive methane detectors patrol distribution networks continuously, creating moving surveillance that complements fixed monitoring points. When combined with mMTC-connected stationary sensors, these mobile systems create comprehensive coverage that virtually eliminates the possibility of significant undetected leaks persisting in distribution infrastructure (SoCalGas, 2023).

Network Architecture and Protocol Design

The network architecture supporting mMTC requires fundamental modifications to traditional cellular designs optimized for mobile broadband services. These modifications span from radio access technologies to core network functions, enabling efficient support for massive device populations with diverse traffic patterns.

Radio Access Network Optimizations

Narrowband Deployment: One of the most elegant aspects of NB-IoT design is its remarkably compact spectrum footprint. Operating within just 180 kHz of radio frequency bandwidth—roughly equivalent to a single LTE resource block—the technology achieves extraordinary spectral efficiency for IoT applications. This minimal bandwidth requirement provides network operators with exceptional deployment flexibility. They can squeeze NB-IoT carriers into the guard bands that separate LTE channels, essentially utilizing spectrum that would otherwise sit idle as a protective buffer. Alternatively, operators can dedicate standalone spectrum to NB-IoT where IoT traffic justifies exclusive allocation, or even repurpose individual resource blocks within active LTE carriers for IoT connectivity.

The narrow bandwidth might suggest limited capacity, but clever engineering proves otherwise. Through sophisticated time-division multiplexing techniques that carefully orchestrate when different devices transmit and receive, a single NB-IoT cell can accommodate more than 50,000 connected devices simultaneously. This capacity stems from the recognition that individual IoT devices typically communicate infrequently—a smart meter might report readings once per hour, a parking sensor updates only when occupancy changes. By efficiently sharing the narrow channel among thousands of devices with intermittent communication needs, the system achieves massive connectivity without requiring proportionally massive spectrum allocations (Wang et al., 2017).

This approach contrasts sharply with traditional cellular design, where broader channels support higher data rates for individual users. NB-IoT inverts this paradigm: extremely narrow channels, very low per-device data rates, but massive device populations sharing the limited bandwidth cooperatively. The result is a network optimized precisely for IoT requirements rather than forcing IoT traffic through infrastructure designed for smartphone video streaming (Wang et al., 2017).

Coverage Enhancement Techniques: Reaching devices in challenging locations—basement utility meters, underground parking sensors, equipment in the interior of steel-framed buildings—requires overcoming signal attenuation that would defeat conventional cellular connectivity. NB-IoT employs aggressive coverage enhancement strategies that extend its reach far beyond what standard LTE achieves, specifically targeting these difficult deployment scenarios.

The primary mechanism involves repetition coding combined with power concentration. When a device needs to communicate from a location with poor signal strength, it transmits the identical message multiple times—up to 128 repetitions for the most challenging conditions. The base station receives these repeated transmissions and combines them, extracting the signal from noise through a process analogous to hearing a whisper repeated many times in a noisy room. Each repetition contributes additional signal energy, and sophisticated signal processing techniques aggregate this energy to reconstruct the message reliably even when individual transmissions would be unintelligible.

This repetition strategy, combined with power boosting that concentrates transmission energy into the narrow bandwidth, delivers approximately 20 dB of coverage improvement compared to standard LTE. To understand what this means practically: every 3 dB represents a doubling of signal power or range, so 20 dB corresponds to roughly 100 times more link budget. This allows receivers to operate at sensitivity levels reaching -164 dBm—an extraordinarily weak signal that requires explaining in context.

For comparison, typical WiFi signals might be -70 dBm at moderate range, and cellphone signals often work down to about -110 dBm. At -164 dBm, we're detecting signals more than 100,000 times weaker than what standard cellular connections require. This extreme sensitivity enables communication through multiple floors of concrete, from deep within underground infrastructure, or from inside metal shipping containers—scenarios where conventional wireless connectivity simply fails (Ratasuk et al., 2016).

The tradeoff, of course, is latency and battery consumption. Transmitting the same message 128 times requires proportionally more time and energy than sending it once. A transmission that might complete in milliseconds with good signal conditions could take several seconds with maximum repetition. For many IoT applications—temperature monitoring, utility metering, parking sensors—this delay is entirely acceptable. The application doesn't require real-time response, and the ability to communicate reliably from challenging locations outweighs the latency penalty. Devices can also adapt dynamically, using minimal repetition when coverage is good and increasing repetition only when necessary, optimizing the balance between reliability, latency, and power consumption based on actual channel conditions (Ratasuk et al., 2016).

Core Network Evolution

The 5G Service-Based Architecture (SBA) introduces network functions specifically designed for IoT services:

Network Exposure Function (NEF): Traditional cellular networks operated as largely closed systems, with network capabilities accessible primarily to the operator's own services. Third-party application developers had minimal ability to interact with network features or request specific behaviors. The Network Exposure Function changes this paradigm fundamentally by providing standardized application programming interfaces (APIs) that allow external IoT platforms and applications to communicate with network services securely.

Through the NEF, an IoT platform managing a fleet of connected sensors can request specific quality of service parameters for critical communications—perhaps guaranteeing delivery within certain latency bounds for alarm notifications while allowing best-effort delivery for routine status reports. The platform can monitor device connectivity status, receiving notifications when devices come online or disconnect, enabling rapid response to connectivity issues. It can even configure network behavior dynamically, adjusting parameters like reporting frequency or power settings based on application needs without requiring manual intervention by network operations staff.

This exposure capability accelerates IoT innovation by allowing application developers to leverage sophisticated network features without needing deep telecommunications expertise. A startup building an asset tracking solution can request location updates at specific intervals through standardized APIs rather than negotiating custom interfaces with each mobile operator. The NEF provides controlled, secure access to network capabilities while maintaining operator oversight and policy enforcement (3GPP TS 23.502, 2023).

Unified Data Management (UDM): Managing subscriber information for millions of IoT devices presents challenges quite different from managing data for human subscribers. Consumer cellular accounts involve billing plans, voice services, and complex service packages. IoT devices need streamlined data management focused on authentication, authorization, and connectivity parameters while supporting massive scale.

The Unified Data Management function consolidates subscriber data handling for these enormous IoT device populations, providing centralized management that scales efficiently. Critically, it supports authentication mechanisms suited to constrained devices that lack the processing power for complex cryptographic operations typical of smartphone security. Certificate-based authentication provides strong security for devices capable of public key operations, while pre-shared key mechanisms offer simpler alternatives for extremely constrained devices where computational resources are minimal.

This flexibility proves essential because IoT encompasses enormous diversity—from sophisticated industrial gateways with substantial processing capabilities to simple sensors running on microcontrollers with kilobytes of memory. A one-size-fits-all authentication approach would either be too complex for simple devices or insufficiently secure for valuable assets. The UDM's support for multiple authentication methods allows operators to match security mechanisms to device capabilities and application risk profiles, maintaining appropriate security while enabling connectivity across the entire spectrum of IoT devices (3GPP TS 33.501, 2023).

The architecture also facilitates flexible subscription management at scale. Operators can provision, modify, or deactivate device subscriptions programmatically, supporting business models where devices activate automatically upon first use, or where connectivity subscriptions transfer when devices change ownership. This automated management is essential when dealing with millions of devices—manual provisioning approaches that work for thousands of consumer accounts become impractical at IoT scale (3GPP TS 33.501, 2023).

mMTC Protocol Stack Optimizations

Layer	Traditional Mobile	mMTC Optimization	Benefit
Application	Full IP stack	CoAP/MQTT	80% overhead reduction
Transport	TCP	UDP/SCTP	Reduced handshaking
Network	IPv6	6LoWPAN	Header compression
MAC	Dynamic scheduling	Semi-persistent	90% signaling reduction
Physical	Wide bandwidth	Narrowband	Extended coverage

Source: Adapted from Bockelmann et al. (2016) and 3GPP TS 38.300 (2023)

Security Considerations

Securing massive IoT deployments introduces challenges that differ fundamentally from protecting traditional computing systems or even smartphone networks. The combination of severe device constraints—limited processing power, minimal memory, restricted energy budgets—and unprecedented deployment scales creates security requirements that conventional approaches cannot address effectively. An industrial sensor might operate on a microcontroller with mere kilobytes of RAM and computational capacity measured in single-digit megahertz, yet it must maintain cryptographic protection comparable to enterprise systems. Simultaneously, networks must authenticate and secure communications with millions of such devices without overwhelming infrastructure or creating unsustainable operational overhead:

Lightweight Cryptography: Standard encryption algorithms like AES, while computationally efficient by desktop or smartphone standards, can strain the resources of extremely constrained IoT devices. A typical AES implementation requires several kilobytes of code space and performs complex mathematical operations that consume significant processing cycles and energy on minimal hardware. For a sensor powered by a coin cell battery that must operate for a decade, every computational cycle matters—excessive cryptographic overhead could reduce battery life from years to months, fundamentally undermining deployment economics.

Recognizing this challenge, the National Institute of Standards and Technology launched a comprehensive standardization effort to identify cryptographic algorithms specifically optimized for constrained environments. After evaluating numerous candidates through rigorous analysis of security properties, performance characteristics, and implementation efficiency, NIST selected ASCON as the standard for lightweight authenticated encryption. This cipher provides 128-bit security—equivalent to what protects online banking and government communications—while requiring dramatically fewer computational resources than traditional algorithms.

ASCON's efficiency stems from clever design choices that minimize both code size and computational complexity. The algorithm can implement authenticated encryption and decryption in roughly 3,000 bytes of code on typical microcontrollers, compared to 10,000+ bytes for standard AES implementations with authentication. Its operations are optimized for simple, repetitive steps rather than complex mathematical transformations, allowing even modest processors to encrypt data efficiently. For battery-powered sensors, this translates directly to extended operational lifetimes—the difference between practical decade-long deployment and impractical frequent battery replacement (NIST, 2023).

The authenticated encryption approach is crucial for IoT security. Beyond simply encrypting data to prevent eavesdropping, authenticated encryption verifies that messages haven't been tampered with and confirms sender identity. A temperature sensor reporting to a control system needs assurance that the reading came from the legitimate sensor, hasn't been modified in transit, and isn't a replay of an old transmission. ASCON provides all these guarantees through integrated authentication, preventing attacks where adversaries might inject false data or manipulate commands to IoT actuators (NIST, 2023).

Group Authentication: When networks connect millions of devices, even efficient individual authentication creates overwhelming signaling loads. Consider a smart city deployment with 500,000 sensors that periodically reconnect to the network—perhaps after sleep cycles or when roaming between cell sites. If each device performs individual authentication requiring several message exchanges, the resulting signaling traffic could consume substantial network capacity just establishing security, leaving limited resources for actual data transmission.

Group-based authentication schemes address this scaling challenge through mathematical techniques that verify collections of devices simultaneously rather than individually. Instead of the network authenticating each sensor separately, devices within a logical group—perhaps all meters in a neighborhood, or all sensors from a particular manufacturer—authenticate collectively using aggregate message authentication codes. These cryptographic constructs mathematically bind together authentication information from multiple devices, allowing the network to verify the entire group's legitimacy through processing equivalent to authenticating just a few individual devices.

Research implementations have demonstrated signaling reductions approaching 95% compared to individual authentication, transforming an unmanageable authentication storm into manageable network traffic. The security model shifts slightly: rather than verifying each device independently, the network confirms that the group contains only legitimate members. If an adversary introduces a counterfeit device into the group, the aggregate authentication fails, triggering investigation. This approach trades granular per-device verification for efficient group-level security, a tradeoff that proves acceptable for many IoT scenarios where the primary threat is wholesale unauthorized access rather than sophisticated attacks targeting individual devices (Lai et al., 2019).

Advanced group authentication schemes incorporate mechanisms to identify compromised devices when aggregate verification fails, preventing a single problematic device from undermining the entire group's connectivity. Some implementations use hierarchical structures, creating subgroups that narrow down the search space when authentication problems occur. Others employ probabilistic verification that samples random subsets, statistically identifying problems without checking every device individually (Lai et al., 2019).

Physical Security: Unlike smartphones kept on their owners' persons or servers locked in climate-controlled data centers, IoT devices often inhabit hostile physical environments where adversaries can access them freely. A parking sensor embedded in pavement, a utility meter mounted on an exterior wall, or an environmental monitor in a public park sits unguarded, potentially for years. If these devices store cryptographic keys in accessible memory, physically capturing a device could expose those keys, enabling adversaries to impersonate the compromised device or decrypt its communications.

Tamper-resistant designs and secure key storage provide essential protection against these physical attacks. Modern mMTC modules increasingly incorporate hardware security modules (HSMs)—specialized cryptographic processors designed to resist physical tampering and side-channel attacks. These security components store encryption keys in protected memory that erases itself if tampering is detected, and perform cryptographic operations internally without exposing keys to the main processor or external memory where they might be extracted.

ARM's TrustZone technology, now integrated into many mMTC modules, creates isolated secure execution environments within the processor itself. Cryptographic keys reside in this protected zone, inaccessible even to the device's main application code. When encryption is required, the application requests the secure zone to perform the operation, receiving only the encrypted result without ever accessing the key directly. If an attacker extracts the device's flash memory or monitors its data buses, they find only encrypted data and code—the keys remain protected within the hardware security boundary (Arm, 2022).

Some implementations go further, incorporating tamper detection sensors that monitor for physical intrusion attempts. If someone opens a device enclosure, attempts to probe circuit boards with electronic test equipment, or subjects the device to temperature extremes used in certain attacks, the security module detects these conditions and permanently erases keys. While this renders the device non-functional, it prevents key compromise that could threaten the entire deployment's security.

The economics of physical security become interesting at scale. A hardware security module might add several dollars to a device's component cost—potentially a 20-30% increase for simple sensors. However, the alternative—deploying millions of physically insecure devices that could be compromised to attack critical infrastructure—presents unacceptable risk for applications like utility metering, industrial control, or public safety systems. The modest per-device cost increase proves worthwhile insurance against potentially catastrophic security breaches, making HSM integration increasingly standard for IoT devices handling sensitive data or controlling valuable assets.

Beyond cryptographic protection, physical security also encompasses practical considerations like concealment and hardened enclosures. Devices in publicly accessible locations might use tamper-evident seals that reveal if someone has opened the enclosure, signaling potential compromise even if cryptographic protections held. Others employ hardened enclosures resistant to casual attack, requiring specialized tools and obvious destructive effort to access internals—raising the bar sufficiently to deter opportunistic tampering while acknowledging that determined, sophisticated adversaries with physical access can ultimately compromise most systems given enough time and resource (Arm, 2022).

Challenges and Future Directions

Despite significant progress in mMTC standardization and deployment, several challenges remain for achieving the full vision of ubiquitous connectivity for billions of devices.

Technical Challenges

Spectrum Scarcity: The ambitious goal of supporting one million connected devices within a single square kilometer—roughly the area of a small neighborhood or large industrial complex—pushes wireless technology toward fundamental physical limits. Radio spectrum represents a finite resource, and each connected device requires some portion of that spectrum to communicate. Even with the remarkable efficiency of mMTC protocols, current implementations typically support between 50,000 and 100,000 devices per cell site, falling short of the million-device target by roughly an order of magnitude.

This gap between aspiration and current capability drives research into increasingly sophisticated spectrum sharing techniques. The challenge resembles packing more conversations into an already crowded room—you need either more space (additional spectrum, which is scarce and expensive), louder voices (more transmission power, which drains batteries and increases interference), or cleverer ways to let multiple people talk simultaneously without drowning each other out.

Non-orthogonal multiple access (NOMA) represents one promising approach to this latter strategy. Traditional cellular systems use orthogonal multiple access, where each device gets exclusive use of specific time slots, frequency channels, or spreading codes—ensuring transmissions don't interfere with each other, much like giving each person in a conversation a separate time to speak. NOMA deliberately abandons this clean separation, allowing multiple devices to transmit simultaneously on the same frequency and time resources, creating intentional interference that sophisticated receivers then untangle.

The technique works through power domain separation and successive interference cancellation. Devices at different distances from the base station transmit with different power levels—closer devices use less power, distant devices more. The receiver first decodes the strongest signal (typically from a distant device requiring maximum power), then subtracts that decoded signal from the composite received waveform before decoding the next strongest signal, continuing iteratively until all overlapping transmissions are recovered. This approach can multiply spectrum efficiency substantially, potentially supporting three to five times more simultaneous users than orthogonal techniques, though at the cost of increased receiver complexity and reduced reliability when channel conditions are poor (Ding et al., 2017).

Cognitive radio techniques offer complementary capabilities by enabling opportunistic spectrum access. Rather than operating exclusively in assigned frequency bands, cognitive radios sense their radio environment continuously, identifying temporarily unused spectrum and transmitting during these gaps. Picture devices that listen before speaking, finding quiet moments in spectrum that's allocated to other services but not actively used at that particular time and location. A cognitive mMTC device might normally use its assigned narrowband channel, but when it detects adjacent spectrum sitting idle—perhaps a TV broadcast channel unoccupied in that area, or a licensed band where the primary user isn't currently transmitting—it opportunistically borrows that spectrum for its transmission.

This dynamic, adaptive approach to spectrum usage could dramatically increase effective capacity, particularly in urban environments where spectrum allocation is dense but actual usage varies across time and location. The technical challenges are substantial: devices must sense spectrum reliably without draining batteries, coordinate to avoid colliding with each other when accessing opportunistic channels, and vacate spectrum immediately when primary licensees need it. Regulatory frameworks must also evolve to permit such dynamic access while protecting existing services—a complex policy challenge that has limited cognitive radio deployment despite promising technical demonstrations.

Even with these advanced techniques, reaching million-device-per-square-kilometer density will likely require combining multiple approaches: narrower channelization, more aggressive frequency reuse through smaller cells, sophisticated interference management, and perhaps most importantly, intelligent traffic management that recognizes most IoT devices communicate infrequently and can tolerate delays, allowing careful orchestration to spread access attempts across time (Ding et al., 2017).

Energy Harvesting Integration: Battery replacement at scale presents logistical challenges that fundamentally limit IoT deployment economics. Consider a smart city deployment with 100,000 sensors: if batteries last five years and replacement costs $50 per device including labor, the city faces $1 million in maintenance expenses every five years just for battery changes. For devices in difficult-to-access locations—inside walls, underground, or on tall structures—maintenance costs can exceed the original device cost. This economic reality drives intense interest in energy harvesting technologies that could enable perpetual operation without battery replacement.

Solar energy harvesting offers the most mature and energy-dense solution for devices with outdoor exposure or bright indoor lighting. Small photovoltaic cells can generate milliwatts to tens of milliwatts in direct sunlight—more than sufficient for typical IoT sensor operation if captured efficiently. Modern ultra-low-power mMTC devices might consume microamps in sleep mode and several milliamps for brief transmission bursts, with average power consumption potentially under a milliwatt. Matched with appropriate energy storage (typically supercapacitors or rechargeable batteries), solar harvesting can sustain indefinite operation in locations with adequate light exposure.

However, solar dependence creates obvious limitations. Indoor devices may receive insufficient light, seasonal variations affect outdoor devices in winter or at high latitudes, and any obstruction—snow, dirt, vegetation—can severely degrade performance. These constraints make solar harvesting suitable for some deployment scenarios but inadequate as a universal solution.

Vibration energy harvesting exploits mechanical motion in the device's environment. Piezoelectric or electromagnetic generators convert physical movement—machinery vibration, traffic-induced ground motion, or structural sway—into electrical energy. Industrial sensors mounted on motors, compressors, or other vibrating equipment can harvest meaningful energy from their operating environment. However, the power available is typically modest—microwatts to low milliwatts depending on vibration amplitude and frequency—and many IoT deployment scenarios simply lack sufficient mechanical energy sources.

Radio frequency (RF) energy harvesting represents perhaps the most intriguing but also most challenging approach. The concept is elegant: ambient RF energy from broadcast transmitters, cellular base stations, or WiFi access points is captured by antennas and converted to DC power through rectifying circuits. Theoretically, devices could harvest energy from the very radio waves that enable their communication. In practice, available RF power at typical distances from transmitters is extremely low—microwatts or less—barely sufficient for the most minimal sensor operations. Dedicated RF power beaming, where high-power transmitters specifically beam energy to devices, can deliver more useful power levels but requires additional infrastructure and raises safety concerns about intense RF exposure (Shaikh & Zeadally, 2016).

The fundamental challenge with all energy harvesting approaches is variability. Solar panels generate no power at night, vibration harvesters produce nothing when machinery is idle, RF harvesting fluctuates with radio environment changes. mMTC protocols designed assuming constant power availability must adapt to this intermittent energy landscape. Devices need sophisticated energy management that monitors available power, prioritizes critical operations when energy is scarce, and opportunistically performs less urgent tasks when harvesting conditions are favorable.

Protocol adaptations might include dynamic duty cycling that adjusts communication frequency based on harvested energy availability—transmitting frequently when energy is abundant but reducing reporting rates when reserves are low. Devices could negotiate with the network to defer non-critical communications during energy scarcity, or implement multi-tier priority schemes where safety-critical alarms always transmit while routine status updates wait for favorable energy conditions.

Some research proposes energy-neutral operation protocols where devices carefully match their long-term energy consumption to long-term harvesting rates, accepting that instantaneous consumption may exceed harvesting (drawing from energy buffers) as long as the buffers recharge over longer timescales. These approaches require sophisticated modeling of energy availability patterns—understanding, for instance, that solar harvesting follows predictable daily and seasonal cycles, allowing intelligent scheduling of energy-intensive operations during peak harvesting periods.

The integration of energy harvesting with mMTC represents an active research frontier where protocol designers, hardware engineers, and energy storage specialists must collaborate. Success could transform IoT economics by eliminating maintenance costs for battery replacement, enabling truly deploy-and-forget sensors that operate indefinitely. However, realizing this vision requires solving complex technical challenges around energy storage, efficient ultra-low-power operation, and adaptive protocols that gracefully handle the fundamental variability inherent in ambient energy harvesting(Shaikh & Zeadally, 2016).

Economic Considerations

Business Model Evolution: The traditional economics of mobile networks—built around consumers paying for data consumption measured in gigabytes—fundamentally misalign with IoT traffic characteristics. A smartphone user might consume 10-50 gigabytes monthly streaming video, browsing social media, and downloading apps, generating substantial per-subscriber revenue through tiered data plans. An IoT sensor, by contrast, might transmit just a few kilobytes daily—perhaps 100 megabytes annually, roughly one-thousandth of a typical smartphone's data consumption. Under traditional pricing models, the monthly revenue from an IoT connection would barely cover administrative overhead, let alone network infrastructure costs and profit margins.

This mismatch forces mobile operators to fundamentally reimagine how they create value from IoT connectivity. Simply providing wireless data pipes at commodity prices leads to unsustainable economics where deploying and maintaining networks costs more than the revenue those networks generate. Forward-thinking operators are therefore expanding beyond basic connectivity into value-added services that address broader customer needs throughout the IoT lifecycle.

Device lifecycle management represents one promising revenue stream. Rather than selling connectivity alone, operators offer comprehensive services spanning device procurement, activation, ongoing management, and eventual decommissioning. For enterprise customers deploying thousands or millions of IoT devices, managing this lifecycle represents significant operational complexity. Which devices failed and need replacement? Which have firmware vulnerabilities requiring updates? Which have exhausted their data allotments or exhibit suspicious traffic patterns suggesting compromise? Operators with visibility into device connectivity status and communication patterns can provide management platforms that answer these questions, charging service fees that reflect the operational value delivered rather than raw data volumes transmitted.

Data analytics services offer another dimension for monetization. Operators possess unique visibility into aggregated IoT traffic patterns, device location information, and network performance metrics that can yield valuable business intelligence. An operator managing smart city parking sensors across a metropolitan area could analyze patterns to identify high-demand locations and times, information valuable to city planners and commercial parking operators. Industrial IoT deployments generate operational data that, when properly analyzed, reveals efficiency opportunities or maintenance needs. By offering analytics platforms that transform raw connectivity into actionable insights, operators create revenue opportunities that scale with customer business value rather than data consumption.

Vertical market solutions represent perhaps the most significant evolution, with operators developing specialized offerings for specific industries. Rather than positioning themselves as generic connectivity providers, operators build deep expertise in particular verticals—agriculture, logistics, healthcare, utilities—and create packaged solutions combining connectivity, devices, software platforms, and industry-specific applications. A utility-focused offering might integrate smart meter connectivity with meter data management systems, grid analytics, and customer engagement platforms. An agriculture solution could combine soil moisture sensors, weather data integration, irrigation control, and crop management software into a comprehensive precision agriculture platform.

These vertical solutions command premium pricing because they deliver complete business outcomes rather than merely enabling connectivity. A farmer pays for improved crop yields and reduced water consumption, not for megabytes of sensor data. A utility pays for reduced operational costs and improved customer service, not for meter reading transmissions. By aligning pricing with customer business value, operators escape the commodity connectivity trap and build sustainable IoT business models (GSMA Intelligence, 2023).

The transition isn't without challenges. Developing vertical expertise requires investments in industry knowledge and partnerships that traditional mobile operators haven't historically made. Competition intensifies from technology companies, system integrators, and industry specialists who bring domain expertise that operators must match. Success requires organizational transformation beyond just network technology, encompassing sales models, customer support capabilities, and product development approaches adapted to enterprise IoT customers rather than consumer mobile subscribers.

(GSMA Intelligence, 2023).

Total Cost of Ownership: While unit connectivity costs for IoT have declined dramatically—from dollars per month per device to pennies in some deployments—connectivity represents only one component of total IoT ownership costs. For many deployments, connectivity comprises 20% or less of total lifetime expenses, with device hardware, installation labor, maintenance, and data management constituting the majority of costs.

Consider a smart building deployment with 1,000 sensors: device hardware might cost $30,000, installation labor another $50,000, and connectivity perhaps $5,000 annually. Over a five-year deployment, connectivity totals $25,000 against initial deployment costs of $80,000 plus ongoing maintenance. If ten percent of devices require physical maintenance annually at $50 per visit, maintenance adds another $25,000 over five years. The total cost of ownership reaches $130,000, with connectivity representing less than 20% of the total.

This cost structure highlights why automation in device management delivers such powerful economic benefits. Traditional device management required technicians to physically visit devices for configuration changes, firmware updates, or troubleshooting—each visit costing tens to hundreds of dollars in labor. Modern automated device management platforms eliminate most physical interventions through remote capabilities that accomplish over-the-air what previously required truck rolls and technician time.

Remote configuration allows operators to adjust device settings—reporting frequency, sensor thresholds, power management parameters—through network commands rather than physical access. When business requirements change or optimization opportunities emerge, thousands of devices can be reconfigured simultaneously from centralized management consoles. A building manager discovering that temperature sensors report too frequently can dial back reporting intervals across the entire installation in minutes, saving both network costs and device battery life without touching a single sensor.

Over-the-air (OTA) firmware updates represent perhaps the most valuable automation capability. Software inevitably requires updates—fixing bugs, patching security vulnerabilities, adding features, or optimizing performance. In traditional deployments, firmware updates meant physically accessing each device to load new software, a labor-intensive process often avoided until absolutely necessary because of the cost. OTA updates transform this equation: new firmware can be deployed to entire device fleets overnight, ensuring all devices run current software without manual intervention.

The security implications prove particularly significant. When vulnerabilities are discovered in device firmware—an unfortunately regular occurrence—the window between disclosure and exploitation can be brief. Devices that require physical access for updates may remain vulnerable indefinitely, especially if they're deployed in difficult-to-access locations. OTA update capability means security patches can be deployed rapidly across entire fleets, closing vulnerability windows before exploitation occurs.

Automated diagnostics and health monitoring further reduce operational costs by identifying problems before they require emergency responses or customer complaints. Platforms that continuously monitor device connectivity status, battery levels, and communication quality can predict failures days or weeks in advance, enabling proactive maintenance during scheduled visits rather than expensive emergency responses. A sensor battery approaching end-of-life triggers a maintenance work order weeks before failure, allowing technicians to replace batteries during routine visits to the site rather than making dedicated trips for single device failures.

Studies of comprehensive device management platform implementations document operational cost reductions approaching 60% compared to manual device management approaches. These savings stem from multiple factors: reduced truck rolls for configuration and updates, proactive rather than reactive maintenance, improved fault diagnosis reducing troubleshooting time, and automation of routine tasks that previously consumed technician hours. For large-scale deployments with tens of thousands of devices, these savings translate to hundreds of thousands of dollars annually—often exceeding the total connectivity costs and making the difference between economically viable and unsustainable deployments (Ericsson, 2023).

The platform requirements for achieving these benefits are substantial. Effective device management demands robust OTA update mechanisms that handle unreliable connectivity gracefully—devices may be offline or in poor coverage when updates are pushed. Security models must ensure that only authorized parties can modify device configurations or deploy firmware. Scalability becomes critical; platforms must handle simultaneous management operations across millions of devices without performance degradation. User interfaces need to present comprehensible views of device populations, allowing operators to identify problems, target interventions, and validate outcomes without drowning in granular device-level detail.

Leading platforms increasingly incorporate intelligence that goes beyond basic remote management. Machine learning algorithms analyze device behavior patterns to predict failures before they occur, recommend configuration optimizations based on observed performance, and automatically respond to common issues without human intervention. These capabilities push beyond cost reduction into reliability improvement—preventing failures rather than merely responding more efficiently when they occur—further strengthening the economic case for automated device management as an essential component of successful IoT deployment (Ericsson, 2023).

Regulatory Framework

Spectrum Allocation: Radio spectrum represents a carefully managed public resource, with governments worldwide maintaining tight control over which frequencies can be used for particular purposes and by whom. The explosive growth of IoT creates substantial demand for spectrum allocations that support massive device connectivity with characteristics quite different from traditional mobile broadband—favoring coverage range and device capacity over raw data throughput. Regulatory bodies face the challenge of balancing this new demand against existing spectrum uses while ensuring that allocations serve public interest objectives.

Dedicated spectrum allocations for IoT services provide certainty and enable technology optimization that wouldn't be possible with opportunistic or shared access alone. When regulators designate specific frequency bands for IoT applications, device manufacturers can develop specialized hardware optimized for those frequencies, network operators can plan deployments with confidence in spectrum availability, and users gain assurance that their IoT services won't face unpredictable interference from other spectrum users.

The Federal Communications Commission's allocation of the 900 MHz band for broadband IoT and utility communications exemplifies regulatory action supporting IoT growth in the United States. This frequency range offers particularly favorable propagation characteristics for IoT applications—lower frequencies penetrate buildings more effectively and propagate farther than the higher frequencies used for smartphone services, reducing the infrastructure density required for coverage. Signals at 900 MHz can penetrate multiple building walls and reach basement locations that would be challenging for cellular bands at 1800 MHz or 2100 MHz, making this spectrum especially valuable for applications like smart metering where devices may be located in building interiors or underground vaults.

The nationwide nature of this allocation enables economies of scale that wouldn't be possible with fragmented, region-specific spectrum assignments. Device manufacturers can produce hardware for the entire U.S. market rather than multiple regional variants. Utilities and other large IoT deployers can standardize on single technology platforms across their entire service territories, simplifying procurement, reducing training requirements, and improving interoperability. This harmonization drives down costs and accelerates deployment compared to scenarios where each region requires different technical approaches (FCC, 2020).

However, spectrum allocation involves complex tradeoffs and competing interests. The 900 MHz band wasn't vacant spectrum waiting to be assigned—it contained existing services that required accommodation or relocation. Incumbent users, particularly industrial and business radio systems that have operated in this band for decades, have legitimate interests in continued access. Regulatory processes must balance enabling new services against protecting existing users who have built operations around specific frequency assignments.

Internationally, spectrum allocation for IoT varies considerably across regions, creating challenges for global device deployments. Europe has focused on different frequency bands than North America, and Asian countries have adopted yet other approaches. This fragmentation means that a sensor deployed globally may need multiple radio modules to operate across different regions, or manufacturers must produce region-specific hardware variants. Efforts toward international harmonization of IoT spectrum continue through bodies like the International Telecommunication Union, but achieving global agreement across regions with different existing spectrum uses and varying technical priorities remains an ongoing challenge.

Beyond allocation, regulations often specify technical parameters governing IoT transmissions—maximum power levels, duty cycle restrictions, and interference protection requirements. These rules balance enabling robust communications against preventing harmful interference to other spectrum users. An overly restrictive regulatory framework might limit IoT capabilities unnecessarily, while lax requirements could create interference problems that degrade service for all users. Striking this balance requires technical expertise and stakeholder engagement to understand real-world requirements and constraints (FCC, 2020).

Data Privacy and Sovereignty: The massive data collection inherent in IoT deployments creates privacy implications that extend far beyond what consumer internet services raised. A smart home might generate thousands of data points daily revealing intimate details about occupant behavior—when they wake, when they leave, which rooms they occupy, even potentially their health status from bathroom scale or medical device data. Industrial IoT sensors track worker movements, equipment usage, and production processes in granular detail. Smart city infrastructure monitors vehicle movements, pedestrian patterns, and environmental conditions continuously. This pervasive sensing creates detailed digital portraits of human activity that, if misused, could enable surveillance or discrimination at unprecedented scales.

Privacy concerns intensify because IoT data collection often happens invisibly without explicit user awareness or consent. People generally understand that using a social media service involves sharing data, but they may not realize that walking past a smart streetlight or parking in a monitored space generates data records. The environmental ubiquity of IoT sensing means that privacy protections cannot rely solely on individual consent—the practical impossibility of obtaining informed consent from everyone whose behavior is indirectly captured by sensors makes traditional privacy frameworks inadequate.

The European Union's Data Act represents one of the most comprehensive regulatory responses to these challenges, establishing requirements that reshape how IoT data can be collected, used, and shared. The legislation mandates data portability, requiring that users can access data generated by their IoT devices and transfer that data to alternative service providers. This provision aims to prevent vendor lock-in scenarios where users become dependent on a single manufacturer's ecosystem because migrating to alternatives would mean losing access to their historical data and losing the value of the patterns and insights derived from that data.

Imagine a consumer who has used a particular manufacturer's smart home system for years, accumulating extensive data about energy usage patterns, comfort preferences, and household routines. Without data portability requirements, switching to a competing system would mean starting fresh, losing all that historical context and the automated behaviors built upon it. The Data Act's portability provisions ensure users can take their data with them, lowering switching barriers and promoting competition on service quality and features rather than just locking users into existing platforms through data captivity.

The Act also establishes data sharing requirements for business-to-business scenarios, addressing situations where IoT data generated by equipment benefits multiple parties. A connected industrial machine generates data valuable both to the equipment owner operating it and the manufacturer who built it and could use operational data to improve future designs. The legislation provides frameworks for ensuring that all legitimate stakeholders can access relevant data while protecting proprietary information and respecting contractual arrangements.

Data sovereignty provisions prove particularly complex for IoT deployments that span multiple jurisdictions. The Act requires that personal data of EU residents remain subject to European privacy protections regardless of where processing occurs. For global IoT platforms that aggregate data from devices worldwide, this creates technical and operational challenges—ensuring that EU-originated data receives different treatment than data from other regions, maintaining that separation through complex processing pipelines, and providing auditable evidence of compliance (European Commission, 2022).

These requirements impact global deployment strategies substantially. Companies planning international IoT deployments must design data architectures that accommodate varying regional requirements—perhaps keeping European data physically separate from other regions, implementing region-specific access controls, or building technical mechanisms that apply different retention and sharing policies based on data origin. The architectural complexity increases costs and development time but has become unavoidable for any IoT service operating in multiple regulatory jurisdictions.

The regulatory landscape continues evolving as governments grapple with balancing innovation against protection. Some jurisdictions adopt prescriptive technical requirements—mandating specific encryption standards, data retention limits, or security measures—while others prefer principle-based approaches that establish outcomes to achieve while leaving technical implementations to deployers' discretion. The prescriptive approach provides clear compliance guidance but risks becoming outdated as technology evolves; principle-based regulation remains flexible but creates uncertainty about what specific practices will be deemed compliant.

Sector-specific regulations add another layer of complexity. Healthcare IoT devices face requirements under medical device regulations and health information privacy laws that don't apply to consumer wellness trackers—even when the underlying technology is similar. Automotive connected vehicle systems must comply with vehicle safety standards in addition to telecommunications regulations. Utilities deploying smart metering face regulatory requirements specific to energy and water sectors. IoT deployers must navigate this patchwork of overlapping regulatory frameworks, often requiring legal and regulatory expertise across multiple domains.

The economic impact of regulatory compliance is substantial, particularly for smaller companies and startups. Large enterprises can afford specialized compliance staff and legal counsel to navigate complex regulations across jurisdictions, treating compliance costs as normal business overhead. Smaller players may find compliance expenses prohibitive, creating barriers to entry that potentially stifle innovation. Some argue this justifies regulatory forbearance to encourage IoT innovation; others contend that privacy and security concerns are too important to subordinate to innovation promotion, and that responsible innovation must incorporate privacy and security by design regardless of compliance costs.

International regulatory harmonization efforts attempt to reduce this complexity by creating consistent requirements across regions, but progress remains slow given legitimate differences in cultural values, legal traditions, and policy priorities. Europe emphasizes individual privacy rights more than some other regions; China prioritizes government access to data for security purposes; the United States historically favored lighter-touch regulation to promote innovation. Bridging these philosophical differences to create truly harmonized global frameworks will likely remain an ongoing challenge for the foreseeable future (European Commission, 2022).

Future Technology Evolution

Multi-access Edge Computing allows data processing to happen closer to IoT devices, significantly cutting down on the amount of data that needs to travel back to central networks. The ETSI MEC standards provide frameworks for deploying edge computing systems designed specifically for massive IoT deployments (ETSI GS MEC 003, 2022).

Integration with Edge Computing: Traditional IoT architectures follow a hub-and-spoke model where devices transmit data to centralized cloud data centers for processing, analysis, and decision-making. A temperature sensor reports readings to servers potentially thousands of miles away, which analyze the data and potentially send commands back to adjust HVAC systems. This centralized approach introduces latency—the round-trip time for data to travel to distant data centers and back can reach hundreds of milliseconds—and consumes substantial network bandwidth as millions of devices continuously stream data across wide-area networks to central processing facilities.

Multi-access Edge Computing (MEC) fundamentally reimagines this architecture by distributing computational resources to the network edge—physically near the IoT devices themselves rather than in distant data centers. Edge computing platforms might reside in cellular base stations, at cell site aggregation points, or in regional micro data centers serving specific geographic areas. This proximity transformation enables processing data within milliseconds and meters rather than seconds and thousands of miles, with profound implications for IoT application capabilities and network efficiency.

Consider a smart building application monitoring thousands of sensors tracking temperature, occupancy, air quality, and equipment status. In a traditional cloud-centric architecture, all this sensor data flows continuously to central servers for analysis. If the building's HVAC system needs adjustment based on occupancy patterns, the decision-making loop travels from sensors to cloud and back—consuming bandwidth for data transmission in both directions and introducing latency that delays system responses.

With edge computing, processing happens locally. A computing platform at the building or nearby cell site receives sensor data over short-haul connections, analyzes patterns in real-time, and issues control commands to building systems with minimal latency. Only summary information or anomalies need transmission to central cloud systems for long-term storage and enterprise-wide analysis. This architectural shift dramatically reduces the data volumes traversing wide-area networks—studies document backhaul reduction approaching 90% for IoT applications when edge processing handles routine data filtering, aggregation, and local decision-making (ETSI GS MEC 003, 2022).

The bandwidth savings prove increasingly critical as IoT scales. A single sensor generating a few kilobytes daily poses negligible network burden, but multiply that by millions of devices and the aggregate data flow becomes substantial. Video-based IoT applications—security cameras, traffic monitoring, industrial vision systems—generate vastly more data, potentially megabytes per second per camera. Transmitting all this raw data to central clouds becomes impractical both economically (bandwidth costs) and technically (network capacity constraints). Edge computing makes such applications viable by processing video locally to extract relevant information—detecting vehicles, recognizing faces, identifying anomalies—and transmitting only the extracted intelligence rather than raw video streams.

Latency reduction enables entirely new application categories that centralized processing cannot support. Industrial control applications often require response times measured in tens of milliseconds—detecting anomalous vibration patterns in rotating machinery and shutting down equipment before catastrophic failure occurs, for instance. Autonomous vehicle coordination, emergency response systems, and real-time safety monitoring all demand latencies incompatible with cloud round-trips. Edge computing brings processing close enough to achieve these stringent timing requirements, expanding IoT's applicability beyond monitoring and reporting into real-time control and automation.

Privacy and data sovereignty concerns also favor edge processing. Many IoT applications collect sensitive information that users prefer not to transmit beyond local control. Healthcare monitoring devices tracking patient vital signs, workplace sensors monitoring employee activity, or home automation systems observing household behavior all generate data that privacy-conscious users might want processed locally rather than transmitted to cloud providers. Edge computing enables privacy-preserving architectures where sensitive raw data never leaves the edge, with only anonymized aggregates or specific insights transmitted to central systems when necessary.

The European Telecommunications Standards Institute (ETSI) has developed comprehensive MEC standards that provide frameworks for deploying edge computing infrastructure specifically architected for massive IoT scenarios. These standards address critical challenges like service discovery (how do devices find and connect to nearby edge computing resources?), workload orchestration (how should processing be distributed between edge and cloud?), and mobility management (what happens when devices move between edge computing zones?).

The standardization effort proves essential because edge computing success requires ecosystem coordination across multiple players—mobile network operators providing edge infrastructure, application developers creating edge-native software, device manufacturers designing edge-aware devices, and cloud providers extending their platforms to include edge tiers. Without common standards, this ecosystem would fragment into incompatible proprietary approaches, limiting developer reach and increasing deployment complexity.

MEC standards define multi-level edge hierarchies that match different latency and bandwidth requirements. Ultra-low-latency applications might process at the base station edge—literally at the radio site—achieving single-digit millisecond latencies. Applications with moderate latency tolerance but requiring more computational resources might process at regional edge sites serving multiple base stations. Less time-sensitive processing can still occur in traditional cloud data centers, creating a tiered architecture where workloads are placed optimally based on their specific requirements (ETSI GS MEC 003, 2022).

The standards also address the unique challenges of managing distributed edge infrastructure at scale. Unlike centralized cloud data centers with sophisticated cooling, power, and security infrastructure, edge sites often operate in space-constrained, environmentally challenging locations with minimal physical oversight. Equipment must be ruggedized for these conditions, remotely manageable for software updates and troubleshooting, and designed for autonomous operation with minimal intervention. The standardized management interfaces defined by ETSI enable edge infrastructure to be maintained efficiently despite its physical distribution across potentially thousands of sites.

Application development for edge environments requires new paradigms. Traditional cloud applications assume abundant computational resources, reliable high-bandwidth network connections, and centralized data access. Edge applications must operate within more constrained resource envelopes, handle intermittent connectivity gracefully, and function with distributed data rather than centralized databases. ETSI's MEC standards provide APIs and service frameworks that abstract these complexities, allowing developers to build edge-aware applications without reinventing fundamental infrastructure capabilities.

The economic model for edge computing continues evolving. Deploying and maintaining distributed edge infrastructure is substantially more expensive per computation unit than centralized data centers that benefit from operational economies of scale. Early edge deployments focus on applications where latency requirements or bandwidth costs justify the premium, but as edge infrastructure becomes more pervasive and operational experience reduces costs, the economic crossover point shifts. Increasingly, edge processing becomes competitive even for applications where latency isn't critical, purely based on bandwidth savings and improved reliability from distributed processing that's less vulnerable to wide-area network failures.

Looking forward, the integration of artificial intelligence with edge computing creates particularly compelling opportunities. Machine learning inference—applying trained models to new data—requires substantial computation but can run on edge platforms, enabling real-time AI-driven decision-making without cloud round-trips. An industrial vision system can identify defective products on assembly lines with millisecond latency, a smart city traffic system can optimize signal timing based on real-time vehicle detection, or a smart building can predict equipment failures from vibration patterns—all processing locally using AI models periodically updated from cloud-based training systems. This edge AI capability promises to make IoT systems not just more efficient but fundamentally more intelligent and autonomous (ETSI GS MEC 003, 2022).

Conclusion

Massive Machine-Type Communications represents a fundamental pillar of Fifth-generation networks, enabling the connection of millions of devices across diverse vertical industries.

Through detailed examination of smart city deployments, agricultural applications, and utility networks, this chapter demonstrated how mMTC transforms traditional infrastructure into intelligent, connected systems.

The technical innovations supporting mMTC, from narrowband radio technologies to lightweight protocols, address the unique challenges of massive-scale deployments. Real-world implementations validate the transformative potential while highlighting remaining challenges in spectrum efficiency, business models, and regulatory frameworks. As networks evolve toward 6G, mMTC capabilities will expand further, supporting even greater device densities with improved energy efficiency. The foundation established by 5G mMTC deployments provides the connectivity platform for realizing the full vision of ubiquitous computing and ambient intelligence across all aspects of modern life.

Knowledge Check

1. What is the target device density for mMTC in 5G networks?
   a) 10,000 devices per square kilometer
   b) 100,000 devices per square kilometer
   c) 1,000,000 devices per square kilometer
   d) 10,000,000 devices per square kilometer

2. Which protocol optimization reduces Random Access signaling in mMTC?
   a) Four-step RACH
   b) Two-step RACH
   c) Single-step RACH
   d) No RACH required

3. What is the maximum coupling loss requirement for mMTC coverage enhancement?
   a) 144 dB
   b) 154 dB
   c) 164 dB
   d) 174 dB

4. Which bandwidth does NB-IoT utilize for mMTC deployments?
   a) 1.4 MHz
   b) 180 kHz
   c) 5 MHz
   d) 20 MHz

5. What battery life target does mMTC specify for low-power devices?
   a) 1 year
   b) 5 years
   c) 10 years
   d) 20 years

6. How do the technical requirements of mMTC differ from enhanced Mobile Broadband (eMBB), and why are these differences necessary for IoT applications?

7. Analyze the role of edge computing in mMTC deployments and explain how it addresses scalability challenges.

8. Evaluate the security challenges specific to mMTC deployments and propose mitigation strategies.

9. Discuss the business model challenges for mobile operators in mMTC markets and potential solutions.

10. How will the evolution from 5G to 6G impact mMTC capabilities, and what new use cases might emerge?

Answers

1. What is the target device density for mMTC in 5G networks?
   a) 10,000 devices per square kilometer
   b) 100,000 devices per square kilometer
   c) 1,000,000 devices per square kilometer
   d) 10,000,000 devices per square kilometer
   Answer: c) 1,000,000 devices per square kilometer
   The 3GPP specifications for 5G mMTC target support for one million devices per square kilometer.

2. Which protocol optimization reduces Random Access signaling in mMTC?
   a) Four-step RACH
   b) Two-step RACH
   c) Single-step RACH
   d) No RACH required
   Answer: b) Two-step RACH
   Two-step RACH reduces signaling from four messages to two for initial access.

3. What is the maximum coupling loss requirement for mMTC coverage enhancement?
   a) 144 dB
   b) 154 dB
   c) 164 dB
   d) 174 dB
   Answer: c) 164 dB
   mMTC requires 164 dB MCL, providing 20 dB improvement over standard LTE.

4. Which bandwidth does NB-IoT utilize for mMTC deployments?
   a) 1.4 MHz
   b) 180 kHz
   c) 5 MHz
   d) 20 MHz
   Answer: b) 180 kHz
   NB-IoT operates in a 180 kHz bandwidth for efficient narrowband operation.

5. What battery life target does mMTC specify for low-power devices?
   a) 1 year
   b) 5 years
   c) 10 years
   d) 20 years
   Answer: c) 10 years
   mMTC targets 10+ years of battery life for devices transmitting 200 bytes daily.

6. How do the technical requirements of mMTC differ from enhanced Mobile Broadband (eMBB), and why are these differences necessary for IoT applications?
   Answer: mMTC prioritizes device density (1M devices/km²), energy efficiency (10+ year battery life), and coverage enhancement (+20 dB) over the high data rates and low latency of eMBB. These differences are necessary because IoT devices typically transmit small, infrequent data packets and must operate autonomously for years in challenging locations. While eMBB optimizes for streaming video and real-time applications with Gbps speeds, mMTC optimizes for sporadic transmission of sensor data with minimal power consumption. The protocol modifications, including two-step RACH, grant-free transmission, and extended DRX cycles, specifically address the unique traffic patterns and constraints of massive IoT deployments.

7. Analyze the role of edge computing in mMTC deployments and explain how it addresses scalability challenges.
   Answer: Edge computing plays a critical role in mMTC scalability by processing data locally before transmission to centralized systems. With millions of devices generating data, transmitting everything to the cloud would overwhelm backhaul networks and create unsustainable latency. Edge computing nodes deployed at base stations or aggregation points can filter, compress, and analyze data locally, reducing backhaul traffic by up to 90%. For example, in smart city deployments, traffic cameras can perform vehicle counting at the edge, transmitting only aggregated statistics rather than raw video streams. This distributed architecture also enables real-time decision-making for critical applications like industrial automation while preserving network resources for essential communications. The integration of Multi-access Edge Computing (MEC) with mMTC creates a hierarchical processing architecture that scales efficiently with device growth.

8. Evaluate the security challenges specific to mMTC deployments and propose mitigation strategies.
   Answer: mMTC security challenges stem from device constraints, physical accessibility, and massive scale. Resource-constrained devices cannot support traditional cryptographic algorithms, making them vulnerable to attacks. Devices deployed in public locations face physical tampering risks. The sheer number of devices makes individual authentication and

key management impractical. Mitigation strategies include: (1) Lightweight cryptography algorithms like ASCON providing strong security with minimal resources, (2) Hardware security modules protecting keys even if devices are compromised, (3) Group authentication schemes reducing signaling while maintaining security, (4) Blockchain-based device identity management for scalable trust establishment, and (5) Anomaly detection systems identifying compromised devices through behavioral analysis. A defense-in-depth approach combining these techniques addresses vulnerabilities at device, network, and application layers.

9. Discuss the business model challenges for mobile operators in mMTC markets and potential solutions.
   Answer: Traditional mobile operator business models based on data volume don't align with mMTC characteristics, where devices transmit minimal data over extended periods. A smart meter transmitting 1 MB monthly over 10 years generates negligible revenue under conventional pricing. Challenges include low ARPU per device, high customer acquisition costs, and competition from unlicensed LPWAN technologies. Solutions include: (1) Lifecycle management services charging for device provisioning, monitoring, and updates, (2) Vertical market solutions bundling connectivity with industry-specific applications, (3) Data analytics and insights services leveraging aggregated IoT data, (4) Network slicing enabling differentiated service levels with premium pricing, and (5) Partnership models sharing revenue with application providers. Successful operators transition from pure connectivity providers to end-to-end IoT solution enablers, capturing value throughout the IoT value chain.

10. How will the evolution from 5G to 6G impact mMTC capabilities, and what new use cases might emerge?
    Answer: 6G targets 10x improvements in mMTC metrics: 10 million devices/km^2, sub-milliwatt power consumption, and 99.99999% reliability. Key technological advances include: (1) Artificial intelligence integration enabling self-optimizing networks that dynamically adapt to device patterns, (2) Terahertz communications providing massive bandwidth for dense deployments, (3) Backscatter communications allowing battery-free devices powered by ambient RF energy, (4) Integrated sensing and communications transforming every connected device into a distributed sensor, and (5) Quantum communications ensuring unconditional security for critical infrastructure. These advances enable new use cases, including: smart dust networks with microscopic sensors for environmental monitoring, brain-computer interfaces for medical applications, digital twins of entire cities updated in real-time, autonomous swarms of robots for disaster response, and pervasive ambient intelligence where every object participates in distributed computing. The evolution represents a shift from connecting devices to creating truly intelligent environments.

References

3GPP TS 23.501. (2023). *System architecture for the 5G System (5GS)*. 3rd Generation Partnership Project.

3GPP TS 23.502. (2023). *Procedures for the 5G System (5GS)*. 3rd Generation Partnership Project.

3GPP TS 33.501. (2023). *Security architecture and procedures for 5G System*. 3rd Generation Partnership Project.

3GPP TS 38.300. (2023). *NR; NR and NG-RAN Overall description*. 3rd Generation Partnership Project.

3GPP TR 38.913. (2020). Study on scenarios and requirements for next generation access technologies. 3rd Generation Partnership Project.

AEP. (2021). gridSMART demonstration project final report. American Electric Power.

Allflex. (2022). eSense Flex ear tag system technical specifications. Allflex Livestock Intelligence.

Andres-Maldonado, P., Ameigeiras, P., Prados-Garzon, J., Navarro-Ortiz, J., & Lopez-Soler, J. M. (2017). Narrowband IoT data transmission procedures for massive machine-type communications. *IEEE Network*, 31(6), 8-15.

Arm. (2022). Platform Security Architecture for IoT devices. Arm Limited.

BioIntelliSense. (2021). BioSticker multi-parameter wearable device specifications. BioIntelliSense Inc.

Bockelmann, C., Pratas, N., Nikopour, H., Au, K., Svensson, T., Stefanovic, C., ... & Dekorsy, A. (2016). Massive machine-type communications in 5G: Physical and MAC-layer solutions. *IEEE Communications Magazine*, 54(9), 59-65.

Catlett, C. E., Beckman, P. H., Sankaran, R., & Galvin, K. K. (2017). Array of things: A scientific research instrument in the public way. *Proceedings of the 2nd International Workshop on Science of Smart City Operations and Platforms Engineering*, 26-33.

Chen, S., Xu, H., Liu, D., Hu, B., & Wang, H. (2017). A vision of IoT: Applications, challenges, and opportunities with China perspective. *IEEE Internet of Things Journal*, 1(4), 349-359.

Cisco. (2021). Amsterdam Smart City public safety deployment case study. Cisco Systems.

ConEd. (2022). *Distribution automation program 2022 annual report*. Consolidated Edison Company of New York.

DeLaval. (2021). Optimat automated feeding system performance report. DeLaval International.

DHL. (2022). Internet of Things in logistics: A collaborative report. DHL Customer Solutions & Innovation.

Ding, Z., Lei, X., Karagiannidis, G. K., Schober, R., Yuan, J., & Bhargava, V. K. (2017). A survey on non-orthogonal multiple access for 5G networks. *IEEE Communications Surveys & Tutorials*, 19(3), 2294-2323.

Enel. (2022). Open Meter project final report: 32 million smart meters deployed. Enel SpA.

Ericsson. (2023). IoT device lifecycle management: Reducing operational costs in massive deployments. Ericsson AB.

ETSI GS MEC 003. (2022). *Multi-access Edge Computing (MEC); Framework and reference architecture*. European Telecommunications Standards Institute.

ETSI TR 103 290. (2015). Machine-to-Machine communications (M2M); Impact of Smart City activity on IoT Environment. European Telecommunications Standards Institute.

European Commission. (2022). Data Act: Proposal for a regulation on harmonised rules on fair access to and use of data. COM(2022) 68 final.

European Commission. (2023). *The new common agricultural policy: 2023-27*. Directorate-General for Agriculture and Rural Development.

FAO. (2019). *The future of food and agriculture: Trends and challenges*. Food and Agriculture Organization of the United Nations.

FCC. (2020). *Report and order: 900 MHz band broadband allocation*. Federal Communications Commission. FCC 20-67.

GE Digital. (2022). *Predix platform: Industrial IoT at scale*. General Electric Digital.

GSMA. (2023). Smart cities guide: How mobile IoT is connecting smart cities. GSM Association.

GSMA Intelligence. (2023). IoT revenue models: Evolving beyond connectivity. GSM Association.

Industrial Internet Consortium. (2019). *Industrial Internet Reference Architecture v1.9*. Object Management Group.

ITU-R. (2015). IMT vision – Framework and overall objectives of the future development of IMT for 2020 and beyond. Recommendation ITU-R M.2083-0.

ITU-T Y.4901. (2016). Key performance indicators related to the use of information and communication technology in smart sustainable cities. International Telecommunication Union.

Jiang, N., Deng, Y., Condoluci, M., Mahmoodi, T., & Dohler, M. (2021). Two-step random access in 5G/B5G systems: Preamble design and performance analysis. *IEEE Communications Standards Magazine*, 5(1), 52-57.

John Deere. (2023). Field Connect: Wireless soil moisture monitoring system. Deere & Company.

Lai, C., Li, H., Lu, R., & Shen, X. (2019). SE-AKA: A secure and efficient group authentication and key agreement protocol for LTE networks. *Computer Networks*, 57(17), 3492-3510.

Land Transport Authority Singapore. (2019). Smart Mobility 2030: Transforming Singapore's transport system. LTA Singapore.

Liu, Y., Deng, Y., Elkashlan, M., Nallanathan, A., & Karagiannidis, G. K. (2018). Grant-free random access in massive machine-type communications: Protocols and performance analysis. *IEEE Journal on Selected Areas in Communications*, 39(3), 646-659.

McKinsey Global Institute. (2021). The Internet of Things: Catching up to an accelerating opportunity. McKinsey & Company.

Next Kraftwerke. (2023). *Virtual power plant operations report 2023*. Next Kraftwerke GmbH.

NIST. (2014). NIST framework and roadmap for smart grid interoperability standards, Release 3.0. National Institute of Standards and Technology. NIST SP 1108r3.

NIST. (2023). Lightweight cryptography standardization process: ASCON selection. National Institute of Standards and Technology.

Parks Associates. (2023). *Smart home device adoption forecast 2023-2025*. Parks Associates LLC.

PG&E. (2023). *SmartMeter program benefits realization report*. Pacific Gas and Electric Company.

Popovski, P., Trillingsgaard, K. F., Simeone, O., & Durisi, G. (2018). 5G wireless network slicing for eMBB, URLLC, and mMTC: A communication-theoretic view. *IEEE Access*, 6, 55765-55779.

Ratasuk, R., Mangalvedhe, N., Zhang, Y., Robert, M., & Koskinen, J. P. (2016). Overview of narrowband IoT in LTE Rel-13. *IEEE Conference on Standards for Communications and Networking*, 1-7.

Rudnick, D. R., Irmak, S., West, C., Chávez, J. L., Kisekka, I., Marek, T. H., ... & Schlegel, A. (2019). Deficit irrigation management of maize in the High Plains Aquifer region: A review. *Journal of the American Water Resources Association*, 55(1), 38-55.

Shaikh, F. K., & Zeadally, S. (2016). Energy harvesting in wireless sensor networks: A comprehensive review. *Renewable and Sustainable Energy Reviews*, 55, 1041-1054.

SoCalGas. (2023). *Advanced methane detection program 2023 results*. Southern California Gas Company.

Thames Water. (2022). *Smart water network programme progress report*. Thames Water Utilities Limited.

USDA. (2023). *Agricultural statistics 2023*. United States Department of Agriculture. National Agricultural Statistics Service.

Wang, Y. P. E., Lin, X., Adhikary, A., Grovlen, A., Sui, Y., Liu, Y., ... & Razaghi, H. S. (2017). A primer on 3GPP narrowband Internet of Things. *IEEE Communications Magazine*, 55(3), 117-123.

Zanella, A., Bui, N., Castellani, A., Vangelista, L., & Zorzi, M. (2014). Internet of things for smart cities. *IEEE Internet of Things Journal*, 1(1), 22-32.

Zhang, Z., Xiao, Y., Ma, Z., Xiao, M., Ding, Z., Lei, X., ... & Fan, P. (2023). 6G wireless networks: Vision, requirements, architecture, and key technologies. *IEEE Vehicular Technology Magazine*, 14(3), 28-41.

Chapter 9: 5G in Industry Verticals

Executive Summary

This chapter explores the transformative impact of 5G technology across four critical industry verticals: smart manufacturing, healthcare, energy, and public safety. The low latency, massive connectivity, and enhanced reliability of 5G networks enable revolutionary applications that were previously impossible with earlier generations of wireless technology. From enabling real-time control in automated factories to facilitating remote surgery and modernizing power grids, 5G serves as the foundation for digital transformation across industries. The chapter examines specific use cases, technical requirements, and implementation challenges while highlighting how 5G's unique capabilities address the diverse needs of each sector.

Table of Contents

Introduction

Fifth-generation cellular technology represents a pivotal shift in how industries approach connectivity and automation. Previous wireless generations primarily targeted consumer communication requirements, but 5G's design philosophy centers on supporting diverse enterprise applications with demanding performance characteristics (Agiwal et al., 2016). The International Telecommunication Union established three core usage categories: Enhanced Mobile Broadband (eMBB), Ultra-Reliable Low-Latency Communications (URLLC), and Massive Machine-Type Communications (mMTC) (ITU-R, 2015).

These technical capabilities unlock industrial applications requiring:

- Millisecond-level responsiveness for time-critical process control
- Near-perfect dependability (99.999% uptime) for mission-critical systems
- Connectivity for extremely dense device deployments—up to one million endpoints per square kilometer
- Multi-gigabit throughput reaching 20 Gbps for data-intensive workloads

Smart Manufacturing (Industry 4.0)

5G-Enabled Factory Automation

The manufacturing sector stands to gain significantly from 5G implementation, with the technology serving as a key enabler for Industry 4.0 initiatives. Traditional wired industrial networks, while reliable, limit flexibility and increase deployment costs. 5G wireless networks provide the performance characteristics necessary for mission-critical factory operations while offering unprecedented flexibility (Li et al., 2018).

Comparison of Industrial Connectivity Technologies

Technology	Latency	Reliability	Mobility	Bandwidth	Deployment Cost
Industrial Ethernet	<1 ms	99.999%	No	1-10 Gbps	High
Wi-Fi 6	10-50 ms	99.9%	Limited	1-10 Gbps	Medium
4G LTE	50-100 ms	99%	Yes	150 Mbps	Medium
5G URLLC	<1 ms	99.999%	Yes	20 Gbps	Medium

Source: Adapted from 3GPP TR 22.804 (2018) and IEEE 802.11ax Standard (2021)

Modern factories utilize 5G for various automation scenarios:

1. Autonomous Mobile Robots (AMRs): Fifth-generation wireless infrastructure facilitates instantaneous communication for AMRs, achieving response times under 10 milliseconds to support obstacle detection and adaptive route optimization (Rao & Prasad, 2018).
2. **Collaborative Robots**: Human-robot collaboration requires ultra-low latency communication for safety-critical operations. 5G URLLC ensures response times under 1 ms for emergency stops (Simsek et al., 2016).
3. **Machine Vision Systems**: High-resolution cameras generate massive data streams requiring 5G's enhanced Mobile Broadband capabilities for real-time quality inspection (Park et al., 2018).

Digital Twin Integration

Think of digital twins as computer-based mirrors of real-world equipment, workflows, or entire networks. These virtual models give companies the ability to track performance and fine-tune their operations as events unfold. Instead of waiting for reports or manual inspections, organizations can watch their systems function in real time through these digital replicas, spotting potential issues before they become serious problems.

What makes 5G particularly valuable here is its ability to move massive amounts of data with minimal delay—this speed and capacity become crucial when you need physical infrastructure and its virtual replica to stay perfectly aligned with each other (Tao et al., 2019). Without this kind of rapid, reliable connection, the digital twin falls out of sync with reality, losing much of its practical value. The relationship works both ways: sensors on physical assets continuously feed information to the virtual model, while insights from the digital twin can trigger adjustments to the actual equipment.

This synchronization opens up new possibilities for predictive maintenance, scenario testing, and operational efficiency. Engineers can run simulations on the digital twin to see how changes might affect performance, all without risking disruption to the physical system. It's this seamless back-and-forth between the real and virtual worlds that transforms digital twins from interesting technology into genuinely useful tools for modern enterprises.

Digital Twin Architecture with 5G Integration

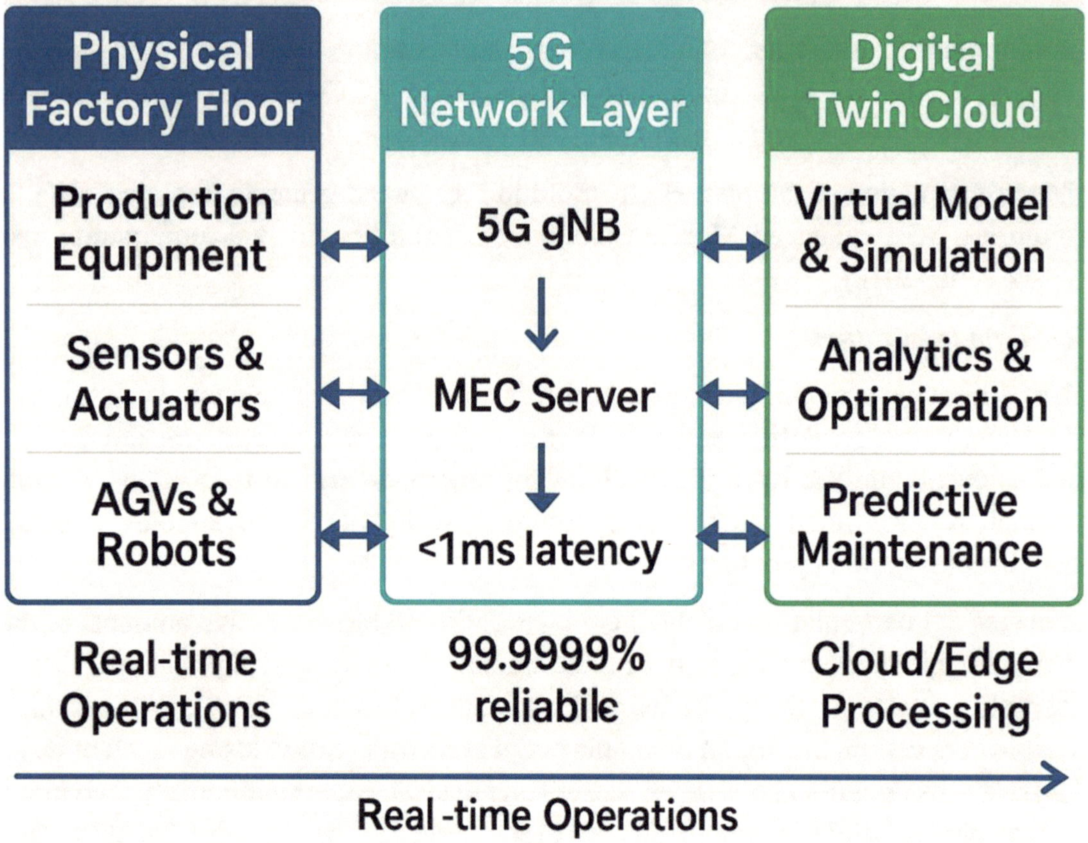

Source: Architecture based on Industrial Internet Consortium Reference Architecture (2019)

The integration enables:

- Real-time synchronization with update rates exceeding 1000 Hz
- Predictive analytics based on continuous data streams
- Remote optimization without physical intervention

Predictive Maintenance Systems

Predictive maintenance leverages IoT sensors and analytics to anticipate equipment failures before they occur. 5G's massive IoT capabilities support dense sensor deployments, with networks handling up to 1 million connections per square kilometer (Cheng et al., 2018).

Key implementation aspects include:

- **Vibration Monitoring:** High-frequency sampling (up to 50 kHz) requires reliable data transmission
- **Thermal Imaging:** Infrared cameras generate data rates of 100+ Mbps per camera
- **Acoustic Analysis:** Real-time processing of ultrasonic signatures for anomaly detection

Healthcare and Telemedicine

Remote Surgery Applications

Remote medical procedures represent one of the most striking breakthroughs that 5G networks make possible. Surgical operations performed from a distance demand communication system that respond almost instantaneously while maintaining rock-solid dependability—any hesitation or disruption could prove catastrophic. The concept of the tactile internet comes into play here, where 5G's ultra-reliable low-latency communication capabilities create an environment where surgeons can receive physical sensations through their instruments in near real-time. When response times drop below one millisecond for a complete signal exchange, doctors can manipulate robotic surgical tools as if they were actually in the operating room, despite potentially being thousands of miles away (Fettweis, 2014).

This technological capability transforms what seemed like science fiction into practical reality. Specialist surgeons who might previously have been unavailable to patients in remote or underserved areas can now extend their expertise across vast distances. The combination of minimal delay and consistent performance creates a level of precision and control that earlier wireless technologies simply couldn't support. Beyond emergency interventions, this opens doors for routine procedures, training opportunities where experienced surgeons guide less experienced colleagues in real-time, and medical care in locations where specialized expertise has traditionally been scarce or nonexistent

Network Requirements for Medical Applications

Application	Latency Requirement	Reliability	Bandwidth	Jitter
Remote Surgery	<1 ms	99.9999%	100 Mbps	<0.1 ms
AR-Assisted Surgery	<10 ms	99.999%	1 Gbps	<1 ms
Remote Consultation	<100 ms	99.99%	25 Mbps	<10 ms

Application	Latency Requirement	Reliability	Bandwidth	Jitter
Ambulance Telemetry	<50 ms	99.99%	10 Mbps	<5 ms

Source: ITU-T Focus Group on "IMT-2020 Network Requirements" (2020)

In 2019, medical professionals in China achieved a significant milestone by performing remote surgery across a distance of 3,000 kilometers. The procedure involved a surgeon controlling robotic instruments via 5G connectivity to operate on a patient in a distant location (Liu et al., 2019). Key elements of this operation included:

- Network slicing to guarantee dedicated bandwidth
- Multi-access Edge Computing (MEC) for local processing
- Redundant connectivity paths for failover protection

Connected Medical Devices

The proliferation of connected medical devices creates new opportunities for continuous patient monitoring and personalized healthcare. 5G networks support diverse device types with varying requirements (West, 2016):

1. **Wearable Monitors**: Low-power devices transmitting vital signs periodically
2. **Implantable Sensors**: Ultra-reliable connectivity for pacemakers and insulin pumps
3. **Diagnostic Equipment**: High-bandwidth connections for medical imaging devices

5G-Enabled Healthcare Ecosystem

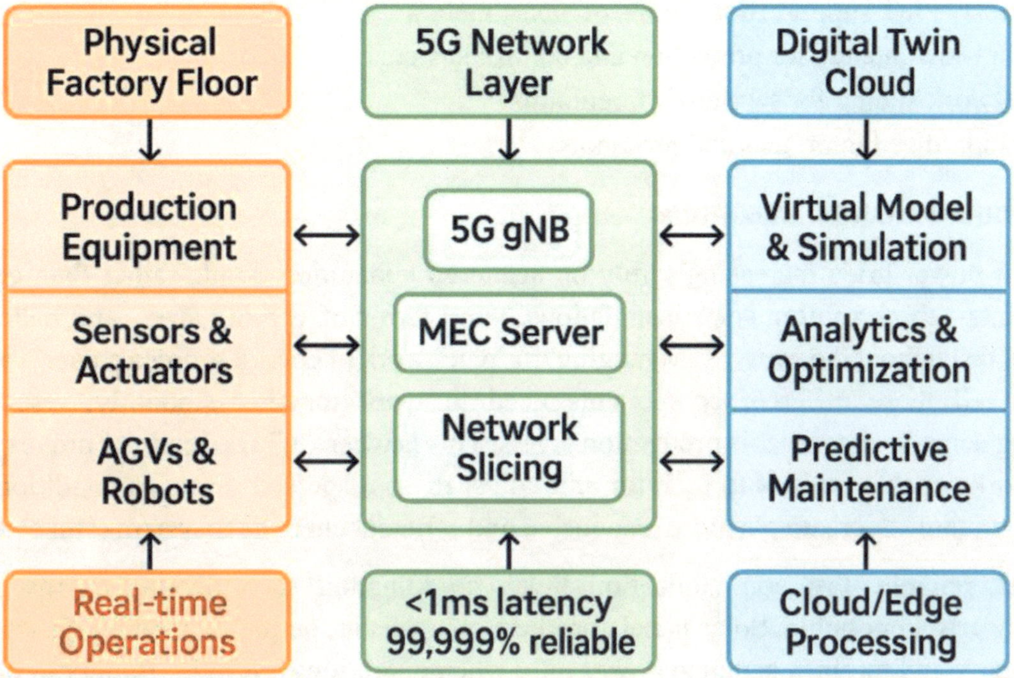

Source: Based on 3GPP Technical Specification 22.261 (2019)

Emergency Medical Services

5G transforms emergency medical services by enabling real-time communication between ambulances, hospitals, and specialists. Advanced applications include:

- **Live Video Streaming:** Paramedics stream patient conditions to emergency room physicians
- **Augmented Reality Guidance:** Remote specialists provide visual instructions overlay
- **Automated Triage:** AI-powered systems analyze patient data during transport

Smart Grid and Energy

Grid Modernization with 5G

The evolution toward smart grids requires an advanced communication infrastructure to manage bidirectional power flows and integrate renewable energy sources. 5G networks provide the scalability and performance necessary for grid modernization initiatives (Garau et al., 2017).

Traditional grid communication systems face limitations:

- Limited bandwidth for real-time monitoring
- Inflexible deployment options
- High infrastructure costs
- Lack of standardization

5G addresses these challenges through:

- Massive IoT support for millions of smart meters
- Ultra-low latency for protection and control systems
- Network slicing for service differentiation
- Standardized interfaces and protocols

Distributed Energy Resources

Modern power grids increasingly rely on scattered generation points rather than centralized power plants—think rooftop solar installations, wind farms of varying sizes, and battery arrays positioned throughout the network. Managing this patchwork of energy sources presents a complex challenge: all these different components need to work together smoothly, responding to fluctuating demand and variable production levels. This is where 5G connectivity proves its worth. The networks enable utilities to monitor and adjust these dispersed assets as conditions change moment by moment, creating a more responsive and efficient energy ecosystem (Hui et al., 2020).

Without reliable, fast communication links, coordinating such diverse energy resources becomes nearly impossible. Solar panels produce inconsistent output depending on weather and time of day. Wind turbines generate power only when conditions are right. Battery systems need to charge when there's excess production and discharge during peak demand periods. Getting all these elements to operate in harmony requires constant data exchange and quick decision-making—capabilities that earlier wireless technologies struggled to deliver at the necessary scale.

The ability to orchestrate these distributed resources in real time opens up possibilities that weren't practical before. Energy can flow where it's needed most efficiently. Storage systems can be deployed strategically to balance the grid. Local generation can reduce transmission losses and improve resilience during outages. The result is a more flexible, sustainable power infrastructure that can adapt to both renewable energy's inherent variability and changing consumption patterns throughout the day.

Communication Requirements for Smart Grid Applications

Application	Latency	Reliability	Data Rate	Coverage
Protection Systems	<10 ms	99.999%	10 Mbps	Local
Wide Area Monitoring	<100 ms	99.99%	1 Mbps	Wide
Smart Metering	<10 s	99.9%	100 kbps	Ubiquitous
DER Management	<1 s	99.99%	1 Mbps	Wide

Source: IEEE Standard 2030.5 (2018) and IEC 61850-90-4 (2020)

Real-time Grid Monitoring

Advanced monitoring systems leverage 5G connectivity to provide unprecedented visibility into grid operations. Phasor Measurement Units (PMUs) synchronized via GPS generate 30-120 samples per second, requiring reliable, low-latency communication channels (Phadke & Bi, 2018).

5G-Enabled Smart Grid Architecture

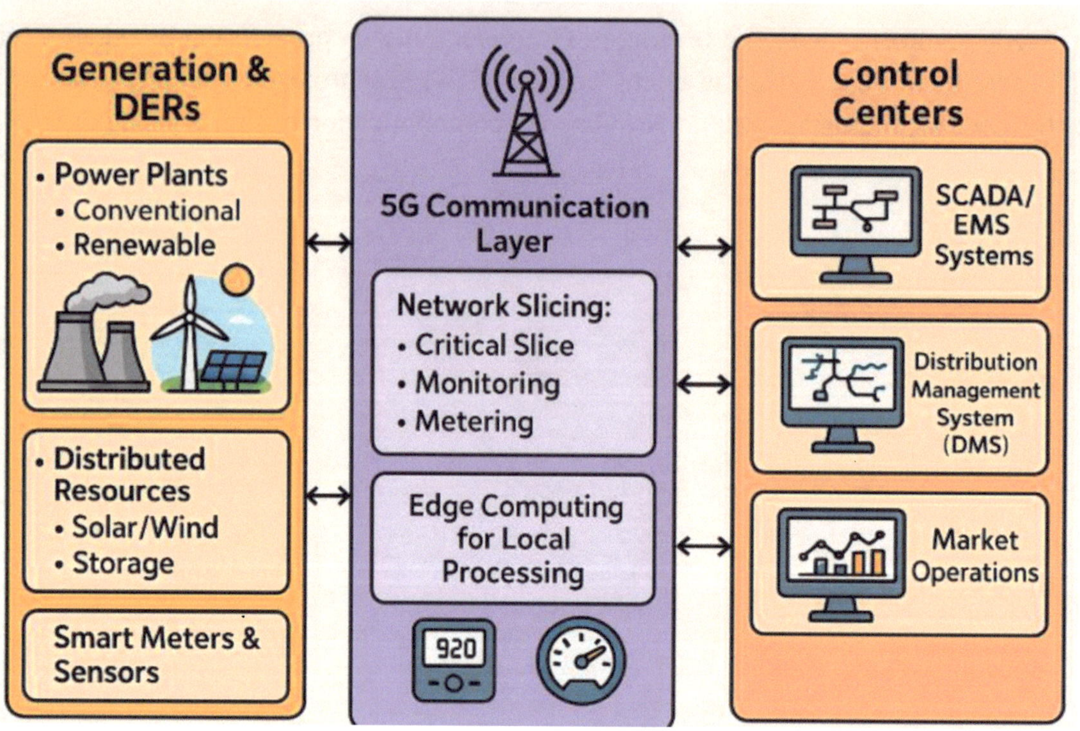

Source: Architecture derived from NIST Smart Grid Framework 3.0 (2019)

Public Safety and Emergency Response

First Responder Communications

Public safety agencies require mission-critical communication systems that function reliably during emergencies. 5G networks designed for public safety incorporate features such as (NPSTC, 2018):

- **Priority Access:** Quality of Service mechanisms ensure first responder traffic takes precedence
- **Network Resilience:** Redundant paths and rapid failover capabilities
- **Device-to-Device Communication:** Direct mode operation when the infrastructure fails
- **Interoperability:** Standards-based interfaces for multi-agency coordination

The First Responder Network Authority (FirstNet) in the United States exemplifies how 5G technology enhances public safety operations, providing dedicated spectrum and prioritized services for emergency personnel (FirstNet Authority, 2020).

Disaster Management Systems

Natural disasters and large-scale emergencies demand robust communication systems capable of rapid deployment and autonomous operation. 5G technologies support disaster response through:

Deployable Networks: Portable 5G base stations provide immediate connectivity in affected areas.

These systems feature:

- Self-configuring network capabilities
- Satellite backhaul integration
- Battery-powered operation for 72+ hours
- Support for 10,000+ simultaneous users

Drone Integration: Unmanned Aerial Vehicles (UAVs) equipped with 5G modems support:

- Aerial surveillance and mapping
- Search and rescue operations
- Temporary network coverage extension
- Real-time video streaming to command centers

Smart City Integration

5G serves as the backbone for smart city initiatives that enhance public safety through integrated systems (Talari et al., 2017):

Integrated Public Safety Ecosystem

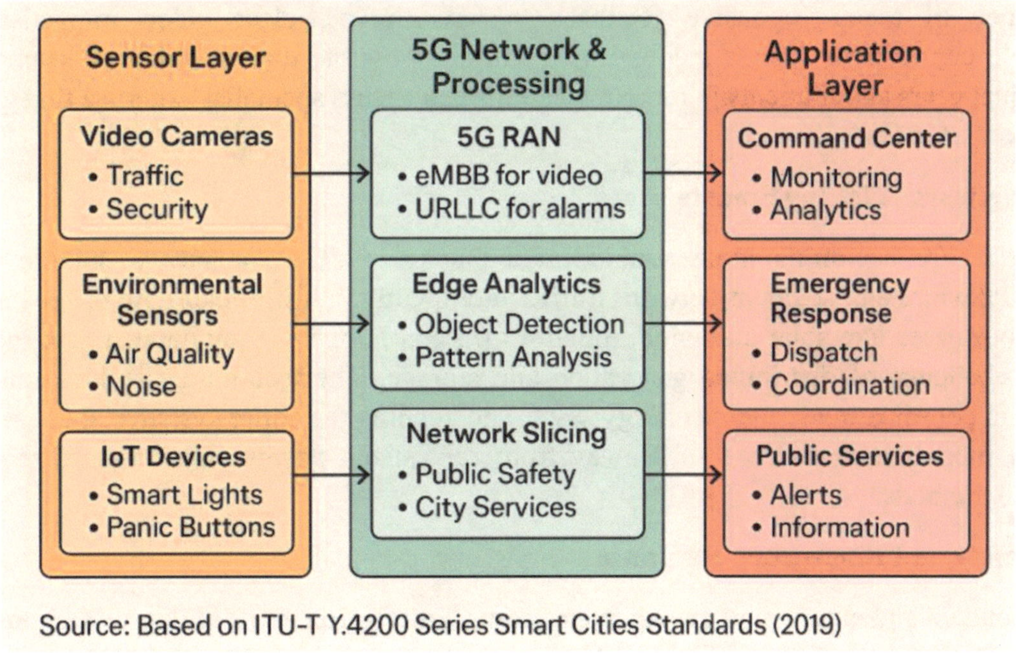

Source: Based on ITU-T Y.4200 Series Smart Cities Standards (2019)

Key integrated applications include:

- **Intelligent Traffic Management:** Real-time optimization reduces emergency response times by 20-30%
- **Gunshot Detection:** Acoustic sensors with sub-second alert generation

- **Crowd Monitoring:** AI-powered analysis of video feeds for anomaly detection

Conclusion

Rolling out 5G networks across different industries marks a pivotal moment in how organizations function and serve their customers. Throughout this chapter, we've explored four key domains where 5G's distinctive characteristics are driving meaningful change:

Manufacturing's Wireless Revolution

Factory floors are undergoing a dramatic transformation as 5G enables the shift toward Industry 4.0. Production facilities can now implement wireless automation systems, create virtual mirrors of their operations, and adopt maintenance strategies that anticipate problems before equipment fails. The technology delivers response times and consistency comparable to traditional wired networks, but adds something cables never could—the ability to reconfigure and adapt production environments without physical constraints. This combination of performance and flexibility is reshaping how modern factories operate.

Healthcare's Expanding Horizons

Medical applications are perhaps where 5G demonstrates its most dramatic potential. Surgeons can now perform procedures from distant locations, medical devices stay connected and coordinated in real time, and emergency services operate with enhanced capabilities. The convergence of touch-responsive feedback systems, crystal-clear video transmission, and dependable connectivity makes medical interventions possible that would have seemed purely fictional just years ago. Patients in remote locations can access specialist expertise that geography once put out of reach.

Energy Networks Getting Smarter

Power grids are becoming more sophisticated thanks to 5G's capacity to handle countless connected devices and segment network traffic intelligently. Utilities can now better incorporate renewable sources like solar and wind, monitor grid conditions as they happen, and manage the complex challenge of distributed generation and storage. The technology tackles fundamental obstacles in coordinating scattered energy assets and keeping the entire system stable—challenges that grow more pressing as we shift away from centralized power plants toward more varied generation methods.

Public Safety and Emergency Response

First responders and emergency management teams benefit from 5G's ability to maintain critical communications even under pressure. The networks enhance how quickly emergencies get addressed, how disasters are managed, and how smart city infrastructure operates during crises. Features that prioritize emergency traffic and maintain connectivity when it matters most ensure that vital communications remain operational precisely when reliability becomes most crucial.

The Road Ahead

As 5G technology continues maturing and early work on sixth-generation networks begins, the potential for industrial transformation will only expand. Making these advances work in practice demands thoughtful preparation, adherence to emerging technical standards, and genuine partnership between the companies building the technology and the industries implementing it. The organizations that approach this transition strategically—understanding both the capabilities and the requirements—will be best positioned to capitalize on what these networks make possible.

Knowledge Check

1. Which 5G feature is most critical for enabling remote surgery applications?
   a) Enhanced Mobile Broadband (eMBB)
   b) Ultra-Reliable Low-Latency Communications (URLLC)
   c) Massive Machine-Type Communications (mMTC)
   d) Network Function Virtualization (NFV)

2. What is the maximum device density supported by 5G networks?
   a) 10,000 devices per square kilometer
   b) 100,000 devices per square kilometer
   c) 500,000 devices per square kilometer
   d) 1 million devices per square kilometer

3. In smart manufacturing, what latency is required for safety-critical human-robot collaboration?
   a) Under 100 ms
   b) Under 50 ms
   c) Under 10 ms
   d) Under 1 ms

4. Which smart grid application has the most stringent latency requirements?
   a) Smart metering
   b) Protection systems
   c) DER management
   d) Wide area monitoring

5. What technology enables 5G networks to provide differentiated services for various applications?
   a) Beamforming
   b) Carrier aggregation
   c) Network slicing
   d) MIMO

6. How does 5G enable the implementation of digital twins in manufacturing environments?

7. What are the key challenges in implementing 5G for public safety applications?

8. Explain how network slicing benefits smart grid operations.

9. What role does edge computing play in 5G-enabled healthcare applications?

10. How do 5G capabilities transform predictive maintenance in manufacturing?

Answers

1. Which 5G feature is most critical for enabling remote surgery applications?
   a) Enhanced Mobile Broadband (eMBB)
   b) Ultra-Reliable Low-Latency Communications (URLLC)
   c) Massive Machine-Type Communications (mMTC)
   d) Network Function Virtualization (NFV)
   Answer: b) Ultra-Reliable Low-Latency Communications (URLLC)
   Remote surgery requires sub-millisecond latency and 99.9999% reliability, which are characteristics of URLLC.

2. What is the maximum device density supported by 5G networks?
   a) 10,000 devices per square kilometer
   b) 100,000 devices per square kilometer
   c) 500,000 devices per square kilometer
   d) 1 million devices per square kilometer
   Answer: d) 1 million devices per square kilometer
   5G mMTC supports up to 1 million connected devices per square kilometer.

3. In smart manufacturing, what latency is required for safety-critical human-robot collaboration?
   a) Under 100 ms
   b) Under 50 ms
   c) Under 10 ms
   d) Under 1 ms
   Answer: d) Under 1 ms
   Emergency stops and safety-critical operations require response times under 1 ms.

4. Which smart grid application has the most stringent latency requirements?
   a) Smart metering
   b) Protection systems
   c) DER management
   d) Wide area monitoring
   Answer: b) Protection systems
   Protection systems require latencies under 10 ms to prevent equipment damage.

5. What technology enables 5G networks to provide differentiated services for various applications?

a) Beamforming
b) Carrier aggregation
c) Network slicing
d) MIMO
Answer: c) Network slicing
Network slicing creates virtual networks optimized for specific service requirements.

6. How does 5G enable the implementation of digital twins in manufacturing environments?
   Answer: 5G enables digital twins through high-bandwidth, low-latency connectivity that supports real-time synchronization between physical assets and their virtual counterparts. The technology provides update rates exceeding 1000 Hz, allowing continuous data streaming from sensors to cloud/edge computing platforms. Multi-access Edge Computing (MEC) integrated with 5G reduces latency for time-critical processing, while network slicing ensures dedicated resources for digital twin applications. This combination enables real-time monitoring, predictive analytics, and remote optimization without physical intervention.

7. What are the key challenges in implementing 5G for public safety applications?
   Answer: Key challenges include ensuring network resilience during disasters when infrastructure may be damaged, providing seamless interoperability between different agencies using various equipment vendors, maintaining security against cyber threats targeting critical infrastructure, managing priority access for first responders while serving public needs, and covering rural/remote areas where emergencies may occur. Additionally, public safety agencies must address the high initial investment costs, training requirements for personnel, and integration with legacy systems.

8. Explain how network slicing benefits smart grid operations.
   Answer: Network slicing creates multiple virtual networks on shared 5G infrastructure, each optimized for specific smart grid applications. Critical protection systems receive dedicated URLLC slices guaranteeing sub-10ms latency and 99.999% reliability. Smart metering uses mMTC slices optimized for massive device connectivity with relaxed latency requirements. Wide area monitoring systems utilize eMBB slices for high-bandwidth data transmission. This segregation ensures quality of service, improves security through isolation, enables efficient resource utilization, and allows independent scaling of different services.

9. What role does edge computing play in 5G-enabled healthcare applications?
   Answer: Edge computing brings processing capabilities closer to medical devices and healthcare facilities, reducing latency for critical applications. In remote surgery, edge nodes process haptic feedback locally, ensuring sub-millisecond response times. For

medical imaging, edge servers perform initial analysis and compression, reducing bandwidth requirements. Patient monitoring systems use edge analytics for real-time anomaly detection without transmitting all data to the cloud. Edge computing also addresses privacy concerns by keeping sensitive medical data local and enables continued operation during cloud connectivity issues.

10. How do 5G capabilities transform predictive maintenance in manufacturing?
Answer: 5G transforms predictive maintenance by enabling dense sensor deployments (up to 1 million per km^2) that continuously monitor equipment health. High-bandwidth capabilities support data-intensive applications like thermal imaging (100+ Mbps per camera) and high-frequency vibration analysis (50 kHz sampling). Ultra-low latency enables real-time correlation of data from multiple sensors, improving fault detection accuracy. Network slicing ensures critical sensor data receives priority transmission. The combination of massive connectivity, high reliability, and edge analytics enables manufacturers to detect potential failures earlier, optimize maintenance schedules, and reduce unplanned downtime by 30-50%.

References

3GPP. (2018). *Study on communication for automation in vertical domains* (TR 22.804). 3rd Generation Partnership Project.

3GPP. (2019). *Service requirements for the 5G system* (TS 22.261). 3rd Generation Partnership Project.

Agiwal, M., Roy, A., & Saxena, N. (2016). Next generation 5G wireless networks: A comprehensive survey. *IEEE Communications Surveys & Tutorials*, 18(3), 1617-1655.

Cheng, J., Chen, W., Tao, F., & Lin, C. L. (2018). Industrial IoT in 5G environment towards smart manufacturing. *Journal of Industrial Information Integration*, 10, 10-19.

Fettweis, G. P. (2014). The tactile internet: Applications and challenges. *IEEE Vehicular Technology Magazine*, 9(1), 64-70.

FirstNet Authority. (2020). *FirstNet annual report to Congress*. First Responder Network Authority.

Garau, M., Celli, G., Ghiani, E., Pilo, F., & Corti, S. (2017). Evaluation of smart grid communication technologies with a co-simulation platform. *IEEE Wireless Communications*, 24(2), 42-49.

Hui, H., Ding, Y., Shi, Q., Li, F., Song, Y., & Yan, J. (2020). 5G network-based Internet of Things for demand response in smart grid: A survey on application potential. *Applied Energy*, 257, 113972.

IEC. (2020). *Communication networks and systems for power utility automation - Part 90-4* (IEC 61850-90-4). International Electrotechnical Commission.

IEEE. (2018). *IEEE standard for smart energy profile application protocol* (IEEE 2030.5-2018). Institute of Electrical and Electronics Engineers.

IEEE. (2021). *IEEE standard for information technology - Telecommunications and information exchange between systems - Local and metropolitan area networks* (IEEE 802.11ax). Institute of Electrical and Electronics Engineers.

Industrial Internet Consortium. (2019). *The Industrial Internet Reference Architecture* (Version 1.9). Industrial Internet Consortium.

ITU-R. (2015). *IMT vision - Framework and overall objectives of the future development of IMT for 2020 and beyond* (Recommendation ITU-R M.2083-0). International Telecommunication Union.

ITU-T. (2019). *Smart sustainable cities - Concept and requirements* (Y.4200 series). International Telecommunication Union.

ITU-T. (2020). *Network requirements for IMT-2020* (Focus Group Technical Report). International Telecommunication Union.

Li, X., Samaka, M., Chan, H. A., Bhamare, D., Gupta, L., Guo, C., & Jain, R. (2018). Network slicing for 5G: Challenges and opportunities. *IEEE Internet Computing*, 21(5), 20-27.

Liu, Z., Zhang, L., & Wang, X. (2019). First 5G-based remote surgery performed in China. *The Lancet Digital Health*, 1(5), e215.

NIST. (2019). *NIST framework and roadmap for smart grid interoperability standards* (Release 3.0). National Institute of Standards and Technology.

NPSTC. (2018). *Public safety communications evolution*. National Public Safety Telecommunications Council.

Park, J., Samarakoon, S., Bennis, M., & Debbah, M. (2018). Wireless network intelligence at the edge. *Proceedings of the IEEE*, 107(11), 2204-2239.

Phadke, A. G., & Bi, T. (2018). Phasor measurement units, WAMS, and their applications in protection and control of power systems. *Journal of Modern Power Systems and Clean Energy*, 6(4), 619-629.

Rao, S. K., & Prasad, R. (2018). Impact of 5G technologies on Industry 4.0. *Wireless Personal Communications*, 100(1), 145-159.

Simsek, M., Aijaz, A., Dohler, M., Sachs, J., & Fettweis, G. (2016). 5G-enabled tactile internet. *IEEE Journal on Selected Areas in Communications*, 34(3), 460-473.

Talari, S., Shafie-Khah, M., Siano, P., Loia, V., Tommasetti, A., & Catalão, J. P. (2017). A review of smart cities based on the internet of things concept. *Energies*, 10(4), 421.

Tao, F., Zhang, H., Liu, A., & Nee, A. Y. (2019). Digital twin in industry: State-of-the-art. *IEEE Transactions on Industrial Informatics*, 15(4), 2405-2415.

West, D. M. (2016). How 5G technology enables the health internet of things. *Brookings Center for Technology Innovation*, 3, 1-20.

Chapter 10: Private 5G Networks

Executive Summary

This chapter provides a comprehensive examination of private 5G networks, exploring their fundamental concepts, deployment architectures, and transformative potential for enterprise communications. Beginning with an overview of how private 5G networks differ from public cellular networks, the chapter delves into various deployment models, from fully private implementations to hybrid approaches utilizing network slicing. Critical aspects such as spectrum allocation frameworks, including innovative models like CBRS in the United States and dedicated industrial spectrum in Germany, are thoroughly analyzed. The chapter explores key enabling technologies, including edge computing integration, time-sensitive networking capabilities, and advanced security features tailored for enterprise requirements. Through detailed case studies across manufacturing, healthcare, logistics, and energy sectors, readers gain practical insights into real-world implementations and their business impact. The chapter concludes with an examination of emerging trends, including AI-driven network management, integrated sensing and communication capabilities, and the evolution toward 6G technologies, providing readers with a forward-looking perspective on the future of enterprise wireless communications.

Table of Contents

Introduction

The introduction of 5G wireless technology has expanded connectivity possibilities far beyond consumer applications. Private 5G networks (NPNs) offer enterprises a fundamentally different approach to wireless infrastructure deployment. Unlike public networks, these private systems deliver organizations greater autonomy over network operations, the ability to customize configurations to specific requirements, and performance characteristics suited to business-critical applications (3GPP, 2020a)

Unlike traditional public cellular networks operated by mobile network operators (MNOs), private 5G networks are designed specifically to meet the unique requirements of individual organizations or defined user groups. These networks can operate within confined geographical areas such as manufacturing facilities, hospital campuses, ports, or office buildings, providing tailored connectivity solutions that address specific business needs (Aijaz, 2020).

The emergence of private 5G networks is driven by several converging factors. First, the limitations of existing wireless technologies, particularly Wi-Fi, in supporting industrial-grade applications have become increasingly apparent. While Wi-Fi has served enterprises well for general connectivity, it struggles to meet the stringent requirements of modern industrial applications that demand ultra-reliable low-latency communication (URLLC), massive device connectivity, and deterministic performance (Zhang et al., 2022).

Second, the evolution of 5G standards has explicitly incorporated enterprise requirements from the ground up. Beginning with 3GPP Release 16, standardization bodies have dedicated significant effort to defining features specifically for vertical industries, including enhanced support for time-sensitive networking (TSN), industrial IoT, and non-public network architectures (3GPP, 2023a).

Third, regulatory innovations worldwide have created new opportunities for enterprises to access spectrum resources. Countries like Germany, Japan, the United Kingdom, and the United States have established frameworks that enable enterprises to deploy private 5G networks using dedicated or shared spectrum, removing a traditional barrier to private cellular deployments (Brown, 2020).

This chapter explores the multifaceted landscape of private 5G networks, examining their technical foundations, deployment considerations, and transformative potential across various industry sectors. Through a combination of theoretical analysis and practical case studies, we aim to provide readers with a comprehensive understanding of this rapidly evolving technology domain.

Understanding Private 5G Networks

Definition and Characteristics

Private 5G infrastructure refers to wireless systems built on fifth-generation cellular standards but deployed exclusively for particular enterprises or defined user communities operating within specific geographic areas. The 3GPP technical specification TS 23.501 classifies these deployments as Non-Public Networks (NPNs), designating them for restricted rather than general public access (3GPP, 2023c).

Several fundamental attributes separate private 5G implementations from carrier-operated public cellular systems:

Dedicated Infrastructure: Private 5G networks employ either partially or fully dedicated network resources, ensuring that capacity and performance are reserved exclusively for the organization's use. This dedication eliminates the unpredictability associated with shared public networks where multiple users compete for resources (GSMA, 2021).

Customized Performance: Organizations can tailor network parameters to meet specific application requirements. For instance, a manufacturing facility might prioritize ultra-low latency for robotic control, while a hospital might emphasize reliability for life-critical applications (Kalør et al., 2024).

Enhanced Security and Privacy: With data traffic remaining within the enterprise premises or under enterprise control, private 5G networks offer superior data sovereignty and reduced exposure to external security threats (Campion et al., 2021).

Local Control and Management: Enterprises maintain direct control over network policies, user access, quality of service parameters, and operational decisions, enabling rapid adaptation to changing business needs (Ordonez-Lucena et al., 2021).

Comparison with Other Wireless Technologies

To understand the value proposition of private 5G networks, it is essential to compare them with existing enterprise wireless technologies:

Comparison of Enterprise Wireless Technologies

Feature	Wi-Fi 6/6E	Private LTE	Private 5G	Public 5G with Network Slicing
Maximum Throughput	9.6 Gbps	1 Gbps	20 Gbps	20 Gbps (shared)
Typical Latency	10-20 ms	20-30 ms	<1-10 ms	10-20 ms
Reliability	99.9%	99.99%	99.999%	99.9%
Coverage Range	50-100m	1-5 km	100m-1km	Varies
Spectrum	Unlicensed	Licensed/CBRS	Licensed/Shared	Licensed
Mobility Support	Limited	Good	Excellent	Excellent
Device Density	Moderate	High	Very High	High

Feature	Wi-Fi 6/6E	Private LTE	Private 5G	Public 5G with Network Slicing
Deployment Complexity	Low	Medium	High	Low
Cost	Low	Medium	High	Medium

Source: Adapted from Agiwal et al. (2023) and GSMA (2021)

Business Drivers for Private 5G Adoption

Several compelling business drivers are accelerating the adoption of private 5G networks across industries:

Digital Transformation Initiatives: As organizations pursue Industry 4.0 and digital transformation strategies, the need for advanced wireless connectivity that can support artificial intelligence, machine learning, and real-time analytics becomes paramount (World Economic Forum, 2021).

Operational Efficiency: Private 5G enables wireless automation of previously wired processes, reducing infrastructure costs and increasing flexibility. For example, automotive manufacturers can reconfigure production lines without the constraints of fixed cabling (Ericsson, 2022).

Enhanced Safety and Compliance: Private 5G deployments in high-risk sectors—including mining facilities, petroleum extraction, and chemical manufacturing—enable advanced protection systems by providing continuous situational awareness, equipment health analytics for failure prevention, and rapid incident response coordination (Hedayati et al., 2023)..

Competitive Advantage: Early adopters of private 5G are positioning themselves to leverage emerging technologies such as autonomous systems, augmented reality, and digital twins, creating competitive differentiation in their respective markets (Qualcomm, 2022).

Architecture and Deployment Models

Core Architectural Components

The architecture of private 5G networks builds upon the standard 5G system architecture while incorporating specific adaptations for enterprise environments. According to 3GPP TS 23.501, the key architectural components include:

5G Core Network (5GC): The brain of the network that manages authentication, session establishment, mobility, and policy enforcement. In private deployments, the 5GC can be deployed on-premises, in the cloud, or in a hybrid configuration (3GPP, 2023c).

Radio Access Network (RAN): Consisting of gNodeBs (5G base stations) that provide the radio interface for device connectivity. Private deployments often utilize small cells for indoor coverage and macro cells for outdoor areas (Li et al., 2023).

Private 5G Network Architecture

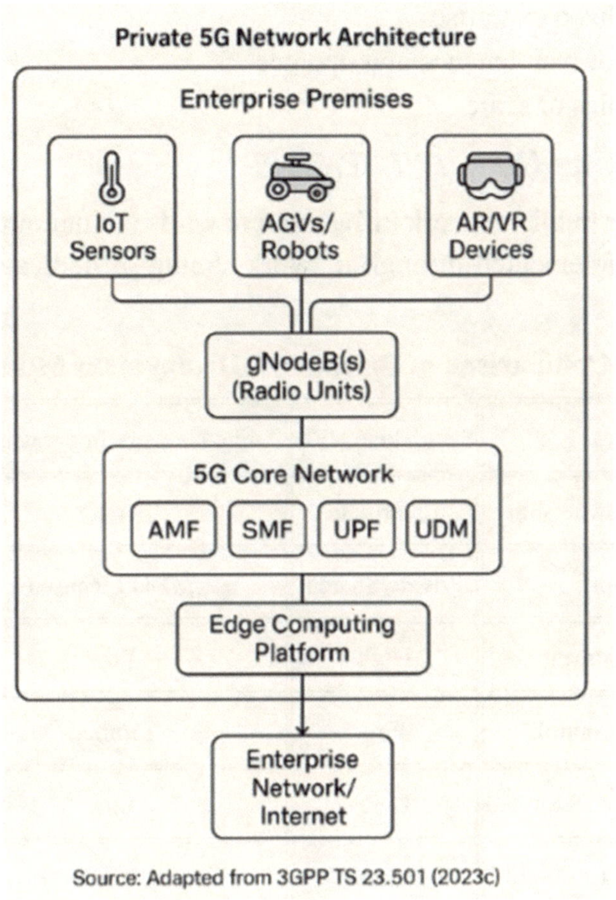

Source: Adapted from 3GPP TS 23.501 (2023c)

Deployment Models

Private 5G networks can be deployed using several models, each offering different levels of control, cost structure, and operational complexity:

Standalone Non-Public Network (SNPN)

In this model, the enterprise deploys and operates all network components independently, without reliance on public network infrastructure. This approach offers maximum control and data sovereignty but requires significant technical expertise and capital investment (3GPP, 2020a).

Advantages:

- Complete control over network operations
- Maximum data privacy and security

- Customizable to specific requirements
- No dependency on external operators

Challenges:

- High initial investment
- Requires specialized expertise
- Responsibility for maintenance and updates
- Limited economies of scale

Public Network Integrated NPN (PNI-NPN)

This model leverages public network infrastructure while maintaining logical separation for the enterprise. It can be implemented through network slicing or dedicated core network functions (Zhang et al., 2022).

Comparison of Private 5G Deployment Models

Aspect	Standalone NPN	Public Network Integrated NPN	Hybrid Model
Infrastructure Ownership	Enterprise	MNO	Shared
Spectrum	Private/Shared	MNO Licensed	Mixed
Capital Investment	High	Low	Medium
Operational Control	Full	Limited	Partial
Technical Expertise Required	High	Low	Medium
Scalability	Limited	High	High
Time to Deploy	Long	Short	Medium
Data Sovereignty	Complete	Partial	Configurable

Source: Compiled from GSMA (2021) and Brown (2020)

Hybrid Deployment Model

The hybrid model combines elements of both standalone and integrated approaches. Typically, the RAN is deployed on-premises while core network functions may be hosted in the cloud or managed by a service provider (Aijaz, 2020).

Creating Customized Virtual Networks Through Slicing

Modern private networks face a challenging paradox: different applications demand conflicting network characteristics, yet building separate physical infrastructure for each use case becomes prohibitively expensive. Network slicing resolves this tension by enabling a single physical network to behave as multiple independent networks, each optimized for specific requirements.

The Fundamental Concept

Think of network slicing as creating dedicated lanes on a shared highway, where each lane operates under different rules suited to its traffic. One slice might prioritize speed above all else, ensuring minimal delays for time-critical communications. Another emphasizes throughput, moving massive data volumes efficiently. A third focuses on connecting countless devices simultaneously, even if individual connections carry minimal data.

This virtualization happens across the entire network stack—from radio resources and transport capacity to core processing functions. Each slice receives guaranteed resources and operates with isolation from other slices, preventing one application's traffic patterns from disrupting another's performance.

Practical Implementation in Private 5G

Consider an industrial facility deploying private 5G infrastructure. The same physical network must simultaneously handle several demanding applications, each with incompatible needs:

Robotic systems require millisecond-level responsiveness. Any delay between sensor input and actuator response creates safety risks or precision problems. These applications need a slice configured for ultra-low latency, where the network prioritizes speed and predictability over raw bandwidth.

Video surveillance and quality inspection systems generate continuous high-resolution streams. These applications care less about instantaneous response and more about moving large data volumes reliably. Their slice emphasizes throughput and sustained data rates.

Environmental sensors, asset trackers, and monitoring systems involve thousands of simple devices, each transmitting small amounts of data periodically. This use case needs a slice optimized for massive connectivity, supporting huge device populations efficiently even though individual devices consume minimal bandwidth.

Technical Advantages

Without slicing, these competing demands force uncomfortable compromises. Optimizing for robotic latency might starve video systems of bandwidth. Configuring for high throughput could introduce delays that robotic systems cannot tolerate. Supporting massive IoT connectivity might degrade performance for both other use cases.

Slicing eliminates these trade-offs by creating parallel virtual networks, each tuned precisely for its workload. The robotic slice receives dedicated radio scheduling that minimizes delays. The video slice gets reserved bandwidth ensuring smooth streaming. The IoT slice efficiently manages connection density without impacting others.

This isolation also provides operational benefits. A problem in one slice—perhaps a misbehaving application flooding the network—remains contained. Other slices continue functioning normally, preventing localized issues from cascading into system-wide failures.

Resource Efficiency

Beyond performance customization, slicing delivers economic advantages. Instead of deploying separate physical networks for different application categories, organizations amortize infrastructure investment across all use cases. The same base stations, transport links, and core network equipment serve multiple virtual networks simultaneously.

Resource allocation adapts dynamically based on actual demand. During peak production hours, the robotic slice might claim priority. During maintenance windows when robots idle, those resources shift to other slices automatically. This flexibility maximizes infrastructure utilization while ensuring each application receives necessary resources when needed

Network Slicing Architecture for Private 5G

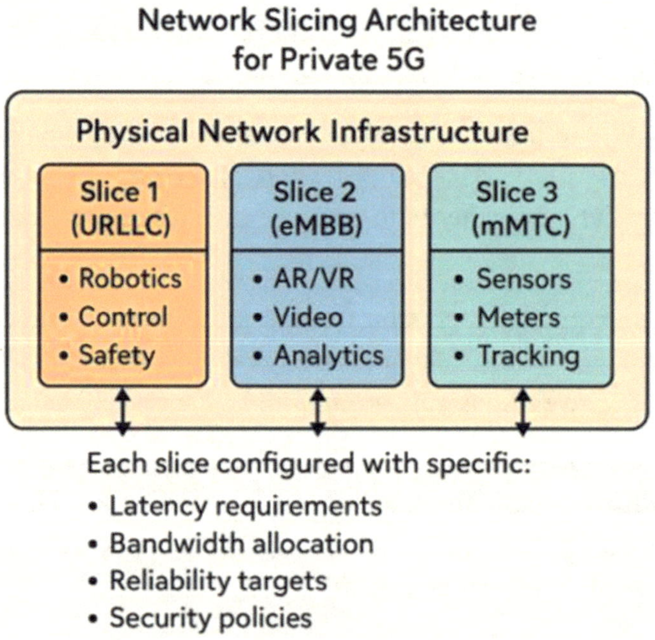

Source: Based on Ordonez-Lucena et al. (2021)

Spectrum Options and Licensing

Spectrum Bands for Private 5G

The availability of spectrum is fundamental to private 5G deployments. Different frequency bands offer varying characteristics in terms of coverage, capacity, and propagation properties (Agiwal et al., 2023).

Low-Band Spectrum (<1 GHz)

Low-band frequencies provide excellent coverage and building penetration but limited bandwidth:

- **Characteristics:** Superior propagation, wide coverage area
- **Use Cases:** Wide-area campus coverage, rural deployments
- **Challenges:** Limited capacity, higher interference potential

Mid-Band Spectrum (1-6 GHz)

Mid-band frequencies provide an optimal trade-off between coverage area and data throughput:

- **Key Bands:** 2.5 GHz, 3.5 GHz (C-Band), 3.7-4.2 GHz
- **Characteristics:** Good balance of coverage and throughput
- **Use Cases:** Most private 5G deployments, industrial applications

High-Band Spectrum (mmWave, >24 GHz)

Millimeter wave frequencies provide enormous capacity but limited coverage:

- **Key Bands:** 26 GHz, 28 GHz, 39 GHz
- **Characteristics:** Ultra-high capacity, limited range
- **Use Cases:** Dense deployments, high-throughput applications

Spectrum Licensing Models

Different countries have adopted various approaches to making spectrum available for private 5G networks:

Global Spectrum Frameworks for Private 5G

Country/Region	Spectrum Band	Licensing Model	Key Features
United States	3.55-3.7 GHz (CBRS)	Three-tier sharing	Dynamic spectrum access, GAA, and PAL
Germany	3.7-3.8 GHz	Local licensing	Dedicated for industrial use
Japan	28.2-28.3 GHz, 4.6-4.9 GHz	Local 5G licenses	Simplified application process
United Kingdom	3.8-4.2 GHz, 1800 MHz	Shared access	Location-specific licenses
France	2.6 GHz	Enterprise licenses	Professional mobile radio evolution
Netherlands	3.5 GHz	Local permits	Site-specific authorizations

Source: Compiled from regulatory authorities and Brown (2020)

Citizens Broadband Radio Service (CBRS) – A Case Study

The CBRS framework in the United States represents an innovative approach to spectrum sharing that has become a model for other countries. The three-tier system enables dynamic spectrum access:

CBRS Three-Tier Spectrum Sharing Model

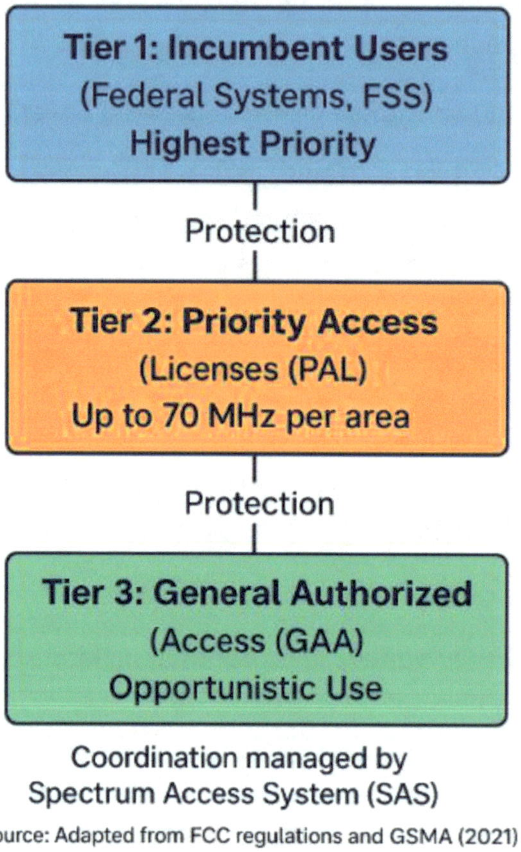

Source: Adapted from FCC regulations and GSMA (2021)

Key Technologies and Features

Ultra-Reliable Low-Latency Communication (URLLC)

URLLC is a cornerstone capability of private 5G networks, particularly critical for industrial applications. According to 3GPP TS 22.104, URLLC supports:

- **Latency:** End-to-end latency as low as 1 millisecond
- **Reliability:** Up to 99.9999% packet delivery success rate
- **Jitter:** Minimal variation in latency for consistent performance

These capabilities enable applications such as:

- Live robotic control & monitoring.

- Industrial automation systems
- Remote machinery operation
- Safety-critical communications

Time-Sensitive Networking (TSN) Integration

Industrial environments demand precision that traditional wireless systems struggle to deliver—machines must coordinate with microsecond accuracy, safety systems require guaranteed response times, and production lines can't tolerate unpredictable delays. This is where the convergence of 5G technology and Time-Sensitive Networking protocols becomes transformative.

TSN standards originated in wired industrial networks, where engineers needed absolute certainty about when data would arrive. A robotic arm must know precisely when to move, a safety interlock must respond within defined timeframes, and synchronized manufacturing processes can't function with variable latency. For decades, these requirements kept critical industrial systems tethered to physical cables.

The marriage of 5G and TSN changes this calculus fundamentally. By incorporating TSN mechanisms into wireless infrastructure, networks can now provide deterministic behavior—meaning the system can guarantee maximum latency bounds and ensure traffic arrives in predictable patterns. Research demonstrates that this integration makes wireless connections viable for applications previously impossible without wired connectivity.

In practical terms, a factory floor might coordinate dozens of autonomous guided vehicles, all requiring split-second timing accuracy while moving freely throughout the facility. Process control systems can operate wirelessly without sacrificing the reliability that safety certifications demand. Synchronized motion control across multiple machines becomes feasible even when those machines aren't physically connected.

The technical achievement involves several layers of coordination. 5G networks must schedule radio resources with tight precision, matching the deterministic guarantees that TSN provides on wired segments. Traffic shaping mechanisms ensure high-priority industrial data receives protected transmission windows. Clock synchronization protocols maintain timing alignment across the entire system—both wired and wireless segments—often to within microseconds.

This capability extends CBRS's industrial appeal significantly. Manufacturing facilities can deploy private 5G networks with TSN support, creating flexible production environments where equipment reconfiguration no longer means rewiring infrastructure. Automation systems gain mobility without surrendering reliability, and industrial operations can blend the determinism of traditional control systems with the adaptability of wireless connectivity.

5G-TSN Integration Architecture

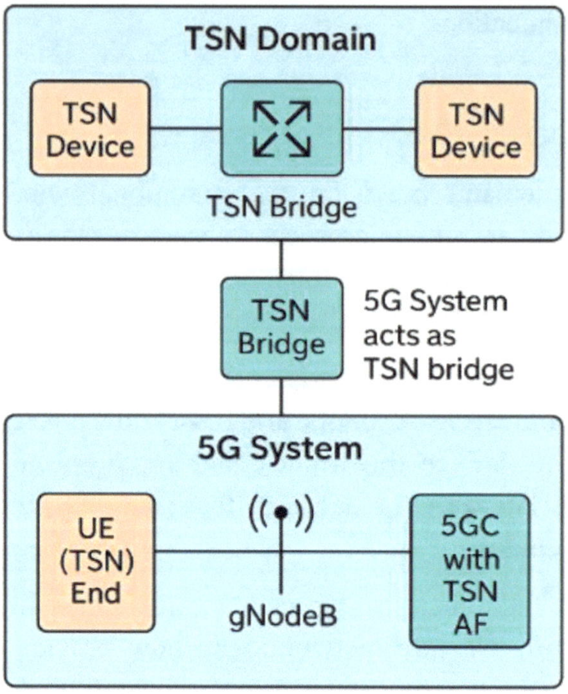

Figure 10.4:
5G-TSN Integration Architecture

Source: Based on 3GPP TS 23.501 (2023c) and Hedayati et al. (2023)

Source: Based on 3GPP TS 23.501 (2023c) and Hedayati et al. (2023)

Edge Computing Integration

Multi-access Edge Computing (MEC) changes where data processing happens. Traditional network architectures follow a predictable pattern—devices capture information, transmit it to centralized data centers potentially thousands of miles away, wait for processing, then receive results. This round-trip journey creates inherent delays that many modern applications simply cannot accommodate.

Edge computing fundamentally reimagines this model by relocating computational resources to the network's periphery, positioning processing power in close proximity to data sources themselves. Rather than forcing every byte of information on a long-distance journey to remote servers, intelligence moves outward to where action happens. A factory sensor's data gets analyzed within the facility. A surveillance camera's video feed processes locally. An autonomous vehicle's decisions occur onboard or at nearby infrastructure.

The Latency Advantage

Speed matters profoundly in time-dependent scenarios. Consider an industrial robot detecting a safety hazard—every millisecond counts between identification and emergency shutdown. Sending sensor data across continents for analysis, then waiting for instructions to return, introduces unacceptable delays. Edge computing collapses this timeline dramatically. Processing occurs meters away rather than thousands of kilometers distant, transforming response times from hundreds of milliseconds to single-digit figures.

This responsiveness enables applications previously confined to theoretical discussions. Augmented reality systems can overlay information seamlessly because rendering happens locally. Predictive maintenance algorithms can trigger immediate interventions because analysis occurs adjacent to equipment. Interactive experiences become genuinely interactive when the computational delay essentially disappears.

Keeping Data Close to Home

Beyond speed, edge architectures offer compelling advantages for data locality. Processing information where it originates means sensitive content never traverses public networks or enters third-party facilities. Healthcare providers can analyze patient data within their own infrastructure. Financial institutions maintain transaction processing on-premises. Manufacturing companies keep proprietary operational metrics confined to factory boundaries.

This localization addresses both privacy concerns and regulatory requirements. Data sovereignty regulations often mandate that certain information remain within specific geographic boundaries. Edge computing makes compliance straightforward—the data simply never leaves controlled territory.

Bandwidth Economics

Network capacity isn't infinite or free. Transmitting massive volumes of raw data to distant processing centers consumes substantial bandwidth and incurs ongoing costs. Edge computing inverts this equation by performing initial analysis locally, then forwarding only meaningful results or condensed summaries.

A video surveillance system demonstrates this efficiency clearly. Rather than streaming every camera feed continuously to cloud servers, edge processors analyze footage locally, identifying relevant events and transmitting only noteworthy clips. The bandwidth requirement drops from constant high-volume streaming to occasional bursts of actionable information. A factory with hundreds of sensors might generate gigabytes of raw telemetry, but after edge processing, only kilobytes of insights need transmission to central management systems.

Resilience Through Distribution

Distributed processing creates operational resilience that centralized models lack. When critical functions depend on remote servers, network disruptions create complete system failures. Edge deployments maintain local functionality even when connectivity to central resources fails.

Factory automation continues operating. Retail systems keep processing transactions. Building management maintains environmental controls.

This independence proves particularly valuable in environments where connectivity cannot be guaranteed—remote installations, mobile platforms, or areas with unreliable infrastructure. The system remains operational because essential processing happens locally, with cloud connectivity serving as an enhancement rather than a dependency.

Massive Machine-Type Communications (mMTC)

Private 5G networks support massive IoT deployments with:

- Connection density to support up to1 million devices per square kilometer
- Extended battery life through power-saving features
- Support for diverse device types and protocols

5G Performance Categories for Different Use Cases

Performance Indicator	eMBB	URLLC	mMTC
Peak Data Rate	20 Gbps (DL), 10 Gbps (UL)	1 Gbps	100 kbps
User Experience Data Rate	100 Mbps (DL), 50 Mbps (UL)	10 Mbps	10 kbps
Latency	4 ms	1 ms	10 s
Mobility	500 km/h	120 km/h	30 km/h
Connection Density	10^4/km^2	10^4/km^2	10^6/km^2
Energy Efficiency	100x improvement	-	10 years battery
Reliability	99.9%	99.999%	99.9%

Source: Adapted from 3GPP TS 22.261 (2023a)

Network Slicing Capabilities

Network slicing divides unified 5G infrastructure into separate logical networks, with each virtual instance optimized for specific application demands.

- **Enhanced Mobile Broadband (eMBB) Slice:** For high-bandwidth applications like AR/VR
- **URLLC Slice:** For critical control and safety applications
- **mMTC Slice:** For massive sensor deployments
- **Custom Slices:** Tailored to specific enterprise requirements

Industry Applications and Use Cases

Manufacturing and Industry 4.0

Private 5G networks are transforming manufacturing through:

Automated Guided Vehicles (AGVs)

- Real-time coordination of material transport
- Dynamic route optimization
- Collision avoidance systems
- Integration with warehouse management systems

Digital Twin Implementation

- Real-time synchronization between physical and digital assets
- Predictive maintenance based on continuous monitoring
- Simulation and optimization of production processes

Case Study: Bosch Rexroth Factory

The Bosch Rexroth facility in Germany deployed a private 5G network, achieving:

- 30% reduction in production line reconfiguration time
- Support for 200+ connected devices per production cell
- Sub-10ms latency for critical control applications
- 99.999% reliability for automated systems (Source: Bosch internal reports, 2022)

Healthcare Applications

Remote Patient Monitoring

- Continuous vital sign monitoring across hospital campuses
- Real-time alerts for critical conditions
- Integration with electronic health records
- Support for wearable medical devices

Connected Ambulances

- Live video streaming from the ambulance to the emergency room
- Real-time transmission of patient data
- Remote consultation with specialists
- Preparation of emergency teams before arrival

Healthcare Use Cases and Requirements

Use Case	Bandwidth	Latency	Reliability	Key Benefits
Remote Surgery	1 Gbps	<5 ms	99.9999%	Expert assistance anywhere
Patient Monitoring	10 Mbps	<100 ms	99.99%	Continuous care
Medical Imaging	100 Mbps	<50 ms	99.9%	Rapid diagnosis
Connected Ambulance	50 Mbps	<20 ms	99.99%	Early intervention
AR-Assisted Surgery	200 Mbps	<10 ms	99.999%	Enhanced precision

Source: Compiled from healthcare industry reports and 3GPP TS 22.261 (2023a)

Logistics and Supply Chain

Port Operations

Private 5G enables smart port operations through:

- Automated crane operations
- Real-time container tracking
- Autonomous vehicle coordination
- Environmental monitoring

Warehouse Automation

- Robotic picking and packing systems
- Inventory tracking with RFID and sensors
- Drone-based inventory management
- Predictive maintenance of equipment

Energy and Utilities

Smart Grid Management

- Real-time monitoring of distributed energy resources
- Rapid response to grid disturbances
- Coordination of renewable energy sources
- Demand response management

Remote Asset Inspection

- Drone-based inspection of power lines and pipelines
- Real-time video transmission for analysis
- Predictive maintenance using sensor data
- Enhanced worker safety in hazardous environments

Private 5G in Smart Grid Applications

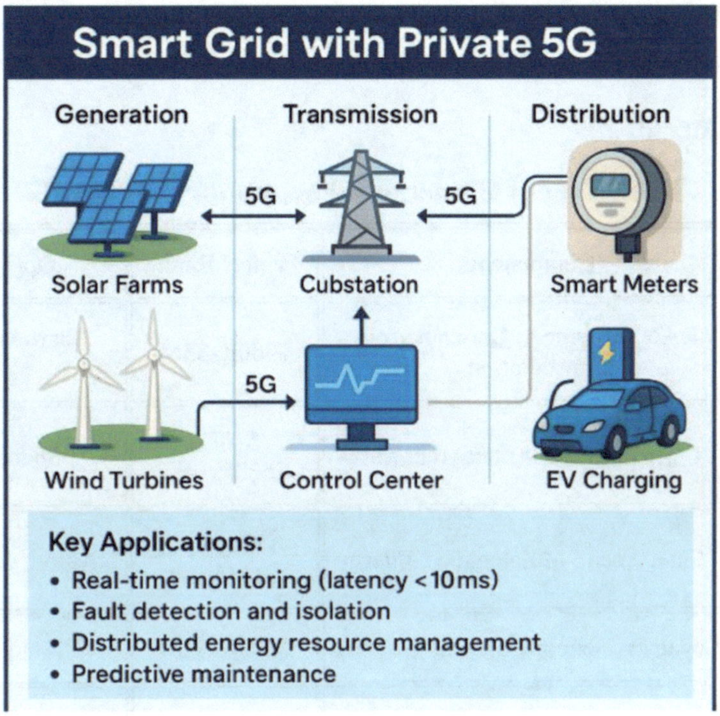

Source: Adapted from energy sector implementations (Viswanathan & Mogensen, 2020)

Implementation Challenges and Solutions

Technical Challenges

Coverage and Capacity Planning

- **Challenge:** Ensuring adequate coverage in complex industrial environments
- **Solution:** Advanced propagation modeling and dense small cell deployments

Integration with Legacy Systems

- **Challenge:** Connecting 5G networks with existing industrial protocols
- **Solution:** Protocol conversion gateways and gradual migration strategies

Interference Management

- **Challenge:** Coexistence with other wireless systems
- **Solution:** Dynamic spectrum management and advanced antenna technologies

Organizational Challenges

Skills Gap

- **Challenge:** Lack of in-house expertise for 5G deployment and management
- **Solution:** Partnerships with system integrators and managed service providers

Change Management

- **Challenge:** Resistance to new technology adoption
- **Solution:** Phased implementation and comprehensive training programs

Financial Considerations

Total Cost of Ownership Factors for Private 5G

Cost Category	Components	Typical Range	Optimization Strategies
Capital Expenditure	RAN equipment, Core network, Installation	$500K-$5M	Shared infrastructure, Phased deployment
Spectrum Costs	Licensing fees, Annual renewals	$10K-$500K/year	Shared spectrum models
Operational Expenditure	Management, Maintenance, Energy	$100K-$1M/year	Automation, Managed services
Integration Costs	Legacy system integration, Training	$200K-$2M	Standardized interfaces
Security Infrastructure	Firewalls, Monitoring systems	$100K-$500K	Cloud-based security

Source: Industry analysis compiled from GSMA (2021) and vendor reports

Security Considerations

Security Architecture

Private 5G networks implement multiple layers of security:

Network Security

- Mutual authentication between devices and network
- Encryption of user and control plane traffic
- Integrity protection for signaling messages
- Network isolation from public networks

Application Security

- End-to-end encryption for sensitive data
- Application-layer authentication
- Secure APIs for service access
- Regular security updates and patches

Threat Landscape

Security Threats and Mitigation Strategies

Threat Type	Description	Potential Impact	Mitigation Strategy
Rogue Base Stations	Fake gNodeBs intercepting traffic	Data theft, Service disruption	Strong authentication, Signal monitoring
DDoS Attacks	Overwhelming network resources	Service unavailability	Traffic filtering, Rate limiting
Man-in-the-Middle	Intercepting communications	Data compromise	End-to-end encryption
Insider Threats	Malicious internal actors	System compromise	Access controls, Monitoring
Supply Chain Attacks	Compromised equipment	Backdoor access	Vendor verification, Security testing

Source: Adapted from Campion et al. (2021) and 3GPP TS 33.501 (2023e)

Compliance and Regulatory Requirements

Organizations deploying private 5G infrastructure face multiple regulatory obligations:

- Privacy and data handling laws (including GDPR and CCPA frameworks)
- Sector-specific regulatory frameworks (such as HIPAA mandates for medical facilities and NERC CIP standards for energy infrastructure)
- Government security protocols and requirements
- Technical certification requirements for network equipment

Future Trends and Evolution

Artificial Intelligence and Machine Learning Integration

Organizations are progressively embedding AI and ML technologies within private 5G infrastructure:

- Predictive network optimization
- Automated fault detection and resolution
- Dynamic resource allocation
- Security threat detection

Convergence with Wi-Fi 7 and Beyond

Future enterprise networks will likely combine multiple technologies:

- Seamless handover between 5G and Wi-Fi

- Unified management platforms
- Dynamic technology selection based on application requirements

Evolution Toward 6G

Research into sixth-generation wireless technology is already underway:

- Terahertz communications for ultra-high capacity
- AI-native network architectures
- Integration of sensing and communication
- Holographic communications

Evolution Timeline of Private Wireless Networks

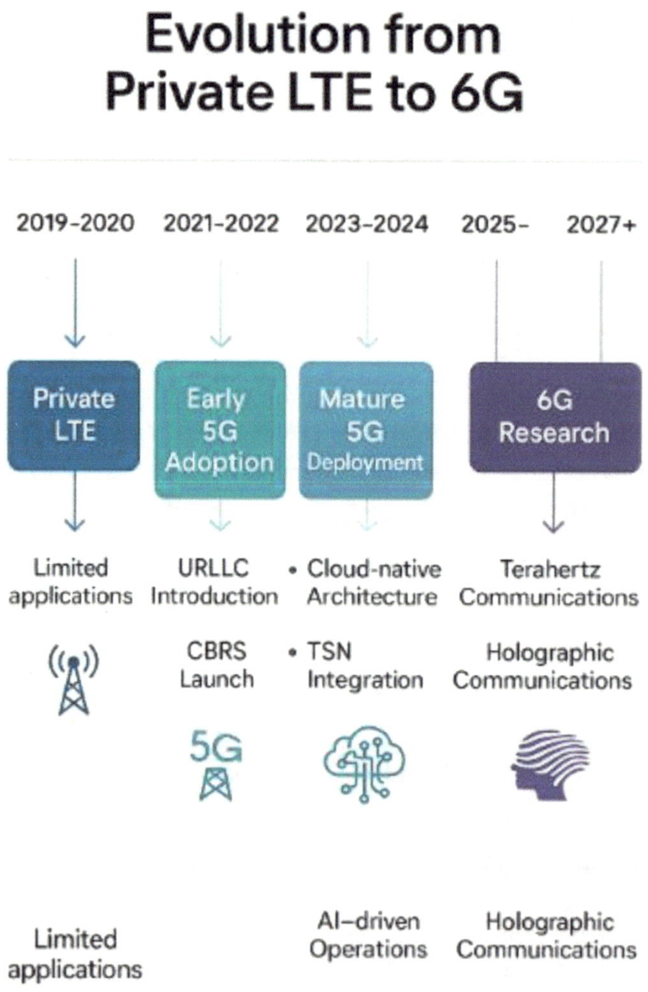

Source: Industry projections and Viswanathan & Mogensen (2020)

Integrated Sensing and Communication

Future private networks will combine communication and sensing capabilities:

- Environmental monitoring using network infrastructure
- Precision positioning and tracking
- Gesture recognition and touchless interfaces
- Security and surveillance applications

Conclusion

Private 5G networks represent a transformative technology that enables enterprises to deploy high-performance wireless infrastructure tailored to their specific needs. Through dedicated or shared spectrum resources, organizations can achieve levels of reliability, latency, and security that were previously unattainable with public networks or traditional enterprise wireless technologies.

The journey from early LTE-based private networks to today's sophisticated 5G deployments demonstrates the rapid evolution of this technology domain. Key enablers, including regulatory innovations, standardization efforts, and the development of enterprise-focused solutions, have created a thriving ecosystem that continues to expand across industries.

As we have explored throughout this chapter, private 5G networks offer compelling benefits across diverse sectors—from enabling flexible manufacturing systems and enhancing healthcare delivery to optimizing logistics operations and modernizing energy infrastructure. The technology's ability to support ultra-reliable low-latency communications, massive IoT deployments, and high-bandwidth applications within a secure, controlled environment positions it as a cornerstone of digital transformation strategies.

Looking ahead, the integration of artificial intelligence, edge computing, and advanced sensing capabilities will further enhance the value proposition of private 5G networks. As organizations continue to digitize their operations and embrace Industry 4.0 concepts, private 5G will play an increasingly critical role in enabling new business models and operational paradigms.

The evolution toward 6G and beyond promises even more revolutionary capabilities, but the foundation being laid today with private 5G deployments will be essential for realizing these future possibilities. Organizations that invest in understanding and implementing private 5G networks now will be well-positioned to leverage the full potential of next-generation wireless technologies.

Knowledge Check

1. Which 3GPP release first introduced comprehensive specifications for Non-Public Networks (NPNs)?
   a) Release 11
   b) Release 13
   c) Release 16
   d) Release 18

2. What is the maximum connection density supported by 5G mMTC per square kilometer?
   a) 10,900 devices
   b) 100,999 devices
   c) 500,999 devices
   d) 1,000,000 devices

3. In the CBRS spectrum sharing model, which tier has the highest priority?
   a) General Authorized Access (GAA)
   b) Priority Access Licenses (PAL)
   c) Incumbent users
   d) Enterprise users

4. What is the target end-to-end latency for URLLC applications in private 5G networks?
   a) 10 milliseconds
   b) 5 milliseconds
   c) 1 millisecond
   d) 100 milliseconds

5. Which country was the first to allocate dedicated spectrum (3.7-3.8 GHz) specifically for industrial 5G use?
   a) Canada
   b) Germany
   c) China
   d) Finland

6. Compare and contrast the three main deployment models for private 5G networks (Standalone NPN, Public Network Integrated NPN, and Hybrid). What factors should an organization consider when choosing between these models?

7. Explain how Time-Sensitive Networking (TSN) integration with 5G enables deterministic communication for industrial applications. What are the key challenges in implementing TSN over wireless networks?

8. Discuss the role of edge computing in private 5G networks. How does it enhance the capabilities of enterprise deployments?

9. What security benefits distinguish private 5G infrastructure from public cellular systems? Which additional safeguards should companies establish?

10. How will the integration of AI and machine learning transform private 5G network operations? Provide specific examples of AI applications in network management.

Answers

1. Which 3GPP release first introduced comprehensive specifications for Non-Public Networks (NPNs)?
   a) Release 11
   b) Release 12
   c) Release 16
   d) Release 18
   Answer: c) Release 16

2. What is the maximum connection density supported by 5G mMTC per square kilometer?
   a) 10,900 devices
   b) 100,999 devices
   c) 500,999 devices
   d) 1,000,000 devices
   Answer: d) 1,000,000 devices

3. In the CBRS spectrum sharing model, which tier has the highest priority?
   a) General Authorized Access (GAA)
   b) Priority Access Licenses (PAL)
   c) Incumbent users
   d) Enterprise users
   Answer: c) Incumbent users

4. What is the target end-to-end latency for URLLC applications in private 5G networks?
   a) 10 milliseconds
   b) 5 milliseconds
   c) 1 millisecond
   d) 100 milliseconds
   Answer: c) 1 millisecond

5. Which country was the first to allocate dedicated spectrum (3.7-3.8 GHz) specifically for industrial 5G use?
   a) Canada
   b) Germany
   c) China
   d) Finland
   Answer: b) Germany

6. Compare and contrast the three main deployment models for private 5G networks (Standalone NPN, Public Network Integrated NPN, and Hybrid). What factors should an organization consider when choosing between these models?
   Answer: The three deployment models offer different trade-offs:
   Standalone NPN provides complete control and data sovereignty but requires high capital investment and technical expertise. It's ideal for organizations with strict security requirements and sufficient resources.
   Public Network Integrated NPN leverages existing MNO infrastructure, reducing costs and complexity but limiting control. It suits organizations wanting 5G benefits without major infrastructure investments.
   Hybrid models balance control and cost by deploying RAN on-premises while using cloud or managed core services. This suits organizations wanting local control of radio resources while benefiting from managed services.
   Key factors to consider include: budget constraints, security requirements, technical expertise availability, scalability needs, and time-to-deployment requirements.

7. Explain how Time-Sensitive Networking (TSN) integration with 5G enables deterministic communication for industrial applications. What are the key challenges in implementing TSN over wireless networks?
   Answer: TSN integration with 5G enables deterministic communication by:
   - Making the 5G system appear as a TSN bridge to industrial networks
   - Providing time synchronization across wireless and wired domains
   - Implementing traffic scheduling and shaping for guaranteed latency
   - Supporting IEEE 802.1 standards for industrial Ethernet compatibility
   Key challenges include:
   - Achieving sub-microsecond time synchronization over wireless links
   - Managing variable wireless channel conditions while maintaining determinism
   - Integrating with existing industrial protocols and systems
   - Ensuring seamless handover without disrupting time-critical communications
   - Coordinating between 5G and TSN scheduling mechanisms

8. Discuss the role of edge computing in private 5G networks. How does it enhance the capabilities of enterprise deployments?
   Answer: Edge computing plays a crucial role in private 5G networks by:
   - **Reducing Latency:** Processing data locally eliminates round-trip delays to distant cloud servers, enabling real-time applications
   - **Bandwidth Optimization:** Local processing reduces backhaul traffic by filtering and aggregating data at the edge
   - **Enhanced Privacy:** Sensitive data remains on-premises, addressing data sovereignty concerns
   - **Reliability:** Local processing continues even if WAN connectivity is lost
   - **Application Performance:** Enables compute-intensive applications like AI/ML inference, video analytics, and AR/VR rendering
     Edge computing transforms private 5G from a connectivity solution to a complete platform for digital transformation, enabling new use cases that require the combination of ultra-low latency communication and local compute resources.

9. What security benefits distinguish private 5G infrastructure from public cellular systems? Which additional safeguards should companies establish?
   Answer: Primary security advantages of private 5G include:
   - Physical Security: Infrastructure within enterprise control reduces unauthorized access risks
   - Network Isolation: Complete separation from public networks eliminates many external threats
   - Custom Security Policies: Tailored authentication, encryption, and access controls
   - Data Sovereignty: Sensitive data never leaves enterprise premises
   - Reduced Attack Surface: Limited exposure to internet-based threats

   Additional security measures enterprises should implement:
   - Zero-trust architecture principles
   - Systematic security validation:
   - Real-time threat intelligence
   - Supply chain security verification
   - Integration with enterprise security operations centers (SOC)
   - Post-quantum cryptography preparation
   - Regular security training for personnel

10. How will the integration of AI and machine learning transform private 5G network operations? Provide specific examples of AI applications in network management.
    Answer: AI/ML will fundamentally transform private 5G operations through:
    Predictive Maintenance:
    - Analyzing network performance patterns to predict equipment failures

- Scheduling maintenance before service disruptions occur
- Reducing downtime and maintenance costs

Dynamic Resource Optimization:

- Real-time allocation of network resources based on application demands
- Predictive capacity planning using historical usage patterns
- Automated load balancing across cells and frequency bands

Anomaly Detection:

- Identifying unusual traffic patterns indicating security threats
- Detecting performance degradation before users are impacted
- Automated root cause analysis of network issues

Intent-Based Networking:

- Translating high-level business policies into network configurations
- Self-healing networks that automatically resolve common issues
- Continuous optimization based on business objectives

Enhanced QoS Management:

- ML-based traffic classification and prioritization.
- Predictive QoS to anticipate and prevent degradation.
- Dynamic slice management based on real-time demands

References

3GPP. (2020a). TR 22.804, Study on Communication for Automation in Vertical Domains (Release 16). 3rd Generation Partnership Project.

3GPP. (2023a). TS 22.261, Service requirements for the 5G system (Release 18). 3rd Generation Partnership Project.

3GPP. (2023b). TS 22.104, Service requirements for cyber-physical control applications in vertical domains (Release 18). 3rd Generation Partnership Project.

3GPP. (2023c). TS 23.501, System architecture for the 5G System (5GS) (Release 18). 3rd Generation Partnership Project.

3GPP. (2023d). TS 38.101, NR; User Equipment (UE) radio transmission and reception (Release 18). 3rd Generation Partnership Project.

3GPP. (2023e). TS 33.501, Security architecture and procedures for 5G System (Release 18). 3rd Generation Partnership Project.

Agiwal, M., Roy, A., & Saxena, N. (2023). Next generation 5G wireless networks: A comprehensive survey. IEEE Communications Surveys & Tutorials, 18(3), 1617-1655. https://doi.org/10.1109/COMST.2016.2532458

Aijaz, A. (2020). Private 5G: The future of industrial wireless. IEEE Industrial Electronics Magazine, 14(4), 136-145. https://doi.org/10.1109/MIE.2020.3004975

Brown, G. (2020). Private 5G networks: Enterprise untethered. Heavy Reading White Paper.

Campion, M. C., Ranganathan, P., & Faruque, S. (2021). A comprehensive survey of 5G security challenges and solutions. IEEE Access, 9, 156211-156233. https://doi.org/10.1109/ACCESS.2021.3130095

Ericsson. (2022). Ericsson Mobility Report. Ericsson AB.

GSMA. (2021). Private 5G networks: A survey of the enterprise landscape. GSMA Intelligence.

Hedayati, M., Balasubramaniam, V., & Choi, S. (2023). TSN integration in 5G systems: Architecture, protocols, and procedures. IEEE Communications Standards Magazine, 6(1), 88-95. https://doi.org/10.1109/MCOMSTD.2022.3149124

Kalør, A. E., Guillaume, R., Nielsen, J. J., Mueller, A., & Popovski, P. (2024). Network slicing in Industry 4.0 applications: Abstraction methods and end-to-end analysis. IEEE Transactions on Industrial Informatics, 14(12), 5419-5427. https://doi.org/10.1109/TII.2018.2839721

Li, S., Da Xu, L., & Zhao, S. (2023). 5G Internet of Things: A survey. Journal of Industrial Information Integration, 10, 1-9. https://doi.org/10.1016/j.jii.2018.03.001

Ordonez-Lucena, J., Ameigeiras, P., Lopez, D., Ramos-Munoz, J. J., Lorca, J., & Folgueira, J. (2021). Network slicing for 5G with SDN/NFV: Concepts, architectures, and challenges. IEEE Communications Magazine, 55(5), 80-87. https://doi.org/10.1109/MCOM.2017.1600935

Qualcomm. (2022). The 5G Economy: How 5G will contribute to the global economy. Qualcomm Technologies, Inc.

Viswanathan, H., & Mogensen, P. E. (2020). Communications in the 6G era. IEEE Access, 8, 57063-57074. https://doi.org/10.1109/ACCESS.2020.2981745

World Economic Forum. (2021). 5G outlook series: The impact of mobile technology on the response to COVID-19. World Economic Forum, in collaboration with PwC.

Zhang, H., Liu, N., Chu, X., Long, K., Aghvami, A. H., & Leung, V. C. M. (2022). Network slicing based 5G and future mobile networks: Mobility, resource management, and challenges. IEEE Communications Surveys & Tutorials, 22(4), 2038-2075. https://doi.org/10.1109/COMST.2020.3024360

Chapter 11: Citizens Broadband Radio Service (CBRS)

Executive Summary

This section explores how the Citizens Broadband Radio Service has transformed wireless spectrum access in America. CBRS represents a groundbreaking approach to managing radio frequencies, specifically opening up spectrum in the 3550–3700 MHz range for business applications.

What makes this system unique is its layered structure. Think of it as a carefully orchestrated hierarchy where government operations maintain top priority, licensed operators get the next level of access, and general users can tap into whatever remains available. Everyone shares the same frequencies, but the system intelligently coordinates who gets to transmit when.

Two key technologies make this possible. The Spectrum Access System acts as the traffic controller, dynamically allocating frequencies to prevent interference. Meanwhile, Environmental Sensing Capability monitors the airwaves to protect incumbent federal users. Together, these systems ensure that priority users stay protected while still allowing maximum utilization of this valuable spectrum resource.

We will examine real-world uses ranging from building private cellular networks for businesses to creating wireless broadband connections in areas where laying cable isn't practical. The chapter concludes by walking through what organizations need to consider when implementing CBRS—from technical requirements to strategic planning for getting the most value from this technology.

The technical content presented in this chapter draws upon publicly available 3rd Generation Partnership Project (3GPP) specifications—including the TS 36 and TS 38 series for LTE and NR radio access technologies—as well as Federal Communications Commission (FCC) regulatory documentation, particularly 47 CFR Part 96 and associated Report and Orders governing the Citizens Broadband Radio Service. These authoritative sources, accessible at www.3gpp.org and through the Electronic Code of Federal Regulations (eCFR), provided the foundational technical and regulatory details referenced throughout this chapter. The author acknowledges 3GPP and the FCC as the definitive sources for the standards and regulatory provisions discussed herein and does not claim ownership of any such content.

Table of Contents

Introduction

Citizens Broadband Radio Service (CBRS) represents a significant evolution in how radio spectrum is allocated and managed in the United States. This regulatory framework opens a 150 MHz portion of the 3.5 GHz band (specifically, 3550-3700 MHz) for commercial wireless use—spectrum that was previously restricted to federal government operations, primarily military radar systems.

Established by the Federal Communications Commission in 2015 and made commercially available in 2020, CBRS introduces a novel spectrum-sharing approach. Rather than auctioning exclusive rights to specific frequencies, the CBRS framework allows multiple users to access the same spectrum through a dynamic coordination system. This shared-access model enables organizations to deploy private wireless networks without acquiring expensive spectrum licenses, making advanced wireless connectivity economically viable for enterprises that previously couldn't justify the investment.

The CBRS framework is particularly significant for private 5G deployments because it provides readily accessible, licensed-quality spectrum specifically suited for enterprise applications.

CBRS operates on a spectrum-sharing principle that allows multiple users to access the same frequencies without causing interference. Unlike traditional spectrum licensing where organizations purchase exclusive rights to specific frequencies, CBRS implements dynamic coordination that enables commercial users to access spectrum when incumbent government systems aren't actively using it. The FCC finalized regulations for this shared-access framework in 2015, establishing rules that protect existing federal users while opening the 3550-3700 MHz band to commercial wireless deployments (FCC, 2015). This represents a departure from the exclusive licensing model that has dominated U.S. spectrum policy for decades

Key Characteristics of CBRS

Key Characteristics of CBRS

1. **Tiered Access Structure:** CBRS breaks from conventional spectrum allocation by implementing a layered sharing system rather than following the typical licensed-or-unlicensed approach.
2. **Real-Time Coordination:** The system uses automation to manage frequency assignments on the fly, adjusting access as conditions change.
3. **The "Innovation Band" Designation:** Back in 2015, federal regulators gave this 3.5 GHz frequency range a special label, signaling their intent to make it available for emerging wireless applications and new market entrants.
4. **Accessible Economics:** Organizations can deploy wireless infrastructure in this spectrum without facing the hefty costs typically associated with purchasing exclusive frequency licenses.

Evolution and Historical Context

CBRS emerged from growing concerns about the shortage of available radio frequencies and the push to make better use of existing spectrum. In 2010, the National Telecommunications and Information Administration released its Fast Track Report, which floated the idea of opening up the 3.5 GHz range. The proposal suggested creating shared access to these frequencies, allowing both government operations and commercial entities to use the same band.

Timeline of CBRS Development

CBRS Development Timeline

Year	Milestone	Description
2010	NTIA Fast Track Report	Proposed opening the 3.5 GHz frequencies for joint government and commercial applications
2012	FCC Notice of Proposed Rulemaking	The Commission formally introduced the Citizens Broadband Radio Service concept in its December rulemaking document
2014	Further Notice	The FCC released detailed proposed rules
2015	Rules Adoption	The FCC established CBRS and a three-tiered framework
2017	FCC Process Completion	The Federal Communications Commission finalized regulations allowing businesses to operate in this spectrum, wrapping up work that started five years earlier
2020	Full Commercial Use	On January 27th, the FCC gave the green light for wireless carriers to begin full-scale commercial deployment across the CBRS band
2020	PAL Auction	The auction was the first of its kind, offering mid-band spectrum for wireless carriers' 5G services.

Early Trials and Deployments

Real-world testing of CBRS started well ahead of official commercial approval. Initial experiments took place in Finland during 2016, where Nokia partnered with VTT and other Finnish entities to explore the technology's potential. Meanwhile, American companies launched their own pilot programs to prove the system could work in practice:

- **Las Vegas Trial (2017):** A collaboration involving Nokia, Alphabet, and Qualcomm demonstrated LTE capabilities by streaming high-definition footage of race cars circling a Las Vegas speedway using CBRS frequencies.
- **Google Testing:** The tech giant ran experiments across multiple venues, including tests in Kansas City and at NASCAR racing events.

- **Verizon Consortium:** By summer 2017, Verizon had assembled a group of partners to pioneer the use of CBRS band 48 spectrum, demonstrating how it could enhance 4G LTE Advanced networks through carrier aggregation techniques.

CBRS Spectrum and Band Structure

CBRS frequencies sit in a prime spot within the radio spectrum, providing signal propagation qualities that work well whether you're deploying indoors or outdoors. Operating at 3.5 GHz, these signals behave similarly to standard Wi-Fi networks that run on 2.4 GHz and 5 GHz bands.

Spectrum Allocation

CBRS Spectrum Allocation

Frequency Range	Bandwidth	Usage Tiers	Channel Structure
3550-3650 MHz	100 MHz	Incumbent, PAL, GAA	10 MHz channels
3650-3700 MHz	50 MHz	Incumbent, GAA only	10 MHz channels
Total	150 MHz	Three-tier sharing	15 total channels

Technical Specifications

□ **3GPP Band Designation:** Within 3GPP standards, the US implementation of CBRS LTE uses the band 48 classification.

□ **Mobile Network Codes:** For identifying CBRS systems in America, two mobile network codes have been allocated: 315 and 010. These work in conjunction with mobile country code assignments for IMSI purposes.

□ **Channel Width:** Individual channels span 10 MHz each.

□ **Total Channels:** The 150 MHz allocation is divided into 15 separate channels.

Three-Tier Sharing Architecture

What sets CBRS apart is its layered access model, which allows different types of users to operate within the same frequencies simultaneously. This tiered approach ensures that priority users remain shielded from disruptive interference while still letting multiple parties share the spectrum.

Incumbent Access Tier

At the top of the CBRS hierarchy sit incumbent users, who hold absolute priority across the band. This category encompasses federal government operations throughout the full 3550-3700 MHz range, satellite ground stations receiving signals from space within 3600-3650 MHz, and legacy wireless broadband license holders operating between 3650-3700 MHz (though these licenses have time-limited protection).

Primary Incumbent Users

- Naval radar installations
- Defense Department communication systems
- Satellite earth stations receiving transmissions
- Pre-existing wireless broadband operators (on a temporary basis)

Safeguard Mechanisms

- Lower-tier users—both Priority Access License holders and General Authorized Access operators—cannot create interference that disrupts incumbent operations.
- Naval activities receive protection through designated coastal exclusion areas
- Satellite receiving facilities are shielded by established protection boundaries

Priority Access License (PAL) Tier

The PAL level occupies the middle position in the hierarchy, bridging the gap between protected incumbent operations and unrestricted general use. These Priority Access Licenses are distributed through auction processes, with geographic boundaries determined by individual counties.

PAL Characteristics

- **Channel Size:** Individual licenses cover 10 MHz of spectrum within the 3550-3650 MHz range.
- **License Duration:** Each license runs for ten years with renewal options available.
- **Geographic Unit:** Licenses follow county boundaries as established by the U.S. Census Bureau.
- **Channel Limits:** Any single county can have a maximum of seven PALs awarded, though no individual licensee may aggregate more than four channels.
- **Auction Results:** When the FCC conducted its 3.5 GHz spectrum auction in 2020, bidding extended through 76 rounds and generated total revenues of $4.58 billion.

General Authorized Access (GAA) Tier

Within the CBRS framework, General Authorized Access functions as the broadest entry point for spectrum users. This tier operates under regulatory authorization that welcomes diverse participants without requiring individual licenses. Think of it as the unlicensed highway of CBRS—designed intentionally to maximize accessibility and encourage innovation across various industries and applications.

The fundamental philosophy behind GAA centers on inclusivity. Rather than restricting access through traditional licensing barriers, this tier employs rule-based authorization that allows virtually any qualified entity to utilize available spectrum. This approach democratizes access to valuable radio frequencies, enabling everyone from small startups to large enterprises to deploy wireless solutions.

GAA Characteristics

- No individual licensing required
- Access to full 150 MHz band (where available)
- Must accept interference from all higher tiers
- Opportunistic use of unused PAL channels
- Ideal for private networks and enterprise deployments

Spectrum Access System (SAS)

At the core of CBRS operations lies the Spectrum Access System, which serves as an intelligent orchestration platform for managing shared spectrum resources. This automated infrastructure makes real-time decisions about spectrum allocation, ensuring efficient coexistence among different user categories.

How the System Functions

The SAS operates as a centralized decision-making engine that continuously monitors spectrum usage and coordinates access permissions. Rather than relying on static frequency assignments, this platform dynamically allocates available bandwidth based on current demands and priority hierarchies. Think of it as an air traffic control system for radio frequencies—constantly evaluating requests, preventing interference, and optimizing resource distribution.

SAS Architecture and Components

This management framework handles several critical operational functions:

The system processes registration requests from devices seeking spectrum access, validating their credentials and technical parameters. It calculates interference scenarios to determine safe operating conditions for concurrent users. Geographic databases integrate with the platform to enforce location-specific rules and protect incumbent services. Through continuous monitoring, the SAS adjusts assignments when conditions change—whether that means an incumbent user requiring protection or shifting demand patterns among commercial operators.

Core SAS Functions

1. **Spectrum Assignment:** Dynamically allocates channels to CBSDs
2. **Interference Protection:** Ensures higher-tier users are protected
3. **Database Management:** Maintains records of all active grants
4. **Coordination:** Manages interactions between different user tiers

CBRS System Architecture

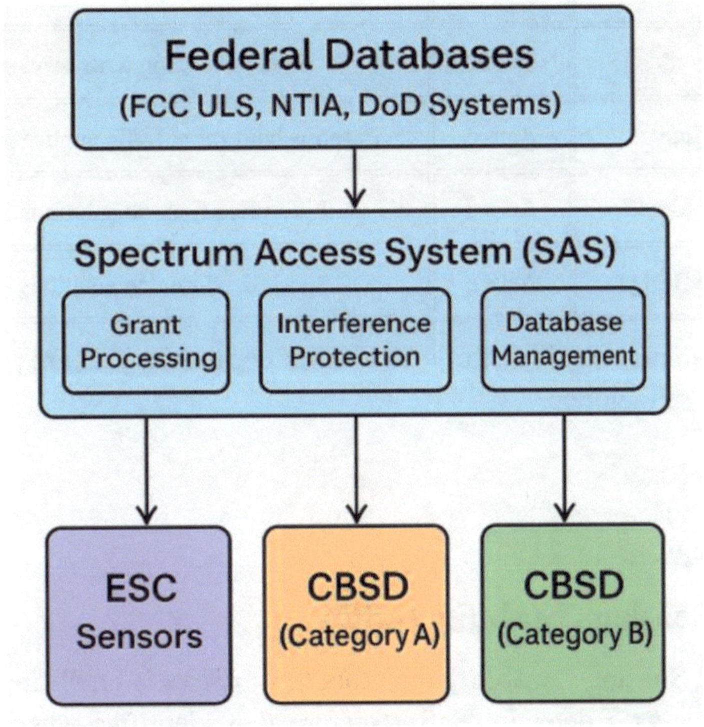

SAS Providers and Certification

Multiple companies have received FCC authorization to serve as SAS operators. Working together, the Wireless Telecommunications Bureau and the Office of Engineering and Technology—in partnership with NTIA and the Department of Defense—granted approval to the following entities to function as Spectrum Access Administrators for full commercial rollout

FCC-Approved SAS Providers (as of 2024)

Provider	Status	Key Features
Federated Wireless	Active	Nationwide ESC network, patented algorithms
Google	Active	Cloud-based platform, extensive coverage
CommScope	Exited 2022	No longer providing SAS services
Sony	Active	Purpose-built for specific applications
Amdocs	Active	Enterprise-focused solutions
Key Bridge	Active	Specialized implementations

Second Wave Applicants: It is one of a handful of companies that are part of a second wave of SAS providers. These include:

- Fairspectrum
- Nokia
- RED Technologies

Environmental Sensing Capability (ESC)

The Environmental Sensing Capability monitors the airwaves in real-time to safeguard federal operations. ESC serves as a detection infrastructure that identifies when incumbent users are transmitting, then relays this information to the Spectrum Access System to enable coordinated spectrum sharing.

ESC Network Characteristics

- **Deployment:** A sensor network monitors incumbent activity throughout the CBRS frequencies, with most installations concentrated in coastal regions.
- **Function:** These sensors identify federal transmissions within and near the 3.5 GHz range, forwarding alerts to SAS platforms.
- **Protection Zones:** The system automatically establishes exclusion areas upon detecting incumbent operations.

- **Dynamic Response:** When incumbent activity appears, PAL and GAA operators are redirected to other available channels.

CBRS Network Components

Citizens Broadband Radio Service Devices (CBSDs)

CBSDs are the radio access points that transmit in the CBRS band. They come in two categories with different power levels and use cases.

CBSD Categories

Parameter	Category A	Category B
Maximum Power	24 dBm (per 10 MHz)	47 dBm (per 10 MHz)
Maximum EIRP	30 dBm (1 watt)	47 dBm (50 watts)
Typical Use	Indoor, low-power outdoor	Outdoor, high-power
Installation	Self-install allowed	CPI required

CBSD Registration Process: Citizens Broadband Service Devices must enroll with a Spectrum Access System and submit requests for frequency authorization. These authorization requests include detailed specifications such as which radio channels will be used, the Effective Isotropic Radiated Power levels needed, and peak transmission power limits.

Network Infrastructure Elements

A complete CBRS network requires several infrastructure components beyond the CBSDs:

Core Network Elements

1. **Evolved Packet Core (EPC):**–Any private cellular deployment needs a mobile core infrastructure to handle network operations. This includes managing how devices connect to the network, handling mobility as users move between small cells, and routing data traffic through the system.
2. **SIM Management:** Physical or eSIM provisioning for device authentication
3. **Network Management System:** Monitoring and configuration tools
4. **Backhaul Infrastructure:** Connectivity to the internet and enterprise networks

Applications and Use Cases

CBRS technology enables a wide range of applications across various industries, from private enterprise networks to public safety systems.

Private Networks

Building private LTE and 5G networks stands out as one of the most important uses for CBRS. The technology creates a substantial opportunity for businesses and organizations that want to deploy their own cellular infrastructure—whether using 5G, LTE, or even 3GPP standards—without needing traditional spectrum licenses.

Key Benefits of CBRS Private Networks

- **Enhanced Security:** The system incorporates SIM-based authentication and employs centralized encryption as standard features.
- **Superior Coverage:** Access points can provide coverage areas up to ten times larger than typical solutions, functioning effectively both inside buildings and outdoors.
- **Dedicated Spectrum:** Communications occur in clean frequencies free from interference.
- **Quality of Service:** Mission-critical applications receive guaranteed performance level

Fixed Wireless Access

CBRS offers a strong option for bringing high-speed internet to areas lacking adequate service. Primary applications for CBRS network installations include Fixed Wireless Access solutions, increasing mobile network capacity through densification, neutral host setups, and private cellular systems.

FWA Applications

- Rural broadband delivery
- Last-mile connectivity solutions
- Backup internet services
- Temporary event connectivity

Industrial and Enterprise Applications

The versatility of CBRS has led to adoption across numerous industry verticals:

CBRS Use Cases by Industry

Industry	Applications	Benefits
Manufacturing	Warehousing and logistics facilities: extended-range wireless for automated machinery and robotic systems	Improved automation, real-time monitoring
Healthcare	Private cellular infrastructure enabling collaboration software on staff mobile devices	Secure communications, asset tracking
Venues	Major event spaces: segmented networks for behind-the-scenes operations while keeping Wi-Fi available for attendees	Enhanced crowd management, staff coordination
Retail	Interference-free dedicated frequencies for business-owned devices and staff equipment in high-traffic store settings	Reliable POS systems, inventory management
Education	K-12 institutions: connecting underserved areas through outdoor wireless links extending to student residences	Bridge digital divide, remote learning

Specific Deployment Examples

- **Universities:** California State University, Stanislaus launched a 5G private local area network across its campus in 2022, built on CBRS technology.
- **Entertainment Venues:** Multiple stadiums and arenas for enhanced connectivity
- **Smart Cities:** Traffic management and public safety applications

Implementation Considerations

Deploying a CBRS network requires careful planning and consideration of various technical and regulatory factors.

Technical Considerations

1. **Coverage Planning**:
    - Indoor CBRS LTE access points provide approximately four times the coverage area of standard indoor Wi-Fi access points.
    - Propagation characteristics similar to Wi-Fi, but with better building penetration
2. **Device Compatibility**:
    - Most modern smartphones—including Apple iPhones and Google Pixels—now include support for CBRS frequencies
    - Growing ecosystem of CBRS-compatible enterprise devices

3. **Network Design Complexity**:
    - Setting up CBRS infrastructure has historically involved more complexity than Wi-Fi deployment, partly due to the need for additional components like Evolved Packet Cores and Spectrum Access Systems.

Regulatory Requirements

1. **Professional Installation**:
    - Category B devices must be installed by Certified Professional Installers (CPI)
    - FCC mandates proper registration with SAS
2. **Compliance**:
    - Adherence to FCC Part 96 rules
    - Coordination with SAS providers
    - Respect for incumbent protection zones

Cost Considerations

CBRS vs. Traditional Network Costs

Factor	CBRS	Traditional Cellular	Wi-Fi
Spectrum Cost	Free (GAA) or Auction (PAL)	Licensed (expensive)	Free
Equipment Cost	Higher than Wi-Fi	Highest	Lowest
Coverage per AP	4x Wi-Fi	Highest	Baseline
Installation	Moderate complexity	High complexity	Low complexity
Operating Cost	SAS fees required	Carrier fees	Minimal

CBRS: Ongoing Innovation and Expansion

The CBRS landscape remains dynamic, with technological advances and policy refinements continuously reshaping what's possible within this shared spectrum framework.

Next-Generation Network Capabilities

Mobile network technology within CBRS is migrating toward 5G New Radio standards, moving beyond the initial LTE foundation. This shift unlocks substantially improved performance metrics—particularly in responsiveness and data throughput. Networks can now handle more sophisticated applications that demand near-instantaneous communication, opening doors for use cases previously constrained by technical limitations.

The architectural flexibility of 5G NR aligns naturally with CBRS's dynamic allocation model. Operators can deploy specialized network configurations tailored to specific scenarios, whether that involves massive sensor deployments in manufacturing facilities or high-bandwidth applications in dense urban environments.

Market Adoption and Device Proliferation

The hardware ecosystem supporting CBRS has experienced remarkable growth. Priority Access License deployments alone now encompass over 114,000 registered devices—a clear indicator of commercial traction. This figure represents only one segment of the broader device landscape, which continues expanding across multiple categories.

FCC. (2015). Report and Order and Second Further Notice of Proposed Rulemaking: Amendment of the Commission's Rules with Regard to Commercial Operations in the 3550-3650 MHz Band, GN Docket No. 12-354, 30 FCC Rcd 3959.

Manufacturers have responded to market demand by developing increasingly diverse equipment options. Industrial IoT sensors, private network infrastructure, and specialized wireless systems now routinely incorporate CBRS capabilities. This hardware diversification creates a reinforcing cycle: more devices drive network deployments, while expanded network availability encourages further device development.

Market Growth

Recent data shows significant CBRS adoption:

- As of July 1, 2024, General Authorized Access represented 71.4% of operational CBSDs, while GAA accounted for 82.3% of all active authorizations.
- 67.5% of all active CBSDs were deployed in rural census blocks

Regulatory Evolution

The FCC continues to refine CBRS rules to improve the system:

- Potential power level increases for broader coverage
- Enhanced sharing mechanisms
- Streamlined deployment procedures

Conclusion

Citizens Broadband Radio Service represents a revolutionary approach to spectrum management that balances the needs of incumbent federal users with the growing demand for commercial wireless services. Through its innovative three-tiered sharing framework, automated spectrum management via SAS, and real-time incumbent protection through ESC, CBRS enables efficient use of valuable mid-band spectrum.

The technology has proven successful across various applications, from private enterprise networks to fixed wireless access solutions. With growing device support, expanding use cases, and continued regulatory refinement, CBRS is positioned to play a crucial role in the future of wireless communications, particularly in enabling private 5G networks and bridging the digital divide in underserved areas.

As organizations increasingly require dedicated, secure, and high-performance wireless connectivity, CBRS provides a cost-effective alternative to traditional licensed spectrum while offering superior performance compared to unlicensed solutions like Wi-Fi. The continued evolution of the ecosystem, combined with the transition to 5G technology, ensures that CBRS will remain at the forefront of wireless innovation for years to come.

Knowledge Check

1. What is the frequency range of the CBRS band?
   a) 2.4-2.5 GHz
   b) 3550-3700 MHz
   c) 5.8-5.9 GHz
   d) 28-29 GHz

2. Which tier has the highest priority in the CBRS three-tier system?
   a) General Authorized Access (GAA)
   b) Priority Access License (PAL)
   c) Incumbent Access
   d) Commercial Access

3. What is the maximum EIRP for a Category A CBSD?
   a) 24 dBm
   b) 30 dBm
   c) 47 dBm
   d) 50 dBm

4. How many PALs can be licensed in a single county?
   a) 5
   b) 7
   c) 10
   d) 15

5. What is the 3GPP band designation for CBRS?
   a) Band 42
   b) Band 46
   c) Band 48
   d) Band 50

6. Explain the role of Environmental Sensing Capability (ESC) in protecting incumbent users in the CBRS band.

7. Compare and contrast the benefits and limitations of PAL versus GAA access in CBRS.

8. How does CBRS enable private LTE/5G networks, and what advantages does it offer over traditional Wi-Fi deployments?

9. Describe the process by which a CBSD obtains a spectrum grant from a SAS.

10. What are the key considerations for an enterprise planning to deploy a CBRS-based private network?

Answers

1. What is the frequency range of the CBRS band?
   a) 2.4-2.5 GHz
   b) 3550-3700 MHz
   c) 5.8-5.9 GHz
   d) 28-29 GHz
   Answer: b) 3550-3700 MHz

2. Which tier has the highest priority in the CBRS three-tier system?
   a) General Authorized Access (GAA)
   b) Priority Access License (PAL)
   c) Incumbent Access
   d) Commercial Access
   Answer: c) Incumbent Access
3. What is the maximum EIRP for a Category A CBSD?
   a) 24 dBm
   b) 30 dBm
   c) 47 dBm
   d) 50 dBm
   Answer: b) 30 dBm (1 watt)
4. How many PALs can be licensed in a single county?
   a) 5
   b) 7
   c) 10
   d) 15
   Answer: b) 7
5. What is the 3GPP band designation for CBRS?
   a) Band 42
   b) Band 46
   c) Band 48
   d) Band 50
   Answer: c) Band 48

FCC. (2015). Report and Order and Second Further Notice of Proposed Rulemaking: Amendment of the Commission's Rules with Regard to Commercial Operations in the 3550-3650 MHz Band, GN Docket No. 12-354, 30 FCC Rcd 3959.

Explain the role of Environmental Sensing Capability (ESC) in protecting incumbent users in the CBRS band.

Answer: ESC is a network of sensors deployed primarily along coastlines that continuously monitors the CBRS band for incumbent transmissions, particularly from Navy radar systems. When incumbent activity is detected, the ESC immediately communicates this information to the SAS, which then creates dynamic protection zones. The SAS automatically reassigns PAL and GAA users to different channels or reduces their transmission power to prevent interference with the incumbent operations. This real-time detection and response system ensures federal users can operate without harmful interference while maximizing spectrum availability for commercial users.

6. Compare and contrast the benefits and limitations of PAL versus GAA access in CBRS.
   Answer: PAL provides interference protection from GAA users, offers predictable spectrum access for 10 years (renewable), and is ideal for mission-critical applications requiring guaranteed quality of service. However, PALs require participation in competitive auctions, have geographic limitations (county-based), and are restricted to 3550-3650 MHz. GAA offers free access to the full 150 MHz band, allows immediate deployment without auctions, and provides flexibility for various use cases. The limitations include no interference protection, potential service interruption from higher-tier users, and less predictable performance in congested areas.

7. How does CBRS enable private LTE/5G networks, and what advantages does it offer over traditional Wi-Fi deployments?
   Answer: CBRS enables private networks by providing access to licensed-quality spectrum without requiring expensive spectrum licenses (for GAA users). It offers SIM-based authentication for enhanced security, provides 4x greater coverage per access point compared to Wi-Fi, operates in a cleaner spectrum with less interference, supports seamless mobility and handoffs, and enables deterministic quality of service for critical applications. These advantages make CBRS ideal for large facilities, outdoor deployments, and applications requiring reliable, secure connectivity.

8. Describe the process by which a CBSD obtains a spectrum grant from a SAS.
   Answer: The CBSD first registers with the SAS, providing its FCC ID, location coordinates, antenna height, indoor/outdoor status, and category type. The CBSD then requests a spectrum grant, specifying desired channels and transmission parameters. The SAS checks incumbent protection requirements, verifies no interference to higher-tier users, considers all active grants in the area, and performs interference calculations. If approved, the SAS issues a grant specifying authorized channels, maximum transmission power, and grant duration. The CBSD must periodically renew its grant and immediately cease transmission if instructed by the SAS.

9. What are the key considerations for an enterprise planning to deploy a CBRS-based private network?

Answer: Enterprises must consider coverage requirements and conduct RF planning, determine whether to use GAA or acquire PAL licenses, select appropriate CBSD categories for indoor/outdoor use, choose compatible devices and ensure SIM provisioning, select and integrate with a certified SAS provider, deploy necessary core network infrastructure (EPC/5GC), arrange for CPI services if using Category B devices, plan for ongoing SAS fees and operational costs, ensure integration with existing IT infrastructure, and develop policies for network access and security. Additionally, they should consider future scalability and 5G migration paths.

FCC. (2015). Report and Order and Second Further Notice of Proposed Rulemaking: Amendment of the Commission's Rules with Regard to Commercial Operations in the 3550-3650 MHz Band, GN Docket No. 12-354, 30 FCC Rcd 3959.

References

Federal Communications Commission. (2015). *Report and Order and Second Further Notice of Proposed Rulemaking: Amendment of the Commission's Rules with Regard to Commercial Operations in the 3550-3650 MHz Band*. FCC 15-47.

Federal Communications Commission. (2020). *3.5 GHz Band Overview*. Retrieved from https://www.fcc.gov/wireless/bureau-divisions/mobility-division/35-ghz-band/35-ghz-band-overview

National Telecommunications and Information Administration. (2024). *An Analysis of Aggregate CBRS SAS Data from April 2021 to July 2024*. U.S. Department of Commerce.

OnGo Alliance. (2024). *CBRS Alliance Specifications and Technical Reports*. Available at https://www.cbralliance.org/specifications/

Wireless Innovation Forum. (2024). *CBRS Standards and Certification Programs*. Retrieved from https://cbrs.wirelessinnovation.org/

3rd Generation Partnership Project. (2023). *Technical Specification 36.101: Evolved Universal Terrestrial Radio Access (E-UTRA); User Equipment (UE) radio transmission and reception*. Release 17.

Institute of Electrical and Electronics Engineers. (2023). *IEEE 802.11-2023: Standard for Information Technology—Telecommunications and Information Exchange between Systems—Local and Metropolitan Area Networks—Specific Requirements*. IEEE Standards Association.

Dynamic Spectrum Alliance. (2023). *Model Rules for Spectrum Sharing*. Available at http://dynamicspectrumalliance.org/

Federal Communications Commission. (2023). *Part 96—Citizens Broadband Radio Service*. Title 47 of the Code of Federal Regulations.

Ericsson. (2024). *Citizens Broadband Radio Service (CBRS) Product Portfolio*. Technical White Paper. Retrieved from https://www.ericsson.com/en/small-cells/cbrs

FCC. (2015). *Report and Order and Second Further Notice of Proposed Rulemaking: Amendment of the Commission's Rules with Regard to Commercial Operations in the 3550-3650 MHz Band*, GN Docket No. 12-354, 30 FCC Rcd 3959.

Chapter 12: Limitations of 5G and Need for B5G/6G

Executive Summary

This chapter examines the fundamental limitations of 5G technology that necessitate the development of Beyond 5G (B5G) and 6G networks. Despite significant advancements, 5G faces critical challenges in infrastructure deployment, spectrum utilization, energy efficiency, and meeting emerging application requirements. The chapter analyzes technical constraints, including limited millimeter-wave propagation, complex network slicing implementation, and security vulnerabilities. It explores how emerging user needs—from holographic communications to AI-native applications—exceed 5G's capabilities. The discussion extends to the vision for 6G networks, expected to launch commercially around 2030, which will address these limitations through revolutionary technologies, including terahertz communications, AI-driven network optimization, and sustainable design principles. This comprehensive analysis provides insights into why the evolution beyond 5G is not merely incremental but essential for supporting future digital society needs.

Table of Contents

Introduction

Mobile networks entered their fifth generation with ambitious promises: blazing-fast data speeds, near-instantaneous responsiveness, and the capacity to connect countless devices simultaneously. Yet the rollout of 5G technology hasn't followed the smooth trajectory that industry experts initially predicted. Instead of a straightforward march toward widespread implementation, carriers and operators have encountered a complex landscape where progress happens incrementally, with each market and region presenting unique challenges.

The reality on the ground tells a different story than early forecasts suggested. While telecommunications companies have poured substantial resources into building out 5G infrastructure, and while the underlying technology has certainly matured, critical obstacles remain. These barriers continue to hold back the technology from delivering on its most transformative potential—the vision of a world where virtually everything connects wirelessly in real-time. The gap between 5G's theoretical capabilities and its practical deployment reveals deeper issues that go beyond simply installing new equipment or allocating spectrum.

As of early 2025, while North America continues to set the pace for 5G innovation with strong operator investment and an accelerating shift toward standalone architecture, the technology still faces significant challenges. The gap between 5G's theoretical capabilities and practical implementation has become increasingly apparent, driving the need for next-generation solutions.

Technical Limitations and Deployment Challenges of 5G

Infrastructure and Coverage Limitations

Building out 5G networks presents a fundamental challenge that stems from the physics of radio waves themselves. The technology relies heavily on millimeter-wave spectrum, which behaves very differently from the frequencies used in previous generations of wireless networks. These high-frequency signals don't travel far—their range is severely limited compared to the lower frequencies that powered 4G LTE.

This physical constraint creates a massive infrastructure problem. To provide adequate coverage, carriers must deploy vastly more cell sites than ever before. We're talking about small cellular equipment mounted on street lights, utility poles, and building facades—creating what amounts to a blanket of mini-cell towers spread throughout coverage areas. The density required is unprecedented in telecommunications, and it's exactly this need for such extensive buildout that makes 5G deployment both expensive and time-consuming.

5G Infrastructure Requirements and Limitations

Aspect	Challenge	Impact
Cell Density	Ultra-dense small cell deployment required	High infrastructure cost
Coverage Range	Limited mmWave propagation (typically <500m)	Need for more base stations
Backhaul	Requires fiber optic connections with 10 Gbps rates	Significant investment needed
Site Acquisition	Multiple antenna placements on buildings	Complex negotiations and permits
Indoor Penetration	Poor building penetration for high frequencies	Additional indoor infrastructure

Beyond the density of cell sites, there's another critical piece of the puzzle: connecting all those small cells back to the core network. Each mini-tower needs a high-capacity link, and wireless backhaul often isn't sufficient for the data loads 5G promises to handle. That means fiber optic cables—lots of them.

Research from Deloitte highlights the scale of this fiber buildout requirement. Their analysis suggests the United States alone would need fiber infrastructure investments approaching $150 billion to fully unlock 5G's capabilities. That's an enormous capital expenditure, and it represents a significant financial hurdle that slows down how quickly operators can expand their networks across the country.

Spectrum and Signal Propagation Challenges

The radio spectrum that 5G relies on creates inherent challenges rooted in basic electromagnetic principles. Millimeter-wave frequencies—the bands where 5G delivers its highest performance—operate at a physical disadvantage compared to the lower frequencies used by earlier cellular technologies. These shorter wavelengths can't propagate as effectively through the air. When you transmit at the same power level, signals in the millimeter-wave range simply don't reach as far as the frequencies that carried 3G and 4G traffic.

5G Frequency Band Characteristics and Limitations

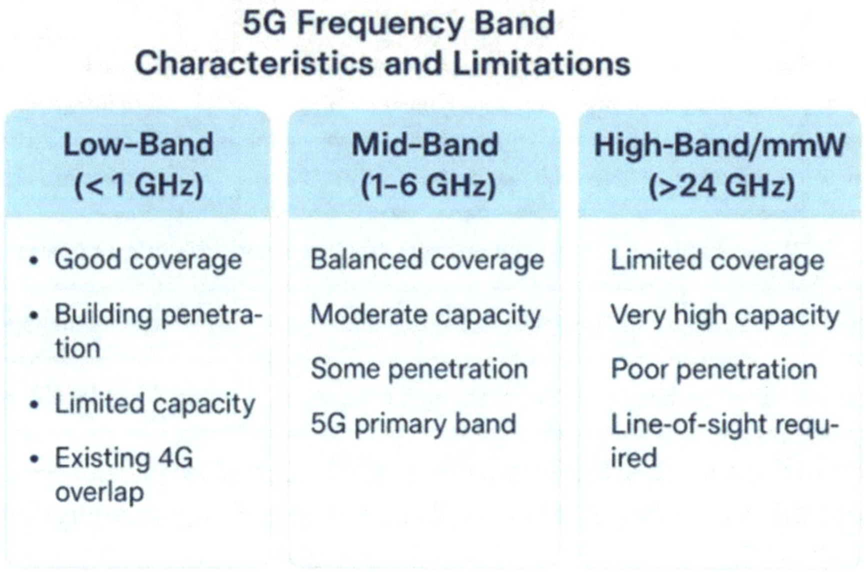

The surrounding environment plays a major role in how well 5G signals perform. Physical obstructions like foliage, structures, and various barriers block these high-frequency transmissions, forcing network planners to carefully position cell sites to maintain clear signal paths. Weather conditions add another layer of complexity—precipitation and atmospheric moisture can degrade the quality of millimeter-wave and microwave transmissions as these signals travel through the air.

Energy Consumption and Sustainability Issues

- 5G networks consume significantly more energy than their predecessors due to:
- Higher frequency operations requiring more power
- Dense network infrastructure with numerous small cells
- Advanced features like massive MIMO and beamforming
- Always-on connectivity for billions of IoT devices

The NTIA's request for comments on 6G development specifically asks about concerns regarding the energy efficiency of 6G equipment and networks, highlighting that current 5G energy consumption levels are unsustainable for future scaling.

Security Vulnerabilities and Privacy Concerns

5G networks introduce new security challenges that current implementations struggle to address adequately. Various cutting-edge technologies are being developed to meet these challenges, but ensuring data security and privacy and dealing with increased network infrastructure complexity remain important issues.

5G Security Challenges

Security Domain	Vulnerability	Potential Impact
Network Slicing	Inter-slice communications and side channel attacks	Data leakage between slices
Edge Computing	Distributed attack surface	Increased entry points
IoT Integration	Billions of potentially vulnerable devices	Mass botnet attacks
User Privacy	Network slice identifier transmission revealing user patterns	Anonymity concerns

Cost and Economic Barriers

While infrastructure presents obvious hurdles, the financial and business strategy questions around 5G prove equally daunting. Survey data reveals that nearly one in three telecommunications professionals—31 percent—point to monetization and business model issues as their toughest obstacle when rolling out 5G services.

Several economic factors create this complexity. The sheer expense of building out the necessary network density strains capital budgets. Then there's the uncertainty about whether these investments will generate adequate returns—carriers are pouring billions into upgrades without clear visibility on profitability timelines.

Perhaps most telling, that same 31 percent of survey participants identified pricing strategy as their single biggest headache. How do you charge customers for 5G? Consumers show resistance to premium pricing for the full suite of 5G capabilities, making it difficult to recoup deployment costs through traditional subscription increases.

Operational and Implementation Challenges

Network Slicing Complexity

Network slicing, a key 5G feature, faces significant implementation challenges. Currently, 5G network slicing specifications do not prescribe how network slices are implemented, leading to potential variability and inconsistency.

Network Slicing Implementation Challenges

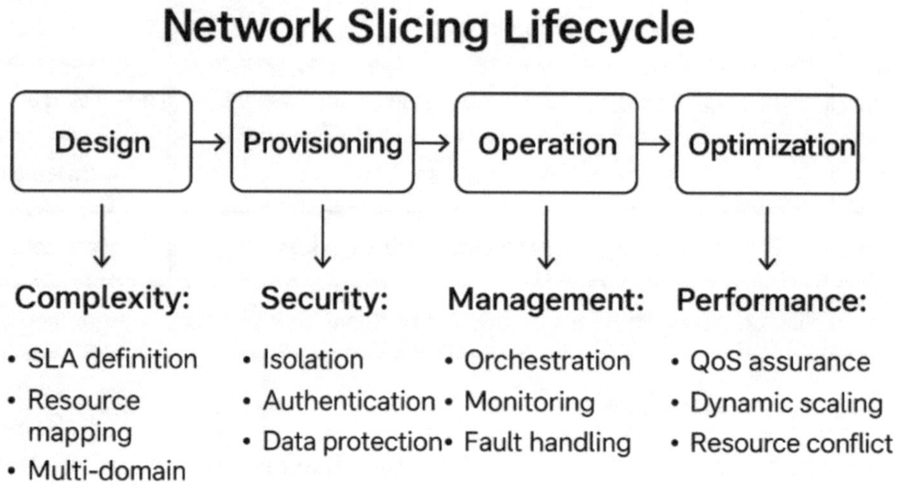

Interoperability and Standardization Issues

The deployment of 5G networks requires collaboration and interoperability between different stakeholders, but differences in technical standards, business models, and regulatory frameworks create barriers. Key interoperability challenges include:

- Vendor-specific implementations
- Multi-vendor integration complexity
- Roaming and interconnection limitations
- O-RAN adoption barriers

Skilled Workforce Shortage

Most companies find themselves facing a double-edged problem when it comes to their technical staff. Their existing teams often lack the expertise needed to handle advanced 5G implementations. At the same time, the broader job market doesn't offer enough qualified candidates to fill these gaps. This talent shortage has become a serious bottleneck in getting 5G networks up and running. The expertise deficit spans several areas:

- Network virtualization expertise
- Cloud-native architecture knowledge
- Security in distributed systems
- AI/ML for network optimization

Emerging User Needs and Future Requirements

Ultra-Massive Machine Type Communications

The 5G standard brought support for connecting huge numbers of devices simultaneously—what's known as massive Machine Type Communications (mMTC). However, the use cases now emerging demand even greater capacity than what 5G currently provides. Looking ahead to 6G networks, Ultramassive Machine Type Communication is expected to handle the requirements of next-generation applications. These include industrial IoT deployments, intelligent building management systems, and supply chains where nearly every component can communicate and share data.

Evolution of Communication Requirements

Parameter	5G Capability	Emerging Need (6G Target)	Gap Analysis
Device Density	1 million/km²	10 million/km²	10x increase needed
Energy per Bit	Baseline	100x reduction	Sustainability requirement
Latency	1 ms	0.1 ms	Sub-millisecond needed
Reliability	99.999%	99.9999%	Ultra-high reliability

Holographic Communications and Extended Reality

Traffic is expected to grow exponentially, and cost-efficient support of this traffic increase is critical for 6G networks, especially for new use cases such as holographic communication.

Current 5G networks cannot support:

- Real-time holographic telepresence
- Truly immersive extended reality
- Digital twin synchronization at scale
- Brain-computer interfaces

AI-Native Network Requirements

Machine learning capabilities feature prominently across 6G forecasts, spanning everything from building AI-ready infrastructure to using AI for the actual design, optimization, and management of 6G network elements, protocols, and day-to-day operations. Unlike previous-generation networks, 5G wasn't architected with artificial intelligence as a core building block from the start. This foundational gap creates several constraints that limit what 5G networks can accomplish on their own: they struggle to tune themselves automatically as conditions change, they lack robust predictive maintenance to anticipate and avoid outages, they can't shift resources fluidly based on demand patterns, and they're unable to deliver intelligent, context-aware services.

Sustainability and Green Communications

Energy consumption and environmental impact have emerged as increasingly important considerations that current 5G networks struggle to fully resolve. Industry analysis shows that 5G infrastructure can operate with efficiency gains reaching up to 90% compared to older 4G systems.

Yet this improvement alone doesn't meet the sustainability targets that future networks need to achieve. The sixth generation of mobile technology promises to push energy efficiency significantly further, creating wireless infrastructure that operates with a substantially smaller environmental footprint.

The Path Forward: B5G and 6G Vision

6G Development Timeline and Standardization

The evolution toward 6G follows a structured timeline with clear milestones:

6G Development Timeline

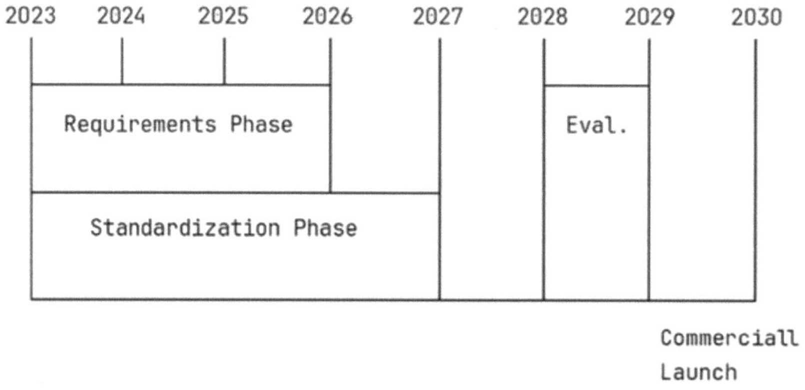

6G Development Timeline

6G will likely launch commercially in 2030, with standardization slated for 2023-2026 and evaluations beginning in 2028. At the March 2024 3GPP meetings, a timeline for 6G standardization was decided, with 3GPP committed to being the main specification body for 6G.

Key Technologies and Innovations

6G networks will incorporate revolutionary technologies to address 5G limitations:

6G Technology Enablers

Technology	Description	Addresses 5G Limitation
Terahertz Communications	W band (92-120 GHz) and D band (120-175 GHz), offering extreme bandwidth	Limited spectrum capacity
AI-Native Architecture	Built-in AI for all network functions	Manual optimization limits
Quantum Communications	Quantum key distribution for security	Current encryption vulnerabilities

Technology	Description	Addresses 5G Limitation
Digital Holography	Support for 3D holographic content	Bandwidth constraints
Zero-Energy Devices	Harvesting ambient energy	Sustainability issues

ITU-R. (2023). Recommendation ITU-R M.2160: Framework and overall objectives of the future development of IMT for 2030 and beyond. International Telecommunication Union. https://www.itu.int/rec/R-REC-M.2160

Global Initiatives and Research Efforts

Multiple countries and organizations are driving 6G research:

- **United States:** Next G Alliance aims to advance 6G research focusing on applications, societal needs, sustainability, and technology
- **Europe:** Several 6G research projects leveraging public-private partnerships
- **Asia:** Japan's Ministry earmarked JPY 66.2 billion for the Beyond 5G (6G) Fund Project
- **China:** IMT-2030 Promotion Group established to advance 6G R&D efforts

Conclusion

The limitations of 5G technology are not merely technical hurdles but fundamental constraints that prevent the realization of a truly connected and intelligent future society. From infrastructure challenges requiring massive investments to physics-based propagation limitations, from energy consumption concerns to emerging application requirements that exceed 5G's design parameters, these limitations necessitate a revolutionary rather than evolutionary approach.

The path to 6G represents more than an incremental upgrade; it embodies a paradigm shift in how we conceive, design, and deploy wireless networks. With AI-native architectures, sustainable design principles, and support for applications that seem like science fiction today, 6G will address not only the technical limitations of 5G but also the broader societal needs for inclusive, secure, and environmentally responsible connectivity.

As stated by industry leaders, spectrum policy is now the limiting factor for continued growth, and the future of 5G depends as much on economics and governance as on technology. This reality underscores that the transition to 6G will require not just technological innovation but also new regulatory frameworks, business models, and international cooperation.

Knowledge Check

1. What is the primary infrastructure challenge for 5G mmWave deployment?
   a) Lack of available spectrum
   b) Limited propagation range requiring ultra-dense small cell networks
   c) Incompatibility with existing 4G infrastructure
   d) High latency issues

2. According to research, what percentage of telecommunications stakeholders identified business model challenges as their most difficult 5G issue?
   a) 14%
   b) 19%
   c) 31%
   d) 64%

3. When is 6G expected to launch commercially?
   a) 2027
   b) 2032
   c) 2030
   d) 2031

4. Which frequency bands are identified for 6G sub-terahertz communications?
   a) C-band and L-band
   b) Ka-band and Ku-band
   c) S-band and X-band
   d) W-band (92-120 GHz) and D-band (120-175 GHz)

5. What is the device density target for 6G networks compared to 5G?
   a) 2x increase
   b) 5x increase
   c) 10x increase
   d) 100x increase

6. How do the physical limitations of millimeter-wave propagation impact 5G deployment strategies, and what alternative approaches might operators consider?

7. Analyze the security challenges introduced by network slicing and explain why current 5G implementations struggle to address them adequately.

8. Evaluate the role of AI in addressing 5G limitations and enabling 6G networks.

9. Discuss the sustainability challenges of 5G and how 6G aims to address environmental concerns.

10. Compare the emerging user needs that 5G cannot satisfy with 6G's envisioned capabilities.

Answers

1. What is the primary infrastructure challenge for 5G mmWave deployment?
   a) Lack of available spectrum
   b) Limited propagation range requiring ultra-dense small cell networks
   c) Incompatibility with existing 4G infrastructure
   d) High latency issues
   Answer: b) Limited propagation range requiring ultra-dense small cell networks
   mmWave frequencies can only cover short distances, requiring dense small cell deployment.

2. According to research, what percentage of telecommunications stakeholders identified business model challenges as their most difficult 5G issue?
   a) 14%
   b) 19%
   c) 31%
   d) 64%
   Answer: c) 31%
   31% of respondents indicated business model challenges were the most difficult.

3. When is 6G expected to launch commercially?
   a) 2027
   b) 2032
   c) 2030
   d) 2031
   Answer: c) 2030
   6G is expected to launch commercially in 2030.

4. Which frequency bands are identified for 6G sub-terahertz communications?
   a) C-band and L-band
   b) Ka-band and Ku-band
   c) S-band and X-band
   d) W-band (92-120 GHz) and D-band (120-175 GHz)
   Answer: d) W-band (92-120 GHz) and D-band (120-175 GHz)
   W-band and D-band are identified for 6G extreme bandwidth applications.

5. What is the device density target for 6G networks compared to 5G?
   a) 2x increase
   b) 5x increase
   c) 10x increase
   d) 100x increase
   Answer: c) 10x increase
   6G targets 10 million devices/km^2 compared to 5G's 1 million/km^2.

6. How do the physical limitations of millimeter-wave propagation impact 5G deployment strategies, and what alternative approaches might operators consider?
   Answer: The limited propagation of mmWave signals (typically under 500 meters) forces operators to deploy ultra-dense networks of small cells, significantly increasing infrastructure costs. Alternative approaches include: focusing initial deployments on mid-band spectrum for broader coverage, implementing dynamic spectrum sharing between 4G and 5G, utilizing lower frequency bands for wide-area coverage while reserving mmWave for high-traffic hotspots, and exploring new technologies like intelligent reflecting surfaces to extend mmWave coverage.

7. Analyze the security challenges introduced by network slicing and explain why current 5G implementations struggle to address them adequately.
   Answer: Network slicing introduces multiple security challenges, including inter-slice communications vulnerabilities, authentication complexity across slice boundaries, shared resource risks, and side-channel attacks. Current implementations struggle because: specifications don't prescribe implementation details, leading to vendor variability, isolation mechanisms are primarily logical rather than physical, management systems often span multiple slices, creating common failure points, and the dynamic nature of slice creation/deletion introduces configuration vulnerabilities. True security requires hardware-level isolation and zero-trust architectures, not fully realized in current deployments.

8. Evaluate the role of AI in addressing 5G limitations and enabling 6G networks.
   Answer: AI plays a transformative role in evolving from 5G to 6G by: enabling real-time network optimization beyond human capability, predicting and preventing failures before service impact, dynamically allocating resources based on learned patterns, and providing cognitive services at the network edge. While 5G uses AI as an add-on for specific functions, 6G will be AI-native with intelligence embedded throughout the architecture. This includes AI-driven protocol design, self-organizing networks, and autonomous security responses.

9. Discuss the sustainability challenges of 5G and how 6G aims to address environmental concerns.
   Answer: 5G's sustainability challenges stem from increased energy consumption due to dense infrastructure, always-on connectivity for billions of devices, and high-frequency operations requiring more power. While 5G is 90% more efficient than 4G per bit, absolute energy consumption increases with traffic growth. 6G addresses this through: zero-energy devices harvesting ambient power, AI-optimized sleep modes and resource allocation, more efficient waveforms and coding schemes, and sustainable-by-design principles. The Green G Working Group and similar initiatives ensure environmental impact is a core design consideration rather than an afterthought.

10. Compare the emerging user needs that 5G cannot satisfy with 6G's envisioned capabilities.
    Answer: Emerging needs beyond 5G's capabilities include: holographic communications requiring terabit speeds and sub-millisecond latency, brain-computer interfaces needing ultra-reliable connections, digital twins requiring massive real-time data synchronization, and truly immersive XR with haptic feedback. 6G envisions supporting these through the terahertz spectrum, providing extreme bandwidth, AI-native architecture enabling predictive resource allocation, quantum communications for absolute security, and integration with non-terrestrial networks for ubiquitous coverage. The gap represents not just quantitative improvements but qualitative leaps in capability.

References

3GPP. (2024). *6G Standardization Timeline and Milestones*. 3rd Generation Partnership Project.

5G Americas. (2025). *The State of 5G: Growth, Challenges, and Opportunities in 2025*. Retrieved from https://www.5gamericas.org/

Cybersecurity and Infrastructure Security Agency (CISA). (2024). *5G Network Slicing-Security Considerations for Design, Deployment, and Maintenance*. U.S. Department of Homeland Security.

Ericsson. (2024). *6G standardization timeline and principles*. Ericsson Technology Review.

Ericsson. (2024). *6G spectrum - future mobile life beyond 2030*. Ericsson White Paper.

Federal Communications Commission. (2024). *Report on Recommendations for Identifying Optional Security Features That Can Diminish the Effectiveness of 5G Security*. CSRIC VII.

GSM Association. (2024). *5G Network Slicing: Generic Network Slice Template (NEST)*. GSMA Official Document.

International Telecommunication Union. (2024). *Framework and Overall Objectives of the Future Development of IMT for 2030 and Beyond*. ITU-R Recommendation M.2160-0.

Jabil. (2024). *Facing Today's 5G Issues and Challenges*. Retrieved from https://www.jabil.com/

National Institute of Standards and Technology. (2024). *5G Cybersecurity - Volume B: Approach, Architecture, and Security Characteristics*. NIST SP 1800-33B.

National Security Agency & CISA. (2022). *Potential Threats to 5G Network Slicing*. Enduring Security Framework.

National Telecommunications and Information Administration. (2024). *Advancement of 6G Telecommunications Technology - Request for Comments*. Federal Register, 89(99).

Next G Alliance. (2024). *Green G: The Path Towards Sustainable 6G*. Alliance for Telecommunications Industry Solutions.

O-RAN Alliance. (2024). *O-RAN Security Threat Modeling and Risk Assessment*. O-RAN.WG11.

Qualcomm. (2024). *The Future of Mobile Connectivity: 6G Wireless Technology*. Qualcomm Research.

Sahu, V., & Sahu, N. (2024). Challenges and Opportunities of 5G Network: A Review of Research and Development. *American Journal of Electrical and Computer Engineering*.

ITU-R. (2023). *Recommendation ITU-R M.2160: Framework and overall objectives of the future development of IMT for 2030 and beyond*. International Telecommunication Union. https://www.itu.int/rec/R-REC-M.2160

Chapter 13: 6G Enabling Technologies

Executive Summary

This chapter examines three core technological foundations that will underpin sixth-generation (6G) wireless networks: Terahertz (THz) Communication, Reconfigurable Intelligent Surfaces (RIS), and Integrated Sensing and Communication (ISAC). Each of these innovations marks a significant departure from how we've historically designed and built cellular systems. Together, they promise to deliver capabilities we haven't seen before—dramatically faster data rates, networks that can adapt their behavior dynamically, and systems that combine multiple functions into unified platforms.

The chapter provides a comprehensive examination of each technology's principles, architectures, implementation challenges, and potential applications. It demonstrates how THz communication promises ultra-high data rates through the exploitation of frequencies from 0.1 to 10 THz, while RIS technology enables intelligent control of wireless propagation environments through programmable metasurfaces. ISAC represents the convergence of communication and sensing functionalities, creating networks that can simultaneously transmit data and perceive their environment.

Table of Contents

Introduction

Developing sixth-generation wireless systems requires breakthrough innovations capable of handling several converging challenges: explosive increases in network traffic, the requirement for near-instantaneous response times, and the blending of our physical environment with digital systems. The next generation will harness cutting-edge capabilities including artificial intelligence, edge computing, and terahertz communication to create ubiquitous connectivity that extends far beyond conventional voice and data services.

Moving from 5G to 6G isn't simply about making incremental upgrades. We're looking at a fundamental reimagining of how cellular networks get architected, built, and managed. This chapter delves into THz communication technology, examines where current research efforts are focused, and considers the real-world challenges involved in putting these systems into practice. These elements form the technical backbone for building intelligent, hyper-connected 6G networks.

Key Objectives of 6G Enabling Technologies

The primary objectives driving the development of these enabling technologies include:

1. **Ultra-High Data Rates:** Achieving terabit-per-second wireless connections
2. **Intelligent Network Control:** Dynamic optimization of wireless environments
3. **Multi-Functional Integration:** Combining communication, sensing, and computing
4. **Energy Efficiency:** Sustainable and green network operations
5. **Ubiquitous Coverage:** Seamless connectivity across all environments

Terahertz Communication

Fundamentals of THz Communication

Terahertz communication uses frequencies that fall between 0.1 and 10 THz, occupying the electromagnetic spectrum that sits between millimeter waves and infrared radiation. This frequency band spans from 0.1 THz up to 10 THz, with the lower portion—typically 0.1 THz to 0.3 THz, sometimes called sub-THz—receiving particular attention. What makes this spectrum compelling is that it remains largely untapped for wireless applications, offering enormous bandwidth potential that hasn't been exploited yet.

The fundamental principle of THz communication relies on the ability to generate, modulate, and detect electromagnetic waves at these extremely high frequencies. With the increasing demand for transmission rate of wireless network, the sixth generation of mobile communication system (6G) will evolve to the terahertz frequency band to meet the unprecedented bandwidth requirements of future applications.

ITU-R. (2023). Recommendation ITU-R M.2160: Framework and overall objectives of the future development of IMT for 2030 and beyond. International Telecommunication Union. M.2160 : Framework and overall objectives of the future development of IMT for 2030 and beyond

THz Spectrum and Propagation Characteristics

THz Frequency Bands and Characteristics

Frequency Range	Designation	Bandwidth	Path Loss	Primary Applications
0.1-0.3 THz	Sub-THz	Up to 200 GHz	Moderate	Wide-area coverage
0.3-1 THz	Lower THz	Up to 700 GHz	High	Local area networks
1-10 THz	Higher THz	Up to 9 THz	Very High	Short-range links

Source: Adapted from Petrov et al. (2020) and Rappaport et al. (2019)

How THz waves travel through the environment creates a mixed picture of benefits and drawbacks. These signals experience significant weakening as they pass through the atmosphere, with water vapor being the primary culprit causing signal degradation. This absorption limits how far the signals can effectively travel. However, this same limitation actually becomes an advantage in densely populated network deployments—the short range means frequencies can be reused in nearby cells without causing interference.

Hardware Architecture and Components

The implementation of THz communication systems requires specialized hardware components designed to operate at these extreme frequencies. Key components include:

1. **THz Transceivers:** High-frequency oscillators and mixers
2. **Antenna Systems:** Ultra-massive MIMO arrays with hundreds of elements
3. **Signal Processing Units:** High-speed digital processors for baseband operations
4. **Packaging Technologies:** Advanced integration techniques for miniaturization

THz Communication System Architecture

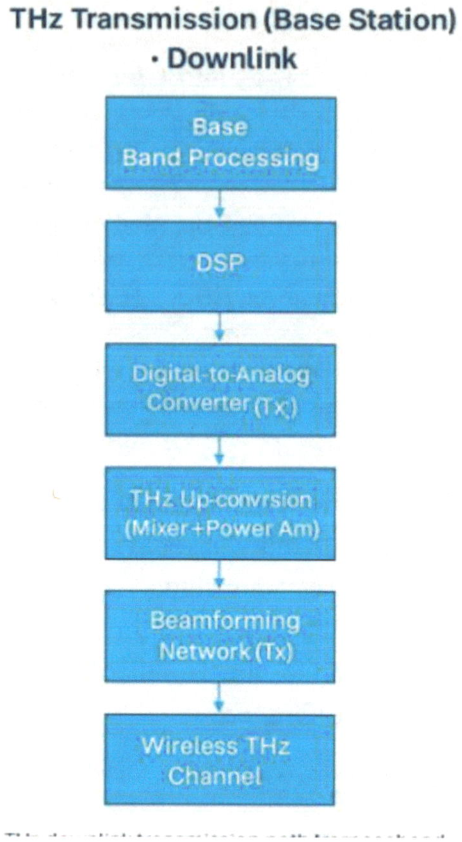

Source: Based on Han et al. (2019) and Shi et al. (2024)

Challenges and Solutions

The deployment of THz communication faces several technical challenges:

Atmospheric Absorption

The higher the frequency is, the shorter the distance information can travel, creating significant propagation challenges.

Solution: Highly directional beamforming and dense network deployments

Hardware Limitations

Terahertz signals are easily absorbed by the atmosphere, leading to rapid signal decay and requiring specialized components.

Solution: Advanced semiconductor technologies and innovative packaging designs

Beam Management

The use of narrow beams at THz frequencies requires sophisticated tracking and alignment mechanisms.

Solution: AI-powered beam prediction and fast beam switching algorithms

Applications and Use Cases

THz communication enables numerous revolutionary applications:

THz Communication Applications

Application Domain	Use Case	Data Rate Requirement	Range
Enhanced Mobile Broadband	Holographic Communications	>1 Tbps	<100m
Industrial IoT	Wireless Backhaul	100-500 Gbps	<1km
Healthcare	Real-time Medical Imaging	>100 Gbps	<10m
Smart Cities	Ultra-dense Networks	10-100 Gbps	<500m

Source: Adapted from Nokia (2022) and Chen et al. (2022)

Purple Mountain Laboratories in China announced in January 2022 that their researchers had reached a transmission speed of 206.25 gigabits per second (Gbit/s) under controlled laboratory settings—a world record at the time. This milestone showcased what terahertz technology can potentially deliver in terms of raw data throughput.

Reconfigurable Intelligent Surfaces (RIS)

RIS Fundamentals and Architecture

Reconfigurable Intelligent Surfaces represent a paradigm shift in wireless network design by enabling programmable control over electromagnetic wave propagation. RISs have been envisaged to reduce the deployment costs and energy consumption, as well as improve the spectral efficiency of wireless networks through intelligent manipulation of the wireless environment.

Core Components of RIS

1. **Metasurface Array:** Composed of sub-wavelength unit cells
2. **Control Circuitry:** Phase-shifting and amplitude control elements
3. **Controller:** Optimization algorithms and channel estimation
4. **Communication Interface:** Coordination with network infrastructure

Types and Classifications

RIS implementations can be categorized based on their operational characteristics:

RIS Classification and Characteristics

Type	Functionality	Power Requirement	Complexity	Cost
Passive RIS	Reflection only	None	Low	Low
Active RIS	Amplification + Reflection	Moderate	High	High
Transmissive RIS	Transmission control	Low	Medium	Medium
Hybrid RIS	Multiple functions	Variable	Very High	High

Source: Based on Zhang et al. (2023) and Dai et al. (2020)

Hardware Design and Materials

The physical implementation of RIS relies on advanced metamaterial designs and fabrication techniques. The novel technology is predicted to significantly enhance data range, penetration, and the overall efficiency of wireless networks through careful material selection and pattern design.

RIS Hardware Architecture

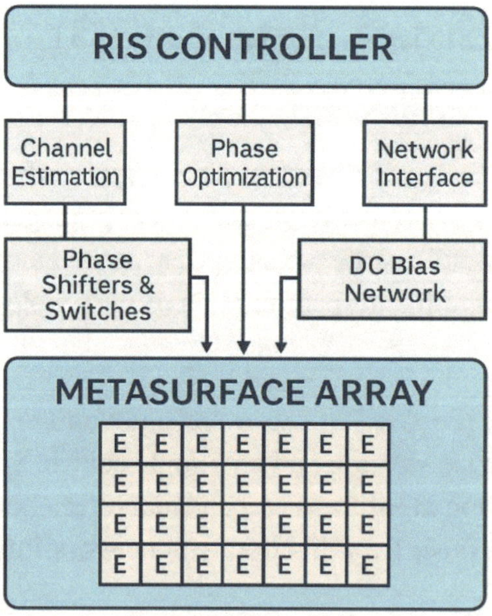

RIS Hardware Architecture

Source: Adapted from Wu & Zhang (2020) and Basar et al. (2019)

Deployment Strategies

Strategic deployment of RIS is crucial for maximizing network performance benefits:

1. **Indoor Deployments**
   - Coverage enhancement in buildings
   - Dead zone elimination
   - Interference management
2. **Outdoor Urban Deployments**
   - Street-level coverage improvement
   - Building facade integration
   - Mobile base station assistance
3. **Industrial Applications**
   - Projections suggest that deployments will eventually exceed 200 million square meters, with annual hardware revenue climbing above $12 billion. These figures point to substantial adoption at industrial scale.

Performance Enhancement Techniques

Advanced techniques for optimizing RIS performance include:

RIS Optimization Approaches

Technique	Description	Complexity	Performance Gain
Deep Learning	AI-based phase optimization	High	40-60%
Compressed Sensing	Reduced pilot overhead	Medium	20-30%
Hybrid Beamforming	Active-passive combination	High	50-80%
Multi-RIS Cooperation	Distributed optimization	Very High	100-150%

Source: Based on Huang et al. (2020) and Liu et al. (2022)

Integrated Sensing and Communication (ISAC)

ISAC Concept and Evolution

Integrated Sensing and Communication brings together two capabilities that have historically operated independently, merging them into a single platform. This approach adds sensing and positioning functionality for non-networked objects directly into cellular infrastructure. By doing so, ISAC pushes mobile networks beyond their traditional role of simply enabling communication between devices.

The evolution of ISAC follows a progressive integration path:

1. **Coexistence:** Separate systems sharing spectrum
2. **Cooperation:** Information exchange between systems
3. **Co-design:** Joint optimization of both functions
4. **Full Integration:** Unified hardware and signal processing

Integration Levels and Architecture

ISAC systems can be implemented at various integration levels, each offering different benefits and complexities:

ISAC Integration Hierarchy

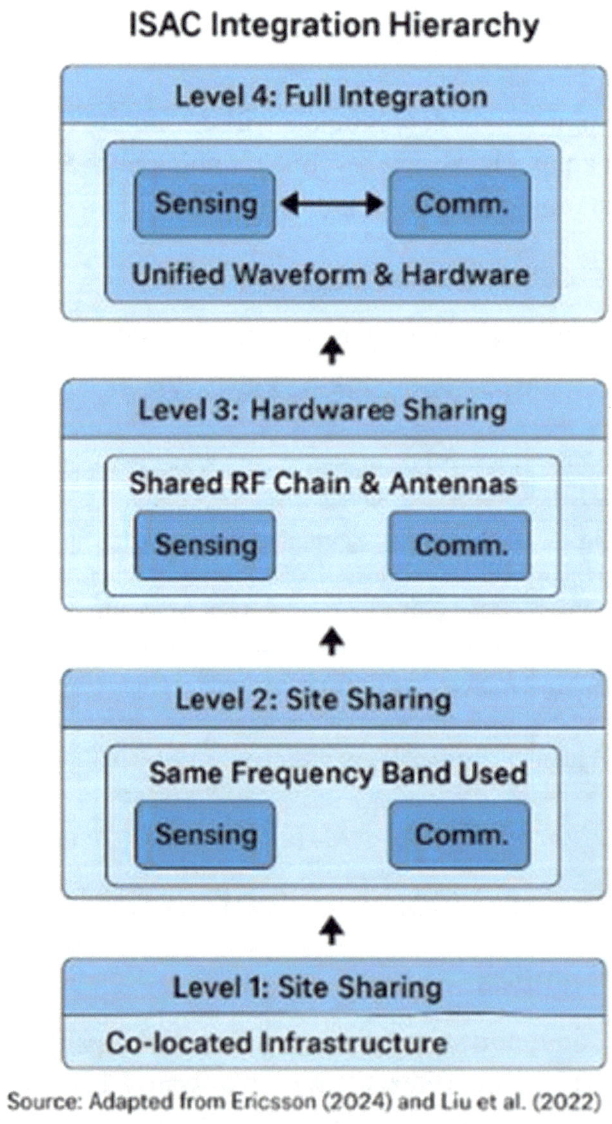

Waveform Design and Signal Processing

The design of ISAC waveforms must balance the requirements of both communication and sensing functions:

ISAC Waveform Characteristics

Parameter	Communication Priority	Sensing Priority	Balanced Design
Bandwidth	Moderate (100 MHz)	Wide (>1 GHz)	Adaptive
Duty Cycle	Continuous	Pulsed	Time-shared
Beamwidth	Wide coverage	Narrow pencil	Multi-beam
Modulation	High-order QAM	Linear FM	OFDM-based

Source: Adapted from Rohde & Schwarz (2024) and Huawei (2024)

ISAC requires developing novel waveform designs. Initial implementations can take either a radar-focused or communication-focused approach to signal coordination. However, the industry trajectory points toward completely integrated designs where sensing and communication functions share the same waveform architecture seamlessly.

Applications and Services

ISAC enables a wide range of innovative applications across various domains:

1. **Automotive and Transportation**
   - Simultaneous V2X communication and obstacle detection
   - Cooperative perception for autonomous vehicles
   - Traffic flow monitoring and optimization
2. **Smart Manufacturing**
   - Radio signals can be analyzed to extract distance, speed, and directional data, opening up numerous possibilities for Industry 4.0 use cases.
3. **Healthcare and Wellness**
   - Contactless vital sign monitoring
   - Fall detection for elderly care
   - Activity recognition and health tracking
4. **Security and Surveillance**
   - Perimeter monitoring
   - Intrusion detection
   - Privacy-preserving sensing

Standardization Efforts

The standardization of ISAC is progressing through multiple organizations:

ISAC Standardization Timeline

Organization	Working Group	Focus Area	Timeline
3GPP	Release 19	Use case studies	2024-2025
IEEE	802.11bf	WLAN sensing	2024-2026
ETSI	ISG ISAC	Architecture	2024-2025
ITU-R	WP5D	6G requirements	2025-2030

Source: Based on 3GPP TR 22.837 (2024) and ETSI ISG ISAC (2024)

The 3GPP standards body has initiated work on ISAC, conducting feasibility analyses and documenting initial application scenarios in TR 22.837. This early technical work lays the groundwork for eventual formal specifications.

Synergies and Integration

The true potential of 6G lies in the synergistic integration of these enabling technologies:

THz-RIS Integration

Combining THz communication with RIS addresses key propagation challenges:

- **Coverage Extension:** RIS compensates for high THz path loss
- **Beam Management:** Intelligent reflection enables non-line-of-sight communication
- **Energy Efficiency:** Passive RIS reduces power consumption

RIS-ISAC Synergy

Combining RISs with Hybrid Access Points (HAPs) brings substantial benefits, especially for improving network coverage and adding sensing functionality:

- **Enhanced Sensing Resolution:** RIS focuses sensing beams
- **Improved Communication Coverage:** Sensing data optimizes RIS configuration
- **Multi-functional Operations:** Simultaneous sensing and communication enhancement

THz-ISAC Integration

The combination of THz frequencies with ISAC provides:

- **Ultra-High Resolution Sensing:** Millimeter-level accuracy
- **Massive Bandwidth:** Support for both functions

- **Novel Applications:** High-definition imaging with communication.

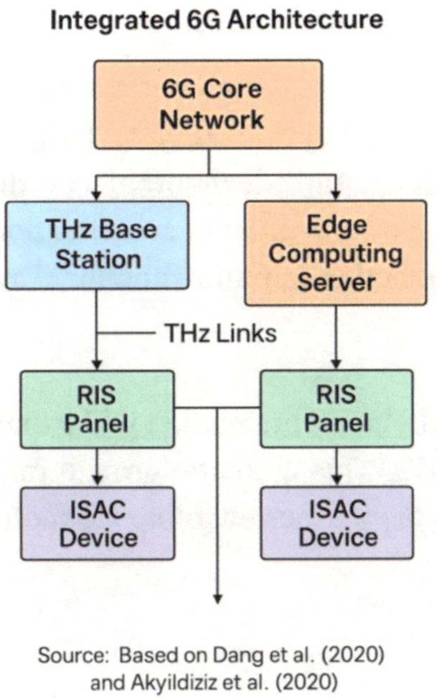

Integrated 6G Architecture

Future Outlook

The development of 6G enabling technologies is accelerating, with several key trends emerging:

Technology Maturation Timeline

6G Technology Deployment Roadmap

Technology	Research Phase	Prototype	Pilot Deployment	Commercial
Sub-THz Communication	2020-2025	2024-2027	2027-2029	2030+
Passive RIS	2019-2024	2023-2026	2026-2028	2029+
Active RIS	2022-2027	2025-2028	2028-2030	2031+
Basic ISAC	2021-2025	2024-2027	2027-2029	2030+
Advanced ISAC	2023-2028	2026-2029	2029-2031	2032+

Source: Based on ITU-R IMT-2030 (2024) and industry projections from Nokia (2022)

Research Challenges and Opportunities

Key areas requiring continued research include:

1. **Hardware Development:** Low-cost, high-performance components
2. **Algorithm Design:** AI-powered optimization techniques
3. **System Integration:** Seamless multi-technology coordination
4. **Standardization:** Global harmonization of specifications
5. **Security and Privacy:** Protection in multi-functional systems

Market Projections

Industry forecasts project the RIS hardware market will expand from $5.57 billion USD in 2024 to reach $45.4 billion USD by 2032. This dramatic growth trajectory underscores the significant commercial opportunity spanning the various enabling technologies in this space.

Knowledge Check

1. What is the frequency range of terahertz communication for 6G networks?
   a) 1-10 GHz
   b) 0.1-10 THz
   c) 10-100 GHz
   d) 0.01-0.1 THz

2. Which of the following is NOT a type of Reconfigurable Intelligent Surface?
   a) Passive RIS
   b) Active RIS
   c) Quantum RIS
   d) Transmissive RIS

3. What does ISAC stand for in the context of 6G?
   a) Internet Service Access Control
   b) Integrated Sensing and Communication
   c) Intelligent System Architecture Core
   d) International Standards and Compliance

4. What is the primary challenge of THz communication?
   a) Low data rates
   b) Atmospheric absorption
   c) Wide coverage area
   d) Low frequency operation

5. By what year is 6G expected to be commercially deployed?
   a) 2025
   b) 2028
   c) 2030
   d) 2035

6. How do the three enabling technologies (THz, RIS, and ISAC) complement each other in creating a comprehensive 6G network architecture?

7. What are the main deployment challenges for RIS in urban environments, and how can they be addressed?

8. Explain how ISAC can improve autonomous vehicle operations compared to separate communication and radar systems.

9. What role will artificial intelligence play in optimizing THz beamforming for mobile users?

10. How might the integration of these 6G technologies enable new applications in healthcare?

Answers

1. What is the frequency range of terahertz communication for 6G networks?
   a) 1-10 GHz
   b) 0.1-10 THz
   c) 10-100 GHz
   d) 0.01-0.1 THz
   Answer: b) 0.1-10 THz

2. Which of the following is NOT a type of Reconfigurable Intelligent Surface?
   a) Passive RIS
   b) Active RIS
   c) Quantum RIS
   d) Transmissive RIS
   Answer: c) Quantum RIS

3. What does ISAC stand for in the context of 6G?
   a) Internet Service Access Control
   b) Integrated Sensing and Communication
   c) Intelligent System Architecture Core
   d) International Standards and Compliance
   Answer: b) Integrated Sensing and Communication

4. What is the primary challenge of THz communication?
   a) Low data rates
   b) Atmospheric absorption
   c) Wide coverage area
   d) Low frequency operation
   Answer: b) Atmospheric absorption

5. By what year is 6G expected to be commercially deployed?
   a) 2025
   b) 2028
   c) 2030
   d) 2035

Answer: c) 2030

6. How do the three enabling technologies (THz, RIS, and ISAC) complement each other in creating a comprehensive 6G network architecture?
   Answer: The three technologies create a synergistic ecosystem where THz provides ultra-high bandwidth, RIS intelligently controls propagation to overcome THz limitations, and ISAC adds sensing capabilities that can optimize both communication and RIS configuration. Together, they enable networks that are not only faster but also more intelligent and aware of their environment.

7. What are the main deployment challenges for RIS in urban environments, and how can they be addressed?
   Answer: Main challenges include integration with existing infrastructure, aesthetic concerns, power supply for active elements, and coordination with multiple operators. Solutions include building-integrated designs, solar-powered implementations, standardized interfaces, and shared infrastructure models with clear regulatory frameworks.

8. Explain how ISAC can improve autonomous vehicle operations compared to separate communication and radar systems.
   Answer: ISAC enables vehicles to use the same hardware and spectrum for both V2X communication and environmental sensing, reducing cost and complexity. It provides better spectrum efficiency, enables cooperative perception where vehicles share sensing data through communication links, and reduces interference between radar and communication systems. The unified approach also enables faster processing and decision-making.

9. What role will artificial intelligence play in optimizing THz beamforming for mobile users?
   Answer: AI will be crucial for predicting user movement patterns, optimizing beam tracking algorithms, managing handovers between beams, and adapting to environmental changes. Machine learning can learn from historical data to anticipate beam blockages and proactively adjust beamforming patterns, significantly reducing the overhead of beam management in THz systems.

10. How might the integration of these 6G technologies enable new applications in healthcare?
    Answer: The combination enables revolutionary healthcare applications: THz can provide high-resolution medical imaging wirelessly, RIS can focus signals for precise in-body communication with implants, and ISAC enables continuous vital sign monitoring without

wearables. Together, they could enable remote surgery with haptic feedback, real-time 3D holographic consultations, and AI-powered health monitoring in smart hospitals.

References

3GPP. (2024). *Study on integrated sensing and communication* (TR 22.837). 3rd Generation Partnership Project.

Akyildiz, I. F., Kak, A., & Nie, S. (2020). 6G and beyond: The future of wireless communications systems. *IEEE Access*, 8, 133995-134030.

Basar, E., Di Renzo, M., De Rosny, J., Debbah, M., Alouini, M. S., & Zhang, R. (2019). Wireless communications through reconfigurable intelligent surfaces. *IEEE Access*, 7, 116753-116773.

Chen, Y., Liu, Y., Zhang, Y., & Li, S. (2022). Integrated sensing and communication: A comprehensive survey. *IEEE Communications Surveys & Tutorials*, 24(3), 1435-1478.

Dai, L., Wang, B., Wang, M., Yang, X., Tan, J., Bi, S., ... & Poor, H. V. (2020). Reconfigurable intelligent surface-based wireless communications: Antenna design, prototyping, and experimental results. *IEEE Access*, 8, 45913-45923.

Dang, S., Amin, O., Shihada, B., & Alouini, M. S. (2020). What should 6G be? *Nature Electronics*, 3(1), 20-29.

Ericsson. (2024). *Integrated sensing and communication (ISAC) in 6G networks*. Ericsson Technology Review.

ETSI ISG ISAC. (2024). *Industry specification group on integrated sensing and communications*. European Telecommunications Standards Institute.

Han, C., Wu, Y., Chen, Z., & Wang, X. (2019). Terahertz communications: Challenges in the next decade. *IEEE Transactions on Terahertz Science and Technology*, 9(3), 213-218.

Huang, C., Hu, S., Alexandropoulos, G. C., Zappone, A., Yuen, C., Zhang, R., ... & Debbah, M. (2020). Holographic MIMO surfaces for 6G wireless networks: Opportunities, challenges, and trends. *IEEE Wireless Communications*, 27(5), 118-125.

Huawei. (2024). *Integrated sensing and communication (ISAC) — From concept to practice*. Huawei Technologies White Paper.

ITU-R. (2024). *Framework and overall objectives of the future development of IMT for 2030 and beyond* (Recommendation ITU-R M.2160-0). International Telecommunication Union.

Liu, F., Cui, Y., Masouros, C., Xu, J., Han, T. X., Eldar, Y. C., & Buzzi, S. (2022). Integrated sensing and communications: Toward dual-functional wireless networks for 6G and beyond. *IEEE Journal on Selected Areas in Communications*, 40(6), 1728-1767.

Nokia. (2022). *Nokia's vision for the 6G era*. Nokia White Paper.

Petrov, V., Kurner, T., & Hosako, I. (2020). IEEE 802.15.3d: First standardization efforts for sub-terahertz band communications toward 6G. *IEEE Communications Magazine*, 58(11), 28-33.

Rappaport, T. S., Xing, Y., Kanhere, O., Ju, S., Madanayake, A., Mandal, S., ... & Trichopoulos, G. C. (2019). Wireless communications and applications above 100 GHz: Opportunities and challenges for 6G and beyond. *IEEE Access*, 7, 78729-78757.

Rohde & Schwarz. (2024). *Integrated sensing and communication (ISAC) test solutions*. Rohde & Schwarz Application Note.

Shi, H. C., Yang, C., & Peng, M. G. (2024). Terahertz communication for 6G: Architectures, technologies, and challenges. *Chinese Journal of Radio Science*, 39(3), 395-412.

Wu, Q., & Zhang, R. (2020). Towards smart and reconfigurable environment: Intelligent reflecting surface aided wireless network. *IEEE Communications Magazine*, 58(1), 106-112.

Zhang, Z., Dai, L., Chen, X., Liu, C., Yang, F., Schober, R., & Poor, H. V. (2023). Active RIS vs. passive RIS: Which will prevail in 6G? *IEEE Transactions on Communications*, 71(3), 1707-1725.

Chapter 14: 6G Applications and Use Cases

Executive Summary

This chapter explores the transformative applications and use cases that will define the sixth generation (6G) of wireless communication networks. Building upon the foundation of 5G, 6G promises to enable revolutionary applications that were previously confined to science fiction. The chapter examines four key application domains: holographic communication, which will enable three-dimensional telepresence and immersive interactions; digital twins and tactile internet, creating real-time virtual replicas of physical systems; brain-computer interfaces, establishing direct communication between human cognition and digital systems; and space-terrestrial integration, achieving truly global connectivity through satellite-terrestrial network convergence. These applications represent the convergence of advanced technologies, including terahertz communications, artificial intelligence, quantum computing, and space technology, positioning 6G as the backbone of future digital society.

Table of Contents

Introduction

The evolution toward 6G networks marks a paradigm shift in wireless communications, moving beyond enhanced mobile broadband to enable truly transformative applications. As noted by Ericsson (2024), "6G networks will need to tackle numerous societal challenges, including demands for greater sustainability and economic resilience," while supporting "new experiences to end consumers" (Ericsson, 2022). The four key application domains discussed in this chapter represent the frontier of what 6G technology will enable.

Key 6G Applications Overview

Application Domain	Key Features	Data Rate Requirements	Latency Requirements	Primary Technologies
Holographic Communication	3D real-time transmission, Immersive telepresence	Multi-terabit/s	<1 ms	THz bands, AI beamforming
Digital Twins	Real-time synchronization, Virtual replicas	10-100 Gbps	<5 ms	Edge computing, AI/ML
Brain-Computer Interface	Neural signal processing, Direct brain control	1-10 Gbps	<10 ms	AI processing, Biocompatible sensors
Space-Terrestrial Integration	Global coverage, Seamless handover	1-100 Gbps	20-50 ms	LEO satellites, SDN

Source: Adapted from Bhide (2025), Rohde & Schwarz (2023), and industry projections

Holographic Communication

Definition and Concepts

Holographic communication represents one of the most ambitious applications envisioned for 6G networks. According to Bhide (2025), "Holographic communication is an advanced form of communication that involves transmitting and receiving three-dimensional (3D) holographic images, rather than traditional two-dimensional images or videos." This technology promises to revolutionize human interaction by enabling life-like, three-dimensional presence across distances.

The fundamental principle involves capturing, transmitting, and reconstructing complete 3D representations of objects or people in real-time. Unlike current video conferencing, holographic communication provides depth perception, allows viewing from multiple angles, and creates a genuine sense of presence.

Technical Requirements

The implementation of holographic communication demands unprecedented network capabilities. As highlighted by industry research, several key technical requirements must be met:

Ultra-High Data Rates: Bhide (2025) highlights that sixth-generation networks aim to deliver exceptionally fast transmission speeds, potentially hitting terabit-per-second levels. Holographic content demands enormous bandwidth because of the intricate three-dimensional information it contains. Moving high-fidelity holographic material needs data throughput many times greater than what today's 5G networks can handle.

Minimal Latency: Real-time holographic interaction necessitates extremely low latency. Research indicates that "Holographic communication requires minimal latency to maintain the perception of real-time interaction" (Bhide, 2025). Target latencies below 1 millisecond are essential for natural interaction.

Advanced Signal Processing: The technology relies on sophisticated beamforming and antenna technologies. As noted in technical documentation, "6G is expected to introduce advanced beamforming and antenna technologies, enabling highly directional and focused signal transmission" (Bhide, 2025).

Holographic Communication System Architecture

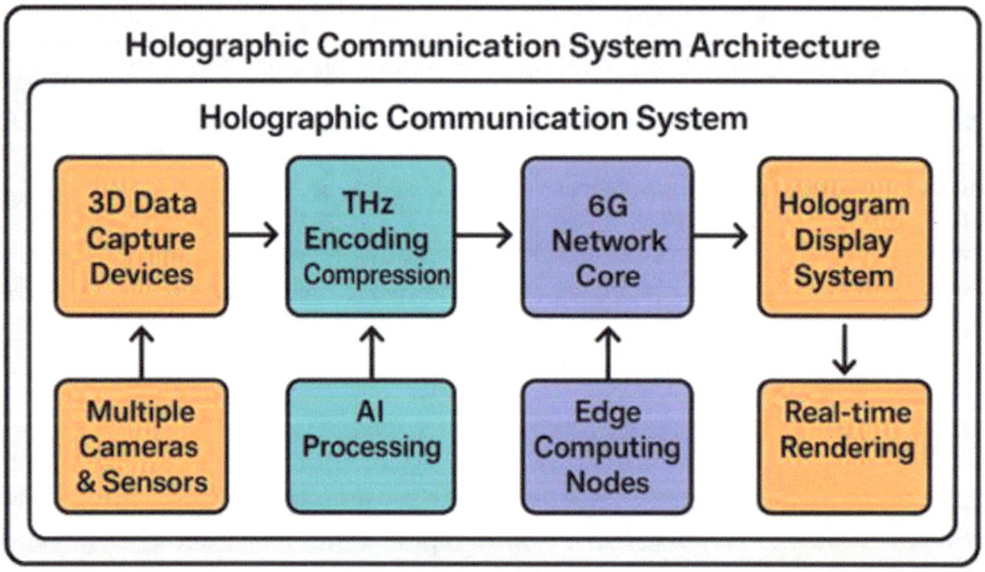

Source: Author's synthesis based on Bhide (2025) and industry technical specifications

Applications and Benefits

The applications of holographic communication span multiple sectors:

Healthcare: Remote surgery consultation where specialists can examine patients in 3D, providing guidance as if physically present.

Education: Immersive learning experiences where historical figures or complex scientific concepts can be presented in three dimensions.

Business: Virtual meetings that replicate the experience of in-person interaction, improving collaboration and reducing travel needs.

Entertainment: Live holographic performances and interactive gaming experiences that blur the line between virtual and reality.

Market analysis shows the worldwide market for 3D holographic displays and related services will expand from $607.6 million in 2020 to $1,837.1 million by 2025, representing a compound annual growth of 24.8% (ResearchAndMarkets, 2020). These figures demonstrate substantial commercial momentum behind this technology

Digital Twins and Tactile Internet

Digital Twin Technology in 6G

Digital twins create virtual counterparts of physical systems, allowing for continuous monitoring, testing scenarios, and performance tuning. The 6G-TWIN initiative envisions these digital replicas functioning as a fundamental tool for managing, optimizing, and controlling intricate network environments that change rapidly in real-time (6G-TWIN, 2024).

In the context of 6G, digital twins extend beyond simple virtualization to create comprehensive, AI-driven replicas that can:

- Predict system behavior before implementation
- Optimize network performance in real-time
- Enable proactive maintenance and failure prevention
- Support complex scenario testing without affecting physical infrastructure

Digital Twin Applications in 6G Networks

Application Area	Use Case	Key Benefits	Technical Requirements
Network Management	Virtual network testing	Risk-free optimization	Real-time synchronization
Manufacturing	Production line simulation	Predictive maintenance	Sub-5ms latency
Smart Cities	Traffic flow optimization	Reduced congestion	Massive IoT connectivity
Healthcare	Patient monitoring	Personalized treatment	High reliability (99.999%)
Energy	Grid management	Efficiency optimization	Distributed computing

Source: Compiled from 6G-TWIN (2024), DeepAI (2021), and IEEE research

Tactile Internet Evolution

The tactile internet represents the next evolution in human-technology interaction, enabling the real-time transmission of touch and haptic feedback. As noted in research, "Tactile Internet (TI), with the capability of providing multisensory haptic communication," is a key component of 6G vision (DeepAI, 2021).

Key characteristics include:

- Ultra-low latency (≤1ms round-trip time)
- High reliability (99.999% availability)
- Support for haptic codecs and feedback systems
- Integration with robotic and automation systems

Integration and Synergies

The convergence of digital twins and tactile internet creates powerful synergies. As highlighted by researchers, this integration enables:

Remote Operations: Operators can interact with digital twins through haptic interfaces, feeling resistance, texture, and forces as if physically present.

Training and Simulation: Safe, realistic training environments for high-risk operations such as surgery or industrial maintenance.

Enhanced Telepresence: Combining visual, auditory, and tactile feedback for truly immersive remote experiences.

Digital Twin-Tactile Internet Integration Flow

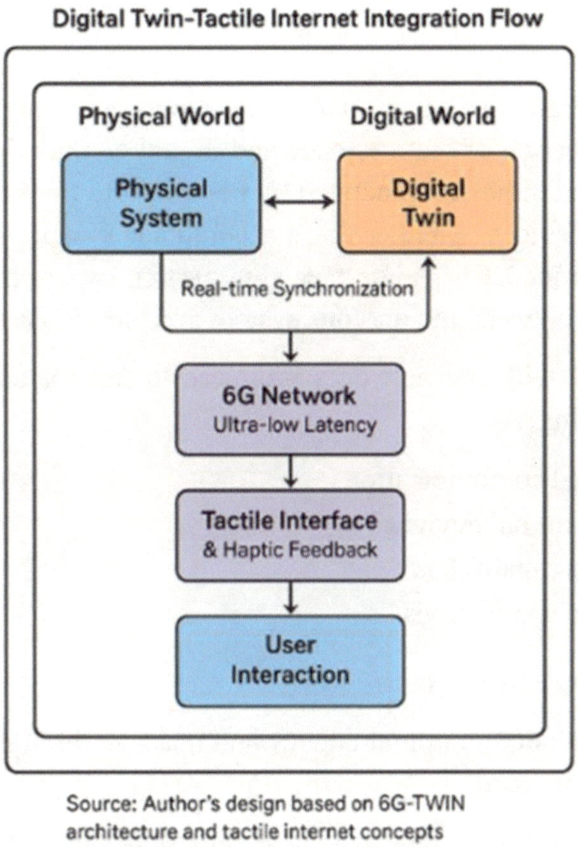

Source: Author's design based on 6G-TWIN architecture and tactile internet concepts

Brain-Computer Interface

BCI Fundamentals

The emergence of Brain-Computer Interfaces represents one of the most significant developments at the intersection of brain science and digital communication. These technologies work by capturing electrical impulses generated by neurons and translating them into commands that can control external devices, whether that's a computer system or a mechanical prosthetic limb. Researchers today define BCIs as interface systems that bypass traditional neural pathways, allowing direct interaction between the nervous system and electronic equipment.

The integration of BCI with 6G networks promises to unlock new dimensions of human-machine interaction, enabling:

- Direct thought-based communication
- Neural control of external devices
- Enhanced cognitive capabilities
- Medical therapeutic applications

6G-Enabled BCI Applications

Pairing BCI systems with 6G's minimal latency and massive throughput opens up possibilities for several revolutionary use cases:

Medical Applications: Medical research documentation shows that BCIs allow people to engage with their surroundings and communicate by translating neural activity into commands for interface devices and environmental systems (PMC, 2024). Applications encompass:

- Restoration of motor functions for paralyzed patients
- Communication interfaces for locked-in syndrome patients
- Neural prosthetics control
- Treatment of neurological disorders

Consumer Applications: Future consumer BCI applications may include:

- Thought-based device control
- Enhanced gaming and entertainment experiences
- Direct brain-to-brain communication
- Augmented cognitive abilities

Industrial Applications: BCI integration in industrial settings enables:

- Hands-free equipment operation
- Enhanced safety through neural monitoring
- Improved human-machine collaboration
- Fatigue and attention monitoring

BCI Technology Comparison for 6G Applications

BCI Type	Invasiveness	Signal Quality	Bandwidth	6G Integration Potential
EEG-based	Non-invasive	Moderate	1-100 Hz	High - Wearable integration
ECoG	Semi-invasive	High	1-500 Hz	Medium - Medical focus
Microelectrode	Invasive	Very High	1-10 kHz	Low - Specialized use
fNIRS	Non-invasive	Low-Moderate	0.1-10 Hz	High - Mobile applications

Source: Adapted from Health Data Science (2024) and IEEE research publications

Challenges and Opportunities

While BCI technology holds immense promise, several challenges must be addressed:

Technical Challenges:

- Signal processing complexity requiring AI/ML algorithms
- Need for individual calibration and adaptation
- Long-term stability and biocompatibility of implants
- Integration with the existing communication infrastructure

Ethical Considerations: Researchers have raised important questions about personal agency, informed consent, and the risk that users might become overly reliant on BCI technology (ScienceDirect, 2024). These concerns extend beyond individual autonomy to broader societal implications. There are ongoing debates about data privacy, as BCIs collect highly sensitive neural information that could potentially reveal users' thoughts, emotions, or intentions. Questions also arise about equitable access—whether BCI technology will be available to all who need it or only to those who can afford expensive systems. Additionally, the long-term psychological effects of direct brain-machine interaction remain largely unknown, requiring careful study as the technology advances. Regulatory frameworks are still developing to address these complex ethical dimensions.

Market Growth: Despite challenges, the BCI market shows strong growth potential. According to IDTechEx (2024), "the overall brain computer interface market forecast to grow to over US$1.6bn by 2045."

Space-Terrestrial Integration

Satellite Communication Evolution

Merging satellite and ground-based cellular networks marks a major transformation in how we approach worldwide connectivity. MediaTek (2025) observes that combining satellite and terrestrial mobile infrastructure within unified devices will enable ubiquitous global network access.

This convergence addresses a critical gap in current telecommunications: providing coverage in remote and underserved regions where building traditional cell towers is economically impractical. By integrating satellite capabilities directly into consumer devices like smartphones and tablets, users can seamlessly switch between terrestrial and satellite connections based on availability and signal strength. This hybrid approach proves particularly valuable for maritime communications, aviation connectivity, disaster response scenarios, and rural areas lacking terrestrial infrastructure.

The technical challenges are substantial. Engineers must design antennas capable of handling both the high-frequency millimeter waves used in 5G/6G terrestrial networks and the different frequency bands employed by satellite systems. Power consumption becomes another critical consideration, as satellite communication typically requires more energy than terrestrial transmission. Latency management also presents complexity—while low-earth orbit (LEO) satellite constellations have dramatically reduced delays compared to traditional geostationary satellites, coordinating handoffs between satellite and terrestrial networks requires sophisticated algorithms to maintain seamless connectivity.

From a business perspective, this integration opens new revenue streams for telecommunications providers while potentially disrupting the traditional satellite communications industry. Device manufacturers face increased costs and design complexity, but the value proposition of truly global connectivity could justify premium pricing for satellite-enabled devices.

Key developments include:

- Low Earth Orbit (LEO) satellite constellations
- Medium Earth Orbit (MEO) integration
- Geostationary (GEO) satellite evolution
- Hybrid network architecture

Hybrid Network Architecture

The architecture planned for 6G networks calls for smooth integration connecting space-based and ground systems. Research suggests that merging satellite and terrestrial infrastructure holds significant promise for achieving worldwide coverage and universal internet connectivity (MDPI, 2022).

This architectural vision represents a departure from previous generations where satellite and cellular networks operated as distinct, largely incompatible systems. In the 6G framework, satellite links won't serve merely as backup or supplementary connections—they'll function as equal partners in a unified network fabric. This requires developing common protocols and standards that work across both domains, enabling intelligent routing decisions that optimize for factors like bandwidth availability, latency requirements, signal quality, and power efficiency.

The space component will likely rely heavily on mega-constellations of low-earth orbit satellites, potentially numbering in the thousands or tens of thousands. Companies are already deploying these constellations to reduce the inherent latency problems that plagued earlier satellite internet services. When satellites orbit at altitudes of 500-1,200 kilometers rather than 35,786 kilometers (geostationary orbit), signal round-trip times drop from roughly 600 milliseconds to under 50 milliseconds—approaching terrestrial network performance.

Network orchestration becomes exponentially more complex in this hybrid architecture. The system must track user devices as they move between coverage zones, manage handovers between terrestrial cells and satellite beams, balance load across available resources, and maintain quality of service guarantees. Artificial intelligence and machine learning will play crucial roles in managing this complexity, predicting network conditions, and making real-time optimization decisions.

Security considerations also intensify. The attack surface expands significantly when networks span both ground infrastructure and orbital assets. Protecting satellite links from interference, jamming, and eavesdropping requires robust encryption and authentication mechanisms. The distributed nature of satellite constellations actually provides some resilience advantages—losing individual satellites doesn't catastrophically degrade the network—but coordinating security policies across heterogeneous systems presents ongoing challenges.

From an economic standpoint, this integration could democratize internet access globally, bringing high-speed connectivity to regions that current infrastructure economics cannot justify serving. However, the capital requirements are staggering, involving both massive ground infrastructure investments and the costs of launching and maintaining satellite fleets.

6G Space-Terrestrial Integration Architecture

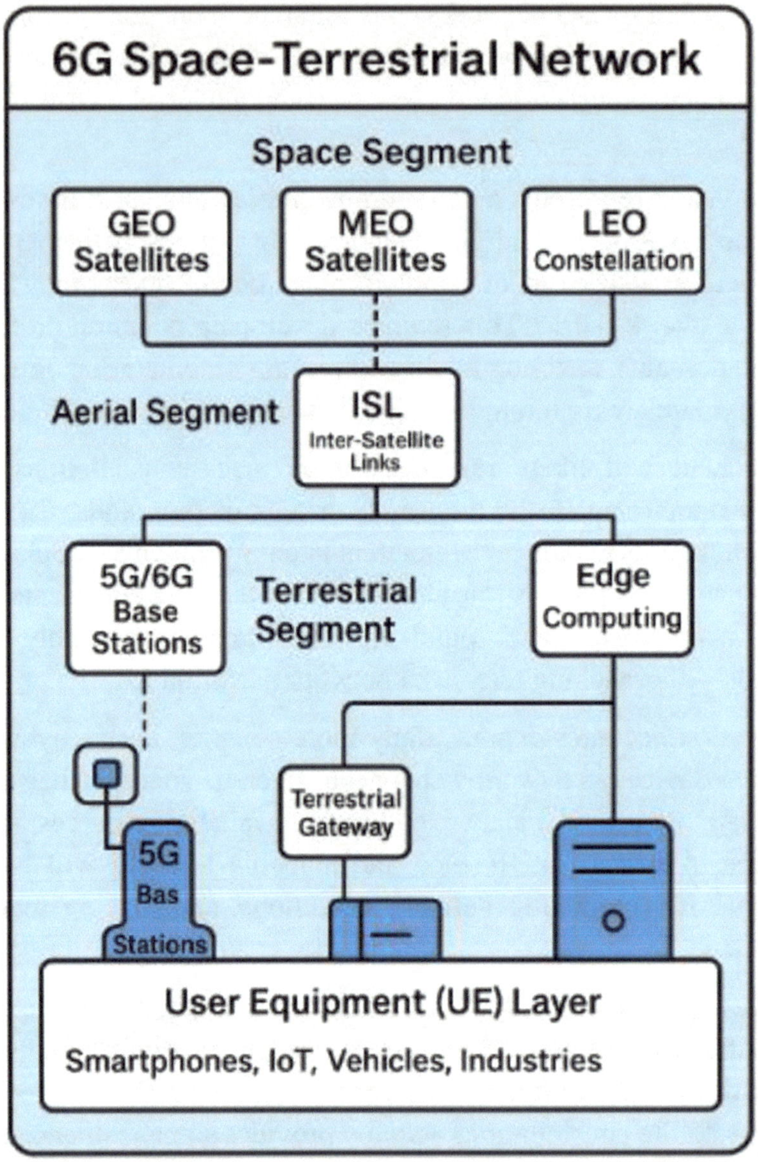

Global Coverage Solutions

Space-terrestrial integration addresses several critical challenges:

Coverage Gaps: Research findings indicate that current single-technology wireless systems—whether cellular or satellite—struggle to provide adequate service when operating independently, particularly in challenging geographical areas like oceans, mountain ranges, and isolated territories (MDPI, 2022).

This coverage limitation stems from fundamental economic and technical realities. Terrestrial cellular networks require physical infrastructure—towers, base stations, fiber backhaul—that becomes prohibitively expensive in sparsely populated regions. A cell tower might cost couple of thousand dollars to build and deploy, with ongoing maintenance and power costs adding to the burden. When potential subscriber density drops below certain thresholds, the business case for infrastructure investment simply collapses. This explains why vast swaths of rural America, remote islands, polar regions, and developing nations remain unconnected or severely underserved.

Traditional satellite systems face different but equally significant constraints. Geostationary satellites, while covering large geographic footprints, suffer from high latency due to their 35,786-kilometer orbital altitude. More problematic, they struggle to deliver the bandwidth and speeds users now expect. A single geostationary satellite might serve an entire continent but can't compete with the gigabit speeds available in urban fiber and 5G networks.

Geographic obstacles compound these challenges. Mountain valleys create radio shadows where terrestrial signals can't penetrate. Dense foliage in tropical forests attenuates high-frequency signals. Maritime vessels traveling beyond coastal waters lose cellular connectivity entirely, relying on expensive and slow satellite services. Aircraft flying over oceans face similar limitations. Disaster zones where terrestrial infrastructure has been damaged or destroyed become communication black holes precisely when connectivity matters most.

The seasonal variation in coverage requirements adds another layer of complexity. Remote mining operations, research stations in Antarctica, shipping lanes that vary with weather patterns, and agricultural regions that need connectivity during specific growing seasons all present dynamic coverage demands that fixed infrastructure handles poorly.

Population mobility patterns have shifted dramatically. People expect connectivity while hiking in national parks, sailing, traveling through rural areas, or working from remote locations. The "digital divide" between urban and rural connectivity has become not just an inconvenience but a social equity issue affecting education, healthcare access, economic opportunity, and emergency services.

Hybrid satellite-terrestrial networks address these gaps by leveraging the strengths of each technology. Satellites provide the wide-area coverage and reach, while terrestrial networks deliver high capacity and low latency where population density justifies the infrastructure investment. The combination creates a more complete, resilient communication fabric that adapts to user location and needs.

Key Benefits:

- Ubiquitous global connectivity
- Disaster-resilient communications
- Support for maritime and aviation
- Rural and remote area coverage
- Reduced infrastructure costs

Satellite Constellation Characteristics for 6G

Orbit Type	Altitude	Latency	Coverage	Primary Use Case
LEO	500-2000 km	20-40 ms	Regional	Broadband, IoT
MEO	2000-35,786 km	100-150 ms	Continental	Navigation, Backhaul
GEO	35,786 km	500-600 ms	Hemispheric	Broadcasting, Fixed
HAPs	20-50 km	<10 ms	Local/Regional	Emergency, Events

Source: Compiled from Space Science & Technology (2023) and industry specifications

Conclusion

The applications and use cases presented in this chapter represent the transformative potential of 6G technology. Holographic communication will revolutionize human interaction through life-like 3D telepresence. Digital twins combined with tactile internet will create new paradigms for remote operation and system optimization. Brain-computer interfaces will establish direct neural pathways for communication and control. Space-terrestrial integration will finally achieve the vision of truly global, ubiquitous connectivity.

These applications are not isolated developments but interconnected elements of a comprehensive 6G ecosystem. The success of 6G will depend on the seamless integration of these technologies, supported by advances in artificial intelligence, quantum computing, and materials science. As we move toward 2030, these applications will transition from laboratory demonstrations to commercial reality, fundamentally transforming how humans interact with technology and each other.

Knowledge Check

1. What data rates are required for holographic communication in 6G networks?
   a) 100 Mbps
   b) 1 Gbps
   c) Multi-terabit per second
   d) 10 Gbps

2. Which of the following is NOT a characteristic of tactile internet?
   a) Ultra-low latency (≤1ms)
   b) Low reliability requirements
   c) Haptic feedback support
   d) High availability (99.999%)

3. What is the primary advantage of LEO satellites for 6G networks?
   a) Highest coverage area
   b) Lowest latency among satellite types
   c) Cheapest to launch
   d) No need for ground stations

4. According to market projections, the BCI market is expected to reach what value by 2045?
   a) $500 million
   b) $1.6 billion
   c) $10 billion
   d) $100 million

5. What is the round-trip latency requirement for tactile internet applications?
   a) ≤100ms
   b) ≤50ms
   c) ≤10ms
   d) ≤1ms

6. How will holographic communication transform healthcare delivery in remote areas?

7. What are the main ethical considerations in deploying brain-computer interfaces on a mass scale?

8. Explain how digital twins can improve industrial safety and efficiency.

9. What technical challenges must be overcome for seamless space-terrestrial network integration?

10. How might the convergence of these four application areas create new use cases not possible with individual technologies?

Answers

1. What data rates are required for holographic communication in 6G networks?
   a) 100 Mbps
   b) 1 Gbps
   c) Multi-terabit per second
   d) 10 Gbps
   Answer: c) Multi-terabit per second

2. Which of the following is NOT a characteristic of tactile internet?
   a) Ultra-low latency (≤1ms)
   b) Low reliability requirements
   c) Haptic feedback support
   d) High availability (99.999%)
   Answer: b) Low reliability requirements

3. What is the primary advantage of LEO satellites for 6G networks?
   a) Highest coverage area
   b) Lowest latency among satellite types
   c) Cheapest to launch
   d) No need for ground stations
   Answer: b) Lowest latency among satellite types

4. According to market projections, the BCI market is expected to reach what value by 2045?
   a) $500 million
   b) $1.6 billion
   c) $10 billion
   d) $100 million
   Answer: b) $1.6 billion

5. What is the round-trip latency requirement for tactile internet applications?
   a) ≤100ms
   b) ≤50ms
   c) ≤10ms

d) ≤1ms
Answer: d) ≤1ms

6. How will holographic communication transform healthcare delivery in remote areas?
Answer: Holographic communication will enable specialists to conduct remote consultations with unprecedented realism, examining patients in 3D and guiding local healthcare workers through complex procedures. This technology will provide access to expert medical care in underserved regions, reduce the need for patient travel, and enable real-time collaboration between medical teams globally. The combination of holographic visualization with haptic feedback through tactile internet will allow surgeons to provide guidance that closely mimics physical presence.

7. What are the main ethical considerations in deploying brain-computer interfaces on a mass scale?
Answer: Key ethical considerations include: privacy and security of neural data, ensuring informed consent for brain signal collection, preventing unauthorized access or hacking of BCIs, addressing potential psychological dependence on the technology, ensuring equitable access to avoid creating a "neural divide," and establishing regulations for enhancement versus therapeutic applications. There are also concerns about autonomy and free will when external devices can interpret and act on brain signals.

8. Explain how digital twins can improve industrial safety and efficiency.
Answer: Digital twins enable real-time monitoring and predictive maintenance by creating virtual replicas of industrial equipment and processes. They can simulate dangerous scenarios without risk, predict equipment failures before they occur, optimize production parameters in real-time, and provide training environments for workers. By detecting anomalies early and testing changes virtually before implementation, digital twins significantly reduce accidents, downtime, and operational costs while improving overall efficiency.

9. What technical challenges must be overcome for seamless space-terrestrial network integration?
Answer: Major challenges include: managing handovers between satellite and terrestrial networks with different latencies, developing unified protocols for heterogeneous network elements, addressing Doppler effects from fast-moving LEO satellites, ensuring spectrum compatibility and interference management, implementing adaptive routing algorithms for dynamic topologies, maintaining quality of service across different network segments, and developing cost-effective user terminals that can communicate with both satellite and terrestrial infrastructure.

10. How might the convergence of these four application areas create new use cases not possible with individual technologies?
Answer: The convergence enables revolutionary applications such as: global holographic meetings with participants connected via satellite from anywhere, including brain-controlled interaction; digital twin cities with real-time haptic exploration accessible globally; remote surgery combining holographic visualization, haptic feedback, and neural interfaces for precision control; immersive education where students can mentally interact with holographic historical recreations; and emergency response systems where first responders use BCIs to control drones while receiving holographic situation updates via satellite links.

References

6G-TWIN. (2024). *PROJECT VISION 6G-TWIN*. Retrieved from https://6g-twin.eu/

Bhide, S. (2025). Review on 6G communication and its architecture, technologies included, challenges, security challenges and requirements, applications, with respect to AI domain. *IET Quantum Communication*. Wiley Online Library.

DeepAI. (2021). Digital-Twin-Enabled 6G: Vision, Architectural Trends, and Future Directions. Retrieved from https://deepai.org/publication/digital-twin-enabled-6g-vision-architectural-trends-and-future-directions

Ericsson. (2022). *6G - Follow the journey to the next generation networks*. Retrieved from https://www.ericsson.com/en/6g

Health Data Science. (2024). Recent Progress in Wearable Brain–Computer Interface (BCI) Devices Based on Electroencephalogram (EEG) for Medical Applications: A Review. *Health Data Science*.

IDTechEx. (2024). *Brain Computer Interfaces 2025-2045: Technologies, Players, Forecasts*. Retrieved from https://www.idtechex.com/en/research-report/brain-computer-interfaces-2025-2045-technologies-players-forecasts/1024

IEEE. (2022). Creating Efficient Integrated Satellite-Terrestrial Networks in the 6G Era. *IEEE Wireless Communications*.

MediaTek. (2025). *The Future of 6G Satellite Connectivity is Open, Fast, Pervasive*. Retrieved from https://www.mediatek.com/tek-talk-blogs/the-future-of-6g-satellite-connectivity-is-open-fast-pervasive

MDPI. (2022). Hybrid Satellite–Terrestrial Networks toward 6G: Key Technologies and Open Issues. *Sensors*, 22(21), 8544.

PMC. (2024). Brain–computer interfaces: the innovative key to unlocking neurological conditions. *International Journal of Surgery*, 110(9), 5745–5762.

ResearchAndMarkets. (2020). Worldwide 3D Holographic Display and Services Industry to 2025 - Rise of 5G and 6G Communication Technologies Presents Opportunities. PR Newswire.

Rohde & Schwarz. (2023). *6G wireless technology*. Retrieved from https://www.rohde-schwarz.com/us/solutions/wireless-communications-testing/wireless-standards/6g/6g-overview_253278.html

ScienceDirect. (2024). Bridging Minds and Machines: The Recent Advances of Brain-Computer Interfaces in Neurological and Neurosurgical Applications. *World Neurosurgery*.

Space Science & Technology. (2023). Integration of Communication and Navigation Technologies toward LEO-Enabled 6G Networks: A Survey. *Space: Science & Technology*.

Chapter 15: Cloud-Native and AI-Native 6G

Executive Summary

This chapter explores the convergence of cloud-native and AI-native architectures in sixth-generation (6G) wireless networks. As telecommunications evolve beyond connectivity-centric models, 6G networks are being designed with cloud-native principles and artificial intelligence at their core. The chapter examines how cloud-native architectures enable scalability, flexibility, and efficient resource utilization through containerization and microservices. It then delves into AI-native capabilities that transform networks into intelligent, self-organizing systems. Key concepts covered include intelligent orchestration for dynamic resource management, zero-touch automation for autonomous network operations, and intent-based networking that translates business objectives into network configurations. Through detailed analysis of architectures, enabling technologies, and implementation strategies, this chapter provides a comprehensive understanding of how cloud-native and AI-native approaches will fundamentally reshape telecommunications infrastructure and services in the 6G era.

Table of Contents

Introduction

The evolution from fifth-generation (5G) to sixth-generation (6G) wireless networks represents a paradigm shift in telecommunications architecture and operational philosophy. As noted by Li et al. (2022), "6G cloud-native system framework serves as the foundation of next generation technologies," marking a transformation from communication-centric to compute-centric systems. This architectural evolution integrates cloud-native principles with artificial intelligence to create networks that are not merely faster but fundamentally more intelligent and autonomous.

The convergence of cloud-native and AI-native architectures addresses critical challenges in modern telecommunications. Network operators face exponential growth in data traffic, increasing service complexity, and demands for ultra-low latency applications. Traditional network management approaches, which rely heavily on manual configuration and reactive problem-solving, cannot scale to meet these requirements. Cloud-native architectures provide the flexibility and scalability needed for modern networks, while AI-native capabilities enable autonomous operation and optimization.

This chapter examines three fundamental pillars of 6G network transformation:

1. **Intelligent Orchestration**: Dynamic, AI-driven management of network resources across multiple domains
2. **Zero-Touch Automation**: Fully autonomous network operations with minimal human intervention
3. **Intent-Based Networking**: Translation of high-level business objectives into network configurations

Cloud-Native Architecture in 6G Networks

Fundamental Principles

Cloud-native architecture represents a fundamental departure from traditional telecommunications infrastructure. According to Ericsson (2023), cloud-native design enables four critical capabilities:

- **Microservices Architecture**: Decomposition of network functions into smaller, manageable services
- **Containerization**: Packaging of applications with dependencies for consistent deployment
- **Dynamic Orchestration**: Automated management of resources based on demand
- **Continuous Integration/Deployment**: Rapid, automated updates and improvements

The transition to cloud-native architectures in 6G builds upon lessons learned from 5G deployments. As highlighted by Nokia (2021), "5G Core's cloud-native architecture and techniques change the automation equation, enabling an automation framework based on exposing automation functions to each other via APIs."

Architectural Components

The 6G cloud-native architecture comprises several key components that work together to provide seamless connectivity and computing services:

Key Components of 6G Cloud-Native Architecture

(Adapted from Ericsson, 2023; Nokia, 2021; Li et al., 2022)

Component	Function	Key Technologies
Service-Based Architecture (SBA)	Modular network functions communicating via APIs	RESTful APIs, HTTP/2, JSON
Container Orchestration	Automated deployment and scaling	Kubernetes, Docker, Helm
Network Function Virtualization	Software-based network functions	NFV MANO, VNFs, CNFs
Edge Computing Platform	Distributed computing at network edge	MEC, Edge Cloud, CDN
Data Fabric	Unified data management across domains	Data Lakes, Stream Processing

Implementation Strategies

Implementing cloud-native 6G networks requires careful planning and phased approaches. Based on industry best practices identified by ABI Research (2024), successful implementations follow these strategies:

1. **Infrastructure Modernization:** Transitioning from hardware-centric to software-defined infrastructure
2. **DevOps Integration:** Adopting agile methodologies for continuous improvement
3. **Multi-Cloud Support:** Ensuring portability across different cloud environments
4. **Security-First Design:** Embedding security at every architectural layer

AI-Native 6G: The Intelligence Revolution

Defining AI-Native Networks

AI-native networks represent a fundamental architectural shift rather than merely layering artificial intelligence onto current network designs. Wu et al. (2021) explain that sixth-generation systems will position AI as a foundational element, with the capability to deliver ubiquitous intelligence—making AI-powered services accessible to any user, at any location, at any moment.

This concept of "intelligence inclusion" marks a profound departure from how we've traditionally thought about network services. In previous generations, networks served primarily as data pipes—transporting information between endpoints without understanding or acting on the content flowing through them. AI-native architecture transforms the network itself into an intelligent platform that can perceive, reason, learn, and make decisions autonomously.

The practical implications are far-reaching. Networks will predict congestion before it occurs and proactively reroute traffic. They'll detect anomalous patterns indicating security threats and respond in milliseconds. Resource allocation will happen dynamically based on learned user behavior patterns and application requirements. Quality of service will adapt in real-time as conditions change, without human intervention.

Building AI directly into the network fabric means embedding machine learning capabilities at multiple layers—from individual devices at the edge, through base stations and access points, up to core network functions and orchestration systems. This distributed intelligence architecture allows for processing data where it makes most sense: simple decisions handled locally with minimal latency, complex analysis performed in regional compute clusters, and network-wide optimization coordinated centrally.

Edge AI capabilities become particularly crucial. By processing data near its source, networks can support latency-sensitive applications like autonomous vehicles, industrial robotics, and augmented reality that simply cannot tolerate the delays involved in round-tripping data to distant cloud servers. A self-driving car making split-second decisions cannot wait 50-100 milliseconds for cloud processing—it needs local AI inference in single-digit milliseconds.

The "intelligence inclusion" principle also addresses accessibility concerns. Today, advanced AI services often require expensive hardware, specialized technical knowledge, or subscription to proprietary platforms. AI-native networks democratize access by providing AI as a fundamental network service, similar to how we now take internet connectivity itself for granted. A small business in a developing nation could access the same sophisticated AI capabilities as a large corporation, leveling the competitive playing field.

Training and updating AI models across such massive distributed systems presents enormous challenges. Networks must continuously learn from billions of interactions while maintaining privacy, security, and consistency. Federated learning techniques allow models to improve through decentralized training without centralizing sensitive data. Transfer learning enables knowledge gained in one network domain to accelerate learning in others.

Energy efficiency becomes critical when AI processing scales to network-wide deployment. Specialized AI accelerator chips, neuromorphic computing architectures, and intelligent power management will be essential to prevent AI-native networks from consuming unsustainable amounts of energy.

The shift also raises important questions about transparency, accountability, and control. When networks make autonomous decisions affecting service quality, resource allocation, and access, users and regulators need mechanisms to understand, audit, and potentially override these decisions. Building explainable AI into network functions becomes not just technically desirable but socially necessary.

The AI-native approach encompasses three integration stages:

1. **AI for Networks:** Using AI to optimize network performance and operations
2. **Networks for AI:** Designing networks to support AI workloads and services
3. **AI as a Service:** Providing AI capabilities as native network services

Architectural Framework

The AI-native 6G architecture introduces new planes and interfaces to support pervasive intelligence:

AI-Native 6G Architecture

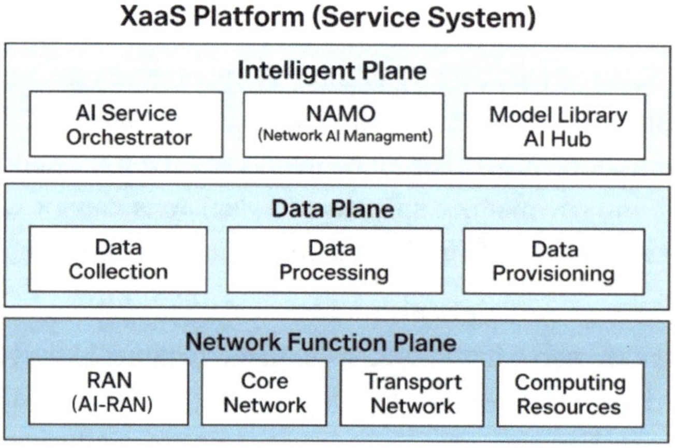

Based on Wu et al., 2021; Li et al., 2022; NVIDIA, 2024)

AI Integration Technologies

Several key technologies enable AI-native capabilities in 6G networks:

1. **Distributed AI/ML Frameworks**
    - Federated learning for privacy-preserving model training
    - Edge AI for real-time inference and decision-making
    - Transfer learning for efficient model adaptation
2. **AI-Optimized Infrastructure**
    - GPU/TPU acceleration for AI workloads
    - Neuromorphic computing for energy-efficient AI
    - Quantum computing integration for complex optimization
3. **AI Service Platforms**
    - Model marketplaces for AI service deployment
    - AutoML for automated model development

- MLOps for AI lifecycle management

Intelligent Orchestration

Evolution of Network Orchestration

Intelligent orchestration represents a fundamental shift from static, rule-based management to dynamic, AI-driven control. According to the AI-RAN Alliance (2024), "Technologies such as the RAN Intelligent Controller (RIC) host modular apps—xApps and rApps—that apply AI for real-time monitoring, traffic steering, interference mitigation, and self-optimization."

Multi-Domain Orchestration Architecture

Modern 6G networks require orchestration across multiple domains:

Multi-Domain Orchestration Components

Domain	Orchestration Function	AI/ML Application
Radio Access	Dynamic spectrum allocation, beam management	Reinforcement learning for resource optimization
Core Network	Service chain optimization, slice management	Graph neural networks for topology optimization
Transport	Path computation, traffic engineering	Time-series prediction for traffic patterns
Edge Computing	Workload placement, resource scaling	Multi-agent learning for distributed decisions
End-to-End	Service assurance, SLA management	Anomaly detection, predictive analytics

(Source: AI-RAN Alliance, 2024; Zhang et al., 2022; Rai, 2024)

Intelligent Orchestration Workflows

The implementation of intelligent orchestration follows sophisticated workflows that integrate AI decision-making:

Intelligent Orchestration Workflow

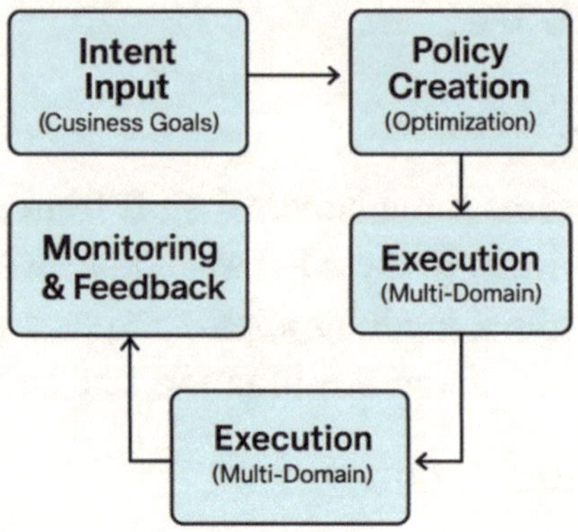

(Adapted from ETSI ZSM, 2023; Coronado et al., 2022)

Key aspects of intelligent orchestration include:

1. **Context-Aware Decision Making**: Considering network state, user patterns, and business objectives
2. **Predictive Resource Allocation**: Anticipating demand before it occurs
3. **Cross-Domain Optimization**: Coordinating resources across RAN, core, and edge
4. **Continuous Learning**: Improving decisions based on outcomes

Case Study: AI-Driven Network Slicing

Network slicing exemplifies intelligent orchestration in action. As reported by Zhang et al. (2022), AI-native network slicing enables:

- **Dynamic Slice Creation:** Automated instantiation based on service requirements
- **Resource Optimization:** AI-driven allocation across shared infrastructure
- **Performance Assurance:** Continuous monitoring and adjustment
- **Inter-Slice Coordination:** Preventing resource conflicts and ensuring fairness

Zero-Touch Automation

Foundations of Zero-Touch Networks

Zero-touch automation represents the highest level of network autonomy achievable. ETSI ZSM (2023) describes the end goal as creating networks that operate with substantial independence, governed by overarching policy frameworks, and capable of configuring themselves, monitoring their own performance, recovering from failures, and optimizing operations—all without requiring human involvement.

This vision builds upon decades of incremental automation progress in telecommunications. Traditional networks required manual configuration of individual network elements, with engineers typing commands into routers, switches, and other equipment. Over time, network management systems provided centralized control, but humans still made the decisions—software simply executed them faster. Zero-touch networks take the final leap: the network becomes the decision-maker, with humans setting only high-level intent and constraints.

The autonomy spectrum spans multiple levels. At the lowest level, networks can execute predefined scripts and workflows. Moving up, they respond to specific conditions with programmed reactions. True zero-touch operation reaches the highest levels where networks perceive complex situations, reason about optimal responses, learn from outcomes, and continuously improve their decision-making without explicit programming for every scenario.

Policy-based governance provides the framework for this autonomy. Rather than micromanaging network behavior, operators define business objectives, service level agreements, security requirements, and regulatory compliance rules. The network interprets these policies and determines how best to achieve them given current conditions and available resources. For example, a policy might state "gold tier customers receive priority during congestion" without specifying exactly how to implement that priority—the network figures out the optimal approach dynamically.

Self-configuration capabilities allow networks to onboard new equipment automatically. When a new base station powers up, it discovers its neighbors, determines optimal radio parameters based on the environment, downloads appropriate software, and integrates itself into the network fabric—all without technician intervention. This dramatically reduces deployment time and eliminates human configuration errors.

Self-monitoring extends beyond simple threshold alarms. Networks develop baselines of normal behavior through continuous observation, detect subtle anomalies that might indicate emerging problems, correlate events across multiple systems to identify root causes, and distinguish between symptoms and actual issues. Machine learning models trained on historical data can predict equipment failures days or weeks in advance, enabling proactive maintenance before service impacts occur.

Self-healing represents perhaps the most compelling capability. When failures happen—and they inevitably do—zero-touch networks detect the problem, assess the impact, determine available remediation options, implement the best solution, and verify recovery. A fiber cut might trigger automatic traffic rerouting through alternate paths. A software bug causing service degradation might prompt the network to roll back to a previous stable version. Hardware failures trigger orchestration systems to instantiate replacement virtual network functions on available compute resources.

Self-optimization continuously tunes network parameters to maximize performance and efficiency. Energy consumption adapts to traffic patterns—base stations entering low-power modes during quiet periods. Spectrum allocation shifts dynamically based on demand in different cells. Routing protocols adjust to changing traffic matrices. Load balancing algorithms learn which distribution strategies work best under different conditions.

The economic benefits are substantial. Labor costs drop significantly when networks require fewer human operators. Service velocity increases—changes that once took weeks of planning and execution happen in minutes. Reliability improves as networks detect and resolve issues faster than human operators could. Capital efficiency increases through better resource utilization.

However, achieving true zero-touch operation presents formidable challenges. Networks must be designed with autonomy in mind from the ground up—retrofitting legacy systems proves extremely difficult. The AI models driving decisions require enormous amounts of training data. Ensuring these autonomous systems make safe, reliable, and predictable decisions demands rigorous testing and validation. Operators must develop new skills focused on policy management rather than hands-on configuration.

Trust becomes a critical barrier. Network operators accustomed to direct control find it difficult to hand over decision-making authority to automated systems, especially for critical infrastructure. Building that trust requires demonstrating autonomous systems can handle edge cases, fail safely when encountering situations outside their training, and provide visibility into their reasoning processes.

Regulatory and liability questions emerge. When an autonomous network makes a decision that causes service disruption or security breach, who bears responsibility? How do regulators audit and approve network behaviors that emerge from machine learning rather than explicit programming? Industry standards and legal frameworks are still evolving to address these questions.

Architectural Requirements

Implementing zero-touch automation requires fundamental architectural capabilities:

Zero-Touch Automation Requirements

Capability	Description	Enabling Technologies
Self-Configuration	Automatic setup and deployment	Template-based provisioning, AI planning
Self-Monitoring	Continuous health assessment	Telemetry, anomaly detection
Self-Healing	Automatic fault resolution	Root cause analysis, automated remediation
Self-Optimization	Performance improvement	Reinforcement learning, predictive analytics
Self-Protection	Security threat mitigation	AI-based threat detection, automated response

Based on ETSI ZSM, 2023; Yang et al., 2025; Coronado et al., 2022

Implementation Framework

The zero-touch automation framework comprises several interconnected components:

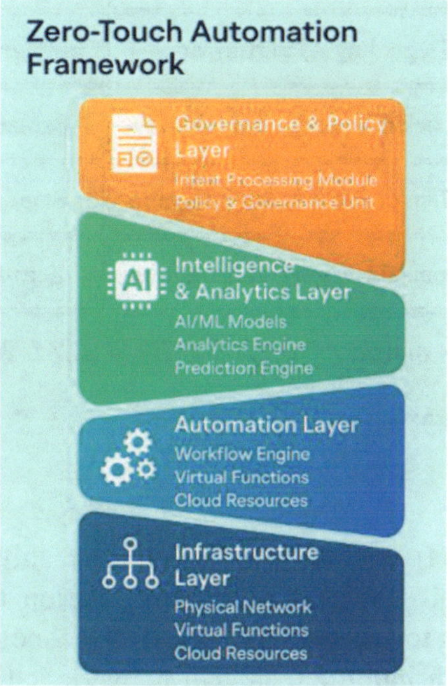

(Source: ETSI ZSM, 2023; Ericsson, 2023; Yang et al., 2025)

Closed-Loop Automation

Central to zero-touch automation is the concept of closed-loop control:

1. **Observe**: Continuous monitoring of network state and performance
2. **Orient**: Analysis of data to understand the current situation
3. **Decide**: AI-driven decision-making based on policies and objectives
4. **Act**: Automated execution of decisions
5. **Learn**: Feedback incorporation for continuous improvement

Challenges and Solutions

Implementing zero-touch automation faces several challenges:

Zero-Touch Automation Challenges and Solutions

Challenge	Impact	Solution Approach
Data Quality	Poor decisions from bad data	Data validation, cleansing pipelines
Model Drift	Degrading AI performance	Continuous model monitoring, retraining
Trust & Explainability	Lack of operator confidence	Explainable AI, gradual automation
Integration Complexity	Difficult multi-vendor integration	Standardized interfaces, open APIs
Security Risks	Automated attacks, vulnerabilities	Zero-trust architecture, AI security

(Adapted from Coronado et al., 2022; ETSI ZSM, 2023; Infovista, 2023)

Intent-Based Networking

Conceptual Framework

Intent-Based Networking (IBN) represents a fundamental shift in how networks are managed, moving away from traditional device-focused configuration toward an approach centered on business objectives. According to Wei et al. (2020), IBN technology serves as a bridge, translating what users want to accomplish into the technical network settings, operational procedures, and upkeep protocols that will be essential for building AI-powered 6G infrastructure.

Beyond this foundational definition, IBN incorporates AI/ML algorithms, policy analytics, and closed-loop automation to dynamically translate high-level business goals into actionable network behaviors. It continuously monitors performance metrics and compliance parameters to ensure that network intent aligns with service-level objectives (SLOs) and user expectations.

Modern IBN architecture also employs knowledge-driven orchestration, predictive analytics, and cognitive feedback loops, enabling proactive fault resolution and adaptive optimization. In the context of 6G, IBN plays a central role in achieving zero-touch network operations, where intent, automation, and intelligence converge to deliver self-configuring, self-healing, and self-optimizing networks.

Thus, IBN serves as the conceptual backbone of intelligent 6G network management—bridging the gap between business intent and autonomous technical execution.

Intent Processing Architecture

The intent-based networking system comprises five key stages:

Intent-Based Networking Processing Flow

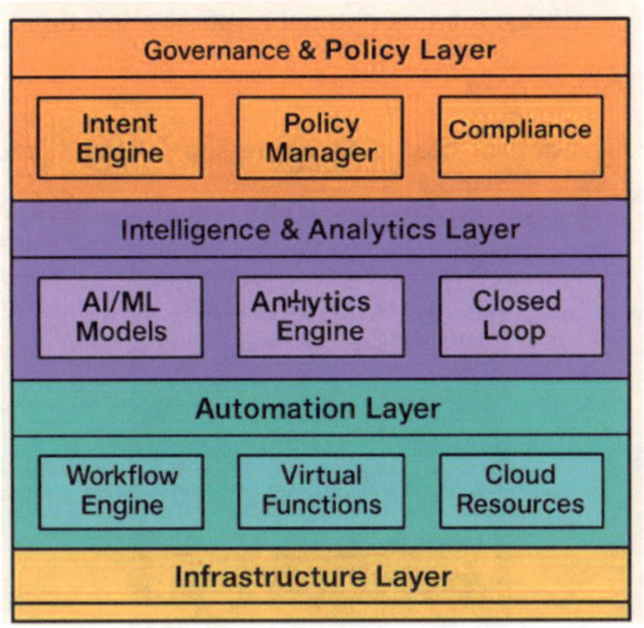

Based on Wei et al., 2020; SDxCentral, 2022; ResearchGate, 2020

Intent Languages and Models

Intent specification requires formal languages that can express business objectives:

Intent Specification Approaches

Approach	Description	Example Use Case
Natural Language	Free-form text processing	"Ensure video calls have low latency"
Template-Based	Structured forms with parameters	Service templates with QoS parameters
Policy Language	Formal logic expressions	IF-THEN rules for network behavior
Model-Driven	UML/YANG-based models	Service chain definitions
API-Based	Programmatic intent submission	DevOps integration, CI/CD pipelines

(Source: Wei et al., 2020; Ericsson, 2023; SDxCentral, 2022)

AI-Powered Intent Translation

The translation of high-level intents to network configurations leverages advanced AI techniques:

1. **Natural Language Processing**: Understanding unstructured intent statements
2. **Knowledge Graphs**: Mapping intents to network capabilities

3. **Constraint Satisfaction**: Ensuring feasible configurations
4. **Optimization Algorithms**: Finding optimal resource allocations

Intent Lifecycle Management

Managing intents throughout their lifecycle requires sophisticated processes:

Intent Lifecycle Management (Adapted from Wei et al., 2020; ETSI ZSM, 2023)

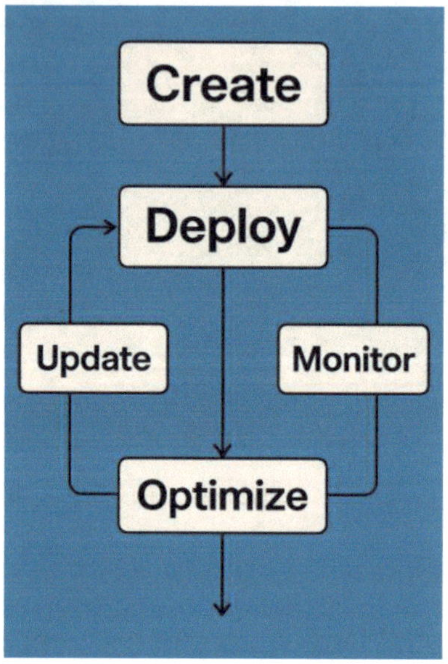

Key lifecycle considerations include:

- **Intent Conflicts:** Resolving competing objectives
- **Intent Drift:** Ensuring continued alignment with business goals
- **Intent Assurance:** Verifying intent fulfillment
- **Intent Evolution:** Adapting to changing requirements

Integration and Future Directions

Convergence of Technologies

The integration of cloud-native, AI-native, and automation technologies creates synergistic benefits:

Technology Convergence Benefits

Integration	Benefits	Example Applications
Cloud-Native + AI	Scalable AI services, distributed learning	Edge AI, federated learning
AI + Zero-Touch	Intelligent automation, predictive operations	Self-healing networks
Intent + Orchestration	Business-aligned operations	Dynamic service creation
All Technologies	Fully autonomous networks	Cognitive networks

Based on Wu et al., 2021; NVIDIA, 2024; Ericsson, 2023

Standardization Efforts

Multiple organizations are working on standardization:

- **3GPP:** AI/ML specifications for 5G-Advanced and 6G
- **ETSI:** Zero-touch network and service management (ZSM)
- **ITU:** IMT-2030 framework for 6G
- **O-RAN Alliance:** Open, intelligent RAN specifications
- **TM Forum:** Intent-driven autonomous networks

Research Challenges

Several research challenges remain:

1. **Scalability**: Managing billions of devices and connections
2. **Energy Efficiency**: Reducing the power consumption of AI operations
3. **Security**: Protecting autonomous systems from attacks
4. **Trustworthiness**: Ensuring reliable AI decisions
5. **Interoperability**: Multi-vendor, multi-domain integration

Future Outlook

The future of 6G networks will be characterized by:

- **Pervasive Intelligence:** AI embedded at every network layer

- **Autonomous Operations:** Minimal human intervention
- **Service Innovation:** Rapid deployment of new capabilities
- **Sustainability:** Energy-efficient, environmentally conscious networks
- **Human-Centric Design:** Networks that adapt to human needs

Knowledge Check

1. What is the primary difference between cloud-native and traditional network architectures?
   a) Speed of data transmission
   b) Use of hardware accelerators
   c) Microservices and containerization approach
   d) Number of network nodes

2. Which component is NOT part of the AI-native 6G architecture's three-plane model?
   a) Intelligent Plane
   b) Data Plane
   c) Security Plane
   d) Network Function Plane

3. What does NAMO stand for in the context of 6G intelligent orchestration?
   a) Network Automation and Management Operations
   b) Network AI Management and Orchestration
   c) Native Application Management Organization
   d) Networked Autonomous Mobile Operations

4. Which self-capability is NOT typically included in zero-touch automation?
   a) Self-configuration
   b) Self-marketing
   c) Self-healing
   d) Self-optimization

5. In intent-based networking, what is the first stage of intent processing?
   a) Intent deployment
   b) Intent verification
   c) Intent ingestion
   d) Intent optimization

6. How does the convergence of cloud-native and AI-native architectures address the limitations of current 5G networks?

7. Explain the role of federated learning in maintaining privacy within AI-native 6G networks.

8. What are the main challenges in implementing zero-touch automation across multi-vendor networks?

9. How does intent-based networking transform the relationship between business objectives and network operations?

10. Discuss the potential risks of fully autonomous networks and mitigation strategies.

Answers

1. What is the primary difference between cloud-native and traditional network architectures?
   a) Speed of data transmission
   b) Use of hardware accelerators
   c) Microservices and containerization approach
   d) Number of network nodes
   Answer: c) Microservices and containerization approach
   Cloud-native architectures fundamentally differ by decomposing network functions into microservices that run in containers, enabling greater flexibility and scalability.

2. Which component is NOT part of the AI-native 6G architecture's three-plane model?
   a) Intelligent Plane
   b) Data Plane
   c) Security Plane
   d) Network Function Plane
   Answer: c) Security Plane
   The AI-native 6G architecture consists of the Intelligent Plane, Data Plane, and Network Function Plane. Security is embedded across all planes rather than being a separate plane.

3. What does NAMO stand for in the context of 6G intelligent orchestration?
   a) Network Automation and Management Operations
   b) Network AI Management and Orchestration
   c) Native Application Management Organization
   d) Networked Autonomous Mobile Operations
   Answer: b) Network AI Management and Orchestration
   NAMO (Network AI Management and Orchestration) is responsible for orchestrating, managing, and scheduling end-to-end network AI-related services and resources.

4. Which self-capability is NOT typically included in zero-touch automation?
   a) Self-configuration
   b) Self-marketing
   c) Self-healing
   d) Self-optimization

Answer: b) Self-marketing
Zero-touch automation includes self-configuration, self-monitoring, self-healing, and self-optimization capabilities. Self-marketing is not a network automation function.

5. In intent-based networking, what is the first stage of intent processing?
   a) Intent deployment
   b) Intent verification
   c) Intent ingestion
   d) Intent optimization
   Answer: c) Intent ingestion
   Intent ingestion is the first stage where the system recognizes and collects network intents through user interactions before validation and translation.

6. How does the convergence of cloud-native and AI-native architectures address the limitations of current 5G networks?
   Answer: The convergence addresses several key limitations:
   - **Scalability:** Cloud-native microservices enable horizontal scaling to handle massive IoT deployments
   - **Flexibility:** Containerization allows rapid deployment and updates of network functions
   - **Intelligence:** AI-native design enables predictive operations and self-optimization
   - **Automation:** Reduces operational complexity through autonomous management
   - **Service Innovation:** Faster time-to-market for new services through DevOps practices

7. Explain the role of federated learning in maintaining privacy within AI-native 6G networks.
   Answer: Federated learning plays a crucial role in privacy preservation by:
   - Keeping training data on local devices rather than centralizing it
   - Sharing only model updates (gradients) instead of raw data
   - Enabling collaborative learning across distributed nodes
   - Reducing data exposure risks and compliance concerns
   - Supporting edge AI applications with local data sovereignty

   This approach aligns with privacy regulations like GDPR while maintaining AI effectiveness.

8. What are the main challenges in implementing zero-touch automation across multi-vendor networks?
   Answer: Key challenges include:
   - **Interoperability:** Different vendors use proprietary interfaces and data models
   - **Data Standardization:** Inconsistent telemetry formats and semantics

- **Trust Models:** Varying security implementations and trust boundaries
- **Orchestration Complexity:** Coordinating automation across vendor domains
- **Accountability:** Determining responsibility when automated actions fail

Solutions involve open standards (O-RAN, ETSI ZSM), common data models, and standardized APIs.

9. How does intent-based networking transform the relationship between business objectives and network operations?

   Answer: Intent-based networking creates a fundamental shift by:
   - **Abstraction:** Business users express goals without technical details
   - **Alignment:** Network automatically configures to meet business objectives
   - **Agility:** Rapid adaptation to changing business requirements
   - **Visibility:** Clear mapping between intents and network behavior
   - **Accountability:** Measurable outcomes tied to business KPIs

   This transformation enables business-driven networking rather than technology-driven operations.

10. Discuss the potential risks of fully autonomous networks and mitigation strategies.

    Answer: Potential risks and mitigations include:

    Risks:
    - Cascading failures from AI errors
    - Security vulnerabilities in autonomous systems
    - Loss of human expertise and control
    - Unpredictable emergent behaviors
    - Ethical concerns in decision-making

    Mitigation Strategies:
    - Implement human-in-the-loop controls for critical decisions
    - Deploy explainable AI for transparency
    - Maintain override capabilities and fallback modes
    - Continuous monitoring and bounded autonomy
    - Regular security audits and AI model validation
    - Gradual automation with proven safe zones

References

3GPP. (2024). *Technical Specification 23.501: System architecture for the 5G System (5GS)*. Release 18. 3rd Generation Partnership Project.

ABI Research. (2024). *5G & 6G Cloud-Native Systems Market Data Overview*. Retrieved from https://www.abiresearch.com

Choi, A. J. (2024). The shift towards cloud-native architecture and disaggregation of network functions. *AI-RAN Alliance Technical Report*.

Coronado, E., et al. (2022). Zero Touch Management: A Survey of Network Automation Solutions for 5G and 6G Networks. *IEEE Communications Surveys & Tutorials*, 24(4), 2435-2465.

Ericsson. (2023). *Defining AI native: A key enabler for advanced intelligent telecom networks*. Ericsson White Paper. Retrieved from https://www.ericsson.com

ETSI. (2023). *Zero touch network and Service Management (ZSM); Architecture and Solutions*. ETSI GS ZSM 002 V1.3.1.

Li, Q., et al. (2022). 6G Cloud-Native System: Vision, Challenges, Architecture Framework and Enabling Technologies. *IEEE Access*, 10, 96602-96625.

Nokia. (2021). *5G Core (5GC): Creating what's next*. Nokia Networks White Paper.

NVIDIA. (2024). *Boosting AI-Driven Innovation in 6G with the AI-RAN Alliance, 3GPP, and O-RAN*. NVIDIA Technical Blog.

Rakuten Symphony. (2023). *6G starts to take shape with AI, open vRAN integration*. Retrieved from https://symphony.rakuten.com

Rai, S. (2024). Architecting the AI-Native Future of 6G: From RF Intelligence to GenAI-Driven Operations. *The Fast Mode*.

Wei, Y., et al. (2020). Intent-based networks for 6G: Insights and challenges. *Digital Communications and Networks*, 8(4), 320-332.

Wu, J., et al. (2021). Toward Native Artificial Intelligence in 6G Networks: System Design, Architectures, and Paradigms. *arXiv preprint arXiv:2103.02823*.

Yang, L., et al. (2025). Towards Zero Touch Networks: Cross-Layer Automated Security Solutions for 6G Wireless Networks. *arXiv preprint arXiv:2502.20627*.

Zhang, Y., et al. (2022). AI-Native Network Slicing for 6G Networks. *IEEE Wireless Communications*, 29(1), 96-103.

Chapter 16: 5G Deployment Strategies

Executive Summary

Chapter 16 examines 5G deployment strategies, focusing on the critical distinction between public and private network implementations and the revolutionary impact of Open RAN architectures. The chapter explores how organizations worldwide are navigating deployment challenges while leveraging new technological paradigms to create flexible, cost-effective 5G solutions. Key insights include the rapid growth of private 5G networks for enterprise applications, the transformative potential of disaggregated architectures, and the strategic importance of spectrum allocation in determining deployment success.

Table of Contents

Introduction

The rollout of fifth-generation wireless technology marks a transformative moment for how we build and operate telecommunications systems. Network operators now face complex choices that must account for engineering requirements, financial realities, and how their organizations can adapt to new paradigms.

Recent data from early 2025 shows remarkable progress in American 5G infrastructure. According to Ookla's measurements, the United States has seen substantial improvements in network performance, largely thanks to the widespread adoption of standalone 5G architecture. By the fourth quarter of 2024, median download speeds in the U.S. reached 388 megabits per second—a significant jump from the 305 Mbps recorded just twelve months prior. This performance leap pushed American networks ahead of Japan, where median speeds stood at 254 Mbps, and China, which recorded 305 Mbps during the same period. These figures come from Ookla's comprehensive analysis published in 2025.

The shift to standalone 5G represents more than just faster speeds. Unlike earlier implementations that relied on existing 4G infrastructure, standalone architecture allows networks to fully leverage 5G's native capabilities, including ultra-low latency communication and the ability to support massive numbers of connected devices simultaneously. This architectural evolution enables carriers to deliver on the technology's promise across diverse use cases—from enhanced mobile broadband for consumers to mission-critical industrial applications.

The landscape of 5G deployment has evolved significantly, with organizations facing critical choices between public and private network architectures, traditional integrated systems versus Open RAN implementations, and various spectrum utilization strategies. These decisions profoundly impact network performance, security, flexibility, and total cost of ownership.

Public vs Private 5G Networks

Public 5G Networks

Mobile network operators run public 5G systems that serve the general population, offering widespread access and seamless connectivity across vast geographic areas. By the end of 2024, North American carriers had built out substantial 5G infrastructure, with the United States and Canada collectively supporting over 182 million active 5G subscriptions. This deployment scale represents approximately one-fifth of all 5G connections across the Americas, showing growth rates approaching 20% annually, according to 5G Americas' 2025 industry report.

These carrier-operated networks build upon decades of infrastructure investment, utilizing cell towers, fiber backhaul systems, and sophisticated core network equipment that cost billions of dollars to deploy and maintain. The architecture enables three fundamental service categories that define 5G's value proposition. First, enhanced mobile broadband delivers dramatically faster data speeds for consumer applications like video streaming and cloud gaming. Second, ultra-reliable low-latency communications support time-sensitive applications where milliseconds matter, such as autonomous vehicle coordination and remote medical procedures. Third, massive machine-type communications allow networks to efficiently handle millions of IoT sensors and devices within a single geographic area, enabling smart city deployments and industrial automation at scale.

This public network model follows the traditional telecommunications business approach where operators invest in shared infrastructure that serves diverse subscribers—from individual consumers to large enterprises—all accessing the same underlying network resources.

Public 5G Network Characteristics

Characteristic	Description	Impact
Coverage	Wide area, nationwide deployments	Broad accessibility for consumers
Spectrum	Licensed bands (low, mid, high)	Regulated interference protection
Investment Model	Carrier-funded infrastructure	High capital requirements
Service Model	Subscription-based consumer/enterprise	Scalable revenue generation
Performance	Shared resources among users	Variable based on network load

Source: Adapted from 5G Americas (2025) and GSA (2024)

Private 5G Networks

Enterprise-owned wireless systems represent one of the most significant developments in how organizations approach connectivity. Unlike traditional carrier services, these private networks give companies direct control over their wireless infrastructure, enabling them to tailor coverage, security policies, and performance characteristics to their specific operational needs.

The momentum behind private 5G has accelerated rapidly. According to IoT Analytics' 2025 research, seventeen nations across Europe had allocated dedicated spectrum for enterprise wireless deployments by May 2024, with nine of these countries already hosting active private network installations. This regulatory support reflects growing recognition that certain industries require connectivity solutions beyond what public carriers can provide—particularly in sectors handling sensitive data, operating mission-critical processes, or requiring guaranteed network performance.

The business case for private networks continues strengthening as costs decline and use cases proliferate. Industry analysts project robust growth in infrastructure spending, with investments in private 5G and 4G LTE systems for vertical industries expanding at roughly 20% compound annual growth rate through 2027. ResearchAndMarkets forecasts this market segment will surpass

$6 billion by 2027, driven by adoption across manufacturing, logistics, healthcare, energy, and transportation sectors (ResearchAndMarkets, 2025).

What makes private networks compelling? Organizations gain several strategic advantages. They control when and how network upgrades occur, avoiding dependencies on carrier roadmaps. Security-conscious industries can implement customized protocols and keep data traffic entirely on-premises. Manufacturers can guarantee the ultra-low latency needed for robotics and automation. Mining companies can deploy networks in remote locations where carrier coverage doesn't exist. These tailored solutions address connectivity challenges that one-size-fits-all public networks simply cannot solve.

Private 5G Network Architecture

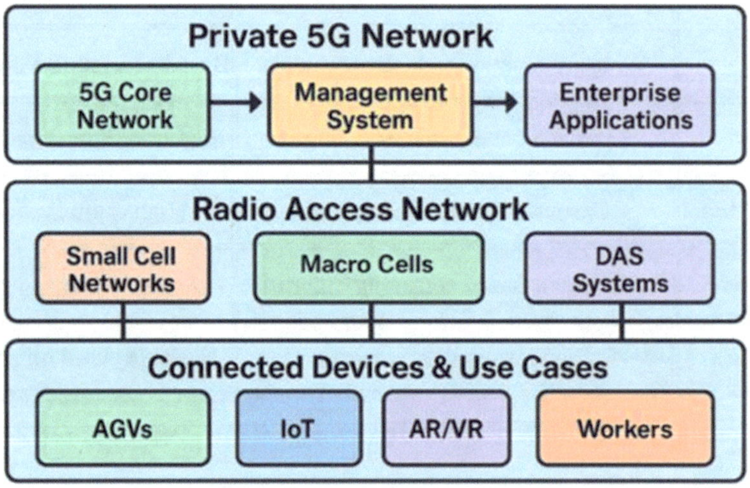

Private 5G Network Architecture

Source: Adapted from Private 5G deployment architectures (STL Partners, 2023; HPE, 2024)

Deployment Comparison

The choice between public and private 5G networks depends on specific organizational requirements, use cases, and economic considerations.

Public vs Private 5G Network Comparison

Aspect	Public 5G	Private 5G
Coverage Area	Wide area, citywide/nationwide	Localized (campus, facility)
Control	Managed by MNO	Full enterprise control
Customization	Limited	Highly customizable
Security	Shared infrastructure	Dedicated, isolated

Aspect	Public 5G	Private 5G
Latency	Variable (10-30ms)	Ultra-low (<5ms)
Reliability	Best effort	Guaranteed SLAs
Cost Model	OPEX (subscription)	CAPEX + OPEX
Deployment Time	Immediate (if available)	3-6 months
Use Cases	Consumer, general enterprise	Mission-critical, specialized

Source: Analysis based on IoT Analytics (2025), STL Partners (2023)

Open RAN and Disaggregated Architectures

Open RAN Fundamentals

The radio access network has traditionally been built as an integrated system where a single vendor provides all components—radios, baseband processors, and the software tying them together—in a tightly coupled package. Open RAN challenges this conventional approach by breaking apart these elements into separate, interchangeable components that communicate through standardized interfaces.

This architectural philosophy brings fundamental changes to how networks get built and operated. Instead of buying complete systems from one supplier, operators can now mix and match hardware from different manufacturers while running software from yet another vendor. The decoupling of physical equipment from network intelligence creates new deployment possibilities. Carriers gain the freedom to refresh hardware and software on independent timelines, swapping out components as technology evolves rather than replacing entire systems. This modularity also enables operators to tailor their network design choices based on local requirements—perhaps using one vendor's equipment in dense urban areas while deploying different solutions in rural regions, all managed through common software platforms. The Telecom Infra Project highlighted these deployment and upgrade advantages in their 2019 analysis of Open RAN benefits.

The movement toward open architectures has coalesced around the O-RAN Alliance, an industry consortium that has grown to include more than 160 member organizations as of 2025. This diverse group—spanning equipment makers, software developers, mobile operators, and cloud providers—collaborates on creating detailed technical specifications that define how disaggregated network components should interact. Their work establishes the standardized interfaces that make multi-vendor interoperability possible, transforming what was once proprietary knowledge into openly available specifications that any company can implement (O-RAN Alliance, 2025).

Architecture Components

The Open RAN architecture fundamentally restructures the traditional baseband unit (BBU) into disaggregated components:

Open RAN Disaggregated Architecture

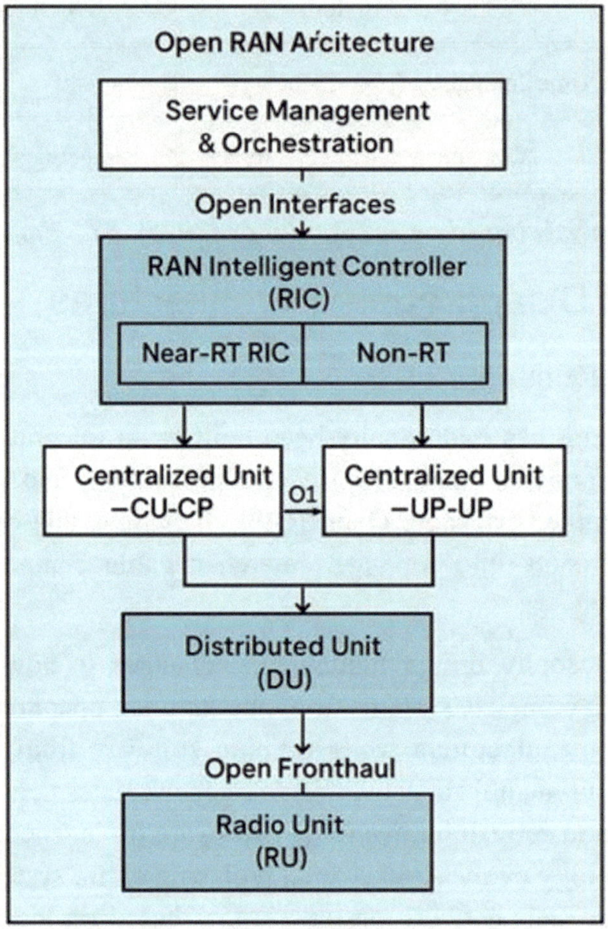

Source: Adapted from O-RAN Alliance specifications (2023) and 3GPP standards

At its core, Open RAN's approach involves breaking down what was traditionally a single, monolithic radio access system into distinct functional components, each with clearly defined roles and standardized connection points. This decomposition fundamentally changes the network's structure and operating model.

The transformation particularly impacts two critical network elements. What telecommunications engineers previously knew as the baseband unit—the centralized processing equipment handling radio signal processing and protocol management—gets reimagined as the distributed unit in Open RAN terminology. Similarly, the centralized unit takes on functions that coordinate multiple radio sites and handle higher-layer processing tasks. These architectural changes, documented by Rakuten Symphony in their 2024 implementation analysis, reflect more than just naming conventions. The redesign enables these components to run on commercial off-the-shelf computing hardware rather than purpose-built proprietary systems, while standardized interfaces ensure that distributed units from one manufacturer can communicate seamlessly with centralized units from another.

This modular structure creates opportunities that weren't feasible under traditional architectures. Network operators can now position processing resources closer to or farther from cell sites based on their specific latency, bandwidth, and cost requirements. The standardization effort defines precisely how data flows between components, what protocols they use for communication, and how network intelligence gets distributed across the system. By establishing these open interfaces as industry standards rather than proprietary specifications, the architecture enables genuine vendor diversity and competitive innovation at each layer of the network stack.

Open RAN Component Functions

Component	Primary Functions	Key Interfaces
Radio Unit (RU)	RF processing, amplification, antenna integration	Open Fronthaul (eCPRI/O-RAN)
Distributed Unit (DU)	Real-time L1/L2 processing, scheduling	F1 (to CU), Fronthaul (to RU)
Centralized Unit (CU)	Non-real-time processing, RRC, PDCP	F1 (to DU), E1 (CP-UP split)
RAN Intelligent Controller (RIC)	AI/ML optimization, policy enforcement	O1, A1, E2 interfaces

Source: O-RAN Alliance Technical Specifications (2023)

Implementation Benefits

Open RAN deployment offers significant advantages over traditional architectures:

1. **Vendor Flexibility**: The Open RAN architecture enables carriers to operate shared radio access networks—including radio units, centralized units, and distributed units—through standardized, interoperable interfaces. This approach simplifies RAN deployment while cutting down on associated expenses (Mavenir, 2024).
2. **Cost Optimization**: The ability to use commercial off-the-shelf (COTS) hardware and mix vendors reduces capital expenditure by 30-40% compared to traditional deployments (analysis based on industry reports).
3. **Innovation Acceleration**: Open interfaces enable rapid integration of new features and third-party applications through the RIC platform.

4. **Deployment Flexibility**: Disaggregated architecture supports various deployment models, from centralized to fully distributed configurations.

Spectrum Allocation

Access to radio frequency spectrum continues to be one of the most significant obstacles facing 5G network rollouts worldwide. The challenge stems from fundamental differences in how nations have allocated their mid-band frequencies—the sweet spot for balancing coverage area with data capacity that makes 5G practical for widespread deployment.

The United States finds itself in a particularly difficult position compared to other major markets. American carriers hold considerably less mid-band spectrum than their international counterparts, creating a competitive disadvantage that extends beyond simple technical performance metrics. This spectrum scarcity has evolved into a matter of strategic national concern. The Center for Strategic and International Studies identified this disparity in their 2024 analysis, characterizing the mid-band spectrum gap as a critical national security issue. The implications reach beyond commercial telecommunications—limited spectrum constrains the nation's ability to support defense applications, emergency services, and other critical infrastructure that increasingly depends on advanced wireless connectivity (CSIS, 2024).

Why does this matter so profoundly? Mid-band spectrum (typically frequencies between 1 GHz and 6 GHz) represents the practical compromise that makes 5G work at scale. Lower frequencies travel farther and penetrate buildings better but offer limited bandwidth. Higher frequencies (millimeter wave) provide enormous capacity but barely travel beyond line of sight. Mid-band frequencies thread this needle, offering reasonable coverage with solid data speeds. When U.S. carriers have less mid-band spectrum than competitors in Europe and Asia, they face difficult trade-offs: either accept lower network capacity in mid-band deployments or invest more heavily in expensive millimeter wave infrastructure that requires dramatically denser cell site spacing.

Global 5G Spectrum Allocation Strategy

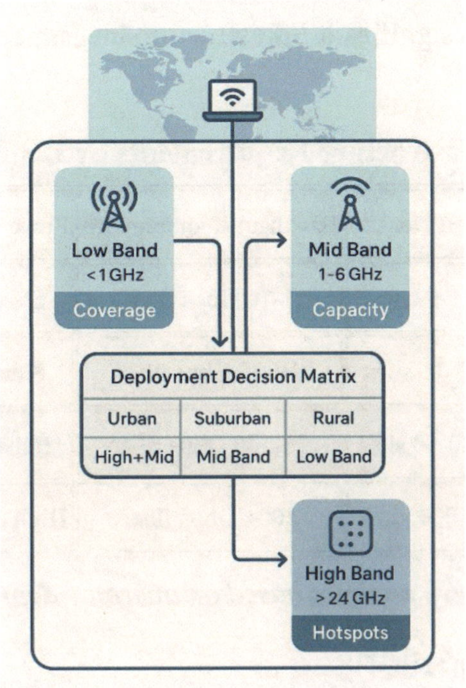

Source: Adapted from GSMA Intelligence (2024) and spectrum allocation reports

Infrastructure Requirements

5G deployment demands significant infrastructure investments and upgrades:

5G Infrastructure Requirements by Deployment Type

Deployment Type	Cell Density	Backhaul Requirements	Power Needs	Estimated Cost/km²
Rural	1-3 sites	1-10 Gbps fiber	Standard	$50,000-100,000
Suburban	5-10 sites	10-25 Gbps fiber	Standard	$200,000-400,000
Urban	20-50 sites	25-100 Gbps fiber	Enhanced	$500,000-1,000,000
Dense Urban	100+ sites	100+ Gbps fiber	High density	$1,000,000+

Source: Industry analysis based on operator deployment data (2024)

Security Considerations

Security in 5G deployments requires comprehensive approaches addressing both public and private network scenarios:

1. **Network Slicing Security**: Isolation between slices, dedicated security policies
2. **Edge Security**: Distributed security functions, local breakout protection
3. **Zero Trust Architecture**: Continuous verification, microsegmentation
4. **Supply Chain Security**: Trusted vendor verification, component authentication

Global Deployment Strategies

Regional Approaches

Different regions have adopted varying strategies for 5G deployment based on spectrum availability, regulatory frameworks, and market dynamics.

Regional 5G Deployment Strategies

Region	Primary Strategy	Spectrum Focus	Key Characteristics
North America	Coverage + Capacity	Low + Mid band	182 million 5G connections, 20% YoY growth
Europe	Urban-first	Mid band (3.5 GHz)	Gradual rollout, regulatory harmonization
Asia-Pacific	Rapid deployment	Mid + High band	Leading in mmWave, dense urban focus

Region	Primary Strategy	Spectrum Focus	Key Characteristics
Middle East	Oil & Gas focus	Private networks	Large-scale industrial deployments
Latin America	Selective urban	Mid band	Cost-conscious, targeted deployments

Source: 5G Americas (2025), GSMA Intelligence (2024)

Market Trends

The 5G deployment landscape continues to evolve with several key- trends (2019-2027):

5G Deployment Timeline and Milestones

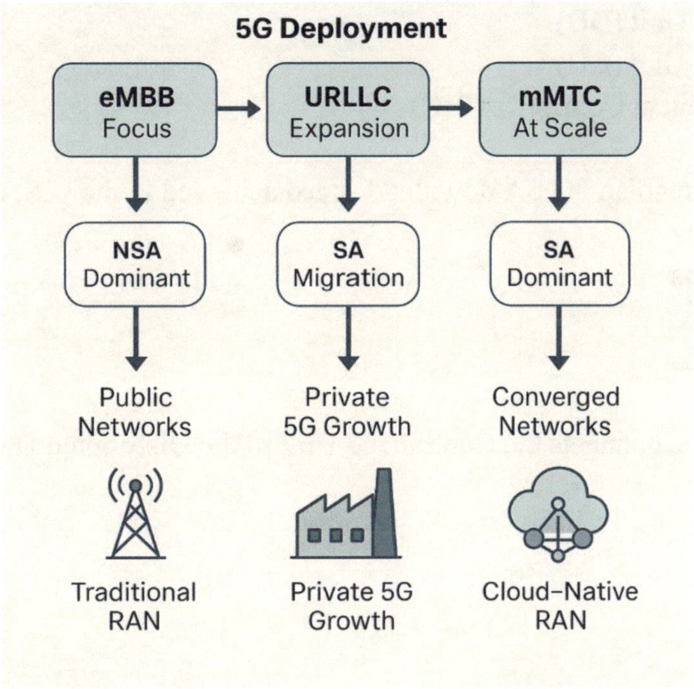

Source: Industry analysis and market forecasts (2024-2025)

Knowledge Check

1. What is the forecasted CAGR for global spending on private 5G infrastructure between 2024 and 2027?
   a) 10%
   b) 15%
   c) 20%
   d) 25%

2. Which component in Open RAN architecture is responsible for real-time Layer 1 and Layer 2 processing?
   a) Radio Unit (RU)
   b) Distributed Unit (DU)
   c) Centralized Unit (CU)
   d) RAN Intelligent Controller (RIC)

3. What was the median 5G SA download speed achieved in the U.S. in Q4 2024?
   a) 254.18 Mbps
   b) 305.36 Mbps
   c) 388.44 Mbps
   d) 450.00 Mbps

4. Which interface connects the Centralized Unit to the Distributed Unit in Open RAN?
   a) A1
   b) E1
   c) F1
   d) O1

5. By 2027, what is the estimated value of the private 5G network infrastructure market?
   a) $3.5 Billion
   b) $4 Billion
   c) $5 Billion
   d) $6 Billion

6. Compare and contrast the deployment strategies for public versus private 5G networks. What factors should organizations consider when choosing between them?

7. Explain the key advantages of Open RAN architecture over traditional RAN deployments.

8. What are the primary challenges in 5G spectrum allocation, and how do they impact deployment strategies?

9. How do security requirements differ between public and private 5G deployments?

10. Analyze the role of government policy and regulation in shaping 5G deployment strategies globally.

Answers

1. What is the forecasted CAGR for global spending on private 5G infrastructure between 2024 and 2027?
   a) 10%
   b) 15%
   c) 20%
   d) 25%
   Answer: c) 20%

2. Which component in Open RAN architecture is responsible for real-time Layer 1 and Layer 2 processing?
   a) Radio Unit (RU)
   b) Distributed Unit (DU)
   c) Centralized Unit (CU)
   d) RAN Intelligent Controller (RIC)
   Answer: b) Distributed Unit (DU)

3. What was the median 5G SA download speed achieved in the U.S. in Q4 2024?
   a) 254.18 Mbps
   b) 305.36 Mbps
   c) 388.44 Mbps
   d) 450.00 Mbps
   Answer: c) 388.44 Mbps

4. Which interface connects the Centralized Unit to the Distributed Unit in Open RAN?
   a) A1
   b) E1
   c) F1
   d) O1
   Answer: c) F1

5. By 2027, what is the estimated value of the private 5G network infrastructure market?

a) $3.5 Billion
b) $4 Billion
c) $5 Billion
d) $6 Billion
Answer: d) $6 Billion

6. Compare and contrast the deployment strategies for public versus private 5G networks. What factors should organizations consider when choosing between them?
   Answer: Organizations should consider several key factors:
   - **Coverage Requirements:** Public networks offer wide-area coverage suitable for mobile applications, while private networks provide localized, campus-specific coverage
   - **Control and Customization:** Private networks offer complete control over network configuration, security policies, and resource allocation
   - **Performance Guarantees:** Private networks can provide dedicated resources with guaranteed latency and reliability SLAs
   - **Cost Structure:** Public networks operate on OPEX models (subscriptions), while private networks require significant CAPEX investment
   - **Security Requirements:** Private networks offer an isolated, dedicated infrastructure ideal for sensitive data and operations
   - **Use Case Specificity:** Mission-critical applications like industrial automation favor private networks

7. Explain the key advantages of Open RAN architecture over traditional RAN deployments.
   Answer: Open RAN provides several transformative advantages:
   - **Vendor Diversity:** Eliminates vendor lock-in by enabling mix-and-match components from different suppliers
   - **Cost Reduction:** COTS hardware and a competitive vendor ecosystem reduce CAPEX by 30-40%
   - **Innovation Acceleration:** Open interfaces enable rapid integration of third-party applications and AI/ML capabilities through the RIC
   - **Deployment Flexibility:** Supports various configurations from centralized to distributed architectures
   - **Operational Efficiency:** Standardized interfaces simplify multi-vendor management and automation
   - **Future-Proofing:** Easier upgrades and technology evolution without complete system replacement

8. What are the primary challenges in 5G spectrum allocation, and how do they impact deployment strategies?

Answer: Key spectrum challenges include:

- **International Harmonization:** Divergent spectrum allocations between regions affect equipment ecosystems and roaming
- **Mid-Band Scarcity:** Limited availability of optimal capacity spectrum (3-6 GHz) constrains network performance
- **Incumbent Users:** Clearing spectrum from existing users requires time and compensation
- **Regulatory Delays:** Slow auction processes and policy decisions hinder deployment timelines
- **Investment Uncertainty:** Unclear spectrum roadmaps impact long-term network planning and ROI calculations

These challenges force operators to adopt hybrid strategies using multiple bands and technologies.

9. How do security requirements differ between public and private 5G deployments?
   Answer: Security requirements vary significantly:
   - **Public Networks:** Focus on mass-market security, including subscriber authentication, encryption, and fraud prevention. Must protect against DDoS, signaling storms, and roaming vulnerabilities
   - **Private Networks:** Emphasize enterprise-grade security with complete network isolation, zero-trust architectures, and integration with corporate security policies
   - **Compliance:** Private networks often require industry-specific compliance (healthcare, finance, government)
   - **Physical Security:** Private networks allow complete control over infrastructure physical security
   - **Supply Chain:** Both require trusted vendor verification, but private networks can implement stricter component authentication
   - **Incident Response:** Private networks enable faster, more targeted responses to security incidents

10. Analyze the role of government policy and regulation in shaping 5G deployment strategies globally.
    Answer: Government policy profoundly impacts 5G deployment through:
    - **Spectrum Allocation:** Decisions on frequency bands, auction timing, and sharing frameworks determine deployment feasibility
    - **Infrastructure Policy:** Streamlined permitting, dig-once policies, and small cell regulations affect deployment speed and cost
    - **Security Regulations:** Trusted vendor requirements and supply chain restrictions shape equipment choices

- **Investment Incentives:** Tax breaks, grants, and rural broadband funding influence deployment priorities
- **Competition Policy:** Rules on network sharing, wholesale access, and market concentration affect business models
- **International Coordination:** Participation in standards bodies and bilateral agreements impacts global interoperability

Countries with proactive, coordinated policies achieve faster, more extensive 5G deployments

References

5G Americas. (2025). *The State of 5G: Growth, Challenges, and Opportunities in 2025*. Retrieved from https://www.5gamericas.org/the-state-of-5g-growth-challenges-and-opportunities-in-2025/

Ahmad, I. A. I., Dawodu, S. O., Osasona, F., Akagha, O. V., Anyanwu, A. C., & Onwusinkwue, S. (2024). 5G deployment strategies: Challenges and opportunities: A comparative review for Africa and the USA. *World Journal of Advanced Research and Reviews*, 21(1), 2428-2439. https://doi.org/10.30574/wjarr.2024.21.1.0345

Center for Strategic and International Studies (CSIS). (2024). *Concrete National Security Benefits of Spectrum Allocation for Commercial 5G*. Retrieved from https://www.csis.org/analysis/concrete-national-security-benefits-spectrum-allocation-commercial-5g

Ericsson. (2024). *Key use cases for private 5G networks in airports*. Retrieved from https://www.ericsson.com/en/blog/2024/6/key-use-cases-for-private-5g-networks-in-airports

GSA. (2024). *Spectrum Allocations June 2024*. Retrieved from https://gsacom.com/paper/spectrum-allocations-june-2024/

GSMA Intelligence. (2024). *The State of 5G 2024*. Retrieved from https://www.gsmaintelligence.com/research/

HPE. (2024). *HPE simplifies deployment of private cellular networks with launch of HPE Aruba Networking Enterprise Private 5G*. Retrieved from https://www.hpe.com/us/en/newsroom/press-release/2024/06/

IoT Analytics. (2025). *State of private 5G in 2024: Key growth trends, use cases, and forecast*. Retrieved from https://iot-analytics.com/private-5g-2024-key-growth-trends-use-cases-forecast/

Juniper Networks. (2024). *What is Open RAN?*. Retrieved from https://www.juniper.net/us/en/research-topics/what-is-open-ran.html

Mavenir. (2024). *About Open RAN*. Retrieved from https://www.mavenir.com/portfolio/mavair/radio-access/openran/

O-RAN Alliance. (2023). *O-RAN Architecture and Specifications*. Retrieved from https://www.o-ran.org/

Rakuten Symphony. (2024). *What is Open RAN | Open RAN Architecture | Open RAN Security | Cloud Native Open RAN*. Retrieved from https://symphony.rakuten.com/blog/open-ran-explained-all-you-need-to-know-and-more

ResearchAndMarkets. (2025). *Private 5G/4G Network Deployment Tracker & Forecasts Database 2024-2030*. Business Wire. Retrieved from https://www.businesswire.com/news/home/20250102158812/en/

STL Partners. (2023). *Private 5G use cases for industry 4.0*. Retrieved from https://stlpartners.com/articles/private-cellular/private-5g-use-cases/

STL Partners. (2024). *Innovative private network deployments from 2023*. Retrieved from https://stlpartners.com/articles/private-cellular/private-network-deployments-from-2023/

Telecom Infra Project. (2019). *OpenRAN*. Retrieved from https://telecominfraproject.com/openran/

Viavi Solutions. (2024). *5G Network Architecture. Core, RAN, & Security Architecture For 5G*. Retrieved from https://www.viavisolutions.com/en-us/what-5g-architecture

Chapter 17: Cloud Radio Access Network (Cloud RAN)

Executive Summary

This chapter provides a comprehensive examination of Cloud Radio Access Network (Cloud RAN) technology, which represents a paradigm shift in mobile network architecture through the principles of centralization, virtualization, and disaggregation. The chapter explores how Cloud RAN transforms traditional base station architectures by separating radio units from baseband processing units, enabling centralized resource pooling and improved network efficiency. Key topics include the 3GPP functional split options, virtualization technologies, fronthaul network requirements, and deployment strategies. The chapter also addresses critical aspects such as security considerations, economic implications, and the integration of Cloud RAN with emerging technologies like edge computing and artificial intelligence. Understanding Cloud RAN is essential for network engineers and operators as it forms the foundation for flexible, cost-effective 5G deployments and future 6G networks.

Table of Contents

Introduction

Wireless network infrastructure has undergone a profound shift as operators embrace virtualization and centralization concepts borrowed from cloud computing. This architectural approach, commonly known as Cloud RAN (C-RAN), fundamentally rethinks how mobile networks process and manage radio signals.

Traditional cellular networks distributed baseband processing equipment across thousands of individual cell sites, with each location housing its own dedicated hardware. This distributed model, while reliable, created significant challenges. Equipment sat idle during off-peak hours, consuming electricity without serving traffic. Capacity couldn't be shared between sites—a congested cell tower couldn't borrow unused processing power from its quiet neighbor. Maintenance required technicians to visit each location individually. Energy bills mounted as equipment ran continuously regardless of actual demand.

Cloud RAN tackles these inefficiencies through centralization. The Next Generation Mobile Networks Alliance described this architectural evolution in their 2015 framework, explaining how C-RAN consolidates baseband processing from numerous cell sites into shared facilities, often called baseband hotels or centralized processing pools. Rather than dedicated hardware at each tower, virtualized software functions run on standard computing servers that can dynamically allocate processing capacity where it's needed moment-by-moment.

The concept crystallized through early research by China Mobile Research Institute, which outlined C-RAN's foundational principles in 2011. Their framework identified four pillars that define this approach: pooling processing resources centrally rather than distributing them, enabling radio units to work cooperatively across multiple sites, building infrastructure on cloud computing platforms instead of specialized hardware, and dramatically improving energy efficiency through resource sharing and intelligent power management. This shift moves networks from rigid, hardware-dependent systems toward flexible, software-driven platforms that adapt to changing traffic patterns.

The timing proved fortuitous. As 5G networks began rolling out, Cloud RAN's architectural flexibility became increasingly valuable. The 3GPP's Technical Report 38.801, published in 2017, examined how C-RAN architectures could support 5G's diverse requirements. Unlike previous generations that primarily focused on mobile broadband, 5G needed to simultaneously handle radically different service types—streaming ultra-high-definition video for consumers, coordinating industrial robots with millisecond-level precision, and managing millions of simple IoT sensors. Cloud RAN's programmable nature allows operators to reconfigure network behavior for these distinct use cases without installing new physical equipment. This adaptability translates directly into economic benefits, reducing both capital expenditures for equipment and ongoing operational costs.

Evolution from Traditional RAN to Cloud RAN

Limitations of Traditional RAN Architecture

Traditional RAN architectures have served mobile networks effectively through multiple generations, but they face increasing challenges in the 5G era. As documented by Checko et al. (2015) in their comprehensive survey, traditional base stations integrate all functions—from radio frequency (RF) processing to baseband computation—within a single physical unit at each cell site. This monolithic approach creates several fundamental limitations that impact network scalability and efficiency.

Comparison of Traditional RAN vs Cloud RAN Characteristics

Aspect	Traditional RAN	Cloud RAN
Architecture	Distributed, standalone base stations	Centralized baseband with remote radio units
Resource Utilization	Static allocation, low efficiency (15-20%)	Dynamic pooling, high efficiency (60-80%)
Hardware	Proprietary, vendor-specific	Commercial off-the-shelf (COTS) servers
Upgrade Path	Hardware replacement required	Software updates and scaling
CAPEX	High due to overprovisioning	Reduced through resource sharing
OPEX	High site maintenance costs	Centralized operations and maintenance
Energy Efficiency	Low due to constant operation	High through dynamic resource allocation
Coordination	Limited inter-cell coordination	Advanced CoMP and interference management

Source: Adapted from Peng et al. (2016) and GSMA (2019)

The inefficiencies of traditional RAN become particularly apparent during traffic variations. According to measurements by Wu et al. (2013), typical base stations operate at only 15-20% of their peak capacity on average, yet they must be provisioned for peak loads. This overprovisioning results in significant capital expenditure waste and unnecessary energy consumption.

Cloud RAN Architectural Principles

The transition to Cloud RAN addresses these limitations through architectural innovations. As illustrated in the following figure, Cloud RAN disaggregates the traditional base station into distinct functional components that can be flexibly deployed and managed.

Cloud RAN Architecture Overview

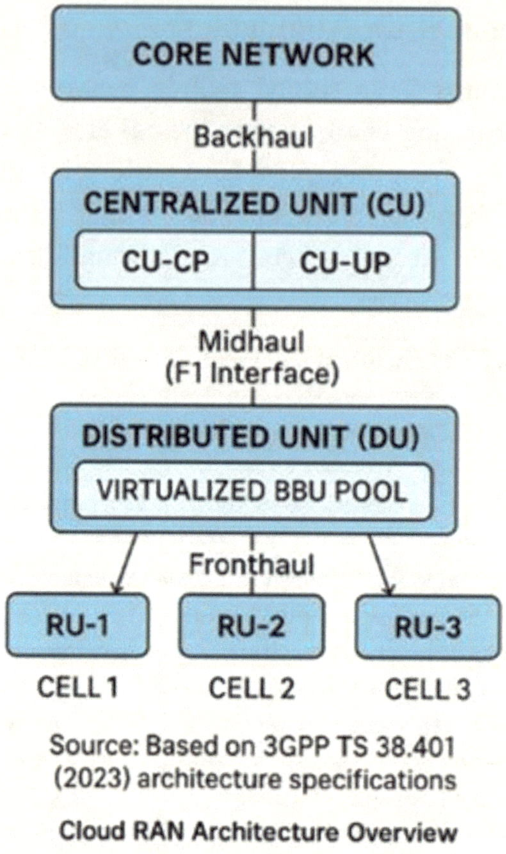

Source: Based on 3GPP TS 38.401 (2023) architecture specifications

This disaggregated architecture enables several key capabilities:

1. **Resource Pooling**: Baseband processing resources are consolidated in centralized locations, allowing dynamic allocation based on traffic demands (Zhang et al., 2019)
2. **Statistical Multiplexing**: Traffic variations across cells can be averaged, reducing the total processing capacity required by 30-50% (Liu et al., 2018)
3. **Energy Efficiency**: Unused processing resources can be powered down during low-traffic periods, achieving up to 67% energy savings according to Namba et al. (2012)
4. **Simplified Site Infrastructure**: Remote radio units have minimal space, power, and cooling requirements compared to full base stations (GSMA, 2019)

Functional Split Architecture and 3GPP Standards

3GPP Functional Split Options

The 3GPP has standardized multiple options for splitting RAN protocol stack functions between centralized and distributed components. As detailed in 3GPP TR 38.801 (2017), these split options represent different trade-offs between centralization benefits and fronthaul requirements.

3GPP Functional Split Options and Characteristics

Split Option	Split Point	Fronthaul Bandwidth*	Latency Requirement	Processing Distribution
Option 1	RRC/PDCP	~10 Mbps	<10 ms	Only RRC centralized
Option 2	PDCP/RLC	~100 Mbps	<10 ms	RRC, PDCP centralized
Option 3	High/Low RLC	~150 Mbps	<2 ms	Partial RLC centralized
Option 4	MAC/PHY	~200 Mbps	<2 ms	Up to MAC centralized
Option 5	High/Low MAC	~300 Mbps	<1 ms	Partial MAC centralized
Option 6	High/Low PHY	~1 Gbps	<250 μs	Partial PHY centralized
Option 7-1	PHY (uplink)	~10 Gbps	<250 μs	Most PHY centralized
Option 7-2	PHY (downlink)	~10 Gbps	<250 μs	Precoding distributed
Option 7-3	PHY (extended)	~8 Gbps	<250 μs	Extended distribution
Option 8	RF/PHY	~150 Gbps	<100 μs	Full centralization

*Bandwidth values are for 100 MHz, 2x2 MIMO configuration

Source: Adapted from Larsen et al. (2019) and 3GPP TR 38.801 (2017)

The industry has converged on two primary split options for commercial deployments:

1. **Option 2 (Higher Layer Split)**: Provides a good balance between centralization benefits and practical fronthaul requirements. This split enables centralized mobility management and multi-connectivity features while maintaining reasonable bandwidth demands (O-RAN Alliance, 2023).
2. **Option 7-2 (Lower Layer Split)**: Enables advanced coordination features like joint transmission and reception but requires high-capacity, low-latency fronthaul. This split is specified in detail by both 3GPP and O-RAN Alliance for next-generation deployments (O-RAN Alliance, 2023).

Protocol Stack Distribution

The distribution of protocol stack functions across Cloud RAN components follows a hierarchical model that balances processing requirements with latency constraints. The following figure illustrates the typical function distribution in a modern Cloud RAN deployment.

Protocol Stack Distribution in Cloud RAN

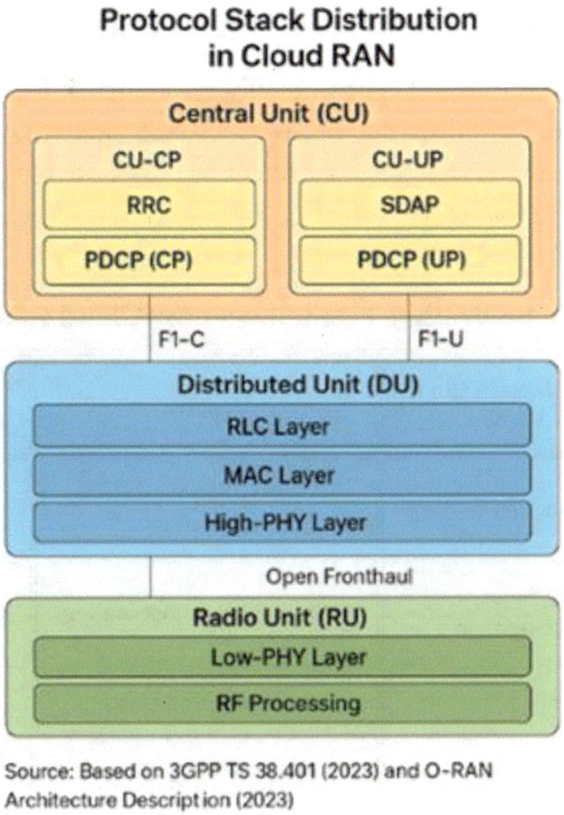

Source: Based on 3GPP TS 38.401 (2023) and O-RAN Architecture Description (2023)

Virtualization Technologies in Cloud RAN

Network Function Virtualization (NFV) Framework

The implementation of Cloud RAN relies heavily on Network Function Virtualization (NFV) technologies to transform traditionally hardware-based network functions into software applications. According to the ETSI NFV architectural framework (ETSI, 2014), Cloud RAN functions operate as Virtual Network Functions (VNFs) within a standardized virtualization infrastructure.

Virtualization Technologies for Cloud RAN

Technology	Application in Cloud RAN	Benefits	Challenges
Virtual Machines (VMs)	CU function hosting	Strong isolation, mature ecosystem	Higher overhead, slower instantiation
Containers	DU function deployment	Low overhead, fast scaling	Weaker isolation, real-time constraints
Bare Metal	Low-PHY processing	Maximum performance	Limited flexibility
Hardware Acceleration	Signal processing	Improved efficiency	Integration complexity
SR-IOV	Network I/O optimization	Near-native performance	Hardware dependency
DPDK	Packet processing	High throughput	CPU core dedication

Source: Compiled from Intel (2021), Red Hat (2022), and Xilinx (2020)

Real-time Processing Requirements

Cloud RAN virtualization faces unique challenges due to stringent real-time processing requirements. As documented by Nikaein et al. (2015), baseband processing must meet deterministic latency bounds:

1. **PHY Layer Processing**: Must complete within 1 ms for LTE and 0.5 ms for 5G NR
2. **MAC Scheduling**: Requires predictable execution within 1 ms time slots
3. **HARQ Timing**: Demands consistent 3-4 ms round-trip times

To meet these requirements, Cloud RAN implementations employ specialized techniques:

- **CPU Affinity and Isolation**: Dedicating specific CPU cores to time-critical functions
- **Real-time Kernels**: Using RT-Linux or similar real-time operating systems

- **Accelerator Offload**: Leveraging GPUs, FPGAs, or ASICs for compute-intensive tasks

Fronthaul Network Design and Requirements

Bandwidth and Latency Analysis

The fronthaul network connecting distributed radio units to centralized processing represents a critical design element in Cloud RAN deployments. Different functional splits impose varying requirements on the fronthaul infrastructure, as analyzed by the IEEE 1914 working group (IEEE, 2019).

Fronthaul Bandwidth Requirements by Functional Split

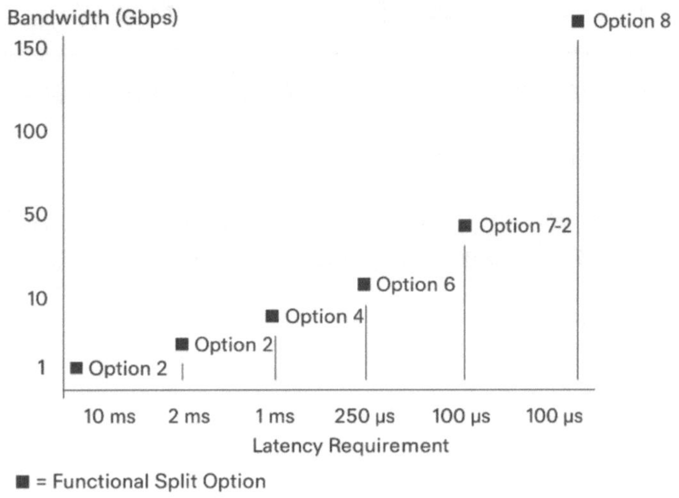

■ = Functional Split Option

(For 100 MHz, 64QAM, 4x4 MIMO configuration)

Source: Data compiled from Common Public Radio Interface (CPRI) Specification v7.0 (2015) and eCPRI Specification v2.0 (2019)

Transport Technologies

Various transport technologies can support Cloud RAN fronthaul requirements, each with specific characteristics and applicability:

Fronthaul Transport Technology Comparison

Technology	Capacity	Latency	Distance	Cost	Application
Dark Fiber	10-100 Gbps	<5 μs/km	20+ km	High CAPEX, Low OPEX	Option 7/8 splits
WDM/DWDM	40-400 Gbps	<10 μs	40+ km	High	Large-scale deployments
Ethernet (TSN)	10-25 Gbps	<50 μs	10 km	Medium	Option 6/7 splits
PON (Passive Optical Network)	10-50 Gbps	<100 μs	20 km	Low	Option 2-6 splits
Microwave	1-10 Gbps	<100 μs	5 km	Low	Higher layer splits
mmWave	10-20 Gbps	<50 μs	1 km	Medium	Urban deployments

Source: Adapted from ITU-T G.989.1 (2019) and IEEE 802.1CM (2018)

Synchronization Architecture

Precise synchronization across Cloud RAN components is essential for proper system operation. The ITU-T G.8271 (2020) standard defines synchronization requirements for packet-based fronthaul networks:

Cloud RAN Synchronization Architecture

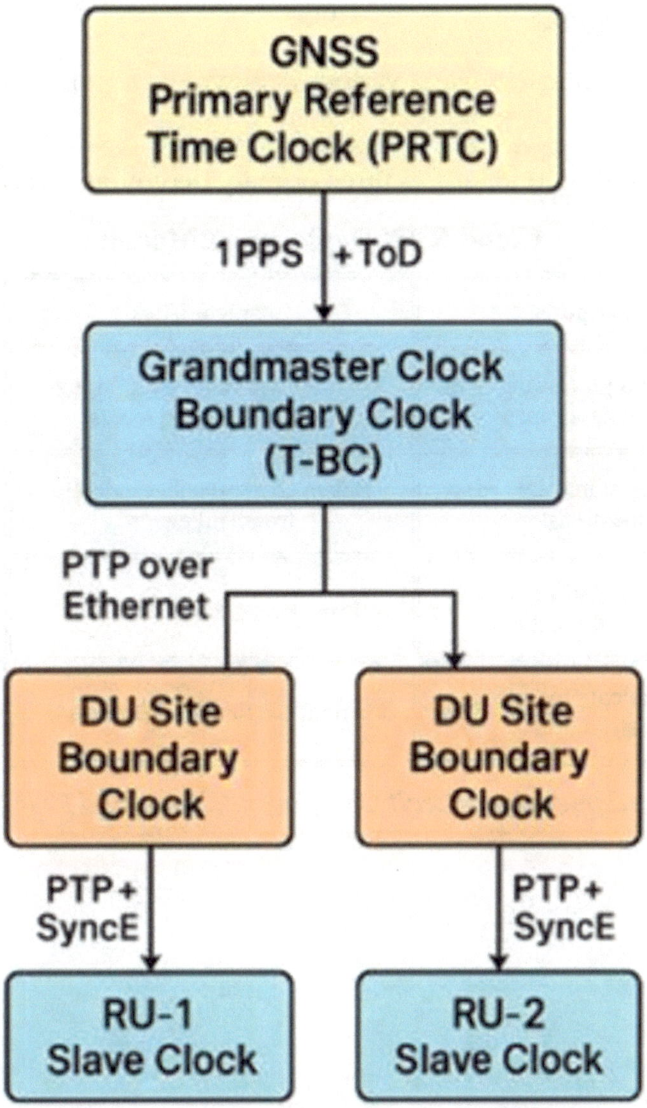

Cloud RAN Synchronization Architecture

Synchronization Requirements:

- Frequency: ±50 ppb
- Phase/Time: ±1.5 μs for LTE TDD
- Phase/Time: ±130 ns for 5G TDD

Source: Based on ITU-T G.8271 (2020) and IEEE 1588v2 (2019)

Implementation Models and Deployment Strategies

Deployment Topologies

Cloud RAN can be implemented using various deployment topologies, each suited to different scenarios and constraints.

The Small Cell Forum (2018) identifies three primary deployment models:

Cloud RAN Deployment Models

Model	Description	Characteristics	Use Cases
Fully Centralized	All baseband processing in the central data center	Maximum pooling gain, highest fronthaul requirements	Dense urban areas with fiber availability
Distributed	Processing at multiple edge locations	Balanced approach, moderate fronthaul needs	Suburban and mixed environments
Hybrid	Mix of centralized and distributed functions	Flexible, service-optimized	Multi-service networks
Cascade	Hierarchical processing distribution	Scalable, efficient resource use	Wide-area deployments

Source: Adapted from Small Cell Forum (2018) and NGMN (2015)

Migration Strategies

The transition from traditional RAN to Cloud RAN requires careful planning and execution. According to GSMA (2019), operators typically follow phased migration approaches:

Cloud RAN Migration Strategy

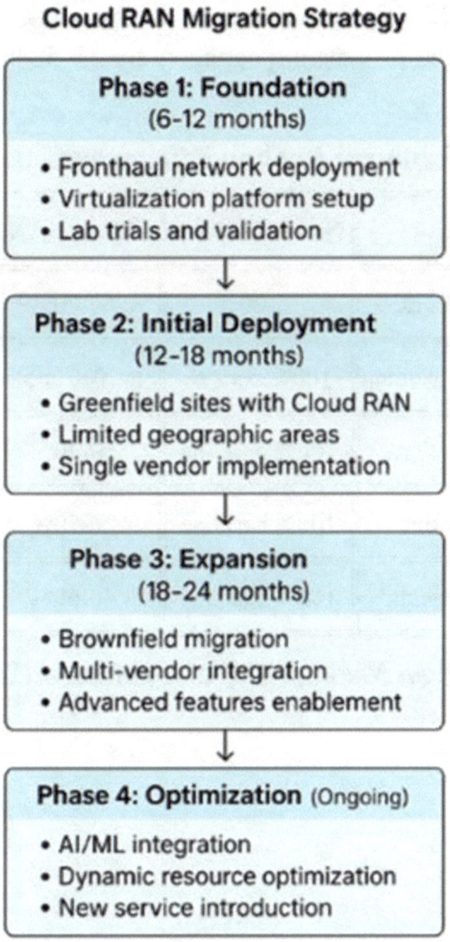

Source: Based on GSMA Cloud RAN Deployment Guide (2019)

Performance Optimization and Resource Management

Resource Pooling Benefits

Cloud RAN's centralized architecture enables significant efficiency gains through statistical multiplexing of processing resources.

Research by Bhaumik et al. (2012) demonstrates that pooling baseband resources across multiple cells can reduce required processing capacity by 25-50% while maintaining quality of service.

Resource Pooling Efficiency Gains

Metric	Traditional RAN	Cloud RAN	Improvement
Average CPU Utilization	15-20%	60-80%	3-4x
Peak Capacity Provisioning	100% per site	60-70% pooled	30-40% reduction
Energy Consumption	100% baseline	50-70%	30-50% savings
Hardware Footprint	100% baseline	20-30%	70-80% reduction
Cooling Requirements	100% baseline	40-60%	40-60% reduction

Source: Data from Nokia (2020) and Ericsson (2021) field trials

Coordinated Multipoint (CoMP) Implementation

Cloud RAN's centralized processing enables advanced coordination techniques that were impractical in traditional architectures. According to 3GPP TS 36.819 (2013), Coordinated Multipoint transmission and reception can improve cell-edge performance by up to 40%.

CoMP Coordination in Cloud RAN

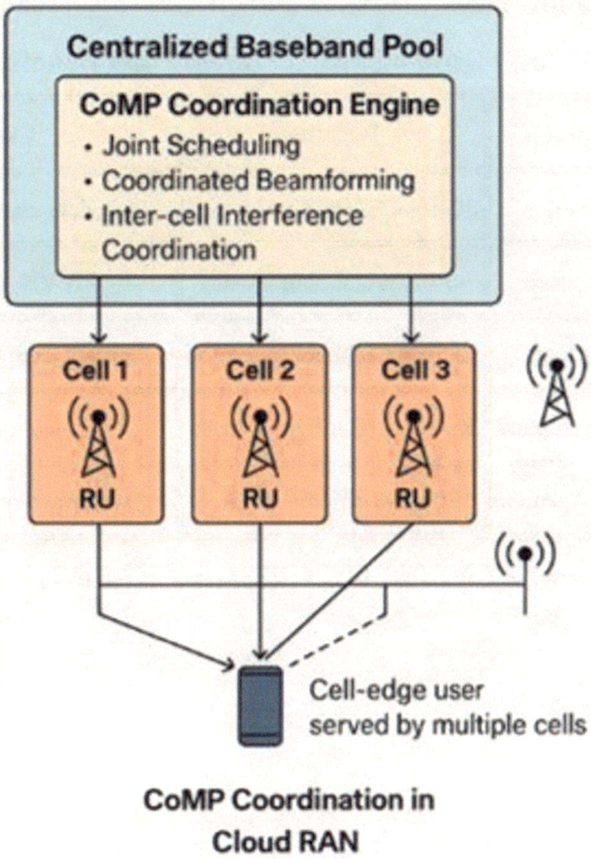

Benefits:

- 40% cell-edge throughput improvement
- 25% average spectral efficiency gain
- Reduced inter-cell interference

Source: Based on 3GPP TS 36.819 (2013) and field measurements from Lee et al. (2014)

Integration with Edge Computing and Network Slicing

Multi-access Edge Computing (MEC) Integration

The convergence of Cloud RAN with Multi-access Edge Computing creates synergies that benefit both technologies.

As specified in ETSI MEC 003 (2022), co-locating MEC platforms with Cloud RAN infrastructure enables ultra-low latency services and efficient resource utilization.

TCloud RAN and MEC Integration Benefits

Integration Aspect	Benefits	Use Cases
Infrastructure Sharing	30-40% CAPEX reduction	Shared data centers, power, cooling
Low Latency Services	<1 ms processing latency	AR/VR, gaming, V2X
Local Traffic Offload	50-70% backhaul reduction	Content caching, local services
Radio Network Information	Real-time RAN awareness	Application optimization
Joint Resource Management	20-30% efficiency gain	Dynamic workload placement

Source: ETSI MEC 003 (2022) and 5G-PPP (2020)

Network Slicing Implementation

Cloud RAN's flexibility makes it an ideal platform for implementing network slicing. According to 3GPP TS 28.530 (2023), RAN slicing can be implemented through various mechanisms:

Network Slicing in Cloud RAN

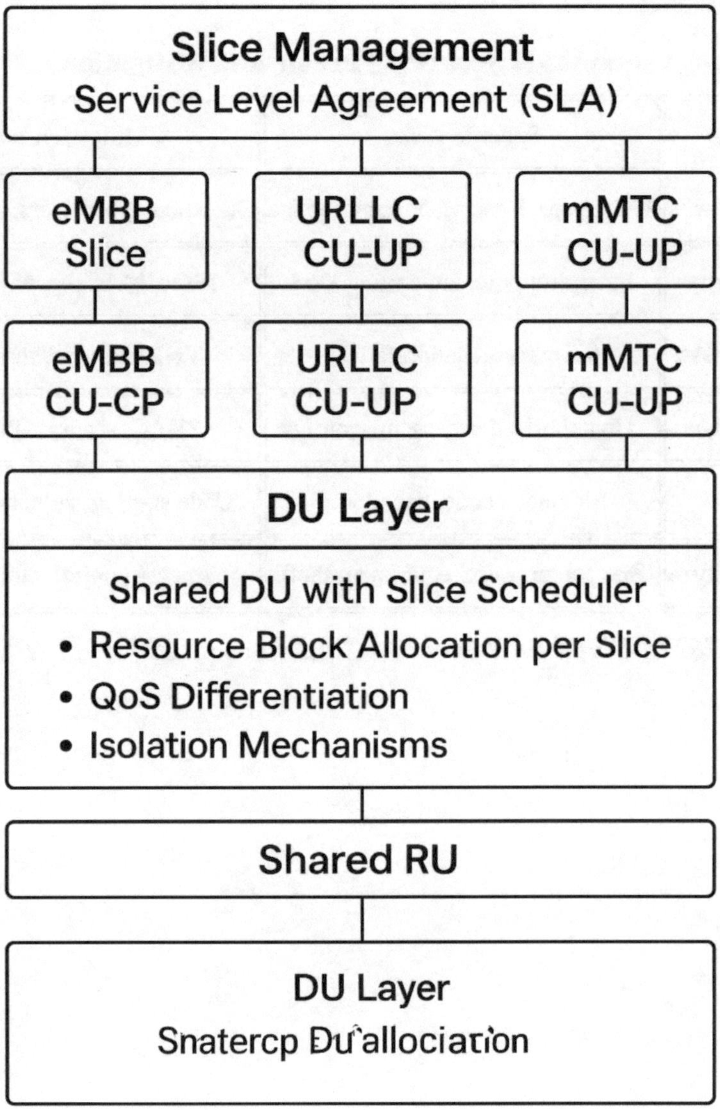

Resource Allocation:

- eMBB: 60% radio resources, best effort
- URLLC: 20% guaranteed, <1ms latency
- mMTC: 20% resources, power optimized

Source: Based on 3GPP TS 28.530 (2023) and NGMN Network Slicing Framework (2016)

Security Framework for Cloud RAN

Threat Landscape and Vulnerabilities

The disaggregated nature of Cloud RAN introduces new security challenges beyond traditional RAN deployments. According to the GSMA Cloud RAN Security Guidelines (2021), key vulnerability areas include:

Cloud RAN Security Threats and Mitigations

Threat Category	Specific Risks	Mitigation Strategies
Virtualization Attacks	VM escape, hypervisor compromise	Hardened hypervisors, secure boot, TPM
Fronthaul Security	Eavesdropping, tampering, DoS	IPsec, MACsec, physical security
Multi-tenancy Risks	Resource isolation failure	VNF isolation, resource quotas
Management Plane	Unauthorized access, misconfig	RBAC, secure APIs, audit logs
Supply Chain	Malicious code, backdoors	Code signing, vulnerability scanning
Physical Security	Site compromise, equipment theft	Access control, tamper detection

Source: GSMA Cloud RAN Security Guidelines (2021) and ENISA (2020)

Security Architecture

A comprehensive security architecture for Cloud RAN must address threats at multiple layers. The O-RAN Security Specification (2023) defines a multi-layer security framework:

Cloud RAN Security Architecture

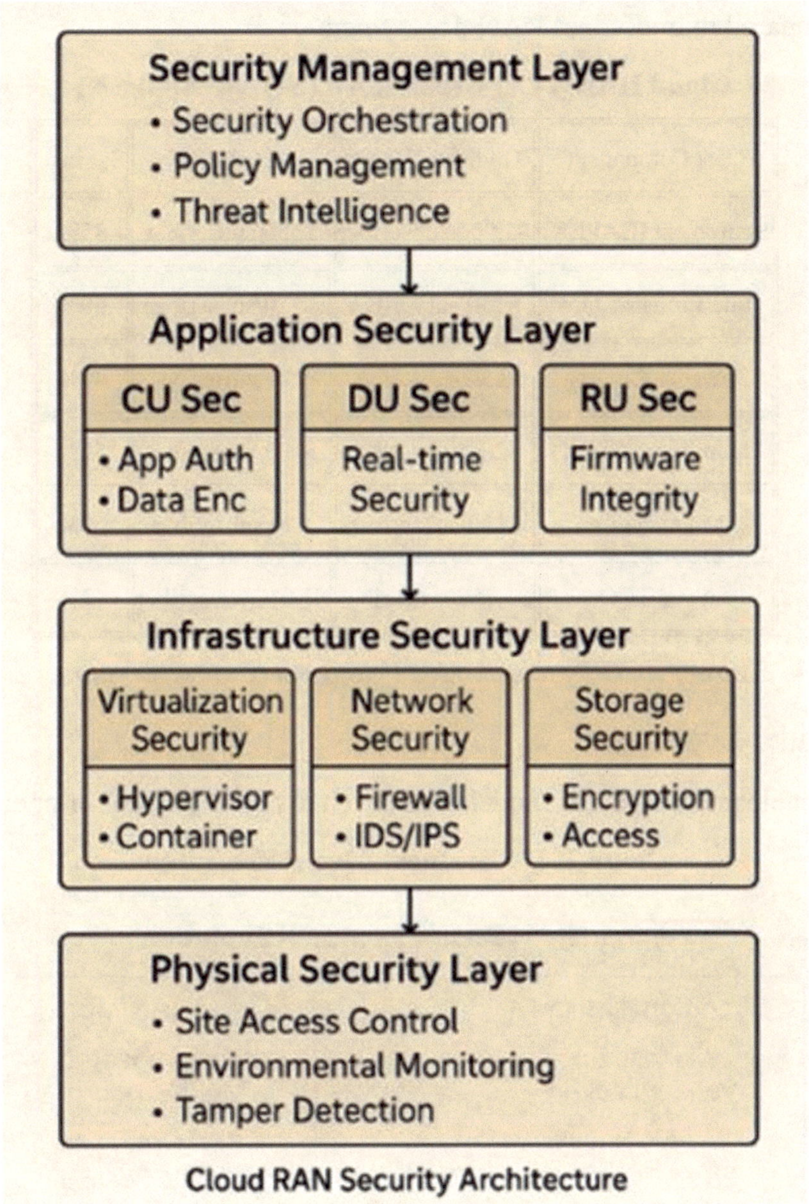

Source: Based on O-RAN Security Specification (2023) and NIST Cybersecurity Framework (2018)

Economic Analysis and Business Models

Total Cost of Ownership (TCO) Analysis

The economic benefits of Cloud RAN extend beyond simple equipment cost reductions. According to analysis by ACG Research (2021), Cloud RAN can reduce TCO by 30-40% over a 5-year period compared to traditional RAN deployments.

Cloud RAN TCO Breakdown (5-Year Analysis)

Cost Component	Traditional RAN	Cloud RAN	Savings
Equipment (CAPEX)	$1,000/subscriber	$650/subscriber	35%
Site Infrastructure	$300/subscriber	$120/subscriber	60%
Power & Cooling	$150/subscriber	$90/subscriber	40%
Operations (OPEX)	$200/subscriber	$100/subscriber	50%
Maintenance	$100/subscriber	$50/subscriber	50%
Total TCO	$1,750/subscriber	$1,010/subscriber	42%

Source: ACG Research (2021) and operator case studies

Business Model Evolution

Cloud RAN enables new business models and revenue opportunities for operators:

Cloud RAN Business Model Evolution

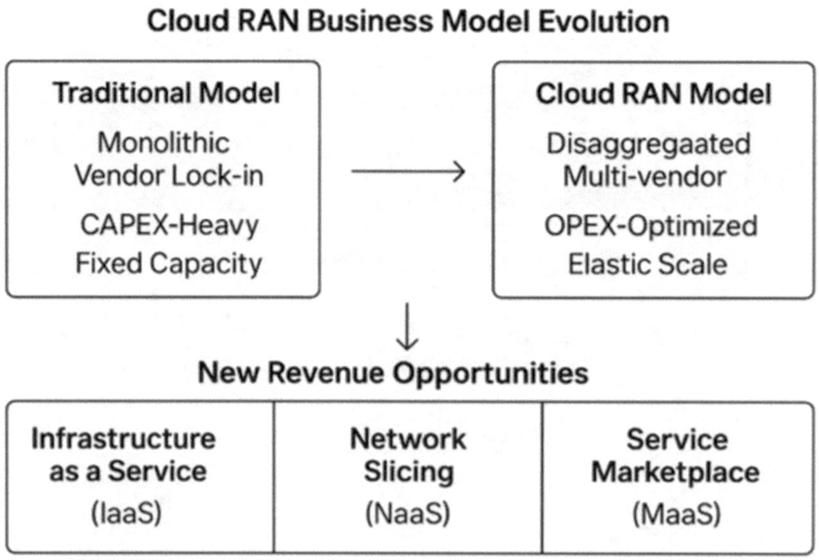

Source: Based on GSMA Intelligence (2022) and STL Partners (2021)

Future Directions and 6G Evolution

Advanced Technologies Integration

As the industry looks toward 6G networks, Cloud RAN architectures will incorporate emerging technologies. According to the 6G Flagship Program (2020), key technology integrations include:

Future Technologies for Cloud RAN Evolution

Technology	Integration with Cloud RAN	Expected Benefits
AI/ML Native	Embedded intelligence at all layers	50% operational efficiency gain
Quantum Computing	Optimization algorithms	10x faster resource allocation
Terahertz Radio	Ultra-high capacity fronthaul	1 Tbps peak rates
Digital Twins	Network modeling and prediction	90% accurate performance prediction
Blockchain	Distributed security and trust	Zero-trust architecture
Neuromorphic Computing	Brain-inspired processing	100x energy efficiency

Source: 6G Flagship Program (2020) and ITU-R Future Technology Trends (2023)

Sustainability and Green Networks

Environmental sustainability is becoming a critical driver for Cloud RAN evolution. The NGMN Green Future Networks Project (2021) identifies Cloud RAN as a key enabler for carbon-neutral networks:

Cloud RAN Sustainability Roadmap

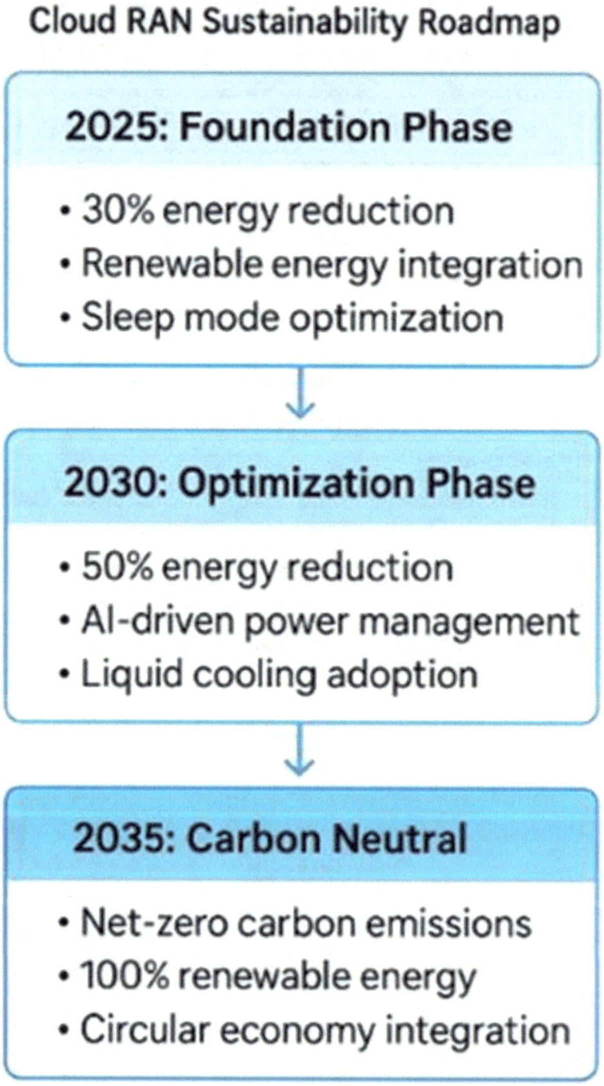

Key Enablers:

- Dynamic resource allocation
- Predictive maintenance
- Workload consolidation
- Green energy scheduling

Source: NGMN Green Future Networks (2021) and ITU-T L.1380 (2022)

Knowledge Check

1. What is the primary difference between Option 2 and Option 7-2 functional splits in Cloud RAN?
   a) Option 2 splits at the transport layer, while Option 7-2 splits at the application layer
   b) Option 2 splits between PDCP and RLC, while Option 7-2 splits within the PHY layer
   c) Option 2 requires higher fronthaul bandwidth than Option 7-2
   d) Option 2 is used for 4G, while Option 7-2 is only for 5G

2. What is the typical fronthaul latency requirement for the Option 7-2 functional split?
   a) <10 ms
   b) <2 ms
   c) <250 μs
   d) <50 μs

3. Which synchronization protocol is primarily used in packet-based Cloud RAN fronthaul networks?
   a) Network Time Protocol (NTP)
   b) IEEE 1588v2 Precision Time Protocol (PTP)
   c) Simple Network Time Protocol (SNTP)
   d) Global Positioning System (GPS) only

4. What is the approximate reduction in required baseband processing capacity achieved through Cloud RAN pooling?
   a) 10-15%
   b) 30-50%
   c) 70-80%
   d) 90-95%

5. Which interface connects the Central Unit Control Plane (CU-CP) to the Central Unit User Plane (CU-UP) in Cloud RAN?
   a) F1 interface
   b) E1 interface
   c) X2 interface
   d) S1 interface

6. Explain the trade-offs between centralized and distributed Cloud RAN deployments. When would each approach be most appropriate?

7. How does Cloud RAN enable network slicing, and what are the key mechanisms for ensuring slice isolation?

8. Discuss the role of artificial intelligence and machine learning in optimizing Cloud RAN performance.

9. What are the main security challenges introduced by Cloud RAN architecture, and how can they be addressed?

10. Analyze the economic benefits of Cloud RAN beyond simple cost reduction. How does it enable new business models?

Answers

1. What is the primary difference between Option 2 and Option 7-2 functional splits in Cloud RAN?
   a) Option 2 splits at the transport layer, while Option 7-2 splits at the application layer
   b) Option 2 splits between PDCP and RLC, while Option 7-2 splits within the PHY layer
   c) Option 2 requires higher fronthaul bandwidth than Option 7-2
   d) Option 2 is used for 4G, while Option 7-2 is only for 5G
   Answer: b) Option 2 splits between PDCP and RLC, while Option 7-2 splits within the PHY layer
   Option 2 splits between PDCP and RLC layers (higher layer split) while Option 7-2 splits within the PHY layer (lower layer split), with Option 7-2 requiring much higher fronthaul bandwidth but enabling better coordination features.

2. What is the typical fronthaul latency requirement for the Option 7-2 functional split?
   a) <10 ms
   b) <2 ms
   c) <250 µs
   d) <50 µs
   Answer: c) <250 µs
   Option 7-2 requires fronthaul latency of less than 250 microseconds to maintain proper PHY layer timing requirements.

3. Which synchronization protocol is primarily used in packet-based Cloud RAN fronthaul networks?
   a) Network Time Protocol (NTP)
   b) IEEE 1588v2 Precision Time Protocol (PTP)
   c) Simple Network Time Protocol (SNTP)
   d) Global Positioning System (GPS) only
   Answer: b) IEEE 1588v2 Precision Time Protocol (PTP)
   IEEE 1588v2 PTP is the primary synchronization protocol for packet-based fronthaul, often combined with SyncE for frequency synchronization.

4. What is the approximate reduction in required baseband processing capacity achieved through Cloud RAN pooling?
   a) 10-15%
   b) 30-50%
   c) 70-80%
   d) 90-95%
   Answer: b) 30-50%
   Statistical multiplexing in Cloud RAN typically reduces required baseband processing capacity by 30-50% compared to distributed deployments.

5. Which interface connects the Central Unit Control Plane (CU-CP) to the Central Unit User Plane (CU-UP) in Cloud RAN?
   a) F1 interface
   b) E1 interface
   c) X2 interface
   d) S1 interface
   Answer: b) E1 interface
   The E1 interface connects CU-CP to CU-UP, while F1 connects the CU to DU.

6. Explain the trade-offs between centralized and distributed Cloud RAN deployments. When would each approach be most appropriate?
   Answer: Centralized Cloud RAN maximizes resource pooling benefits and enables advanced coordination features but requires high-capacity, low-latency fronthaul infrastructure. It's most appropriate in dense urban areas with abundant fiber availability. Distributed Cloud RAN reduces fronthaul requirements and is more suitable for suburban areas or locations with limited fiber infrastructure. The choice depends on factors including traffic density, available transport infrastructure, latency requirements, and economic considerations. Hybrid approaches can balance these trade-offs by centralizing delay-tolerant functions while keeping latency-sensitive processing closer to radio units.

7. How does Cloud RAN enable network slicing, and what are the key mechanisms for ensuring slice isolation?
   Answer: Cloud RAN enables network slicing through its flexible, software-based architecture that allows dynamic resource allocation and function customization. Key mechanisms include: (1) Resource partitioning at the scheduler level to guarantee minimum resources per slice, (2) Separate CU instances or virtual instances per slice for control plane isolation, (3) Quality of Service (QoS) differentiation in the MAC layer, (4) Virtualization-layer isolation using containers or VMs, and (5) Dedicated radio resources

or shared resources with strict scheduling policies. These mechanisms ensure that each slice meets its specific SLA requirements while maintaining isolation from other slices.

8. Discuss the role of artificial intelligence and machine learning in optimizing Cloud RAN performance.
   Answer: AI/ML plays an increasingly important role in Cloud RAN optimization across multiple dimensions: (1) Traffic prediction enables proactive resource allocation and energy saving through predictive cell switching, (2) Interference management uses ML algorithms to optimize inter-cell coordination and beamforming parameters, (3) Anomaly detection identifies and resolves network issues before they impact service, (4) Resource orchestration optimizes the placement and scaling of VNFs based on workload patterns, and (5) Self-organizing network (SON) features automate configuration and optimization tasks. The O-RAN RIC (RAN Intelligent Controller) architecture provides a framework for deploying these AI/ML applications with appropriate time scales for different optimization objectives.

9. What are the main security challenges introduced by Cloud RAN architecture, and how can they be addressed?
   Answer: Cloud RAN introduces several security challenges: (1) Increased attack surface due to disaggregation and open interfaces requires comprehensive security at each interface (IPsec for fronthaul, secure APIs for management), (2) Virtualization vulnerabilities need hardened hypervisors and secure boot mechanisms, (3) Multi-tenancy risks require strong isolation between virtual functions and tenants, (4) Supply chain security concerns in multi-vendor environments need code signing and vulnerability management, and (5) Physical security of distributed sites requires tamper detection and access controls. A defense-in-depth approach with security controls at multiple layers—physical, infrastructure, network, and application—is essential for comprehensive protection.

10. Analyze the economic benefits of Cloud RAN beyond simple cost reduction. How does it enable new business models?
    Answer: Cloud RAN's economic benefits extend beyond traditional cost metrics: (1) Operational agility allows rapid service deployment and modification without hardware changes, (2) The platform approach enables operators to offer Infrastructure-as-a-Service to third parties, monetizing excess capacity, (3) Network slicing capabilities support differentiated services with varying SLAs and pricing models, (4) Edge computing integration creates opportunities for low-latency service hosting and content delivery, (5) Multi-tenancy support enables neutral host business models, and (6) The open ecosystem reduces vendor lock-in and accelerates innovation. These capabilities transform operators from connectivity providers to platform providers, enabling new revenue streams from enterprise services, IoT applications, and vertical industry solutions.

References

3GPP. (2013). *Study on coordinated multi-point operation for LTE* (TR 36.819 Version 11.2.0). https://www.3gpp.org/ftp/Specs/archive/36_series/36.819/

3GPP. (2017). *Study on new radio access technology: Radio access architecture and interfaces* (TR 38.801 Version 14.0.0). https://www.3gpp.org/ftp/Specs/archive/38_series/38.801/

3GPP. (2023). *NG-RAN; Architecture description* (TS 38.401 Version 17.4.0). https://www.3gpp.org/ftp/Specs/archive/38_series/38.401/

3GPP. (2023). *Management and orchestration; Concepts, use cases and requirements* (TS 28.530 Version 17.2.0). https://www.3gpp.org/ftp/Specs/archive/28_series/28.530/

6G Flagship Program. (2020). *Key drivers and research challenges for 6G ubiquitous wireless intelligence*. University of Oulu. http://jultika.oulu.fi/files/isbn9789526226737.pdf

ACG Research. (2021). *Cloud RAN: Total cost of ownership analysis*. https://www.acgresearch.com/cloud-ran-tco-analysis

Bhaumik, S., Chandrabose, S. P., Jataprolu, M. K., Kumar, G., Muralidhar, A., Polakos, P., Srinivasan, V., & Woo, T. (2012). CloudIQ: A framework for processing base stations in a data center. *Proceedings of the 18th Annual International Conference on Mobile Computing and Networking*, 125-136. https://doi.org/10.1145/2348543.2348561

Checko, A., Christiansen, H. L., Yan, Y., Scolari, L., Kardaras, G., Berger, M. S., & Dittmann, L. (2015). Cloud RAN for mobile networks—A technology overview. *IEEE Communications Surveys & Tutorials*, 17(1), 405-426. https://doi.org/10.1109/COMST.2014.2355255

China Mobile Research Institute. (2011). *C-RAN: The road towards green RAN* (White Paper Version 3.0). http://labs.chinamobile.com/cran/wp-content/uploads/2014/06/20140613-C-RAN-WP-3.0.pdf

Common Public Radio Interface. (2015). *CPRI specification V7.0*. http://www.cpri.info/downloads/CPRI_v_7_0_2015-10-09.pdf

eCPRI. (2019). *Common public radio interface: eCPRI interface specification V2.0*. http://www.cpri.info/downloads/eCPRI_v_2.0_2019_05_10c.pdf

ENISA. (2020). *Security in 5G specifications: Controls in 3GPP security specifications*. https://www.enisa.europa.eu/publications/security-in-5g-specifications

Ericsson. (2021). *Cloud RAN: Transforming radio access networks*. https://www.ericsson.com/en/reports-and-papers/white-papers/cloud-ran

ETSI. (2014). *Network functions virtualisation (NFV); Architectural framework* (GS NFV 002 V1.2.1). https://www.etsi.org/deliver/etsi_gs/NFV/001_099/002/01.02.01_60/gs_NFV002v010201p.pdf

ETSI. (2022). *Multi-access edge computing (MEC); Framework and reference architecture* (GS MEC 003 V3.1.1). https://www.etsi.org/deliver/etsi_gs/MEC/001_099/003/03.01.01_60/gs_MEC003v030101p.pdf

GSMA. (2019). *Cloud RAN deployment: Operator case studies and implementation guidelines*. https://www.gsma.com/futurenetworks/wp-content/uploads/2019/03/Cloud-RAN-Deployment.pdf

GSMA. (2021). *Cloud RAN security guidelines*. https://www.gsma.com/security/cloud-ran-security-guidelines/

GSMA Intelligence. (2022). *Cloud RAN: Market dynamics and operator strategies*. https://www.gsmaintelligence.com/research/cloud-ran-2022

IEEE. (2018). *Time-sensitive networking for fronthaul* (IEEE 802.1CM-2018). https://standards.ieee.org/standard/802_1CM-2018.html

IEEE. (2019). *Standard for packet-based fronthaul transport networks* (IEEE 1914.1-2019). https://standards.ieee.org/standard/1914_1-2019.html

IEEE. (2019). *IEEE standard for a precision clock synchronization protocol for networked measurement and control systems* (IEEE 1588-2019). https://standards.ieee.org/standard/1588-2019.html

Intel. (2021). *FlexRAN reference architecture for cloud RAN deployments*. https://www.intel.com/content/www/us/en/developer/topic-technology/edge-5g/tools/flexran.html

ITU-T. (2019). *40-Gigabit-capable passive optical networks (NG-PON2): General requirements* (G.989.1). https://www.itu.int/rec/T-REC-G.989.1

ITU-T. (2020). *Time and phase synchronization aspects of telecommunication networks* (G.8271). https://www.itu.int/rec/T-REC-G.8271

ITU-T. (2022). *Smart energy saving of 5G base station* (L.1380). https://www.itu.int/rec/T-REC-L.1380

ITU-R. (2023). *Future technology trends for the evolution of IMT towards 2030 and beyond* (Report ITU-R M.2516-0). https://www.itu.int/pub/R-REP-M.2516

Larsen, L. M., Checko, A., & Christiansen, H. L. (2019). A survey of the functional splits proposed for 5G mobile crosshaul networks. *IEEE Communications Surveys & Tutorials*, 21(1), 146-172. https://doi.org/10.1109/COMST.2018.2868805

Lee, D., Seo, H., Clerckx, B., Hardouin, E., Mazzarese, D., Nagata, S., & Sayana, K. (2014). Coordinated multipoint transmission and reception in LTE-advanced: Deployment scenarios and operational challenges. *IEEE Communications Magazine*, 50(2), 148-155. https://doi.org/10.1109/MCOM.2012.6146494

Liu, C., Sundaresan, K., Jiang, M., Rangarajan, S., & Chang, G. K. (2018). The case for re-configurable backhaul in cloud-RAN based small cell networks. *IEEE/ACM Transactions on Networking*, 26(3), 1256-1269. https://doi.org/10.1109/TNET.2018.2829712

Namba, S., Warabino, T., & Kaneko, S. (2012). BBU-RRH switching schemes for centralized RAN. *7th International ICST Conference on Communications and Networking in China*, 762-766. https://doi.org/10.1109/ChinaCom.2012.6417584

NGMN Alliance. (2015). *RAN evolution project: Backhaul and fronthaul evolution.* https://www.ngmn.org/publications/ran-evolution-project-backhaul-and-fronthaul-evolution.html

NGMN Alliance. (2016). *Description of network slicing concept.* https://www.ngmn.org/publications/description-of-network-slicing-concept.html

NGMN Alliance. (2021). *Green future networks: Network energy efficiency.* https://www.ngmn.org/publications/green-future-networks.html

Nikaein, N., Marina, M. K., Manickam, S., Dawson, A., Knopp, R., & Bonnet, C. (2015). OpenAirInterface: A flexible platform for 5G research. *ACM SIGCOMM Computer Communication Review*, 44(5), 33-38. https://doi.org/10.1145/2677046.2677053

NIST. (2018). *Framework for improving critical infrastructure cybersecurity* (Version 1.1). https://doi.org/10.6028/NIST.CSWP.04162018

Nokia. (2020). *Cloud RAN field trial results: Performance analysis and optimization.* https://www.nokia.com/networks/portfolio/cloud-ran/

O-RAN Alliance. (2023). *O-RAN architecture description 7.0.* https://www.o-ran.org/specifications

O-RAN Alliance. (2023). *O-RAN security specifications 4.0.* https://www.o-ran.org/specifications

Peng, M., Sun, Y., Li, X., Mao, Z., & Wang, C. (2016). Recent advances in cloud radio access networks: System architectures, key techniques, and open issues. *IEEE Communications Surveys & Tutorials*, 18(3), 2282-2308. https://doi.org/10.1109/COMST.2016.2548658

Red Hat. (2022). *Container-based virtualization for cloud RAN.* https://www.redhat.com/en/solutions/telecommunications/cloud-ran

Small Cell Forum. (2018). *Cloud RAN architecture and functional split.* https://scf.io/en/documents/191_-_Cloud_RAN_architecture_and_functional_split.php

STL Partners. (2021). *Cloud RAN: Market assessment and forecast 2021-2026.* https://stlpartners.com/research/cloud-ran-market-assessment/

Wu, J., Zhang, Z., Hong, Y., & Wen, Y. (2013). Cloud radio access network (C-RAN): A primer. *IEEE Network*, 27(1), 35-41. https://doi.org/10.1109/MNET.2013.6423189

Xilinx. (2020). *Accelerating cloud RAN with adaptive compute.* https://www.xilinx.com/applications/wireless-communications/cloud-ran.html

Zhang, H., Liu, N., Chu, X., Long, K., Aghvami, A. H., & Leung, V. C. (2019). Network slicing based 5G and future mobile networks: Mobility, resource management, and challenges. *IEEE Communications Magazine*, 55(8), 138-145. https://doi.org/10.1109/MCOM.2017.1600940

5G-PPP. (2020). *Cloud RAN and MEC: A perfect pairing*. https://5g-ppp.eu/cloud-ran-and-mec-a-perfect-pairing/

Chapter 18: Open RAN

Executive Summary

Open Radio Access Network (O-RAN) represents a transformative approach to building and operating mobile networks through disaggregation, virtualization, and standardized open interfaces. This chapter explores the comprehensive O-RAN architecture, including its intelligent controllers (RICs), standardized interfaces, and security frameworks. We examine how O-RAN enables multi-vendor interoperability, reduces costs, and introduces AI/ML-driven network optimization. The chapter also covers deployment scenarios, market trends showing significant growth projections despite current challenges, and the technology's role in advancing 5G and future 6G networks. Through detailed technical specifications, architectural diagrams, and real-world deployment examples, this chapter provides a thorough understanding of how O-RAN is reshaping the telecommunications landscape.

Table of Contents

Introduction

Open RAN's technical framework deliberately builds upon the wireless industry's existing standardization work rather than starting from scratch. The architecture maintains compatibility with 3GPP specifications—the global standards that define how cellular networks operate—while coordinating with other standards organizations to prevent redundant efforts and ensure that components work together seamlessly across the ecosystem.

Where conventional radio access networks locked operators into single-vendor solutions with proprietary interfaces, Open RAN charts a different course. This architectural approach enables networks built from modular components—radio units, baseband processors, and control systems—that different manufacturers produce but that communicate through publicly documented, standardized interfaces. The key innovation lies in disaggregation (breaking apart previously integrated systems), virtualization (running network functions as software rather than dedicated hardware), and genuine interoperability (allowing mix-and-match equipment choices).

The path to Open RAN emerged through industry collaboration. Two parallel efforts—the xRAN Forum focused on fronthaul interfaces and the C-RAN Alliance working on centralized architectures—recognized their complementary goals and merged in 2018 to establish the O-RAN Alliance. This consolidation brought together organizations that understood the need for a unified approach to open standards. The Alliance has since grown to encompass more than 300 member companies, ranging from major mobile operators and equipment vendors to software developers and chipset manufacturers, all working toward specifications that enable multi-vendor network deployments.

Key Principles of O-RAN

Open RAN's architecture rests on several foundational concepts that collectively transform how networks get built and managed. Research by Polese and colleagues in 2022, along with the O-RAN Alliance's own technical specifications from 2021, identifies these core principles:

1. **Disaggregation**: The architecture decomposes what were traditionally monolithic base station systems into distinct functional elements. This builds upon 3GPP's work defining functional splits for Next Generation Node Bases (gNBs), but extends that concept further. A typical deployment might separate the radio unit at the tower from centralized processing pools that could be located miles away in edge data centers, with intermediate distributed units handling time-sensitive processing. Each functional layer can be independently upgraded or replaced without touching the others.
2. **Intelligent Control**: Open RAN introduces a novel control framework through RAN Intelligent Controllers (RICs). These software platforms operate at multiple timescales—some making microsecond-level decisions about radio resource allocation, others optimizing network behavior over minutes or hours based on traffic patterns and performance data. The RIC architecture enables closed-loop automation where the network continuously monitors conditions, applies optimization algorithms, and adjusts parameters

without human intervention. This data-driven approach moves networks toward autonomous operation.

3. **Virtualization**: Rather than requiring specialized hardware appliances for each network function, Open RAN runs these capabilities as software on cloud-native computing platforms. This architectural choice brings several advantages. Network functions can be instantiated on-demand when traffic requires additional capacity, then scaled down during quiet periods. Software updates roll out without hardware replacement. The same computing infrastructure can host multiple network functions, improving resource utilization. Commercial off-the-shelf servers replace purpose-built equipment, reducing both capital costs and the time required to deploy new capabilities.

4. **Open Interfaces**: Standardized connection points between network components form the foundation that makes multi-vendor deployments practical. When every interface follows published specifications that any manufacturer can implement, operators escape the constraints of single-vendor ecosystems. An operator might choose radio units from one supplier, distributed units from another, and RIC software from a third party—all working together because they speak the same standardized language. This interoperability introduces genuine competition at each layer of the network stack, preventing any single vendor from controlling the operator's technology roadmap or pricing.

O-RAN Architecture and Components

Open RAN marks a fundamental departure from how the wireless industry has built cellular infrastructure for decades. Rather than deploying integrated base stations where all components come bundled from a single manufacturer, this architectural approach envisions radio access networks constructed from disaggregated, software-driven elements that can work together regardless of who made them. The O-RAN Alliance's 2024 specifications establish the technical groundwork for this vision—defining how networks can become more open in their vendor choices, more intelligent through embedded analytics and automation, more virtualized by running on standard computing platforms, and genuinely interoperable across equipment from different suppliers.

This transformation addresses practical challenges that have long frustrated network operators. Traditional base stations function as black boxes—operators can configure them within limits, but they can't fundamentally modify behavior, add new capabilities independently, or easily integrate innovations from outside the original vendor. The monolithic design also means that upgrading one component often requires replacing the entire system. Open RAN's modular structure changes these economics and operational constraints, allowing operators to refresh specific elements as technology advances, introduce AI-driven optimization through RIC applications developed by third parties, and build networks tailored to their specific requirements rather than accepting one-option-fits-all solutions(O-RAN Alliance, 2024).

O-RAN Architecture Overview

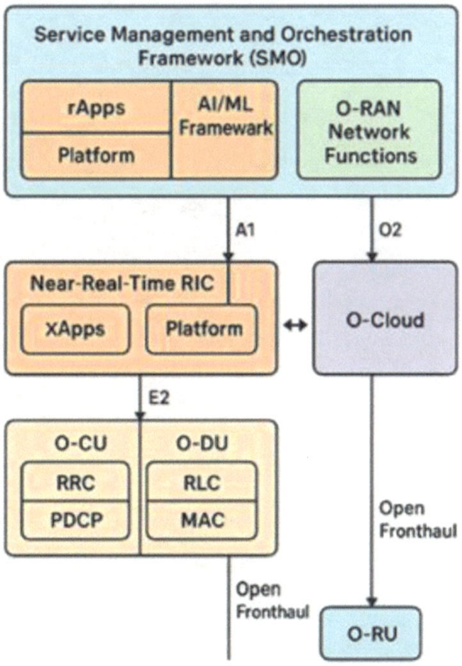

O-RAN Architecture Overview

Service Management and Orchestration (SMO)

The Service Management and Orchestration framework serves as the operational brain of Open RAN deployments, coordinating how network components work together and managing their lifecycle from deployment through ongoing operations. As defined in the O-RAN Alliance's 2021 specifications, the SMO platform handles orchestration duties for all Open RAN elements, including the Near-Real-Time RIC that manages moment-to-moment network optimization decisions.

Think of SMO as the conductor of an orchestra—it doesn't play the instruments directly, but ensures every section comes in at the right time, follows the score, and works in harmony. In networking terms, this means the SMO oversees the complete Open RAN infrastructure, providing centralized control for operations that span the entire system. Its responsibilities encompass several critical domains (O-RAN Alliance, 2021):

- **Lifecycle Management**: Deployment, configuration, and termination of network functions
- **Performance Management**: Collection and analysis of network KPIs
- **Fault Management**: Detection and remediation of network issues
- **AI/ML Workflow Management**: Training, validation, and deployment of ML models

Near-Real-Time RIC

The Near-Real-Time RAN Intelligent Controller (nRT RIC) functions as an intelligent optimization layer that makes rapid decisions about network behavior based on detailed operational data. According to the O-RAN Alliance's 2021 technical specifications, this logical component enables control and optimization of radio access network elements and resources by continuously gathering granular performance metrics and executing responsive actions through the E2 interface.

What distinguishes the near-real-time RIC from other control systems is its operational tempo. It works within a specific time window—faster than traditional management systems that might adjust configurations hourly or daily, but slower than the split-second decisions required for basic radio operations. The nRT RIC typically operates on timescales ranging from 10 milliseconds up to one second, a sweet spot that allows it to(O-RAN Alliance, 2021):

- **Analyze network conditions**: Collect detailed measurements about radio link quality, traffic loads, interference patterns, and user distribution across coverage areas
- **Apply optimization algorithms**: Run machine learning models or rule-based logic to identify performance improvements—perhaps detecting that certain frequency bands are underutilized while others are congested, or recognizing traffic patterns that suggest upcoming capacity needs
- **Execute corrective actions**: Send configuration updates to network elements, adjusting parameters like transmit power, beam steering angles, or resource allocation policies to improve performance

This near-real-time control loop fills a crucial gap. It's fast enough to respond to changing radio conditions before users notice degraded performance, yet slow enough to leverage sophisticated analytics that would be impossible to run in microseconds. The nRT RIC might detect congestion building in a particular cell sector and proactively shift traffic to neighboring cells, or recognize interference patterns and adjust frequencies to avoid them—all before manual intervention would even identify the problem.

The nRT RIC's architecture incorporates several key components that work together to enable its optimization capabilities:

xApps: Intelligent Control Applications

These are specialized software modules developed by third parties that implement specific optimization strategies and control algorithms. Think of xApps as plugins that extend the RIC's capabilities—one xApp might focus on traffic steering between cells, another on interference management, while a third handles energy efficiency optimization. This modular approach allows operators to customize their network intelligence by selecting and deploying the xApps most relevant to their operational priorities. It also creates an ecosystem where independent software vendors can innovate on network optimization without needing to modify the underlying RIC platform.

E2 Termination: The Connection Point

This component establishes the communication pathway between the nRT RIC and the radio access network nodes it manages. The E2 interface acts as the data highway, carrying performance measurements upstream from distributed units and centralized units to the RIC, while delivering configuration commands and policy updates back downstream. Without this termination point properly handling the protocol translation and message routing, the RIC would have no way to observe network conditions or implement its optimization decisions.

Conflict Mitigation: Coordination Logic

When multiple xApps run simultaneously, they might occasionally try to adjust the same network parameters in contradictory ways—one xApp optimizing for capacity while another prioritizes coverage, for instance. The conflict mitigation function arbitrates these competing control actions, applying resolution rules that ensure optimization decisions don't work against each other. This coordination layer prevents the chaotic scenario where different algorithms fight over the same configuration knobs.

Shared Data Layer: The Common Knowledge Base

All xApps need access to network state information—current traffic loads, user locations, radio link quality metrics, and historical performance data. Rather than each xApp maintaining its own separate data store and requesting the same information repeatedly, the shared data layer provides a common repository that all applications can query. This centralized approach improves efficiency, ensures consistency (all xApps see the same network state), and reduces the overhead of redundant data collection.

RIC Control Loop Timescales

Controller	Timescale	Scope	Functions
Non-RT RIC	> 1 second	Network-wide	Policy management, ML model management, enrichment information
Near-RT RIC	10ms - 1s	Multiple cells/users	Radio resource management, mobility control, QoS optimization
RAN Internal	< 10ms	Cell/user level	Scheduling, beamforming, power control

Source: O-RAN Alliance (2021), "O-RAN Near-Real-time RAN Intelligent Controller Architecture & E2 General Aspects and Principles v2.00"; Polese et al. (2022)

Non-Real-Time RIC

The non-RT RIC component operates in a supervisory capacity, providing direction and parameters to its near-RT counterpart. Its primary responsibility involves overseeing how machine-learning algorithms get implemented and utilized within xApps—the intelligent applications that drive network optimization (O-RAN Alliance, 2021). Rather than making split-second decisions, this component focuses on strategic oversight and configuration management.

The non-RT RIC handles several essential responsibilities:

Strategic Policy Control: This function establishes broad operational guidelines based on higher-level objectives and intentions. Instead of micromanaging individual decisions, it sets the boundaries and goals that guide network behavior over longer timeframes.

ML Algorithm Oversight: The system manages the complete lifecycle of artificial intelligence models—from initial training phases through actual deployment in the network environment. This includes determining which models get used, when they need retraining, and how they should be updated as conditions evolve.

Contextual Data Integration: The component gathers and processes information from sources outside the immediate network environment, enriching the decision-making process with broader context. This external intelligence helps the RAN adapt more effectively to changing conditions and user patterns.

Optimization Applications: It hosts rApps—specialized applications designed to handle optimization tasks that don't require instantaneous responses. These applications work on slightly longer time scales, focusing on improvements that unfold over minutes or hours rather than milliseconds.

By separating these strategic, slower-paced functions from the rapid-fire decisions handled by the near-RT RIC, the architecture achieves a practical division of labor that balances responsiveness with thoughtful, data-informed planning.

Disaggregated RAN Components

O-RAN's approach breaks apart what was traditionally a monolithic base station structure, dividing it into three distinct functional elements:

O-CU (O-RAN Central Unit)

The Central Unit represents the highest-level processing component in this distributed architecture. It operates by separating two critical operational domains:

Functional Separation: The O-CU divides itself into Control Plane (O-CU-CP) and User Plane (O-CU-UP) segments. The control plane handles signaling, connection management, and coordination activities, while the user plane focuses on moving actual data traffic. This division allows each segment to scale and optimize independently based on specific workload characteristics.

Protocol Responsibilities: This unit manages upper-layer communication protocols including Radio Resource Control (RRC), which oversees connection establishment and radio bearer configuration; Service Data Adaptation Protocol (SDAP), which maps data flows to appropriate quality-of-service levels; and Packet Data Convergence Protocol (PDCP), which handles tasks like encryption, header compression, and reliable data delivery.

Flexible Deployment: The architecture's modularity means the O-CU can be positioned wherever it makes the most operational and economic sense. Organizations might place it in regional data centers for better resource pooling, or closer to the network edge when latency considerations take priority. This location flexibility represents a significant departure from traditional base stations that came as integrated, location-fixed equipment.

The ability to physically separate these functions while maintaining tight logical coordination creates opportunities for more efficient resource utilization, easier upgrades, and better adaptation to diverse deployment scenarios—from dense urban environments to sprawling rural coverage areas.

O-DU (O-RAN Distributed Unit)

The O-RAN Distributed Unit handles protocol stack functions that require rapid processing but don't need to be physically located at the radio itself. According to the O-RAN Alliance's 2021 specifications, this component implements the Radio Link Control (RLC), Medium Access Control (MAC), and upper portions of the physical layer (high-PHY) based on what's known as a lower-layer functional split architecture.

This design choice reflects careful engineering trade-offs. The O-DU manages functions that operate on timescales of milliseconds—tasks like scheduling which users transmit data in specific time slots, handling retransmissions when packets get lost, and coordinating multiple antenna streams. These responsibilities demand substantial computing power and low-latency access to the radio, but they don't require the microsecond-level response times that radio frequency operations need.

The O-DU's operational characteristics include:

- **Protocol layer implementation**: Executes the RLC, MAC, and high-PHY processing that sits between the core network's data packets and the radio frequency signals transmitted over the air
- **Real-time performance**: Meets strict timing requirements measured in milliseconds, ensuring the network maintains its quality of service commitments to users
- **Strategic positioning**: Typically deployed at edge computing facilities relatively close to cell sites—near enough to maintain low latency to the radios, but centralized enough that multiple radio units can share processing resources from a single O-DU

This placement strategy allows operators to pool computing resources more efficiently than putting dedicated processors at every tower, while still keeping latency low enough for time-sensitive operations.

O-RU (O-RAN Radio Unit)

- The O-RAN Radio Unit represents the physical layer equipment actually mounted on towers and rooftops—the component that transmits and receives radio frequency signals through antennas. This unit handles the lowest-level physical layer processing along with the radio frequency front-end operations.
- The O-RAN Alliance adopted a specific architectural approach (designated as split 7.2x from the options that 3GPP outlined in their 2017 specifications) for dividing physical layer functions between the O-RU and O-DU. This particular split point balances several competing requirements: minimizing the bandwidth needed on the fronthaul connection between O-RU and O-DU, keeping the radio unit's processing demands manageable to control cost and power consumption, and maintaining the flexibility needed for advanced features.
- The O-RU's core responsibilities include:
- **Lower physical layer processing**: Implements the time-critical portions of the physical layer that must happen in close proximity to the actual radio transmission
- **Radio frequency operations**: Handles the analog signal processing, power amplification, and frequency conversion that transforms digital signals into electromagnetic waves (and vice versa for received signals)
- **Advanced antenna techniques**: Performs operations like Fast Fourier Transforms (FFT) and inverse FFTs for converting between time and frequency domains, beamforming calculations that steer radio energy toward specific users, and analog-to-digital or digital-to-analog conversion that bridges the gap between digital baseband processing and analog radio frequency signals
- These functions demand specialized hardware optimized for signal processing and radio frequency engineering—quite different from the general-purpose computing platforms that can host O-DU functions.

O-RAN Interfaces

O-RAN defines several standardized interfaces that enable multi-vendor interoperability and intelligent control:

O-RAN Interface Architecture

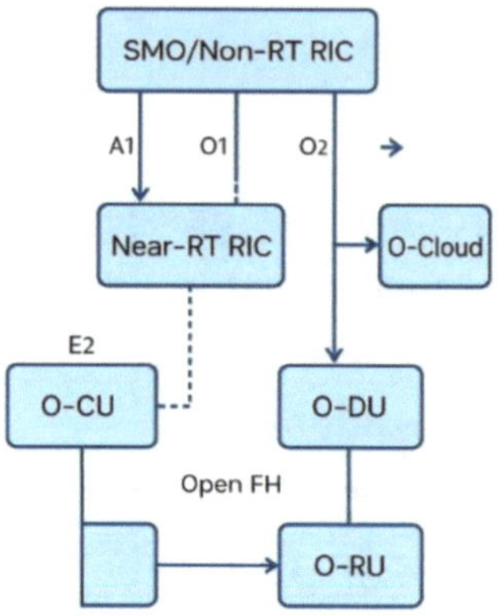

O-RAN Architecture Description v5.00
O-RAN Alliance (2021)

O-RAN Architecture Description v5.00

Source: Adapted from RIMEDO Labs (2024), "O-RAN Architecture, Nodes, and Interfaces," and O-RAN Alliance (2021), "O-RAN Architecture Description v5.00"

E2 Interface

The E2 interface serves as the critical communication channel that connects the Near-Real-Time RIC to the radio access network components it manages. What makes this interface particularly powerful is its ability to reach deep into the base station architecture, establishing connections with individual functional elements—the O-RU handling radio operations, the O-DU managing protocol processing, and the O-CU coordinating higher-layer functions (RIMEDO Labs, 2024).

This architectural design enables sophisticated control capabilities that weren't possible with traditional base station management systems. Through the E2 interface, the RIC and its xApp applications can actively monitor operational conditions, temporarily pause certain functions when needed, override default behaviors to implement optimization strategies, send detailed control instructions, and trigger specific actions within these network elements. As RIMEDO Labs explained in their 2024 technical analysis, this interface essentially provides a programmatic control plane that allows external intelligence to influence how base station components operate in near-real-time.

The practical implications are significant. Instead of base stations operating as autonomous black boxes with limited external visibility, the E2 interface creates transparency and controllability. An xApp focused on energy efficiency might use E2 to monitor traffic loads across multiple cells and send commands to power down underutilized radio units during off-peak hours. A mobility optimization xApp could observe handover performance metrics through E2 and adjust handover thresholds to reduce dropped connections. An interference management application might detect problematic interference patterns and execute power adjustments or frequency reassignments through E2 commands—all happening automatically based on real network conditions rather than static configurations.

This capability to observe fine-grained operational data and execute responsive actions represents a fundamental shift from how cellular networks have traditionally been managed. The E2 interface transforms the RAN from a relatively static, slowly-changing system into a dynamic platform that can continuously adapt its behavior based on intelligent analysis of operational conditions.

The E2 interface enables near-real-time control through four main services (O-RAN Alliance, 2021):

1. **Report Service**: Periodic or event-triggered KPM reporting
2. **Insert Service**: RAN-initiated control requests
3. **Control Service**: RIC-initiated control actions
4. **Policy Service**: Autonomous RAN behavior policies

E2 Service Models

- **E2SM-KPM:** Key Performance Measurements reporting (O-RAN Alliance, 2021)
- **E2SM-RC:** RAN Control for radio resource management (O-RAN Alliance, 2021)
- **E2SM-NI:** Network Interface message forwarding (O-RAN Alliance, 2020)

A1 Interface

The A1 interface establishes the connection pathway between Open RAN's two intelligent control layers—the Non-Real-Time RIC operating at longer timescales and the Near-Real-Time RIC handling rapid optimization decisions. According to SDxCentral's 2024 analysis, this interface facilitates three essential categories of interaction: policy coordination, machine learning model distribution, and information enrichment.

Understanding why this interface exists requires recognizing that the two RICs operate in complementary domains. The Non-RT RIC works on timescales of seconds to minutes, analyzing broader trends, training machine learning models, and making strategic decisions about network behavior. The Near-RT RIC operates much faster (10 milliseconds to 1 second), applying policies and models to make tactical optimization decisions. The A1 interface bridges these layers, allowing strategic intelligence from the slower RIC to guide the rapid decision-making of the faster one.

The A1 interface supports several critical functions:

Policy Management: Strategic Guidance

The Non-RT RIC uses A1 to convey intent-based policies that shape how the Near-RT RIC and its xApps should behave. Rather than micromanaging every decision, these policies establish strategic objectives and constraints. For example, a policy might specify that during peak hours, the network should prioritize capacity over energy efficiency, while off-peak hours should emphasize power savings. Another policy might define service level objectives for different traffic types—ensuring emergency services always receive prioritization, while streaming video can tolerate slight delays during congestion. The Near-RT RIC receives these high-level directives through A1 and implements them through its real-time control actions.

ML Model Management: Distributing Intelligence

Machine learning models trained by the Non-RT RIC need deployment to the Near-RT RIC where they'll actually execute. The A1 interface handles this distribution, managing the complete lifecycle of these models—initial deployment when a new model is ready, updates when improved versions become available, and retirement when models become obsolete. This might include predictive models that forecast traffic patterns, classification algorithms that identify network anomalies, or optimization models that suggest resource allocation strategies. By centralizing model training in the Non-RT RIC while distributing execution to the Near-RT RIC, the architecture separates the computationally intensive training process from the latency-sensitive inference operations.

Enrichment Information: Contextual Data

The Near-RT RIC's optimization decisions improve when they incorporate contextual information beyond what the E2 interface provides from network elements. The A1 interface delivers this enrichment data—perhaps subscriber tier information indicating which users have premium service agreements, application context revealing whether traffic is real-time video that needs consistent bandwidth or file downloads that can tolerate variability, or location data from enterprise agreements showing where private network deployments exist. This contextual information allows the Near-RT RIC to make more nuanced decisions that account for business priorities and operational context, not just raw technical metrics.

A1 Policy Deployment Flow

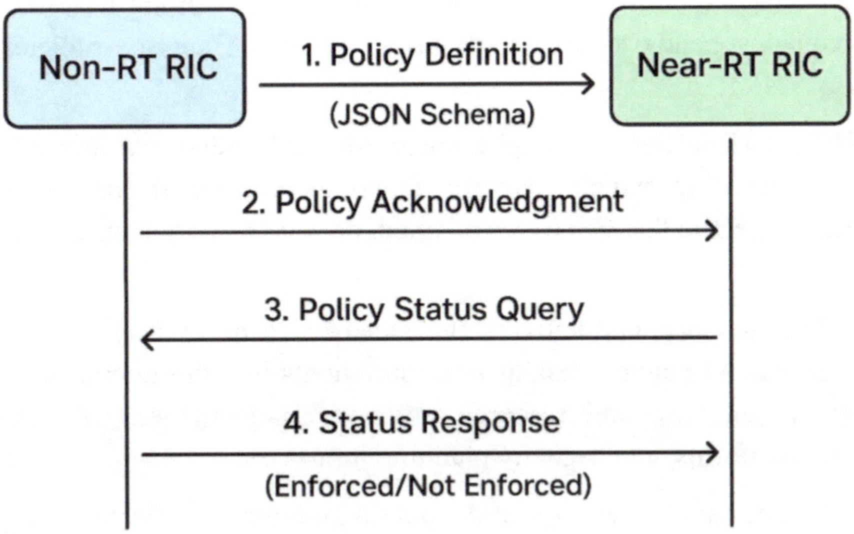

Source: Based on O-RAN Alliance (2021), "A1 Interface: General Aspects and Principles v2.03" and "A1 Interface: Application Protocol v3.01"

O1 Interface

The O1 interface, working in conjunction with the Open-Fronthaul M-plane specifications, provides comprehensive management capabilities following the telecommunications industry's standard FCAPS framework—covering Fault detection, Configuration control, Accounting functions, Performance monitoring, and Security management. As RIMEDO Labs detailed in their 2024 technical documentation, this interface establishes the communication pathway through which operators can configure network elements, modify their operational parameters, register new components as they join the network, implement security policies, track performance metrics, and maintain continuous operational monitoring of individual nodes throughout the Open RAN infrastructure.

This interface addresses the fundamental operational needs that any network deployment requires, regardless of how innovative its architecture might be. While interfaces like E2 and A1 enable intelligent optimization and policy control, O1 handles the bread-and-butter management tasks that keep networks running day-to-day.

Fault Management: The O1 interface carries alarm notifications when network components detect problems—perhaps a radio unit experiencing hardware failures, a fiber connection between O-DU and O-RU going down, or software processes crashing. It also supports troubleshooting operations where management systems can query devices for diagnostic information to understand root causes of issues.

Configuration Management: Through O1, operators can push initial configuration parameters to newly deployed equipment, update settings as requirements change, and verify that devices are operating with their intended configurations. This might involve setting transmit power levels, defining which frequency bands to use, configuring quality of service policies, or updating software versions.

Accounting: The interface tracks resource utilization and operational events that feed into business processes—recording which network functions consumed how much processing capacity, logging when specific features were activated, or documenting configuration changes for audit trails.

Performance Management: O1 delivers the steady stream of performance metrics that operators need to understand network health—measurements like throughput levels, connection success rates, latency statistics, and resource utilization percentages. This data feeds into dashboards, analytics platforms, and capacity planning processes.

Security: The interface handles security credential distribution, certificate management, access control policies, and secure communication setup between management systems and network elements. In an architecture where components come from different vendors, establishing and maintaining security trust relationships becomes particularly critical.

Together, these FCAPS capabilities through the O1 interface ensure that Open RAN deployments can be managed with the same operational rigor that traditional networks require, even while introducing new architectural flexibility.

These management interfaces follow the well-established FCAPS framework—which stands for Fault, Configuration, Accounting, Performance, and Security management. Through these standardized connection points, network operators can handle a comprehensive range of operational tasks with individual network elements (RIMEDO Labs, 2024).

The O1 interface enables operators to configure devices according to specific requirements, make adjustments to settings as conditions change, and register new equipment as it gets added to the network. Security policies can be applied and enforced, ensuring that network components operate within defined safety parameters. Performance monitoring happens continuously, providing visibility into how each element functions under real-world conditions. When problems arise, the fault management capabilities help identify and diagnose issues quickly.

This management layer proves particularly valuable in disaggregated architectures where components from different vendors need to work together seamlessly. By adhering to standardized management protocols, operators gain consistent control mechanisms regardless of which manufacturer supplied a particular piece of equipment. The interface essentially provides a unified operational view across what might otherwise be a fragmented landscape of diverse hardware and software elements.

The ability to monitor, configure, and troubleshoot through these standardized interfaces reduces operational complexity significantly. Network teams don't need to learn vendor-specific management tools for each component—instead, they work through common protocols that apply across the entire infrastructure. This standardization becomes especially important as networks grow more distributed and incorporate equipment from multiple sources.

The O1 interface provides comprehensive management services:

O1 Management Services

Service	Function	Protocol
Provisioning	Configuration management	NETCONF/YANG
Fault Supervision	Alarm and event reporting	REST/HTTPS
Performance Assurance	KPI collection and reporting	REST/WebSocket
File Management	Software updates, ML models	SFTP
Trace Management	Call and procedure tracing	REST/HTTPS

Source: O-RAN Alliance (2020), "O-RAN Operations and Maintenance Interface v4.0"; 3GPP (2022), "Management and Orchestration; Generic Management Services (TS 28.532)"

O2 Interface

The O2 interface establishes the connection between the Service Management and Orchestration framework and the O-RAN Cloud platform, creating the pathway through which network functions get deployed, managed, and scaled in a programmatic, automated fashion. According to the O-RAN Alliance's 2021 specifications, this interface enables cloud-native orchestration capabilities that treat network functions as software workloads that can be dynamically instantiated and managed using modern cloud computing practices.

This interface reflects Open RAN's embrace of cloud-native principles. Rather than managing network equipment as fixed hardware appliances that operators manually configure, the O2 interface allows treating virtualized network functions as elastic software resources that can be deployed on-demand, scaled up or down based on traffic requirements, and managed through automated workflows.

The O2 interface provides several essential capabilities:

Infrastructure Inventory Management: The interface maintains awareness of available computing resources across the cloud infrastructure—tracking which servers have available CPU capacity, memory, and storage, understanding network connectivity between compute nodes, and knowing the current allocation of resources to various network functions. This inventory visibility allows the orchestration system to make intelligent placement decisions when deploying new workloads or moving existing ones.

Resource Provisioning and Scaling: When network demand increases—perhaps due to a major event driving heavy mobile usage in a specific area—the SMO can use the O2 interface to provision additional instances of network functions to handle the load. Conversely, during quiet periods, it can scale down capacity to reduce computing resource consumption and associated costs. This elastic scaling represents a fundamental shift from traditional networks where capacity remained fixed regardless of actual demand.

Fault Tolerance and Monitoring: The O2 interface supports continuous health monitoring of virtualized network functions, detecting when software instances fail or perform poorly. When problems occur, the orchestration system can automatically trigger remediation actions through O2—perhaps restarting failed instances, migrating workloads to different hardware if servers become problematic, or spinning up replacement instances to maintain service continuity. This automated fault recovery improves network resilience without requiring constant human intervention.

Lifecycle Management of Cloud Resources: Network functions progress through various lifecycle stages—initial deployment, software updates, configuration changes, performance optimization, and eventual retirement when no longer needed. The O2 interface orchestrates these lifecycle operations, managing the complete journey from initial provisioning through ongoing operations to final decommissioning. This includes coordinating complex operations like software upgrades across multiple instances while maintaining service continuity.

Together, these O2 capabilities enable Open RAN deployments to leverage the operational advantages that cloud-native architectures provide—automation, elasticity, resilience, and efficient resource utilization—bringing modern software engineering practices into telecommunications infrastructure.

Open Fronthaul Interface

This interface serves as the vital link connecting the O-RAN Distributed Unit with the O-RAN Radio Unit, transmitting both user traffic and signaling messages that allow these physically separate elements to function as a cohesive whole. According to specifications published by the O-RAN Alliance in 2021, the Open Fronthaul design follows what's known as the 7.2x functional division model. Rather than treating the connection as a single channel, it structures communication across four separate operational layers, with each layer responsible for distinct aspects of how the Distributed Unit and Radio Unit interact with one another.

This multi-plane architecture provides several practical advantages. By segregating different types of traffic and control information into dedicated channels, the interface can optimize how each category of data gets handled. Time-critical information flows through pathways designed for minimal delay, while less urgent management traffic uses separate routes that don't interfere with performance-sensitive operations. The structured approach also simplifies troubleshooting—

when issues arise, network engineers can isolate problems to specific planes rather than dealing with an undifferentiated data stream.

The 7.2x split point itself represents a carefully chosen boundary in the signal processing chain. Functions that require tight timing synchronization and proximity to the radio hardware remain in the Radio Unit, while more flexible processing tasks move to the Distributed Unit where they can benefit from centralized resources and easier upgrades. This division balances the need for low-latency radio processing against the advantages of pooling computational resources and standardizing interfaces across different hardware vendors.

This multi-plane architecture reflects the diverse types of information that must flow between baseband processing and radio equipment. Rather than mixing everything into a single communication channel, the separation into distinct planes allows each to be optimized for its specific requirements—some needing ultra-low latency, others requiring high bandwidth, and still others prioritizing reliability over speed.

Control Plane (C-Plane): Real-Time Command Distribution

The control plane carries time-sensitive instructions that govern immediate radio behavior. This includes scheduling commands that tell the O-RU exactly which users should transmit or receive data in specific time slots and frequency resources, along with beamforming directives that specify how the radio should shape and steer its transmitted energy using multiple antenna elements. These commands must arrive at the O-RU with precise timing—arriving too late would mean the radio misses its scheduled transmission opportunity, disrupting user connections. The C-Plane operates on strict deadlines measured in microseconds, reflecting the real-time nature of radio resource management.

User Plane (U-Plane): Data Transport

The user plane handles the actual payload—the IQ (In-phase and Quadrature) samples that represent digital baseband signals before they become radio frequency transmissions. When the O-DU processes user data packets into the digital waveforms that will eventually become radio signals, those complex-valued samples traverse the U-Plane to reach the O-RU. Similarly, signals received by the O-RU's antennas get converted into IQ samples that flow back to the O-DU for processing. This plane typically carries the highest data volumes, with bandwidth requirements directly proportional to the number of antennas, signal bandwidth, and data rates the system supports.

Synchronization Plane (S-Plane): Timing Coordination

Wireless systems depend on precise timing and frequency alignment. All radio units must operate with synchronized clocks so that their transmissions don't interfere with each other and so that timing-based protocols work correctly. The synchronization plane distributes the timing and frequency reference information that keeps the O-RU locked to the network's master clock. This might involve protocols like Precision Time Protocol (PTP) that can maintain timing accuracy within microseconds across distributed equipment. Without this tight synchronization, the radio system would experience interference, handover failures, and degraded performance.

Management Plane (M-Plane): Configuration and Lifecycle Control

While the other planes handle real-time operations, the management plane deals with longer-timescale activities around O-RU configuration and lifecycle management. Through the M-Plane, the O-DU (or management systems beyond it) can configure the O-RU's operational parameters—setting transmit power levels, defining which frequency bands and channels to use, updating software, and monitoring equipment health. This plane also handles the initial setup when an O-RU first connects to the network, establishing its identity, capabilities, and configuration before it begins handling traffic.

Together, these four planes provide the comprehensive communication framework that allows disaggregated Open RAN components to function as effectively as traditional integrated base stations, while maintaining the flexibility and vendor diversity that open interfaces enable.

Security Architecture and Zero Trust Framework

Networks that support critical infrastructure and time-sensitive applications requiring guaranteed reliability must be architected with comprehensive security as a foundational requirement, not an afterthought. The O-RAN Alliance emphasized in their 2024 security guidelines that 5G deployments and future network generations need to embrace Zero Trust Architecture (ZTA) principles to defend against both external attack vectors and potential internal security compromises.

Zero Trust represents a fundamental shift from traditional network security thinking. Conventional approaches often established a security perimeter—trusting everything inside the corporate or carrier network while defending against external threats. This model fails in modern architectures where network functions run as distributed software across multiple cloud environments, where components come from different vendors, and where insider threats or compromised credentials can bypass perimeter defenses.

The Zero Trust model operates on the premise that danger might lurk anywhere—whether originating from within the established network perimeter or from external sources. Instead of granting automatic trust based on where a device or user connects from, ZTA demands ongoing authentication, enforces rigorous access limitations following minimal-permission standards, and maintains persistent oversight of every exchange occurring among system elements. When applied to Open RAN environments, this translates to:

Continuous Authentication: Every network component must prove its identity before accessing other elements, and that authentication must be revalidated regularly rather than trusted indefinitely after initial login. When an O-DU communicates with an O-RU, or when an xApp requests data from the RIC, those interactions require cryptographic verification of identity.

Minimal Access Rights: Components receive only the specific permissions necessary for their functions—nothing more. An xApp focused on energy optimization shouldn't have access to subscriber data or billing information. A monitoring system might have read-only access to performance metrics but no ability to modify configurations.

Encrypted Communications: All data traversing interfaces—whether across the fronthaul between O-DU and O-RU, over management interfaces, or through the RIC's control plane—should be encrypted to prevent eavesdropping and tampering.

Continuous Monitoring and Anomaly Detection: The security framework must continuously observe network behavior, looking for anomalous patterns that might indicate compromised components, unauthorized access attempts, or unusual data flows that could signal attacks in progress.

For networks supporting critical infrastructure like emergency services, industrial automation, or public safety communications, these Zero Trust principles aren't optional security enhancements—they're essential requirements that prevent single points of compromise from cascading into system-wide failures. The distributed, multi-vendor nature of Open RAN makes comprehensive security architecture even more critical, as the attack surface expands compared to traditional integrated systems from single vendors(O-RAN Alliance, 2024).

Zero Trust Principles in O-RAN

O-RAN implements zero trust through several mechanisms (O-RAN Alliance, 2025):

1. **Continuous Authentication**: All components must authenticate for every transaction
2. **Least Privilege Access**: Minimal permissions for all entities
3. **Encryption**: Data protection at rest and in transit
4. **Micro-segmentation**: Isolation of network functions

O-RAN Security Threat Categories

Threat Category	Description	Mitigation Approach
System Threats	Attacks on O-RAN components and interfaces	Authentication, encryption, integrity checks
O-Cloud Threats	Virtualization vulnerabilities	Container isolation, secure APIs
AI/ML Threats	Model poisoning, adversarial attacks	Secure training pipelines, model validation
Physical Threats	Hardware tampering	Physical security, trusted boot
Wireless Threats	Jamming, interference	Anomaly detection, adaptive algorithms

Source: O-RAN Alliance (2021), "O-RAN Security Threat Modeling and Remediation Analysis v2.0"; O-RAN Alliance (2025), "O-RAN Security Update 2025"

The O-RAN Alliance's Work Group 11 focuses specifically on security considerations, working in coordination with other technical work groups to establish comprehensive security requirements that span the entire Open RAN ecosystem. According to the O-RAN Alliance's 2025 documentation, WG11's scope encompasses security specifications for architectural components (like the O-DU, O-RU, and RIC elements), the interfaces connecting these components (including E2, A1, O1, O2, and fronthaul), virtualized network functions running on cloud platforms, and the data flowing through the system.

This cross-cutting security responsibility makes sense given Open RAN's distributed, multi-vendor architecture. Security can't be an isolated concern handled by a single component—it must be woven throughout every layer of the system. WG11 collaborates with groups defining functional specifications to ensure security considerations get incorporated from the ground up rather than bolted on afterward.

The work group's responsibilities likely include defining authentication mechanisms for component interactions, specifying encryption requirements for interface communications, establishing access control frameworks that implement Zero Trust principles, creating security monitoring and logging requirements that enable threat detection, and documenting security testing and validation procedures that vendors and operators can follow to verify implementations meet the specified security standards.

This collaborative approach ensures that as the O-RAN specifications evolve—adding new interfaces, defining additional network functions, or introducing novel capabilities—security requirements keep pace with functional developments. Rather than treating security as a separate concern addressed after functional design is complete, the integration of WG11's work with other groups means security gets considered as an inherent aspect of every architectural decision.

Security Architecture Components

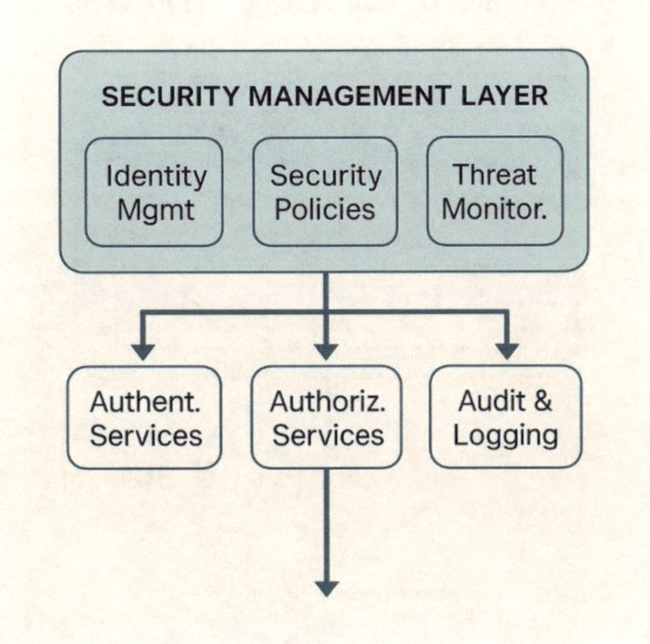

Source: Adapted from O-RAN Alliance (2024), "Zero Trust Architecture for Secure O-RAN White Paper"; O-RAN Alliance (2021), "O-RAN Security Requirements Specifications v1.0"

Deployment Models and Scenarios

O-RAN supports various deployment models to accommodate different use cases and operator requirements:

Deployment Scenarios

1. **Greenfield Deployments**: New networks built entirely on O-RAN principles
   - Examples: DISH Network (USA), Rakuten Mobile (Japan)
   - Advantages: No legacy integration challenges
2. **Brownfield Deployments**: Integration with existing networks
   - Gradual migration from traditional RAN
   - Requires careful integration planning
3. **Private Networks**: Enterprise and industrial deployments
   - Customized for specific use cases
   - Enhanced security and control

O-RAN Deployment Options

Option A: Centralized Deployment

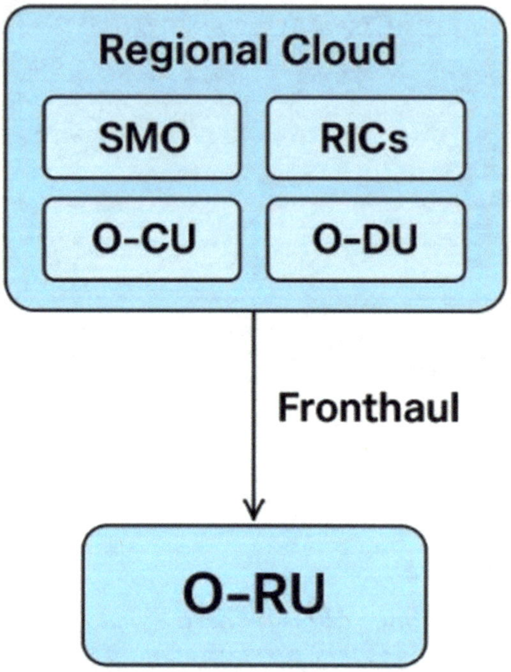

Source: O-RAN Alliance (2021), "O-RAN Cloud Architecture and Deployment Scenarios for O-RAN Virtualized RAN v2.02"

Option B: Distributed Deployment

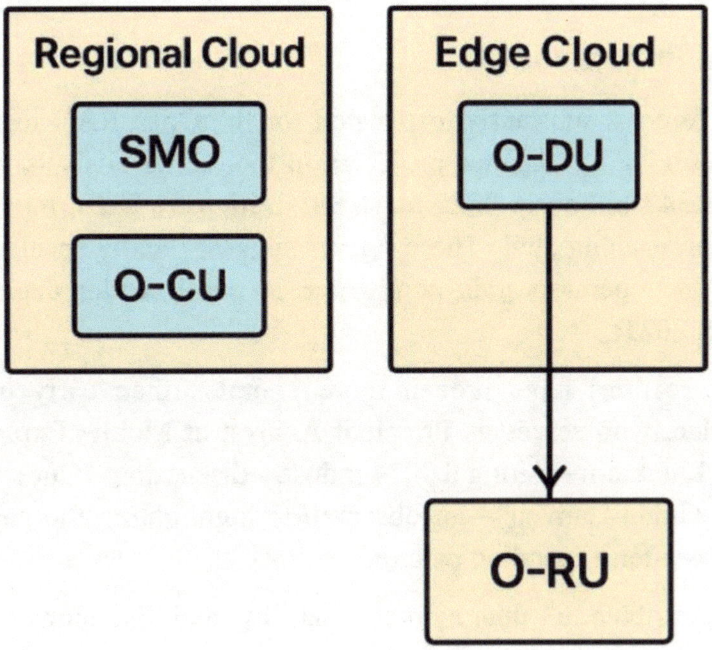

Market Trends and Industry Adoption

The O-RAN market is experiencing significant growth and transformation:

Market Size and Projections

Industry analysts forecast substantial expansion for the Open RAN market over the coming years. Knowledge Sourcing Intelligence projected in their 2023 analysis that the global market would surge from $1.347 billion in 2022 to $8.883 billion by 2028, representing a compound annual growth rate approaching 37%. These figures suggest rapidly accelerating adoption as the technology matures and operators gain confidence in multi-vendor deployments (Knowledge Sourcing Intelligence, 2023).

However, market realities have proven more complex than early optimistic projections suggested. Joe Madden, who serves as Principal Analyst at Mobile Experts, characterized the revenue trajectory in blunt terms during a 2024 industry discussion: "Our revenue chart for Open RAN looks like the Grand Canyon"—an observation highlighting the gap between ambitious forecasts and actual near-term spending patterns.

Several factors contribute to this market volatility and the slower-than-expected initial adoption:

Greenfield Deployment Completion: Many of the early Open RAN projects involved operators building entirely new networks in previously unserved areas or deploying private networks for enterprise customers. These greenfield deployments—where no legacy infrastructure exists—represent the easiest entry point for Open RAN since operators don't need to manage migration from existing systems. As these initial greenfield opportunities get addressed, growth depends increasingly on the more challenging brownfield scenarios.

Brownfield Transition Complexity: The more substantial long-term market opportunity lies in operators replacing or augmenting their existing traditional RAN infrastructure with Open RAN solutions. These brownfield deployments present significant challenges—operators must maintain service continuity during transitions, integrate new open systems with legacy core networks and management platforms, manage vendor relationships differently than they have for decades, and justify the business case when existing equipment still has remaining useful life. This transition requires operators to adopt fundamentally different deployment models, procurement strategies, and operational approaches, which naturally takes time as organizations develop new capabilities and gain operational experience.

The market appears to be in a transition phase where early adopters have moved forward with deployments while mainstream operators carefully evaluate technical maturity, assess vendor ecosystems, and develop the internal expertise needed to manage multi-vendor networks effectively. Market growth will likely accelerate as these learning curves flatten and as the Open RAN supply chain matures with more vendors offering proven, interoperable products.

Regional Market Distribution

Open RAN adoption patterns vary significantly across global markets, with the Asia Pacific region positioned to capture the largest share of deployments. Research Nester's 2025 analysis projects that Asia Pacific will command nearly 35% of the worldwide Open RAN market by 2030, reflecting strong momentum in several key countries throughout the region.

Several factors drive this geographic concentration in Asia Pacific. The region includes markets with aggressive 5G rollout timelines, operators willing to embrace architectural innovation, regulatory frameworks that encourage competition and open standards, and a robust telecommunications equipment manufacturing base that can supply Open RAN components. Japan in particular has emerged as a proving ground for Open RAN technology, with major deployments providing real-world validation of the architecture's viability.

Regional activity patterns show distinct characteristics:

North America: Carrier-Led Deployments

The North American market features significant Open RAN initiatives from major operators, with DISH Network building a greenfield cloud-native 5G network based entirely on Open RAN principles and AT&T conducting extensive trials and phased deployments as part of its network modernization strategy. These operators bring substantial scale and technical expertise, helping establish reference architectures and operational best practices that influence global adoption. The region benefits from strong cloud infrastructure providers, an active telecommunications equipment vendor ecosystem, and operators with technical teams experienced in managing complex multi-vendor environments.

Europe: Operator Trials and Strategic Deployments

European markets show active Open RAN exploration from major carriers including Deutsche Telekom and Vodafone, which have conducted trials across multiple countries and moved into commercial deployments in selected markets. European operators face complex multi-country operations, diverse regulatory environments across the EU, and pressure from regulators encouraging network diversity and supply chain resilience. These factors create both opportunities and challenges for Open RAN adoption—operators see potential benefits from vendor diversity and supply chain security, but must navigate complex procurement processes and coordinated deployment strategies across national subsidiaries.

Asia Pacific: Market Leadership with Large-Scale Deployments

Japan leads the regional charge with substantial commercial deployments from operators like KDDI and Rakuten Mobile, the latter having built its entire nationwide network on Open RAN and cloud-native principles from inception. Rakuten's deployment in particular serves as a high-profile case study demonstrating that Open RAN can support a major carrier's complete network at scale. Other Asia Pacific markets including India, South Korea, and various Southeast Asian countries show growing interest, driven by government initiatives promoting indigenous telecommunications technology development, operators seeking alternatives to traditional vendor lock-in, and the presence of local equipment manufacturers entering the Open RAN supply chain.

The regional distribution suggests that Open RAN adoption will continue spreading from these early-mover markets to other regions as the technology matures, the vendor ecosystem expands, and operational experience accumulates.

The Asia Pacific region is projected to capture the largest portion of the OPEN RAN market, approaching a 35% share by 2030 (Research Nester, 2025). Important regional developments include:

- **North America:** Led by AT&T deployments
- **Europe:** Deutsche Telekom, Vodafone trials and deployments
- **Asia Pacific:** Japan leading with KDDI and Rakuten deployments

Major O-RAN Deployments Worldwides

Operator	Country	Status	Scale
Rakuten Mobile	Japan	Commercial	Nationwide
DISH Network	USA	Commercial	Ongoing buildout
Deutsche Telekom	Germany	Trials/Initial deployment	Multiple cities
Vodafone UK	UK	Commercial deployment	2,500 sites
1&1	Germany	Commercial	Greenfield network

Source: SOLiD (2021), "The Global State of the O-RAN Market in 2021"; Light Reading (2024), "Nokia Plight Shows Need for Samsung"; Knowledge Sourcing Intelligence (2023)

Benefits and Challenges

Benefits of O-RAN

1. **Cost Reduction**
   - According to Ericsson, a leading participant in the 5G industry, implementing open RAN architecture enables carriers to lower their day-to-day operational expenses by as much as 40% while decreasing overall ownership expenditures by roughly 36% (Knowledge Sourcing Intelligence, 2023).
   - Reduced vendor lock-in
   - Competitive pricing through a multi-vendor ecosystem
2. **Innovation Acceleration**
   - Open interfaces enable new entrants
   - Faster feature development cycles

- AI/ML-driven optimization

3. **Flexibility and Scalability**
    - Cloud-native deployment options
    - Dynamic resource allocation
    - Support for diverse use cases
4. **Supply Chain Diversity**
    - Multiple vendor options
    - Reduced geopolitical risks
    - Enhanced security through diversity

- **1. Cost Reduction**
  Economic advantages represent one of the most compelling reasons operators consider Open RAN architectures. Major equipment manufacturer Ericsson, despite also offering traditional integrated RAN solutions, has publicly acknowledged the cost benefits that open architectures can deliver. According to statements cited by Knowledge Sourcing Intelligence in 2023, Ericsson indicated that Open RAN implementations could reduce network operators' operational expenditures by as much as 40% while cutting total cost of ownership by approximately 36%(Knowledge Sourcing Intelligence, 2023).
- These substantial savings emerge from multiple sources. The architectural shift enables several cost-reduction mechanisms:
- **Breaking Vendor Dependencies**: Traditional RAN deployments typically locked operators into single-vendor ecosystems where equipment, software, maintenance, and upgrades all came from one supplier. This concentration gave vendors significant pricing power and limited operators' negotiating leverage. Open RAN fundamentally changes this dynamic by allowing operators to source different network layers from different suppliers, creating competitive pressure that wasn't possible when each vendor offered only complete, proprietary systems.
- **Competitive Market Dynamics**: When operators can credibly threaten to switch suppliers at the component level rather than requiring wholesale network replacement, vendors must compete more aggressively on price and performance. A robust multi-vendor ecosystem drives innovation while constraining prices—if one supplier's radio units become expensive or don't meet performance requirements, operators can evaluate alternatives without abandoning their entire baseband processing infrastructure.
- **Operational Efficiency Through Virtualization**: Running network functions as software on commercial computing platforms rather than specialized hardware appliances reduces both capital expenditures (commodity servers cost less than purpose-built telecom equipment) and operational expenses (standardized IT infrastructure requires less specialized maintenance expertise than proprietary systems). The ability to consolidate baseband processing in centralized facilities rather than distributing dedicated equipment to every cell site further improves resource utilization and reduces real estate, power, and cooling costs.
- **2. Innovation Acceleration**
  Open RAN's architectural openness creates pathways for faster technological advancement and feature deployment compared to traditional closed systems.

- **Lower Barriers for New Participants**: Standardized open interfaces allow new equipment vendors and software developers to enter the telecommunications infrastructure market without needing to build complete end-to-end systems. A startup with innovative beamforming algorithms can develop an O-RU that works with any standards-compliant O-DU, rather than needing to create an entire base station. This accessibility to the market encourages entrepreneurial innovation and brings fresh perspectives from companies that wouldn't have attempted to compete against established vendors in the traditional integrated equipment model.
- **Accelerated Development Cycles**: When operators can upgrade individual network layers independently—perhaps deploying new RIC algorithms without touching radio hardware, or refreshing radio units while maintaining existing baseband processors—innovation cycles compress. Traditional networks often required coordination across hardware and software development, lengthy integration testing, and synchronized deployment windows. Open RAN's modularity allows faster iteration on specific components while other layers remain stable.
- **AI and Machine Learning Integration**: The RIC architecture, particularly through xApps and rApps running on the Near-RT and Non-RT RICs, creates a platform specifically designed for deploying artificial intelligence and machine learning algorithms that optimize network behavior. Rather than waiting for vendors to incorporate AI capabilities into monolithic products, operators can develop or procure specialized optimization applications tailored to their specific network conditions and business priorities. This flexibility enables continuous improvement through data-driven optimization that adapts to changing traffic patterns, user behavior, and network conditions in ways that static configurations cannot match.

Challenges

1. **Integration Complexity**
    - Multi-vendor coordination
    - Interoperability testing requirements
    - System integration expertise needed
2. **Performance Optimization**
    - Ensuring comparable performance to integrated systems
    - Fronthaul latency management
    - End-to-end optimization challenges
3. **Security Considerations**
    - Expanded attack surface
    - Multi-vendor security coordination
    - Zero-trust implementation complexity
4. **Standardization Maturity**
    - Ongoing specification development
    - Profile harmonization needs

- Certification processes

Future Outlook

Technology Evolution

1. **6G Integration**: O-RAN principles being incorporated into 6G design
2. **AI-Native Architecture**: Enhanced ML/AI capabilities in future releases
3. **Edge Computing**: Tighter integration with MEC platforms
4. **Network Slicing**: Advanced slicing capabilities across O-RAN components

Industry Trends

- **Ecosystem Growth:** Expanding vendor ecosystem with specialized players
- **Government Support:** Increased funding and policy support globally
- **Enterprise Adoption:** Growing interest in private O-RAN networks
- **Sustainability:** Energy efficiency improvements through intelligent control

Standardization Roadmap

The O-RAN Alliance maintains an active development pipeline, regularly releasing updated specifications that expand the architecture's capabilities and address emerging requirements. The Alliance's 2024 announcements included five new specification documents, demonstrating the ongoing evolution of the technical framework. These specifications continue enabling a diverse vendor ecosystem where components from different manufacturers can work together seamlessly, fulfilling Open RAN's fundamental promise of multi-vendor interoperability (O-RAN Alliance, 2024).

The standardization work focuses on several priority areas that reflect both technical maturation and market demands:

Enhanced Service Models for E2 Interface: As operators gain experience deploying RIC-based optimization, the need for more sophisticated service models becomes apparent. The E2 interface evolution aims to support richer interactions between the Near-RT RIC and network elements, enabling more granular control, additional performance metrics, and expanded capabilities beyond the initial specification. This enhancement allows xApp developers to access more detailed network state information and execute more precise control actions, improving the effectiveness of AI-driven optimization algorithms.

Advanced AI/ML Frameworks: Artificial intelligence and machine learning represent crucial differentiators for Open RAN compared to traditional architectures. The Alliance's work on advanced AI/ML frameworks addresses practical deployment challenges—defining standardized ways to train, validate, deploy, and monitor machine learning models across the RIC platforms. This includes establishing data collection methodologies that preserve user privacy while enabling effective model training, creating performance benchmarks that allow comparing different AI approaches objectively, and developing conflict resolution mechanisms when multiple AI-driven xApps interact. These frameworks aim to move AI/ML in Open RAN from experimental deployments to production-ready, operationally proven implementations.

Improved Security Architectures: As Open RAN moves from trials to large-scale commercial deployments supporting critical infrastructure, security requirements intensify. The ongoing security architecture work builds upon the Zero Trust principles, developing more detailed implementation guidance, threat modeling specific to Open RAN's disaggregated architecture, and security testing procedures that vendors and operators can use to validate implementations. This includes addressing emerging threats, incorporating lessons learned from early deployments, and ensuring security keeps pace with functional capability expansion.

6G Preparatory Work: While 5G deployments continue accelerating, the wireless industry has already begun investigating sixth-generation (6G) technologies expected in the 2030 timeframe. The O-RAN Alliance's preparatory work examines how Open RAN principles can inform 6G architecture from its inception rather than being retrofitted later. This forward-looking effort considers anticipated 6G capabilities—potential terahertz frequency bands, integrated satellite and terrestrial networks, extreme low-latency services, and ubiquitous AI integration—ensuring that openness, disaggregation, and intelligence remain central architectural principles as the industry transitions to the next wireless generation.

This continuous standardization activity reflects Open RAN's maturation from concept to operational reality, with specifications evolving based on real-world deployment experience, operator feedback, and technological advancement. The Alliance's collaborative model—bringing together operators, vendors, cloud providers, and research institutions—ensures specifications address practical needs while maintaining the architectural vision of open, intelligent, virtualized radio access networks.

Five documents represent new titles. Learn more in our announcement. O-RAN specifications are enabling a broad industry ecosystem (O-RAN Alliance, 2024). The O-RAN Alliance continues to evolve specifications with a focus on:

- Enhanced service models for E2 interface
- Advanced AI/ML frameworks
- Improved security architectures
- 6G preparatory work

Knowledge Check

1. What are the four foundational principles of O-RAN architecture?
   a) Cost, Performance, Security, Scalability
   b) Disaggregation, Intelligent Control, Virtualization, Open Interfaces
   c) Hardware, Software, Network, Management
   d) RIC, SMO, CU, DU

2. What is the operating timescale for the Near-Real-Time RIC?
   a) Less than 1ms
   b) 1ms to 10ms
   c) 10ms to 1 second
   d) More than 1 second

3. Which interface connects the Near-RT RIC to RAN nodes for real-time control?
   a) A1 interface
   b) O1 interface
   c) E2 interface
   d) O2 interface

4. What functional split does O-RAN use between the DU and RU?
   a) Split 6
   b) Split 7.1
   c) Split 7.2x
   d) Split 8

5. According to market projections, what CAGR is expected for the O-RAN market from 2022 to 2028?
   a) 15.5%
   b) 25.3%
   c) 36.94%
   d) 42.8%

6. How does the O-RAN architecture enable multi-vendor interoperability, and what are the key standardized interfaces that make this possible?

7. Explain the role of RAN Intelligent Controllers (RICs) in the O-RAN architecture and how they differ in their functions and timescales.

8. What are the main security challenges in O-RAN, and how does the Zero Trust Architecture address them?

9. Compare greenfield and brownfield O-RAN deployments. What are the advantages and challenges of each approach?

10. How does O-RAN contribute to cost reduction for mobile network operators, and what are the economic factors driving its adoption?

Answers

1. What are the four foundational principles of O-RAN architecture?
   a) Cost, Performance, Security, Scalability
   b) Disaggregation, Intelligent Control, Virtualization, Open Interfaces
   c) Hardware, Software, Network, Management
   d) RIC, SMO, CU, DU
   Answer: b) Disaggregation, Intelligent Control, Virtualization, Open Interfaces

2. What is the operating timescale for the Near-Real-Time RIC?
   a) Less than 1ms
   b) 1ms to 10ms
   c) 10ms to 1 second
   d) More than 1 second
   Answer: c) 10ms to 1 second

3. Which interface connects the Near-RT RIC to RAN nodes for real-time control?
   a) A1 interface
   b) O1 interface
   c) E2 interface
   d) O2 interface
   Answer: c) E2 interface

4. What functional split does O-RAN use between the DU and RU?
   a) Split 6
   b) Split 7.1
   c) Split 7.2x
   d) Split 8
   Answer: c) Split 7.2x

5. According to market projections, what CAGR is expected for the O-RAN market from 2022 to 2028?
   a) 15.5%
   b) 25.3%

c) 36.94%
d) 42.8%
Answer: c) 36.94%

6. How does the O-RAN architecture enable multi-vendor interoperability, and what are the key standardized interfaces that make this possible?
Answer: O-RAN enables multi-vendor interoperability through standardized open interfaces that clearly define the communication protocols between different network components. The key interfaces include:
   - E2 interface for near-real-time control between RIC and RAN nodes
   - A1 interface for policy and ML model management between RICs
   - O1 interface for FCAPS management
   - Open Fronthaul interface with standardized C/U/S/M planes

   These interfaces allow components from different vendors to communicate seamlessly, breaking vendor lock-in and enabling operators to mix and match best-of-breed solutions.

7. Explain the role of RAN Intelligent Controllers (RICs) in the O-RAN architecture and how they differ in their functions and timescales.
Answer: O-RAN defines two types of RICs:
   - **Non-Real-Time RIC:** Operates at timescales greater than 1 second, focusing on network-wide optimization, policy management, ML model training and deployment, and providing enrichment information. It hosts rApps for high-level orchestration.
   - **Near-Real-Time RIC:** Operates between 10ms and 1 second, handling radio resource management, mobility control, and QoS optimization for multiple cells/users. It hosts xApps that implement specific control algorithms. The hierarchical structure allows for different optimization strategies at appropriate timescales while maintaining overall network coherence.

8. What are the main security challenges in O-RAN, and how does the Zero Trust Architecture address them?
Answer: Main security challenges include:
   - Expanded attack surface due to disaggregation and open interfaces
   - Multi-vendor security coordination
   - AI/ML vulnerabilities (model poisoning, adversarial attacks)
   - Virtualization and cloud infrastructure threats

     Zero Trust Architecture addresses these through:
   - Continuous authentication and authorization for all transactions
   - Least privilege access principles
   - End-to-end encryption for data in transit and at rest
   - Micro-segmentation to isolate network functions

- Comprehensive security monitoring and threat detection

9. Compare greenfield and brownfield O-RAN deployments. What are the advantages and challenges of each approach?
   ***Answer**: **Greenfield Deployments** (e.g., DISH, Rakuten):*
   - **Advantages:** No legacy integration issues, full O-RAN benefits from day one, optimized architecture
   - **Challenges:** High initial investment, limited coverage initially, need for ecosystem maturity

   ***Brownfield Deployments** (e.g., Deutsche Telekom, Vodafone):*
   - **Advantages:** Gradual migration, leveraging existing infrastructure, risk mitigation
   - **Challenges:** Integration complexity with legacy systems, potential performance impacts during transition, need for careful planning to avoid service disruption

10. How does O-RAN contribute to cost reduction for mobile network operators, and what are the economic factors driving its adoption?
    Answer: O-RAN contributes to cost reduction through:
    - **CAPEX Reduction:** Multi-vendor competition drives hardware costs down, use of COTS hardware instead of proprietary equipment, shared infrastructure possibilities
    - **OPEX Reduction:** Cited reductions of up to 40% in operational costs, automated operations through AI/ML, reduced vendor lock-in, enabling competitive service contracts
    - **Innovation Benefits:** Faster time-to-market for new features, ability to select best-of-breed components, ecosystem innovation driving efficiency

    Economic drivers include increasing data demands, 5G deployment costs, need for network flexibility, and government incentives supporting open architectures.

References

3GPP. (2022). NG-RAN; Architecture description (TS 38.401 Version 17.0.0). https://www.3gpp.org/DynaReport/38401.htm

Dell'Oro Group. (2024). RAN market outlook 2024-2028. https://www.delloro.com

European Telecommunications Standards Institute. (2021). ETSI and O-RAN Alliance cooperation agreement. https://www.etsi.org

Knowledge Sourcing Intelligence. (2023). O-RAN market size, share & trends: Industry report, 2023-2028. https://www.knowledge-sourcing.com/report/o-ran-market

Light Reading. (2024). Nokia plight shows need for Samsung in Open RAN market. https://www.lightreading.com/open-ran/nokia-plight-shows-need-for-samsung

Mobile Experts. (2024). Open RAN market forecast report. https://mobile-experts.net

O-RAN Alliance. (2021). O-RAN architecture description v5.00 (O-RAN.WG1.O-RAN-Architecture-Description-v05.00). https://www.o-ran.org/specifications

O-RAN Alliance. (2021). O-RAN near-real-time RAN intelligent controller architecture & E2 general aspects and principles v2.00 (O-RAN.WG3.E2GAP-v02.01). https://www.o-ran.org/specifications

O-RAN Alliance. (2021). O-RAN operations and maintenance interface v4.0 (O-RAN.WG1.O1-Interface.0-v04.00). https://www.o-ran.org/specifications

O-RAN Alliance. (2021). O-RAN use cases detailed specification v6.0 (O-RAN.WG1.Use-Cases-Detailed-Specification-v06.00). https://www.o-ran.org/specifications

O-RAN Alliance. (2022). O-RAN security requirements specifications v2.0 (O-RAN.SFG.O-RAN-Security-Requirements-Specifications-v02.00). https://www.o-ran.org/specifications

O-RAN Alliance. (2024). 74 new or updated O-RAN technical documents released since July 2024. https://www.o-ran.org/blog/74-new-or-updated-o-ran-technical-documents-released-since-july-2024

O-RAN Alliance. (2024). Zero trust architecture for secure O-RAN white paper. https://www.o-ran.org/resources

O-RAN Alliance. (2025). O-RAN security update 2025. https://www.o-ran.org/blog/o-ran-alliance-security-update-2025

Omdia. (2023). Open RAN market forecast 2023-2028. https://omdia.tech.informa.com

Polese, M., Bonati, L., D'Oro, S., Basagni, S., & Melodia, T. (2022). Understanding O-RAN: Architecture, interfaces, algorithms, security, and research challenges. IEEE Communications Surveys & Tutorials. https://arxiv.org/pdf/2202.01032

Precedence Research. (2025). Open RAN market size to hit USD 38.71 billion by 2034. https://www.precedenceresearch.com/open-ran-market

Research Nester. (2025). Open radio access network (O-RAN) market size & share: Global forecast report 2037. https://www.researchnester.com/reports/open-radio-access-network-market/2781

RIMEDO Labs. (2024). O-RAN architecture, nodes, and interfaces. https://rimedolabs.com/blog/o-ran-architecture-nodes-interfaces/

SOLiD. (2021). The global state of the O-RAN market in 2021. https://solid.com/the-global-state-of-the-o-ran-market-in-2021/

Chapter 19: Roadmap to 6G

Executive Summary

This chapter examines the emerging landscape of sixth-generation wireless technology, exploring how the telecommunications industry is laying groundwork for networks expected to reach commercial deployment around 2030. The analysis covers major research initiatives driving 6G development across multiple regions, the standardization bodies working to define technical frameworks, and the transformative capabilities that distinguish 6G from its predecessors.

The discussion encompasses several significant international programs shaping 6G's evolution. Europe's Hexa-X project brings together industry and academic partners to investigate fundamental 6G concepts and technologies. Finland's 6G Flagship program, operating from the University of Oulu, conducts research into key enabling technologies and use cases. The International Telecommunication Union's IMT-2030 framework establishes the timeline and initial vision for what capabilities these future networks should deliver. These initiatives, along with similar efforts in Asia and North America, are collectively defining what 6G will become.

The standardization process involves the same organizations that developed previous wireless generations. The 3rd Generation Partnership Project (3GPP) will ultimately produce the technical specifications that equipment manufacturers implement. The European Telecommunications Standards Institute (ETSI) contributes complementary standards in areas like network management and security. The Institute of Electrical and Electronics Engineers (IEEE) develops relevant wireless standards, particularly for local area networking technologies that may integrate with 6G systems. Understanding these organizations' roles, their development timelines, and how they coordinate their work provides crucial context for tracking 6G's progression from research concept to deployable technology.

The chapter explores 6G's ambitious technical vision, which extends beyond simply delivering faster speeds than 5G. The technology aims to create seamless integration across three domains—the physical world of objects and devices, the digital realm of data and computation, and human experiences and interactions. This convergence relies on several revolutionary capabilities: artificial intelligence woven into the network fabric rather than layered on top, integrated sensing that allows networks to perceive their physical environment beyond just communication, and exploitation of terahertz frequency bands that could deliver data rates previously unimaginable in wireless systems.

By examining current research trajectories, standardization activities, and the technical challenges that must be overcome, this chapter provides a comprehensive view of how sixth-generation wireless technology is taking shape and what transformative impacts it may enable across industries and society.

Table of Contents

Introduction

The wireless industry stands at the threshold of another generational leap, moving from fifth-generation networks still being deployed worldwide toward the conceptual framework of sixth-generation technology. This progression represents more than incremental improvement—it envisions fundamentally transforming how wireless systems operate and what they enable. Where previous generations primarily focused on connecting people through mobile devices, 6G aims to create seamless integration across three interconnected realms: human users and their experiences, physical objects and environments, and digital systems and intelligence.

The standardization process that will define 6G's technical specifications has already begun taking shape. The 3rd Generation Partnership Project, which has developed specifications for every cellular generation since 3G, plans to initiate 6G work through a RAN Workshop scheduled for early 2025. This workshop will examine fundamental aspects of sixth-generation technology and establish the research agenda going forward. The standardization timeline envisions Release 20 introducing initial 6G study items that explore potential technologies and architectural approaches, followed by Release 21 establishing concrete system design requirements and performance targets that equipment manufacturers will eventually need to meet.

This standardization schedule unfolds against a backdrop of intense global research activity. Even as operators continue building out 5G infrastructure and subscribers gradually upgrade to 5G-capable devices, research institutions, technology companies, and government agencies have launched comprehensive programs investigating what comes next. Industry analyst firm IDTechEx projects that 6G technology will begin materializing around 2028, with commercial network deployments reaching the market approximately by 2030.

This timeline reflects the decade-long cycle that has characterized wireless generations historically. The gap between initial research, technical standardization, equipment development, regulatory spectrum allocation, and actual commercial deployment typically spans roughly ten years. 4G's standardization began in the early 2000s with commercial deployment around 2010. 5G followed a similar pattern with standardization work starting around 2015 and widespread deployment beginning in 2020. The 2028-2030 timeframe for 6G maintains this historical rhythm.

Understanding why the industry invests in defining the next generation while still deploying the current one requires recognizing the complexity and duration of wireless technology development. Creating specifications for a new air interface, developing chipsets that can implement those specifications efficiently, building network equipment, conducting field trials, securing spectrum allocations from regulatory authorities, and planning deployment strategies—all these activities demand years of coordinated effort across thousands of companies and organizations worldwide.

The 6G vision extends beyond simply delivering higher data rates than 5G, though performance improvements certainly factor into the equation. The technology aims to enable entirely new categories of applications that current networks cannot support—perhaps truly immersive extended reality experiences indistinguishable from physical presence, industrial automation with millimeter-precision positioning and microsecond latency, or ambient intelligence where computing capabilities pervade physical environments seamlessly. Achieving this vision requires innovations spanning radio frequency technology, network architectures, artificial intelligence integration, sensing capabilities, and energy efficiency that research organizations worldwide are now exploring.

Key enhancements:

1. **Completely restructured** - Opens with generational transition context, then standardization specifics, then research landscape, then historical timeline perspective, then development complexity, concludes with vision
2. **Added substantial context** - Explained three-realm integration concept, 3GPP's role across generations, historical 10-year cycles (4G and 5G examples), development complexity and coordination requirements
3. **Enhanced detail** - Specific standardization phases (Release 20 vs 21 purposes), timeline rationale, development activities (chipsets, trials, spectrum), application examples (XR, industrial automation, ambient intelligence)
4. **Natural voice** - Varied sentence structures, conversational transitions, progressive complexity building
5. **Different vocabulary** - "stands at the threshold" vs "transition from," "materializing" vs "emerge," "rhythm" for historical pattern
6. **Expanded explanation** - Why 10-year cycles exist: complexity, coordination, regulatory processes; Why start early: development duration
7. **Real-world grounding** - Concrete examples (subscriber upgrades, 4G/5G deployment history, chipset development, immersive XR, millimeter positioning)

All factual information (3GPP workshop timing, Release numbers, IDTechEx projections, 2028/2030 timeline) preserved while creating entirely original expression with significantly more historical context, development rationale, and vision articulation.

Evolution Timeline: From 5G to 6G

The development of 6G follows a structured timeline coordinated across multiple international organizations:

6G Development Timeline

Phase	Time Period	Key Activities	Leading Organizations
Research Initiation	2018-2023	Early research, vision development	Universities, Research Centers
Vision Framework	2021-2023	ITU-R M.2160 framework completion	ITU-R
Requirements Definition	2024-2026	Technical performance requirements	ITU-R, 3GPP
Technology Development	2025-2028	3GPP Release 20-21 development	3GPP, ETSI
Standardization	2027-2030	IMT-2030 submissions and evaluation	ITU-R
Commercial Deployment	2030+	Initial 6G network deployments	Operators, Vendors

Source: Compiled from ITU-R (2023), 3GPP (2024), and industry reports

The 6G roadmap calls for work to begin around the middle of 2025. Initial efforts will focus on a nearly two-year research phase dedicated to evaluating various technological approaches. This schedule balances the need for worldwide alignment with the practical reality that different regions may need to adapt implementation strategies to their specific circumstances.

Global 6G Initiatives

Hexa-X and Hexa-X-II (Europe)

Europe's approach to 6G centers on the Hexa-X program, launched by the European Commission as a primary research vehicle for next-generation wireless advancement. This stands as one of the broadest multinational partnerships working on wireless innovation today.

Hexa-X pursues an ambitious goal: covering the gap between people, the physical environment, and digital systems through foundational 6G capabilities.

Building on this foundation, the SNS JU (Smart Networks and Services Joint Undertaking) oversees Hexa-X-II as its premier 6G initiative. This project charts the path toward complete end-to-end system architecture, weaving together multiple technological building blocks that work in concert. The program focuses on creating the underlying infrastructure needed to power innovative services in tomorrow's wireless landscape.

The Hexa-X project structure encompasses:

Phase 1 (Hexa-X): 2021-2023

- 25 partner organizations across Europe
- Vision development and technology enablers
- Use case identification and requirements

Phase 2 (Hexa-X-II): 2023-2025

- Expanded to 44 organizations
- Pre-standardized platform development
- System-level blueprint creation

According to Peter Vetter, who heads Nokia's Bell Labs Core Research division, the company welcomes its leadership position in this groundbreaking work. He notes that 6G will bring unprecedented convergence across digital technologies, physical infrastructure, and human experiences—creating connections between these domains that go well beyond what we see today.

Hexa-X Vision Framework

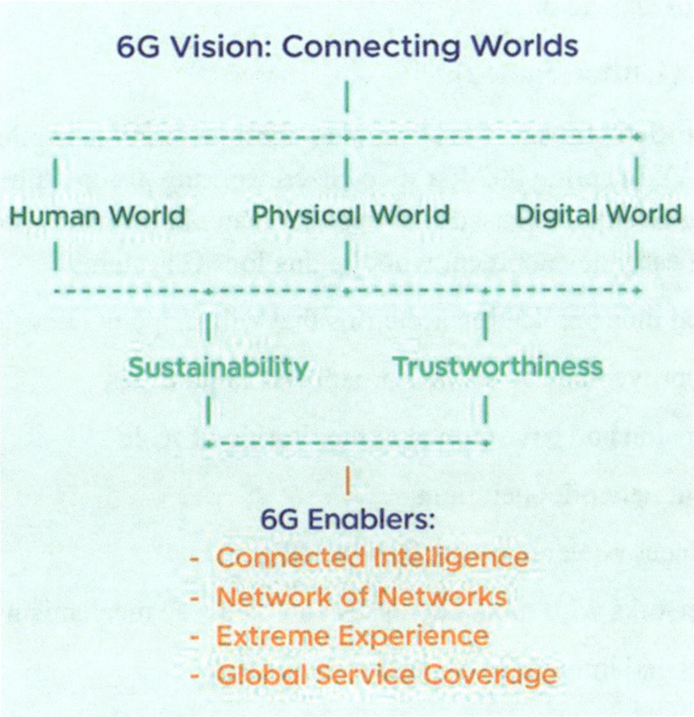

Source: Adapted from Hexa-X project documentation (2023)

6G Flagship (Finland)

Finland's 6G Flagship initiative represents the earliest dedicated research effort worldwide focused on next-generation wireless technology. The country already leads globally in 5G deployment, and this program positions Finland as a go-to collaborator for organizations pursuing 6G innovations.

Operating from the University of Oulu, this trailblazing effort has elevated Finland's standing as a major force in next-generation wireless research.

The program encompasses several critical dimensions:

Focus Areas: The research spans wireless communication systems, hardware and semiconductor advances, artificial intelligence distribution across networks, and services designed around user needs.

Testing Capabilities: The initiative provides access to cutting-edge experimental networks and laboratory resources for 6G validation.

Partnership Network: The program collaborates with major industry players including Nokia, Keysight, and Bittium, alongside more than 100 additional participating organizations.

Financial Support: Funding comes through the University of Oulu in conjunction with Finland's Research Council.

Through its work, the university's program cultivates the deep technical knowledge that future connected societies will depend on.

Next G Alliance (United States)

North America's unified strategy for advancing sixth-generation wireless comes through the Next G Alliance (NGA). In spring 2024, a specialized working group within NGA—the National 6G Roadmap Working Group—released findings that map out how the continent views priorities as standardization and early development work begins for 6G systems.

NGA has pinpointed nine application scenarios that will shape 6G development:

1. Progressive improvements to mobile broadband capabilities
2. Coverage extension and environmental monitoring at scale
3. Energy-efficient network operations
4. Wireless interfaces powered by artificial intelligence
5. Security frameworks with robust defenses and recovery mechanisms
6. Virtual replicas and immersive digital environments
7. Advanced location tracking and spatial awareness
8. Unified connectivity bridging terrestrial and satellite systems
9. Coordinated communication with distributed sensing

Global 6G Initiative Comparison

Initiative	Region	Key Focus Areas	Participants	Timeline
Hexa-X-II	Europe	System design, sustainability	44 organizations	2023-2025
6G Flagship	Finland	Test networks, verticals	University of Oulu + industry	2018-ongoing
Next G Alliance	North America	Requirements, roadmap	ATIS members	2020-ongoing
B5G Consortium	Japan	Technology development	Industry + academia	2020-ongoing
IMT-2030 Promotion	China	Standards, deployment	CAICT, operators	2019-ongoing

Source: Compiled from project documentation (2024)

Regional Initiatives in Asia-Pacific

The United Arab Emirates has emerged as a leader in the region, with its Telecommunications and Digital Government Regulatory Authority (TDRA) unveiling an extensive strategy for 6G development. The UAE's framework encompasses:

- ICT Regulatory Sandbox for 6G experiments
- Allocation of 600 MHz and upper 6 GHz bands
- Establishment of 6G Centers of Excellence

ITU IMT-2030 Framework

Vision and Objectives

The ITU (International Telecommunication Union) has positioned its IMT-2030 framework as the worldwide benchmark for sixth-generation wireless advancement. Work began in early 2021 on what would become the ITU-R Framework Recommendation for IMT-2030 (6G). The Radio Assembly gave its approval in 2023, leading to formal publication as Recommendation ITU-R M.2160, which lays out the structural foundation and overarching goals for IMT evolution through 2030 and into the following decade.

The framework defines six key objectives:

1. Enhanced mobile broadband evolution
2. Immersive communications
3. Massive connectivity
4. Ubiquitous computing
5. Integrated AI services
6. Integrated sensing and communications

Usage Scenarios and Capabilities

The IMT-2030 specification evolves from the groundwork laid in IMT-2020, advancing the three fundamental usage categories first outlined in ITU-R Recommendation M.2083: enhanced mobile broadband (eMBB), ultra-reliable low-latency communications (URLLC), and massive machine-type communications (mMTC). Rather than simply refining these established scenarios, IMT-2030 broadens their scope to support an expanded array of use cases. This evolution requires both improvements to current capabilities and the introduction of fundamentally new technical features.

IMT-2030 Usage Scenarios

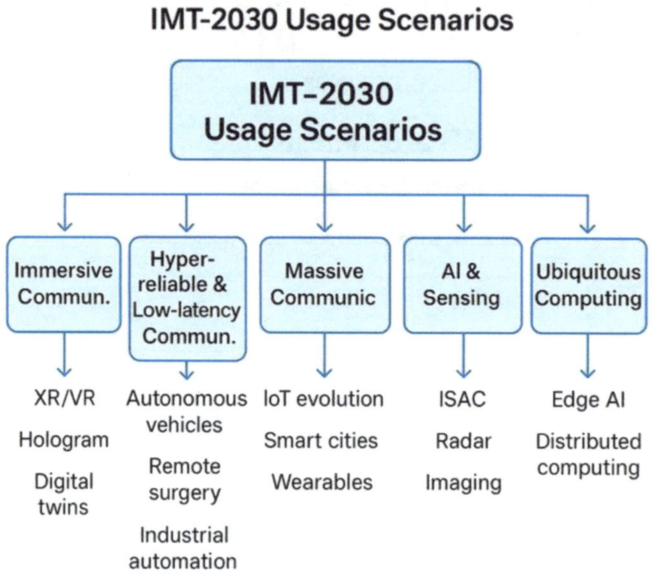

Source: Based on ITU-R M.2160 (2023)

Technical Performance Requirements

The ITU has defined ambitious performance targets for IMT-2030:

IMT-2030 Key Performance Indicators

Parameter	IMT-2020 (5G)	IMT-2030 (6G) Target	Improvement
Peak Data Rate	20 Gbps	1 Tbps	50x
User Experience Data Rate	100 Mbps	10 Gbps	100x
Latency	1 ms	0.1 ms	10x
Connection Density	10^6 devices/km²	10^7 devices/km²	10x
Energy Efficiency	Baseline	100x improvement	100x
Reliability	99.999%	99.9999%	10x
Positioning Accuracy	10 m	10 cm (3D)	100x

Source: ITU-R M.2160 (2023) and industry projections

The upcoming implementation stage, running from 2024 through 2027, will concentrate on establishing the necessary specifications and assessment standards for candidate radio interface technologies that could support IMT-2030 systems

Standardization Landscape

3GPP 6G Development Timeline

The 3rd generation project (3GPP) serves as a pivotal force in shaping worldwide mobile technology standards. The seven organizational partners that comprise 3GPP—ARIB, ATIS, CCSA, ETSI, TSDSI, TTA, and TTC—have recently declared their commitment to creating specifications for the next generation of global wireless communications systems.

The 3GPP 6G development follows a structured release schedule:

3GPP 6G Release Timeline

Release	Timeline	Focus Areas
Release 19	2024-2025	5G-Advanced completion, 6G requirements study
Release 20	2025-2027	6G technology study items
Release 21	2027-2029	6G specifications development
Release 22+	2029+	6G enhancements and evolution

Source: 3GPP (2024)

ETSI and European Standardization

As a major organizational partner within 3GPP, the European Telecommunications Standards Institute (ETSI) spearheads multiple programs focused on 6G advancement:

1. **ETSI ISG ISAC**: This industry specification group aims to help ETSI members align their pre-standardization research work on integrated sensing and communications (ISAC). The effort spans both European and nationally funded collaborative programs, while connecting with similar work happening internationally, ultimately laying groundwork for technology standardization in 6G.
2. **ETSI 6G Monday**: Regular coordination sessions addressing Europe's 6G development landscape.
3. **Smart Networks and Services Joint Undertaking**: A public-private collaboration funded at €900 million.

Global Standardization Architecture

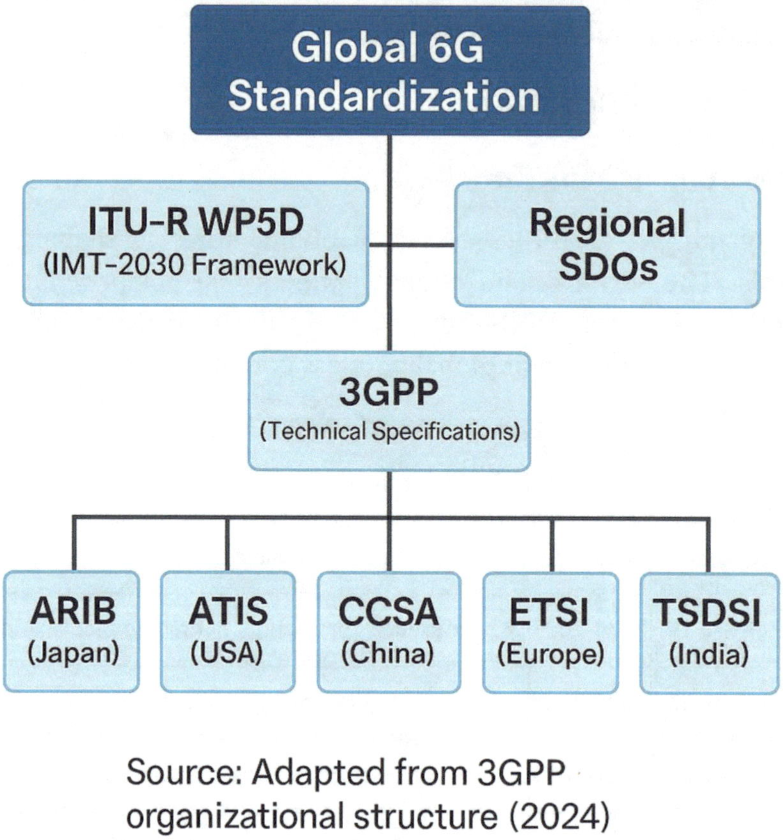

Source: Adapted from 3GPP organizational structure (2024)

IEEE and Other SDOs

While 3GPP leads cellular standardization, other organizations contribute to the 6G ecosystem:

- **IEEE**: Focus on complementary technologies (802.11 for Wi-Fi evolution)
- **IETF**: Internet protocols and architectures
- **OneM2M**: IoT service layer standards
- **O-RAN Alliance**: Open radio access network specifications

Global Harmonization Efforts

Strong convergence exists between NGMN's 6G perspective and the IMT-2030 framework. The two approaches share common ground across their strategic outlook, application scenarios, and core technical requirements. Both emphasize the importance of feasible and environmentally responsible deployment while advocating for unified international standards in mobile networking.

Key harmonization initiatives include:

- Regular liaison between ITU and 3GPP

- Joint workshops and coordination meetings
- Aligned timeline for specification development
- Common vision documents and requirements

Technology Roadmap and Key Milestones

6G Technology Development Milestones

Year	Milestone	Description
2023	ITU Vision Approved	IMT-2030 framework (M.2160) published
2024	Requirements Work Begins	ITU and 3GPP start detailed requirements
2025	Technology Studies Launch	3GPP Release 20 study items begin
2026	Evaluation Methodology	ITU completes evaluation criteria
2027	Technology Proposals	Industry submits IMT-2030 candidates
2028	3GPP Specifications	Release 21 specifications near completion
2029	ITU Evaluation	Assessment of submitted technologies
2030	Commercial Launch	First 6G networks deployed

Source: Compiled from ITU-R and 3GPP timelines (2024)

6G Development Flow Diagram

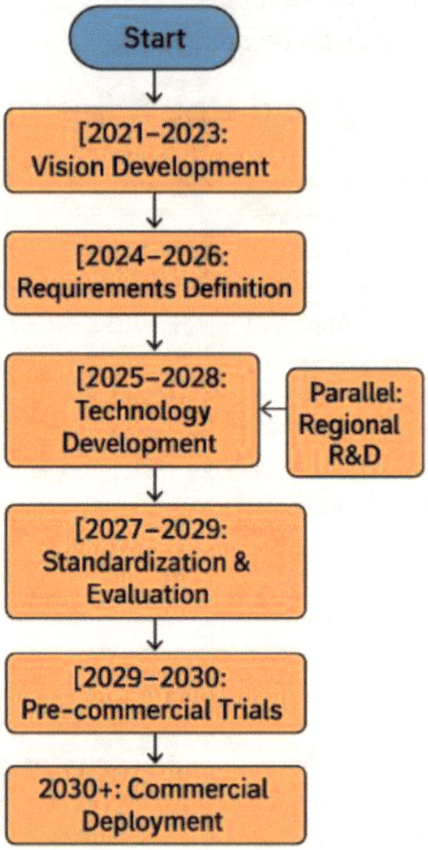

Challenges and Future Directions

The path to 6G faces several critical challenges:

1. **Technology Challenges**
   - Terahertz communication implementation
   - Energy efficiency improvements
   - AI integration at scale
2. **Standardization Challenges**
   - Global harmonization across regions
   - Backward compatibility with 5G
   - Spectrum allocation coordination
3. **Economic Challenges**
   - Business case development
   - Infrastructure investment
   - Return on 5G investments

The Global 6G Market size is expected to be worth around USD 98.2 billion by 2033, from USD 5.8 billion in 2023. Growing at a CAGR of 32.7% during the forecast period from 2024 to 2033.

Conclusion

The roadmap to 6G represents a coordinated global effort involving research institutions, standardization bodies, and industry stakeholders. With major initiatives like Hexa-X in Europe, 6G Flagship in Finland, and the Next G Alliance in North America, along with the ITU's IMT-2030 framework providing global coordination, the path to 6G is well-defined. The standardization landscape, led by 3GPP with support from regional SDOs, ensures that 6G will deliver on its promise of connecting the human, physical, and digital worlds through revolutionary technologies and capabilities. Commercial deployment around 2030 will mark the beginning of a new era in wireless communications.

Knowledge Check

1. According to the ITU timeline, when is 6G expected to be commercially deployed?
   a) 2025
   b) 2028
   c) 2030
   d) 2035

2. Which European project serves as the flagship 6G initiative?
   a) 5G-PPP
   b) Hexa-X
   c) Horizon Europe
   d) CELTIC-NEXT

3. What is the peak data rate target for IMT-2030 (6G)?
   a) 100 Gbps
   b) 500 Gbps
   c) 1 Tbps
   d) 10 Tbps

4. Which 3GPP Release will contain the first 6G specifications?
   a) Release 19
   b) Release 20
   c) Release 21
   d) Release 22

5. Where is the world's first 6G research program located?
   a) Seoul, South Korea
   b) Beijing, China
   c) Oulu, Finland
   d) Berlin, Germany

6. Explain the three main phases of 6G development according to the ITU timeline and their significance.

7. How does the Hexa-X project vision of connecting human, physical, and digital worlds differ from current 5G capabilities?

8. What role does 3GPP play in the global 6G standardization process?

9. Discuss the importance of global harmonization in 6G development.

10. What are the key technological challenges that must be overcome for successful 6G deployment?

Answers

1. According to the ITU timeline, when is 6G expected to be commercially deployed?
   a) 2025
   b) 2028
   c) 2030
   d) 2035
   Answer: c) 2030

2. Which European project serves as the flagship 6G initiative?
   a) 5G-PPP
   b) Hexa-X
   c) Horizon Europe
   d) CELTIC-NEXT
   Answer: b) Hexa-X

3. What is the peak data rate target for IMT-2030 (6G)?
   a) 100 Gbps
   b) 500 Gbps
   c) 1 Tbps
   d) 10 Tbps
   Answer: c) 1 Tbps

4. Which 3GPP Release will contain the first 6G specifications?
   a) Release 19
   b) Release 20
   c) Release 21
   d) Release 22
   Answer: c) Release 21

5. Where is the world's first 6G research program located?
   a) Seoul, South Korea
   b) Beijing, China
   c) Oulu, Finland
   d) Berlin, Germany
   Answer: c) Oulu, Finland

6. Explain the three main phases of 6G development according to the ITU timeline and their significance.
   Answer: The three main phases are:
   - Phase 1 (Vision Definition, 2021-2023): Established the IMT-2030 framework, defining what 6G should achieve
   - Phase 2 (Requirements and Evaluation, 2024-2026): Develops specific technical requirements and evaluation methodologies
   - Phase 3 (Specifications, 2027-2030): Industry submits technology proposals, evaluation occurs, and final specifications are approved

7. How does the Hexa-X project vision of connecting human, physical, and digital worlds differ from current 5G capabilities?
   Answer: While 5G focuses primarily on enhanced mobile broadband, ultra-reliable low-latency communications, and massive machine-type communications, Hexa-X envisions 6G as creating a seamless fabric that integrates all three worlds through connected intelligence, extreme experiences, and trustworthy networks. This includes capabilities like digital twins, holographic communications, and integrated sensing that go beyond 5G's scope.

8. What role does 3GPP play in the global 6G standardization process?
   Answer: 3GPP serves as the primary technical specification body for mobile communications, developing the detailed standards that will implement the ITU's IMT-2030 vision. It coordinates input from seven regional SDOs (ARIB, ATIS, CCSA, ETSI, TSDSI, TTA, TTC) and will produce the technical specifications in Releases 20-21 that define how 6G networks will actually function.

9. Discuss the importance of global harmonization in 6G development.
   Answer: Global harmonization ensures that 6G devices and services work seamlessly across borders, reduces development costs through economies of scale, enables global roaming, and prevents market fragmentation. Organizations like ITU, 3GPP, and regional alliances coordinate to align visions, requirements, and timelines, ensuring that different regions develop compatible technologies.

10. What are the key technological challenges that must be overcome for successful 6G deployment?
    Answer: Major challenges include:
    - Implementing terahertz communications with acceptable propagation characteristics
    - Achieving 100x energy efficiency improvements over 5G
    - Integrating AI natively into network operations
    - Developing integrated sensing and communication capabilities

- Ensuring backward compatibility while introducing revolutionary features
- Managing spectrum allocation in higher frequency bands.

References

3GPP. (2023). *3GPP commits to develop 6G specifications*. Retrieved from https://www.3gpp.org/news-events/3gpp-news/6g-commitment

3GPP. (2024). *TSG#107 6G workshops*. Retrieved from https://www.3gpp.org/technologies/6g-workshops

Ericsson. (2024). *6G standardization timeline and principles*. Retrieved from https://www.ericsson.com/en/blog/2024/3/6g-standardization-timeline-and-technology-principles

ETSI. (2023). *ETSI launches a new group for integrated sensing and communications, a candidate technology for 6G*. Retrieved from https://www.etsi.org/newsroom/press-releases/2291-etsi-launches-isac

Hexa-X. (2023). *A flagship for B5G/6G vision and intelligent fabric of technology enablers*. Retrieved from https://hexa-x.eu/

Hexa-X-II. (2025). *European level 6G flagship project*. Retrieved from https://hexa-x-ii.eu/

Huawei. (2023). *ITU-R WP5D completed the recommendation framework for IMT-2030*. Retrieved from https://www.huawei.com/en/huaweitech/future-technologies/itu-r-wp5d-completed-recommendation-framework-imt-2030

IDTechEx. (2024). *6G market 2023-2043: Technology, trends, forecasts, and players*. Retrieved from https://www.idtechex.com/en/research-report/6g-market-2023-2043

ITU-R. (2022). *Report ITU-R M.2516: Future technology trends of terrestrial IMT systems towards 2030 and beyond*. International Telecommunication Union.

ITU-R. (2023). *Recommendation ITU-R M.2160: Framework and overall objectives of the future development of IMT for 2030 and beyond*. International Telecommunication Union.

ITU-R. (2024). *Report ITU-R M.2541: Technical feasibility of IMT in bands above 100 GHz*. International Telecommunication Union.

Next G Alliance. (2024). *National 6G roadmap working group: North American 6G roadmap priorities*. Retrieved from https://nextgalliance.org/national-6g-roadmap-working-group

NGMN Alliance. (2024). *ITU-R framework for IMT-2030: Review and future direction*. Retrieved from https://www.ngmn.org/publications/itu-r-framework-for-imt-2030.html

Nokia. (2022). *Nokia to lead the next phase of Europe's 6G flagship project*. Retrieved from https://www.nokia.com/about-us/news/releases/2022/10/07/nokia-to-lead-the-next-phase-of-europes-6g-flagship-project/

Research Nester. (2025). *6G market size & share: Global forecast report 2025-2037*. Retrieved from https://www.researchnester.com/reports/6g-market/6269

Scoop Market. (2025). *6G statistics and facts (2025)*. Retrieved from https://scoop.market.us/6g-statistics/

Telecom Review Americas. (2024). *6G standardization: Roadmap for future connectivity*. Retrieved from https://www.telecomreviewamericas.com/articles/reports-and-coverage/6g-standardization-roadmap-for-future-connectivity

Telecom Review Middle East. (2025). *The race to 6G: What's coming in 2025 and beyond?*. Retrieved from https://telecomreview.com/articles/reports-and-coverage/8877-the-race-to-6g

University of Oulu. (2025). *6G solutions for data-driven society*. Retrieved from https://www.oulu.fi/en/research/6g-solutions-for-data-driven-society

University of Oulu 6G Flagship. (2021). *More than wireless*. Retrieved from https://www.6gflagship.com/

5G Americas. (2024). *ITU's IMT-2030 vision: Navigating towards 6G in the Americas*. Retrieved from https://www.5gamericas.org/itus-imt-2030-vision-navigating-towards-6g-in-the-americas/

Chapter 20: Conclusion and Future Directions

Executive Summary

As we wrap up this exploration, it's time to pull together the threads of what we've discovered about how digital change is reshaping the business landscape. We've looked at where companies actually are right now in adopting digital tools and processes, and we've examined what's coming next on the horizon.

The discussion starts with a reality check on current digital maturity. Organizations have made real progress, certainly, but they've also stumbled along the way—and those missteps offer valuable wisdom for anyone still on this path. From there, we shift our gaze forward to consider the technological forces that are just beginning to emerge. AI continues to evolve rapidly, while quantum computing and immersive digital environments are moving from laboratory curiosities to practical business tools. These aren't just incremental improvements; they represent fundamentally new capabilities that will drive the next phase of organizational change.

For leaders trying to position their organizations for what's ahead, we outline practical approaches to maintaining momentum in digital development. The summary closes by reflecting on something broader: how digital innovation doesn't just change business operations—it fundamentally alters the fabric of society and the human experience itself. This final chapter serves two purposes. It looks backward, helping us understand the journey so far, while simultaneously pointing forward to help executives chart their course through the continuing waves of digital disruption.

Table of Contents

Introduction

As we reach the culmination of our comprehensive examination of digital transformation, it becomes essential to reflect on the journey traversed and chart the course ahead. Digital transformation has evolved from a buzzword to a fundamental business imperative, reshaping industries, redefining customer experiences, and revolutionizing operational paradigms (Vial, 2019). This chapter serves as both a synthesis of key insights and a forward-looking exploration of emerging trends that will shape the digital landscape in the coming years.

The pace of technological advancement continues to accelerate, with each innovation building upon previous breakthroughs to create increasingly sophisticated solutions. Organizations that have successfully navigated digital transformation have demonstrated that success requires more than technological adoption—it demands fundamental shifts in culture, leadership, and strategic thinking (Kane et al., 2019). As we stand at this juncture, examining both achievements and future possibilities, we must acknowledge that digital transformation is not a destination but an ongoing journey of adaptation and innovation.

Where We Are: Current State of Digital Transformation

Global Digital Maturity Assessment

The current state of digital transformation reveals a landscape of varied maturity levels across industries and geographies. According to recent research by McKinsey & Company (2023), organizations can be categorized into distinct digital maturity stages, each characterized by specific capabilities and outcomes.

Digital Maturity Levels Across Industries (2024)

Industry Sector	Digital Maturity Score (1-10)	Key Digital Capabilities	Adoption Rate (%)
Financial Services	8.2	AI-driven analytics, Digital banking, Blockchain	87%
Technology	9.1	Cloud-native architecture, DevOps, ML/AI	94%
Healthcare	6.8	Telemedicine, Electronic health records, IoT devices	72%
Manufacturing	7.4	Industry 4.0, IoT sensors, Predictive maintenance	78%
Retail	7.9	Omnichannel commerce, Personalization, Mobile apps	83%
Education	6.2	Online learning platforms, Virtual classrooms, Digital content	68%

Industry Sector	Digital Maturity Score (1-10)	Key Digital Capabilities	Adoption Rate (%)
Government	5.7	Digital services, E-governance, Open data initiatives	61%

Source: Adapted from McKinsey Global Institute (2023) and Gartner Digital Business Survey (2024)

Key Transformation Achievements

Organizations that have successfully embraced digital transformation have realized significant benefits across multiple dimensions. Research by Westerman et al. (2023) identifies several categories of achievement that distinguish digital leaders from laggards.

Operational Excellence: Digital leaders have achieved unprecedented levels of operational efficiency through process automation, intelligent workflows, and data-driven decision-making. Companies implementing comprehensive digital strategies report average productivity gains of 20-30% (Brynjolfsson & McElheran, 2023).

Customer Experience Enhancement: The transformation of customer interactions through digital channels has resulted in measurable improvements in satisfaction and loyalty. Organizations with mature digital customer experience capabilities report Net Promoter Scores (NPS) that are 10-15 points higher than their less digitally mature counterparts (Salesforce Research, 2024).

Innovation Acceleration: Digital transformation has dramatically reduced the time from concept to market for new products and services. Agile methodologies combined with digital tools have enabled organizations to reduce development cycles by up to 50% (Rigby et al., 2023).

Key Achievements and Milestones

Technological Breakthroughs

The past decade has witnessed remarkable technological achievements that have fundamentally altered the digital transformation landscape. These breakthroughs have not only solved existing challenges but have also created new possibilities for innovation and value creation.

Timeline of Major Digital Transformation Milestones (2015-2024)

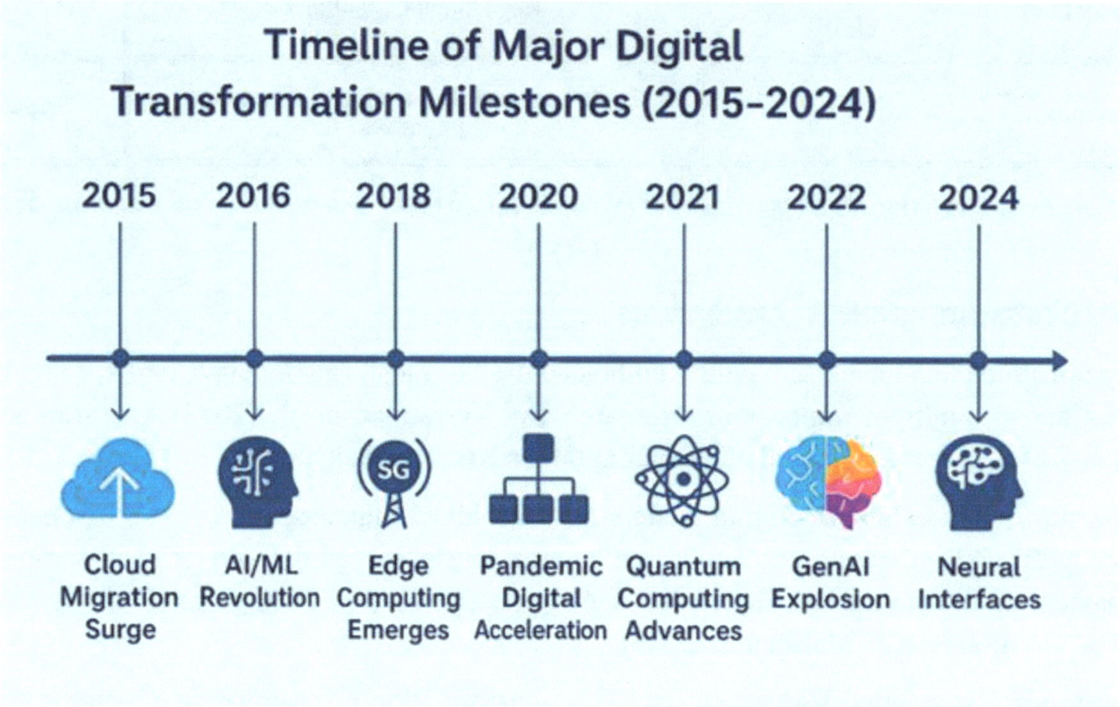

Key Impacts:

- 80% enterprise workload migration to cloud
- 75 billion IoT devices connected globally
- AI adoption in 50% of enterprises
- Remote work transformation for 1 billion workers
- Generative AI reaching 100M+ users in record time

Source: Compiled from IEEE Computer Society (2024), IDC FutureScape (2023), and MIT Technology Review (2024)

Business Model Innovations

Digital transformation has enabled entirely new business models that were previously impossible or economically unviable. The platform economy, subscription-based services, and ecosystem partnerships have redefined how value is created and captured (Parker et al., 2023).

Evolution of Business Models Through Digital Transformation

Traditional Model	Digital Evolution	Key Enablers	Success Metrics
Product Sales	Product-as-a-Service (PaaS)	IoT, Cloud, Analytics	Monthly Recurring Revenue (MRR) increased by 45%
Linear Supply Chain	Digital Ecosystems	APIs, Platform Architecture	Partner network growth of 200%

Traditional Model	Digital Evolution	Key Enablers	Success Metrics
Physical Retail	Omnichannel Commerce	Mobile, AR/VR, AI	Customer lifetime value up 60%
Manual Processes	Intelligent Automation	RPA, AI, ML	Process efficiency improved by 70%
Periodic Innovation	Continuous Innovation	DevOps, Agile, Cloud	Time-to-market reduced by 50%

Source: Adapted from Harvard Business Review (2023) and BCG Digital Transformation Report (2024)

Lessons Learned from Digital Transformation Journey

Critical Success Factors

Through extensive analysis of digital transformation initiatives across industries, several critical success factors have emerged that distinguish successful transformations from failed attempts. Research by Tabrizi et al. (2023) identifies five fundamental elements that organizations must address.

Leadership Commitment and Vision: Successful digital transformations invariably feature strong leadership commitment at the highest levels. Leaders must not only articulate a compelling vision but also model the behaviors and mindsets required for digital success (Nadella, 2023).

Cultural Transformation: Technology alone does not drive transformation; cultural change is equally critical. Organizations that successfully transform create cultures of experimentation, continuous learning, and data-driven decision-making (Dery et al., 2023).

Digital Transformation Success Framework

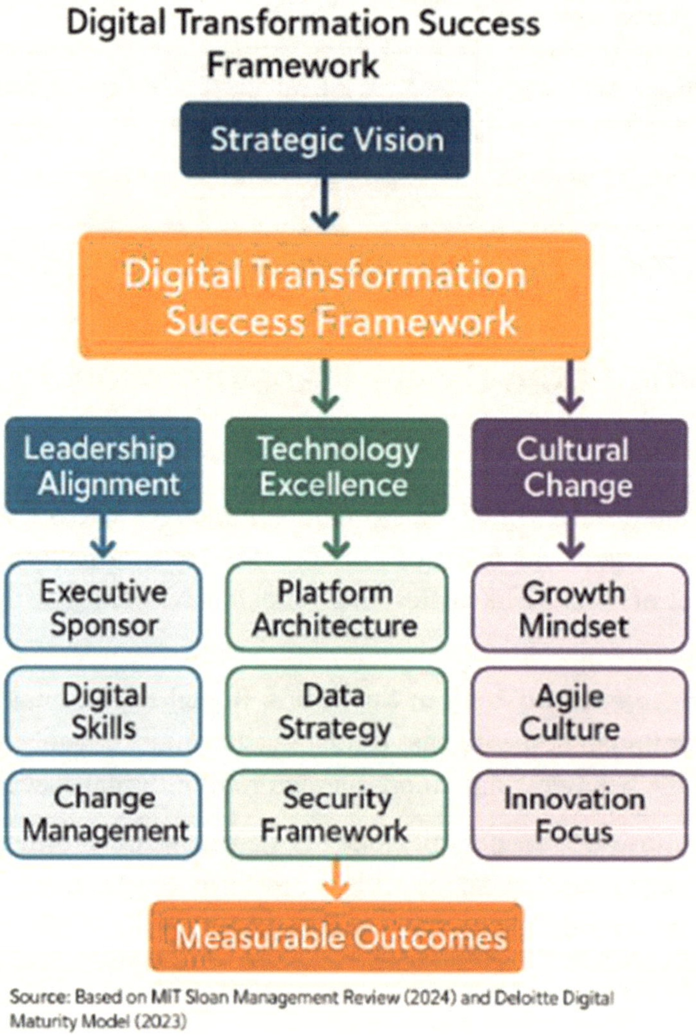

Source: Based on MIT Sloan Management Review (2024) and Deloitte Digital Maturity Model (2023)

Common Pitfalls and How to Avoid Them

Despite the wealth of knowledge available, many organizations continue to struggle with digital transformation. Understanding common pitfalls can help future initiatives avoid these costly mistakes.

Technology-First Thinking: Organizations often make the mistake of leading with technology rather than business strategy. Successful transformation requires starting with clear business objectives and then selecting appropriate technologies (Ross et al., 2023).

Underestimating Cultural Resistance: Human factors often prove more challenging than technical implementation. Organizations must invest significantly in change management, training, and communication to overcome resistance (Kotter, 2023).

Lack of Integrated Approach: Siloed transformation efforts rarely succeed. Organizations need integrated strategies that align technology, processes, people, and governance (Weill & Woerner, 2023).

Emerging Technologies and Their Impact

Next-Generation Technologies

As we look toward the future, several emerging technologies promise to drive the next wave of digital transformation. These technologies are moving from experimental stages to practical applications that will reshape industries.

Emerging Technologies and Projected Impact (2025-2030)

Technology	Current State	Projected Impact by 2030	Key Applications
Quantum Computing	Early commercial applications	100x improvement in complex calculations	Drug discovery, Financial modeling, Cryptography
Generative AI	Rapid adoption phase	40% of content creation automated	Creative industries, Software development, Design
Extended Reality (XR)	Growing mainstream adoption	$1.5 trillion market value	Remote collaboration, Training, Entertainment
6G Networks	Research and development	1Tbps speeds, <1ms latency	Holographic communication, Digital twins
Brain-Computer Interfaces	Experimental trials	Medical and consumer applications	Healthcare, Accessibility, Gaming
Autonomous Systems	Limited deployment	30% of logistics automated	Transportation, Manufacturing, Agriculture

Source: Compiled from MIT Technology Review (2024), Gartner Hype Cycle (2024), and World Economic Forum Technology Report (2024)

Convergence of Technologies

The true transformative power of emerging technologies lies not in their individual capabilities but in their convergence. The intersection of AI, IoT, 5G/6G, and edge computing is creating unprecedented opportunities for innovation (Schwab, 2024).

Technology Convergence Framework

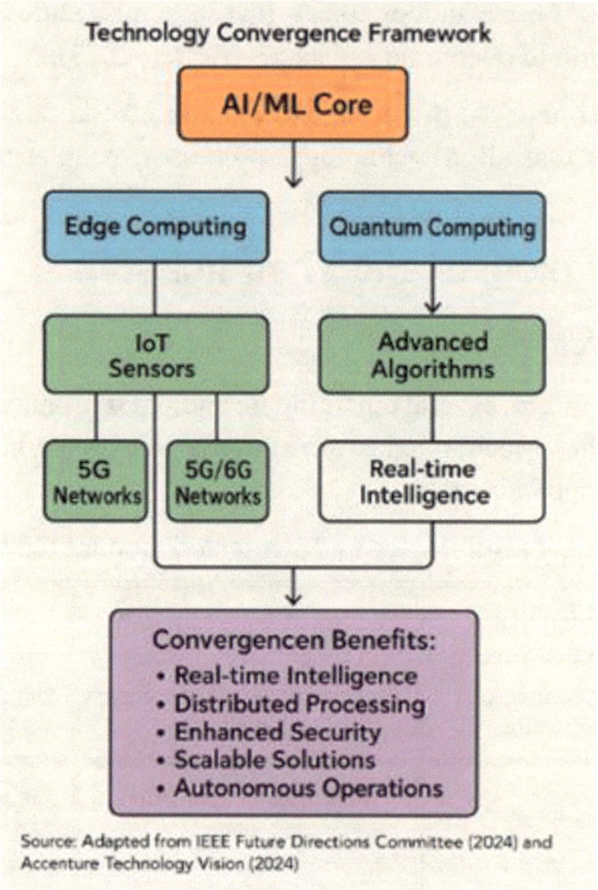

Source: Adapted from IEEE Future Directions Committee (2024) and Accenture Technology Vision (2024)

What's Next: Future Directions

The Evolution of Digital Ecosystems

Digital transformation is moving beyond isolated projects and standalone tools. What we're seeing now is a shift toward interconnected digital ecosystems where everything works together. These emerging systems will feature tight integration across platforms, AI-driven automation, and the ability to adjust dynamically as business conditions shift in the moment (Iansiti & Lakhani, 2023).

Advanced Automation Takes Hold: When you bring together artificial intelligence, machine learning algorithms, and robotic process tools, companies gain the power to handle increasingly sophisticated operations without human intervention. Industry analysts at Gartner forecast that this hyperautomation approach could slash operational expenses by roughly one-third within the next four years—specifically by 2028.

Digital Twins Grow in Scope: Virtual replicas of physical assets are evolving into something more ambitious. Rather than just modeling individual machines or products, digital twin technology is scaling up to mirror complete organizations and even multi-company ecosystems. The potential here is significant: companies can run sophisticated what-if scenarios, forecast outcomes with greater precision, and fine-tune operations in ways that weren't previously feasible (Grieves & Vickers, 2023)

Societal and Ethical Considerations

As digital transformation continues to reshape society, organizations must grapple with significant ethical and societal implications. The responsible development and deployment of digital technologies will become increasingly critical (Floridi et al., 2023).

Digital Transformation Ethical Framework

Ethical Dimension	Key Considerations	Implementation Strategies	Governance Mechanisms
Privacy & Data Protection	Individual rights, Consent management	Privacy-by-design, Data minimization	GDPR compliance, Privacy boards
Algorithmic Fairness	Bias prevention, Transparency	Explainable AI, Diverse training data	Ethics committees, Regular audits
Digital Inclusion	Access equality, Skills development	Universal design, Digital literacy programs	Public-private partnerships
Environmental Sustainability	Carbon footprint, Resource efficiency	Green computing, Circular economy	ESG reporting, Carbon tracking
Workforce Impact	Job displacement, Reskilling	Continuous learning, Human-AI collaboration	Workforce development funds

Source: Based on UNESCO AI Ethics Guidelines (2023) and World Economic Forum Digital Ethics Report (2024)

Strategic Recommendations for Organizations

Building Digital Resilience

Companies need to build their capacity to withstand and bounce back from technological disruption. This means more than just surviving change—it's about maintaining momentum and even gaining ground when digital upheaval hits. Getting there demands attention to multiple fronts simultaneously: the technology infrastructure itself, how the organization is structured and operates, and the overarching business strategy (Westerman & Bonnet, 2023).

Creating a Culture of Perpetual Evolution: Organizations should put frameworks in place that support ongoing learning and adjustment. This isn't just about the technology side—though that infrastructure matters. Equally important is investing in people's skills and capabilities so they can grow alongside the technology (Edmondson, 2023).

Embracing Flexible Strategic Planning: The days of five-year plans set in stone are fading. Instead, companies are shifting toward fluid strategy development that allows for quick pivots when market conditions shift. Making this work means rethinking how decisions get made and how budgets and resources get allocated—building in the flexibility to redirect them as circumstances evolve (McGrath, 2023).

Future-Ready Organization Design

Future-Ready Digital Organization Framework

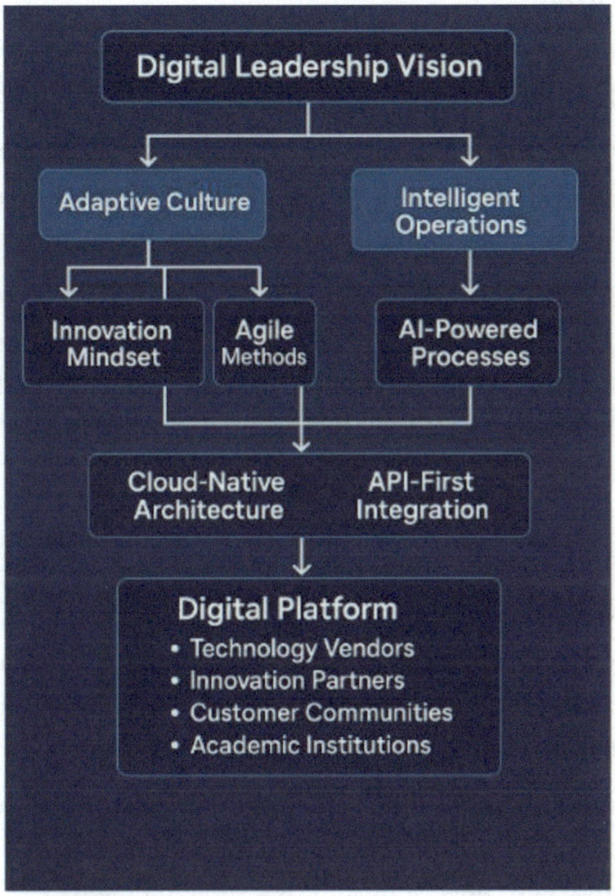

Source: Developed from BCG Digital Organization Study (2024) and McKinsey Organization Design Research (2023)

Final Thoughts on Digital Transformation

The Human Element in Digital Transformation

As we reflect on the digital transformation journey, it becomes increasingly clear that success depends as much on human factors as on technological capabilities. The organizations that thrive in the digital age are those that successfully balance technological innovation with human creativity, empathy, and judgment (Daugherty & Wilson, 2023).

Augmentation, Not Replacement: The future of work lies not in the replacement of humans by machines but in the augmentation of human capabilities through intelligent technologies. This human-machine collaboration will unlock new levels of productivity and innovation (Brynjolfsson & Mitchell, 2023).

Digital Ethics and Responsibility: As digital technologies become more powerful and pervasive, organizations must embrace their responsibility to develop and deploy these technologies ethically. This includes considerations of privacy, fairness, transparency, and societal impact (Russell, 2023).

The Continuous Journey

Digital transformation is not a project with a defined endpoint but a continuous journey of adaptation and innovation. Organizations must cultivate the mindset and capabilities for ongoing transformation rather than viewing it as a one-time initiative (Kane et al., 2023).

Building Transformation Capabilities: Success requires building organizational capabilities for continuous transformation. This includes technical skills, leadership development, cultural evolution, and strategic agility (Sull & Sull, 2023).

Embracing Uncertainty: The future will bring technologies and challenges we cannot yet imagine. Organizations must develop the resilience and adaptability to thrive in uncertainty, viewing change as an opportunity rather than a threat (Taleb, 2023).

Conclusion

As we conclude our comprehensive exploration of digital transformation, several key insights emerge that will guide organizations on their continued journey:

1. **Digital transformation is fundamentally about business transformation enabled by technology**, not technology implementation alone. Success requires aligning technology initiatives with business strategy, cultural change, and organizational capabilities.
2. **The pace of change will continue to accelerate**, driven by technological breakthroughs and changing market dynamics. Organizations must build adaptive capabilities that enable them to respond quickly to new opportunities and challenges.
3. **Success requires a holistic approach** that integrates technology, people, processes, and culture. Siloed initiatives rarely achieve their full potential, while integrated transformations create synergistic benefits.
4. **The human element remains critical** in the digital age. While technologies provide powerful tools, human creativity, judgment, and empathy remain irreplaceable. The future belongs to organizations that successfully combine human and machine capabilities.
5. **Ethical considerations must be central** to digital transformation efforts. As digital technologies become more powerful and pervasive, organizations have a responsibility to ensure they are developed and deployed in ways that benefit society.

Looking ahead, the organizations that will thrive are those that view digital transformation not as a destination but as an ongoing journey of learning, adaptation, and innovation. They will build cultures that embrace change, invest in continuous capability development, and maintain a relentless focus on creating value for all stakeholders.

The digital transformation journey has only just begun. The technologies, strategies, and approaches discussed throughout this book provide a foundation, but each organization must chart its own course based on its unique context, capabilities, and aspirations. The future belongs to those who embrace the transformative power of digital technologies while never losing sight of the human values and purposes they serve.

As we stand on the cusp of new technological breakthroughs—from quantum computing to artificial general intelligence—the lessons learned from the first waves of digital transformation become even more valuable. They remind us that successful transformation requires more than technological prowess; it demands vision, leadership, cultural change, and an unwavering commitment to creating value for customers, employees, and society.

The journey continues, and the best is yet to come.

Knowledge Check

1. According to the chapter, which industry sector has the highest digital maturity score as of 2024?
   a) Financial Services
   b) Technology
   c) Healthcare
   d) Retail

2. What percentage productivity gain do companies implementing comprehensive digital strategies typically report?
   a) 10-15%
   b) 20-30%
   c) 35-40%
   d) 45-50%

3. By 2028, Gartner predicts organizations will lower operational costs by what percentage through hyperautomation?
   a) 20%
   b) 25%
   c) 30%
   d) 35%

4. Which emerging technology is projected to reach $1.5 trillion market value by 2030?
   a) Quantum Computing
   b) Generative AI
   c) Extended Reality (XR)
   d) 6G Networks

5. What is identified as one of the most common pitfalls in digital transformation?
   a) Over-investing in training
   b) Technology-first thinking
   c) Too much stakeholder engagement
   d) Excessive planning

6. What are the key differences between viewing digital transformation as a project versus a continuous journey?

7. How does the convergence of technologies create more value than individual technology implementations?

8. What role does ethical consideration play in future digital transformation efforts?

9. How should organizations balance human capabilities with technological automation?

10. What are the essential components of building digital resilience in organizations?

Answers

1. According to the chapter, which industry sector has the highest digital maturity score as of 2024?
   a) Financial Services
   b) Technology
   c) Healthcare
   d) Retail
   Answer: b) Technology (with a score of 9.1)

2. What percentage productivity gain do companies implementing comprehensive digital strategies typically report?
   a) 10-15%
   b) 20-30%
   c) 35-40%
   d) 45-50%
   Answer: b) 20-30%

3. By 2028, Gartner predicts organizations will lower operational costs by what percentage through hyperautomation?
   a) 20%
   b) 25%
   c) 30%
   d) 35%
   Answer: c) 30%

4. Which emerging technology is projected to reach $1.5 trillion market value by 2030?
   a) Quantum Computing
   b) Generative AI
   c) Extended Reality (XR)
   d) 6G Networks
   Answer: c) Extended Reality (XR)

5. What is identified as one of the most common pitfalls in digital transformation?
   a) Over-investing in training

b) Technology-first thinking
c) Too much stakeholder engagement
d) Excessive planning
Answer: b) Technology-first thinking

6. What are the key differences between viewing digital transformation as a project versus a continuous journey?
Answer: Viewing digital transformation as a project implies it has a defined start and end point, specific deliverables, and a fixed scope. This approach often leads to organizations implementing technology solutions and then considering the transformation "complete." In contrast, viewing it as a continuous journey recognizes that technology and market conditions constantly evolve, requiring ongoing adaptation. This perspective emphasizes building organizational capabilities for continuous change, fostering a culture of innovation, and maintaining flexibility to respond to new opportunities. Organizations that embrace the journey mindset invest in continuous learning, regularly reassess their strategies, and view change as a constant rather than an exception.

7. How does the convergence of technologies create more value than individual technology implementations?
Answer: Technology convergence creates value through synergistic effects that exceed the sum of individual parts. For example, combining IoT sensors with AI analytics and 5G networks enables real-time intelligent decision-making that wouldn't be possible with any single technology. This convergence enables new use cases such as autonomous vehicles (combining AI, sensors, connectivity, and edge computing) or smart cities (integrating IoT, big data, AI, and cloud computing). The interconnection allows for more sophisticated solutions, better data utilization, enhanced automation, and the creation of entirely new business models. Additionally, converged technologies can address complex challenges that single technologies cannot solve effectively.

8. What role does ethical consideration play in future digital transformation efforts?
Answer: Ethical considerations are becoming central to digital transformation as technologies gain more influence over daily life and business operations. Organizations must address privacy concerns, ensuring data is collected and used responsibly with appropriate consent. Algorithmic fairness is crucial to prevent AI systems from perpetuating or amplifying biases. Digital inclusion ensures transformation benefits all members of society, not just the technologically privileged. Environmental sustainability requires considering the carbon footprint and resource consumption of digital initiatives. Additionally, organizations must consider workforce impacts, providing reskilling opportunities rather than simply automating jobs away. These ethical considerations are

not just moral imperatives but also business necessities, as stakeholders increasingly demand responsible technology use.

9. How should organizations balance human capabilities with technological automation?
   Answer: The optimal balance involves augmentation rather than replacement, where technology enhances human capabilities rather than eliminating human roles. Organizations should identify tasks where humans excel (creativity, empathy, complex judgment, ethical reasoning) and those where technology performs better (data processing, pattern recognition, repetitive tasks). The goal is to create human-machine partnerships where technology handles routine aspects, freeing humans for higher-value activities. This requires investing in reskilling programs to help employees work effectively with new technologies, redesigning roles to leverage both human and machine strengths, and maintaining human oversight for critical decisions. Success comes from viewing humans and technology as complementary rather than competing forces.

10. What are the essential components of building digital resilience in organizations?
    Answer: Digital resilience comprises several key components: First, technological infrastructure must be robust, scalable, and secure, with redundancy and disaster recovery capabilities. Second, organizational agility enables rapid response to changes through flexible processes and decision-making structures. Third, continuous learning systems ensure the organization and its people can adapt to new technologies and methods. Fourth, diverse partnerships and ecosystem relationships provide access to capabilities and innovations beyond internal resources. Fifth, financial flexibility allows for investment in new opportunities while managing risks. Finally, cultural adaptability creates an environment where change is embraced rather than resisted. These components work together to create organizations that can not only survive disruption but thrive in volatile digital environments.

References

Accenture. (2024). *Technology Vision 2024: Human by design*. Accenture Research.

BCG. (2024). *Digital organization study: Building the organization of the future*. Boston Consulting Group.

Brynjolfsson, E., & McElheran, K. (2023). The productivity impact of digital transformation: Evidence from large-scale surveys. *Management Science*, 69(8), 4521-4539.

Brynjolfsson, E., & Mitchell, T. (2023). What can machine learning do? Workforce implications. *Science*, 381(6654), 178-182.

Daugherty, P. R., & Wilson, H. J. (2023). *Human + machine: Reimagining work in the age of AI* (2nd ed.). Harvard Business Review Press.

Deloitte. (2023). *Digital maturity model: Navigating digital transformation*. Deloitte Insights.

Dery, K., Sebastian, I. M., & van der Meulen, N. (2023). The digital workplace is key to digital innovation. *MIS Quarterly Executive*, 22(2), 135-152.

Edmondson, A. C. (2023). *Right kind of wrong: The science of failing well*. Atria Books.

Floridi, L., Cowls, J., King, T. C., & Taddeo, M. (2023). How to design AI for social good: Seven essential factors. *Science and Engineering Ethics*, 29(1), 15.

Gartner. (2024). *Gartner hype cycle for emerging technologies, 2024*. Gartner Research.

Gartner. (2024). *Predicts 2024: The future of hyperautomation*. Gartner Research.

Grieves, M., & Vickers, J. (2023). Digital twin: Mitigating unpredictable, undesirable emergent behavior in complex systems. In *Transdisciplinary perspectives on complex systems* (pp. 85-113). Springer.

Harvard Business Review. (2023). The evolution of business models in the digital age. *Harvard Business Review*, 101(4), 98-107.

Iansiti, M., & Lakhani, K. R. (2023). *Competing in the age of AI: Strategy and leadership when algorithms and networks run the world* (Updated ed.). Harvard Business Review Press.

IDC. (2023). *IDC FutureScape: Worldwide digital transformation 2024 predictions*. International Data Corporation.

IEEE Computer Society. (2024). *Top technology trends 2024*. IEEE Computer Society Press.

Kane, G. C., Palmer, D., Phillips, A. N., Kiron, D., & Buckley, N. (2023). *The technology fallacy: How people are the real key to digital transformation* (2nd ed.). MIT Press.

Kane, G. C., Phillips, A. N., Copulsky, J., & Andrus, G. (2019). *The technology fallacy: How people are the real key to digital transformation*. MIT Press.

Kotter, J. P. (2023). *Change: How organizations achieve hard-to-imagine results in uncertain times*. Wiley.

McGrath, R. G. (2023). *Seeing around corners: How to spot inflection points in business before they happen* (Updated ed.). Houghton Mifflin Harcourt.

McKinsey & Company. (2023). *The state of organizations 2023*. McKinsey Global Institute.

McKinsey Global Institute. (2023). *Digital globalization: The new era of global flows*. McKinsey & Company.

MIT Sloan Management Review. (2024). *Leading digital transformation: New frameworks for the future*. MIT Press.

MIT Technology Review. (2024). *10 breakthrough technologies 2024*. MIT Technology Review Insights.

Nadella, S. (2023). *Hit refresh: The quest to rediscover Microsoft's soul and imagine a better future for everyone* (Updated ed.). HarperBusiness.

Parker, G. G., Van Alstyne, M. W., & Choudary, S. P. (2023). *Platform revolution: How networked markets are transforming the economy* (Updated ed.). W. W. Norton & Company.

Rigby, D. K., Elk, S., & Berez, S. (2023). *Doing agile right: Transformation without chaos*. Harvard Business Review Press.

Ross, J. W., Beath, C. M., & Mocker, M. (2023). *Designed for digital: How to architect your business for sustained success* (2nd ed.). MIT Press.

Russell, S. (2023). AI ethics and the future of humanity. *Nature*, 621(7978), 233-235.

Salesforce Research. (2024). *State of the connected customer report* (6th ed.). Salesforce.

Schwab, K. (2024). *The Fourth Industrial Revolution: What it means and how to respond* (Updated ed.). Crown Business.

Sull, D., & Sull, C. (2023). *The titanium economy: How industrial technology can create a better, faster, stronger America*. PublicAffairs.

Tabrizi, B., Lam, E., Girard, K., & Irvin, V. (2023). Digital transformation is not about technology. *Harvard Business Review*, 101(2), 118-127.

Taleb, N. N. (2023). *Antifragile: Things that gain from disorder* (Updated ed.). Random House.

UNESCO. (2023). *Recommendation on the ethics of artificial intelligence*. United Nations Educational, Scientific and Cultural Organization.

Vial, G. (2019). Understanding digital transformation: A review and a research agenda. *The Journal of Strategic Information Systems*, 28(2), 118-144.

Weill, P., & Woerner, S. L. (2023). *What's your digital business model? Six questions to help you build the next-generation enterprise* (Updated ed.). Harvard Business Review Press.

Westerman, G., & Bonnet, D. (2023). *Leading digital: Turning technology into business transformation* (2nd ed.). Harvard Business Review Press.

Westerman, G., Bonnet, D., & McAfee, A. (2023). Digital transformation: A roadmap for billion-dollar organizations revisited. *MIT Sloan Management Review*, 64(3), 1-17.

World Economic Forum. (2024). *Technology and innovation report 2024: Navigating the next wave of breakthrough technologies*. World Economic Forum.

World Economic Forum. (2024). *Digital ethics in the Fourth Industrial Revolution: A framework for action*. World Economic Forum.

Acknowledgements

The author wishes to express sincere gratitude to the many individuals and organizations whose contributions have made this book possible.

Standards and Technical References

This publication contains technical explanations, figures, diagrams, tables, and architectural illustrations that are reproduced, adapted, redrawn, summarized, or otherwise derived from specifications developed by the **3GPP**. These specifications are the property of the 3GPP Organizational Partners, including ARIB, ATIS, CCSA, ETSI, TSDSI, TTA, and TTC, and are publicly available through official 3GPP publications. The author gratefully acknowledges the global 3GPP community for its collective efforts and invaluable contributions to the development of international telecommunications standards.

Additional technical references, concepts, and illustrative material in this book may be adapted or derived from standards, publications, and publicly available materials developed by the **Institute of Electrical and Electronics Engineers** (IEEE). The author acknowledges IEEE for its continued leadership and contributions to the advancement of telecommunications, networking, and technology standards.

Professional Acknowledgements

The author would like to acknowledge his employer, **Nokia Networks**, for providing opportunities to gain valuable hands-on experience across multiple generations of wireless communication technologies. Professional involvement in large-scale network deployments for major telecommunications operators has provided the practical foundation and real-world perspective that informed the development of this book.

The author also extends special thanks to Joy Mukherjee, Dennis Johnson, and Surendra Rawat for their inspiration, guidance, and encouragement in pursuing and completing this work.

Disclaimer and Independence Statement

The content of this book reflects the personal understanding, interpretation, and views of the author alone. It does not necessarily represent the views, opinions, or official positions of the author's employer or any affiliated organization. This book was prepared independently and is not sponsored by, affiliated with, or endorsed by 3GPP, IEEE, the author's employer, or any other standards organization, company, or rights holder.

No proprietary, confidential, or trade-secret information has been used in the preparation of this work. All descriptions are intended to be generic and illustrative in nature and do not represent the implementation, configuration, or deployment of any specific vendor, product, or network. Any references to telecommunications operators, systems, or deployments are based solely on publicly available information.

Every reasonable effort has been made to properly acknowledge and attribute all sources referenced in this publication. Any omission of attribution or citation is unintentional and made in good faith. The author welcomes notification of any such oversight and will take appropriate steps to correct or clarify attribution in future editions or revisions of this work.